MR. CHAIRMAN

The Journal of a Congressional Appropriator

D1711207

Congressman
William Lehman (Ret.)

University Press of America,® Inc.
Lanham • New York • Oxford

4720 Boston Way
Lanham, Maryland 20706

12 Hid's Copse Rd.
Cumnor Hill, Oxford OX2 9JJ

Printed in the United States of America
British Library Cataloging in Publication Information Available

Library of Congress Cataloging-in-Publication Data

Lehman, William
Mr. Chairman : the journal of a congressional appropriator /
William Lehman.
p. cm.
1. United States. Congress. House. 2. Legislators—United States. 3. United States—Politics and government—1981-1989. I. Title: Mr. Chairman. II. Title.
JK1319.L45 2000 328.73'092—dc21 99-049038 CIP

ISBN 0-7618-1559-7 (pbk: alk. ppr.)

™ The paper used in this publication meets the minimum requirements of American National Standard for Information Sciences—Permanence of Paper for Printed Library Materials, ANSI Z39.48—1984

To Joan,

supportive

and

patient

PREFACE

The 100th Congress, the 1987-88 session, was not significantly different than my previous seven terms or my last two before retiring in 1993.

The very averageness of the session, despite its number 100 designation, is what I wanted to capture and relate.

As a legislator in the trenches and not of the leadership who felt more the responsibility than the power of my office, I have a story to tell. As an aging member with the position of an appropriations subcommittee chairman, I held sort of high ground to observe and affect the legislative players and process. The fact is that in both in 1987 and 1988, as every year, as an appropriator I had to pass a spending bill to keep the government operating. It made me a "do it," not "talk it" member. I was pro-active from necessity.

The material is detailed and often trivial but that is what goes into making legislation. Read patiently and learn both the tedium and excitement of trying to make a democratic legislative process function.

Contents

Chapter 1

JANUARY 5, 1987 - MONDAY

This day, January 5, 1987, the day before the opening of the 100th Congress, there is the usual scene of members moving around the corridors of the Capitol and in the House office buildings. Especially active are new members with their families and their retinues. Each group looks like a small parade with the congressman as head drum major. This is the time new members have their big moment. The first time to be sworn in is very heady, yet few have any knowledge about what they are really in for; all, though, appear very sure of themselves.

Visible lobbying on the House Floor aisles can be seen on the Democratic side during the early afternoon session. The lobbying is due largely to the Democratic Caucus having morning sessions even as the House is organizing itself; this is quite unusual since the caucus process ordinarily is completed in December before the full Congress returns in January. Because the Democrats in the House have been in the majority almost exclusively since 1932, the Democratic Caucus is like a legislative body unto itself. The most important meetings of the caucus take place in December of election years. At that time the caucus, in closed session, confirms who serves on what committee and who will or will not continue to serve as chairmen. The most important of these sessions during my terms was in December 1974 when, for the first time, caucus rules were changed to provide secret balloting for committee chairmen. Four longtime chairmen were suddenly dumped and fear was instilled in the remaining chairmen.

There are now two contests pending with promise of real drama. One is for Chairman of the Committee on Science and Technology between Bill Nelson of Florida and George Brown of California. I feel I must support Bill Nelson, as he is a good friend. Also, I would have problems with the Florida delegation if I did otherwise. George Brown, however, is among the brightest people I have known in Washington. The problem with George is his inability to build a support system to get a coalition going for himself. One of my best friends is Don Edwards, Dean of the California delegation, and of course, Don is supporting George Brown. This was going to be an interesting battle especially since Nelson has been up in space as a payload specialist on the 1986 Shuttle Mission 61-C. Some members in the Congress resent his trip and thought it showboating and self-promoting. But, one also has to see it as an act of courage.

Even more controversial is the battle for Chairman of the Armed Services Committee. Les Aspin of Wisconsin, who unseated the previous chairman, Melvin Price (D-IL), in the caucus of the 99th Congress, has disillusioned some of his liberal supporters and is truly worried about surviving as chairman. Even Bob Kastenmeier, a dove and Dean of the Wisconsin delegation, is not sure he is supporting Aspin. Conservative Sonny Montgomery of Mississippi tells me that Aspin should have "quit" as chairman as he has not done anything on the committee in the past year. Sonny is somewhat of a hawk and is not supporting Aspin because he feels Les is anti-defense; Kastenmeier would not support Les because he feels he's too hawkish. Aspin's main challenge is Marvin Leath of Texas. Charlie Bennett of Florida also wants the chairmanship. The first vote in the caucus was on the Steering and Policy Committee's recommendation of Aspin. This recommendation was voted down by a six-vote margin, followed by nominations from the caucus floor. Nominated were Aspin, Nicholas Mavroules of Massachusetts, Charlie Bennett and Marvin Leath. The problem I had with Aspin was that I did not really believe he was sincere in what he said he stood for. He is charming, a good person to be around, and bright, but he vacillates on the issues and I never know from where he is coming. However, I do not believe Marvin Leath is better. Leath is deeply committed to defense, and could be more of a problem than a solution.

There were also tensions within the Energy and Commerce Committee. Chairman John Dingell (MI) was attempting to gain more control over the entire committee and reduce power of the subcommittee chairmen, especially Henry Waxman of California, and James Florio of New Jersey. It is a very powerful committee with much authorizing and investigative jurisdiction, and members like to be on this committee as they often have their names in the media.

When the press asked about the President's budget and what our transportation committee intended to do about cuts in Amtrak and mass transit, I told them we would do the same as last year and replace the cuts in the President's budget. This effort will be difficult but realistically our subcommittee is not going to shut down Amtrak. Since the administration does not provide money for urban mass transit, the subcommittee has to reprogram money from other transportation budget items into mass transit.

The press also wanted my statement on the proposed members' salary increase from $75,000 to $89,500. My personal feeling, as a former businessman, is that when you have good employees the way to keep them is to pay a competitive salary. The increase to $89,500 is reasonable, and could upgrade the quality of members as it will be more in competition with the private sector. If it comes to a vote (and I hoped it did not as voting would put members in a tough position) I will vote for the raise. It is quite difficult to explain to constituents why their Representative in Washington has a hard time living on $75,000 a year, but maintaining two homes can inflict an enormous burden on your budget. Many members can double or even triple the salary in the private sector, and if the congressional salary is not competitive, Congress will consist of people who are either independently wealthy, or others who cannot make that amount of money elsewhere, except as a member of Congress.

JANUARY 6 TUESDAY

I am sworn in today, January 6, 1987, for the 100th Congress.

In the morning the House Democrats had an important caucus. This is the time committee assignments and committee chairmen nominations take place. As to the Appropriations Committee every Democratic committee member that ran was re-elected. The Steering and Policy Committee as usual recommended to the Democratic Caucus the same appropriations subcommittee chairmen that served in the 99th Congress. Only on Appropriations does the caucus vote for subcommittee chairmen. The Appropriations subcommittee chairmen are more important and influential than other subcommittee chairmen and are equivalent in the level of power to full committee chairmen of the authorizing committees; in some cases they are more powerful.

So, I am re-elected as Chairman of the Subcommittee on Transportation of the Appropriations Committee. This is my eighth year as chairman. Because the Speaker of the House has not yet been elected, the regular session which began at noon is presided over by the newly-elected Clerk of the House, Donnald K. Anderson. There are nominations from the Democratic and Republican sides for Speaker, and Jim Wright of Texas is elected with the formality of a roll call vote. Members are then officially sworn in. On the Floor, there are so many noisy families of the members that one cannot hear the proceedings.

A quorum of the House is called because at this point it is impossible to know who is present. This is the first year members' parents are allowed on the Floor, and it is difficult for members to find an empty seat. With the House now organized, the Republicans tried to pass a resolution that would prevent any bill from raising the tax rate this year, and it is done to embarrass Jim Wright and the Democrats. The "question" was defeated and there is no legislation to prevent increasing the personal income tax rate if Congress so desired later.

In the afternoon there are several receptions for new members and their families and guests. I did attend a reception at the Florida House and from there I left with my friend Alice Rivlin of The Brookings Institute and went to the home of Katherine Graham, who was hosting a reception for her brother-in-law, the new Florida Senator Bob Graham, which included many of Miami's power structure people. When Alice Rivlin is with me at receptions people are impressed, just as I am, that she likes being with me. Alice is a world renown economist. [She became Director of the Office of Management and Budget, and is now Vice Chairman of the Federal Reserve.]

Afterwards we went to a fundraiser for Congressman Frank McCloskey of Indiana. McCloskey is very happy as he has won convincingly with about 53 percent of the vote over McIntyre. The previous election, he won by only four actual votes with the same opponent. While there, I met another good friend, Penny Farthing, a member of the law firm Patten, Boggs and Blow, who is lobbying for the proposed new regional airport in Denver. Penny with my help on the subcommittee was instrumental in getting FAA appropriations for the Denver airport, the first regional jetport built in over thirty years.

JANUARY 7 WEDNESDAY

In the morning session on the House Floor, we voted to establish the Investigative Committee on the Iran-Contra problem. I am very pleased that Lee Hamilton will head this committee. Initially, I was reluctant because I thought Dante Fascell of Florida wanted that position; I spoke to Lee about it, and he told me there was no problem between him and Dante.

Also on the Floor the highway bill was put off until January 20. The bill does not take the highway trust fund off budget. In the 1986 legislation, a motion was carried to recommit with instructions to the committee to bring back the bill with language to take the highway trust fund section of the bill off budget.

From time to time the State of Florida highway officials come in - always most anxious to get a larger share of federal money for highways, and always working to have the trust fund taken off budget. I have told them this is not the way to proceed as it throws the federal budget out of whack, and always I have stressed

that I would see that they got their rightful share of federal aid for highways. Public Works Chair Jim Howard (NJ) told me he was not going to fight me this year on taking the trust fund off budget. Perhaps this was because of the controversial rule on his highway bill, and my submitting a statement in the bill supporting the 65 miles per hour speed limit.

In the district there is a problem with the proposed South Florida tri-county commuter rail system, as the CSX railroad wants to charge Dade County $200 thousand a month for the use of its CSX tracks, and the State is willing to pay only $30 thousand a month. I am attempting to put pressure on CSX to bring the price down and, if necessary, I will call on other South Florida members to persuade CSX to be more cooperative, as the commuter rail system is essential.

Another dilemma is the awarding of funding for 80 buses to Metro Dade Transit. Ralph Stanley, Urban Mass Transit Administrator, and an anti-unionist, wanted forty new buses for Metro Transit Authority and forty new buses for private companies in Dade County to see which of the two operated more efficiently. The problem is the unions would not sign off on the 13C clause, and according to the Federal labor law, this was a necessary prerequisite. The Dade County local union is in an untenable position. If they appear selfish and unwilling to sign off, preventing the awarding of new buses into Dade County, the public will be outraged. On the other hand, if they do sign off and obtain the buses, the unions could look like heroes. [As it turned out, they did sign off on the 13C clause, and there was no discernible difference between union and private operators in the operating efficiency of our public transportation system.]

JANUARY 8 THURSDAY

In the Democratic Caucus of the full Appropriations Committee in choosing subcommittee assignments on the third round of choices, I was first in line to choose a vacancy on the Military Construction Subcommittee, but I passed so that Vic Fazio of California, who wanted this assignment to protect a military installation in his district, could have it. Vic is a good ally when it comes to protecting the transportation subcommittee legislation on the House Floor against off-budget resolutions, and I owed him. However, Charlie Wilson of Texas also wanted on Military Construction. The result was that the full Appropriations Committee voted to enlarge the subcommittee by one Republican and one Democrat.

JANUARY 9 FRIDAY

Congress has recessed until Tuesday, January 20, but I am not scheduled to leave for Miami until tomorrow morning. It is quiet on the Hill as most of the members have already left for their home districts.

JANUARY 10 SATURDAY

Arriving in Miami around noon, I was in time for Honey and Al Pallot's luncheon at the Marriott Hotel on the Miami River. Al and his wife Honey have a Beautification of Miami Foundation, and they hold this luncheon annually. Al, I believe, does this partly as an ego trip, but I have found that even when people do things to inflate their ego it often does good for others as well. In this case the awards help stimulate citizens to improve their neighborhoods. I noted that there were no blacks present except Mrs. Thelma Gibson, the widow of Rev. Theodore Gibson, who had been one of Miami's leading black ministers and political leaders. My criticism of Al and the foundation is that no awards were ever given in recognition of the inner city areas or public housing projects. All the recognition went to areas along Brickell Avenue where beautification was already in place. I called this to Al's attention for next year's awards.

Al is one of my good supporters, and in his introduction he bragged about me, saying that unlike Claude Pepper and Dante Fascell, I had no re-election opposition. It was a tactless remark for Pallot to make, but it was well-meaning. I explained to the guests that the fact that I had no opposition did not mean I was more effective, it was just that sometimes it worked that way. Al also said that Florida had three great Congressmen in Washington in Bill Lehman, Dante Fascell, and Claude Pepper. And, it was true that the three of us are very effective. We have the seniority and the committee chairmanships to do an amazing job with our combined efforts and, as Tip O'Neill said, "Bill Lehman, Dante Fascell and Claude Pepper provide the best representation of a metropolitan area anywhere in the country." Together we have a lot of clout.

Sharyn Fallick, my campaign manager, was with me at the luncheon and it was fortunate that we attended, as several meetings were being held in other rooms at the hotel, and many of Miami's downtown power structure people were there. I ran into many friends who are the basis of my fundraising efforts. I even met there the British Ambassador, Sir Anthony Acland, and had a photo opportunity with him.

JANUARY 11 SUNDAY

Relaxation and time spent with family.

JANUARY 12 MONDAY

Ditto

JANUARY 13 TUESDAY

The *Miami Herald* has featured a story today about opposition to the overpass, but my name is not mentioned, and I am glad. This is an ongoing struggle in North Dade between adjacent homeowners and the State of Florida Highway Department regarding the building of a highway overpass over FEC tracks at 203rd Street. The overpass would fly over W. Dixie Highway and the railroad tracks, enabling commuters to avoid the freight train delays. Charlotte Greenbarg is leading this personal vendetta against construction of the overpass. Some homeowners in the Skylake area feel the overpass will diminish the property value of their homes and they do not want their neighborhood invaded by additional traffic. I can certainly empathize with those opposing the overpass in their neighborhood, but the intersection is used by all the people in the North Dade area, and we have to keep up with traffic growth. Opponents of the overpass were even using children as a rationale to prevent the implementation of the overpass. A junior high school is a few blocks away, and the opponents claim that the overpass would be a danger to the children because of the increase in traffic. But the area is very congested, and the overpass is needed to relieve traffic on Biscayne Blvd. It will save lives on the railroad crossing more than threaten the safety of children from the nearby junior high school. [Charlotte eventually moved to North Florida but the traffic congestion is worse than ever.]

John Schelble, my press assistant, is in from Washington, and joined me in a 1:00 meeting with Bill Miller from the Florida Department of Transportation. We discussed the same controversial overpass at 203rd Street and Biscayne and, with the differences now resolved between CSX and the State of Florida over the use of the CSX tracks, we talked about future plans for the tri-county commuter rail. The tri-rail commuter system is another step forward in the modernization of public transportation in Southeast Florida.

From Washington I had arranged to meet today with Dade County Manager Sergio Pereira, the Army Corps of Engineers, and State officials regarding the Sunny Isles Beach Restoration project. The meeting was held at 2:00, in Pereira's office on N.W. lst Street. The Energy and Water Appropriations Subcommittee had put a little over $8 million in federal money in last year's appropriations' bill for restoration of the beaches on Sunny Isles. It took me about twelve years of work to do this appropriation. The problem now was that the State and County had not come forward with their matching funds. The meeting today alerted the county to the urgency of moving quickly on the project so that State funds already allocated could be claimed by the county for Sunny Isles beach restoration.

John's main purpose in coming to Miami was to join me in meetings with editorial boards of Dade County's major newspapers. At least once a year I try to do this with the newspapers to discuss current issues. At today's meeting with the *Miami Herald* editorial board, we talked about the air traffic control system, and I explained that Congress had just passed a supplemental appropriations' bill which would increase the number of fully qualified air traffic controllers to 15,000 in the next fiscal year, and that our transportation subcommittee already had the money appropriated for this.

Meeting with the *Miami News* editorial board, they basically asked the same questions as the *Herald*. They were also concerned with the inefficiency of Metro-Dade Transit. I told them that we need a qualified transit administrator who really knows how to run a transportation system, and mentioned as examples the administrators in Houston and New York with well-run transit operations. I said that "until we have a top notch person, we will not have a quality-run transportation system." I thought I was speaking "off the record," but my adverse comments about the Metro-Dade transportation system were published. I should have been more careful about my remarks, but perhaps it will do some good to criticize Dade transit.

JANUARY 14 WEDNESDAY

This morning I visited an elderly patient at the Greynolds Park Manor Rehabilitation Center regarding Medicare. A photo was taken, and the patient seemed happy at this nursing home, which is a contrast to most people in nursing homes as they usually seem depressed. One problem with Medicare for the elderly is that Medicare does not pay for nursing home care unless the person is actually ill, and then it will pay the medical costs but not the nursing home costs.

Today John and I visited the newspaper offices of Dade's two Jewish newspapers. We had with us materials regarding my recent fourteen-day trip to Israel. At the newly begun *Jewish Tribune*, the reporter interviewing me was ignorant of the appropriations process and how I was involved in it. He had no background information, and it was difficult talking to a reporter who did not know the right or essential questions to ask. I had to spend most of the time explaining background to him. We met next with Fred Schocket, publisher of the *Jewish Floridian*. The Floridian has been in existence for over sixty years and Fred is very knowledgeable on the issues. I spoke to him about my trip to Israel and mentioned the possibility of my going to East Germany and taking with me a Rabbi. That was the first time I had remarked to the press about my upcoming trip, which is being arranged by the American Jewish Committee.

Later, I was at a meeting in North Miami Beach with residents of the Point East Condo, as usual run by Annie Ackerman, a native of Chicago and an icon in Miami's condo political arena. Every few months I get together with Annie and her group. She and her husband were the first Senior Citizen Interns to work in my Washington office. Annie, who is also a good friend, once asked if I could get a page appointment for her friend's grandchild. My own page was already appointed, and since seniority members are allowed only one page from his/her district at a time, I thought my chances of fulfilling Annie's request might be impossible. But speaking with Jack Brooks of Texas who heads the House patronage office, Jack said he would try to work out something, and he did, providing me with an additional appointment. This was the only time I had ever heard of two pages simultaneously.

Approximately 100 people come to these meetings and they are the core of my support system in the condo area. This evening they are interested in why the social security increase (COLA's) was only 1.2 percent while federal employees received a 3 percent raise. Sometimes questions were asked for which I did not have all the answers or information. From these questions I learn what is on my constituents' minds. Another question was whether the 100th Congress would be more liberal or more conservative. I said an indication would be who is chosen to head the Armed Services Committee. If Leath won it would suggest more conservative; and if Aspin won, more liberal.

JANUARY 15 THURSDAY

Today was easy other than a call from Sergio Pereira, the Metro-Dade Manager, who was upset because he read in the *Miami News* today that I was unhappy about the Metro Dade Transit Authority.

JANUARY 16 FRIDAY

Another easy day.

JANUARY 17 SATURDAY

As a guest speaker today at a meeting with some of Miami's black business leaders, I was introduced by the Commissioner of the City of Miami, Miller Dawkins. Their primary concerns were about minority economic development problems in Haiti and Haitian refugees. "The problem with Haiti," I said, "is that the Reagan administration had supported the anti-communist Baby Doc." I also told them that there would be a greater political presence of black Haitians in Miami, and that the Haitians would be playing a more important economic role. But, it is also important that relations improve between the American black community and the Haitians. My comments were well received, and it was a good meeting, with many of my friends there like Raul Masvidal from the Cuban community, Metro Commissioner Art Teele, and attorney George Knox, among others.

JANUARY 18 SUNDAY

This morning Bill Bayer of WINZ interviewed me for his Sunday evening radio program. Bill often calls for an interview as he usually has three politicians taped ahead for his program. A closet Republican, Bill is funny, a good person, and open-minded on the issues. The topic this morning was on the labor unions signing off on the contract for federal money to purchase 80 buses for Metro-Dade transit.

JANUARY 19 MONDAY

As a participant today in the Martin Luther King Day Parade, I decided to ride a horse rather than sit waving in an open car, and practiced to refresh my ability to ride a horse at the City of Miami Police Stables. I hate parades, but I'd rather participate by riding a horse than walking or riding in an open car. On a horse you project a kind of earthy symbol. The only problem with horses in a parade is that someone has to walk behind you with a shovel. The parade began at 10:00 a.m., and went along 62nd Street, but prior to its start the usual snafus occurred: locating the horse, locating the candy I had brought, and locating the backup car with my sign on it. The car with my parade sign was found a half mile back of my horse and me. I have on my cowboy outfit, but I do not think the people know who I am. Senator Lawton Chiles is riding in the car behind me.

Some politicians love parades, but I usually felt that considering the amount of energy and wasted time involved parades did not do anything to help me politically or help the community. I never saw any point to participating in a parade except to show people that you are still alive. This being the Martin Luther King Parade, I felt it is important to be there so that the people know you are interested in their community.

At 5:30 p.m., I left Miami on an Eastern flight headed back to Washington.

JANUARY 20 TUESDAY

In Washington Tad Foote, President of the University of Miami, came to the office with lobbyist Art Roberts, a friend for many years, to speak about additional funding for programs at the University of Miami. I had frequently been effective in gaining grants for the University.

Officials from the City of North Miami, including the Mayor, again came to see me about the ongoing problem of cleaning up the toxic wastes on the Munisport site. The toxic waste was put there by private enterprise waste companies 10-25 years ago, and this should not have been allowed. I told the North Miami officials that the Munisport was contaminated, and that they should make it a city priority to combine local matching funds and super fund dollars to do the cleanup. The Munisport is a very valuable piece of property but cannot be sold with toxic wastes still present, as any potential developers will first want the site cleaned up.

The Turkish Embassy has invited me to a reception this evening in honor of the President of Turkey, Kenin Evren, who is visiting in Washington. Turkey Ambassador Sukru Elekdag invites me to all such events. Joan was with me, as she loves the architecture and splendor of the Embassy, a beautiful mansion on Massachusetts Avenue designed at the turn of the century by a Turkish architect for an American millionaire who supposedly invented the cap for the coca-cola bottle.

The Turkish government is very dependent on our military assistance, and whenever the Embassy has a social affair, they usually invite many Armed Services Committee members and Uniformed

Military people. I was invited as a member on the Foreign Operations Appropriations Subcommittee. (Tomorrow the affair will be written up in the *Washington Post*.)

JANUARY 21 WEDNESDAY

Illinois Republican Governor Thompson, and Richard Durbin of Illinois, a colleague of mine on the appropriations subcommittee, spoke to me about getting the highway bill out "as quickly as possible" because of the need for rapid reconstruction on the highways in Illinois. Thompson is a very capable governor and works well with both Republicans and Democrats.

Speaker Jim Wright and Appropriations Committee Chairman Jamie Whitten are writing a supplemental appropriations bill for the homeless. I have spoken to Dade County Manager Sergio Pereira about the possibility of converting the unused public transit parking garages into temporary housing for the homeless, but this effort at the county level, to my knowledge, was never made.

By the Democratic Caucus I was reappointed today to the Select Subcommittee on Children, Youth and Families. George Miller, who chairs the committee, appreciated that I volunteered to remain on this committee, as not too many senior members want to serve on this select committee. Although I told George that, if he wanted, I would chair a task force subcommittee, it would be fine by me if he wished to give the assignment to a younger committee member, as I have plenty to do on the appropriations committee. For several years I have worked with George on the select committee with emphasis on child care and teenage pregnancy issues, and during that time we held hearings, issued press releases, but no legislation was ever initiated. Select committees are ninety-eight percent useless congressional expenditures.

In the evening Joan and I had dinner at LaColline Restaurant, one of the Hill's better watering places. We ran into Congressman Buddy MacKay of Florida, Greg Farmer, Secretary of Commerce for the State of Florida and his wife Suzanne Collins Farmer. I first met Suzanne fifteen years ago at a political party at Charlie Allen's home in Biscayne Park. Charlie and Sue Allen were classmates of my daughter Kathy at Miami Edison Senior High. Suzanne was a social studies teacher then at Horace Mann Junior High School. After this campaign event I asked her to come to Washington for the summer to be my intern. In Washington she became hooked on politics, quit her teaching job, and came to work for me in the Miami district office; later, she found a staff job on the Hill. Likewise with Greg, I have known him for many years, going back to when he was a bagboy in a local North Miami supermarket. Greg worked for me on re-election campaigns when Suzanne was working in my district office. Many former campaign workers now have positions of power and authority in the staff bureaucracy in Florida and in Washington. Sergio Bendixen, for instance, who led my 1974 campaign is now with Hispanic Television and we are still close friends. It is interesting to see the way young people develop over the years.

JANUARY 22 THURSDAY

For the additional space needed to hold all the participants who were in this morning for the City of North Miami Munisport meeting, we had to go to my subcommittee room. The meeting included Mayor Marco Lafredo, Jr., of North Miami and his key people, staff members from the offices of "Senator" Claude Pepper, Senator Lawton Chiles, and the Environmental Protection Agency (EPA). As mentioned, the Munisport contains acres of potentially valuable land, and North Miami is trying to have the site removed from the EPA superfund list. The superfund list means being targeted as one of the worst toxic waste sites in the country, and since North Miami cannot sell or dispose of the property until it is off the superfund list, there is no way the city can pay off the debt from funds borrowed to buy the property. I am trying to have the EPA give the City of North Miami a break and remove the property from the superfund list. However, not all of the people in the Munisport area want it removed, as they think the land should be better cleaned before removal from the superfund list. And, some environmentalists were sure there were still toxic wastes leaking into the bay waters from this landfill. The land had been used for a dump for many years after the City of North Miami acquired it.

Some progress was made, and I believe we can expedite the necessary review by the EPA, whose officials agreed to report back to me by February 5. I want to help free up the land for the City of North Miami and reduce its many million dollars a year debt service cost.

A newsworthy snowstorm has hit Washington and after our meeting Senator Chiles, Mayor Marco Lafredo and I had photos taken of us shoveling snow and throwing snowballs. We were using this snowstorm coverage as leverage for publicity on the North Miami Munisport problem, and had a House photographer and a *Miami Herald* reporter covering the event. That evening Miami television did use the photo showing us shoveling snow, and said that we were in Washington trying to get help on the Munisport problem. Sometimes you have to use such opportunities for media publicity on an issue.

In the afternoon the Democratic Caucus went back into session to resolve the chairmanship of the Armed Services Committee. On the first two votes, the first eliminated Nick Mavroules of Massachusetts, then Charlie Bennett (FL) was out on the second. On the final vote between Marvin Leath and Les Aspin, I voted for Aspin, not too happily, but I felt he was the lesser of the two evils. I was concerned about the other Jewish members' vote. It would not be wise for all of the Jewish members to vote for one person because the State of Israel is going to need help from whomever is chairman of the Armed Services Committee. Most of my Jewish friends say they will be voting for Aspin, so he does have some Jewish support, but the vote is going to be close.

Back in the office I am working on my first newsletter of the year, targeted to the residents of Sunny Isles to report on our accomplishments with the Sunny Isles beach restoration. The State of Florida and Dade County came up with the matching funds, and all parties have signed the contract. The Army Corps of Engineers will be ready to start the project in March of this year, and the restoration will be financially and environmentally beneficial to the district, as many European tourists use the beaches in that area. We are getting good response on the recent newsletter to the Jewish community mailing list about my trip to the Mid-East. After traveling, I send out a newsletter to my constituents telling them where I went and why. I believe in keeping my district informed of my travels and I have never had any public relations problems regarding these trips. We have not sent out a general purpose newsletter recently, but we soon will on day-care problems.

Word has just come to me on the final vote for the chair of the Armed Services Committee - Aspin had 133 votes and Leath 116. I am glad to be with a winner and I think everything is going to work out all right. Most of our staff left the office by mid-afternoon because of the snowstorm. Pat Thorpe and John Schelble are still here so I asked them to check with the East Wing of the National

Galley to see if the evening's preview exhibition on the "Age of the Sultan Suramin the Magnificent" was still scheduled. It was, so Joan and I went to see the art exhibit. It was a wonderful exhibit but, unfortunately, because of the snowstorm, only about one-tenth of the people showed up, and arrangements had been made for approximately 800 guests.

Joan and I sat with such interesting people as Mr. & Mrs. David Dunn. David works for the Patton, Boggs and Blow law firm, and I have known him for many years even back when he was in love with a Dante Fascell staffer named Edie from North Carolina. Also at our table were Senator Al Gore, and a young lady reporter with *Life Magazine*. *Life* was doing a story on whom the next Democratic and Republican candidates might be for the presidential primaries. [The *Life* story said that Al Gore would want to run for the Democratic nomination in 1992 or 1996, and he is doing all the right things and is an ideal candidate.] It was a pleasant moment with lots of lively conversation. I have always enjoyed going to these previews in the East Wing as it is a very beautiful setting and the food, by Windows Catering, is always delicious.

JANUARY 23 FRIDAY

I spent most of the morning at the Navy Dental Yard Clinic having minor surgery. The Clinic is a huge facility only about ten minutes from my townhouse, and it gives me a sense of security to be able to go there and have them check on me once in awhile. I have to maintain very good dental care because of my surgical operation in 1982 for throat cancer and the fact that dental problems could be serious because of the radiation I had. It is much more convenient for me to use the Navy dentists in Washington than those at Memorial Sloan Kettering in New York where my surgery was done.

One of the conversations we had last evening at the art exhibition was about Speaker Jim Wright's proposal of a fifty-cent gas tax. I did not know about his proposal, but today I saw Jim coming into the Member's Dining Room and congratulated him on his trial balloon. I told him I was for it and would support him on the issue. He thanked me but said he really did not see it happening. We both knew it was needed if we were ever to get our budget close to being balanced. Our failing infrastructure also needs additional revenue to make repairs and do maintenance.

JANUARY 24 SATURDAY

Last evening after the dental surgery I did not feel very well, and so I mostly just stayed around the house. This morning when I awakened most of the soreness from the extracted tooth was gone, but I thought I had an antibiotic pill stuck in my throat, as my throat was bothering me. I called the Capitol Physician's Office and there was a doctor on duty (Saturday), who told me to come in to be examined. The pill had indeed stuck in the esophagus and made a small ulcer, so the doctor put me on liquid medication instead of pills. It is good to know that even on a Saturday morning you can walk into a doctor's office and get treated. For me there is a good medical support system here.

That evening our Washington office had its staff party at the Phoenix Court Restaurant. Everyone showed up, and it was a nice event. Most of the staff have been with me ten years or more and are really good people; we are like a family.

JANUARY 25 SUNDAY

My neighbor, lobbyist Maurice Rosenblatt and I dined this evening at the Four Seasons; following dinner we went to a movie in Georgetown. Washington was like a winter wonderland, very quiet, and the streets covered with snow seemed eerie, with a rural atmosphere - unlike a world power center. The only other cars on the street were four wheel drives and police cars. On our way home around 10:00 p.m., you could see hundreds of young people around George Washington University playing in the snow.

JANUARY 26 MONDAY

Due to the snowstorm most of the government offices are closed. I went to the office and the only staff person present is Pat Thorpe. It is very quiet here and in the district office. Joan and I may go back to Miami this afternoon, but first I will try to complete a couple of newsletters. One for the Jewish list on the rescue of Esther Debra Benchoam, and the other on daycare center programs for which we are trying to introduce legislation.

JANUARY 27 TUESDAY

Most of the staff came in this morning. Jeff Berkowitz of the Jewish Federation in Miami was in to see me with Jorge Mas, a Cuban-American leader from Miami. The American Israel Public Affairs Committee (AIPAC), and the Cuban-American Foundation are trying to combine their programs for more effectiveness. Jeff is working to move some of the more moderate of the influential Cubans to work with the Congressional Democratic leadership, and is also exploring ways to bring the Jewish and Cuban leadership in South Florida closer together. The problem is that many Jewish members of Congress voted against aid to the Contras, which is a strong issue with the Cuban-American Foundation. It will be interesting to see how these two groups work together, as one group is so ultra right-wing and AIPAC members, except on Israel security, are usually liberal. I will be meeting with both groups tomorrow at a luncheon.

I also had visitors from the Dade County School Board. They usually come to Washington once or twice a year, and this year Rosa Feinberg, the new member of the school board, was with the group. We had a group photo taken outside in the snow.

For the last two days security has been in full force around the Hill in preparation for the President's State of the Union Address tonight. Considerably more concern is shown this year over terrorist activities than ever before. A meeting was held in the Democratic Caucus Room in the Cannon Building to alert members to the dangers of terrorism. The Chief Security Officer and Sergeant-At-Arms, Jack Russ, lectured on how to be especially careful with our automobiles parked in the underground parking area, and how lethal a few sticks of dynamite can be. We were told to remove all the insignia on our automobiles to avoid being recognized as a member. All decals came off the cars, and even the name tag over my parking spot was removed.

The only vote on the Floor today was the supplemental appropriations' bill on aid for the homeless. Other than that things are quiet. I played tennis at the Army/Navy Club with my tennis buddies, Bob Kastenmeier, Don Edwards, and U.S. Appeals Court Judge, Abner Mikva. The indoor court was available to us from 2:00-3:00, not much time, but better than nothing. We usually play at Haines Point, but the plastic bubble that covers those courts was blown down with the storm. It is very difficult to reserve a court at the Army/Navy Club, especially for more than one hour, but we had a good time. I like to buy the club's sweatshirts and occasionally swipe a towel.

Patty Diaz, a case worker in the district office, was very instrumental in getting a mother out of Cuba so she could spend the last days of her son's life with him. He is a Marielito and is in a hospital in Miami dying from AIDS. Patty was able to cut through the bureaucratic red tape to enable the mother to get the necessary documents to come to the United States. She is due to arrive in Miami today. Channel 7 is also involved and we may have stories tomorrow in the *Miami News* and the *Miami Herald.* John Schelble was a little unhappy with me because in speaking to the media I gave most of the credit to Patty, who really did all the work. John felt that I should take the credit. But, as I told John, I did not feel right taking all the media attention for something that Patty really did and not give her the recognition. I only provided some assistance by making one or two phone calls.

I then called Penny Farthing of the law firm, Patton, Boggs and Blow, to let her know that I had a gallery ticket for her to the President's State of the Union Address this evening, and she was thrilled. Later I went to the Democratic Study Group election to vote on our regional representative, and cast my vote for Larry Smith, my colleague from South Broward County, who had told me that he wanted this position. One person I saw there was former member Frank Thompson (D-NJ) who served with me on the Education and Labor Committee. Frank was an outstanding congressman, and well liked by the members, but he had a drinking problem. In 1980, he was trapped in the ABSCAM sting operation and went to prison, and we lost a good member. Frank was one of the founders of the Democratic Study Group, which was formed about twenty years ago as a liberal arm of House Democrats to prevent control of the Democrats by the moderates and conservatives. The DSG became a factor in anti-Vietnam war legislation and was in the forefront of civil rights legislation. Chairing the Study Group often becomes a stepping stone to Chairman of the Democratic Caucus and on up the leadership line.

When I was first in Washington, Phil Burton from California was Chairman of the Democratic Study Group, and at that time it was a highly visible organization that influenced the Congress in many ways. As time went on it diminished in its quality and accomplishments, especially as the Democratic Caucus became more liberal. I used to be more active in this group but now I don't have much time for these peripheral organizations. Being chairman of a subcommittee on appropriations does not leave much time for anything else.

The President has just finished his State of the Union Address. Before the speech, members played musical chairs and moved around a lot. Joe Kennedy was saving a seat for his uncle, Senator Ted Kennedy; I sat next to my friend Phil Sharpe of Indiana. The speech was not very impressive. Basically the members are fond of President Reagan but don't take him seriously anymore. He is an aging President and has lost his omnipotence. A funny thing happened during Reagan's speech. With the statement that he was going to ask the Democratic leadership to cut the defense budget by $50 billion over the next three years, Reagan expected people to be unhappy, but Democrats applauded and this threw him off balance for a minute. He is still obsessed with the Sandinistas, and with the strategic defense initiatives, and uses his same patriotic symbols, but most of the American people still like him. The President apologized for the Iran arms sale fiasco, and in the same passive voice said that "mistakes were made," but never saying who the hell made the mistakes.

After the speech, a couple of media people were expecting me to call. I gave a statement to the *Miami News* and spoke with Hal Cessna of WIOD Radio for a live statement over the air. Leaving the House Floor I ran into the very charming Adele Graham, wife of Senator Bob Graham of Florida, who was escorted by Jerry Berlin and his wife Gwen. Jerry to me is somewhat of a mystery person who turns up everywhere and seems to know everyone. He is a political "junkie" and raises lots of money for Democratic candidates at receptions held at his beautiful home in Southwest Dade, but I have never really understood his own financial base.

The National School Board Association held its reception this evening. As a former member of the Dade County School Board and then its chairman before my election to Congress in 1972, I felt obligated to attend, but once there I received the wrong name tag, which said "Richard Lehman." No one noticed, however, as most were too busy eating. It was an extremely crowded affair, open to the staff, and many staff members, especially interns, attend for the food and I don't blame them, but it becomes like a "food orgy" type reception.

Bob Kastenmeier was at the reception and asked where I was going for the evening. Telling him that Penny Farthing and I were having dinner together at LaColline's, I asked him to join us. Bob insisted that we go "dutch" before agreeing to come along, and so we did. After dinner I returned to the office and phoned John Downey, a friend and a former Peace Corps director I had met in

Malaysia. I wanted information about Malaysia manufacturing cars for export in case there were some possible business arrangements that he knew about in which my son, Bill, might be interested. Leaving the Peace Corps, John now works for the International Catholic Migration Commission in the Philippines, training Vietnamese refugees to resettle in the United States. He said he would get back to me with names for Bill to contact in Malaysia regarding automobile manufacturing.

I made progress today on my trip to East Germany with Rabbi Neuman. The East German Ambassador Gerhard Herder, and Klaus Gysi, Minister for Cultural Affairs, will now be meeting with us very soon.

JANUARY 28 WEDNESDAY

This morning I went directly to the Senate side for a breakfast meeting with the Florida Department of Reserve Officers Association. I met Colonel Boaz Brandmarker who lives in the Biscayne Gardens Condo, and I mention this particularly because it is unusual to have a Jew so much involved as a reserve officer. Also present was a former colleague Bob Sikes who had been Dean of the Florida delegation. Sikes is an old man now, and does not look like the same man who dominated the Florida delegation in the old and powerful days of the conservative, southern Democrats. I was there mainly because the reserve officers of the Coast Guard are included and our transportation subcommittee deals with the Coast Guard Reserve.

On the way into the meeting I saw the newly elected Senator, and feisty liberal Barbara Mikulski (D-MD) and it was good seeing her again. Last evening after the State of the Union Address, she spent most of her time among the House members rather than with her new Senate colleagues. Barbara is on the Senate Appropriations Committee and will be on Appropriations Foreign Operations Subcommittee, so I will be seeing her quite a bit.

At the office I called Marianna Fernandez in Hialeah, who is the cousin of the Cuban Marielito who is dying of AIDS. His mother is now in Miami from Cuba, and I will see the family when I go to Miami. This was a good deed but I really did not personally have much to do with bringing the mother here. The family, however, was most appreciative. Patty Diaz in our district office, who deserves most of the credit, will be on Channel 51 this morning. She is very nervous, but I am happy that she is to be recognized for her hard work in bringing the mother here.

Today I had two luncheon meetings, one with the Petroleum Marketers Association, and the other with a Miami Cuban and Jewish leadership group. At the Petroleum luncheon, I had only one constituent there, a Miami Shores resident, who was also head of the association. We spoke for a while, and I soon left after picking up a few business cards for future Florida fundraisers. Leaving that luncheon, I headed for the Members Dining Room, where Dante Fascell and Larry Smith were hosting the Miami Cuban and Jewish leadership luncheon. This was an effort to reconcile the differences between the two groups, and to pull them together in the community. It was a good turnout, but again I did not stay long as I had to return to the office for a scheduled legislative staff meeting.

Lately it has been difficult and a little frustrating trying to schedule all the staff together at once to go over the issues with which I have to deal. I need to visit the Air Traffic Controllers Center in Oklahoma City, but I do not want to miss any votes to do this. The staff will have to work out the dates when I can be away. This trip is important because funding for air traffic controllers is a big issue in our transportation appropriations subcommittee. The staff was waiting for me when I got to the office, so we went right into our meeting. In addition to the Oklahoma City trip, we spoke about the newsletters to go out on the home nursing care problems we have in Miami and public housing legislation.

My son Bill had a call last week that said one of his employees was going to be kidnapped and held for $20,000 ransom. I called the House Sergeant-at-Arms, Jack Russ, to see what type of precautions we should take in this type of situation. Fortunately it all blew over.

JANUARY 29 THURSDAY

In the office this morning not all of the staff are in, and some won't be coming in at all because of the weather. Living on the Hill is very convenient for me especially when the weather is like it is now, making the road conditions hazardous. My townhouse is only two blocks away from my office, so I can walk to work. Most of the staff live in the suburbs, except for Pat Thorpe, who also lives close to the Hill. The storm has not interfered much with my activities, as last evening I was at three receptions, none of which I enjoyed very much. The Delta Airlines reception was a big disappointment, as was the American Red Cross reception for the author who is writing a book about the American Red Cross. The third reception, hosted by the American Association of Retired People (AARP), was jammed with people. Many members go because they are afraid to miss group events involving elderly voters. I personally think AARP is overrated and, as an organization, it really does not do much to get out the vote at election time. It does, however, initiate some letter-writing campaigns that bother members who do not vote for pro-AARP issues, but in my district AARP does not have much political clout.

John Schelble wants me to spend more time with the news people and television media, and less on newsletters. This will be more prestigious for him. I feel it is perhaps more important for me to get out the newsletters to my district. Yesterday, we had two stories in the *Miami News*, which few people in my area read, but many do read my newsletters. One article about the State of the Union Address contained my remark about the President's statement that "mistakes were made," and my response: "But who the hell made the mistakes." The other story was about the Cuban mother who arrived in Miami to see her dying son. The *Miami Herald* would not print the story unless it could use names and say "dying from AIDS." We were against releasing that information so the *Herald* refused to run the story.

Sharyn Fallick and I have been looking into the possibility of using the Reserve Officers Club as a backup location for our Washington fundraiser. We are trying to find the best possible place and would prefer the Folger Library. The Reserve Officers Club does have the space, but not the elegance of the Folger. To help with the Folger I spoke to Sid Yates, Chairman of Appropriations Subcommittee on the Interior, who has appropriation jurisdiction over the Folger Library as a branch of the National Endowment for the Arts. Sid said he would help. Although the cost would be about two thousand dollars, compared to the Reserve Officers Club, whose fee is between one and two hundred dollars, the Folger has the atmosphere that we are seeking.

A Close-Up group from Notre Dame High School was in. The Carol City Senior High group did not show. Notre Dame High is a private school and the children live mostly in the northeast area of our district. They are nice young people and their questions concerned nuclear weapons and the deterioration of the public schools. Afterwards we went to the Rayburn Cafeteria for lunch and then had photographs taken, which our office will mail to each of them at their homes. We do this cafeteria bit with all the Close-Up groups. I try to be as involved as possible, to leave them with a good feeling about what their visit is all about.

At noon at the Independent Life Insurance Company luncheon meeting, I met the Southeast Florida representative, and we exchanged cards. I saw Harry Teeter, a big supporter and lobbyist for trauma legislation, who has been helpful to me on several occasions, especially in relation to our effort to establish a shock trauma center in Miami; he also supports the funding of shock trauma research at the Centers for Disease Control in Atlanta. In a collaborative effort, we have worked to include in our Transportation bill the transfer of $10-$15 million from the Department of Transportation to the Department of Health and Human Services to be earmarked for the Center for Disease Control in Atlanta for trauma research. Trauma is the number one cause of death for people between 15 and 30 years of age.

3:00 p.m., Bill Bolger, legislative liaison and head of the Air Transportation Association came to the office. The Federal Aviation Administration (FAA) is behind schedule in awarding a $2 billion contract portion of the automated air traffic system contract, and the FAA is required to pay about $70 million to the losing bidder for bid preparation cost. Because the software is slow to develop, the FAA is unable to obligate available appropriation money for the NAS (National Aviation Systems) Plan. The big problem now is determining when the software will be available. It seems IBM, one of the two competitors, is falling behind substantially in its computer software, and will eventually lose the bid. Hughes, IBM's main competitor, will win the bid.

Another problem the subcommittee has is that some want the FAA taken off budget and perhaps recreated as a private corporation so that the FAA would be less subject to politics. Over $4 billion is in the FAA trust fund, and the FAA staff is trying to obligate it as fast as prudently possible. Just throwing money into the NAS Plan or any other program of the FAA is not going to resolve the problems. Our subcommittee does not tell the FAA to whom to award a contract but, nevertheless, if the subcommittee had a serious objection to a bidder, then the FAA would certainly hesitate to contract with that party. Our subcommittee stays out of micro-managing the FAA and I believe the FAA should remain a governmental agency. As the saying goes, "If it ain't really broke, don't fix it." And, for this year at least, I do not believe anything is going to happen on this. The meeting reinforced my knowledge on high-technology regarding the FAA's problems that I will be dealing with this year. It was interesting and made for much complex thinking, as I am not a computer expert or scientist or engineer.

Sharyn called about our fundraiser in Washington. We now have the Folger Library for April 7, at a cost of $2,500, and about two months to put it together. Then, Hal Cessna from WIOD called and said that my statement to him after the State of the Union Address was the best he had and, of course, I was pleased. He also asked if I had a comment on the members' pay raise that was coming up for a vote in the Senate, but I am not commenting on Senate legislation; when the legislation comes to the House, I told Cessna, I will then take a position. I see no point in being a lightning rod at this time by indicating my support for the pay raise.

JANUARY 30 FRIDAY

Sergio Bendixen and I had breakfast together in the Longworth Cafeteria this morning. Sergio is like a son to me; I am somewhat his mentor and he, in some ways, is my mentor. Sergio was very instrumental in my being on the Appropriations Committee by working for the Steering and Policy Committee victory for John Breaux (D-LA). So after John won the Region 12 slot, he used his position on Steering and Policy to support my effort to get on Appropriations and to defeat Andy Ireland of Florida, my competitor who actually had support from six of eleven Florida Democrats. A short time later Andy switched to the Republican party, but I am not sure if this was the reason. This morning Andy joined Sergio and me at breakfast, as we were always good friends.

Sergio told me about the Steve Pajcic campaign for governor of Florida in which Pajcic had been the Democratic nominee defeated by Republican Bob Martinez. He spoke highly of Pajcic and of how well Pajcic performed despite the loss, saying that Pajcic would probably run again for governor in four years. Sergio asked about Bill Nelson who also has the governorship of Florida in mind four years from now, and I told him that Nelson was fine with me and that I liked him as a congressional colleague.

On the way back to the office, we ran into Bill Natcher from Kentucky, who insisted on taking Sergio and me to his office to show us his collections of buckeyes and other knickknacks, including bells from all over the world; his office is a mini-museum. Bill is 76 years old, quite a character, and a fascinating man. He has not missed a vote in the 37 years he has been in Congress. This has become an obsession with him and the first thing he advises new members is to "miss an unimportant early vote." Bill keeps a daily journal which he said was for his grandchildren, and the journal cannot be read until his death. The rumor is that the journal contains some very revealing information, including Bill's idea about what really happened in the Kennedy assassination. Members will approach Bill on the House floor and ask if they are in his journal for that day. The journal will probably be very revealing.

Returning to the office Sergio told me a great deal more about the Pajcic campaign. He also thinks that Jack Kemp will pick up many of the Bush people, and will continue to gain strength for the Republican nomination. We ended with my promising to help his nephew who is hoping to be admitted to Georgetown University.

I then went to the Capitol Physician's Office because I hurt my hand yesterday when I fell playing tennis. The doctor took an x-ray and thought I may have broken a small bone in my wrist and, "as a precautionary measure," he put on a hand cast almost up to my elbow. Now I am wondering if he put the cast on for that reason, or because on Saturday's the doctors are just tired of my coming in. In any case, my right hand will be immobilized for about a week.

Seeing Silvio Conte (R-MA), ranking minority on Appropriations, I told him that despite time running out for the vote deadline, Jim Wright had decided to bring the pay raise up for a vote. I had just read that information in the morning *Washington Post* and Silvio had not known about it. He said, "Oh shit! That son-of-a-bitch! He didn't have to do that and make the members vote on this pay raise. Wait till I call Tip O'Neill. Tip will say the same." Despite the deadline expiration of automatically creating a pay raise, I will vote for the pay raise to show my independence. The vote for a raise makes a member look a little ridiculous to most constituents in the congressional district, but there is another constituency in Washington — your colleagues. A bold vote makes a good image for a member among other members. Colleagues admire such a vote. There is also the message that says a member is strong enough in his district to vote the way he chooses, and that kind of independence is something that people in Washington respect.

The Ryder Trucking Company invited me to play in a pro-celebrity golf tournament. I reminded them that I was a tennis player, not a golfer. Ryder said if it ever held a tennis tournament I would be the first called. I am invited to many charitable functions but I usually don't go. I am not going down to the retreat in Greenbrier with most of the Democrats this weekend, although many of my friends are going. Sometimes they are more partisan Democrat than I am. I try to go with what my responsibilities are, and I do what I have to for the Democrats, but I don't go flat out "Democrats above all." I do want to keep the Democrats as the majority in the House, for if we ever lost this majority, which has never happened since I have been in Congress, then I will lose my chairmanship. The chairman has a lot more authority than the ranking member of the minority party.

There are many good Republicans in the House and I like to see them re-elected. Naturally some Republicans are better than some Democrats, so I don't get carried away with these retreats such as Greenbrier. The retreat is about two-thirds recreational, and if Joan enjoyed going or if we had young children, it would be pleasant to spend time there horseback riding, or some other recreational activity. I do, however, enjoy participating in the Democratic Presidential Convention(s).

The next two weeks beginning Monday the 9th are going to be a little stressful. Joan is coming to Washington on February 6, and we have tickets for the play, "Les Miserables," on the 7th at the Kennedy Center. The House is not in session beginning the week of February 9, and that means my plans have to change. I have to reschedule to leave Washington Tuesday, February 10, go to Oklahoma City on February 11, and fly back to Miami on February 14. There is much rescheduling to do.

January is still too soon to start the subcommittee hearing process and unless we have to come back on February 15, to vote on the pay raise, we will be out for two weeks. Nothing is happening on the Hill now as the committees have not been organized. By late February the committees will be organized and our subcommittee will be ready to hold hearings. Some office appointments will now be cancelled because I will be in Florida or traveling.

In the evening I got with close friend Susan Perry, legislative director for the American Bus Association, for a reception in the Rayburn Building. Sue first came to Washington to work with Senator McCarthy from Minnesota, and is politically very well informed. She is also a good friend of Jim Howard (D-NJ), Chairman of the Public

Works and Transportation Committee, and that makes her a good connection for me as I have to work with Jim constantly on the appropriations' process. Quite often I have joined Sue and Jim having breakfast together in the Rayburn Cafeteria and managed to resolve some problems related to our respective committees.

At the Rayburn Building reception held by the Caucus on Population Planning for the new Chairman of the Congressional Family Planning Caucus, Jim Moody of Wisconsin, Warner Fornos, Executive Director of the Population Planning Council, told me he had just returned from Miami where he met with the *Miami Herald* editorial board. A problem for the Population Planning Council is that the population-concerned lobbyists cannot deliver the votes on the House floor on family planning legislation. Warner said that when the editorial board asked whom he thought the best members in the Florida delegation were, he seemed to take particular delight in telling me that his answer was "Bill Lehman and Dante Fascell."

Afterwards, Sue and I attended a reception for Mike Reed who is retiring from Congressman Bill Gray's Budget Committee staff. Gray also serves on our Transportation Subcommittee. Mike had been his associate staff person for the subcommittee and been very effective in working on legislative language regarding "minority business opportunities" contracts in Transportation Department spending. Gray was the master of ceremonies and when he introduced me, I said that "behind every great staffer there is a great congressman," and everyone seemed to like the twist on the usual cliché. Several other staff members were there, including Art Roberts' wife, Rosalie, who now works for Bill Gray, and Foreign Operations subcommittee staff, Bill Scheuch, a good friend with whom I had taken overseas trips.

Also present was Appropriations Chair Jamie Whitten. Fiscally conservative, Jamie is reluctant to give the appropriations staff the 3-percent automatic raise. One member on the staff whose wife works for the Department of Labor said that his wife, who receives automatic raises, was now earning $10,000 more than he is.

JANUARY 31 SATURDAY

At the Navy Yard Dental Clinic this morning, I had a temporary crown put on my tooth. The doctor said I needed a permanent crown, but I will have to have it done in Miami. The clinic dentist would have liked to put on the permanent crown, but if the Navy Yard Dental Clinic did that type of work, it would be deluged with congressional requests. The Navy Yard Dental Clinic has a hard time meeting all demands, but the dentists there do a commendable job, and they are very meticulous.

From Miami on Friday, February 13, I will fly commercial to Oklahoma City. The FAA Administrator Admiral Donald Engen will fly me back to Miami in his FAA jet. This will save much time returning to Miami. Going with me from our subcommittee will be Democrats Bob Carr of Michigan and Richard Durbin of Illinois; Dave McCurdy and Mickey Edwards both members from Oklahoma, will meet us in Oklahoma City. I appreciate Dave and Mickey's offers of various hospitalities but I just want to go in and out. For me this is a trip only because of the 50 percent drop-out rate among the candidates in the air traffic controllers school, and I want to find out why.

One problem I have with the cast is that I write many handwritten notes to my staff and the notes I am now writing look as though I had a stroke or that they had been written by an elementary student. I also add a lot of handwritten postscripts on my letters. The only consoling thing is that the bubble on the tennis court at Haines Point is still down, so I can't play tennis anyway this week.

Dr. Moynihan in the Capitol Physician's Office was telling me about all the precautions the office took for the President's State of the Union Address. There were several ambulances, evacuation helicopters, and though there is no trauma unit in the Capitol itself, all of the surrounding units were very well prepared for violence.

Chapter 2

FEBRUARY 1, 1987 SUNDAY

My good friend John Buchanan and I had lunch together today. John, a liberal Republican who was defeated last September in the Alabama Republican Primary, had with him a person by the name of Roswell Falkinberry, a relative of one of my boyhood friends in Selma. In the general election, Ben Erdrich, a Jewish Democrat from Birmingham, defeated the far right Republican who had defeated John. I knew Ben's father Stanley when I was at the University of Alabama, and my father was a good friend of Ben Leader, Ben's grandfather. Ben frustrates me because he is a liberal Jew but votes like a redneck ultra conservative just to stay elected. I do not like to see young members vote against their convictions just to get a sixty-five-percent vote next time around. Liberal members who do this still often lose because they dishearten the people who did believe in the member but then become too disillusioned to vote.

FEBRUARY 2 MONDAY

First thing this morning I learned that a colleague, Sala Burton, died Sunday evening. (Sala was the widow of Congressman Phil Burton of California, who died while in office in 1983. Sala won by "special election" in California to fill the vacancy caused by her husband's death.) Don Edwards, Dean of the California delegation, my tennis buddy and close friend, was arranging the testimonial honors and other speeches for Sala. I gave a one-minute speech, and was very pleased to learn that everything I said was well understood and my statements had been taken down correctly by the House reporter, despite the slur in my speech. The speech had continuity and cohesiveness, and this was the first time I had spoken off-the-cuff since my mouth surgery. Following my surgery I have been reluctant to go to the Well, an area just below the Speaker's podium, to speak. This is real progress for me. The following is the speech in its entirety:

> "Mr. Speaker, I thank my friend, the gentleman from California. This House has often been referred to as sort of a fraternity. If this fraternity had a housemother, as fraternities do, Sala was the personification of that kind of person. First impressions are not always the most reliable, but the first impression I had of Sala Burton is one that I still carry in my memory, and it has been reaffirmed and reconfirmed ever since I came here, ever since I have known her. Fourteen years ago I came up to Washington on a dreary, dark late November evening after I had been elected for the first time. I was alone and uncertain. I did not know where to check in. I was over at the Skyline Inn, which is not the most cheerful place in the world to be alone, and there was a note there for me to call Sala Burton. I called Sala Burton, and she introduced herself. She said to me, "Come over to the house tonight for dinner." I went over to their home on Constitution Avenue. It was bright and cheerful. I was made welcome in Washington. It was uplifting, it was rewarding, and it was the beginning of a long-time admiration on my part for Phil and for, especially, Sala. Thank you again, Sala."

A plane will be leaving Thursday morning to take a Congressional delegation to California for the funeral services, but this would be a hard trip for me to go and return the same day. I wish I could travel with the other 150 members, but I need to conserve my energy and a twelve-hour trip will be very strenuous. I spoke with Congressman George Miller of California, a close friend of the Burtons, and he said he understood why I could not make the trip. I then told him about Penny Farthing, a close friend to Sala and a lawyer lobbyist, who wanted to fly with the Congressional delegation to the funeral. George said he would see if he could arrange this, but I really do not see this happening because, ordinarily, private citizens cannot fly on military planes and I doubt seriously if George can do this.

Meeting with Miguel Recarey, President of International Medical Center, the largest HMO in South Florida, I learned he is trying to buy Av-Med, another HMO in Dade County, which operates out of the Dadeland area but has members in my district. Miguel talked and I just listened. When he finished I assured him that I had no problem with what he wanted to do, but I suggested that he also meet with Metro-Dade County officials. [He later became a fugitive from justice.]

The doctor's office called to see whether the wrist cast was on too tight. I went in to have it checked, and it was fine. It is nice to have a doctor call you before you call him. Because the cast is on my right hand, I cannot write memos to the staff, so I am using a small hand recorder. There is a rule change in the Capitol Physician's Office. Until now, I could get free all the vitamin and food supplement pills I needed. Now the only pills I can get free are multivitamins. The other food supplement pills which I am taking because of my chewing and swallowing problems, a result of my surgery, now have to be bought on the outside.

Stopping by the Senate Page luncheon, I met a Carol City High School senior named Richard Coasum who had scored 1150 on his college boards and was applying to Harvard and the University of Florida. He was a very bright, eager African-American who was going to succeed and this was good to see. We had a photo taken to be sent to one of the neighborhood Miami newspapers, and other than Richard the students were anglo-white mid-America high school eager beavers. I was late for a luncheon on the Senate side for the Florida Congressional Delegation, whose guests were officials from the Florida Association of Housing and Redevelopment - and the public housing staff of the State of Florida. None of the guests were Dade County representatives, and I found this most disappointing, because Dade has serious public housing problems.

Encountering colleagues Bill Ford (D. Michigan), Chairman of the House Post Office and Civil Service Committee and Bill Clay of Missouri, also a senior member on that committee, I asked about the pay raise, as they are still working on the legislation, and told them that when it came to a vote I would be supportive. But they already knew I would be.

Larry Smith, a deputy Whip and my colleague from South Broward County, called and asked how I would be voting on the pay raise. I told him that I admired the positive statement he made about the pay raise and that he could count on me. Larry told me that all the Democratic members in Southeast Florida will make a solid vote for the pay raise. This is the type of vote on which we need to stick together. If all of us vote the same way no one in particular gets hurt by whatever public hostility may arise for members voting themselves a pay raise.

3:00, Lottie Hines and her group came in. Lottie is a citizen leader in Liberty City who represents the Public Housing Tenants Association. For these meetings in our office we usually provide too much food or too few people or vice versa. About forty people were expected and only eight showed. The others apparently got lost somewhere between Miami and Washington. In discussing the housing problem, she said that when people move out of public housing projects the Miami Housing Authority did not move quickly enough to rent the apartments. Consequently, the vacant apartments are vandalized, everything is ripped out, and then the apartments are boarded up. Lottie wants the housing authority to have people move into the vacated apartments immediately. I told her we need to have a meeting with the Miami Housing Authority to tell Little HUD to let the Tenants Association immediately select a family to move into the apartment "as is," with reconditioning done with the apartment occupied.

Our office is to arrange a meeting later this month in Miami with Lottie's group and Little HUD officials. I suggested that the media attend the meeting to report any reluctance of the housing authority people to comply with the proposal, and to report about what happens to a housing unit once it is abandoned. Destruction is very costly and there are then no funds for repairs.

Next in was Metro-Dade Transit lobbyist Dennis Vierra, who reported that the Metro-Dade Transit and the Urban Mass Transit Administration (UMTA) were together making progress on the environmental impact statement necessary before construction begins on the Metromover extensions. I told him about the problem of the empty garages in North Dade, pointing out especially the garage at the

Martin Luther King station, and suggested that he find out if there was another use for the garages, such as housing for the homeless. It did not seem right to have these $5 million garages go almost totally unused. This causes a problem, as people will complain that the garages are a waste of tax dollars, and I feel a particular responsibility, as the garages were built with money I earmarked in the jobs bill as a member on the transportation subcommittee during the last years of the Carter Administration.

John and I went over proofs of the daycare newsletter, including photos of the Senate Daycare Center. The newsletter is to encourage support for legislation to be proposed by the Children, Youth and Families Select Committee. I think people are interested in the care of children at this time especially people in Miami because of what happened a few months ago. A mother had to leave her two pre-school children for an hour to work at a Dade County public school lunchroom. Upon returning, she found that her children had been asphyxiated in an automatic clothes dryer. The children's names had been on a waiting list for subsidized daycare for two years.

Miami Herald reporter and political editor Tom Fiedler had a story in today's *Herald* about the aging Florida delegation. Six members over 65 years of age are in the Florida delegation: "Claude Pepper, Charlie Bennett, Sam Gibbons, Bill Chappell, Dante Fascell, and Bill Lehman." The article said that I had the only "safe" seat from being taken over by Republicans should any one of us retire.

In the Senate Caucus Room at an evening gathering of the American Association of Airport Executives and Chairmen of Airport Operators Council, the nation's top airport executives were there, along with the FAA Administrator Admiral Engen, and Dick Judy, Director of Miami International Airport. Dick asked about the possibility of including language in my bill this year to upgrade Tamiami Airport. I told him I would try to help, just as we had done in the past for Opa Locka Airport. Dick wants to set up a satellite FAA school in Opa Locka to train American and overseas air traffic controllers - especially those from Central and South America. Hearing that I was going to Oklahoma City to look at the FAA school, he wanted to go with me, but I was not sure this was a good idea. Dick is very aggressive, too much so at times.

The National Transportation Safety Board officials were also at the meeting. National Transportation Safety Board Chairman Jim Burnett talked about the problems with Eastern Airlines, saying that Eastern would have to become cost competitive and that their labor union must see the handwriting on the wall. Eastern's labor will have to accept the same levels of pay as their competition. I like Jim because when he testifies before our subcommittee hearings, he is so knowledgeable, and gives short, cogent answers. The usual lobbyists were there like Cliff Madison of California, who works for the Los Angeles rapid transit system, and Ed Stimson for the General Aviation Manufacturers Association. Ed is a loyal and good friend despite the fact that I have legislation in the bill restricting general aviation in controlled airspaces. I only stayed about twenty minutes but it was a worthwhile stop.

FEBRUARY 3 TUESDAY

This morning I took our two interns to breakfast: Mark Korvas, a student from Barry University, who lives next door to me in Biscayne Park, and Neil Roberts, a young black student from the University of Houston - both bright young people. I took them through the Speaker's chambers and onto the House Floor, and for a photo opportunity in front of the Capitol, and then to the Members Dining Room for breakfast. They had a good time and said they hoped to be members of Congress some day. I enjoy these meetings with our college interns and it leaves an impression on them and something to talk about when they get home.

After the breakfast, I met with "Close Up" students from Miami Country Day School in Miami Shores and the Carol City Senior High School. The Carol City students were from lower income families, mostly African-American and Hispanic. We had a group question and answer period in the transportation subcommittee room; the students asked about the vote on the pay raise, and I told them I was going to vote for it and why. They seemed well satisfied with the meeting, and afterwards I took them through the Rayburn Cafeteria line and told them to get whatever they wanted, and told the cashier to send the bill to me.

Mid-morning Wayne Merry from the East German desk at the State Department came in as a prelude to tomorrow's meeting with East German Ambassador Herder and Minister Klaus Gysi of the East German Cultural Affairs Department. This is all in preparation for my forthcoming trip to East Germany with the first Rabbi to be allowed to live in East Germany and serve the Jewish community since World War II. Wayne chiefly wanted to review other subjects that may come up during my visit such as trade, corporate exchanges and tourism. Following our meeting, I went to the House Floor where we voted on the veto override of the clean water bill, and by a large margin, the House overrode the President's veto.

On the Floor I spoke to two of the members about possible page appointments for high school students who had applied to me for a page appointment. One applicant was the son of my cousins, Lynn and David Barton of Nashville, Tennessee. I gave that request to Congressman Bill Boner from Nashville who knows the family. He thinks he can probably give young Barton a job in his office. I also spoke to Larry Smith about helping another young man with a page appointment, as he is from Larry's district. These were both summer page applicants, and I have already made commitments for the next two summers. I do not like disappointing these young people but I am allowed only one page per summer. When possible I try to find them a job with members in whose districts they live. Being a Congressional Page is a highly regarded, highly competitive, and prestigious position for students in their junior year of high school, and having held this position is impressive on a student's college application.

A *Federal Times* reporter came in about the Leave Sharing legislation for government employees. We included this legislation in the appropriations continuing resolution in the last Congress, which allows Federal employees, facing a personal or medical crisis and having exhausted their sick leave, to use sick and annual leave donated from other employees. It was a very good piece of legislation which I had originally initiated as a demonstration project in the Appropriations Subcommittee on Treasury, Postal Service and General Government. The idea of the legislation came about by happenstance. In August of 1986, while visiting the IRS office in North Dade on one of my customary visits to Federal agencies that work with cases from our district office, I asked Gary Krevat if there was anything I could do for him and his office. He then told me about the Chiles's. Thirty-five-year-old Shannon Chiles, terminally ill with cervical cancer, had used all of her and her husband Joe's 240 hours of annual paid leave during Shannon's operations and chemotherapy treatment. Shannon had been diagnosed with this illness after giving birth to her second child in 1985. Both Shannon and her husband worked for this IRS office and Krevat was Shannon's supervisor. My staff and I went to work almost immediately on writing legislation for a pilot program to see how it would work and what it would cost to have federal employees donate their sick and annual leave. Since this was in August, there were only six working weeks left before Congress adjourned for the year, and I wanted to introduce the leave sharing legislation before the break. I knew that time was crucial both for the Chiles's and for me to figure out a way to get this particular legislation introduced. After failing at having the amendment attached to a civil service bill, I attached it to the appropriations continuing resolution, a $567 billion catchall spending measure. I then approached several members of Congress who chaired key committees, and received indications of their support. To gain even more leverage support, two other demonstration projects for leave sharing were added to the amendment.

When the spending measure passed, with the demonstration project for the Chiles's intact, I was thrilled, and in a phone interview from my district office with States News Service, I said, "I didn't think we had a chance," which was repeated in the newspaper account on the Shannon Chiles story. [Later, the *Miami News* reported that IRS workers all over the Southeast donated more than $17,000 and almost 6,000 hours of leave to the Chiles's in less than one year.]

An interesting thing happened on the House Floor today - some parliamentary maneuvers on the pay raise vote. The pay raise would automatically go into effect unless the House voted not to do so by February 5. Some members wanted the House to adjourn before bringing up the Homeless bill, but a small group of Republicans wanted the bill brought to the Floor so that the anti-pay raise language, in the Senate version of the Homeless bill, would then be part of the House bill. What happened first was a division vote, a non-recorded vote on whether the House should adjourn. This vote was three to one for adjournment. The person in the Chair at that time was Acting Speaker Steny Hoyer of Maryland. When the division vote was announced, Steny said, "The House is now adjourned," and he then quickly vacated the Chair. This, of course, left the Republicans with their mouths open. The Republicans were going to ask for a roll-call vote but now they must wait until tomorrow. The time, however, will first expire as the vote would have had to take place before midnight February 5. That is how we will get our pay raise. It was a back-door scheme to have the pay raise without a vote, and it was fun to watch.

In my one-minute speech on the House Floor today to protest the nuclear test explosion today in Nevada, I called it "trigger happy" because the Defense Department should have waited until the test ban expired before exploding a nuclear device. Seeing George Miller on the Floor, I gave him a condolence letter to give to John Burton, Sala's brother-in-law. George again said he understood how difficult a trip it would be for me to fly out to California and back the same day, and also told me that he had been unable, as I suspected, to gain permission for Penny Farthing to fly with the Congressional delegation to Sala's funeral.

Much had to be done today. I have been working with my colleague Pete Stark of California in an attempt to obtain a chiropractor's license for my cousin, Beth Marx, who now lives in Pete's Oakland district. At noon I met Lottie Hines of Liberty City and her people to take them to the Members Gallery so they could watch the session on the House Floor. I also walked over to the Members Gallery to see John Stembridge and his entourage of human rights activists. Adele Liskov has done a good job in handling the John Stembridge agenda for me, so I did not have to listen to his speeches. John is a former Mayor of North Miami, and I often run into him in the district. When I am having breakfast at Neighbors Restaurant in North Miami, John comes over to the table and I can't get rid of him. He tries to do so much good but is over-dedicated and difficult to listen to so frequently. Adele said he is like flypaper, "You just can't shake him." He is, however, right on the issues, and today he spoke about the problems in Haiti.

Sergio Bendixen has again asked me to get in touch with Father George from Georgetown University in an effort to get his nephew, who is from Peru, into the school. Father George is the Georgetown University lobbyist specializing in Federal legislation. Our subcommittee has helped Father George with funding for a battery-powered bus demonstration project. When I got Father George on the phone, he began telling me he had just seen Esther Debra Benchoam who was applying to the Georgetown University Law School. He is trying to help with her admission even though her admission test scores are not high. Debra is the twenty-year-old political prisoner I helped free from an Argentine prison and who has subsequently become my surrogate daughter. Apparently Father George has not received all the necessary paperwork from Sergio's nephew, and I will leave that message with Sergio.

Following my brief meeting with Richard Meed from the Southeast Mortgage Company of Miami, Sonny Billie came in about the environmental and educational problems of Miccosukee Indians that live out on Tamiami Trail. A Mr. Lupo was in next about an extension of his Federal employment until June, before he is forced into retirement with the Customs Office in Miami. We went to Appropriations Subcommittee on Treasury, Postal Service, and General Government to see if Tex Gunnels or Bill Smith, two subcommittee staff members, could intercede with Customs to grant him an extension. Lupo is a member of Rabbi Max Lipschitz's Beth Torah congregation in my district. The Customs Office may be pushing him around, but I believe he is also a nuisance to them. Then Susan Kellon from the *Federal Times* came in with a photographer for an interview and photo for the *Federal Employees* newspaper. The interview was about Shannon Chiles, and this should be a good story and of real interest to Federal employees nationwide.

Patrice Rosemond from our district staff is in Washington, and we walked over to the Cannon Building to meet with the new black Representative from Mississippi, Mike Espy. I wanted Espy to meet Patrice because I have asked him to be the honored guest at my annual Black Leadership Meeting in Miami in April, and Patrice is putting this event together.

Many calls come in to our Washington office from constituents. Most of these calls asking for help should be directed to the district office, but I try to handle them, making a call back from Washington, which seems to make a very good impression on constituents. Since my arm has been in a cast, I have been exercising in the Rayburn Building Gym on the stationary bicycle and treadmill. It is fun to see who is doing what there. Jim Florio [future Governor of New Jersey] was a professional boxer twenty years ago and even has a broken nose to show for it. He tackles the boxing bag as if he were still in training for a welterweight championship and goes through all the motions of a professional fighter. Most of the younger members play basketball; there are so many that they play ten at a time - ten play and ten sit out. The gym has more members now than ever. Less paddleball is played and none of the people that played paddleball fourteen years ago when I first came to the Congress are playing it today. In fact, most of the members who were here fourteen years ago are now only in the steam room.

Indiana member Lee Hamilton was in the gym, and told me about his new job heading the Special Task Force for the Iran-Contra Investigation. He said that just because Israel suggested that we ship arms to Iran did not mean that we had to sell them everything Israel suggested. Lee, a member on the Foreign Affairs Committee, is Chairman of the Subcommittee on Europe and the Mid-East. Next to Dante Fascell, Lee is the most powerful member in the House on foreign affairs authorizing legislation. He is also highly respected and well liked, and many members watch how Lee votes on controversial issues as his vote is like a weather vane.

Appropriations Foreign Ops Chair Dave Obey called this afternoon and asked if I wanted to go to Central America during the February recess on a fact-finding mission. I told him that I had already made plans to take some of my subcommittee members out to Oklahoma City to visit the Air Traffic Controllers School.

Later I went to see Tom Luken, head of the authorizing subcommittee on Amtrak, to set up an appointment for Jack and Sid Langer of the City Gas Company. [Luken is the member with whom the Langers should meet to help settle their claim against the Federal Railway Administration. This claim has been hanging around for about seven years, and I had been telling the Langers for just about all of that time to get a sign-off from the authorizing committee chairman, who was Jim Florio at that time, and they never did. Now I am trying to have them do it with present chairman Tom Luken of Ohio. The Langers hire expensive Washington lawyers who charge them a huge fee and never finish the job. Amtrak built a station near City Gas's tank farm and then City Gas had to move the tanks because their insurance rates escalated. Maybe it is true that that is the reason the move was made, or maybe not.]

5:30 p.m., I went to a reception in the Russell Senate Office Building for a reception given by the Council for a Liveable World and its Peace PAC. Jerry Grossman heads the PAC and has supported me in the past. Many senators were there, and as I was walking in the senators were walking out to vote. Apparently the Senate is in session late tonight. It was interesting to see the Senators there I knew who had once served in the House, such as Paul Sarbanes of Maryland and Max Baucus of Montana. I also met Senator Howard Metzenbaum of Ohio who asked for my help in selling his Mustang automobile that he had left at his condo on Miami Beach.

Going to the Senate side, I ran into Jack Kemp and told him that I had been speaking to Sergio Bendixen and that Sergio had said, "In 1988, Jack would be the one to watch." With President Reagan losing his popularity, Vice President Bush's polls went down and the Bush vote would shift to Kemp rather than to Dole. Kemp said, "Dynamics are hard to predict, but I've made up my mind that it is going to be either up, over or out in 1988 for me."

It has been a very active day for me, constituent oriented, talking to people every few minutes, and I can't believe all that has happened today.

FEBRUARY 4 WEDNESDAY

At 8:30, I attended an Eastern Airlines breakfast hosted by Eastern's new President, Bill Bakes, who formerly was President of Texas Air. Several years ago when Bill was President of Texas Air, I helped him on an appropriation bill by not defeating bill language that would have prevented Texas Air from going into Chapter Eleven. I may have antagonized the pilots union by not complying with their demands, but I did not believe such legislative language should be part of our appropriations bill. I did what I thought was right at the time. In Bakes's speech this morning he discussed the problems of getting Eastern Airlines' costs down. The best example was that Eastern was paying baggage handlers $42,000 a year, twice as much as competing companies, but the most troubling problem for him, he said, is building morale among workers and gaining their trust.

The old Eastern Airlines management under Frank Borman had lost the confidence of the employees, and Eastern's now very controversial CEO Frank Lorenzo inherited the problem. Lorenzo does not have a handle on controlling the costs of Eastern Airlines, but he asked for a meeting with the Florida Delegation. Both Senators and most of the Representatives were at the meeting. Lorenzo asked us not to do anything but to give him some time to build a system that could be reconstituted in South Florida to maintain the workforce there. He said that the Eastern facilities in Miami were so tremendous and valuable that they could not be replaced elsewhere for millions of dollars. There were some hostile questions from Senator Pepper and from Larry Smith, who is anti-Eastern management and who has many Eastern employees living in his South Broward district.

After the breakfast, I joined the Select Committee on Children, Youth and Families, who needed me for a quorum in the committee's Democratic Caucus. Chairman George Miller asked me to remain as Chair of the Task Force Subcommittee on "Prevention Strategy," as I had said that I would like to relinquish the chair of that task force because I don't have the time to devote. This day the quorum was never obtained so the Caucus was re-scheduled.

East German Ambassador Gerhard Herder and East German Minister of Cultural Affairs, Secretary Klaus Gysi, came in at 10:30 a.m. The East German government is now rebuilding the once famous 6,000-seat capacity synagogue in East Berlin and they want me to make this trip to East Germany. They do not foresee any problems in providing a visa for Rabbi Neuman whom the American Jewish Committee has selected to serve in East Germany. The visa will be a multiple entry visa so that the Rabbi can go back and forth between East and West Germany as often as he chooses. Herder and Gysi are hoping that I will go, and are planning visits for me to various places such as the old Jewish cemetery and old Jewish communities that still survive in East Germany. After the meeting I took Gysi to the House Floor. The House was not in session, but he spoke with some of the House pages. We entered the Speaker's Chambers, and Gysi was given a notepad which read, "From the Speaker's Room," and we all had a photo opportunity with Speaker Jim Wright. Gysi seemed very impressed with the special treatment he received.

Members are beginning to come to me with transportation appropriation requests. Charlie Rose of North Carolina wants airport money for one of the smaller airports in his district; Bill Boner from Nashville also wants airport money. I spoke to Pete Stark about the status of my cousin Beth Marx's California chiropractor's license. He was to review her test scores and try to help, as she had failed part of the exam. My son Bill told me that he received a call from the House Sergeant-at-Arms staff regarding security after the threatening phone call Bill received at his office. I called Sid and Jack Langer to get things going with their meeting with Tom Luken regarding the Amtrak problem. And Congressman Claude Pepper called to accept my invitation to join Joan and me Saturday evening to see the play "Les Miserables." Claude said he was looking forward to going with us.

Larry Smith told me that he had a page position for Maryann Osmand's grandchild who had applied for a page position with my office. Maryann lives at Point East Condo, which is in our district. Since Annie Ackerman, the condo leader at Point East, had asked me to arrange this, I was very pleased that it turned out so favorably. And Bill Boner called to let me know that young Barton would be his summer page. Bill wanted to do this because he will be leaving the House and running for Mayor of Nashville and wants our transportation subcommittee to appropriate about $200,000 for a study on the rapidly expanding Nashville Airport. Indirectly, through Larry Smith and Bill Boner, I was able to please not only the students, who are very deserving, but also all those involved with the requests.

2:00 p.m., I was in a meeting in Senator Graham's office in the Hart Building with Lucy Hand and Marsha Runningen from my staff. Senator Graham and his staff wanted to discuss the issues he should be aware of in my 17th district. I told him about problems we were concerned with in transportation, especially the ceiling limitations on the highway and the FAA trust fund. I told him about problems with public housing in our district in the Liberty Square and Carver Public Housing Projects as well as in the Carol City Villa Housing Project, and said that I would be visiting some of these areas when I go back to Miami next week. I also mentioned the tri-county rail problem as to the State being able to use highway trust funds to subsidize the Tri-County Rail in repairing I-95. Talking with Bob Graham is a pleasure, as he seems to have his feet on the ground. His staff is very competent, some of them having worked with him in the Florida Governor's office.

Seeing the Calder sculpture in the atrium of the Senate Hart Building for the first time, I was very impressed. Leaving the Senate building, I had time before returning to the Floor for a possible vote to have lunch with Lucy and Marsha at the Brasserie. This is the first time in a long while I am able to do a lunch like this in a work day. Back in the office I spoke to the *Ft. Lauderdale News* about the public housing problems in Carol City.

My next appointment with Gerard Jonti, a Haitian working for the Miami Chamber of Commerce, concerned a problem he had with the Federal government and the way he was laid off from his employment. At the time, Jonti was living and working in New York, so I got Congressman Major Owens of New York from Jonti's old district on the phone, and arranged a meeting between them. He does have a justifiable complaint, and I was glad to be of help. Jonti now lives in my district and works for the New York Life Insurance Company.

At the gym I exercised on the bicycle for about ten minutes. On the bicycle next to me was my good friend Butler Derrick from South Carolina. I especially like his ex-wife Suzanne, with whom Joan and I traveled when Butler and I have gone on codels together. There is a lot of activity in the gym with many people using the new equipment and "pumping iron." I saw Andy Jacobs whose ex-wife Martha is the sister of Senator Gary Hart's wife Lee. Andy still has lunch with Martha once a week and is hoping, if Gary Hart is reelected, to find Martha a job in the White House and not worry about nepotism. I said to him, if the Kennedy's could do it then why not Gary.

Leaving the gym, I saw Bill Nelson in his jogging outfit. He came to the breakfast this morning in the same running attire, and it seems to me he is spending more time getting into better physical condition than he is working. More members now are in the gym than I have ever seen over the past fifteen years. Physical fitness is really big these days, and will probably remain so.

I went to the Appropriations front office to ask staffer Ed Powers [who died two years later of AIDS] whether the Appropriations Committee would pay for my travel to East Germany. Ed is very familiar with the authorization process for members' overseas travel, and he assured me that there would not be a problem. Ed formerly was on the staff of Appropriations Foreign Ops Subcommittee, but when Dave Obey became chairman of that subcommittee, Ed was moved to Appropriations front office, where he has a close relationship with Appropriations Chair Jamie Whitten. With a new chairman, a move such as this is not unusual.

It was on a Congressional Delegation (CODEL) with Ed Powers in 1986 to East Berlin that I met our U.S. Ambassador to East Germany, Francis Meehan. Meehan was the first to bring to my attention the lack of and need for a Rabbi in East Germany and the difficulties of arranging this. I told the Ambassador that I was very interested in helping to bring this about, and that I would see what I could do to help.

When I got back to the States, Eugene Dubow of the New York-based American Jewish Committee flew down to meet with me. He had heard of my visit with Ambassador Meehan and of my interest in placing a Rabbi in East Germany. Eugene has been struggling with this cause since 1983, ever since he and an AJC delegation went to East Germany and met with Peter Kirchner, president of the East Berlin Jewish community. A year after their meeting, the East German Government did give permission for an American rabbi to visit in East Germany on the High Holy Days, but would not allow a rabbi to stay and serve the Jewish community on a continual basis. The Jewish community wanted a rabbi who would have a permanent place in their community, not just one who came over from West Berlin for special occasions. Dubow had found Rabbi Neuman, who is from New York, but he has not yet been successful in persuading the East German government to let him stay.

Penny Farthing and I went this evening to a fundraiser for Jim Jontz, the newly elected Democrat from Indiana who pulled an upset victory in a Republican district in Indiana. The event was held at Victor Kamber's interesting home, which is filled with various types of art - some strange and some very nice. Victor heads the Kamber Group and helps in Congressional campaigns as well as lobbies for special interests, especially organized labor. When Victor puts on a fundraiser, he brings in his special interest people such as the Association of American Meat Producers, who were there. One does not usually see these groups at other fundraisers, and I will speak with Sharyn about possibly using Victor to help with my fundraisers.

FEBRUARY 5 THURSDAY

We are not in session now so it will be a quiet day. The pay raise will be on hold for a while, but surprisingly many members are speaking out for the pay raise. Our office has received lots of mail on this issue. I drafted a very brief letter thanking people for contacting us regarding the pay increase and then briefly explained my views on the issue. In a Rayburn Building corridor surrounded by reporters was New York Governor Mario Cuomo. Mario definitely has a special aura, and made a big impression yesterday talking to the Banking Committee about the homeless problems in New York and around the country.

Richard Durbin from Illinois, a member on our transportation subcommittee, called to complain about the date change of our hearing to February 19, with the Secretary of Transportation. Dick is also on the Budget Committee and was to be in California for a meeting on the 19th, and wanted us to reschedule. I explained that we could not reschedule Secretary Dole as it was the only time she could make the hearing. He was unhappy, but I said I would arrange for him to have a photo opportunity with the Secretary. I'm very fond of Dick, a valuable member of our subcommittee.

At noon I attended the Seabreeze Award Ceremony. The cosmetic company Seabreeze was giving an award to Diana (Ana) Gomez from my district, who is totally deaf. Other disabled, mostly hearing impaired, people were there. What was so interesting about Ana was that her mother speaks only Spanish and her father speaks only English and Ana has to use two different types of sign language to communicate with her parents. I had understood that Miss America was going to be at the luncheon, and I mentioned this to a young lady standing nearby. She said, "I'm Kellye Cash and I'm Miss America. How about taking a picture with me." She was Johnny Cash's niece and I had my photo taken with her and with Ana Gomez.

During my last year's trip in November/December to Sri Lanka, I met with three members of the International Executive Service Corp., which is funded by approximately $6 million earmarked by our Foreign Operations Subcommittee to help small businesses. This group is headed by retirees who go overseas to help third world businesses, and with the small amount of money they receive, they do a lot of good in over thirty third world countries. I hope to eventually develop a newsletter on these working retirees and the good that they do.

In a call to Al Moore, head of Little Hud in Miami, I arranged a public housing meeting to try to solve the vandalism problem of vacant public housing units. Then Jim Mayera, a freelance writer from North Miami, stopped by the office unannounced. He had just come from the National Institutes of Health (NIH) and was writing a story for the *Miami News* about people in Miami with AIDS who are taking a drug to combat this disease, which the Food and Drug Administration (FDA) has not approved. He said Medicare disability does not take effect until twenty-five months after diagnosis, and the average lifespan after diagnosis of AIDS is only sixteen months. We went to see Mike Stephens, chief staff on Appropriations Health and Human Services Subcommittee, to provide him with additional information on what is taking place with these unfortunate AIDS victims, and John Schelble will get a media release on this story.

Esther Kurtz from the American Israel Public Affairs Committee (AIPAC) came to my office to explain the agenda for the Sunday evening event AIPAC is holding at the LaColline Restaurant on Capitol Hill. At least a dozen House members have been invited, and we will be joined by about fifty of AIPAC's major donors.

In the evening I went to the American Psychological Association reception for Silvio Conte (R-MA). The association had expected the House to be in session when scheduling the event, and it was not. Only about one fourth of the people expected were there, and I was the only member. I did not stay very long as it was not much of a reception in comparison to the one I attended several years ago for Silvio in Ted Kennedy's home in Virginia.

CBS Broadcast called about the T-CAS System for air-collision avoidance which our subcommittee is funding in the FAA appropriation. The Pilots Association had told CBS to get in touch with me. The T-CAS is a very technical piece of equipment, and I was very careful with what I said to CBS as I wanted any information or statements to be totally accurate. Following the phone conversation with CBS, I called Tom Kingfield, staff director of our Appropriations Transportation Subcommittee, suggesting that we try to get the FAA to move faster with the installation of the T-CAS.

FEBRUARY 6 FRIDAY

Several phone calls have come in regarding the sick leave system we worked out for Shannon Chiles. Bill Gradison of Cincinnati was having a similar problem with his Federal employees, and I explained to him the procedure we used to get this done. Seeing Dante Fascell, I told him I had asked a leading question about Israel to Lee Hamilton, head of the Iran-Scam Task Force of the House Investigation Committee. I wanted to get Dante's reaction, and Dante, who is Chairman of the Foreign Affairs Committee, also assured me that Israel would not have a problem with the Iran-Contra chaos.

FEBRUARY 7 SATURDAY

Joan and I saw "Les Miserables" at the Kennedy Center this evening with Peggy Gordon, our house guest from Miami Beach, who was escorted by Senator Claude Pepper. As we stood

in the lobby before taking our seats, many people came up to greet Pepper and to thank him for all that he had done. It was like a receiving line, and I had never seen so much admiration for any member since being in Washington. Foreign Ops Subcommittee Chair Dave Obey was also at the theater with his wife Joan and their boys - quite a lovely family.

FEBRUARY 8 SUNDAY

This morning I stopped by Pete Stark's house, two blocks from my townhouse, and announced to him that "We are going to the American Cafe for brunch." Pete's newest lady friend Debbie, who was once an intern in his office, joined us at the cafe, as did Dante Fascell. We talked about going to Pete's house in Eastern Shore, Maryland when summer comes to play tennis on his private court. The weekends I like to keep in touch with such friends and colleagues as Pete Stark, Don Edwards, and Dante, not only for company, but because as members we share a common bond. Don Edwards also has a lovely place on the Eastern Shore, and I will be visiting him this summer. I also saw Sam Gejdenson of Connecticut and asked if he was going to the AIPAC dinner this evening. Gejdenson said he would be there, but he could only stay about an hour because he had to return to his district for a meeting.

Later in the afternoon Joan, our house guest Peggy, and I went to the Navy Museum for a celebration honoring the America's Cup winners. Bill Lowery of California, a Republican member on Appropriations, hosted the event because the race was in his district. It was a nice celebration but we did not stay very long.

We went next to the AIPAC dinner for members at LaColline. Close friends from Miami were at the dinner including Jerry Berlin and Harvey Friedman. About twelve members from Congress and approximately 100 other people were there. The AIPAC contributors wanted to meet some of the members they had helped elect to urge them to hold firm on their supportive position on Israel. This included both Democrats and Republicans. Foreign Ops Chair Dave

Obey, who I very much admire, was there, and everyone was in good spirits. Each member made a speech and I suggested that we make this an annual affair.

FEBRUARY 9 MONDAY

For several hours now I have been working on a potential newsletter on "How a Bill Becomes a Law." We did a newsletter several years ago on how my Appropriations Transportation Subcommittee bill became a law, and explained the appropriations process. This newsletter will explain how a bill becomes a law in the general sense. Leaving the office to see the Speaker's appointment secretary, I am hoping to encourage Jim Wright to make a trip to Miami in June for a fundraiser for the South Florida Democratic Party.

In the evening at a reception for the Sri Lanka foreign minister held at the residence of the Sri Lankan Embassy, I found it interesting that the Soviet Ambassador Yuri Dobryin was at this very modest reception. There was also Richard Murphy, ranked second to Secretary Schultz in our State Department. I believe they attended because the United States is trying to obtain base rights for our Navy in Sri Lanka, and I am sure the Soviets would not like to see that happen. I met Richard in 1978 when he was an Ambassador to Manila in the Philippines, meeting Joan and me at the plane and putting flower leis around our necks when we arrived in Manila. He has come up through the Foreign Service Office ranks and been one of our Mideast peace negotiators.

I complained to the foreign minister that I was displeased with the way the Israeli representatives in Sri Lanka had been treated and the unfavorable comments about Israel made in their Parliament during my visit to Sri Lanka last December. I said there was no call for the negative comments, especially after the President of Israel had visited their country on a goodwill mission. I did not want to make a big issue there because at that time Richard Murphy was a negotiator in the Mideast. He was in a good mood as he had just learned that the threatened execution of the American hostages in the Mideast had been postponed. It was a reception at which to be. My friend and colleague Charlie Wilson of Texas said to me that "these little countries like Sri Lanka do not have the strength to support Israel in any meaningful way and only the United States can do so in a broad-based manner."

FEBRUARY 10 TUESDAY

James Emery, Administrator for the St. Lawrence Seaway, and Larry Coughlin, ranking minority member on our subcommittee, came in for their 10:00 a.m. appointment. The problem with the St. Lawrence Seaway is that in last year's legislation the funding for the Seaway was put on budget. In the past it was off budget and came under the jurisdiction of our subcommittee. I have no motivation to keep it off budget as I prefer to see all such independent agencies on budget. The Seaway will have a problem with lack of funds if it does not get an appropriation supplemental bill or a bill to reverse the authorizing legislation, giving it the right to keep the revenue generated from the U.S. portion of the St. Lawrence Seaway. The Seaway is not a very large part, but a very complicated part of our jurisdiction in the Transportation Appropriations Subcommittee. Carl Purcell (R-MI), in particular, has a provincial interest in the St. Lawrence Seaway, as the steel industry is large in the Midwest and a great deal of revenue is lost to the Seaway because of the lack of steel exports. And, we do not send much manufactured products through the Seaway anymore as most Seaway cargo is now agricultural products.

Ray Kudisch, who represents Racal-Milgo Corporation in South Florida, came in about potential legislation that would give the "Baby Bells" (Southern Bell, New England Bell), the right to manufacture electronic products, which they do not now have under Judge Green's ruling to separate the Baby Bells from AT&T. A movement is in Congress to permit them to manufacture, but this would handicap the Racal-Milgo's electronic equipment firm in its sales to AT&T. Ray thanked me for not cosponsoring the proposed bill. Then Elton Gissendanner from South Florida came in to discuss beach restoration problems in Sunny Isles. Elton was concerned about the new super-highrise hotel that the Sheraton Hotel chain wants to build at the north end of Sunny Isles. He also wanted me to know he may be trying for a federal position in the near future and may need a letter of recommendation from me. As a former working veterinarian in Miami, Elton took care of our pets. He later became Mayor of North Miami, and was always a decent man. I like him, and told him I would gladly write the letter of recommendation.

We put a statement in the *Congressional Record* today regarding Jewish condo leaders going to Little Havana and meeting with leaders there to "build bridges" for better relations between South Florida Jews and Cuban-Americans. It is quite dispiriting to see our communities so polarized and fragmented, as is much of our country, and any effort to pull everyone together should only help. You have to start somewhere.

At the Arts Caucus luncheon in the Longworth Building, the luncheon was held to elect either Bob Carr of Michigan or Ted Weiss of New York as the new chair of the Arts Caucus. I voted for Carr, and he won. The previous two chairmen had come from the East, and I believed it was time for someone other than from New York; also, Carr is on my transportation subcommittee. Though Carr may know something about the theater (and he may be a frustrated actor) he does not know much about the visual arts. The election drew a big attendance, but I could not stay long as I had to catch a plane to Miami.

I found out why the Soviet Ambassador and the State Department's Richard Murphy were at the Sri Lankan Embassy Reception Monday evening. It seems the Sri Lankans are having problems with the Tamils in the north of their island country where a revolt is happening. Sri Lanka needs military aid and both the United States and the Soviets want base rights in Sri Lanka. Certainly the Soviets would want to stop us from getting this, especially in such ports as Colombo on the Indian Ocean.

FEBRUARY 11 WEDNESDAY

In Miami this morning, I went first to the district office and then to the Highland Oaks Junior High School to talk to a social studies class. I do not do this for the students as they don't care, but because Norma Schmidt, a teacher at Highland Oaks is a loyal supporter. She has been a great help to me in Miami Shores and has come out for me on many occasions when some of her Miami Shores friends and neighbors have been opposed to positions I have taken. The students in her class asked the usual questions on how members get elected, on the pay raise, on Nicaragua, etc. At one time, students asked more questions about abortion and marijuana, but not now.

That evening Joan and I attended a party on Miami Beach given by one of my supporters, Joe Kantor, a big banker in Miami. The party was for his wife who was a nightclub singer thirty-five years ago. Joe rented a nightclub for the party so that his wife could sing again to an audience. He has been a steady supporter, so I was obligated to go; and when I wanted to leave early, he insisted that I stay for his wife's performance. I did stay and she was good. Several of my supporters were there, and it was good to be at a local social event among these people as opposed to just seeing them as lobbyists in Washington.

FEBRUARY 12 THURSDAY

At the district office I made several calls to Washington and learned that the public housing information I had given Senator Graham and his staff may have triggered some action. Senator Graham was in Miami today checking on public housing, and it may have preempted us in what we had planned for this Friday regarding problems with Carol City public housing. Leaving the office in the early afternoon, I went home to rest and to get ready for my trip late this afternoon to Oklahoma City. I did not want to make this trip, but I had to because this is where the Air Traffic Control School is located and the school is one of the FAA's big problems. If I am going to be responsible for FAA financing, I have to find out why there is such a high dropout rate at the school.

When I arrived in Oklahoma City at 9:30 p.m., Dave Carmichael, Assistant to Jim Richardson of the Aeronautical Center, met me at the airport and we went directly to the hotel where they had arranged the usual VIP welcome.

FEBRUARY 13 FRIDAY

Today marks almost six years since the air traffic controllers walked out and the FAA has had to rebuild almost from scratch the safety management of our airways. The process has been slow and difficult. We have been fortunate, despite the increase in air passenger service, that there have been so few air traffic fatalities - though the number of near-misses has increased. At 8:00 a.m., I started my tour by first going to the FAA warehouse, a very efficient and very automated facility.

Next was a visit to the laboratories and the classrooms.

The FAA last year admitted that there were still too few controllers who were "full performance" (fully trained) - about 64% of the total compared to 80% before the strike. There are some high-density airports such as O'Hare in Chicago where the controllers are even below the national average. Therefore, in 1987, in our transportation appropriations part of the omnibus continuing resolution we mandated that by September 30, the FAA must have at least 15,000 controllers and a certain percent had to be full performers. But writing legislation does not automatically produce results. I made this visit so that I could see up close what was happening and to help quicken the recovery of our air traffic system. The visit did not remove all my concerns but what I saw and learned were somewhat reassuring.

The quality of applicants selected for the Air Traffic Controllers Academy was first rate, and those I encountered were extremely bright and motivated. To be a good controller requires a special kind of three-dimensional conception and a great deal of concentration. To my surprise, those enrolled in the academy were not being taught how to operate the control towers or the enroute stations. For that they are sent to "on the job training" at centers and stations. The students told me they were living in a pressure cooker much like a Marine bootcamp. The attrition rate caused by rigid entry standards in the academy has reduced the failures in the field to less than 10 percent. This saves the taxpayers money and prevents personal disruption to those who find too late that they cannot cut it as air traffic controllers. After about two years in the field the controllers are back at the academy to receive radar and other instructions and then return to a station to serve as full performers.

I also saw the full performers being trained at the academy to become instructors. The cycle is continuous because after the age of thirty-five, the controllers' operating efficiency diminishes. High-density airport control towers such as O'Hare are duplicated in the academy so people from O'Hare can be tested and trained to deal with the difficulties they may encounter at that location. A unique operation occurs in the use of the physically disabled who work at the academy as simulated or "ghost" pilots, giving the handicapped an opportunity to work under highly-motivated conditions. They are in mockup cockpits in one room and communicate with air traffic controllers at their screens in a separate room. As I left the academy, FAA Administrator Admiral Engen said to me, as words of caution, that the human mind is still the weakest link in our safety and that air-traffic control is very labor intensive. He was so right, as all the training and all the computer fail-safe backups can never completely overcome human fallibility. But within the limits of technology, our dedication and commitment, the FAA is being responsible to both the safety and the growth of our airways.

Later in the afternoon I joined Admiral Engen and flew back to Miami in his FAA jet. It took five hours to arrive in Oklahoma City flying commercially and only two and a half hours to return on his private jet. It is an ideal way to travel. Accompanying me to Oklahoma City were members from my subcommittee - Bob Carr and Richard Durbin - and Dave McCurdy, a member from Oklahoma. It was a worthwhile venture and a good learning experience. This was strictly a business trip and I never saw inside the Oklahoma City limits. As a favor to Lany Narot, the widow of our Rabbi and a frequent visitor to Washington, I did stop at a famous boot store to buy a pair of lavender cowboy boots that Lany had asked me to bring back.

FEBRUARY 14 SATURDAY

At the district office this afternoon a *Miami Herald* freelance writer, Norma Orovitz came in. Norma is doing a story on specific people and how they manage their offices. She was surprised that I did not use my desk more, preferring instead to work from a medium-size table in my office. I have no idea if and when this story may appear in the *Miami Herald*, but it was fun working with Norma.

Herb Stettin had a reception this evening at his super-sumptuous home. Herb is a lawyer friend in Southwest Miami, and these receptions are both social and political as many of the guests are politicians or affluent people who have contributed to my past campaigns, and I like to keep in touch with them. Herb and his wife had their home built at a cost of about $2 million. The builder was Ron Ager and the architect was Alfred Browning Parker, both longtime friends of mine. Herb is a former judge who went back to the more lucrative profession of practicing law.

FEBRUARY 15 SUNDAY

This morning Jeff Mell and I presided at Haulover Beach for an Asthma Walk-a-thon promoted by activist Ruth Rosen. The proceeds will go to the asthma foundation in Denver. We paid homage to Ruth and to the condo leaders who were there, and acknowledged various politicians such as Marge McDonald, Mayor of North Miami Beach; State Representative Mike Friedman; and several mayors from the North Dade area. It was the kind of event that one has to do.

FEBRUARY 16 MONDAY

In Miami the Federal offices are closed today in celebration of President's Day, but I put in a few hours at the office. In the evening I attended a fundraiser for Senate Majority Leader, Robert Byrd, at the home of Jerry and Gwen Berlin. The purpose of the fundraiser was to show Jewish support for Senator Byrd and to encourage his continued support for Israel. The goal was to raise $10-15,000. I thought this sum rather modest, as Byrd could play his fiddle in the Democratic Club in Washington, and raise $25,000 anytime he wanted. Jerry Berlin has been supportive of me as have the other AIPAC people at the fundraiser, i.e., Sam Adler, his son Mike, and attorney Bob Traurig.

Jerry Berlin introduced me, and I introduced Congressman Larry Smith; Larry Smith introduced Senator Bob Graham; and Graham introduced Senate Majority Leader Byrd. Byrd is a powerful Senate member but seemed a little uncomfortable. He is a simple West Virginia country boy - a coal miner's son with very simple tastes - and was here in a very elaborate home filled with mostly very wealthy, sophisticated Jews. Surprisingly, the event raised approximately $50,000.

Sharyn and I will go over a list of people to invite to my Miami fundraiser, including some people here this evening and also past Saturday evening's reception at the home of Herb Stettin. It was strange that the two houses, Berlin's and Stettin's, where these receptions were held are next to each other at the other end of the county from where I live.

FEBRUARY 17 TUESDAY

It has been busy today at the district office. My first meeting was with Paul Walker, a business agent for the Carpenters Union in Dade County, concerning violation of the Davis-Bacon Act, a federal labor law requiring that all labor of Federal Government contract jobs be paid the equivalent of union scale. Next were officials from the Veterans Hospital and then a husband and wife, both Coast Guard employees, came in about the new Coast Guard reorganization and the plan to relocate some Miami Beach-based employees. This couple had just transferred from another government agency to the Coast Guard to be in South Florida and they were in a real dilemma, as the husband is not in the best of health and the move would not be beneficial. Admiral Yost, generally pessimistic, had called to warn me that this was a problem, so I knew this was coming, and told them I would look into the matter when I was in Washington.

At 10:00 a.m., as I met with Bill Guralnik, Director of the Miami American Jewish Committee, Guralnik told me that his office would provide more than $1,000 for Adele Liskov on my staff to go to East Germany with us. Bill thought I had performed a miracle to get as far as I had with the East German government, but it really was not all that difficult and I am getting more credit than I deserve. We also talked about plans to open communications between the black community and the condo groups - busing some condo residents to the black community to the Davis Restaurant on N.W. 62nd Street, and busing the black leaders from Liberty City to Essen Deli in the Point East area. 11:00, I was at the Biscayne Gardens Women's Club, a WASP group of elderly women from a middle class, modest neighborhood, and one of the last remnants in my district in old Miami. I enjoy my visits with this club, as it reminds me of the Miami I used to know. They seemed happy to see me, but I only stayed about twenty minutes. They had questions mostly about social security, and concerning the Congressional pay raise, I told them that I would vote for the raise if it came to a vote and they did not make a big issue about it. Asking about AIDS, they expressed concern about the breakdown of morals. It was rather funny as they were embarrassed to say the word "condom" when talking about people handing them out. When I spoke I used the word "condom" and they seemed relieved that I said it first and broke the ice.

Sharyn has turned out letters for the Washington fundraiser and I will spend time signing and putting personal notes on some.

FEBRUARY 18 WEDNESDAY

At the beginning of each new year, in January, the President sends to Congress a large and detailed document estimating the cost of running the government for the upcoming fiscal year, asking for specific appropriations or funding for government agencies and programs.

For the beginning of my responsibility as Chairman of the Appropriations Subcommittee on Transportation, I will hold hearings (as will the twelve other appropriations subcommittee chairmen) on the budget requests for the Department of Transportation and its related agencies and programs. To justify the President's budget requests, the Secretary, Administrators and other important officials of the Department of Transportation and its related agencies testify as witnesses before our Transportation Subcommittee. Those agencies include:

Department of Transportation

Office of the Secretary
Coast Guard
Federal Aviation Administration
Federal Highway Administration
National Highway Traffic Safety Administration
Federal Railroad Administration
Urban Mass Transportation Administration
St. Lawrence Seaway
Research and Special Programs Administration
Office of the Inspector General

Transportation Related Agencies

Architectural & Transportation Barriers Compliance Board
Aviation Safety Commission
National Transportation Safety Board
Interstate Commerce Commission
Panama Canal Commission
U.S. Railway Association

We also hear testimony from members of Congress and other interested individuals and organizations. The questions vary from year to year, but for the most part questioning from our subcommittee is rather routine except for pressing concerns that the subcommittee members may have regarding the agencies. A great deal of emphasis is routinely placed by our subcommittee on the safety and operating efficiency of these agencies. We hear about the new technology and start-up programs that the agencies hope to justify for funding, and in many instances we will appropriate more than some agencies request in order to enhance the success of these projects.

I left Miami Wednesday for Washington to further prepare for the beginning of our hearings, spending most of the time on the plane going over questions that will be asked at our first hearing of the year which is always with Department of Transportation Secretary Elizabeth Dole. When I arrived at Washington National Airport around noon, an office staffer was there to meet me; in the car on the way to the office, I read and signed as much mail as possible before arriving there.

Lucy Hand and Greg Dahlberg were waiting for me and for the next two hours we went over my opening statement and the problems we may or may not have with the prepared questions. The questions were primarily the same as last year. The main problems we anticipated in the questions were that, as in previous years, no requests were for any funds for Amtrak or for the subsidizing of urban mass transit, which starts our committee off with a $3.6 billion shortfall. The big media event in the hearing will be the drug problem - not only concerning air traffic controllers but also with the random mandatory drug testing for Federal Railroad Administration, and Conrail personnel.

4:30 p.m., I met with the Florida Chapter of the National Association of Postmasters, including the Hallandale Postmaster who was a member of my daughter Kathy's class in Miami Edison High School. Every time I meet a classmate of Kathy's who remembers her well, it gives me satisfaction to know that she is not forgotten.

In the evening I went to a couple of receptions - neither very interesting. One was for a former colleague who has now served for six years as head of the Democratic Congressional Campaign Committee, and who strangely is leaving to work for Charles Walker and Associates - a basically Republican lobbying group in

Washington. At the National Press Club reception for SANE, an anti-nuclear group, Soviet Ambassador Dobryin was to be there but did not show. His second ranking Embassy official did attend and made amusing comments about the ridiculousness of the anti-Soviet television show called "Amerika" being shown now. The only colleagues I saw were Senator Paul Simon and Rep. Lane Evans, both of Illinois. Betsy Berg, the daughter of Lany Narot, was with me, and afterwards we went to dinner. Betsy is with a speaker's booking group in New York, and is in Washington hoping to engage some celebrity speakers for her company.

FEBRUARY 19 THURSDAY

At the start of our transportation hearing this morning, the other Democratic members were Marty Sabo and Bob Carr. Also present was Appropriations Committee Chairman Jamie Whitten, our first witness. Jamie spoke with concern about the problems in Mississippi and the airports in his area that he sometimes sees threatened by less Federal funding. Present on the Republican side were Larry Coughlin of Pennsylvania, Frank Wolf of Northern Virginia, and new member Tom DeLay of Texas.

The Secretary of Transportation Elizabeth Dole, our star witness, is as gracious as always. Her opening statement includes the budget requests for each transportation agency, with individual agency hearings to follow; but before she began to speak on this, Secretary Dole apologized to the subcommittee and remarked that she was a "bit breathless" because of a traffic jam that ensnarled her coming to the hearings and so had to turn around and go in a different direction. I thought this rather amusing, and said, "The Transportation Secretary has transportation problems!" Secretary Dole and I have a good working relationship, and the fact that I helped her with transferring authority from the FAA at the Washington National and Dulles Airports to a new Metropolitan Washington Airports Authority has really made her a friend. She has to defend the administration's positions even when there are no funds requested in the budget for Amtrak or sufficient money for urban mass transit. One disparity we have is that I thought she jumped the gun on mandatory random drug testing for DOT personnel. Mandatory drug testing meant that transportation employees - specifically airline pilots, railroad workers, air traffic controllers, and other selected DOT employees - could be randomly tested without cause. The Democrats on our subcommittee were also not in favor of mandatory testing because organized labor is in opposition, and our Democrats are usually in step with organized labor.

Addressing the Secretary, I said that "the requirement for random testing is especially controversial and raises some significant constitutional issues, and I know many labor leaders believe that your proposed solution is overkill." Asked if she could explain how pervasive the drug and alcohol problems were in each of the major work force sectors to justify random testing, the Secretary answered that she could not. I think Secretary Dole agreed to the mandatory random drug testing because she wanted to be out front on any Federal compulsory anti-drug resolution and did not want to be caught napping. Other than the fact that she is taking the administration line, naturally not recommending funding for mass transit and Amtrak, we do not have major differences. Last year the Secretary's big problem was antiterrorism and the year before it was seatbelt legislation. This year it is drug testing. Each year the Department of Transportation has to have a highly visible program that appeals to the public and the media.

We also differed on increasing the 55 mph speed limit in rural areas. It was my opinion and one that I expressed at the hearing that if you raised the speed limit to 65, people were going to go 75, and that is a very dangerous speed even in the rural areas. I felt that more people would be injured and there would be more fatalities at the greater speed. The fact that we were losing 120 people a day in highway accidents is considerably more than a trivial consideration in my opposition to the speed limit increase. Also factored in to my equating increased speed with an increased accident ratio was my experience as a former automobile dealer.

On the other side, the rationale was that if you redeploy the police from the rural interstates, with fewer violators, and assign them to urban interstates, the manpower impact would be negligible and would possibly save lives. The police thought their resources were being wasted on the low-fatality interstates. Although the administration was taking no actual position on the proposal, it was clear from the Secretary's remarks that DOT was principally favorable to a more flexible policy of relaxing the speed limit in some rural areas. Her comments today were that the administration had accepted the "concept" in terms of the governors having more flexibility to raise the speed limit on some rural interstates, where the volume of traffic was perhaps 10,000 vehicles or less per day. I will hold further questioning on this issue for Diane Steed, Administrator of the National Highway Traffic Safety Administration.

In the afternoon I met with Miami Southeast First National Bank officials, one of whom is trying to get his daughter a page position for the summer. Unfortunately many of these requests come to me too late for a summer page appointment. The bank official does not live in my district so I took him across the corridor to the office of Dante Fascell, in whose district he lives, and Dante's staff is going to try to help him. Afterwards we had a photo opportunity, and I will send the photo to my son Bill as he does business with the Southeast First National Bank.

When they left, I went to see Mike Stevens, chief staff on Appropriations Subcommittee on Health and Human Services, and his assistant Bettilou Taylor about a lady I met on the airplane to Miami last week. She came to me weeping as she had just buried her son who had committed suicide. Her son worked at the National Institutes of Health, and she was upset about the treatment and harassment he received from some people who work there, and who she said falsified some of his research data. Mike said there would be questions about this at the next NIH hearing. I wrote to the mother explaining what actions we were taking in the hope it would make her feel better that someone was trying to do something to protect the memory of her son. I was following my rule of taking care of my constituents.

People from Budget Rental Cars came in about their parking car lot at the Washington National Airport. The lot is being removed by the Virginia Highway Department, but when I called the FAA they said that in about two weeks the FAA would have other space available for Budget to park its cars, and this seemed to satisfy the Budget people. One reason I was glad this worked out so well is because Silvia De Leon of the Akin, Gump, Strauss, Hauer & Feld law firm that represents Budget has always been very supportive of me.

At the Florida House for the High Speed Rail Commission reception this evening, the former Chairman of Miami's Chamber of Commerce Dave Blumberg was there, and I like to keep in touch with Dave, an old personal friend from Dothan, Alabama. Some

TGR (French High Speed Rail Authority) officials from France were there. When in France in 1983, I took the high-speed rail and what a fascinating ride! One other reception that I attended was for the American Women of Radio and Television. I saw my good friend Penny Farthing of Patton, Boggs and Blow, and television's Maria Shriver. It was a good affair and the food was great. Between the two receptions, I will not need dinner before my flight to Miami this evening.

FEBRUARY 20 FRIDAY

Arriving in Miami last evening at 11:00, and rising early this morning for the meeting in Carol City, I was a little tired. Hopefully something constructive can develop from this meeting on the Carol City public housing facility and its community center, a $500,000 building which hasn't been used. Representatives from Miami's Little HUD and from HUD's regional headquarters in Jacksonville were there, and joined by top officials from Metro Dade County Public Safety; Dade County School Board; Metro Dade Parks Department; the head of the Tenants Association; private citizen John Smith, who heads the "We Care for Carol City" group; and two reporters, representing the *Sun Sentinel* and the *Miami Herald*. Having reporters present meant that I had to produce.

First, I wanted them to know what I could do as their representative in Congress, and started by telling them that I would try to arrange funding to provide for the federal portion of the cost of activating the community center, but to accomplish this, I said, would take cooperation among the Public Safety Department, Little HUD, and the Parks Department. The police have said that this area in Dade County has the highest crime rate and is the most dangerous in the Northwest section of Dade County. To turn this neighborhood around there must be a viable community center with activities and ongoing community development. The place looked a lot better today since my last visit in December. At that time it was in shambles with trash strewed all around. Today the center was air conditioned, lights were on, and it was cleaned up in front. The Dade County Housing Authority had really tried to improve the surroundings. It will be interesting to see how the story plays in the media.

Patrice and Bernie Torra from my North Miami Beach office were with me, and they will follow through until I return. The next meeting will be at John Smith's office in the Cloverleaf Bowling Building. I promised I would be in Miami Friday, March 14, to update them on what I am trying to do. We must have an educational program in place as soon as possible and a children's program by the summer to prevent any additional degradation of this area. I feel a real responsibility to the community to do something to help, and I think we made some progress.

It has come to my attention that people in Little Havana are gathering a petition for me to go to Cuba to obtain the release of a political prisoner who has been in jail for over twenty years. I may be the only one in the Florida delegation that Castro may listen to because I am the only one who has not been hard-lining him and who would be willing to go to Cuba. These are the types of situations I try to avoid, but sometimes I can work them through successfully. In this case, I may be able to save a life, but sometimes a situation is so volatile that I cannot really pursue it. The next steps will be to speak to Mickey Leland of Texas, who is a friend of Castro, and then meet with the Cuban Interest Section at the Czechoslovakian Embassy in Washington. From meeting with the Cuban Interest Section I want to see if Cuba will give me a response as to what I may accomplish in trying to free this prisoner.

Sharyn has given me several hundred letters to sign for my April fundraiser in Washington. If I know the person personally, I write a postscript. Signing all these letters is an aggravation but a necessity for raising money, and the letters will need to go out by the end of February. I pay special attention to each letter, as many people on our fundraiser list have changed addresses or have new jobs, and some companies have either merged or been taken over by other companies, and I want to be sure each letter is correct. I spoke with Lucy today about the complimentary tickets to the fundraiser and there is always a question as to how many staff people we need there. Our cost per person is $100.00, and the more we have of important Hill staff present the better. It is especially appealing to the lobbyists who want to talk to Appropriations front office staff and the staffs of Appropriations subcommittees.

Secretary Dole called at my district office to thank me for the quality of the hearing we held the previous Thursday. We paid each other compliments and said we hoped to work together. Secretary Dole is very smooth and professional, and it had been more of a love-in than a hearing. The only member who may have given her a hard time was Bob Carr, an adversary type, but he was not too tough.

There is not much we can do with our budget this year as it is like last year's budget. We receive the budget from the Administration through the Secretary and rework it within possible limitations to serve the best needs of the country. This often means reducing the obligation ceiling of the highway trust fund and transferring those outlays to mass transit and Amtrak.

FEBRUARY 21 SATURDAY

Signing letters and writing postscripts for the fundraiser, it occurred to me to invite some of our Miami contributors to Washington. Sharyn and I can work on writing a separate letter, as there are many Miami people that often contact me in Washington, and I would like to include them.

Bill Bayer of WINZ Radio called wanting me to do a taping tomorrow for his Sunday evening broadcast. I told him I just did a taping about three weeks ago, so he only did a short tape about the Iran crisis. In the interview, I said it will get worse before it gets better, and that regarding President Reagan, it will really be up to the Congress to govern the country. It is sad that in the last two years of Reagan's term he was an irrelevant President, running out of power before his term expires. Unfortunately our past few presidents went the same way, and maybe we need a woman president like Prime Minister Thatcher of England. It seems that women are more stable leaders than men and perhaps it is something in the "macho" self-image with which men need to sustain themselves.

FEBRUARY 22 SUNDAY

At the airport on my way back to Washington, there is another snowstorm in the Washington area which is causing many changes and delays. It is very disconcerting to fly back and forth between Miami and Washington in the winter.

FEBRUARY 23 MONDAY

Because of the snowstorm, not all of the staff was able to get in to the office and none of my appointments have shown. The Florida PTA people did not come, and I have an appointment this afternoon with the Deputy of the Secretary of Defense about Israel's Lavi aircraft. I am wondering if he will make it. It is a quiet time at the office. Greg Dahlberg is at the subcommittee office and he will have the questions for me for tomorrow's hearing on the National Transportation Safety Board. It will be interesting to see the questions on mandatory drug testing, especially for airline pilots.

I always like to start my week by getting in shape playing tennis on Monday's. Today I played with my colleague tennis buddies indoors at the Army/Navy Club. On the Hill, mostly everything is closed, even the Rayburn Cafeteria and the barber shop. These last two snowstorms have really tied up Washington.

This evening I attended the reception for Florida Governor Bob Martinez, but only two or three members were there for this very modest reception but with good crabcakes. The Governor is quite impressive and I said to him that he was the first Governor to provide State aid for the Metromover in downtown Miami. As a former Tampa Mayor, Martinez said he knew what the problems were. He was very knowledgeable, very personable and I was quite impressed. I think he will do all right and feel I can work with him.

FEBRUARY 24 TUESDAY

It is 9:00 a.m., and no one is in the office, as yet, except me. I think the staff is too conscious of the weather conditions and perhaps carrying it too far by not being at the office. Every other office has people in so I think I will have a talk with Carolyn Cornish, our office manager.

This morning I met with the Parks Service officials from Florida and with a constituent from Dade County who is helping with the Carol City Community Center project. Afterwards, one of my legislative assistants, Nadine Berg and I met with representatives of the Dade County School Board Food Service. They want assurance that I will cosponsor a federal assistance bill for the schools' food service programs in the coming year. The federal government is supposed to reimburse school systems for this service, and I usually automatically cosponsor these kinds of bills. The problem is that Florida does not have a member on the Education and Labor Committee so Florida people come to me for help on education issues.

The budget request for the National Transportation Safety Board is $23.6 million. NTSB's primary function is to make safety recommendations based on its investigations and studies to Federal, State and local government agencies and to the transportation industry regarding actions that should be taken to prevent accidents. At our hearing today, we really did not find out much more than we already knew. The NTSB is following very closely the air-traffic control problem and the number of people needed as full performance controllers, and monitoring the types of railroad safety devices we need to avoid another Amtrak accident as the one recently in Chase, Maryland. National Transportation Safety Board Administrator, Jim Burnett, is one of the best witnesses as his answers are short and direct. When asked what he considered the most serious transportation safety problem confronting us to date, his response was that when more than 40,000 people still die every year in motor vehicle traffic accidents, "highway safety is still the single most serious transportation problem." He said there was no single solution, but they would continue to work on safety-belt education, support for drunk driving programs, and continue to enforce the monitoring of vehicle defects.

After the hearing a *New York Times* reporter, who had been a friend of my deceased colleague Ben Rosenthal, questioned me about urban mass transit. John Schelble, my press assistant, was also at the interview. The reporter had been talking to Urban Mass Transit Administration (UMTA) Administrator, Ralph Stanley, and Ralph as usual had been criticizing the way discretionary funds were used for construction of new-start programs in the urban mass transit system. Stanley had said that the administration's hands were tied by Congress and UMTA had to obligate money regardless of real needs. The reporter asked me to justify the appropriations process regarding urban mass transit, especially for new starts. Our subcommittee has been appropriating in this manner for years and has greatly helped the Metro Dade transit system. I gave him the usual answers, Metro Dade has a good system, which will be even better in the future. As I told the reporter, I actually inherited the plans for the system when I became an appropriations chairman and the route was a compromise to get votes from Liberty City and Hialeah to pass the referendum necessary to build the system.

When the reporter left, John was a little upset because during the interview I harshly criticized Mayor Suarez of Miami for being frustrated because the City of Miami did not have its own transit system. I also told the reporter that members try to help each other and anytime I could earmark a justifiably good project, especially one that deals with highway safety, I would do so regardless of the member's party. John tells me that I am too honest when dealing with reporters and that I should be more circumspect and a bit more careful. Maybe I should, but I just shoot from the hip on these answers and let the chips fall where they may. Perhaps I am a little irresponsible because as chairman of the subcommittee I have a responsibility to protect the image of the members on our committee, and I should try not to be so cavalier.

Milton and Joyce Toppel came in at 4:30. They are entrepreneurs, originally from New Jersey then Puerto Rico, who own highly successful mega supermarkets called X-tra, and they were in Washington for the American National Grocers Association meeting. The Toppels' first store opened in New Jersey and now there are a number of stores, one located across from my son Bill's automobile dealership in North Dade. They were concerned about the possibility of federally mandated employee benefits such as maternity leave and other proposed legislation to protect employees, which would be very costly to their business. My own son Bill has been pressuring me about these same problems. Telling them about Bill, I said that I certainly understood their concerns and that I was strongly considering all sides of the issue.

After the Toppels, I met with Steve O'Toole, General Motors legislative liaison, and reiterated concerns my son Bill had expressed about the need to reorganize General Motors. Bill complained about the duplication and anachronistic setup of the General Motors organization, saying that there are too many tiers of people that he has to go through to get results. General Motors has to be more responsive to the dealers. Afterwards I went hastily to two receptions. First, was the National Wholesale Grocers Association, where I met people to be followed-up for my Washington fundraiser. You have to appear at these events and get your name marked off as attending. I saw the Toppels again, and the wife of old friend Glen Woodward from Winn Dixie in Jacksonville, who told me that Glen could not make it. I did not see anyone from Publix Supermarkets, but it was a huge event held in the Longworth Cafeteria, so it is possible that others were there that I knew and I just could not locate them in the crowd.

Leaving the Longworth Building, I headed for the Rayburn Building for a reception that the new Florida member Bill Grant was hosting for the Florida Public Service Commission. I greeted Dick Sewell from Florida Power and Light, and we were happy to see each other. Dick told me that the Port St. Lucie nuclear plant was doing very well and that there were no problems, which was very encouraging. In the 1970's, I had visited Port St. Lucie because of the big controversy concerning the installation of the nuclear power in that area. I felt the plant was safe and in the long run less dangerous than some fossil fuel plants.

Joan had come back to Washington with me, and together we attended the 25th Anniversary celebration of the NBC Today Show. Held at the Willard Hotel, this was the big event of the evening, and all the NBC celebrities were there, i.e., Jane Pauley, Bryant Gumbel, etc. Other celebrities included George and Barbara Bush, Tip O'Neill, Secretary of State George Schultz, top officials from the National Transportation Safety Board, and Joan Claybrook with Ralph Nader's Public Citizens Group. I complained to Joan Claybrook about all the cheap shots she and her organization had made about the salary increase, and she disarmed me by telling me she had heard about so many good things that I had done, such as appropriating money for the Center for Disease Control in Atlanta. Many of our subcommittee members and other colleagues were there, such as Pat Schroeder of Colorado who supplied a bit of gossip that George Bush was going to be in trouble when the Tower Report on Iran Contra came out and that he may even be faced with impeachment. We will see if that is true, as George and Barbara did not seem at all perturbed this evening. The company and the food were just great, and it seemed to be a good time for all.

FEBRUARY 25 WEDNESDAY

We had our first full Appropriations Committee hearing this morning and Chairman Jamie Whitten warned us about the Gramm-Rudman legislation limitations on spending this year. Everyone knows that we will not meet the Gramm-Rudman limits this year - a 1985 law that sets a timetable for achieving a balanced budget. We will see how Jamie figures out how our appropriations subcommittees will be allocated funds. The appropriations process is difficult.

Our hearing today with the Interstate Commerce Commission (ICC) went well. The ICC is the regulatory agency for interstate surface transportation to ensure that competitive, efficient, and safe transportation services are provided to meet the needs of shippers, receivers, passengers, and consumers. Their budget request is $48 million, and it went very smoothly. Before the hearing Greg Dahlberg and I went over some of the questions, and a big problem with the ICC is that there is a good chance the ICC will be sunseted (closed) before the end of this year and phased into the Department of Justice and into the Transportation Department. Heather Gradison is the chairperson, and a pleasant witness. She is the young wife of Rep. Bill Gradison of Ohio and they have started a new family. In my concern for the employees, I asked, "If the President's proposal goes through to sunset the ICC, how many of the employees would be transferred, and how many would be terminated?" The information she provided revealed that the President's proposal suggests that out of 750 employees, 249 would go to the Department of Transportation, 16 to Justice, and 9 to the Federal Trade Commission, which meant that 476 positions would be abolished or terminated. Of these 476 positions, there was talk of the "early out" option and the chairperson's expressed desire to "make certain that our people are treated fairly." The only Democrat present was Dick Durbin, but the Republicans were there in full force.

Early afternoon I went to the memorial service at the Statuary Hall in the Capitol for Sala Burton. I wanted my California friends and her family to know that I cared enough to be there even though I had arrived a little late. It was the kind of event I could not afford to miss. A reception was to follow the tribute, but I did not attend as I left to pick up Joan for the Chesapeake

Festival at the Jefferson Island Club. The Jefferson Island Club is an old organization originated by Franklin D. Roosevelt as a retreat in Chesapeake Bay where members go and meet together quietly without being under the eyes of the public and press. Mostly now the most active members of this club are from the Defense and the Armed Services Committees, and always there is excellent food such as Maryland oyster stew and crabcakes.

Staying only about an hour at the Jefferson Island Club, Joan and I debated going to the Mississippi Gumbo Festival in the Longworth Building, but Joan has to maintain a low-salt diet, so we skipped it. I also chose not to attend the Richard Gephardt (D- Missouri) reception at the Mayflower Hotel because I did not want to align myself at this time with any of the candidates for the Democratic nomination and Gephardt is going to run. We decided instead to have dinner in downtown Chinatown at a restaurant called the Mongolian, one of Tony Chang's new restaurants. I had helped Tony years ago with some of his employees' visa problems, and he always treats me very well when I patronize his restaurants.

FEBRUARY 26 THURSDAY

My first appointment this morning was with a legislative liaison from the Florida Governor's Office in Washington. I knew what her concerns were even before she arrived. She asked about the issues of offshore oil drilling, the 55 mph speed limit, and the problem of coal replacing oil as an energy source. She was rather attractive and I had fun teasing her about the issues, and asked if she wanted us to go further in debt to increase the petroleum reserves. She is a Republican, and I put her on the spot. She does not want to increase the deficit, but she does want to increase the petroleum reserves. Asking her from where she wanted me to take the money, she of course had no answer.

Our subcommittee hearing began today with witness John Melcher, the Inspector General of the Department of Transportation. The Office of Inspector General of the Department of Transportation conducts and supervises audits and investigations to promote efficiency and effectiveness and provides a means to keep the Secretary of Transportation and

Congress fully and currently informed of programs and deficiencies in the administration of transportation programs and operations. Their budget request is for $30.1 million. We learned about the cheating on exams at the FAA Aviation School in Oklahoma City, and bid rigging on federal highway construction contracts. Bid rigging is when bidding companies get together before bidding and set guidelines so no one bids too cheaply. We also learned about the disadvantaged business enterprise frauds, and the uncovering of transit authorities' schemes involving kickbacks, inflation of charges, and fraud and embezzlement. Substantiated cases were singled out, such as an FAA employee's misuse of FAA aircraft to transport personal items, and the use of unsafe trucks and violations of Federal, DOT, and Office of Occupational Safety and Health Administration regulations by a motor freight carrier. Penalties and enforcement action were taken in both instances. It was a good, informative hearing, and I felt we learned a great deal.

5:30 at the Florida Bankers Association reception in the Speaker's Dining Room, the only person from Miami was the Southeast Bank representative, who was also the President of the Florida Bankers Association. I did not stay very long but felt I had to make an appearance. Minority Leader Bob Michel was there. Members said they want to see cuts in the interest rate.

Colleague Howard Berman from Burbank, California, came in about the noise problem Burbank is experiencing, and asked that our subcommittee mandate the FAA not to fund the Burbank Airport unless it changes takeoff and landing patterns flying over the residential areas in his district. I told Berman that the action he was asking me to take, withholding funds for the Burbank Airport, really belonged in the authorizing jurisdiction of the Public Works Aviation Subcommittee and not in the appropriations process. Another case of people buying houses by airports, then complaining about the noise.

Lucy and others on my staff briefed me on what was said on television regarding the Iran-Scam and the Tower Report, and then provided me with further details on the report. Reporters will probably meet me at the airport today in Miami, and I want to be informed. Before I left for Miami, the Opa Locka Chief of Police came in with a representative from the Opa Locka community to see about obtaining Justice Department funds to deal with crime in Opa Locka. Opa Locka has the highest rate of drugs and homicides in the county. We will work to obtain money for a demonstration program in that area, and I will speak to Neal Smith, a good friend and Chairman of Appropriations Subcommittee on Commerce, State, and Justice.

When I arrived in Miami, Jeff Mell met me at the airport and we went directly to a groundbreaking ceremony at the Concord Two Building in my district. The building's developer, Bill Landa, is a contributor to my campaigns. Dade County Commissioner Barry Schrieber introduced me and in my brief remarks, I said it was good to have new commercial development in North Dade. Some congratulated me on the William Lehman Causeway, but Barry had to say that the County paid for part of it. It was true, but Barry always has to take cheap shots, probably jealous that a member of Congress has more prestige than a county commissioner. I used to play tennis with Barry on his court in the back of his house in North Miami Beach, and I always won. My winning bothered him also. He was always asking about my cancer operation. One day he asked my son Bill how I *really* was feeling, and Bill said to him, "Well, who won the tennis match?" Barry replied, "Your father did." Bill said that should answer your question. I understand Barry's ambition so we get along.

FEBRUARY 27 FRIDAY

Last evening I was interviewed by WIOD and WINZ radio stations, and in the *Miami News* today I was quoted saying that I thought Reagan should talk to his wife about his present staff problems. This morning I taped a half-hour show called "Newsmakers" for Channel 4. Two people from Channel 4 and Tom Fiedler, political editor for the *Miami Herald*, were there. The show has a good audience and will be aired Sunday. Their questions were primarily on the Tower Report. I said that the White House should get rid of all their staff people and have Jerry Ford back as a White House advisor as he has all the experience, knowhow and credibility. Afterwards I went to the Spanish radio station and met some Contra refugees from Nicaragua and a reporter was trying to get a photo of me with the Tower Report in my hand. Then I was interviewed about my observations on the Contra report and I told them that if the State Department was going to delegate power they had better be sure to whom they delegate, and then follow up to see what happens. Most of what I said had already been said in the media and by other members of Congress.

FEBRUARY 28 SATURDAY

Sharyn and I spent about three hours in the campaign office going over the list of possible Miami people to invite to the Washington fundraiser. We have about 100 names, and about ten or fifteen percent will be followed up with a phone call. Much later, Joan and I attended a reception at the Westview (Jewish) Country Club at the invitation of our friend Peggy Gordon. It was fun, and I met people there that may be helpful to my fundraising campaign.

Chapter 3

MARCH 1, 1987 - SUNDAY

Today Joan and I attended the wedding of Ellen Kempler, my daughter's best friend, and Ken Rosen, past president of Temple Israel and a wealthy real estate developer. The ceremony was held at Ken's home in Coconut Grove, with many politicians among the guests. It was a very lovely affair, including the reception, and Joan and I were happy to be there. Afterwards I attended a Daily Bread meeting held in a warehouse in the Brownsville area, and was presented with an appreciation plaque. Archbishop McCarthy was also there. My affiliation with this organization goes back several years, and I have seen the good that the organization does by collecting extra food from food brokers, supermarkets and restaurants, then redistributing the food to the needy. From there, I left for the airport for my flight back to Washington.

MARCH 2 MONDAY

At the Washington office this morning were North Miami City

Manager Larry Casey, and North Miami Council Members John Hagerty, Bill Carr, and Shelly Gassner, concerned about the Munisport and the fact that it is still on EPA's toxic waste superfund list. Presently I am waiting for the EPA to respond to my recent letter as to the status of this case. I do not want to legislate the removal of the Munisport from the toxic waste list, but I will if I have to. It would be better, however, if the removal was done administratively after proper investigation. I believe it was put on the list improperly, but once on, it is very difficult to be removed because by doing so you run the risk of being accused of endangering the environment.

Our subcommittee staff and I are going over questions for the Coast Guard hearing. We have a new Coast Guard commandant this year, Admiral Paul Yost, and I think he will be more flexible than the previous commandant, Gracey. The problem this year is that Coast Guard funding from the Department of Defense, which amounted to approximately $3 billion over the past few years, is going to be more difficult to come by. The Coast Guard is also going to have problems with their funding request for two new icebreakers, and other efforts it wants to undertake. The three primary missions of the Coast Guard are maritime law enforcement, maritime safety, and military readiness. The Coast Guard feels very oppressed as it does not have the recognition it feels it deserves, and by the military is treated like a stepchild. This is a uniformed service without the funds of other uniformed services. They actually are better off being under the auspices of the transportation appropriations subcommittee rather than the defense appropriations subcommittee as their numbers are small in comparison to the other uniformed services. Our subcommittee is, therefore, better able to give them the appropriate attention and recognition merited. The Coast Guard hearing is tomorrow, but many members of our subcommittee have other meetings, so a full contingent will not be present.

My tennis buddies and I had a good game this afternoon, and in order for me to play I postponed a scheduled meeting with the U.S. Ambassador to Italy Max Rabb, who has entertained me several times on my previous trips to Italy, and been very gracious. I will see him tomorrow, and also Jessie Trice, Director of the Family Health Center in Miami whom I also rescheduled. Tennis keeps me healthy. Later, John Schelble and I worked on the newsletter: "How Our Laws Are Made," and hopefully it will be finished by the end of the week. We try to have a newsletter out about once a month, but it is usually about every two or three months.

MARCH 3 TUESDAY

At 8:00, I was at a breakfast reception at the Phoenix Park Hotel, hosted by Maurice Rosenblatt, a lobbyist, friend, and neighbor. Bill Holayor from the machinists union was at the breakfast, as was Graham Claytor, President of Amtrak. This was basically a pep meeting about increasing the gas tax to help build the infrastructure of the country. A portion of the new revenue would also be used to reduce the deficit. Public Works Committee Chairman Jim Howard, and Dick Sullivan, Chief of Staff on the Public Works Committee, are pushing for this tax, which would start at ten cents a gallon and increase in increments to fifty cents a gallon. A real pipe dream, you might say.

Back on the Hill by 9:00, I stopped in at the Select Committee's hearing on child abuse but could not stay long as I had my own hearing at 10:00 with the Coast Guard. Adele is covering the Foreign Operations hearing for me as all three hearings are scheduled simultaneously. The President's budget request for the Coast Guard is $2.72 billion, and the hearing went very well. Admiral Yost is as I conjectured more forthcoming than was Commandant Gracey. In answer to my questions on what specific objectives are established for the Coast Guard for the next three years, the Admiral said that the top priorities were drug interdiction, military preparedness, maritime safety and reduction in some operating costs and more user fees revenue. The biggest "headaches," he said, were in personnel strength to operate the new on-line equipment. (Included in the President's budget were funds for 800 additional employees). After further questioning on personnel shortfall, I yielded to my subcommittee colleagues the greater part of the morning session for questions that they had for Admiral Yost. His answers to their questions, though, were very long and drawn out, so we did not move as fast as we should.

We recessed at noon, and I went to the Capitol to meet with the Greater Miami Chamber of Commerce to discuss plans for the Florida Congressional Weekend. Bernie Jacobson of the Fine and

Jacobson law firm presided. Old friend Walter Revell, head of an engineering firm in Miami, attended, as did most of the congressional members from South Florida. The group would like the Florida delegation to come to Miami in early May for a chamber of commerce meeting and to showcase Miami at the same time. The meeting went very well, with the Florida delegation agreeing to a cooperative effort.

At the office I met with the U.S. Ambassador to Italy, Max Rabb, who is always fun to be with. The Ambassador is asking for additional funds not only for his embassy but for embassies around the world, and told me that he spends about $4 thousand out of his own pocket every month just to support the American Embassy in Rome. I said I would try to help and to just point me in the right direction.

The Coast Guard hearing resumed at 2:00. In 1982, the Coast Guard's South Florida Task Force was established to combat the drug trade. I asked Admiral Yost to comment on the report last fall that the Federal officials who run the task force acknowledged that after 4-1/2 years, they had barely made a dent in the drug trade, and that more cocaine was being smuggled through Florida than ever before. (Since the task force was established, the percentage of the nation's cocaine being smuggled through Florida had increased by 10 percent.) The Admiral stated that when the task force was formed marijuana was the drug of the day. "Now," he said, "it's cocaine, which poses a more difficult problem since most of it comes in by air and air interdiction is much more complex, expensive and difficult to combat." When asked how effective the Coast Guard had been in alleviating the problem, he said that without knowledge of exactly how much drugs are being shipped, "it is very difficult to get a measure of how effective you are in interdicting, but with the supply of marijuana down along the East Coast, this could be seen as a measure of effectiveness, and of how productive the Coast Guard had been during the last three years they had spent in the Caribbean." The price of cocaine, he said, was down and therefore the supply was up, and the Admiral acknowledged, in all candor, that the Coast Guard was not doing that good a job in interdicting cocaine, adding that he was not sure the Coast Guard was going to do much better than they were doing now. I said to him that was about the most candid answer we have had in a long time.

Leaving ranking minority member Larry Coughlin (R-PA) as acting chair, I came out briefly to meet with Jessie Trice from the Family Health Center in Miami. Most of the subcommittee members are missing from the hearing today, including Marty Sabo of Minnesota who is tied down by the Defense Appropriations Subcommittee and Budget Chairman Bill Gray of Pennsylvania, who can't break away from the Budget hearings.

Following the hearing, which ended at 4:00, I met with Graham Claytor, President of Amtrak, and offered him encouragement for funding in 1988. Then Sam Rabin, a constituent from North Miami Beach came in. Sam is an old friend and told me about his problems in Miami. I took a break and went to the gym and then to a reception for the Security Industry, where I met the industry representative from Palm Beach, Florida.

In the evening, Washington lawyer Janet Studley and I attended the reception for Donn Anderson, our newly elected Clerk of the House. The event was held at the Sheraton Grand Hotel, and the place was jam-packed. On the upper level of this same hotel, the Short Line Railroads reception was being held, and I saw Lucy from my staff and Ray Chambers, a lobbyist friend. Janet and I left the Sheraton Grand for a reception at the German Embassy residence in honor of the Lord Mayor of West Berlin. The residence is exquisite, and officials from West Berlin that I had met last year on my codel to Germany were there, along with our Ambassador to Belgium, Geoffrey Swaebe, whom I met in Brussels on a previous trip. Most of them knew that I was going to East and West Berlin the following month.

MARCH 4 WEDNESDAY

During this second day of the Coast Guard hearings, I had ranking member Larry Coughlin ask most of the justification questions. First, however, I did go into the issue of the shrinkage of parts inventory in Coast Guard warehouses. The Coast Guard loses parts worth millions of dollars due to obsolescence and also has no record of the shrinkage due to the disappearance of parts in warehouses. I told Admiral Yost our committee wanted physical inventory taken at least once a year to track parts inventory and that, unlike this year when the Coast Guard can shed no light on inventory shrinkage, next year I wanted an acceptable answer.

After the hearing, representatives of the Florida Civilian Employees of the Coast Guard were in to see me about the proposed Coast Guard reorganization. Many were afraid of being transferred, and I assured them that our office could deal successfully with their problems on an individual case basis. Then I did a live T.V. broadcast for Miami's Channel 7. The broadcast was made outdoors next to the LaColline Restaurant on N. Capitol Street, and I was asked about the President's speech that is being given tonight. A special hookup is attached so that the studio audience in Miami can ask questions, and I am equipped with an earphone to respond. I said that "the President is more a symbolic than a real president, and that Secretary of Treasury Jim Baker is running the country."

In the evening I stopped by two receptions, the Michigan Road Builders Association, hosted by Bob Carr of our transportation subcommittee, and the Kennedy Chapter of B'nai B'rith. Afterwards, with Congressional Budget Director Alice Rivlin, I went to the Hyatt Regency for the reception of my good friend Representative Charlie Rangel of New York. We could not stay until Charlie arrived, but we did speak with his wife Alma. From there we went to the Motion Pictures Association Building for the Jack Valenti dinner reception in honor of the new CEO's of the Walt Disney Company. Valenti is President of the Motion Pictures Association of America. The two young men who took over the company, Jeffrey Katzenberg and Micheal Eisner showed their new movie, "The Tin Man," and I was delightedly surprised to be invited. Some of the guests included *Washington Post* Editor, Ben Bradlee and his girlfriend Sally Quinn, my colleagues Pat Schroeder of Colorado and Dan Rostenkowski of Chicago. Top people from Florida were also there such as my colleague Dante Fascell and his wife Jean Marie. We watched the President's speech on the Iran-scam and then all the members went to the phones to call their local media. Many guests then left without seeing the film, but it was a fascinating evening.

MARCH 5 THURSDAY

Our subcommittee hearing this morning was on the St. Lawrence Waterway Development Corporation, a wholly-owned government corporation responsible for the operation, maintenance and development of the U.S. portion of the St. Lawrence Seaway between Montreal and Lake Erie. The President's budget request is for $12 million. The Seaway's initial cargo was grain out and iron ore back, but not anymore as the principal commodity is now only grain, and about 60 percent of all commodities traveling through the Seaway are outgoing. The corporation would like to have the authorization legislation revised so that they can keep the revenue generated from the U.S. portion of the St. Lawrence Seaway and become more self-sustaining.

At noon full Appropriations Chairman Jamie Whitten had the 13 subcommittee chairmen meet in his front office to brief us on the forthcoming Supplemental Appropriations Bill, granting extra funds to Federal agencies to respond to unforeseen emergencies or to fund new activities. The main concern and discussion was, however, about the possibility of an amendment being offered to eliminate the congressional pay raise when the supplemental bill comes to the Floor. Following the meeting we had our subcommittee hearing on the transportation function in the supplemental bill, and learned of funds in the bill recommended for the Federal Aviation, the Federal Highway, and the Federal Railroad Administrations. I now needed to get a commitment from the Federal Railroad Administration that proceeds from the preference shares in the legislation would be used for building the Tri-County Commuter Rail in South Florida. Preference shares is a back-door procedure that I am using to obtain two percent government funds for South Florida's Tri-County Commuter Rail System.

4:00, Al Drissler, a former State Department official, came in. Al, from the office of Dennis Neill, a lobbyist representing foreign governments, is hoping to get into Stanford University, and asked if I would write a letter of recommendation for him. I was happy to do so as Al is a good friend; I got to know him well when we traveled on codels together when he was with the State Department. Then, officials from the Department of Defense came in. Under Secretary of Defense Zakov and his Deputy spoke to me and Adele Liskov, my staff assistant on Appropriations Foreign Operations Subcommittee, about the problems of the Lavi fighter planes being made in Israel. The U.S. Defense Department is trying to convince Foreign Operations Subcommittee members that it would be in Israel's best interest, and our country's interest in saving money, if Israel dropped production of the Lavi and continued to use U.S. F15's and F16's. Israel could then upgrade the technology on those fighters and spend more resources on some of its ground forces, especially the Israeli-invented antiballistic weapons.

Israel's throwing money into the Lavi program is preventing the Israeli Defense Force (IDF) from funding pilots for the same number of training hours as previous. A few years ago their pilots were flying many more hours than U.S. pilots and now Israel's pilots are flying fewer hours than ours. The qualitative difference depends on the number of hours a pilot flies, the more the better. This is something Israel must reestablish for its continued security in the Mideast. I had heard all of this when I was in Jerusalem last year, so the information the Defense Department officials are providing is not new to me.

Today is strange as all year we have not had as many votes, only about seven or eight, the number we have had today. The homeless bill is on the Floor today, and we don't expect to adjourn until around 7:30. The South Florida Associated General Contractors are honoring the Florida Congressional Delegation this evening at the Florida House, but I doubt if I will make it.

MARCH 6 FRIDAY

My only morning appointment was at 11:00 with Roosevelt Richardson, Jr., from Miami Dade Community College, regarding the National Youth Program. After telling me of his concerns, I walked him over to meet with the staff on Appropriations Subcommittee on Labor, Health, Education and Human Services, who informed him on the present status of the program. That afternoon, I spoke to a *New York Times* reporter about Elizabeth Dole's proposal to form a committee of private citizens to figure out ways to subsidize Amtrak. My only comment was that I did not have a problem with the Secretary's proposal; however, Elizabeth may appoint a committee but it may come back with answers she did not want to hear, such as recommending for more Federal subsidy into Amtrak for better operating efficiency.

In the gym, members were laughing and joking about the Presidential race. Les Aspin was kidding some Republicans, saying "We ran Mondale against you in 1984 and the least you can do is reciprocate and run Bush against us in 1988, so we can go ahead and win." They all think Bush is a Republican Mondale, but we will see.

Our office did a lot of press today on the problems of the deportation case in the Justice Department's Office of Special Investigation (OSI). The OSI investigates cases where Nazi war criminals may have entered the United States by giving false information. They cannot prosecute the individual for any overseas criminal acts that he/she may have committed, but they can have the individual deported. The case that consumed much of my attention and effort was of concentration camp chief Karl Linnas. Linnas was chief of a concentration camp in Tartu, Estonia, from 1941 to 1943, and was responsible for the physical abuse and execution of hundreds of civilians. He was tried and convicted in absentia by the Soviet Union in 1962 and sentenced to death by a firing squad.

Linnas had been working as a draftsman on Long Island when he was tracked down in 1979 by the Office of Special Investigations. The OSI presented the argument that Linnas misrepresented his role in the atrocities when he entered the United States on May 17, 1951, and received citizenship on February 5, 1960. Deportation proceedings were brought against Linnas, and he was ordered to be deported in 1985.

I had just written a letter to Attorney General Edwin Meese, co-signed by Senators Lawton Chiles (D-FL), John Danforth (R-MO), and Rep. Bill Green (R-NY), informing the Attorney General of our exasperation at the delayed action in this case, and ordering Linnas's immediate deportation. In strengthening my position I stated the facts: that the case had been heard by a federal district judge, twice by the 2nd Circuit Court of Appeals, twice by an immigration judge, twice by the Board of Immigration Appeals and rejected three times by the U.S. Supreme Court, and that the result had been the same at every step. Furthermore, no American judge had questioned the evidence or failed to conclude that Linnas participated in the war crimes. My letter will also be circulated to members of Congress.

Following the interview with *Miami News* reporter Larry Lipman, the story was written up in the next day's edition with the headline: "Lehman wants Nazi camp chief deported." The article summarized much of what was in our letter to the Attorney General, including my vehement comments that Linnas did not deserve any more delays and that a lot more consideration had been given to him than he gave to hundreds of men, women and children killed in the Holocaust. The only reason the Department of Justice is asking for this delay is because Linnas is being deported to a country (Estonia in the Soviet Union) that Meese and Buchanan say could possibly execute him. Linnas was being defended by outgoing White House communications chief Patrick Buchanan and Buchanan had also unsuccessfully sought to block the extradition to Israel of accused mass murderer John Demjanjuk. (Buchanan wanted Linnas tried in the United States, West Germany or Israel, but not deported to the Soviet Union.) But the main person standing in the way of Linnas' deportation is Ed Meese, and, as I said to Lipman, "I don't think that is Meese's job."

Alabama member Bill Dickinson came to the office about funds for Auburn University in Alabama for an airway science program. Our subcommittee had put in a good deal of money for airway science for the University of North Dakota because Senator Mark Andrews, R-North Dakota, former chairman of the senate subcommittee, wanted to help the University of North Dakota. An Auburn alumnus now from my district had asked me to help, and I had him get in touch with the Auburn member from Alabama who happened to be Bill Dickinson. Bill gives a very hawkish, austere impression, and Lucy of my staff was concerned about him. However, he is a real southern gentleman and just about charmed the hell out of Lucy. He didn't press for anything - just stated his problem. I told Bill to have Senator Shelby or Heflin from Alabama talk to Senator Lautenberg, Chairman of the Senate Transportation Appropriations Subcommittee to work with us, and that we would try to assist the University. What is so funny is that Lucy who was afraid of Bill's influence now thinks he is wonderful and will do anything to help him. You just can't beat these southern members when it comes to handling people as they have a very gracious way about them.

The American Public Transportation Association (APTA) had its reception this evening. The affair was held at the Marriott Hotel, with public transportation representatives from all over the country there, including Miami but I was the only member from Congress at the gathering. They were very appreciative of my presence and I went away with a $1,000 honorarium for my daughter's memorial scholarship fund at FIU.

MARCH 9 MONDAY

Dade County School Board Superintendent Leonard Britton, and Tee Greer, the Deputy Superintendent, came in this morning. They are interested in converting the Liberty City Metro Rail garage into a bus maintenance garage for the Dade County Public School System. I told them I would look into it.

After my usual Monday morning tennis, I was back at the office for a meeting with Eli Feinberg (formerly administrative aide for Senator Richard Stone of Florida), a lobbyist friend from Miami who wants a Customs office setup at the Tamiami Airport. I took Eli to speak with Tex Gunnels, Chief of Staff on Appropriations Subcommittee on Treasury, Postal Service, and General Government, and I think we made some progress with Tex. Corporate jets and private planes fly from the Bahamas and other Caribbean Islands and land directly at Tamiami Airport, and this proposed Customs office would be primarily for the convenience of these corporate jets.

Various transit authority officials from around the country have been in to see me about their problems. Representatives from the Jacksonville Chamber of Commerce have problems regarding funding for their "Skyway" Rail System; people from Austin, Texas, and the San Francisco Bay area transit were also among those with problems - all looking for funds. I listened but made no real commitments.

Two surprise parties were held this evening for colleagues Dante Fascell at 70 years of age and John Myers of Indiana, at 60, the ranking Republican on Appropriations Subcommittee on Energy and Water Development. I brought them both a T-shirt which said, "Just because it's my birthday doesn't mean I have to tell you how fucking old I am." They enjoyed the T-shirts but didn't wear them at their birthday parties. Leaving the Hill with Debra Benchoam, who had accompanied me to the parties, I headed for the U.S. Chamber of Commerce building where I was to do a taping with Julian Bond for Gannett Studios for the American Black Forum on Channel 6 in Miami. The program airs very early in the morning and probably won't have much of an audience, but I like Julian Bond and readily agreed to participate. They were not ready for us when we arrived, so Debra and I went out to dinner and when we returned everything was in place. We talked for fifteen minutes and then the usual questions from the Contra situation to mass transit. The questions were not necessarily about black issues but mainstream issues of the day. I learned from Julian that one of my old colleagues, Andy Young, Mayor of Atlanta, is now considering running for Governor of Georgia. I asked Julian if he would like to be mayor of Atlanta and he said, "No," that he enjoys being in the state legislature.

MARCH 10 TUESDAY

The American Trucking Association had a breakfast reception for me this morning at their headquarters two blocks from my townhouse. My old friend Bill Cable, a lobbyist and a former staffer on Education and Labor when I was on that committee, was the master of ceremonies. Following a question and answer period, which consisted of the routine questions on the 55 mph speed limit and various transportation issues, I received yet another $1,000 honorarium for my daughter's education fund at FIU. Very seldom do I take honorariums paid directly to me unless for reimbursement of travel expenses. When the honorarium is payable to the educational fund at FIU, this allows me to keep the memory of my daughter alive, and also to help young students become English teachers, as was Kathy.

Leaving the breakfast, I returned to the Hill for the hearing of the Select Committee on Children, Youth, and Families, and introduced the witness from the University of Miami. The hearing was on child care, and from the dais I spoke of the North Dade Tenants Association's concern with vacated apartments in public housing, and the lack of child care centers which causes a major problem for welfare mothers in the public housing projects. Because these mothers do not leave their children to work, many attract the wrong kind of unemployed males who hang around the women in the projects. Responsible people living in public housing want a child care center to help young mothers get out of the house and into the workforce to improve their own conditions and to create a better public housing environment.

We had a relatively short transportation subcommittee hearing on the Panama Canal Commission, the operating arm of the Panama Canal. The President's budget request is for $467 million, and the chief witnesses are William Gianello, Secretary of Defense Representative for Panama Canal Affairs, and Dennis McAuliffe,

Administrator of the Commission. The Panama Canal hearings are usually a waste of time. Although the Panama Canal Commission goes through the appropriation's process, the funds are already in a special Panama Canal Commission Fund coffered by tolls and other revenue sources indigenous to the Canal. It does not use tax dollars and is, for all practical purposes, self-sufficient. Both Gianello and McAuliffe in their presentations requested the support of the Administration's legislation to convert the Panama Canal Commission from the appropriation's process to a revolving-fund agency. I did give these witnesses a hard time on the lack of inventory control by telling them that most of the government agencies, compared to most businesses, do not seem to have good inventory management, and that there are infrequent physical inventories to check against computer records. "You cannot depend just on computer cards to determine what you have on hand," I said, but it is rather disheartening, as none of these agencies under the Department of Transportation seems to have much inventory control. They do not take a physical inventory of their supplies though they stock millions of dollars' worth of materials. I hope the commission has good security. We soon adjourned.

The American Public Transportation Association is still in town and people are continually coming in from various transportation entities to see me. Jim Copeland and Cecil Barnard from BART (Bay Area Rapid Transit) came in about future financing problems; then Ben Gilford, Director of the Metro-Dade Transit, had a problem. The decision Gilford must make is whether Metro-Dade Transit will drop its original full-funding contract. The contract will say that Metro-Dade Transit cannot start the extensions on the Metromover until there is a dedicated source of revenue, and this Dade County does not have. Metro-Dade Transit has to make a judgement call on whether to give up the full-funding contract to eliminate the precondition requiring a one cent sales tax that cannot pass a referendum in Dade County. My hope is that we can de-legislate the condition of the full-funding contract for Metro-rail. Gilford says that Dade County is also working with me to have Ralph Stanley release the specs on the private vs. public bus demonstration project to permit the Department of Labor to sign off on the Fair Labor Act.

Hector Alcalde, a Washington lobbyist for the Jacksonville Port Authority, came in for help on a federal highway project to the port in Jacksonville. These days are rather hectic. Many people are in town wanting to meet with me and, in addition to the hearings, this means a lot of time consumption. I don't even have the opportunity to return phone calls as I am immersed in the hearings. The one consolation is that people are sending in checks for our fundraiser before we even make phone calls. Sharyn is happy about this but soon she will begin making calls.

MARCH 11 WEDNESDAY

This morning our subcommittee marked up the supplemental appropriations on the section dealing with transportation appropriations. The markup sessions are for the committees' preparation of a bill for Floor action by editing, amending and drafting language. The draft of the bill is literally "marked up." On my suggestion, the markup on our transportation function of the bill was closed to the public, including lobbyists. We appropriated $5 million of new money into the FAA Air Traffic Controllers Academy in Oklahoma City to build simulated air towers in which to train radar operators for overcrowded airports, as in Los Angeles and Cleveland; the trainees will now have firsthand supervision and the capability to practice their skills right at the academy. One million dollars of new money was also marked for the National Highway Traffic Safety Administration, of which $150 thousand will go to Dade County, which needs this financial shot-in-the-arm for Metro-Dade's trauma network, my pet project and the main reason I included funds for the National Highway Traffic Safety Administration. The balance of the money went to the Center for Disease Control in Atlanta for the study of trauma research.

The Amtrak hearing followed the markup, and we talked about the ridiculousness of Amtrak having to deal each year with a non-funding request from the Administration. There were two witnesses: John Riley, Federal Railroad Administrator, and Graham Claytor, President of Amtrak. In John's opening remarks, he said that despite improvements, Amtrak still projects an operating loss in excess of $600 million in the next fiscal year. The Administration's position was that with the present budget deficit, the country could not afford to continue subsidizing Amtrak.

I knew Riley from when he was administrative assistant to Senator Dave Durenberger (R-MN), Chair of the Senate Public

Works Committee. During a break in the hearing, Riley took me aside and told me that as FRA Administrator he had to go through the motions of supporting the administration's position even though he did not believe in it. Riley believes that the administration should support Amtrak and provide federal funding, but he could not voice that opinion in a public hearing. The FRA Administrator is an appointed position, and as such Riley has no choice but to support the administration or lose his job.

Our committee did do some tough questioning on the recent Amtrak/Conrail accident that happened this past January 4, in Chase, Maryland - one of the worst accidents in Amtrak's history. (Of the 600 people aboard the Amtrak train, 15 died and about 350 were injured.) I found interesting and alarming Riley's comments regarding the accident. He said that both Conrail employees came on duty and were "eyeballed" and talked with by a supervisor who had undergone a special training program in recognizing drug symptoms. In this case, the supervisor did not recognize the symptoms and cleared both employees for duty. They tested positive several hours later, but it was not established that the men were impaired at the time of the accident. This was yet another agency voicing the need for mandatory drug and alcohol testing of transportation employees. Substance abuse is a big issue this year.

Public transportation in our country should be the safest and most efficiently-run system in the world, and I reminded Riley that, "compared to the high-speed Japanese trains, or the high-speed French trains, Amtrak is not nearly as smooth a ride in the Northeast Corridor." I told Riley that I believed both the Amtrak and Conrail trains were exceeding the required speed limit when they collided, and asked him why the automatic brake did not work to slow down the train. Riley commented that the train was actually going at a slower speed than usual and if it had been going at the normal limit of 125 mph, the automatic brake would have kicked in. He went on to explain how they monitor for speed by using "speed guns," similar to what state troopers use, and the Amtrak trains have recorders that you can pull out to check if the engineer was speeding. He said occasionally you catch somebody but it is not an endemic problem. We continued the hearing in early afternoon and finished all the Amtrak questions. Tomorrow we deal with the Federal Railroad Administration questions.

On the Floor today we voted to eliminate aid to the Contras, which passed with a 230-196 margin, but not by enough to override a veto. Dan Mica, Buddy MacKay and I were the only members from Florida who voted to cut off aid to the Contras. Most of the Florida members still vote the Cuban-American position on these issues. Prior to the vote, our Washington and Miami offices received hundreds of calls from mostly Latin Americans with such messages as, "if Congressman Lehman does not support aid to the Contras, we will see that he doesn't get reelected." The staff finally had to stop answering the phones until the rash of calls ceased. As always, though, I voted according to my convictions. Pragmatically, voting otherwise does not convince the other side, and only disillusions those who support my stand.

Late in the afternoon I joined the Foreign Operations Subcommittee for the markup on the foreign operations portion of the supplemental bill. Chairman Dave Obey (D-WI) only has money for the Philippines and for the U.S. portion of U.N. aid to Angola. Other requests rightly will wait for the 1988 Appropriations Bill. Obey agreed that the $50 million to the Philippines were essential. Charlie Wilson (D-TX), a member on foreign ops, told an interesting story about his recent trip to Afghanistan where he spent time with the Afghan freedom fighters. When he was leaving Afghanistan, after being with them for several days, the freedom fighters asked Charlie if there was anything they could do, and Charlie said he would like to talk to some of their war prisoners. They brought him two Afghan pilots who had been trained in Russia and had been part of the Afghan government supported by the Soviets. Charlie spoke with the pilots and they gave him the usual answers and requested that he not make their position anymore untenable than it already was, presently held as "traitors" to their country. After the pilots left, Charlie asked the freedom fighters if he could speak to some of the captured Soviet prisoners. They replied: "There are none, but if we could know ahead of time, we will save you a few until you get here."

The Florida State Society had its reception this evening, and I attended even though I stayed only briefly. I feel I have to attend these kinds of events just to keep the Florida connection. I also had a few minutes, between a phone call and a vote, to attend the Association of American Vintage and Wine Institute reception. The food and wine were excellent, and I left wanting to stay longer. There are several things that I am scheduled to do today but cannot; I don't have time. I will miss the T.V. press conference on the Contra vote, and also my meeting with representatives from the United Nations Association. The staff will have to fill in for me as I must chair the subcommittee. Even when I yield the questioning to Larry Coughlin, the ranking Republican on our subcommittee, I still remain. The other Democrats on our subcommittee really don't want to spend much time at the hearings unless they have particular questions to ask. They say they will help chair the hearings but are not there when I really need them. Since their actions pretty much mirror my own under the preceding chairman, I may get annoyed at times, but it's usually seasoned with understanding.

MARCH 12 THURSDAY

My morning started off with an interesting meeting with the Florida Sheriffs Association. Their biggest problem now is the Haitians that are dealing and using crack cocaine up and down the State. It is not just a Miami or South Dade problem, as these sheriffs are from central and northern Florida. When the Haitians are arrested, the counties do not have the space or cells to hold them, and the federal authorities won't take them. I told the group that the repeat offenders should be incarcerated in the Immigration Naturalization Service (INS) facilities in Krome, and they are going to look into my suggestion as a possible solution.

Afterwards, I met with representatives from the Joint American-Israel Committee. It is an organization comprised of well-to-do Jewish middle-aged women from all over the country, and they wanted to know about the adverse effects of the Jonathan Pollack spy scandal, and how it would affect the funding for Israel this year. "So far," I said, "I have seen no signs that the scandal will affect funding for Israel." [And, this remained true.] A reporter from *Roll Call*, a Capitol Hill newspaper, interviewed me on "my favorite restaurant" in Washington. They are doing a survey, the results of which will appear in Monday's issue, and I am curious as to what it has to say.

Our second day of hearings with the Federal Railroad Administration and John Riley as witness, began at 10:00. Our subcommittee staff director Tom Kingfield is back at work almost completely recovered from a distressing back ailment. With Tom's return, we will now be running efficient hearings, and I am really glad to have him back. With the FRA, the questions continued on the influence of drugs and alcohol use of railroad workers, as well as safety devices and accident rates. Riley is a very good witness - open and forthright - and never more so than when speaking of Conrail's alcohol and drug program. He expressed his "unhappiness" with Conrail's program and said they had not executed the "Operation Red Block" agreement with labor - the voluntary prevention program developed by railroad labor and management. He then rated Conrail's program close to the bottom. (It is clear that the Chase, Maryland, accident has had an impact on John and the agency, and Conrail's involvement in it.) It is almost a repeat of yesterday's hearing on Amtrak, except for the revelation of how extensive "equipment tampering" has become. John indicated that tampering with railroad safety equipment has reached epidemic proportion, and is a serious threat to the public safety. FRA had found 74 instances where essential safety devices were disabled in locomotive cabs, and this apparently was just the tip of the iceberg. "It is so easy," he said, "to remove a tape from a whistle; to remove a block of wood from a dead man's control; so easy to turn that switch that has been turned off and put it back in the 'on' position. It is so easy to drive a screwdriver through the circuit to short-circuit it and then pull it out."

They were finding employees that were not only irresponsible, but careless and not in insignificant numbers. He proposed that, as a deterrent, jurisdiction over the employees be given to the FRA. The agency does have enforcement jurisdiction over the railroad companies, but no enforcement jurisdiction over the employees who actually run the trains.

With my subcommittee hearing over, I went to the Foreign Operations markup where we reported out the foreign operations part of the half a billion dollars supplemental bill, most of which went to Central America and the Philippines. I spoke to Dave Obey about the possibility of Sam Nunn of Georgia, Chair of the Senate Armed Services Committee, and Rep. Bill Gray of Philadelphia, as a Democratic Presidential ticket. "Not a bad idea," he said. In the afternoon Majority Leader Richard Gephardt of Missouri came to see me, and I told him I would do what I could to help him in his presidential bid. Still hanging loose, I don't want to support anyone at this time. "If I decide to help anyone else," I said to Gephardt, "I will let you know at once." In the meantime, I will help him anyway I can in the Miami area.

Calling Bill Guralnik, Director of the American Jewish Committee in Miami, I wanted to know if the AJC would be funding some of Adele's trip expense to East Germany and also about agenda items for tomorrow with the condo leaders going into Liberty City to meet with the black leadership. Bill will be there as his group is actually sponsoring the Black-Jewish relations meeting, and I feel good about my involvement in this effort.

My plane for Miami this evening is an hour late, par for Eastern. I seem to see the same people traveling back and forth like Leo Zefferedi, who goes to and from Washington every weekend. Leo is a former member who lives in Biscayne Park, and is now a lobbyist for the laborers union. Senator Claude Pepper is also on this flight. I arrived home about 9:00 p.m.

MARCH 13 FRIDAY

This morning I met with friends Al Moskovitz and Nancy Pollock, at the Neighbors Restaurant in North Miami. Al has a problem with an AID (Agency for International Development) program for a foreign assistance development that he wants to set up in Guatemala. AID has eliminated his project from consideration and he wants them to reconsider his proposal. For a year now I have told him that he should allow me to arrange an appointment with him and Peter McPherson, AID Administrator, or an AID legislative liaison official. But sometimes people just go through all these expensive lawyer lobbyists in Washington because of the perception of some special power that they have, when I can get more results by just walking them over to a member or staff person, as I did when bringing together Eli Feinberg and Tex Gunnels of the Subcommittee on Treasury and Post Office concerning a Customs office at Tamiami Airport.

Patrice and I drove out to the Carol City Public Housing Recreation Center. There was representation from the Police Department, Dade County School Board, Parks Department, Department of Public Safety, the Tenants Association and officials from Little HUD in Miami. John Smith from the North Dade Chamber of Commerce and the Jaycees from North Miami were also there. The Carol City Child Care Center will make a big difference in this community and I am very pleased with what we are accomplishing here.

Our next stop was at the meeting which I had put together with the Jewish condo leaders and the black leadership. The meeting was held at the Davis Restaurant on N.W. 62nd Street in the Liberty City area, and the idea for this gathering came to me in January when the condo leaders went to Little Havana, and I thought then that the condo leaders also needed to go into the Liberty City area. Today I had some apprehension because I feared some of the condo leaders would raise the issue of Rev. Farrakhan of Chicago or Rev. Jessie Jackson and the fact that none of the leadership in the black community had spoken out against Farrakhan's and Jackson's antisemitic statements. There was good representation from both sides and everyone behaved. Reporters were there from the *Miami Herald*, the *Miami Times* (a black newspaper), and two Jewish newspapers. I was a little embarrassed as every time someone was introduced they said something nice about me, and I wanted them to be more complimentary to each other.

We left the Black-Jewish leadership luncheon and headed for Edison High School's athletic field to meet Dick Judy, Administrator for Miami International Airport. From there, Dick and I went to the heliport, which was presently under construction at the Miami International Airport. A *Miami Herald* reporter was there to meet us, and I was quite impressed as the new heliport operations reached out 100 miles in every direction and looked like something from the 21st Century. We flew by helicopter to the Opa Locka Airport in my district where we saw the new proposed Executive Airport Building under construction. I believe it will be one of the finest executive airports in the country. Dick has a lot of plans for Opa Locka and my job is to keep these construction start-ups on the high priority list for FAA facility funding.

This ends my workday. All three events today were covered by different *Miami Herald* reporters.

MARCH 14 SATURDAY

The Congressional Arts Competition is being held today at the North Miami Museum. Each year our congressional office expends much time and effort for an art competition among high school students. The high school art teachers submit their students best work to a panel of judges. When the judges make their selections the first place winning art and artist are flown to Washington and the exhibit is placed in a corridor of the Capital. Our campaign fund pays for the artist's trip. The exhibits for the second, third, and fourth place winners are placed in our three offices, one in Washington and one each in our two district offices. The students are also given plaques, and each high school student who enters the competition gets a certificate. Unfortunately not many high school teachers promote this event and only about half the schools enter.

Back at the district office I met with Mary Santucci who was running for the village council in Bal Harbour. Bal Harbour is not in my district but Mary and her husband are good friends and supporters. It was amazing how little she knew about campaigning. I told Mary she would need to get a telephone bank organized, and to raise several thousand dollars. [To my knowledge, Mary was never elected to the Bal Harbour Village Council.]

MARCH 15 SUNDAY

The Milt Littman Foundation breakfast was held today at Turnberry, with all the "condo commanders" from North Dade there, and others like Mayor Clark of Metro and Ralph Renick, a former Channel 4 anchorman. I gave the wrap-up statement, complimenting the Littman's on their philanthropic endeavors. Although I feel at times the Littman's are somewhat self-promoters, they are kind and generous, and provide at least a dozen scholarships for high school graduates. Some of the condo people who were at the Davis Cafeteria for the Black-Jewish Leadership gathering came up to me and said that they were a little disappointed that the *Miami Herald* did not feature the story on their meeting - especially considering the time and effort put forth. I reasoned that the *Herald* did not give us a write-up because there really wasn't any hard news to report. It was more a "love-in" than a news story even though the *Herald* sent a reporter and a photographer. There could have been hard news had I raised the question as to why the black leadership did not speak out against Farrakhan and Jessie Jackson, but I did not want the meeting to go in that direction. The only write-up the *Herald* gave us was on my trip in the helicopter with Dick Judy, and that was in today's edition of the *Miami Herald Neighbor's* section.

On the plane back to Washington, my seatmate was an officer from AmeriFirst Bank in Miami, who was also head of the AmeriFirst PAC, and we got on very well talking politics for most of the trip. I suggested the Democratic ticket of Sam Nunn and Bill Gray for 1988. He said he had worked for Bob Dole and was very much in favor of Dole on the Republican ticket.

MARCH 16 MONDAY

I started off by having breakfast with my cousin Marx Leva in the Members Dining Room, and he brought me up-to-date on family matters. Marx is a prominent Washington lawyer, and in addition to family, we enjoy talking politics. On my return to the office, we had a short staff meeting regarding my schedule, which has me very busy - not only in Washington but also in Miami. Afterwards, I called Tex Gunnels about the status of the Customs office and immigration service at the Tamiami Airport, and then Carol Woodward at the Agency for International Development (AID) of the State Department regarding the schedule for my forthcoming East Germany trip. A little later, I went to the Appropriations front office in the Capitol to confirm that Appropriations Chair Jamie Whitten had signed the letter authorizing the trip.

Back at the office I called the Coast Guard liaison and asked if it would be possible for my family to fly with me to Nantucket on the Coast Guard plane. They don't think it will be a problem. At 2:00, I attended a State Department press conference on Child Survival. AID's Peter McPherson headed the conference, and is really up-to-speed on the children situation in Southeast Asia. Adele from my staff was also there. I spoke about fifteen minutes on child survival, immunization, family planning and the oral rehydration program, and I was the only one to mention family planning.

Representatives from the National Endowment for Democracy were in about their program. I sent them to Adele as there isn't much I can do for them as their area of interest really falls under Neal Smith's State Department Appropriations Subcommittee. At 3:30, Dr. Edwin Carlson from St. Petersburg came in. Carlson heads an organization in North Florida called VOCAL (Victims of Child Abuse Law). Then Bill Ratchford, a lobbyist for Washington Mass

Transit (WMATA), came in to talk about the hearing tomorrow on WMATA and its problems. Bill is a former transportation committee colleague, and has invited me to use his home on Cape Cod on Memorial Day recess. Howard Foreman, Chairman of the Broward County Commission, was my next appointment. Howard is a friend from Hallandale and I knew him well when I represented that area; even though I am no longer his congressman, he still refers to me as such.

In the afternoon Tom, Lucy and I reviewed the questions for tomorrow's WMATA hearing. I spoke to Public Works and Transportation Chairman Jim Howard to see if he needed me on the Floor Wednesday to speak in favor of the 55 mph speed limit. When the conference report on the surface transportation bill comes to the Floor, a separate vote will be held on the 55 mph speed limit.

Sharyn is in from Miami to do the fundraiser, and we will go out to dinner this evening and discuss the details of our event. I will have a lot of paperwork to take home this evening.

MARCH 17 TUESDAY

The Florida Congressional Delegation's breakfast meeting this morning was with the Florida Association of Counties. The event was held at the Florida House, and Harvey Ruvin was there from the Dade Metro Commission, and we are always glad to see each other. Jerry Berlin reminded me to write a letter to Leonard Abess, a faithful contributor to my campaign, as I was unable to attend his recent party in Miami.

9:00 a.m., Bob Tallon, President of Florida Power & Light and Dick Sewell, FP&L's Washington representative and lobbyist came in. FP&L wants a new Metrorail station built on the main system over its property on the north side of the Miami River. This is a new endeavor that FP&L is undertaking to develop its property, which has nothing to do with the utility business. Before the hearing, I took Tallon and Sewell to meet with Ralph Stanley. Stanley is the Urban Mass Transit Administrator and the one to make the decision on whether there will be federal funding for the new Metrorail station. Stanley said that he thought FP&L's proposal was "a good idea," and if Metro-Dade would make a funding request to the Urban Mass Transit Authority (UMTA), he would commit to a feasibility study, at UMTA's expense, on the possibility of establishing an additional Metrorail station in connection with the FP&L development.

We went into the WMATA (Washington Metropolitan Area Transit Authority) hearing with questions going to Ralph Stanley and to Carmen Turner, General Manager of WMATA. Carmen is a very able, competent woman and runs the Washington Metrorail Transit System very efficiently. Carmen and Ralph had program contention as well as dollar-figure differences in relation to the amount of money it would take to complete the 89 miles of WMATA. Carmen was requesting $250 million and Ralph was obdurate in his defense of the Administration's budget proposal of $130 million as sufficient to cover WMATA's needs. Much of the friction centered around WMATA's failure and/or reluctance to provide to the Project Management Oversight Consultant the requisite information to support their estimates. Stanley explained that because they did not have WMATA's estimates, figures were compiled based on the completion cost of Phase 1. I think both parties came to the hearing prepared to do battle, so I gave hard directions to WMATA and UMTA to get their acts together and work out any differences and then get back to us with a common ground proposal as to how much future federal money would be feasible to finish off the Washington area Metrorail through this 89.5 mile original segment. WMATA is also talking about 13.9 additional miles after the original segment, and that will probably take new legislation beyond the Stark-Harris bill which authorizes the present Washington Area Metrorail. There may be some funds remaining in the authorization bill but only for additional short segments.

It was a very good hearing. We usually finish before noon, but as WMATA gets longer so do the hearings. We went from 10:00 to noon, reconvened at 2:00, and ended at 4:00, with UMTA and WMATA on considerably more agreeable terms. Chairing the hearing, however, prevented me from attending the Foreign Operations Subcommittee's hearing where former White House Chief of Staff and now Treasury Secretary Jim Baker testified. I also missed the Select Committee on Children, Youth and Families hearing. But I really had wanted to be present for Secretary Baker's testimony.

We had about an hour and forty-five minutes for lunch. During that time, I met Florida Power & Light's Board of Directors at a meeting in the Capitol, and then stopped briefly at a luncheon hosted by Congressman Steve Solarz of New York for the Foreign Minister of Turkey. I am a good friend of Turkey Ambassador Sukru Elekdag, and one of these days I will visit Turkey again. It was a run-run deal for both of these functions.

Later, Cindy Ybarra of the United Teachers of Dade came in about school problems, but I had to tell her that I had momentary tunnel vision and had put on hold any problems other than transportation until the hearings were completed. I did, however, speak with Eli Feinberg and Tex Gunnels about the pending project of establishing a Customs office at Tamiami Airport. Gunnels said that if Tamiami has a Customs office then it needs to also have INS there. I learned that for a small airport, such as Chalk on the MacArthur Causeway and the Opa Locka Airport, immigration could be served by the Customs office. Customs would have jurisdiction to handle the immigration service should the Customs office be willing to put in an 8-hour day at Tamiami Airport.

On the Floor there were several suspension bills. I gave a few magazine articles to some of my colleagues that I thought might be of interest to them. I do a lot of reading and clip items that I think some members might enjoy and even articles about them that they may not have seen. One article on karate I gave to Bill Chappell of Florida and an article on Afghanistan I gave to Charlie Wilson. I make friends on the Floor by doing this.

I visited Dante Fascell in his office, which is directly across from mine. Dante was serving Irish coffee in celebration of St. Patrick's Day. He may be having an operation on his nose, which may be serious. I told Dante that if it was critical he should go to Sloan Kettering in New York, where I had my throat surgery, as they have the best and most experienced physicians. I hope Dante takes my advice, but mostly I hope that this is not serious. [Apparently it wasn't because, to my knowledge, Dante never had the operation.]

On my way into the National Education Association reception in the Cannon Building, I saw Budget Committee Chairman Bill Gray in his office, which was right across from where the reception was being held. I kidded him about the Democratic ticket of Nunn and Gray and he said, "Boy, if you're my friend, you will quit talking about this," but he really did enjoy hearing it. I also saw George Miller, a member on the Budget Committee, and apologized to him for not making the Children, Youth and Families hearing. I missed the Amalgamated Transit Union reception, and I had already turned down the Dr. Brazelton invitation. Dr. Brazelton is from the University of Chicago and is the number one expert on childhood development. Senator DeConcini's wife hosted the reception, but I just couldn't make it. When you start off at 8:00 in the morning and go to 8:00 in the evening you are just not ready to go to a quasi-formal dinner. It has been very busy and I enjoy it, but the demands do not give you much flexibility.

MARCH 18 WEDNESDAY

George Reagle and Diane Steed from the National Highway Traffic Safety Administration met me for breakfast this morning. We talked about problems of the Metro-Dade Trauma Network, and George said it wasn't nearly as bad as the *Wall Street Journal* made it out to be. I knew this to be true. He assured me that the system was working very well, and asked how I wanted the $150,000 that I had put in the supplemental appropriations bill for Metro Dade to be spent. Later in the year he wants me to accompany him to other cities and view trauma outreach programs which benefited from our appropriated $10 million for the Center for Disease Control in Atlanta.

We began the Urban Mass Transit Administration hearing this morning with UMTA Administrator Ralph Stanley as a witness, and it went very well. The budget request was for $1.5 billion, including $130 million for WMATA to continue construction of the Washington Metro system. I asked Ralph why the Administration's budget request reflected a decrease in spending, when other transportation programs were increasing. The Gramm-Rudman restrictions were a consideration, he said, and the need to set Federal priorities such as the Coast Guard's and the Federal Aviation Administration's increased responsibilities for drug interdiction. The drug war is indeed playing a major role in our budget considerations. We finished the morning session at noon. During the recess, I went over to have a photo taken with Speaker Jim Wright. Afterwards, John Schelble and I did a taping in front of the Capitol Building for Channel 7 in Miami on the Public Works Bill which maintains the 55 mph speed limit.

1:30, I met with C.D. Ward, chief Washington legislative liaison for the Martin Marietta Company which has a systems management contract to deal with the FAA NAS (National Air Space) Plan. This is a $1 to $2 billion contract which will run over five years and Martin Marietta is the systems engineer to supervise the NAS Plan. There was some disagreement with the contract as to how well Martin Marietta was performing, and C.D. was very concerned about any penalties his company may incur with the FAA.

The UMTA hearing continued at 2:00 with questions to Ralph Stanley regarding the full funding contract and the Draft Environmental Impact Statement that Metro-Dade submitted for UMTA's review on the north/south extensions to the Metromover. If UMTA finds the Impact Statement acceptable, the environmental process could be completed by the end of July. (No Federal funds can be obligated to these kinds of projects until the environmental process is complete.) Ralph was cooperative and it may be smooth sailing if Metro-Dade can reply with valid answers to any comments UMTA may have on the draft statement. The hearing got as far as the justification questions before we adjourned at 3:30. We finish up tomorrow morning.

On the House Floor during general debate on the 55 mph speed limit, Jim Howard, who is managing the amendment, gave me a few minutes to debate, and I spoke in favor of maintaining the 55 mph speed limit. The staff had prepared my speech. I read half and the rest I spoke extemporaneously. I prefer not reading speeches and do much better just speaking out about an issue and on the 55 mph speed limit, I was well enough informed to do so. The amendment lost by ten votes, but the full Public Works Bill passed. Now we will see if the President signs the bill.

Energy Committee Chair, John Dingell, was on the Floor, and I told him that my grandson Sean had applied for a summer intern position at Los Alamos Laboratories in New Mexico. He said, "Just bring me the information and I will make the phone call." I think he will be able to secure the position for Sean. Also on the Floor was former Florida Senator George Smathers whom I hadn't seen for a long time, as he had retired years earlier. George was first a congressman from South Florida back in the late 1940's, and then a senator. In the time he was a member of the House of Representatives his congressional district was Palm Beach, Broward and Dade Counties.

In the gym I spoke with Tom Downey of New York, who is interested in building a twenty mile chain-link fence for safety purposes along the commuter rail system in his district. I told him to document what the effort required, and to state in writing to me that Jim Howard had no objection to his proposal. I always want written documentation on such matters, not just word of mouth, as Jim will raise hell at the Rules Committee hearings saying that I was trying to legislate an appropriation's bill. With the indication of Jim's approval in writing, I can justify my actions. We almost had a paddle ball game today in the gym with Bob Kastenmeier of Wisconsin and Jake Pickle of Texas, but as everyone got busy our schedules were changed, and we could never get together. I like to play paddleball and we used to play quite often; now it's mostly tennis.

The campaign donations have been coming in quite regularly. We have approximately $25,000 and we haven't used the phones as yet. I took Sharyn to the dinner and musical tribute sponsored by the American Society of Composers And Publishers (ASCAP), held this evening at the Radisson Hotel. It was a wonderful event, honoring Lena Horne, and the best was the ASCAP Board of Directors performing their own songs to Lena. It was amazing how these elderly, mostly Jewish composers from the past could sing, play piano and perform so well in their late years. Morton Gould was the Master of Ceremonies, Sammy Cahn and Tony Bennett were there and then Lena, in her own unique style, rambled on for about half an hour. She is an amazing looking woman for 70 years of age. Many important people from the Congress were there such as Senator Durenberger of Minnesota and his wife Penny, Senator Metzenbaum of Ohio, and Senator Lautenberg of New Jersey. Senator Lautenberg was complaining about Florida Senator Lawton Chiles's tough stance on some of the transportation appropriation problems in his Senate subcommittee. Senator Lautenberg is one of the important senators whose signature I wanted on the letter to Attorney General Edwin Meese regarding Linnas's deportation. I took this opportunity to speak with him about it, and he told me he was negotiating some other matter with Attorney General Meese and did not want to "muddy things up."

MARCH 19 THURSDAY

This morning I went to the Longworth Building for the Dave Obey meeting. Martin Sabo of Minnesota and Jim Moody of

Wisconsin were there. Obey spoke about the trade bill and legislative problems in the Ways and Means Committee, and sought advice on how to deal with Ways and Means Chairman, Dan Rostenkowski. He also mentioned the problem of new taxes in the future, especially payroll taxes.

We wrapped up the UMTA hearings with Ralph Stanley and all went well. Stanley is anxious for me to get Dade County to apply for a preliminary engineering study for the new Metrorail station that Florida Power & Light want to put over its property on the Miami River. The study will cost about $1 million to complete, and I'm not about to stop Stanley from spending UMTA money to determine the feasibility of building such a station.

After the hearing a *Miami Herald* reporter wanted a statement on the Alcie Hastings impeachment process in the Judiciary Committee. The situation is rather sad. I do not know whether he is guilty or not, but he went through one trial process in 1983 and was acquitted. Despite his acquittal, a special judicial investigating committee of the U.S. Circuit Court of Appeals concluded that Alcie had "lied and fabricated" evidence at the trial. Under procedures of a 1980 judicial discipline law, the judges recommended he be impeached, and the U.S. Judicial Conference sent the recommendation to the Judicial Committee of the House of Representatives. [This was to be the longest impeachment process in America's history.]

A *Ft. Lauderdale News* reporter spoke to me about how the Florida delegation voted on Contra aid. I told him that, in addition to myself, I thought Dan Mica may have voted against Contra aid because, as a member on the Steering and Policy Committee, Dan would want to support the leadership and Speaker Jim Wright. Whether the reason was true or not, Mica did vote as I predicted. I was also televised by Channel 7 in Miami on what I would do if I were President. "More forthcoming, less evasive, and more candid," was my response. Channel 7 also aired my interview on the 55 mph speed limit and my statement: "I don't know why some of the Western State Senators are anxious to raise the speed limit when their ancestors traveled out West in slow covered wagons and succeeded pretty well." To my surprise, some of my colleagues told me that my speech on the Floor in support of maintaining the speed limit was on public radio.

At 4:15, I met with Professor Henrietta Waters of Barry University and also with the Child Welfare League of America.

Professor Waters is a lovely individual, very bright, and we will continue to work on the problems of child care. Plans are in preparation for hearings in Miami on child care centers sometime in May. Then, the Florida House Supervisor David Wilson came in, and we spoke about Senator Lawton Chiles not looking too well, and I said that Lawton had to learn to relax. David told me that Lawton reads the *Bible* every morning to relax and to remove tension. I said perhaps he should read *Playboy* instead, as it may do him more good. Lawton is so fanatical about living the pure life and doing the right thing; he is already working very hard for his reelection which is two years away and he doesn't really have a problem but is just running as though he does. As Chairman of the Senate Budget Committee and Chairman of Appropriations Subcommittee on Labor, Health and Human Services, his plate is too full. I fear that Lawton may run into trouble medically, but hopefully not, as he is a good Senator.

Afterwards, meeting with Ambassador Rosene of Israel in the office of Howard Berman of California, with other Jewish members from the House Foreign Affairs Committee, we discussed the problems of Israel's new policy toward South Africa, and the fact that Israel should not commit to any new contracts with South Africa for arms shipment. The problem is, however, that the members do not like the implication that the old contracts would be in effect and could last for several more years. Members there were trying to impress on the Israeli Embassy officials that Israel would have to make a clean break with South Africa if it was going to join the free world in its position on South Africa, including the sanctions that this country has imposed. Of course Israel is in a little different position in its almost friendless world, in that other than the United States and the Netherlands, it has a friend in South Africa. It is difficult to break from the relationship and be even more alone. However, I do not think Israel is in a position to have any choice if it is to maintain any broad-base support in the United States, considering the amount of military and economic aid now going to Israel.

MARCH 20 FRIDAY

Greg Dahlberg on my subcommittee staff, and Lucy and I met this morning with Tom Lukins, Chairman of the Subcommittee on

Surface Transportation of the Public Works and Transportation Committee, the authorizing jurisdiction for Amtrak. We went over some of the problems in our own subcommittee, and talked about John Dingell's letter asking us in the supplemental bill to de-fund the task force appointed by Secretary Dole to study ways in which to reduce or eliminate federal subsidies to Amtrak. We know that the group Secretary Dole nominated to undertake this study is noted for wanting to eliminate federal subsidies, which would wipe out Amtrak. This new Amtrak Commission is loaded with people that are pro-private sector and anti-Amtrak, and could really be a problem. I have already gone on the hearing record condemning the manner in which the commission was established, but before taking further action, I will wait for suggestions from Amtrak on how to rearrange the charter of this commission to create a more balanced membership, by including labor members, for instance. We can then call Secretary Dole and see if she can be convinced to adjust the present bias of this commission, or our subcommittee will de-fund it.

We also discussed problems on the flight service stations that some members want to maintain. These members want us to mandate the maintenance of their district's flight service stations in the supplemental bill. I don't think we can realistically do this, however, and still have the programs under the new technology that we are trying to implement. Barbara Vucanovich of Nevada and Roy Dyson of Maryland have flight service stations in their areas and they want to protect them even though they only serve private pilots.

Lloyd Neville, the legislative liaison for the Israeli Embassy, was in the Rayburn Cafeteria this morning. Neville was at the meeting yesterday in Berman's office with the Israeli Ambassador, and seeing me in the cafeteria, he approached me and asked what I thought of the meeting. I told him that Israel would just have to cut "cold turkey" its relationship with South Africa if it wanted to maintain credibility. The Israelis should not only turn down any new contracts with South Africa but they will have to cancel any existing contracts as well. Neville knows Israel has this problem and has been talking to Appropriations Foreign Operations Subcommittee Chair Dave Obey, and Budget Committee Chair Bill Gray.

MARCH 21 SATURDAY

Late this afternoon Greg, Lucy, and I met to go over again Secretary Dole's new charter commission. I have received a call from Jim Snyder, head of the Transportation Workers Union opposing this task force, and another letter from authorizing Chairman John Dingell wanting me to strike it in the full Appropriations Committee. Calling Larry Coughlin, ranking minority member on our subcommittee, I told him of my plans; Larry said he would call Secretary Dole on Monday and alert her to what I had in mind. I don't want to blind side her. Graham Claytor, President of Amtrak, is also to call me. Secretary Dole will have a few days to put labor people on this commission and then maybe redirect the commission to not entirely eliminate the subsidy to Amtrak, but perhaps find ways in which to improve Amtrak operations.

It has been difficult reaching Peter McPherson, my contact at the AID office in the State Department, as I need information about the AID Program on St. Kitts on which Al Moskovitz had an opportunity to bid. Peter and I kept missing each other's calls, and when we finally spoke he said to write him a letter regarding Al's problem and he would try to have the bids reopened.

Leaving the Hill, I went to George Washington Hospital to see Sue Perry, who was doing well following her surgery. Sue is a good friend and a lobbyist for the American Bus Association, and while visiting with her she told me she was worried about the surface transportation bill and what it may or may not do to her independent or private bus operators.

MARCH 22 SUNDAY

It has been a relatively nonpolitical weekend for me. I had breakfast with my former employee and good friend Sergio Bendixen, who now is a Washington-based political consultant. Sergio is the media consultant to the Bruce Babbitt Campaign for President. We talked politics, and with him pushing for Babbitt for the Democratic nomination, he seemed to think that Jack Kemp would be the Republican nominee. He does not think that Gary Hart will make it, largely because of the character issue enveloping Gary.

At the gym both yesterday and today there were few of my colleagues around. I played tennis at Haines Point with Jo Deutsch's girlfriend, Theresa Williams. Jo is the sister of Marjorie Deutsch, who worked in my Washington office as an intern several summers ago. Marjorie had a brain tumor just like my daughter Kathy. While she was working in my office, I helped Marjorie find a job in Washington, but soon after, she had a reoccurrence and now is very ill. I visit Marjorie often on my returns to Miami, and always bring her gifts from my trips overseas.

Jo is a legislative liaison and lobbyist for the Flight Attendants Association and worked with me on legislative language in my bill regarding flight attendants. Theresa is a computer programmer for the National Academy of Sciences, and is very athletic. She likes to play tennis on Saturday afternoon, and I play her for the exercise and to keep in practice. While Theresa and I played, Jo watched. Sonny Montgomery of Mississippi was also there. Later, he said to me, "Boy, those are two good-looking women." I said, "Yes, they are my girlfriends and they are lesbians and you haven't had good sex until you have had two lesbians making love to you at the same time." He didn't believe me, but he wanted so badly to believe it. Montgomery is a 69 year old bachelor and he thinks a lot about women. A funny story about Sonny is that he was complaining that some of his women friends were getting tired of him. I told him the way to fix that was the next time he had a woman come to see him at his apartment to give her $100 and tell her that it was just walking around money. Two days later he got back to me and said, "You know, that $100 was the sexiest thing I ever did."

The rest of the day was spent catching up on my reading, writing lots of notes for Sharyn for the fundraiser and to the staff.

MARCH 23 MONDAY

After breakfast in the Members Dining Room with Laura Liebman, the daughter of a constituent who is an AIPAC leader, we had a photo taken on the Capitol steps to send to her parents.

My tennis buddies and I played a good game today. Afterwards, at the Foreign Operations Subcommittee hearings on the Refugee Assistance Program and the Peace Corps. I questioned the witness about the reduction of aid to refugee programs in Israel, and told him about my experiences in

Pakistan with the Afghanistan refugees. During the Peace Corps hearing, I said to a witness that the Peace Corps needs to follow up on some of its projects to find out what happens to these efforts after the Peace Corps volunteers leave. I asked Loret Ruppe, Director of Peace Corps, about the motorcycle accidents that the Peace Corps volunteers were having on back country dirt roads, and suggested that they get horses instead; she said some are doing so. I left the hearing and returned to my office to go over with Greg tomorrow's questions for Diane Steed, Administrator of the National Highway Traffic Safety Administration.

MARCH 24 TUESDAY

The Florida Association of Realtors were in this morning. This group has never contributed to my fundraisers, so I did not have them on my list of invites. They had heard about the upcoming fundraiser and asked me about it. I took the name of their Washington legislative representative, and told them I would have an invitation sent.

At 9:30, I met with George Miller and the Select Committee on Children, Youth and Families. Pat Schroeder of Colorado, Lindy Boggs of Louisiana, and myself are the three chairs of the committee task forces. In the wake of Gramm-Rudman, we lack sufficient funds to hire a staff person for each of the task forces, as we have had previously, and this has caused a problem. So, we decided to keep the task forces and use the full committee staff as resource people. Miller's office is full of photos, pictures and memorabilia and, next to Florida Senator Claude Pepper's, it is one of the most interesting offices.

10:00 a.m., we had the National Highway Traffic Safety Administration hearing with Diane Steed. The President's budget request is for $90 million. This time Steed was not wearing such a low-cut dress, and it wasn't nearly as much fun, as she is quite good looking, and very well endowed. She also works very hard and is quite safety conscious. "All of your hard work is negated by the raising of the speed limit 10 mph," I somewhat lectured. As an opponent of the 10 mph increase, I was disappointed that she did not oppose raising the speed limit from 55 to 65 mph. She also had no data to determine exactly what percentage of fatalities was attributable to speed, and this was a major point with me. I expressed concern that raising the speed limit to 65 miles an hour was tantamount to doing away with the speed limit. "Even though it was not 100 percent enforced, we saved a hell of a lot of lives," I said. We should have data now as to how many lives the 55 miles an hour speed limit has saved. I told her that even if we go to 65, NHTSA should maintain a month to month kind of monitoring system on what is happening where the 65 miles an hour speed limit goes into effect, and whether it is actually enforced. The rest of the hearing went well, with questions on safety features such as airbags, seat belts, and the like. We finished at 3:00, and the justification questions will be done tomorrow.

At noon I went to the Florida AFL-CIO private hearing in the Longworth Building. The two Florida senators and most of the Florida members were present. National Machinists President Bill Holayor and Charlie Bryant, head of Eastern's Machinists Union, were there. Charlie followed me to the office to complain about the "terrible things" that were happening to Eastern Airline's labor force and the violations that were occurring against organized labor. The machinists are in a rather bad fix with Frank Lorenzo who is running Texas Air International, which owns Eastern Airlines, and is trying to squeeze organized labor out of Eastern. Charlie said that Eastern Airlines lost 200 pilots to Northwest Air, but I don't know how true this is.

I didn't have time to make the Anti-Defamation League's Israel Mission Reunion. There were no votes on the Floor yesterday and today, and at 3:00, John Schelble and I got together in the office to discuss tomorrow's meeting with the Presidents of the CSX Railroad and the Florida East Coast Railroad. I want more freight traffic taken off the Florida East Coast tracks because FEC runs down through our main constituency - not only causing a noise problem, but creating and endangering auto traffic. This is really an exercise in frustration and futility but it is an effort that I have to make; perhaps this will at least generate good press.

Metro-Dade Commissioner and Transit Committee Chair Clara Oesterle called to tell me that the Department of Labor had signed off on the 13C Fair Labor Act regulation so that Dade County can receive the eighty extra buses on the demonstration project of the private sector comparability to the public sector. I already knew about this, but she was happy and I told her that she should have Metro-Dade request UMTA to do a feasibility study of the proposed station on the Miami River that Florida Power & Light wants to have built. Ralph Stanley told me that all UMTA needed was such a request.

Elizabeth Dole did get back to Larry Coughlin regarding the Amtrak proposal. Larry told Secretary Dole that the review board she had appointed was so loaded with right wingers that it had no validity and that Conte, ranking Republican on the full Appropriations Committee, as well as John Dingell and myself, were very concerned. Telling her that the commission would be de-funded when the matter came before our full committee tomorrow, Larry said Secretary Dole did not seem that anxious or concerned about it. We have not heard from Amtrak, but I am in a definite position and not as blind sided as the Secretary. I intend to make a motion to de-fund the Amtrak review commission unless its charter is changed to become more balanced. This may take place tomorrow, but I don't think I will antagonize her as much as I did last year when I reduced the amount of funding the Secretary's office requested, which got her very upset. I did this to get her attention on other matters about which our subcommittee was concerned. And so far this year, I have been able to deal comfortably with Secretary Dole.

Everett Williams and his friend Tom Stevenson of Lon Worth Crow Realtor and Mortgage Company came in at 4:30. I knew Everett as he lives in Miami Shores and was a member of the Miami Shores Village Council. It was a good meeting, with a definitive legislative agenda wish list from Lon Worth Crow.

In the evening Sharyn and I attended the reception of the National Association of Retail Druggists. The small gathering on the top floor of the Madison Building had no pharmacists there from Dade County, and hardly any members because of other events being held. Although small in numbers, the event was well organized, having the excellent Ridgewell Catering Service, and Sharyn made good contacts. From the Madison Building, we went to the Hay-Adams Hotel where Bill Gray held his super fundraiser. There were a number of members in attendance and all the heavy hitter lobbyists were there. It was also very crowded, and we skipped the dinner, leaving after the reception. Sharyn and I both made many contacts with lobbyists for our fundraiser, e.g., Morris Amitay, Stuart Eisenstat, Dennis Neill and many others from both labor and industry. When you attend a leadership reception such as Bill Gray's you don't just see one group of lobbyists but all the PAC's. I really believe attending these events is the most productive way to lay the foundation for any fundraiser.

MARCH 25 WEDNESDAY

9:00 a.m., I was in a meeting with the Vice President of CSX Railroad and Ray Wycoff, President of FEC, to run through the situation of moving the FEC tracks out of the heart of our district. I think it is a pipe dream, but I do have to go through the motions; it was indeed an exercise in futility. There is, however, a big noise problem. Overpasses need to be erected, which the residents will hate to see, as they conceive every overpass as bringing more traffic into their area. Despite the fact that the residents are unhappy with the thought of this construction in their neighborhood, progress has to be made to keep up with growth in South Florida. The FEC has spent a great deal of money improving its right of way and is not about to give it up; plus, the CSX tracks cannot accommodate FEC freight. They were very nice and I did the best I could, but I don't expect much success on this.

Charlie Bryant from the Eastern Machinists Union in Miami came in upset as usual by Texas Air's Frank Lorenzo's treatment of Eastern employees, saying that Lorenzo was actually trying to cut Eastern back to an Atlantic seaboard airline and deunionize Eastern Airlines. He also said that many of the older machinists were leaving and the new people coming on board were not well trained and did not stay very long. For the moment the only thing I could tell him to do was to give me a set of questions for the FAA hearings in regard to Eastern's lack of safety requirements.

Then the President of the Florida Medical Association, with my old friend Dr. Jay Groff of Miami came in about the costs of medical malpractice insurance; Jay is usually frustrated by Florida regulatory bureaucracy. Afterwards, I went to the Close-Up group meeting but soon turned the group over to Nadine from my staff, while I went to my hearing. About twenty minutes later Nadine brought the group to the subcommittee hearing where they listened to questions on shock trauma, emergency medical service and the issues we had with Highway Safety and Traffic. Today only Tom Delay (R-TX) and Larry Coughlin (R-PA) on our subcommittee were at the hearing to ask questions, and they were there only for a few minutes. By noon, we had finished all the general questions, and will finish the justification questions tomorrow.

During lunch I met with chain smoker Ray Barnhart, Administrator for the Federal Highway Administration, who will appear before our subcommittee tomorrow morning. Barnhart wanted to go over questions and problems pertaining to the FHA, but mainly he wanted to let me know that he would have to leave the hearing about noon. The hearing will begin tomorrow morning at 9:30, but the Republicans will be in New York in the afternoon so we will have a sort of "rump" hearing with the Federal Highway Administration. I will most likely be the only member there for most of the day and in the afternoon Barnhart's assistants will be the witnesses.

In the afternoon I went to the supplemental appropriations markup in the full Appropriations Committee and did some photographic opportunities for my newsletter on how legislation is made in the appropriations' process. As to the transportation chapter of the supplemental bill, the main thing we did was remove the funding from the blue ribbon panel that was appointed by Secretary Dole, as I had threatened in the full committee. I made a motion that the Department of Transportation could not spend money on the appointed commission, explaining that the panel was loaded with anti-Amtrak people and that the charter was extremely one-sided in its outlook on the way to deal with Amtrak. I also, on the transportation function, had to defend against amendments that were offered in regard to directing the FAA on air space. There were other amendments in support of maintaining certain flight service stations in various parts of the country, but these are the standard problems which we overcame as usual.

The big question in the full Appropriations Committee concerned nuclear weapons testing. Anti-nuclear weapons testing won, but will probably be "knocked out" later in the House/Senate conference. Another big question was maritime. Maritime jurisdiction is in the Commerce Subcommittee under Neal Smith and I voted with Neal to change the Merchant Marine Commission's subsidy provisions to help U.S. ocean shipping. Members voted according to the area they represented and which organized labor organization they favored. The full committee markup has no court reporter so we have no hearing records. I was happy with what I accomplished today at this hearing especially regarding Amtrak and eliminating the task force appointed by Secretary Dole. We will rearrange the charter and with the ranking minority member Larry Coughlin, we will work out a more equitable foundation from which to work.

When there is a supplemental appropriations bill many members call me with requests as they all want a piece of the action and don't want to wait for the annual appropriations bill to have matters resolved. Today I spoke with Clay Shaw (Representative, Ft. Lauderdale) and the Mayor of Pompano about problems with the Pompano Airport. I also received calls from North Carolina members about the Raleigh-Durham Airport and from Roy Dyson of Maryland about his airport problems.

MARCH 26 THURSDAY

This morning I was at the Sheraton Grand Hotel speaking to the National Head Injury Foundation. The Vice President's son and Chairman of the Board, Jerry Bush, introduced me. I met Marilyn Spivak from Florida there and Rep. Chet Atkins of Massachusetts. Senator Howard Metzenbaum of Ohio was there, and spoke about his wife who suffered a head injury in an automobile accident, and said that she still has problems. Spivak had come to my office earlier and I had her get in touch with my Alabama college buddy E.M. Friend, whose wife Hermione has been in a coma for several months from a head injury received in a highway accident. The Foundation made me feel very welcome, due in large part to the funds I had provided for the National Science Foundation to do its study on trauma and then $10 million a year to the Center for Disease Control in Atlanta to implement its trauma research program.

Back at the office Tom Kingfield briefed me on the hearing today with Ray Barnhart, Administrator of the FHA, going over certain safety factors that should be addressed by Barnhart. The hearing went smoothly, though, and we finished all the justification questions by early afternoon. At 2:00 p.m., I was on a flight to Miami.

MARCH 27 FRIDAY

The media is to be at the district office this morning to meet with the condo group petitioning for the freedom of a Cuban political prisoner approaching his 27th year in prison.

Looking back on Wednesday's full Appropriations Committee markup, I remembered Silvio Conte (R-MA) at the meeting who had just undergone an operation for prostate cancer. He thanked everyone for their concern and said how much he appreciated hearing from the members when he was in the hospital. Sid Yates and Charlie Wilson, both good friends of mine, were at the meeting, and Sid was moaning that he doesn't travel much anymore as his wife is ill; Charlie was moaning because he had a bad cold and a fever and was up late the night before. Charlie is in his fifties and has a twenty-eight year old girlfriend. He is probably trying to keep up with her and doesn't have the energy anymore.

MARCH 28 SATURDAY

I just wrote a letter to Ellen Kempler thanking her for the beautiful job she did in introducing me to her group "Results," a lobbying organization for hunger and poverty. After my speech they announced the twenty winners, two of whom were from my district, and I presented them with a plaque and a bottle of champagne, and placed a blue ribbon like a Hawaiian lei around their necks. It was a very good event. In her introduction, Ellen talked about the heart valve that I smuggled into the Soviet Union. Jeff Mell had given her a copy of the news story that was reported a few years ago after my visit to the Soviet Union.

To tell about the heart valve episode, we have to go back to October 1985. The opening scenario is a speeding taxi cab zooming through the streets of Tbilisi, the capital of Soviet Georgia, with my Washington aide Adele Liskov, a State Department interpreter, and me, holding on for dear life to a small box containing a $2,000 synthetic heart valve, which I had just smuggled into the Soviet Union, and hoping that the taxi driver is not a KGB agent. Telling the taxi driver to stop at the nearest telephone booth, the interpreter got out of the taxi, cautiously entered the telephone booth, and dialed our contact person. The contact gave him an address and said to "Look for a woman in red standing next to a short man. They will know who you are." Well, what could go wrong did go wrong: The interpreter was given the wrong address! We then wondered what to do next. We had not told the cab driver anything of our mission, but under the circumstances I felt that if anybody could help us, he could. The questions remained, however. Could we trust him? Could he be a KGB agent? We reasoned that anybody who drove the way he did must be trustworthy, since it was not possible for anyone to have followed us. And so we confided in our cabbie, who was in reality an Armenian who communicated in fractured French and handled the streets of Tbilisi like a New York gypsy cab driver. As it turned out, had it not been for our cab driver we might never have found our "lady in red," and accomplished our mission. Sometimes it's the unforeseen elements which lead to either success or failure in the best of plans. In this case, we got lucky.

This drama was set in motion during the summer of 1985, when Hachig Seyranian, a Soviet emigre from Niagara Falls, New York, received a phone call from a brother still living in the Soviet Union. The brother's twenty-two year old ailing daughter, Vartitar, needed a heart operation but was unable to get an artificial heart valve in the Soviet Union. Seyranian was able to purchase a heart valve in New York, but could not find anyone to deliver it. (Several friends returning to the Soviet Union for visits refused to take the valve because they feared it would cause them problems at the border and persons familiar with the Soviet mail system said all packages arriving in the country are opened and their contents often intercepted.)

So, Seyranian took his problem to the State Department, and they told him of my planned codel to the Soviet Union. When the story was told to me, I agreed to undertake the mission, but not before asking myself, what would my daughter Kathy want me to do? The rest, of course, is history. I simply slipped the valve into my briefcase and walked in.

I vowed to make no mention of this to the press until I received word of Vartitar's operation, that she was well on her way to complete recovery, and that the Seyranian family in Russia would be safe from state security forces. So for two months I kept quiet and when the story broke it made news on a national scale. Some of the headlines were as follows: "A Secret Mission of Mercy"; "A Smuggler in a Good Cause"; "Florida Congressman Becomes Secret Agent ...," etc. I felt an overwhelming sense of fulfillment at the thought of my having helped to save a life. These are the moments in Congress that I find truly rewarding.

MARCH 29 SUNDAY

Last evening Joan and I went to dinner with some old friends, the Davis's. Joe Davis is a hard rock Republican conservative. Even though he does not believe in the way I vote, he told me that he hears such good things about me from all of his friends who are also conservatives, about what a conscientious good job I'm doing and what a good Congressman I am. It was the first time he had ever said anything to me about my activities in the Congress, and it was nice to hear.

On the flight back to Washington today my seatmate would not stop talking. He was with Floral Importers, and is scheduled to meet with me on Tuesday, along with other members of the Floral Importers Association.

MARCH 30 MONDAY

This morning I met with Pam Bethel, who is seeking a magistrate position in Miami. I know her mother and father who were both with the Dade County school system, and it was more a social call than anything else, but I did write several letters of recommendation for her.

At tennis with my House buddies and Judge Mikva, who proudly informed us that last night he became a grandfather, and I am sure this is why he did not play very well; we did, however, have a good game. Kastenmeier and Mikva had gone to the Grid Iron Club Dinner and were criticizing Jim Wright's poor taste remarks about Barbara Mikulski being in the centerfold of *Playboy* magazine. Apparently the star of the show was President Reagan. They were amazed at the President and his ability to handle his own role there and the jokes that he told. They also talked about the problem of Mary Rose Oakar of Ohio, a once rising star being groomed for the next Chair of the Democratic Caucus, who suddenly is knee-deep in scandal involving an alleged lesbian lover who lives in New York but was kept on her office payroll. I thought at the time that Mary Rose would have a hard time getting reelected to Congress. [This was not the case, but she never served as Chair of the Democratic Caucus.]

Back at the office Charlie Wilson called and invited me to the Sri

Lanka Embassy for dinner on April 7, but it is the same night as my fundraiser. There will be many events going on that evening, and I do not know how we are going to get people to come to our fundraiser. I think it will be a success, but I will probably have to hand out a few more complimentary tickets. A representative from the Family Research Council came in at 3:30. He was running down the list of people on the Children, Youth and Families Select Committee and trying to find out how his organization, soon to specialize in data information, could be of use to our select committee. He was a nice young man trying to make a job for himself with a new organization, and I helped him as much as I could.

Richard Bolling, former Chairman of the Rules Committee, has written me a very nice letter. Bolling was a very strong leader in the House, and had retired a few years ago. Through the district office, I was able to get an immigration matter solved for one of his friends. I didn't even know about the case, and I was very flattered by his handwritten letter, as he is very well respected on the Hill.

MARCH 31 TUESDAY

This morning in a meeting with the Florida Association of Floral Importers, Jim Hill, the gentleman I met on the plane, was in the group, as was their lobbyist in Washington, who told me that he would be coming to our fundraiser. The Importers explained to me how important they were to Miami as they employ 2,500 people and are the largest air freight loaders coming to and shipping from Miami. They asked that I watch for any trade restrictions on imported flowers, and I assured them that I would. I then went to the hearing of the full Appropriations Committee to hear testify Treasury Secretary Jim Baker and the Director of the Office of Management and Budget, Jim Miller.

The only votes today were a huge override of the President's veto on the Surface Transportation Authorization bill. Last evening Lawton Chiles told me that in the Senate the bill would not be overridden because Treasury Secretary Baker had enough chips to call in from the time he was Majority Leader in the Senate to sustain the veto.

The Bolivian Ambassador came in concerning foreign aid, and with him was my old colleague Jim Symington from Missouri, who is now a lawyer lobbyist. Later, I met with Mickey Leland of Texas and some of the Jewish members regarding the Falasha Jews. Mickey had just returned from Ethiopia, and has a plan to airlift Falasha Jews to visit Jerusalem. This will all have to be approved by the Ethiopian government.

In the evening I took my secretary Wynne Frank to the Floral Importers reception in the Cannon Building, where we each picked up two beautiful floral arrangements. Afterwards I attended the fundraiser for Senator Don Reigel (D-MI), sponsored by Patton, Boggs and Blow. Sharyn was there, as were many lobbyists, but I stayed only briefly, leaving to pick up my special friend Alice Rivlin, Director of the Congressional Budget Office, for the University of Miami dinner honoring Dante Fascell and the Florida Congressional Delegation. The dinner was fine except for Tad Foote, President of the University of Miami, who was boringly long winded in his speech.

Chapter 4

APRIL 1, 1987 - WEDNESDAY

It is 8:30 a.m., and my good friend and tennis buddy from Dade County, John Grabowski and his family are at the office. Grabowski, a Polish army liberator of concentration camps in WWII, has relatives visiting from Poland, and they are interested in seeing the sights in Washington. Walking them over to the Capitol, I saw John Dingell, Chairman of the Energy and Commerce Committee. I am still waiting for John to let me know about the status of my grandson Sean's application for an intern position at Los Alamos. John told me he should be hearing shortly as to whether Sean's application was accepted, and I was glad he brought the subject up before I did.

The hearing this morning was with the Department of Transportation's Research and Special Programs Administration, with a budget request for $22.7 million. RSPA is responsible for the safe transport of toxic materials throughout the country. Administrator Cindy Douglas is an attractive witness, but her answers are too long and she takes far too much time. The fact is the RSPA is still disorganized in administering the transport of toxic materials. The Federal guidance provided by RSPA to the state and local agencies is often ignored, so the regulatory responsibilities have become very fragmented, causing inconsistencies and diverse regulations being administered by different federal, state, and local agencies. Nevertheless, most hazardous materials are transported safely to their destinations. I hope, however, that the next Administrator has better answers to our questions, as I was dissatisfied with Cindy's responses.

During the lunch break two students from my district, Lisa Einhorn and Alberta Worzanack, visited the office. They are in Washington attending the Young National Leadership Conference, and Lisa's sister was the recipient a few years ago of my daughter's Memorial Scholarship Fund at FIU. After the usual photo opportunity, I took them over to spend the first half hour at our afternoon hearing with the Architectural and Transportation Barriers Compliance Board. The Board's responsibility is to ensure that all persons, particularly the disabled, have easy access to our Federal and federally-funded buildings, and of the twenty-three board members, six are required to be disabled. The agency cannot do much with only a $2 million budget and it is the smallest agency with which we deal. Their agenda is of little substance, but it does have a great deal of human interest. I asked questions about accommodations for wheelchairs and for the blind getting on airplanes and on rapid mass transit. Some airlines permit a wheelchair person to go from their seat to the restroom in the aircraft once it is in flight, but most do not. The typical "boarding" chair is designed for boarding, not for independent movement within the aircraft. Passengers are taken on the aircraft in the boarding chair. The boarding chair is then removed and placed back in the airport facility, with the wheelchair probably parked some place on the plane. And while that person is on the plane, he is immobile until the plane lands.

Charles Hauser, Chairperson and witness for the ATBCB, indicated that a few air carriers did have on-board collapsible chairs, but that the size and weight of the wheelchairs and the fact that the restroom doors and the restroom itself had to be wider than usual to be accommodating were major constraints. The Air Carrier Access Act of 1986, will help to rectify this problem. I also made reference to mass transit in Japan and in the Soviet Union and the fact that in those countries the blind, by raised surface markers on the platform, can line up with where the doors are supposed to be on the car when the train stops.

Back at my office J.D. Williams, a flamboyant Washington lobbyist lawyer whom I like, wants me to write to the Interstate Commerce Commission (ICC) asking for reconsideration of ICC's refusal to submit to Congress the merger between Southern Pacific and Santa Fe Railroads. I will probably do so because John Dingell, Chairman of the Committee on Energy and Commerce, who manages the authorization of this legislation, has sent me a copy of a similar letter that he has written to the ICC. If my approach to the ICC is completely neutral and objective, I do not see any harm in asking them to do this. But, if the merger goes through, it would eliminate most of the Southwest rail competition.

We just received a $500 check from Citizens Southern Bank of Georgia, and Sharyn tells me the money is steadily coming in. Nine fundraisers are being held the same evening, and about ten other socially attractive events. I do not know how many people will actually attend our fundraiser, but we now have enough to cover our overhead expense. Anna Thaxton from our district office is in Washington for the fundraiser, and I took her this evening to a reception in honor of Transportation Secretary Elizabeth Dole. The affair was at Tyson's Corner in McLean, Virginia, and the Secretary was, as always, very gracious. Much jewelry and mink coats adorned the wives of the Northern Virginia real estate developers. I spoke to many of the guests, including Shirley Ybarra of DOT, and lobbyist J.D. Williams, about Amtrak's blue ribbon committee, and advised Shirley to have the matter settled before it reached the House Floor; also discussed was the Southern Pacific and Santa Fe merger.

APRIL 2 THURSDAY

Lobbyist David Osterhaus and the President of UNISIS Corporation, which does business with the FAA, came in this morning. I have known David since he was an Air Force escort officer on the codels to Europe for the Interparliamentary Union meeting ten or twelve years ago.

The hearing this morning was with the Office of the Secretary. Jim Burnley, the Deputy Secretary of Transportation, was the witness. I do not think anything has gotten the attention of the Congress in recent months more than flight delays, which have increased substantially in the last year. The airlines blame the FAA and the air traffic control system; others point to airline scheduling. I told Burnley of my experience with the flight out of Miami that departs around 5:30 p.m. to Washington National. I had been taking that Sunday flight for some time, and for a while they were flying 727's, which meant that I would end up in Baltimore, because the flight would be delayed past 10 p.m. So, departing from Miami a couple of Sundays ago, as usual, the plane was two hours late. I asked the ticket agent if the plane would be landing at Washington National, to which she replied: "Yes, we have gotten smart. We only use 757's on our 5:30, two-hour flight to Washington National because we land them after 10 p.m." The delays are so prevalent, I said to Burnley, that Eastern can no longer use 727's even on a two-hour flight from Miami to Washington National.

Airports are like a zoo, once airlines cancel a flight. I have seen everything from shoving matches to fist fights. "I feel sorry for the airline personnel," I lamented. Burnley said he has heard many people refer to modern day airports as looking like "bus stations of old." "I wish they did look like bus stations," I said. "One way to fix this, that I think would be a terrible tragedy," he said, "would be to re-regulate and have fewer passengers on the airplanes and fewer airplanes in the skies. We would not have as many delays and there would not be as many angry people in the airports." I told him that was not a feasible alternative. He agreed.

For lunch, I had an omelet and picked up a dozen eggs at the Egg Producers luncheon hosted by Kiki De La Garza of Texas and Chairman of the Agriculture Committee. I stopped at an event for the South Florida Hadassah group and then on to another luncheon hosted by Glenn Anderson, Dean of the California delegation, where members received a carry-out sack of California foods. In the afternoon I managed to play tennis for over an hour with Judge Mikva, my colleague Howard Coble of North Carolina and House Chaplain Jim Ford. Howard won with everyone; he is a little too good for us. On the next court was Supreme Court Justice Scalia, and I was surprised to see him playing on a public court.

APRIL 3 FRIDAY

No hearings today, which allowed me time to meet with Terry Peel, chief staff on Appropriations Foreign Operations Subcommittee, to organize the itinerary for our trip to East Germany. I also spoke to the East German Embassy about visas for Rabbi Neuman and Gene DuBow of the American Jewish Committee. Today there are several irons in the fire: plans for the East German trip, the transportation hearings, and John Schelble is telling me that our newsletter on health care and the prevailing problems in nursing homes is now ready for mailing to our constituents. The Health Care Financing Administration (HCFA) is the oversight for Medicare in the Atlanta regional office, and our office has a problem with HCFA's rejection of too many cases. Blue Cross/Blue Shield and Aetna also have problems with health care in nursing homes.

My friend Caroline Brown, a Washington schoolteacher and an activist in educational politics, is in the office for our dinner date. It has been a long time since I have seen her, and I am looking forward to our evening.

APRIL 4 SATURDAY

I broke a toe on my townhouse staircase and it hurts quite a bit. Since it is the weekend and I cannot go to the Capitol Physician's Office, I am keeping it elevated and taking aspirin. Joan and I had tickets this evening to see Leonard Bernstein conduct the National Symphony Orchestra at the Kennedy Center, and I felt well enough to go. Arriving late, we could not get balcony seats but we did get good seats down front. We spent intermission in my colleague Sid Yates's Kennedy Center office, as Sid is on the Advisory Board of Trustees for the Kennedy Center.

APRIL 5 SUNDAY

Joan and our good friends from Miami, Al and Esther Green, are in town, and we spent a really nice evening together dining at the Westwood Country Club with Dr. Everett and Marion Gordon.

APRIL 6 MONDAY

The first thing I did this morning was to have my toe examined at the Capitol Physician's Office. The doctor x-rayed and confirmed that the toe was broken and, in fact, the top joint was shattered in several places like a piece of glass. He sent the x-rays to Bethesda Naval Hospital to determine whether I needed a cast or pins; later in the day the doctor called with the results Bethesda, and I did not need either a cast or pins. He is to x-ray my toe again in about five days before I leave for Europe.

I went to Don Edwards's office to tell him sadly I would not be playing tennis today, as I do look forward to our tennis games. The rest of the morning was not too active, so I went home early and propped up my foot. In the evening I felt well enough to go with Joan and the Green's to Senator Bob Graham's party in the Hart Building to meet Jimmy Buffett on "Save the Manatees." Afterwards, we attended a beautiful party in the Cannon Caucus Room sponsored by the pharmaceutical company Schering-Plough out of Memphis. The featured cuisine was Memphis barbecue and seafood.

APRIL 7 TUESDAY

My first appointment this morning was with Jack Langer from City Gas. Jack is still trying to recover $1 million or so from Amtrak. We resolved the problem in the House but his lawyers have not been able to protect him in the Senate version. Barbara Warden from the Garment Workers Union was in next about textile and apparel legislation; her husband Dick represents the United Automobile Workers. Barbara asked for my support of the Gephardt protectionist amendment, but I had to tell her that at present I did not want to commit to any additional protectionist amendments. My intentions are to keep all options open and see what happens on the trade bill.

NBC's Sallie Forman came in for assurance that I would stay neutral on the NBC takeover of the Channel 4 affiliate in Miami; I told her I would maintain my neutrality throughout the proceedings. Afterwards, I spoke at length with *Miami Herald* reporter Ricardo Zaldivar, supplying information on my proposed trip to East Germany. If the trip is successful, he wants to have all the background information in place.

The fundraiser this evening at the Folger was a huge success - both financially and socially - with attendance close to two hundred. Elizabeth Dole came, which pleased me. Guests from Miami came up for the event - Al Moskovitz, Nancy Pollock, my younger son Tom, Jack Langer, Eli Feinberg, and Sidney Alterman, owner of a large trucking company in Opa Locka; Alterman's son Rick and my son Tom are good friends. Don Edwards and George Miller were among many of my colleagues there, including members on my subcommittee. I will write to thank all of them. Three hundred pounds of stone crabs flown up from Miami disappeared in the first hour, and the caterers were excellent. Greg from the transportation subcommittee said, "You maintained your reputation for putting on the best fundraising party on the Hill." We did better than $80,000, which was more than expected. It was exhausting, but also exhilarating.

APRIL 8 WEDNESDAY

This morning, I started with the Foreign Operations Subcommittee hearings on the Mideast regional programs and Richard Murphy's testimony. (Murphy is the former Ambassador from the Philippines who greeted Joan and me on the taxi runway with a flower lei when we first visited there.) The last time I saw him was at the Sri Lanka Embassy party in February. During the hearing my questions to him were about the Philippines, President Cory Aquino's illness, the status of the Tamils in Sri Lanka, and the danger of the Syrian military at some point reaching a critical mass. Murphy thought that any attempt by Syria on Israel would be suicidal.

Harry Belafonte was also a witness, and he was wonderful, speaking primarily about the hardships people suffered in Africa from malnutrition and dysentery. I interjected with how the United States had increased military systems programs in South Africa and cut back on UNICEF, and how obscene I thought this was. Nodding his head and saying that he agreed, he then told us about children he had seen in Angola who had stepped on U.S.-made landmines and about other parts of Africa where children were dying in their mother's arms. It was interesting how much more effective he was when he put down his papers and just talked, than when he read his material.

Feisty Dick Judy, Director of Miami International Airport, and Hector Alcalde, its Washington lobbyist, came in. Apparently, officials from Eastern Airlines and Texas Air want to schedule flights to Buenos Aires, which would be devastating to Pan American Airlines. I do not know why Dick is involved in these kinds of issues, with one airline going against another. (Pan American representatives are scheduled to meet with me tomorrow.) I told Dick I would think about his problem, but that I could not at this time make a commitment. This is one issue I will steer clear of, and it is unfortunate that the director of an airport is less than neutral in this competitive situation.

J.T. Griffin, head of the Florida Citrus Association, came in about support for additional funds for fruitfly eradication efforts. And then Jacques Despinossa, a Haitian radio talk show host and hustler from my district, was in about "getting South Florida Haitians ready to vote." Patrice in our Northwest district office will help, and I told Jacque to get in touch with Patrice, as she would have my consent to set up a tent in front of the 79th Street office for voter registration.

I was tired this evening, but I did meet Joan and Nancy Pollock at the National Gallery reception for the film premier of "Suleyman the Magnificent," the Turkish sultan who lived during the 1400's. While they watched the film, I sat outside and caught up on my reading of the *Wall Street Journal* and *Congressional Record*. Afterwards, we took Nancy to the airport and then Joan and I went to dinner.

APRIL 9 THURSDAY

The day began with Mark and Carol Press from my district regarding the overpass on Ives Dairy Road and West Dixie Highway at 203rd Street over the railroad tracks, which would be built in front of their house. Then Rosemary Murray and Don Taylor from Pan Am came to tell the other side of the story about Eastern and Texas Air moving in on Pan American. I listened, but continued my resolve to stay out of this fight. Next, Nancy Sellick from the Center for Responsive Politics came in for an interview on my attitudes and feelings toward Congress. During the interview the bells sounded, so I had to get to the Floor for a vote. Majority Leader Tom Foley selected her for this project, and what I did not answer orally I will have Marsha from my staff complete. I just do not have the time to fill out all the detailed questionnaires that these well-meaning persons sometimes want.

Back at the office Marsha, my legislative aide, was meeting with the Communication Workers of America representatives, while waiting for my return. They were seeking support for legislation that would assure employees that the government would prevent supervisors from "eavesdropping" on employees' phone calls without notification. I told them that I would look into the matter and get back to them. Before making any commitment to this group I first want to check with Bell South, as I do not want to be caught in the middle of a fight between Bell South and the CWA. When they left, Joel Williams from the Savannah Foods Industry, came in asking for my support of the trade bill that contains export help for the sugar industry in this country.

Still trying to wrap things up before my overseas trip, I am not getting as much done as I would like, as members continue to come in to discuss special projects they want in my bill now that we are nearing the end of our hearings. I tell them to speak to Jim Howard, Chairman of the authorizing Committee on Public Works, and then to write me a letter saying that Howard doesn't object. This does not mean we can appropriate for the request, but, if so, I will not have a problem with the authorizing committee.

The budget, which I supported, passed on the House floor today. It will be a bit tough on our transportation bill this year, but I hope we can preserve the $2 billion we have for the subsidy of public mass transit. The problem will be the additional billion needed for the FAA, and this puts the squeeze on us. The budget bill allocates for all the subcommittee appropriations. I do not know how Chairman Whitten will divide up among each subcommittee the Appropriations allocation, but I hope he takes care of transportation. I think he will look out for health and human services before transportation.

We have a problem in Miami. The Government Service Administration (GSA) is making available to Dade County five acres of land. Metro-Dade wants to use the five acres to build a prison center. The city of Opa Locka is opposed. The situation in Opa Locka is bad enough with residents moving away, we certainly do not need a prison to make it worse, especially since the land can be used by private enterprise to help stabilize the area. I went to the Subcommittee on Treasury, Postal Service and General Government, which funds GSA, and asked the staff to see what could be done to stop Metro-Dade. Then, in my call to the Department of Justice, I was told that papers submitted by Metro-Dade were not in proper order, which fortunately means that private enterprise will probably get the land since the April 15 deadline will pass before GSA can transfer the property to Metro-Dade.

Silvio Conte is still ill from his operation for prostate cancer. I took him the food supplement, Ensure Plus, which helped me following my surgery.

Joan and I had dinner at Le Gaulois, and because I praised Le Gaulois in the Roll Call survey and said it was my favorite restaurant, they really pulled out the red carpet for us. We saw old friends, Carolyn Alper and her friend, Mickey, there. Carolyn, a native Washingtonian, is an artist.

APRIL 10 FRIDAY

This morning Joan and I, accompanied by Terry Peel, chief staff on Appropriations Foreign Operations Subcommittee, and Adele Liskov, my associate staff on Foreign Ops flew off to New York to catch our Pan American flight to London. Elizabeth Dole happened to be on the same flight. When we arrived in New York, our connecting flight was soon to depart, but we got the VIP treatment. Jerry DiSilva from Pan Am was at Kennedy Airport to meet us and made sure our baggage got on the connecting flight. I will be writing a letter of appreciation to him and to his boss. We are now about three hours out, and the flight has been very pleasant.

On the plane I was reading about Senator Paul Simon (D-IL) who was quoted as saying he would announce in May his candidacy for president. This came as no surprise to me, as Simon had called me about a week ago and asked if I would again support him in his presidential bid. I told him "No" because, after he dropped out of contention to support Babbitt, I gave my word that I would probably not make a commitment until the Democratic Presidential Convention, and suggested to Paul that he not run, as I thought it was not the wise thing to do after once dropping out of the race.

Simon's initial presidential boom got started in January 1985, the night of Reagan's second inauguration. That evening I was asked in a television interview who I thought would be a strong Democratic presidential candidate for 1988, and I named "Paul Simon of Illinois," because Paul had defeated, in a state that gave Reagan a landslide victory, the most formidable candidate Charles Percy, a seated and popular Republican senator at that time. Paul did well in the Iowa caucus and the New Hampshire primary and from there a kind of boom developed. I think his timing is wrong now, and I hope he withdraws his candidacy. It looks as though Al Gore is also going to run. I even spoke to John Dingell about running for the presidency, but Dingell said, "I am too happy to take on anything like that right now."

When we arrived at Heathrow, there to meet us was Matt Bouce from the American Embassy. Matt comes from a suburb of Detroit, and is your typical Foreign Service officer - young, Ivy League, and very nice. We are staying at the Grosvenor House for this short stopover in London, and when we got to the hotel there was a message from John, my press assistant. John had learned through United Press International (UPI) that the American Jewish Committee had broken the story even though they had agreed to wait until Wednesday when we expect it to be official that the Rabbi will be approved to serve in East Germany. That threw us off a bit because the *Miami Herald* reporter, Ricardo Zaldivar, had agreed to hold the story until Wednesday. John had no choice but to tell Ricardo to go ahead and run the story. I was disappointed because I wanted the story to appear after we reached a firm agreement. The main thing I did not want to occur was to have the story come out before it actually happened and run the risk of upsetting the East Germans.

Later, I felt less anxious about the matter and relaxed, due largely to Larry Wheeler legislative liaison of the Hughes Corporation who had managed to get me tickets to the "Phantom of the Opera" this evening, when all other sources had failed to come up with the tickets.

APRIL 11 SATURDAY **THRU APRIL 17**

Trip to the German Democratic Republic

As we departed from Heathrow this morning the airport was very crowded and hectic, but once on the plane and in flight, we were all able to relax. We are en route to East Germany to continue negotiating with the East German government for a rabbi to serve in East Berlin to the few small Jewish communities in the German Democratic Republic for the first time since the end of World War II. We went through customs in Hamburg and then flew to Berlin from Hamburg. Berlin is an international city, divided after World War II.

In Berlin another foreign service officer, Wayne Merry, met us at the airport. Wayne is the charge d'affaires of the East German desk at the State Department, and flew over from the States especially for this project. Also to meet us was Ken Pitterly, the "Control Officer" assigned from the U.S. Mission in West Berlin. We had the same chauffeur when I was here a year ago last April, and today we had use of the Ambassador's Mercedes.

Our accommodations were at the excellent Kempinski Hotel, and we ate in the hotel restaurant where I dined on my previous visit, and the food is superb. In the evening we went to hear the Berlin Philharmonic Symphony, one of the finest orchestras in the world, but the conductor, unfortunately, was Von Karian, a Nazi sympathizer. The concert was not all that great, and I had difficulty staying awake after the long and early day from London. The one good thing was that the concert lasted only about an hour and a half with no intermission. Tomorrow we will be briefed at the U.S. Mission before going to the Nazi Documentation Center which houses the most extensive collection of Nazi data. Much of the data housed at the center is furnished to our Department of Justice's Office of Special Investigations in Washington. I had initiated the original appropriations for the Special Investigations several years ago.

The trip is moving along on schedule, and we are getting good Embassy support. It is not quite as comfortable as going with a Congressional CODEL, but then neither are we tied down to a large group of people. We took Ken Pitterly and Wayne Merry to dinner at the Kempinski, and they enjoyed it. Ken is somewhat of a nerd, and Wayne is a super-cultured know-it-all, but I think he will be all right. So far we have been getting along, and they have been quite accommodating.

APRIL 12 SUNDAY

Across the street from the Kempinski Hotel is the Jewish Community Center where we were supposed to meet Haim Golinsky, head of the West Berlin Jewish Community. Golinsky did not show, but sent one of his representatives to meet with us. We learned that there are now 5-6,000 Jews in Berlin, and most of them are emigres from the Soviet Union. Tight security is necessary there since many Berliners are still hostile to Jews and to the State of Israel. Before World War II, nearly 400,000 Jews lived in pre-divided Berlin. The Center is not open today, Sunday, and I heard one Jewish American from California told to come back tomorrow. It is quite an impressive building and a good community center for children from kindergarten through high school. There are two rabbis at the center and about twenty rabbis in all of West Germany.

Leaving the Jewish Center, we went to see the Polansky Memorial, constructed in memory of those in the German resistance who, in July 1944, tried to overthrow the German government. Most of those "resisters" were executed. There were many German families who lost relatives in the uprising. It is surprising that I had not seen this memorial on my two previous trips to Berlin.

A blister has broken out on my foot, and I have to watch to make sure it does not get infected. I may have to go to the Mission headquarters to have it examined. There is no American consulate or embassy in West Berlin and, because of the unusual status of West Berlin, the equivalent of a consulate or embassy is called a Mission.

APRIL 13 MONDAY

At the U.S. Mission headquarters, my friend John Kornblum was in charge of the base, as the General was out. John was the Control Officer when I was here last April, and he has a very important position. We had met again in Washington last month at a reception for the Lord Mayor of West Berlin at the West German Embassy. It was good to see him again, but he did not give us much information that we already did not know. We talked about automobiles more than anything else. John is a classic-car and Detroit Tigers fanatic. He gave me a book of the 105 classic cars, which was a lot of fun because that was from my heyday in the automobile industry back in the 1950's, and he can recognize cars even better than I can.

Following our U.S. Mission visit, we spent time in several department stores, and the prices had almost doubled from last year when I was here. I only bought a few souvenirs and ordered a few tee-shirts from the U.S. Mission Army base. My toe was giving me trouble so I went to the U.S. military headquarters where a nurse from Scotland was just wonderful. After medicating the toe, she redressed it and gave me medication to reduce the swelling. It feels much better now, and I should get back to the States in good shape. Leaving the base and checking out of the Kempinski hotel, we went to a lodge for lunch with Ken Pitterly and the others. Joan met us there with Diane, the young American Chief of Protocol for the Mission, who was taking Joan around. The main thing I remember about the lunch was the fresh white delicious asparagus that I had not seen since I was a child. They were just like my mother used to serve, and it brought me back many years. The entire meal was wonderful, and a nice way to wrap up the West Berlin visit.

Around 2:00 we departed for East Germany. Instead of going through Checkpoint Charlie directly into East Berlin, we went through Checkpoint Bravo, which took us from West Berlin and into East Germany, rather than into East Berlin. Since we would be traveling outside East Berlin into other parts of East Germany, we required a different passport control procedure due to the lack of total recognition by the United States of East Germany as a country. Instead of driving from one side of Berlin to another, we had to drive about an hour in order to enter at a different part of East Berlin. Passing through areas of East Berlin that were not part of the tourist route, we came across areas that were still bombed out, and passed by buildings with bullet holes and shrapnel embedded in them. It is said that Berlin received more tonnage of bombs than any other city in Germany.

East Berlin is surely different from West Berlin. For one thing, it is the old, original Berlin and has a grander character to it than the more modern, Americanized West Berlin. Although dreary, I found fascinating the original Berlin Prussian architecture. It was early afternoon when we arrived at our hotel, the newest hotel in East Berlin. At the American Mission, our Ambassador to East Berlin, Francis Meehan, was in the United States but Alan Thompson, the charge d'affaires, made us feel right at home. He gave us the usual briefing about the situation in East Berlin, especially how, as he saw it, the purpose of our mission was to "bring in" the Rabbi. He discussed the problems, what angles we could pursue, and the steps we should take with East German Minister Klaus Gysi and with the Jewish community. In Dresden we will meet with the elder of the East German Jewish community who will have an important role in the decision to accept this particular Rabbi.

At the hotel that evening, Minister Gysi entertained our group in a first-rate restaurant's private dining room. The meal was superb and all the right toasts were made; we got along just fine. We did not speak much about the issues, and it was a more congenial relationship than we had established when Gysi was in Washington. Dinner went from 7-9:00. We had arranged for Rabbi Neuman and AJC's Eugene Dubow to meet us at the hotel at 10:00, not thinking that the dinner would be that late. Minister Gysi was not expecting us to meet with the Rabbi and Dubow until the next morning, so, not wanting to get into an embarrassing situation, I went up to my room around 9:30, telling Terry Peel to call me when the Rabbi arrived at the hotel. With us now are Terry Peel, Adele Liskov, and Wayne Merry from the East German desk. At about 10:00, the Rabbi and Gene Dubow arrived, and we assembled in the hotel bar for a good strategy meeting. The Rabbi was very definite in what he wanted, the two basic prerequisites being to have a multiple visa, not just conversation about it, but something established, and an acceptable housing situation. I told him I would give it my best shot.

APRIL 14 TUESDAY

This morning our group went directly to the Office of Minister Gysi, who spoke to us about human rights and the GDR, plus a lot of propaganda. When I tried to pin him down as to the multiple visa for the Rabbi, he said he could not do anything until the Jewish community made a formal request to him. He explained that the government would not make a decision for the Jewish community, but would respond to a request from the community for a rabbi to be invited. (This exercise was designed to show us that the government did not encroach on the autonomy of the Jewish community.) He handed out mementos, one of which was a beautiful piece of Meissen porcelain for Joan. Joan was out sightseeing with a young woman named Irene Runge, a prominent member of the East Berlin Jewish community. Irene was born in New York after her German parents fled Germany before the war. During the McCarthy era they moved back with Irene and settled in East

Berlin. Irene has adjusted and made her life there as a sociologist at Humboldt University, having written and had published a book in German about New York; she and Joan are getting along quite well.

Following our meeting with Gysi, we met with the Minister of Trade. There we heard about the U.S. trade barriers with East Germany. The problem of course is the Berlin wall, and as long as the wall is up a human rights problem will exist. There is difficulty to lowering trade barriers between our country and East Germany, although, to me, it is detrimental to both countries to maintain these barriers, and I hope we can work out better trade arrangements; I believe it would help the East German government to turn more westward and not look to the Soviet Bloc. The Minister of Trade was quite cordial.

We then went to the Metropol Hotel for lunch, and it took over two hours for us to be served. The main course was not served until the Chargé told us we would be meeting the Foreign Minister in fifteen minutes, whether the meal was served or not. Everything was then served immediately, and the food was worth the wait. The delay may have been a response to the bureaucracy from people working in a socialistic society; in any case, the food was very good. The Foreign Minister was a tough old bird. I mentioned to him that I hoped he would help Klaus Gysi expedite the necessary visa for Rabbi Neuman. He did not know about the visa for the Rabbi, and complained to us about the inability of the East German delegation in Washington to move about freely in the United States. Wayne Merry quickly corrected him on that. Wayne said to me later that the foreign minister was actually trying to get something from me in return for helping us with the visa, but he was really asking for something that was already provided.

In the evening, our group went to a Seder in the Jewish community's cultural center, which was attached to the huge old synagogue destroyed on Kristallnacht. The East German government says the temple will be restored. The religious service was held in the front and the Seder was in the back of the building in the Jewish community culture room.

APRIL 15 WEDNESDAY

Arriving in Dresden today, we first did a quick sightseeing tour and then attended a luncheon hosted by the Dresden Jewish community. Its leader, 79-year-old Helmut Aris, President of the Association of Jewish Communities of the GDR, was to have been deported from Dresden to a concentration camp on the very day that the allies fire-bombed Dresden so devastatingly. He fled from the train station and, as he said, "It was a tragedy that so many people in Dresden were killed that day in order to save the concentration camp victims who were to be shipped out the same day." Aris stayed in Dresden during the first couple of years of the war because he was an expert metallurgical engineer and knew how to run his family's metal business, and Germany needed him for that. At the luncheon were Rabbi Neuman from Champagne, Illinois, but originally from Germany, Eugene Dubow of the New York-based American Jewish Committee, and a visiting cantor from Budapest.

After lunch, I went back to the hotel and called *Miami Herald* reporter Ricardo Zaldivar to inform him on what we had accomplished, and suggested that he call Rabbi Neuman and Gene Dubow for additional information. I am not yet sure that Ricardo will have a story because, although we are all in agreement in principle, it is not yet a "done deed." There are three groups of players - the East German government with Minister Klaus Gysi, the American Jewish Committee, and the East German Jewish community, and it may take another couple of weeks for us to work this out. The goal is to have the Rabbi in East Germany by September for the High Holy Days. If anything can move the Rabbi to come to East Germany, it would be the need for common ground on which young Jews can come together to relate and communicate. Many have drifted off into the mainstream and have lost the Jewish interaction and contacts. The Rabbi's and my motive is to bring them back into the Jewish community and make them a unit as they were once, especially among the young people from mixed marriages.

That evening our group was the guest of Klaus Gysi at the Dresden Opera. Sitting in the center box, the President's box in the balcony, we had the finest seats in the house. The rebuilt Dresden Opera House is beautiful, quite breathtaking. Our delegation, our translator, and Minister Gysi's aide were also there. In a conversation with Rabbi Neuman, I said I would like to meet with his son in Washington to tell him that his father may be moving to Germany, and the Rabbi quickly responded, saying, "Don't do that until I tell him that I have made up my mind, as I want him to think he has a role to play in my decision." I got the definite feeling that Rabbi Neuman had made up his mind to come to East Germany as soon as the details are worked out even though he has not said so. After the opera some of our group went to a German wine cellar and had a good time. Dresden is a remarkable city, and I would like to visit here again.

APRIL 16 THURSDAY

Early this morning we left for Leipzig. The drive is very beautiful along the Elbe and we were able to see the old German way of life, which has not been modernized with shopping malls. Heavy industrialization is all along the river. Minister Gysi's representative is on this trip, and seems to be a fine young man; he had "hung out" with our group last evening at the wine cellar. I gave him a cowboy shirt that I had brought with me, and he really seemed to like the gift. Doing for a staff person, I thought, is more productive than presenting Gysi with yet another gift.

We are now making plans to meet in Washington with Gene Dubow, Ambassador Herder and possibly Wayne Merry in about two weeks. First I expect to be with Secretary of State George Schultz at a dinner party hosted by New York Congressman Jim Scheuer at his home, and I am arranging to have the Secretary briefed on our trip prior to seeing him at the dinner. I understand also that Ambassador Ridgeway is interested in knowing what is happening in the East Bloc countries, and perhaps she can help us.

APRIL 17 FRIDAY

Yesterday was extremely busy as they put us on another "killer" but productive schedule. We did stop in Meissen to shop, and I bought a couple of plates as gifts for my grandchildren. The Meissen factory is very interesting with lots of young people as employees. We had to go into the city of Meissen to shop and buy merchandise because nothing could be purchased at the factory.

When we reached Leipzig, the Leipzig District Council had arranged a luncheon for us on the top floor of the tooth-shaped

University building, appropriately called the Wisdom Tooth Building. Leipzig is very much into trade and the ancient Leipzig Trade Fair is being rejuvenated. Our hosts wanted to do all they could to impress upon us the importance of re-establishing an American presence in Leipzig. I told them I would try to arrange for a Congressional delegation to come to Leipzig for a future trade fair and to work on the possibilities of relaxing some of the trade restriction pressures that the United States has on the DGR. The Leipzig luncheon was interesting, but not really fascinating.

Following the luncheon, they gave us more sightseeing that I wanted: the town hall, the rebuilt parts of the city, and the concert hall, which is their big showplace and one of the finest such halls in the world. It cost about 130 million marks (around $79 million) to build, and no other country would put such state funds into a concert building. The most rewarding was the fact that in all the world Leipzig probably has the finest organs and acoustics of any major concert hall, and I do not know if a building of this magnitude could ever be built again. The young organist performed a Mendelssohn piece for us, as we sat in the front balcony. We were the only ones in the hall and the magnificence of his rendition practically blew my mind.

We went through other older buildings and then down into a wine cellar where Bach used to spend time. We went by the synagogue for a short visit with some of the survivors of the Jewish community who were there. Only four or five people were present, and thus had difficulty making a minion (ten Jewish men). This was a city that had 6-8,000 Jews and 17 synagogues before World War II. The DGR has just spent $35,000 on fixing up the old synagogue and they are very proud of how it looks. At this point I am rather tired. We got back to the hotel at 5:00, the same time we were to be ready to go to the Bach concert at the Bach St. John Church. Klaus Gysi and his young aide driven down from Berlin in four hours of heavy traffic to attend the concert with us. Gysi was also tired. He and I decided to let the group go on to the concert, including Joan and Gysi's wife, while we just stayed around the hotel to have a quiet time.

First, he arranged a private dining room where we had snacks and talked; then I suggested that we go for a massage in the hotel sauna, and he agreed. Although it was his country, it was funny that I was "in control," as he did not know how to arrange for saunas and massages. It was the best thing we did. There was only one masseuse, a pretty young woman by the name of Kristiana, and I was first. When done, I waited for Gysi in the fitness club bar to join me for a drink. We sat for over an hour talking to the very attractive masseuse, who now served as barmaid, and she and Minister Gysi were having a great time together as she flattered him with how impressed she was with his importance in the DGR. We did not talk about the Rabbi problem but about girls, the business enterprise problems, families, etc., and it was nice. He found out that Kristiana's sister worked in East Berlin, and I have a feeling he will look her up. He is 75 years old but still has ideas. About 9:30 p.m., the group returned and joined us for another light summer meal in the hotel's private dining room.

APRIL 18 SATURDAY

Leaving the hotel at 7:00 a.m., we said our farewells, and were off to the airport for our flight to Paris. The main thing Gysi (who never admits it but was a Jew) said to me just before I left was that he was going to work out the details, and inside of four weeks, "you will see the cable from me which will be the finalization of the arrangements to bring the Rabbi to East Berlin, ... because I see how desperately the people there need him."

As we entered the West Berlin sector, the cars pulled off to the side of the road and we got out and into cars driven by officials from West Berlin assigned to meet us. So, we had left Leipzig in cars provided by the East German government, and when we got to a checkpoint outside the West Berlin area, we had to get into cars provided by the American Mission in West Berlin. From there we continued on to the airport, where the plane was on time. It seems the flights in Europe are more on schedule than in the United States; also, the European airports seem more civilized. The security check, as well, is very reassuring, and a lot better than in the United States. They search everything and everyone, and don't take any chances. Of course there was a down side - not one shop was open at the airport to buy anything, not even a cup of coffee.

(PARIS)

Arriving in Paris, after the damp dull cold it was warm and the sun was shining; I didn't even need a suit coat. We went to the Crillion Hotel and into another civilization. An old friend, John Berg from the U.S. Embassy, met us at the airport. John and I first met in 1975 on my first codel to Europe. I had told the State Department that I wanted to meet with the Jewish community in Marseilles to see how they were faring, and the Embassy sent John Berg who took me to the synagogue that Saturday morning. What I remember was that there were three services going on at the same time: Orthodox, Sephardic, and Conservative. John was working for the American Embassy in Paris but was a stateless person. Although working for the Embassy, he was not an American citizen and had no citizenship papers. [Later, some of my colleagues and I began to work on John's problem, and several years later he came to the United States and acquired his citizenship.] Now he has quite a responsible position at the Embassy, overseeing the Senators and/or Congressmen, and other VIPs, who come to Paris, and he is the most efficient control officer at the Paris Embassy.

The best U.S. embassy commissary anywhere is at the Paris Embassy. Members and their wives when in Paris shop at the commissary as the prices are about half what you find in Paris shops or in the United States. Today, several Senators' wives were buying in the commissary. In the evening Joan and I took Adele and Terry to dinner. It was the first time I had taken anyone to dinner where it cost $100 a person, but I think it is worth it when you have people who have worked as hard as they have to make this trip a success.

APRIL 19 SUNDAY

John Berg drove us to the airport for our flight back to the States. Reflecting on the trip - at the Jewish Community Center in West Berlin there was 24 hour security. At the Jewish Center in East Berlin, security was not necessary as street crime and terrorism do not happen in the communist or socialist countries.

On board the plane was my colleague liberal Representative Claudine Schneider from Rhode Island, and we sat together for a while. She had been over to make a speech in French to the French nuclear energy officials, and had also been to the Soviet Union to work out a cooperative satellite broadcast. Claudine is a remarkable woman - smart, good looking and votes right - an asset to the membership of the House. The fact that she is a Republican does not mean a thing.

Tonight, back in Washington, I spent about two hours at the office getting things in order and catching up on correspondence before the jet lag hit me. The work that didn't get done I took home with me. This is the underside of being away for an extended period.

APRIL 20 MONDAY

The day started off slow, so I went first to see the House physician who said that my foot was coming along just fine. Later that morning Eli Feinberg came in about the Tamiami Airport customs problem, and then Dr. Manny Papper, an old friend and the former Dean of the University of Miami School of Medicine. Manny had his colleague from Venezuela with him, another anesthesiologist, who has a problem with the IRS and the INS. I am still catching up on correspondence, but I managed a few hours with Tom Kingfield going over questions for tomorrow's subcommittee hearing. I saw Terry Peel; he also is still tired from the trip. On the conference table in my office are all the presents I brought back, and tomorrow Carolyn and I will go through and figure out what to give to whom. Everyone seems happy to have me back.

A *Miami Herald* reporter called, wanting information on the role I played in preventing the prison from being built in Opa Locka. I also talked to a reporter in Kansas City who wanted to know about my relationship with Secretary Dole and my appraisal of her capabilities, especially as a campaign person who would help her husband in the Republican primaries. I said probably the biggest asset Senator Dole has is his wife, Elizabeth.

That evening, Joan and I dined at the home of Pete Stark for some Chinese cooking. Pete has his own Chinese chef, Sam, who prepared the meal, and it was delicious. It was just the three of us. We talked about politics and life, and it was quite a relaxing, enjoyable evening. Pete is a very wealthy, liberal Democrat, and as Chairman of the Subcommittee on Health for the Ways and Means Committee, he does a good job. He, at my request legislated Medicare benefits for Hospice.

APRIL 21 TUESDAY

The FAA hearing was today. The first hour was with the General Accounting Office and its investigation of the FAA's ongoing programs and activities to further modernize, automate and consolidate our National Airspace System (NAS). Although the GAO endorsed the FAA's budget request, it was critical of practically every phase of the program - from schedule delays to implementation strategy to the maintenance technician work force. (It is, however, the job of the GAO to find problems.)

I said to the GAO representatives, "As I listen to you, sometimes I think of the FAA's NAS plan as an impossible dream. We are, after all, only human, with all the frailties we have as people; and, as you say, despite some of the delays, FAA is doing more things right than they are doing wrong." The goal of the FAA's NAS program is to get the aviation industry under a high degree of technological control, a wonderful idea, but the implementation is a tremendous task, especially when the FAA is trying to put so much together in a limited period of time.

The remaining morning and two-hour afternoon sessions were with FAA Administrator Admiral Donald Engen. We covered about half the general questions, but the main question I tried to pin the Admiral down on was the comparison percentage of the full-performance air traffic controllers on board this year with last year's percent and numbers. In an effort to speed rebuilding the system after the 1981 controllers' strike, in which President Reagan fired 11,400 striking controllers, Congress mandated that the FAA have 15,000 air traffic controllers by the end of September 1987, of which 70 percent must be full-performance controllers (FPCs).

This year the FAA is not using the same yearly percentage criteria to measure as it did last year by including the assistant controllers, which gives a false high percentage of full- performance controllers. There are approximately 1,500 assistant controllers who are excluded from becoming qualified as air traffic controllers. In figuring the 70 percent FPCs, the FAA excluded the assistant controllers which reduces the amount against which you have full performance controllers. "In order to meet the 15,000 goal," I remarked, "you include the air traffic assistants, but in order to meet the 70 percentage mark, you knock off the 1,500 assistants and, of course, that increases the percentage margin of the full performance controllers, because you have 13,500 instead of 15,000." The Admiral indicated that they were not trying to reach their goals by shenanigans or by being sneaky. "No," I stated, "it is all out there." We resume tomorrow morning at 10:00.

After the hearing, I returned to the office and Carolyn and I divided the gifts that I brought back from my trip, though still a little tired from jet lag. I received a call from Hal (Hap) Bader. In the used car business I had known his parents as customers, and now he wants my help with Rep. Morris K. "Mo" Udall of Arizona. There is a company in Udall's district with a Defense Department contract in the Philippines and Hap wants some of it subcontracted to his company in North Miami. What it means is approximately 200 jobs in my district. So I will try.

APRIL 22 WEDNESDAY

This morning I had breakfast in the Members Dining Room with Marcel and Donna Infeld, a very interesting young couple from North Miami Beach, and children of survivors of the Holocaust. I really enjoyed being with them.

At the FAA hearing, we are about halfway through, and it has been rough. We raised a lot of issues, especially on the transference of Washington National and Dulles International Airports to the new Virginia Airport Authority, and continued on the issue of the lack of progress in new full performance air traffic controllers. From yesterday's hearing, Admiral Engen was to clarify the information regarding the percentages of the full performance level controllers. The "Members are getting restless," I said, in reference to an article in the *Washington Post* about the frustrations of the Members on flight delays, and on what they read in their hometown newspapers about the near-misses; and, "as yet," I noted, "we cannot show, in my mind, a significant improvement in the actual number of operational controllers." Admiral Engen stated that people perceive that the air traffic controller is responsible for near or mid-air collisions. "That is not true," he said. "Pilots are responsible for near or mid-air collisions." He said that 3 percent of operational errors, as opposed to 13 percent of pilot deviations, result in near mid-air collisions, and that we need to view the entire system as dependent upon the people who use it as well as the people who control it.

"Lots of things we do on the Floor, and elsewhere in politics, or anywhere, are not based so much on facts as on perception," I said. "Just as people perceive near-misses as a controller error, and it is really a pilot error, people also believe if the fired air traffic controllers from the 1981 strike were brought back, they would prevent these abominable delays that my colleagues are talking about." As long as they perceive that this is what is going to count, that is what is going to make for the votes on the Floor and the FAA will have to deal with perceptions as realities. I told him how imperative it was that he realize the situation that our committee will be facing when we go to the Floor, which is that unless there is a significant improvement in the controller situation, beyond what he had presented to us so far, I did not think we were going to have the ammunition to oppose another Molinari-type amendment on the Floor to rehire the fired controllers. I wanted to show between now and the time that we went to the Floor, that the attrition rate was down, the operational and full performance level controller numbers were up, and the number of delays was down, and so indicated to Admiral Engen that he would have to provide this information to us, if we were going to be able to provide him with the same kind of operational freedom that he had today.

During the two-hour lunch break, I met the U.S. Ambassador to East Germany, Francis Meehan, to brief him on my visit to East Germany. Meehan was very nice and had about the same evaluation of Klaus Gysi as a flaky Communist bureaucrat as I did. Trying to meet with all my appointments, it is rather difficult, with hearings from 10:00 to noon and in the afternoon from 2-4:00. We had only one vote today, the only vote this week so far, and having no roll call votes helps with our hearings, as each vote means a twenty to thirty minute interruption. At 2:00, I appeared at the hearings of the Appropriations Subcommittee on Labor, Health and Human Services, to introduce as one of the witnesses,

Sister Jeanne O'Laughlin, President of Barry University. This was fun, as I enjoyed introducing Sister Jeanne, who is planning a dinner in Miami for Joan and me.

Much of the afternoon FAA hearing was devoted to questions on the consolidation and modernization of the flight service stations system, and we adjourned at 4:00. After the hearing, two professors from George Mason University in Northern Virginia and members on the Amtrak Study Commission, Richard Fink and Dan Witt, came in to stress the merits and benefits of the Amtrak study group. Following the professors, an old friend from the United Automobile Workers stopped in hoping for my support on the Gephardt protectionist trade bill amendment for automobile workers, but I made no promises to him. At 5:00, Miami retail representatives came in. Old friend, Peggy Hurst, from Burdines, D.C. Olin from K-Mart, and Terry Covone from Spiegel, all urged me not to vote the Gephardt amendment because it would raise costs for the retirees in my district. I probably won't vote for the Gephardt bill, but I would support Ways and Means Chairman Dan Rostenkowski's less protective substitute trade bill.

I spoke to my grandson Sean, a freshman at the University of Hawaii in Honolulu, and he suddenly is reluctant to take the summer job in Los Alamos. It puts me in an awkward position, but I think I can talk him into taking the job especially after Buck Thompson in Los Alamos talks to him.

In the evening, I went to a reception at the home of Warren O'Reilly. A former music critic for the *Washington Post*, O'Reilly now lives in Miami and is an aging homosexual. The people there were turn of the century types - elderly, cultured, over the hill, and mostly central Europeans. Staying only briefly, I left to pick up Joan for the ballet. Earlier Pete Stark had given us his box tickets, but once at the ballet we managed to sit through only the first two acts, as we were still tired from the trip and the jet lag.

APRIL 23 THURSDAY

The FAA hearing resumed at 10:00 a.m. Finishing the general questions, we started on the justification questions, getting about ten pages into the questions before recessing. We have to be back Monday to finish the FAA hearings because the supplemental appropriations bill will be on the Floor this afternoon.

After a quick lunch, I was back on the Floor for general debate on the supplemental bill. There were fifteen votes, and I think this was the highest number we have had anytime this year. My voting record is still at 100% - not missing a single vote or quorum call; part of this is just good luck and that I have not been ill. Because of the votes, I had to stay close to the Floor nearly all day, but I did manage between votes to get to the gym for a shower.

The supplemental bill on the Floor was moving slowly and, finally, we got to the transportation chapter about 8:00. There were several amendments pending that I persuaded the members to withdraw regarding flight service stations, Amtrak, and highway demonstration projects grants. In the supplemental, $8.6 million were earmarked for closing 55 flight service stations that the FAA had targeted for consolidation, and the closures were opposed by some of the members in whose districts the stations were located. I rose in opposition to the amendment offered, though later withdrawn, by Roy Dyson of Maryland, to remove the funds earmarked for the closures. Roy has a flight service station in his Salisbury district. "None of us like to see Federal facilities moved from our districts," I stated, and told of the hearing today with FAA Administrator, Admiral Engen, and his testimony that he was going to look at certain of the flight service stations with regard to using them as an adjunct or a satellite facility, and what the criteria would be. To pacify these colleagues I offered assurance that when the Federal Aviation Administrator came before our subcommittee again on Monday, we were going to again request that he look at the remaining flight service stations, to see if it was possible to use them as satellite units.

My colleague from California, Norman Mineta, Aviation Subcommittee Chairman of the Authorizing Committee on Public Works and Transportation, who supports the closings, then rose, saying that a report would be forthcoming from the General Accounting Office, which hopefully would indicate that the new equipment was performing adequately and doing the job expected - providing to the pilot community timely information that is equal to if not better than what pilots have now. As he said, close to $350 million had already gone into the research and development of this new equipment, and in terms of long-term savings, it was important that the consolidation program go forward.

At the end, though, we got sandbagged on Jim Traficant's Youngstown, Ohio, flight service station consolidation amendment. Traficant is kind of crazy, but he had the Democrats behind him. I tried but failed to defeat his amendment. As Appropriations Chairman Jamie Whitten should have but did not help me, although I explained that this amendment would be detrimental to the consolidation and modernization of the FAA's air traffic control system.

It is hard to close down a federal facility in a member's district when he gets emotional about it. The "ayes" carried on a voice vote. I should have called for a recorded vote, but that meant keeping my colleagues on the Floor even longer, and I reasoned that perhaps later I would be able to take the amendment out in conference. But this victory for Traficant left me with a bad taste in my mouth because last year in the subcommittee's 1987 Appropriations Bill we were able to defeat all eleven amendments offered on the Floor. Maybe I should have tried to defeat this amendment and called for a roll call vote even at the risk of aggravating some of my colleagues.

APRIL 24 FRIDAY

After a late night on the Floor I was home about 1:30 a.m., and up early today to head back to Miami on the 8:15 flight. Jeff met me at the Miami airport with a message from the accounting firm of Coopers and Lybrand that they had gotten me an extension on my income tax return. This had been necessary because of my being out of the country on April 15. Our Medicare Newsletter on nursing homes has stirred up a lot of interest in the district. People are calling in with case problems about nursing homes, and this has created more work for our staff; it also means we have created an effective newsletter.

Reflection on yesterday and what happened on the House Floor was very interesting. Traficant, though more or less unstable, rolled us. Jamie Whitten did not do much to help by promising Traficant he would support him, as did the Speaker. I have to remember this and not let it happen again, especially with our 1988 bill. The leadership screwed me and I'll remember that.

APRIL 25 SATURDAY

Our annual black leadership brunch was held this morning at Turnberry, and it was very successful. Patrice has been putting this event together for several years now, and she does a really wonderful job. That evening Joan and I went to the very elaborate Bar Mitzvah of the son of Eli and Lisa Timoner, at the Intercontinental Hotel. Many of the guests were contributors to my Miami fundraiser, so I had the chance to thank them personally.

APRIL 26 SUNDAY

This morning Joan and I attended the wedding of Harvey Ruvin, Metro-Dade Commissioner. The event was held in South Dade at the Signature Club, which is owned by Jerry Berlin, and it was quite a grandiose affair with close to one thousand guests, including Metro Commissioner Barry Schreiber who did the service. Many of the politicians, entrepreneurs, and power structure people who were there I had seen last night at the Bar Mitzvah. I also saw sentimental friends and condo supporters from North Dade like Dave Sampson and Rose Ruban. These two events were good places to be, and I didn't even have to perform. I received good comments about my trip to East Germany, both last evening and today. This afternoon I will fly back to Washington.

APRIL 27 MONDAY

We finished our FAA hearings, the last of the agencies to appear before our subcommittee. The only nonsubcommittee member at the hearing today was John Murtha (D-PA), who wanted to be sure the FAA was not closing his Johnstown, Pennsylvania, flight service facility. Murtha came to testify, but we learned that the FAA was leaving his facility open as a satellite operation, and that satisfied him. Tomorrow we begin the outside witnesses hearings, which will be long, drawn out, and quite strenuous.

Officials from the Florida Rural Electrification Administration are here for their annual visit. The President of the North Dade

Chamber of Commerce, who also works for Southern Bell, came to see me about South Florida hosting a future America's Cup contest, which would really be something for South Florida. Dave Bochaney at the White House called to ask how I intended to vote on the trade bill, and I told him that I would probably vote for the bill, which pleased him. Dave is the House Legislative Liaison at the White House, and the only good friend I now have at the White House.

The Florida Chamber of Commerce had its reception this evening, and it was much more elaborate this year than in the past. The event was held at the Sheraton Grand Hotel. I stayed about twenty minutes speaking with several people from my area who were there, such as Charlie Rice, President of Barnett Bank, Arnold Friedman, a nursing home owner from Hialeah, and Dick Sewell from Florida Power and Light.

Leaving the hotel, I headed for the Brasserie where Rabbi Neuman, his son Mark, and Adele from my staff, were waiting for me. Rabbi Neuman and his son had come down from New York. We talked about the problems in East Germany, and I believe we made some progress. Mark is very protective of his father, and the Rabbi is still uncertain. I believe, however, that we left the restaurant with a commitment from the Rabbi to go over for the High Holy Days, and stay six weeks to see if he can accommodate himself to all the uncertainties. If he finds that it is possible to live there and to accomplish what he envisions for the young people, then he may stay. There are various dynamics that take place in that Marxist country, and when you have people who are trying to be both Jew and accommodating to communism, there exists a difficult situation to manage, whether as a congregation or as a Jewish community. One thing I did was talk to Mark and quote from Tennyson's "Ulysses" that A'Tis not too late to seek a newer world." He was quite interested in the poem and wrote down the name. When I get home, I will send him a copy of the poem, whose message was to let his aging father have a chance for another adventure in life.

APRIL 28 TUESDAY

At the Florida Chamber of Commerce breakfast this morning, most of the Florida Delegation members were there, and I sat next to the energy conservation person from the University of Florida, who told me how to insulate a house very reasonably by just putting builders' aluminum foil up in the attic instead of having a complicated insulation job. I may have saved several hundred dollars this morning just on home expenditures. I also met people from Burdines and the President of the Tallahassee Chamber; before leaving, I spoke to Senator Bob Graham and updated him on the new problem at the Munisport in North Miami. Bob too thinks that the Munisport has been mistakenly placed on the EPA superfund list. I have, of course, been trying to have it taken off the EPA toxic waste list. But, last week I received adverse comments from Joe Fleming, an environmental lawyer, and from Maureen Hurwitz, citizen activist from North Miami, that more study needed to be done before we take it off the list. I passed this information on to Graham, who still was in favor of removal, but said he wanted to speak to me further about the problem, and about how to find the right buyer for the right development for that particular site.

Today we had the first of our Public Witnesses, and it will be three long days. Jack Langer from City Gas Company and Sid Alterman of Alterman Trucking Company from Miami were among the witnesses this morning. We finished the day pretty much on schedule by holding everyone to their scheduled ten minutes. During the noon break, I went to the Florida delegation luncheon hosted by the Women's Division of the Jewish Federation. My friend Sue Stevens from the New York-based division and Mark Talisman, head of the Washington Federation office, were the organizers. All of my Florida colleagues who were there made a brief speech, and I spoke for a few minutes about my trip to Germany and about working on appropriations for Israel.

APRIL 29 WEDNESDAY

First on the schedule was a meeting with the Army Corps of Engineers, who estimate that construction on the Sunny Isles beach restoration will begin this summer; a ceremony will be held to "kick off" the event. Afterwards I went to the Capitol where Representative Pat Schroeder was introducing legislation to reimburse federal employees for adoption costs. I am one of the originators of these adoption amendments, but I was not able to stay for the press conference.

During the hearings of the Public Witnesses, we had many interrupting roll call votes, and finished at 1:00 p.m., an hour past our normal schedule. I will have lunch in the office as people will be coming in to see me.

APRIL 30 THURSDAY

Yesterday I was hassled on the Floor about the Gephardt amendment, but I am holding firm. Voting against the amendment, I did so because I felt the wrong message was being sent to the wrong people, and that it would be counterproductive. The amendment passed, however, by four votes and strangely enough, today, no one as usual asked for a separate vote in the full House after the committee rose. I guess the administration did not want to bother turning the people around, and now they have an excuse to veto the entire trade bill. I did vote for final passage. Late this afternoon I will fly back to Miami for the early Friday morning start of the Greater Miami Chamber of Commerce Weekend for the Florida Congressional Delegation.

Chapter 5

MAY 1, 1987 - FRIDAY

The Greater Miami Chamber of Commerce has asked the Congressional Delegation and other guests to assemble downtown at the Pavilion [now Intercontinental] Hotel. So, at 7:30 this morning I met Sharyn at Neighbors Restaurant in North Miami and headed for the Pavilion. Many prominent Miami leadership people were there, and we all walked over to the Metromover station and rode to the Government Center. We were shown slides and movies of Miami, and then given a presentation on Miami's economy. At noon we took the Metrorail to the Hialeah Race Course for lunch in the Clubhouse. Sharyn and I shared a table with lobbyist Priscilla Perry and Dante Fascell's wife, Jean Marie, and it was good to see Janet Studley from the Holland and Knight law firm there, along with House Democratic Whip Bill Gray, Mike Reed of Senator Chiles's staff, Washington lobbyist friend Jeff Trammel (7th generation Floridian), Dave Walker from Bell South, and my long time friend, A.J. Montenari, who runs a home for troubled youths in Hialeah. County Manager Sergio Pereira was there and happy that he got his eighty buses for the private sector versus public sector competitive program. That news was released today.

I was sort of a hero, as the talk was about the present and future benefits of the Metrorail, and how I was responsible for providing the system. Channel 4 interviewed me about the Tri-County Rail System and about the future of the Metromover. Walter Revell with an engineering firm in Miami and Dick Sewell of FP&L came up to me and said that most people do not know just how responsible I am for mass transit. But I had plenty of praise. I spoke with attorney Rep. Tom Tew who said good things about my son Tom. Tew is handling a case on which my Tom is also working. [Tom is now managing partner of Tew's firm.]

The Greater Miami Chamber put on a better show than I had anticipated. Everything went so smoothly, and the Chamber members were so gracious and accommodating, leaving everyone in a good mood. Attorney Bernie Jacobson, President of the Greater Miami Chamber of Commerce and chief organizer of the event, really did a beautiful job.

Medicare informed me yesterday that IMC (International Medical Center) was going out of business. Apparently that HMO has legal problems and Medicare shut them down. We expect a great many calls from people who have this IMC coverage, but the main people to be hurt are IMC employees who now will be out of jobs.

Al Moskovitz and I played tennis at 4:00, and this was the first time I played since the East Germany trip; my bad toe held up pretty well. At 6:00, Joan and I went to the Southeast Bank reception, followed by a party at the Metro-Dade Cultural Center in honor of the Florida Congressional Delegation. It was the best party food I had in a long time, and the entertainment was impressive - five bands and four or five shows. Everything was set up on the large outside patio. I spoke with Armando Codina, a successful Cuban-American businessman who asked for an office appointment, Phil Bakes from Eastern Airlines, and several people who will be helpful to me in my re-election campaign. This was quite a wonderful day for Miami and for me.

MAY 2 SATURDAY

With no morning or afternoon district office appointments the day has been very relaxing. In the evening, Joan and I attended the formal Military Dinner at Vizcaya. The guests were escorted in by officers from every branch of our armed services - Coast Guard, Navy, Air Force, Army, and Marines. There was much pomp and ceremony and the food was excellent. The caterer, Gene Singletary, did a really fine job. The guests at our table included the commanding officer of Homestead Air Force Base, the County Manager Sergio Pereira, and the Metro Commissioner Clara Oesterle. Clara always is fun to talk to as she makes candid remarks about her fellow commissioners as well as other local officials. I made several good contacts - especially with the more influential, well-to-do Cuban-Americans in our community with whom I need to improve relations. Joan and I got home about 11:00.

MAY 3 SUNDAY

This morning I went to the Wilshire Towers Condominium's Social Club. I told them a little about my trip to East Germany, and answered their many questions on Medicare. My friend, Bernard Levy, was the organizer, and it was a good meeting but I could not stay long as I had a flight to catch.

Back in Washington, I met with Sue Perry, Vice President of Congressional Affairs of the American Bus Association, and she told me of her problem stemming from the public transportation charter people who testified before our subcommittee, and the fact that their testimonies caught her organization by surprise. I feel bad for her, as she just had a major malignancy operation and now she is worried about her job. Sue was not at the hearing and no one notified her of the opposition that was to appear before our subcommittee. Maybe I can help her in our mark-up. The private bus charters that Sue represents think that competitive charters from subsidized public transportation is unfair, and I will ask my subcommittee colleagues Bob Carr and Dick Durbin to help on this.

MAY 4 MONDAY

Today has been the easiest I have had in a very long time. Not having to deal with the hearings all day is like getting out of a pressure cooker. In the morning, I played tennis with Judge Mikva, Don Edwards, and Sonny Montgomery. In the afternoon, I was back to my regular office routine. I had only two meetings, one with Beth Dubin of the Florida Juvenile Diabetes Foundation, and the other with Reese Taylor, former chairman of the Interstate Commerce Commission. Reese is seeking the position of president of the Association of Port Authorities, and he wants me to lobby my colleague Norman Mineta for him, in case Mineta had any objections to him filling the position.

In the evening I was at Alice Rivlin's home for dinner. She cooked, and it was very lovely. Alice is still with Brookings Institute, and we talked about lots of things - some personal, some political. Of the presidential candidates she likes Bob Dole the best, and she agreed with me on the Gephardt protectionist amendment. I was home by 9:30 p.m.

MAY 5 TUESDAY

I met this morning with Richard Schwartz, head of the National Boating Association. He is the husband of actress Sally Jane Heit, a friend of Marvelle Colby, who is my good friend. I did not promise him anything but told him we would try to help with funds for boating safety, depending on budget restraints.

1:00, I met with lobbyist Roger Lemaster and his client from South Florida, Phil Shailor, Vice President of Alamo Rent-A-Car. They were concerned about the off-airport car rental and their company's inability to have fair access to the Washington National airport. I told them I would see what I could do.

My 2:00 appointment was with Charlie Bryant, President of the Machinist Union in Miami, and his people from the machinist union of Eastern Airlines who are trying to buy time to recapture their company from Texas Air. I think this is already a *fait accompli*, and that they are wasting their time. While I waited for my 3:00 appointment with Maryland Governor Donald Schaefer and Cong. Steny Hoyer, who want to talk about transportation problems in Maryland, the bells rang, so I was off to the House Floor to vote on the Aspin substitute amendments to the Armed Services Committee's defense authorization bill. Much of the conversation on the Floor included jokes about the Gary Hart affair. It was everything from "tailgate" to "where's the beef," and of course the "beef is in the rice." I spoke with Mickey Leland on the Floor about getting a Cuban prisoner out of Castro's prison. I think Mickey has lost interest, as he suggested that I call Mayor Andy Young (a friend of Castro's) in Atlanta, which I did.

Back in the office Governor Schaefer, Steny and their Maryland cohorts were waiting for me. We discussed the Western Maryland Turnpike, funds for the Washington-Baltimore Parkway, and the need for Section III transit funds for the City of Baltimore. The Governor does a good job, and I like to work with him and Steny. I will see if our subcommittee can provide Interstate Transfer and Section III funds and still be under the budget restrictions.

In the evening I stopped by the Cannon Caucus Room for a reception hosted by the International Association of Machinists and Aerospace Workers; and then to the Rayburn Building for a reception in celebration of Texas Congressman Henry Gonzalez's 71st birthday and his 34th anniversary as an elected public official; following that I attended the reception honoring the appointment of Michigan Congressman David Bonior as Chief Deputy Whip; and the last of my reception hopping was for Senator Jeff Bingaman of New Mexico held in the upper floor of my townhouse that I lease to the law firm of Patton, Boggs and Blow. I had dinner later with my good friend Penny Farthing, a partner with that firm.

This was a busy day - all the votes on the DOD authorization amendments, my office appointments going long, and the many receptions.

MAY 6 WEDNESDAY

I sat through the Foreign Operations hearings on foreign military sales for over an hour. Foreign military credit sales create foreign debts to our country that are not ever going to be paid. We move these unpayable debts around from private sector to public to balloon notes. We call this debt restructuring.

MAY 7 THURSDAY

At breakfast in the Member's Dining Room with Illinois Senator Paul Simon, we discussed his presidential campaign plans. There is not much else going on today, other than more votes on the Department of Defense authorization bill. There will be more votes tomorrow, which I will miss for the first time this year, as I am leaving soon for the airport for an early afternoon flight to Miami. This evening in Miami the American Jewish Committee is honoring me at a dinner at the Omni Hotel.

In Miami at the Omni, the dinner started pretty much on schedule, around 7:30. Dave Fleeman, President of the AJC and an old friend, gave me a great introduction and awarded me with a plaque, one of the nicest I have ever received. I said a few words about my involvement with the American Jewish Committee in Miami on Jewish/Black relations and on what we are trying to do by getting Rabbi Neuman into East Germany. We also had a good panel discussion that included two representatives from the *Miami Herald*, one from the *Miami News*, one from Channel 10, and me.

Westinghouse lobbyist Priscilla Perry was there, and we talked about her problems regarding contracts for the extensions of the Metromover.

MAY 8 FRIDAY

At the district office this morning there were eight different groups waiting for me: people from the Juvenile Diabetes Foundation; the Women League of Voters; individuals worried about the change in the minimum wage law; people with Medicare problems; a lady from the social security office who cannot retire because she falls in the crack between her social security benefits and the federal employment benefits; and people from the Lake Stevens area who want me to do something about widening N.W. 57th Avenue to six lanes.

I went to see Dr. Groff, my ENT specialist around noon, and got good news - no reoccurrence. That evening I attended a reception at the law firm of Hughes, Herbert and Read on Brickell Avenue in celebration of State Representative Ron Silver joining the firm as a partner. Alvah Chapman, Chairman of the Board of Knight-Ridder was there, and I spoke to him about the *Herald's* exposure of Gary Hart's careless involvement with Donna Rice. I said that if Hart was that unstable it is better that he not run for president.

MAY 9 SATURDAY

This Saturday morning I met with the Ministers and Laymen's group at the Caanan Baptist Church on Biscayne Boulevard and 76th Street. George Ellis, a good friend who always supports me in the black community, gave a good introduction, and I spoke briefly. I primarily wanted to let them know I was aware of their support and appreciated it. What this group really wants is to have a black member of Congress from South Florida, but I do not think they now have enough blacks in any one district to accomplish this. It would take some very good reapportionment in 1992 to be able to get enough blacks in one area to have a chance for a black congressional member. In the four South Florida districts, blacks remain pretty much a minority, although in the 17th District they do represent close to fifty percent of the registered Democrats.

At a dinner party this evening at Grace and B.B. Goldstein's, many of my old supporters were there, and also new people whom I can count on as potential supporters. I worked the party just as I would a political event. Everyone seemed to be pleased and proud that I am an old friend and also a member of congress.

MAY 10 SUNDAY

Around noon I had brunch at my son Bill's house; at 3:00, I played tennis with Al Moskovitz; and at 5:30, I was on a flight back to Washington.

MAY 11 MONDAY

Today is very quiet, as Monday's usually are. I had only one office appointment, and that was with someone who wanted me to cosponsor the Armenian genocide bill. There were about five votes on the Floor today, and I missed about eight votes last Thursday and Friday while in Miami. This will bring my average down to a little over ninety percent so I will be careful not to go below this percentage.

Thursday, I am going up to New York for my annual follow-up examination at Sloan Kettering. There are no votes that day because of the funeral for Stuart McKinney of Connecticut. I knew he had AIDS but no other members wanted to believe it.

On the House Floor I told Pat Schroeder about my conspiracy theory that the woman, Donna Rice, from Miami was really a guided missile pointed at Gary Hart and the *Miami Herald* by someone who did not like either Hart or the *Herald*. Who did not like them both was organized labor, and in this way labor could kill two birds with one stone. What gave me this notion was that Donna Rice's lawyer, Tom McAliley, is a labor lawyer from Miami and also a friend of mine. Later in the day Representative Bill Clay from Missouri told me the same conspiracy theory so my story was coming full circle.

MAY 12 TUESDAY

My appointments started at 9:00 this morning with Andy Manatos, a lobbyist for Greece, about aid to Greece. I told him I would try to help in the Foreign Operations bill. At 9:30 I met with Xie Xide, President of Fudam University in Shanghai, and Gerald Cassidy, a Washington lawyer lobbyist representing the school. They were seeking American Schools and Hospitals Abroad funds in our Foreign Operations bill for the University, sort of a useless pork barrel program heavily concentrated in Lebanon.

At 10:00, I met with the Florida Association of Realtors who asked questions about the FHA and the proposed banking legislation. There were about twelve Miami people at this meeting, and many of them I knew from past associations and business dealings. Some of our children even went to school together. It was like a reunion.

Dave Obey called, asking for my support if he should make a run next session for Chair of the Budget Committee. Dave and I are to meet tomorrow to discuss what I can do about getting people to help him. His competition will probably be Marvin Leath of Texas and Leon Panetta of California.

11:00, I met with the Florida Sierra Club and the Everglades Coalition representatives about the Kissimmee River project and how to bring the river back to its original condition. I told them to have spokesmen from Tom Lewis's district get in touch with Lewis because they will need his support before the House will do anything.

11:30, Jerry Aspland, President of ARCO Marine, came in. Aspland was concerned about the Carr amendment on the payback provisions regarding merchant marine tankers built with federal subsidy, which restricts the use on coastal service. Some now want to pay back the subsidy and use these large tankers from Alaska to other American ports to better compete. It is a very complex issue with labor and industry split on both sides of the issue. I believe that the larger tankers will be more efficient and less labor intensive. I will listen to both sides, but will probably stick with Neal Smith, Chair of the Appropriations Subcommittee on Commerce, Justice, State, and Judiciary, who has jurisdiction over this though the Merchant Marine is part of the Department of Transportation.

At 2:00 I met with David Weinstein, Acting Executive Director of the Holocaust Memorial Council, of which I am a member. Dave brought me up-to-date on the Holocaust Memorial activities in the United States. 2:30, Sue Perry of the American Bus Association came in about the proposed charter bus regulations, which she opposes as her association wants to prohibit public buses from competing with the private sector if public buses use federal subsidy. This also means that in the off-peak hours public buses cannot pick up this additional revenue. There is no right or wrong on this issue. I would, however, like to see how well the private sector continues to perform before letting the public sector compete, since the private sector has been doing the job adequately and cost effectively so far.

Besides my appointments, the day has been filled with votes on the defense authorization, especially votes on the Strategic Defense Initiative (SDI) amendments, which I oppose as big technological pork barrel. Many reduction amendments passed, and I hope we can accomplish a decent compromise with the Senate in conference.

In the evening I took Wynne Frank from my staff, and Katherine Karpoff from Norman Mineta's staff to the Directors Guild of America's reception. The Congressional Arts Caucus sponsored the affair. We met actor/directors, Woody Allen and

Sydney Pollack, opponents of the colorization of the old black and white films to be reshown on television. One thing I remember about Woody Allen is that he is physically very deceiving. He seems very small but is quite solid and muscular, as I found out when I put my arm around his shoulders for a photo opportunity. Woody also seemed very unhappy he had to be there.

MAY 13 WEDNESDAY

This morning, I attended a breakfast meeting with the Florida League of Financial Institutions, and afterwards met with my grandson, John Lehman's class from New York. I took John and his friends to our subcommittee room, then to the Capitol to meet House Speaker Jim Wright, then back to the Rayburn Cafeteria for a snack, and then to their bus. I had one hour to do the whole bit, and I think they had a good time.

Dave Obey called for a meeting in his office at 11:30 with some of his supporters to launch his campaign for chairman of the Budget Committee. I received my list of fifteen people to contact and so far the responses are soft but favorable.

At noon the Jewish committee members met for lunch with the Israeli Minister of Absorption, Yakov Tsur, in Sid Yates's subcommittee office. Sid is also dean of the House Jewish members. Minister Ysur spoke about the increased number of Soviet refugees and the need for assistance, and we will see what can be done through refugee assistance funds in our Foreign Operations Subcommittee.

1:30, I met with Eric Peterson of the United Bus Owners of America, who had the same concerns as Sue Perry regarding UMTA charter bus regulations. Peterson represents the charter bus operators and they are worried about competition if new regulations come into effect permitting the public transit to compete with the private charters. After Peterson, Dr. and Mrs. Arthur Levine from my district came in. The Levine's are very nice, and have been loyal supporters of mine for a long time; it was a courtesy visit, and I was quite glad to see them. Lottie Hines also came by with representatives from the Tenants Council of Dade County with the usual difficult problems about public housing.

People are contacting me about transportation problems in

their districts. Bill Chappell from Florida has a radar problem at the airport in Gainesville, Al Swift has a highway problem in the State of Washington, and this is what we run into as we approach the mark-up session of the transportation subcommittee.

That evening I was on the shuttle to New York.

MAY 14 THURSDAY

I got to Dr. Strong's office early but had to wait a few hours because he was called into surgery. When I did see him, he gave me a clean bill of health. At 2:00, I was on the shuttle back to Washington.

Back in my office were Tom Beris and Joe Ratchet from Miami. They work for IMC, but are no longer paid as IMC is now in bankruptcy, and want me to call the heads of the Florida insurance department to urge them to continue HMO insurance funds so that the employees still working for IMC could be paid. I need to consider the best way if any to go about this. I met next with Adele, Al Moskovitz, and people from AID (Agency for International Development) regarding Al's project on St. Kitts. I am still trying to keep the door open for Al's project.

To show support for the working mothers on my staff, I joined Marsha, Nadine and Adele at the ribbon-cutting ceremony for the Senate Day Care Center playground. All three have children at the center. While there I spoke with the Quaker Oats representatives, who subsidize the center.

After the Day Care ceremony, I went to the Capitol for the Government Division Reception of the United Jewish Appeal, and then to Dick Sullivan's 70th birthday celebration. Dick is Chief of Staff on the Public Works Committee. His reception was held at the Federal Express office, and I thought what a great place to have this type of event. I saw my friend Federal Express legislative liaison Sandy Dickey there, and Federal Express staff people were happy to see me and appreciated a member showing up.

MAY 15 FRIDAY

Today has been fairly easy. The only meeting I had was with a family of constituents from North Miami, Maureen Harwitz, her husband Dr. Daniel Harwitz and their two boys. Maureen is an environmental activist, and she appealed to me to stay out of the Munisport toxic waste issue. I had already decided that I would now do just that.

Amtrak had been calling me, as its President Graham Claytor is trying to get GMAC to finance the purchase of ten locomotives built in the GMAC plant in Illinois, and wanted my help. GMAC wants Amtrak to pay one point over prime. I think Amtrak should pay only a half point over prime. My own son only pays three-quarters of a point over prime for his GMAC floor plan on Buicks. I do not see why Amtrak which is practically guaranteed by the government has to pay more over prime than automobile dealers. I think I can help on this reduction.

Ellen Kempler and her "Results" group which deals with world hunger will be coming in from Miami this evening, as will my son Bill for the car import dealers convention. I will have lots of company over the weekend.

MAY 16 SATURDAY

Bob Carr and I had breakfast this morning to discuss our subcommittee bill. I will try to raise re-election funds for him in Miami.

In the evening Ellen Kempler and I had dinner with Mr.& Mrs. Robin Lloyd. Robin is the NBC reporter at the White House, who has also been covering Nicaragua, and it was interesting talking to him. He told me that the Reagan administration was now going to claim that the Boland amendment - which limited aid to the Contra's - only applies to the State Department, CIA, and Defense Department, and did not apply to the National Security Council. Therefore, whatever the National Security Council did was not under the jurisdiction of the legislation of the Boland amendment. This was to be their escape route for any kind of effort they may be hatching for Contra aid. Another thing he said was that President Duarte of El Salvador was "dead in the water," and in a few years El Salvador will be back the way it was. Duarte may be the best democrat they have, but he is ineffective. So, in a few years the Army leader Colonel D'Aubison will be back in power with the death squads active again. There is no way any country in Central America now or in the foreseeable future will have a democratic election in the same manner that elections are held in this country or in Western Europe as it is just not part of their culture. [I was wrong on Nicaragua.]

MAY 17 SUNDAY

Bill and I went this evening to the Hyundai reception at the Willard Hotel. One million dollars were raised from the Hyundai dealers for a memorial to American casualties in the Korean War. We left the Willard and went across 13th Street to a *Sports Illustrated*-sponsored reception at the Marriott Hotel for the American Association of Car Import Dealers. We met other dealers there that both Bill and I knew.

MAY 18 MONDAY

This morning Bill and I had breakfast with Congressman Mineta and representatives from Hyundai and Mitsubishi, and then met later in the office of Julian Dixon of California, head of the Congressional Black Caucus, regarding black minority opportunities for Hyundai dealerships, and Julian made quite an impression. At 3:30, Congressman Bill Richardson of New Mexico was at the office about the too-narrow road problem from Los Alamos to Santa Fe, where nuclear waste is transported. I'll try to help with a highway demonstration project in my bill.

I then met with Ellen Kempler, Gail Neumann, Kathleen Gordon and Clea Sucoff from the "Results" group. This citizen's lobby on world-wide hunger spoke about the problems of overseas hunger. If one needs convincing about world poverty, this is the group to do it. They are so articulate, knowledgeable and dedicated to their cause. Afterwards, I took them to the Gallery to watch the House in session, and then to the East Front of the Capitol for a photo.

In the early evening, Bill, Ellen and I attended two receptions - both at the Marriott Hotel. We went first to the upper level of the hotel for the Auto Dealers and Drivers for Free Trade PAC's reception, and then to the Grand Ballroom for the

American International Automobile Dealers Association reception. I was somewhat a hero at this reception as they all knew that I voted against the Gephardt amendment, which to defeat was critical for them as the amendment proposed raising tariffs and limiting the import of foreign cars. I picked up a list of those in attendance for future fundraising. Frank Bolton and Jim Evans, both auto dealers in North Dade were there and were especially cordial to me. We did not stay long, as Bill and Ellen had a flight back to Miami, and I had a dinner engagement with Janet Studley.

Janet and I always have a good time together. She took me to the recently opened Italian restaurant, Bice, and told me about her new romance with Senator Mitchell of Maine, who was getting a divorce. This was interesting since the senator still lives at home with his wife when he is in Maine. I gave her the best advice that I could as I think she is in for some problems, but none that she can't resolve.

MAY 19 TUESDAY

This morning I went to a breakfast reception at the National Democratic Club honoring Congressman Bill Nelson, and then to the Cannon Building for the AIPAC breakfast reception. There was a huge turnout. By 9:00, I was at the office for my first appointment with representatives from the Sacramento Metropolitan Chamber of Commerce about their light rail system. And at 10:00, as Chairman of the Task Force on Prevention Strategy of the Children, Youth and Families Select Committee, I had a press conference with the American Psychological Association.

Afterwards, AIPAC representatives met with me on various problems concerning Israel, especially the sale of new replacement weapons to Saudi Arabia. Then lobbyist Hector Alcalde came in with a client about the Port Authority bridge in Jacksonville.

A busy morning, but the best thing to happen was a phone call from my grandson Sean who told me he had worked out his problems with the people at the University of Hawaii, and he will definitely be taking the intern position at Los Alamos this summer.

After lunch I met with Al Savage, Executive Director of the Buffalo Niagara Frontier Transit Authority, Ray Gallagher, Chairman of the Board who promised me a football signed by all the Buffalo Bills players, and Dennis Vierra who represents Dade County Metrorail. Dennis told me that Dade's environmental impact statement was moving right along and that by October everything should be in place to begin work on the Metromover extensions.

I had a visit from Wayne Merry of the State Department's East German Desk about our meeting tomorrow at the East German Embassy. One of two things we have to do is have Ambassador Herder get the documentation from Gysi defining on paper what the DGR is going to do for the Rabbi. The other is to find out what happened to the letter promised us inviting a congressional delegation to the Leipzig Fair in September.

My 3:00 appointment with Bill Hamilton, Director and Faye Wattleton, President of the Planned Parenthood of America, was about support on restructuring the Mexico City language, which eliminates U.S. grants on family planning abroad. The Mexico City language puts regulations on our overseas non-profit organizations that are more restrictive than those enforced in this country in regard to abortion. I need to turn around about four people on the Foreign Operations Subcommittee before I can ask Dave Obey to put it in our bill. If I can guarantee that members like John Porter and Silvio Conte will vote contrary to the way they voted in 1985 then I think Obey will put the language in his mark-up.

Something rather amusing happened today on the House Floor. Representative Barbara Boxer of California asked me if I could put some legislation in our transportation bill this year prohibiting the airlines from sending planes overseas for overhauling, especially to Taiwan, because her district is losing airline maintenance jobs. She already has been in trouble with Israeli supporters by voting against foreign aid, because the bill contained aid to El Salvador's military junta. "Israel overhauls airplanes from all over the world including U.S. airlines," I said; and she replied, "Oh no, you're not bringing Israel into this?" I was just teasing her.

3:30, Tunisian Ambassador Habib Ben Yahia came in for our

annual visit. The Ambassador is very articulate, and every year he comes in for about thirty minutes to brief me on the situation in Tunisia. Leslie Pantin, a top Cuban-American community leader in Miami, also stopped in for a short visit.

I then went to see Tex Gunnels, staff on the Post Office and Treasury Subcommittee about the language that the Metro-Dade Airport Authority wanted in the Treasury Appropriations bill that would provide for customs officials at Tamiami Airport.

Grumman Corporation has been helpful with my fundraiser and once manufactured buses for Urban Mass Transit. At their reception this evening in the Rayburn Building, I saw a plaque that said "NAS," which I mistakenly thought referred to what Grumman's was doing on the NAS plan for the FAA. I quickly learned, however, that the "NAS" plaque at Grumman's really stood for Naval Air Station.

Later, Joan and I went to the Corcoran Gallery of Art for the "Gala Salute to Congress and the Arts." This black-tie affair was sponsored by the American Arts Alliance, and on hand were a host of celebrities. We shared a table with Senator Chiles and his wife Rhea; Edward Villella, Director of the Balanchine Ballet in New York; and Bernie Jacobson of the Fine and Jacobson law firm in North Florida. The most interesting person there was actress Kitty Carlisle. Senator Claiborne Pell of Rhode Island was there, as were Representatives Sid Yates and Bob Carr.

MAY 20 WEDNESDAY

This morning Adele and I went to the East German Embassy on Massachusetts Avenue, N.W., to meet with Ambassador Herder and Wayne Merry about the problem of Rabbi Neuman going to East Germany. I told Ambassador Herder that we would like some documentation soon and he said we would have it in about two weeks, and that everything was moving along on schedule. I also asked why we had not received a letter from the people in Leipzig regarding the congressional delegation being invited to their trade fair this year. I had mentioned the trade fair to Tom Foley and Sam Gibbons and they would like to have an invitation. East Germany is very much interested in trade and I have put out the bait, but they have not really nibbled.

In a phone conversation with Rabbi Neuman in Champaign, Illinois, the Rabbi said he would have definite plans by Fall. I have to do something on the East German situation within a month or it will stall. At the meeting Wayne Merry told me he was being transferred to Athens. Many State Department people are moving around this summer so we really have to move faster.

Again I went to see Tex Gunnels about bill language on the Tamiami Airport situation. Tex said there would be language in the bill telling Customs to put their people at the Tamiami Airport, but not how many or under what particular circumstances. Dick Judy should be happy.

Members are getting in touch with me about the interstate-highway transfer funds to be earmarked in our markup. We have about three times as many requests as we have funds available.

We finished the DOD authorization bill on the Floor today, and I voted against all the Contra amendments. I did vote for final passage as the bill contains strategic weapons limitations and also reduces the strategic defense initiative funding. I saw George Miller who told me that the Select Committee on Children, Youth and Families would be holding hearings in Miami the first week in June. He now has to get back to me with an exact date.

At 1:30 I spoke to sixth grade students from North County Elementary School, who asked lots of questions - especially about the car business. But the high point of their visit was probably when I took them to the Rayburn Cafeteria and let them buy whatever they wanted. I really enjoyed watching them pick out food - some chose three or four desserts.

It is 3:00, and except for votes I am free until the 6:00 American Truckers Association reception honoring Bob Carr.

Joan and I had a great time at Alice Rivlin's this evening. Alice hosted a reception for her sister who works for AID (Agency for International Development), and she is moving to Bangladesh to serve as AID Administrator. An interesting group of people from Southeast Asia was there. Alice was funny in telling that her son wants her to run for President, which really is the highest compliment a son could pay to a mother.

MAY 21 THURSDAY

The Select Committee on Children, Youth and Families held its hearing this morning on "Alternative Reproductive Technologies: Implications for Children and Families." This was all about surrogate mothers and test tube babies. I had my photo taken with one of the lawyers who testified in regard to surrogate mothers, and I may be doing a newsletter on the subject.

Neal Smith, Chairman of the Subcommittee on Commerce, Justice, State, and the Judiciary, spoke to me about his codel to the Soviet Union in July, but I told him I would not be able to go with him this time. I like traveling with Neal and he has a good group going, but I think I should go back to South Florida, take it easy, and do a little politicking.

Late this afternoon Joan and I left for Nantucket aboard a two-engine Coast Guard jet. The plane could seat approximately fifteen people and we had it all to ourselves - just the two of us. It was super red carpet transportation but once we arrive the Coast Guard will keep me quite busy. We met my son Tom and his wife Amy there who flew in on a commercial airline. We had to wait an hour for them as their flight was late, so we used the time to visit the airport manager in the control tower to see about their need for radar. In regard to instrument landings, this airport is the second busiest in Massachusetts. They do have an ILS (Instrument Landing System) but they also need radar. The radar will cost less than one million dollars and would make this airport a lot safer. The manager is going to get in touch with his Congressman Gerry Studds and perhaps I can do something in our markup if Gerry requests.

MAY 22 FRIDAY

This morning the Coast Guard took us by van to a huge Air Force helicopter. We flew over Otis Air Force Base and were shown the lighthouse and the helicopter pads. Landing at Otis,

I thought how pathetic to see the base housing once used for 50,000 troops in WWII now being used by the Coast Guard at a mere ten percent of that number, and the unused housing just falling apart. It looked like a ghost town. We then drove to Woods Hole where we had lunch at the Coast Guard base and were given a tour of the Coast Guard Station. The Coast Guard is trying to recondition housing in all the stations in the Cape Cod area.

MAY 23 SATURDAY to May 26 TUESDAY

We spent Saturday on Martha's Vineyard and visited the electronic station transmitter at Break Point, the Coast Guard housing, and the Grant Point Lighthouse Station where we lunched on gourmet food. For about six hours we were with Captain Collins and the crew going over Coast Guard problems at Martha's Vineyard. Sunday and Monday we took it easy, and Tuesday we were picked up at the Nantucket airport and flown back to Washington. I got back to the office about 4:30 in the afternoon.

MAY 27 WEDNESDAY

This morning I went to see Tex Gunnels about a matter concerning Allen Brice from Brice Southern Elevator, who is being harassed by the IRS. Occasionally we do have people in business who are harassed by the IRS, and often it is not their fault but rather an overzealous IRS person who is acting above and beyond the call of duty.

Mostly I have been dealing with various little problems in the office, such as souvenir caps I had ordered to hand out to constituents visiting in Washington. The ones I received are marked, "Made in Taiwan," so now I cannot give them to our visiting constituents. This is one of the small but important things we have to watch out for. Fred Flynn, an attorney representing Hero Communications in Hialeah, came in about problems with the export of satellite discs. I asked him to find out exactly what the problem was and why the Commerce Department was giving him a hard time while letting others export. He will get back with me.

Speaker Jim Wright called a meeting this afternoon with the Democratic Majority Leader, the Democratic Whip, and all thirteen subcommittee chairmen on Appropriations. He told us he wanted to start moving appropriation legislation, but I told him I would not move my bill until I had a better knowledge of what the Budget Committee will allocate the transportation function in the House version of the bill. After the meeting, I saw Bill Gray on the House Floor and he told me he would have the Budget Conference Report out in about two weeks. Maybe Gray can get us better numbers in conference with the Senate than the numbers in the House bill.

Lynn Helms, former head of the FAA, met me in the Members Dining Room and spoke about an advisory group he had put together for Martin Marietta to extend the NAS plan (National Air Space) into foreign countries. He is now doing some overseas promotion for Martin Marietta.

Lou Gerber, the lobbyist for Communication Workers of America, came to the office to ask that I cosponsor the Don Edwards bill, which called for putting a beeper on phone calls when an employer overhears employees' phone conversations. I would vote for the bill if it came to the Floor, but I did not think the issue was that important. Then Aviva Meyer, who runs Project Interchange, was in. Project Interchange takes mixed cultural and racial groups to Israel. I am having a Black-Jewish luncheon a week from Friday in Miami, maybe we can raise enough seed money to send two Blacks with two Jews to Israel for about $8,000. Our campaign fund could also contribute.

MAY 28 THURSDAY

My first meeting today was with trade union representatives. Gary Ferrar from Amalgamated Clothing and Textile Workers Union and Nick Bonano from the International Ladies Garment Workers Union wanted me to endorse the textile and footwear trade bill; Pedro Mirones from Suave Shoes came in about the same bill. I told them all that I would support the bill when it came to the House Floor, but I was not at this point going to cosponsor as I had some reservations. If the bill was going anywhere I would support it, but I did not want to antagonize people on either side of the issue for a bill that would not get to the House Floor. I felt that the textile and shoe industries were doing all right. There are fewer people working in those businesses but production has been climbing steadily.

The main meeting today was a follow up of yesterday's meeting of the appropriations subcommittee chairs. Chairman Whitten announced our 302B allocations. I had to speak out, as others did, that if we had to live within these 302B allocations there would be no special projects money for members' requests, and there would be severe cuts in national programs such as federal subsidies for public transportation. We did gain $155 million more than the original allocation, and Dave Obey transferred funds to Transportation from the Foreign Operations allocation because he wanted to be at the Foreign Ops' Senate level, and the Legislative Subcommittee transferred to us $15 million from its allocation. We now have a level of funding with which we can work.

I want to keep in my markup valuable special projects and projects for certain members that have special needs in their districts. What will probably happen is a reduction in the subsidies of Section 9 for mass transit because Section 9 does not have strong support among the House members, and the only constituency for Section 9 seems to be the American Public Transportation Association.

MAY 29 FRIDAY

The day is slow except for House Coast Guard legislative liaison Commander Guy, who came in to go over the problems we reviewed on our trip to Nantucket. This evening my cousins, Marx and Shirley Leva, and I will go to the marine barracks to watch the Drill Parade.

We just hired a new receptionist, Barbara Zalinski, a Michigan State graduate, and I think she will work out fine. My secretary Wynne is glad to have her, as she has been doing both her job and filling in as receptionist.

MAY 30 SATURDAY

Joan and I went this evening to a party for Florida State Senator Jack Gordon. Myra McPherson, his new wife gave the party and many Washington media people were there such as David Brody, Richard Cohen, and others. Jack has a new young wife and I do not know if he can handle her as she sure is a live wire.

MAY 31 SUNDAY

Sergio Bendixen and I had brunch together this morning. Sergio is really busy now running the Babbitt campaign, and it was fun talking politics. Sergio thinks Babbitt has a good chance to come in first in Iowa, but I think he is dreaming. He told me some things about the Gary Hart problem and Tom Fiedler's role. When Hart saw Tom Fiedler, a political reporter for the *Miami Herald*, outside the house where he was having his extramarital affair, he knew that his campaign was over. [Tom, who has the credibility that other investigative reporters do not have, told me later that this was one assignment he was not proud of.]

Chapter 6

JUNE 1, 1987 - MONDAY

Sonny Montgomery, Chairman of the Committee on Veterans Affairs, asked me to accompany him and the Veterans Affairs Committee staff to the White House for President Reagan's signing of the Veterans Education Bill. The ceremony was short with the President thanking Sonny for the bill. Later Sonny and I played tennis and had a good time, as we won as partners against Judge Mikva and Bob Kastenmeier. Don Edwards no longer plays tennis with us, and we are trying to find out whether it is physical or just that he is too busy.

Bob Kunst from my district came in concerning AIDS. Bob is an admitted homosexual, who occasionally runs for the Florida Senate on the gay rights issue. He gets a few votes, but it is more a public relations effort on his part. He has little or no substance, and does not really do much about the problems of his own colleagues in the gay community.

Sharyn, who is in town for our fundraiser breakfast on Wednesday, spoke to me about launching her own business, and I gave her advice about some pitfalls of owning your own business from my past experience. It is not as simple as one might think. In the evening I took her and Wynne to the Aircraft Owners and Pilots Association reception at the Watergate, as neither had ever been to the Watergate.

JUNE 2 TUESDAY

My schedule is now straightened out for the coming weeks. We are trying to get organized on the Carol City Community Center, as they do not have all of the essentials in place to open. We got a $500 check from my son Bill and $500 from our campaign, which I will give to Al Moore, head of Little HUD in Miami, as the first payment on lights for the basketball court. The basketball court at the Carol City housing complex is very popular with the teenagers who live in that area, and during the day it is a good way to keep them off the streets. If the court is lighted, this would also be a good way to keep them off the streets at night. They need other things of course, like tennis courts and an indoor activities center, but this is a start.

GMAC executives met with me later in the morning to put together a deal for the purchasing and financing of the General Motors locomotives for Amtrak. This is the matter about which Amtrak so urgently needed me. I think now a compromise on the interest rate is all worked out. At noon I attended the luncheon of the Population Institute held in the Rayburn Building; at 2:00 I met with Anita Epstein and Paul Berger, both from a prestigious Washington law firm, regarding the proposed resolution to include the Armenian tragedy in the Holocaust Memorial. (In the 1920's the Armenians suffered under the Turks.) I am not a cosponsor of this resolution, and apparently most of the survivors of the Holocaust in the Jewish community do not want to be placed in the same category as the Armenians, as the Armenians were in a different kind of situation from the Jews. It was interesting talking to Anita Epstein as she and her mother are survivors of the concentration camps.

On the House Floor, I went up to Barney Frank from Massachusetts and shook his hand for publicly acknowledging a few days ago that he was a homosexual. Several members approached me saying that I had done the right thing and that they would do the same. The members, though, hesitate to do so publicly.

JUNE 3 WEDNESDAY

The Washington law firm of Gerald Cassidy and Associates sponsored a lovely fundraiser breakfast for me this morning. The event was held at their offices on 15th Street in downtown Washington in a beautiful old building which had just been renovated to include a gorgeous atrium, and the offices were very eloquently decorated. Sharyn and I picked up $2,000 in checks from the firm and its clients, with a promise of $2,000 more, making it a $4,000 fundraiser.

I was back on the Hill by 9:00, for Dave Obey's meeting with the supporters of his campaign for Chair of the Budget Committee. His effort is moving along but, as yet, nothing is really happening. On the House Floor we had a few votes, but none as strange as the vote yesterday on the Persian Gulf resolution, requiring the Department of Defense to report to Congress, within seven days of the bill's enactment, threats U.S. forces would face in the Persian Gulf under the administration's program of reflagging Kuwaiti oil tankers for U.S. protection against Iraqi and Iranian forces. The votes against came from liberals and ultra conservatives. Ultra liberals such as Don Edwards, Sid Yates, and Bob Kastenmeier did not vote "yea" because they said it violated the War Powers Act, which requires the president to report to Congress before sending U.S. forces into hostile situations. That was too fine a legal difference for me so I voted for the resolution, but I can understand their concerns. Sometimes we have some really strange votes on the Floor where the super liberals and super conservatives are the only ones either voting for or against a piece of legislation.

Returning from the Floor I checked with Tex Gunnels to be sure everything was okay with the Tamiami airport language on the customs officials to be stationed there, and it was. I expect the language will now remain in the bill in the full appropriations committee markup. At the office, staffer Mike Stephens from Appropriations Subcommittee on Health and Human Services came in and wanted to know if we had room for another intern, no pay, for a friend of his brother's from Great Britain. It will be difficult to find space in the office what with the three new interns we already have, and they are using makeshift desks. But I promised Mike I would get back to him.

In the afternoon Norman Goldenberg from Miami, a member of the National Pest Control Association, came in concerned with the proposed legislative limitations on polygraph tests and with family leave for childbirth legislation pertaining to small company employees. I told him I was opposite his opinion but I would probably support some kind of compromise. Next to arrive was Peter Kyros regarding high speed rail and suggested that I visit Spain to look at the equipment there. Peter is a former member of Congress from Maine and now represents Spanish equipment manufacturers that want to supply Amtrak. Perhaps in the Fall if I have the time I will take a group to Spain to look at the equipment and see if it applies to our Amtrak needs.

Then Representative Bob Mollahan of West Virginia came in about two projects for his area. One is for a University of West Virginia study on a highway corridor and the other is an airport priority listing for a taxi strip at the Charleston airport.

Back on the House Floor I saw for the first time a draft of the Budget Conference Report. A little more allotment is provided for the transportation function, but I do not know if that necessarily will filter down to our own subcommittee or to other areas of function of the budget.

That evening I attended a reception at the National Democratic Club for Ed Boland of Massachusetts, and then to the Florida House for a farewell party for Floridian, Janet Patten, sponsored by her colleagues at Textron. Janet is opening her own consulting firm.

JUNE 4 THURSDAY

This morning I met with Edie Wilkie, wife of my good friend and colleague, Don Edwards, and Caleb Rossiter from the Arms Control and Defense Caucus. Edie has worked for various peace organizations and was very much involved with the Members of Congress for Peace Through Law organization, which has now changed its name and direction. They want me to put language regarding Costa Rica in the Foreign Operations Subcommittee markup, on how the peace organizations want economic security funds spent for development instead of Costa Rica using security funds to pay debt interest or to build up the infrastructure of the military. Edie wants to support Costa Rican President Oscar Arias by increasing AID and economic security funds to the 1986 level, which were cut back $30 million in 1987 by the administration. The cutback was due to Costa Rica wanting to negotiate with the Sandinistas, and this was the administration's way of sending President Arias a tough message.

People from Parsons, Brinckerhoff, Quade & Douglas, an Arizona engineering firm came in around 10:30 with Alan Wulkan. I knew Alan from his former position as legislative liaison for Metro-Dade Transit. Parsons, Brinckerhoff, Quade & Douglas have money problems regarding a light rail system in Salt Lake City, and Alan is to get back to me. I then walked over to the Capitol to meet with staff on Appropriations VA, HUD and Independent Agencies Subcommittee concerning the 1987 application for a $6 million grant for Little HUD in Miami. Miami's Little HUD's records and operations are in such a mess that a suit was filed by the Dade State Attorney's office claiming the Miami agency is a public nuisance. The Atlanta regional office is in the midst of an investigation that should be completed by July 1. Until then no federal funds will be released to Miami's Little HUD for comprehensive modernization. I am hoping the subcommittee can offer some help on this.

On the Floor I tried to recruit some members on the Children, Youth and Families Select Committee to come to Miami for the hearing on June 22. George Miller, chairman of the select committee, was supposed to come but he has other commitments. I do not need George to chair the hearing, because as Chairman of the Task Force on Prevention Strategy and the ranking Democrat on the committee, I can; but unless one or two members besides myself attend, the committee will not pay the expenses of the staff needed to set up the hearing. I will also be embarrassed because I had to cancel a hearing once before in Miami.

This is a committee I would really like to leave to give other committee Democrats a chance to move up in rank. My plate is full and sometimes running over as Chairman of the

Subcommittee on Transportation Appropriations and as a member on the Foreign Operations Subcommittee. Nadine and Marsha, my legislative assistants, both have small children and are very interested in this select committee, and have been urging me to stay on it.

Mayor Tom Bradley called from Los Angeles about funds in our bill for the Los Angeles rapid mass transit system, and I tried to assure him that everything would be all right. The Secretary of the Department of Transportation made a request for $51 million yesterday to assist air traffic controllers, and I spoke to radio stations in Miami this morning about what I thought our subcommittee action would be. "Fifty million dollars will not help our air traffic," I said, "and it will be several more years before new air traffic controllers are trained." A radio station in New York called, and I told them the same thing. This has been a busy media day for me, as I also spoke to an AP reporter on this.

My flight to Miami was delayed and I did not arrive in Miami until 1:00 a.m.

JUNE 5 FRIDAY

Before our Black-Jewish leadership luncheon at noon today, I met with Arlene Gray, Project Director for the Daily Bread Food Bank. We went over her speech for the luncheon, with the primary points of emphasis on hunger and public transportation. We discussed her effort to have a joint Black-Jewish volunteer task force to help distribute food gathered for this project. A great amount of food in this program is distributed to various organizations, many of which are for poor Blacks and elderly Jews.

The luncheon meeting was held at the Beth Torah Synagogue on 163rd Street in North Miami Beach, and it was a little short on blacks but enough to be representative. Point East Condo leader, Annie Ackerman, was there. Annie did not look well, but she is still active. Ben Gilford, the new head of the Metro-Dade Transit System, was our first speaker, and had a good reception. Arlene then gave her presentation, which was also well received. We now have a committee of four that will arrange for volunteers to distribute the food. As the final speaker, I told them that I would be working to send representatives of both groups on a trip to Israel in 1988, and that maybe the following year we would plan a trip to the Sahara or South Africa. "Two thousand dollars will be donated from our campaign," I said, and suggested that the rest could be gotten through local organizations that I had already contacted. The meeting worked out very well.

JUNE 6 SATURDAY

Since I am in Miami for only a couple of weekends a month, Saturday is often the only day I have to meet with constituents in the district office. Most of the staff are in the office as though it is a weekday, which is the usual procedure when I am in town. The first of our appointments began at 10:00 with Charlotte Greenbarg. Charlotte is obsessed with the overpass planned by the Florida Department of Transportation to be built on 203rd Street and Ives Dairy Road. She said the people who live there do not want the overpass. This I knew from Mark and Carol Press who met with me in Washington two months ago. I also knew that the State Highway Department needed the overpass to relieve traffic on Biscayne Boulevard being held up by the railroad crossing. Ives Dairy Road is the shortest East-West distance between I-95 and U.S. 1, Biscayne Boulevard. I told Charlotte that I would arrange for a meeting in my office with a representative of the Federal Highway Administration so that she and her group could present its opposing argument. I did not say I would support them but only agreed that I would let the FHA know that many people in my district have indicated their opposition to the proposed overpass. I know eventually we will need this overpass to reduce the traffic congestion.

Then lovely Nancy Maldonado, a former recipient of my daughter's Memorial Scholarship Award at FIU, came in. Nancy worked as a waitress at Clifford's Restaurant until she graduated from Florida International University and is now a teacher at North Miami High School. We had our photo taken, and I promised to visit her class at North Miami High next fall.

JUNE 7 SUNDAY

Today I gave the commencement address before the South East College of Osteopathic Medicine. The ceremony was held at the Gusman Cultural Center on East Flagler Street, and I was awarded an Honorary Doctorate Degree. At 5:30, I was on the flight back to Washington.

JUNE 8 MONDAY

I had a courtesy visit from the new FAA Administrator nominee, Allan McArtor. Greg and Lucy were present, and we talked about a half hour regarding current and long-term problems of the FAA. After McArtor's visit, Tom, Greg, Lucy and I went over the thirty or forty amendments in disagreement in the transportation section of the supplemental appropriations conference bill. Most of the disagreements are already worked out by House-Senate committee staff, but there are several open questions such as the problem of Amtrak on one of its routes, and the flight service station in Youngstown, Ohio.

At 4:30, my good friend Stu Eizenstat, Director of Domestic Affairs during the Carter administration, came in regarding the Foreign Operations part of the emergency supplemental of the 1988 Appropriations Bill. Stu is concerned about the Export-Import Bank funding, especially if there is a $200 million dollar recision in the supplemental. He also wants funds earmarked in the 1988 bill for Morocco, and is working with Israeli Foreign Minister Shimon Peres who is helping Morocco in the interest of Israel. Stu represents the Ex-Im Bank and I will probably support him on both issues.

I spoke with *Miami Herald* editor and columnist, Carl Hiaasen, about a case involving the Immigration Naturalization Service and a 19 year old woman who did not have a driver's license as a means of identification and was about to lose her job at Burger King. We went to Burger King management and to the INS office in Miami to resolve the matter, and she will now be allowed to keep her position.

There are two receptions that I will skip this evening. One is for Byron Dorgan of North Dakota at Yolanda's Restaurant. Yolanda's is an excellent restaurant, but when my daughter Kathy was alive, she and Joan and I went there for lunch. Kathy had a severe seizure at the restaurant and I have bad feelings about going back there as it reminds me of how ill Kathy was. The other reception is Jamie Whitten's annual fundraiser being held at the Roof Top Terrace of the Hotel Washington. I have been to about five of his fundraisers, and I think I can get away with not going to this one.

This week is going to be rough with both the transportation subcommittee markup and the full appropriations supplemental markups. And, looking at tomorrow's office appointments, someone is scheduled to meet with me every thirty minutes.

JUNE 9 TUESDAY

Today began with one of the fastest fundraisers I have ever attended - a breakfast at the Reserve Officers Association headquarters honoring Florida Congressman Charles Bennett. It began at 8:00 and everyone was gone by 8:30. More and more fundraisers are now being held in the morning or midday as the evenings are just overloaded with these events. I stopped in at the hearing of the Select Committee on Children, Youth and Families, which started at 9:00, and tried again to convince a few Republicans to attend our hearing in Miami. I have one or two possibilities.

Opa Locka Mayor Robert Ingram from my district was in about the crime and drug problems in Opa Locka. I now have documentation for Congressman George Crockett from Michigan, Chairman of the Crime and Criminal Justice Subcommittee of the Judiciary Committee, which should induce him to make a call to the Justice Department urging the release of crime prevention funds now being withheld. Opa Locka has the highest crime rate in Dade County, and help is long overdue and crucial. Mayor Ingram also put in a request for an abandoned building, once occupied by a Federal agency, that could now be used by the City of Opa Locka. Before I can go to the GSA with this request, the Mayor must submit a statement to me outlining the proposed use for this building.

1:00, Joseph Nicholson came in bemoaning the fact that the company he was working for is going out of business. This country is no longer making rail cars, and he is now looking for a job. 2:00, I met with Peter Defazio (D-OR), who wanted to be sure that the Northbend Municipal Airport in Oregon was on the list of airport priorities in our bill. Then Los Angeles Transit Administrator, John Dyer, and lobbyist friend, Cliff Madison, came in with an update on the progress of the Los Angeles metrorail and the need for additional funds. This is going to be one of L.A.'s big years for funds, but it must realize there is going to be considerable competition for this year's transit appropriations.

Eugene Dubow wants me to meet the new chairman of the American Jewish Committee this afternoon. And Francis Meehan called regarding the Rabbi's move to East Germany. The Ambassador had received a cable from Klaus Gysi which stated that there were a few problems but to be patient as everything will work out okay. I told him I would wait until after the July 4 recess, but that any later I would have to take action. I am hoping that the Rabbi's visa is then in hand so that he may freely travel in and out of the GDR.

Clay Shaw (R-FL) had his fundraiser/reception this evening. The reception was on the Hill at Anton's Loyal Opposition - not much of a reception really, but I always enjoy attending events for my Florida colleagues. I left to attend the private viewing of Andrew Wyeth's drawings and watercolors at the National Endowment for the Arts. The DuPont Corporation sponsored the exhibition and reception, and it was one of the most beautiful and enjoyable events that I had been to in a while.

JUNE 10 WEDNESDAY

The Florida Congressional Delegation met this morning in Charlie Bennett's office to nominate him as our representative at the 200th Bicentennial Constitutional Anniversary Meeting in Philadelphia, in July; Dante Fascell was named alternate. The House went in session at 10:00 a.m., which had me running back and forth to vote. Dr. Edward Truppman, President of the American Association for Accreditation of Ambulatory Plastic Surgery Facilities, and a resident in my district, came in about problems regarding medical legislation. I did not have much time to talk to him although I should have taken the time, as he is a loyal supporter. His main concern was that he wanted plastic surgeon patients to receive the same kind of Medicare/Medicaid benefits as other surgeons' patients.

At 11:30 Jim Miller, Director of the Office of Management and Budget (OMB), came in with his aide and went through the same unrealistic bullshit about the privatization of Amtrak and the reduction or elimination of federal subsidy for mass transit. The Office of Management and Budget goes through the same charade every year and always receives the same answers. Lucy Hand and Tom

Kingfield were with me, and we wasted thirty minutes just talking to Miller about what will be in our bill. He knows and I know that the bill will pass and will probably be lumped into a continuing resolution. I told him that the President will have on his desk on the 24th of December a tax bill together with all the appropriations bills in one package, which the President has to sign or close down the government. Miller left a bit frustrated.

The Appropriations Supplemental Conference was held today on the Senate side to accommodate Senator John Stennis, Chairman of the Senate Appropriations Committee, who just recently had his leg amputated. At noon, I met with my subcommittee counterpart, Senator Frank Lautenberg, and staff from both subcommittees, to work out the differences in the appropriations transportation section of the supplemental bill. We settled all but a couple of items, one dealing with the flight service station in Youngstown, Ohio. We will have to arrange some compromise as the amendment offered by Jim Traficant from Ohio did pass on a vote in the House. I told Lautenberg that I did not want to win or to lose on this, but that I just wanted to get by without too much hassle on the problem. The other item left unsettled was a small disagreement on the Montreal Amtrak route from New York to Montreal which runs on the Boston and Maine Railroad right of way. The problem is Amtrak uses the right of way, but the Boston Montreal Railroad does not well maintain the railbed.

At 2:00, I met with Congressman Bob Carr, Al Dellibovi the Acting UMTA Administrator, Amtrak representatives, Tom Kingfield, and Jeff Jacobs from Congressman Silvio Conte's staff. The meeting was an effort to reach a compromise on the new regulation that would prohibit the federally funded public transit properties from competing with private sector franchised charter buses. There is a need periodically to charter public transit properties when there are no available private sector properties, especially for the handicapped, the elderly and for special occasions and events. At the same time it is not fair for the publicly funded properties to take business away from the transit companies that are privately operated. Therefore, we are trying to work out bill language that will prevent Bob Carr from offering tomorrow an amendment in our subcommittee markup that will prohibit any funds for the implementation of the regulation prohibiting federally funded public transit properties from competing with private sector franchised charter buses. This is the type of compromise that will take a lot of energy before parties can come to an agreement.

Then Jim Fox, Jim Rich and Ralph Krebs from Shell Oil came in about the expiration of offshore oil drilling rights off the Gulf Coast of Florida. I have mixed feelings about this; it is the same old question, whether to continue offshore oil drilling in Florida and perhaps damage the ocean environment, or do we remain more dependent on Mideast oil and maybe have long lines at the service stations, as we once had. I'll come down on the side of the environment as usual.

Miami Herald Publisher Dick Capen called, wanting to meet with me in Miami regarding my experiences on the East Germany trip, especially with Klaus Gysi and what is happening now regarding the Rabbi's visa. He also wants to play tennis, since Merritt Steirheim, Manager of Metro-Dade, told him that I was good.

I saw George Crockett from the Judiciary Committee and gave him the information that Mayor Ingram had given me documenting Opa Locka's need to be included in the Department of Justice's crime prevention and grants program. I hope Crockett will follow up, but I will also check with the Justice Department to see where the grant now stands.

At 5:00 Tom, Greg, Lucy and I went over the notes for the subcommittee markup. We finished about 8:00, and with a little smoke and mirrors and by moving around a couple hundred million of FAA appropriated but not-obligated funds, we were able to score these FAA funds back into the 1987 budget allotment. We then made an assumption that transportation will also receive $275 million for the Coast Guard in the Department of Defense (DOD) appropriation bill, and with all of this we came within the 302B allocation for transportation appropriation imposed on our subcommittee. Also the Federal Railroad Administration is going to sell preference shares on the open market at the market value, which we hope will bring in about $450 million and will reduce our outlays by that amount. This, of course, will help us with the Senate because the Senate counts outlays differently from the House. We did a good job, and were even able to keep in the "pork barrel" projects requested by members.

JUNE 11 THURSDAY

Prior to our subcommittee's markup, I went over the markup notes with Larry Coughlin to be sure he knew what was in the markup, although his staff already knew. At 10:30 a.m., we began the Transportation Subcommittee markup, and voted to close it to the public so that we could move faster. Not many changes or amendments were offered, but there were several interruptions for Floor votes. We finished about 2:30, with no major changes. The bill contains $10.7 billion in discretionary funds plus $15 billion in contract authority for highways and airport facilities. After the markup I met with the press in my office and also made phone calls to the media in Miami about the bill.

Patrice from the district office called about problems in Miami with the federal grant money for Metro-Dade Little HUD. The Carol City Recreation Center may not be able to reopen because the entire public housing project to which the recreation center is connected may be closed.

On the House Floor Dan Rostenkowski handed me an envelope that had a $1,500 check from the imported car dealers PAC. Perhaps this was for standing with Dan in opposing the Gephardt amendment in the Ways and Means trade bill. I never asked him for it, but he seems to want to help those who stayed with him on a tough issue. Colorado member Pat Schroeder was nearby, and I told her about the conversation I overheard in a Miami Howard Johnson's about her running for the presidency and how she was coming across as too much of a "know-it-all." Pat asked for the names of the people I had overheard so that she could have her public relations people talk to them, and she really seemed to appreciate my working with her. Also on the Floor, Republican Nancy Johnson of Connecticut said she is definitely coming to Miami for the Select Committee hearing on June 22, as will Nadine Berg and John Schelble from my office staff. Democrat Tom Sawyer of Ohio also indicated that he would come.

Adele and I are working on the Foreign Operations Subcommittee legislation, and one thing we want to accomplish is to eliminate the sale of artillery shells to Saudi Arabia. When I saw Dave Obey on the Floor, he agreed to take this out in his subcommittee markup. Ambassador Meehan called to offer his assistance in putting together the arrangements for a congressional delegation, led by Sam Gibbons from the Committee on Ways and Means and Majority Leader Tom Foley, to visit the Leipzig Fair. Apparently the East Germans are very sensitive about inviting people and then being rejected. East Germany is going to have to learn how to deal with that problem.

Stopping by the subcommittee office on Commerce, State and Justice, I told the staff that I would not be making the trip to the Soviet Union even if we were out of session for the long July 4th holiday. Though most of my work with the transportation appropriations bill is now "over the hump," we still have the full committee markup and the Floor action.

JUNE 12 FRIDAY

I was invited downtown for breakfast this morning to meet with the National Outdoor Advertising Association. Vernon Clark was there and six of his employees, all women. After the breakfast I was handed a $1,000 honorarium and Vernon extended an invitation to me to come to Palm Springs anytime during the coming year and receive another honorarium. We sat and talked politics and discussed presidential candidates. I also left on the table my notes from yesterday's markup, but got a call from the restaurant saying that they were found.

At the Washington Airport for my flight to Miami, I saw Miami attorney John Smith whom I had met last night at the American Bankers Association and Senator Steve Symms of Idaho. I got the two of them together. Smith is a partner in the Steel, Hector law firm and Steve, a conservative Republican, is going to Miami to talk to the Miami Cuban community. I like Steve, but of course our voting patterns are different.

Arriving in Miami early afternoon, I was met by staffer Bernie Torra, and we drove to the *Miami Herald* building for my appointment with Publisher Dick Capen. This was the first time Bernie had been in a newsroom, and he was quite impressed with being on the fifth floor of the *Miami Herald*. I had been there so many times that it did not have that much of an impact on me.

From home I made phone calls to Washington about minor scheduling problems for next week. Later in the afternoon I played tennis at the Miami Shores Country Club with 39 year old Dick Green, and I won.

JUNE 13 SATURDAY

This morning I went to the Point East Condo to visit with Annie Ackerman, who is now walking using a walker, and not doing too well. We talked politics and she said that she liked Dukakis for president but neither of us is committed to any one candidate. After Annie I went to the district office and handled some routine matters - wrote thank you letters, reviewed messages, filled out forms and the like. Jeff will be representing me today at condo leader Max Watner's funeral. He will also represent me at a presentation this weekend at another condo association.

In the afternoon I played tennis with Art Hill, a prominent black attorney in my district. Art is President of People's Commercial Bank, and a Republican, and wanted me to hire his daughter as an intern; unfortunately our summer slots are all filled, and he asked too late.

Chip Bishop, APTA's (American Public Transit Association) public relations director, called to invite me to address their convention in North Carolina in August. I do not know whether I can schedule this as I am to spend time with my grandsons Sean and Matt in New Mexico in August. Also, I think it would be very valuable for me to visit San Diego to view the best trauma network in the country, and then write a newsletter on the kind of trauma system Metro-Dade should pursue.

An item was in today's *Miami News*, Martin Lucoff's column, regarding my appointment to a four-year term on the Washington Metropolitan Airport Authority. The article was rather humorous, saying that now I would have to run for two more terms in order to fill my commitment to the Washington Metro Airport Authority. This is really a Northern Virginia Airport Authority as the two airports, Dulles and Washington-National, are in Virginia.

On Father's Day, our family had dinner at the Miami International Airport. Through Dick Judy's liaison office, I arranged for a private dining room on the seventh floor of the new section of the airport. The tables were beautifully decorated and the dining room caterer went all out for the fourteen members of my family who were there. Dick Judy really did a wonderful job.

After dinner the head tour guide took us by shuttle bus to the main control tower and we spent about an hour in the Terminal Radar Air Traffic Control Center. The FAA people who took us through were very attentive, and it made for quite an unusual Father's Day. I did spend time in the actual FAA operations, and the more I see of it the more I understand what is going on; and yet, it is still too technical for me to fully comprehend. I also learned that very few of the controllers there came through the training center in Oklahoma City, but drifted into the job either through the Army or through other airport jobs.

JUNE 14 SUNDAY

I had an early afternoon flight back to Washington, but I did manage before leaving to get together with Al Moskovitz for tennis. Al told me about another AID project on which he wants my help. This time the project is in the West Indies.

JUNE 15 MONDAY

This morning I started off by having coffee with Bob Rogers and his family in the Members Dining Room. Bob is the Regional Hyundai Director in Atlanta. I took them on a brief tour onto the House Floor, and then to the East front for a photo.

At noon I hosted a luncheon in the Gold Room of the Rayburn Building for the Ethiopian Resettlement Program in Israel. Sharing the head table with me was a representative from the Israeli Embassy, and a representative from the United Jewish Appeal in New York. The UJA raises private money for the resettlement program. We talked about the increase this year of people coming out from the Soviet Union, Iran and Ethiopia in comparison to last year. We discussed Romania, one of our country's most favored trading nations, and the fact that although they are not very good to the Jews that are still living in Romania, the country does cooperate with Israel in allowing Soviet Jews to fly there and then go on to Israel. Of course, this is what Israel wants because if Soviet Jews fly first into Vienna about half will split to go to places other than Israel, and that defeats the purpose of the visa. Since Romania is a most favored nation and accepts the Soviet Jews, it would be good to send a message asking Romania not to oppress Jews that are there, and yet be so circumspect in our message that it would not destroy the relationship Israel has with Romania for Soviet Jews.

Afterwards I played tennis at the Army/Navy Club with Sonny Montgomery, Bob Kastenmeier and the House Chaplain, Dr. James Ford. When I got back to the office I canceled my invitation to the Ecuadorian Embassy because it is too far from Capitol Hill and would cause me to miss other engagements.

I took Janet Studley, Len Rappaport, and Lany Narot, who arrived in Washington this morning from Miami, to the J.C. Penney reception in the Rayburn Cafeteria, and from there we went to the NYNEX (NY Baby Bell) reception in the Cannon Caucus Room. Senator George Mitchell, who is dating Janet Studley, was there, and sat at our table for a while. I spoke to Lee Hamilton (D-IN) and teased him about being the first to mention "impeachment" on a Sunday newscast in regard to the Iranscam that his select committee is investigating.

It was a busy evening, as I had arranged with Dave Bocknay on the White House staff to take Wynne, Len, Lany and me on a private tour of the White House. Dave spent an hour showing us around. In the midst of the tour, a rather surprising incident occurred. As Dave opened the door to a little room in the West Wing of the White House, inside were three generations of a Japanese family sitting there by themselves eating a Burger King carry out. Dave did not know what to make of it, and neither did the White House staff, as no one had bothered explaining their presence there. Forty-five years ago when we were at war with Japan, this would have been one of the most absurd scenes one could ever imagine; and now a Japanese family has taken over one of the situation rooms in the West Wing of the White House.

JUNE 16 TUESDAY

I met Len Rappaport and Lany Narot in the office, and we went to the Senate Dining Room for breakfast. At 10:00, I was to meet with former Congressman Jim Symington, but he did not show. One of Jim's law partners, Mike Ferrell, came instead, with people from the El Salvador Chamber of Commerce. Mike formerly worked in our office as a legislative assistant, and then as general counsel on the Census and Population Subcommittee when I became chairman of that subcommittee. They wanted to be sure that U.S. aid to El Salvador did not end up in the government's hands but that it benefitted the economy, especially small businesses that are struggling to survive.

El Salvador's problem is that the Duarte reforms have crippled private enterprise and the Chamber wants to be sure the United States is not supporting an anti-business socialist corrupt Marxist government. The Chamber members were primarily coffee exporters and brought me several packages of coffee, which I will take home to Joan. Afterwards Evan Katzman, the grandson of Ben Sachs, a North Dade supporter of mine especially on pharmaceutical legislation, came in. Evan is a computer genius, looking for a high-tech job in Washington, and I got him an appointment with the FAA research staff.

11:30, Larry Coughlin and I met with Senator Frank Lautenberg in the Senate Appropriations Committee room. Since I seemed to know more of the details than Frank, I was pretty much in control of the meeting. We went over the amendments in disagreement that staff had resolved in the supplemental appropriations committee conference. Most of it was inconsequential, but one sticking point was what to do with Jim Traficant's flight service station. We ended up receding to the Senate with language by the House to accept the FAA court order that the Youngstown, Ohio, flight service station could only be closed by congressional action. We also worked out the differences on Senator Leahy and Rep. Conte's wishes to provide $5 million to recondition the Amtrak run on the roadbed for the Boston-Montreal Railroad which has deteriorated.

On the House Floor Charlie Wilson told me about an interesting trip he is planning to India and Pakistan this October. He wants to go to Pakistan near the Chinese border for five days and stop in Sardinia, Crete and Turkey on the way. It sounds like an ideal trip. Although Charlie is not a subcommittee chairman, I will try to help him put the trip together. So far the Appropriations Committee chairman is not authorizing any overseas travel for nonsubcommittee appropriations chairmen. It is one of Jamie Whitten's hangups.

Also on the Floor, Pete Stark told me he was interested in the letter that I received from Ted Slack, an old friend and former Dade County School Board member, which stated that in last year's tax bill if a child was sent to camp as a form of day care the costs would be tax deductible; but if the child went to a camp that was educational in concept it would not be tax deductible.

He said he would try to change this in the bill this year and would let me know.

We finally passed a labor-industry construction bill. There were five or six amendments which weakened the bill, and I voted against it. I was not happy with the amendments or the bill, but Marsha on my staff committed me to the labor position early in the year. I told both Marsha and Nadine that from now on they were not to endorse or list me as a cosponsor on any bill until I give them the word to do so.

Although I have cosponsored labor bills in the past, I do not feel that labor is in the same position it was a few years ago, because management is not the enemy. The enemy is foreign competition. In order to protect American industry from labor inflated costs, labor and management must stop being adversaries. I do represent a consumer district and my constituents are more concerned about costs than labor rights.

JUNE 17 WEDNESDAY

Our first markup in the full Appropriations Committee began this morning at 9:OO with the Subcommittee on Energy and Water Development, and lasted about an hour. Tom Bevill from Alabama, chairman of the subcommittee, guided his bill through the markup.

At our office we had an extended staff meeting on issues dealing with appropriations markups and the forthcoming hearing in Miami on Children, Youth and Families. I invited Deborah Levy, a Presidential Scholar from North Miami Senior High School to "sit in," and she was quite impressed with my handling of the various issues.

At Appropriations' Democratic Caucus, I reported the status of our subcommittee's House-Senate mini-conferences to the full Appropriations Committee Chairman, telling him that our subcommittee had worked out all differences except for language on the Boston and Maine Railroad, and that this too would be worked out during the afternoon between the staffs. Whitten seemed very satisfied with my report, especially in the knowledge that we were under the 1987 budget figures on both outlays and budget authorities.

Tex Gunnels has agreed to change language that was added to

the bill originating in the Subcommittee on Treasury, Postal Service and General Government regarding the Customs Office Station at Tamiami Airport. The added language stated that Metro-Dade would have to pay part of the expense at the airport and I did not think this was fair as Dade County generates a lot of customs revenue for the Customs Office. Tex said he would remove that portion of the language before the end of the full committee markup and before the bill reached the House Floor.

He wanted reassurance from me that the $5 million that was now disputed between the Customs Office and the Department of Transportation was being resolved fairly. I told him that in our supplemental bill for 1987, we stated that the $5 million would not be transferred to the Coast Guard until such time as the General Accounting Office reported that the disputed $5 million belonged under the Coast Guard's authority. We spent a lot of time discussing such legislative turf.

I wish I could remember all of the conversations that I have on the House Floor because some of these conversations and many of the things that I do on the Floor or in the gym are done on a one to one basis when people consult me on issues and I do the same, and we agree on certain ways that we can help each other with various problems. For instance, I spoke to Bob Mrazek on the Floor about the best way to get his material in our bill this year. Companies like Hazeltine Corporation in his district, who made the Microwave Landing Systems for the FAA, did not get funding for the MLS in the bill last year but could perhaps get in this year. I told him that if he wanted this, he would have to be at the hearing procedure when this came up. Unfortunately, last year he never appeared at the right time to answer questions that would have supported his request. He said he would try to adjust his time to the process.

And Bill Grant, a member from the Florida Panhandle, spoke to me on the Floor about getting together with Sid Yates, Chairman of the Subcommittee on the Interior, and getting $800 thousand for wilderness land in North Florida. Yates has already marked up his bill but maybe he can insert language in the full committee markup. The new members do not yet know how to be on top of the process, so the bills slide by in our subcommittee and afterwards it is very difficult to go back and make changes. If a member wants or requests funds after all the "line items" of the bill are completed, then those funds have to be taken from other members' allotments, and this can make some members very unhappy.

Speaking to Don Edwards, I tried to get him to play tennis with us again, but he said his eyes are giving him trouble. I asked if he could read the names on the House voting board and he said that he could not and that he was really having a vision problem. It is sad because he was our leader on the tennis court. Because I am pressed for time, I can't get back to the office to meet with Mrs. Henry Harris's, so the staff will meet with her. Mrs. Harris's husband is a former councilman from North Miami Beach, but he is now in federal prison convicted on several counts of embezzlement. His wife is hoping to have Henry moved to a halfway house in Miami for him to serve the balance of his time. I remember Henry when he was a councilman. He was a bit flaky, but his wife is a decent, good individual. We will help all we can.

Mickey Leland (D-TX) also talked to me on the Floor about a very successful black businessman who supplies new buses and feels he was discriminated against in the bidding process with the Chicago Transit Authority. They are now scheduled to meet with me, my subcommittee staff, and UMTA representatives, on Thursday at 2:00 in the subcommittee room, to see if there was a problem in the bidding process and, if so, how we could handle it.

At 5:00, I attended the Independent Bakers Association fundraiser reception in honor of Senators Hollings from South Carolina and Lugar from Indiana. Most of the "Famous Bread" on the sample table was gone by the time I got there, but I did get to meet the Washington legislative liaison of the association; perhaps he will be able to help later with my fundraiser. Afterwards, I went to the Washington Chapter of the Women in Transportation Seminar in the Rayburn Building, where Jim Howard, Chairman of the Public Works and Transportation Committee, was being honored. I enjoyed seeing many of my friends from this organization, that two years ago presented me with an honorary plaque.

The National Legislative Education Foundation, in conjunction with the House Democratic Caucus, held its dinner this evening in the Rayburn Building. A very youthful looking Ted Koppel was the guest speaker, and he had his attractive eighteen year old daughter with him. Staying only for the reception, I left for a quiet dinner at LaColline's restaurant.

JUNE 18 THURSDAY

Full Appropriations Committee markups began this morning on the Interior, the District of Columbia, and the Legislative Subcommittees, with each taking about thirty minutes. Since then it has been busy on the Floor with the State Department authorization bill.

The meeting with Mickey Leland and his friend concerning a bid that he made on public transit buses for the City of Chicago started at 2:00. It seems Mickey's friend had been the only bidder, and because of certain bidding specifications by the Chicago Transportation Authority when there is only one bid, the Chicago Transit wanted to eliminate the one bid and reopen the bidding process. UMTA officials think that the entrepreneur runs a very respectable company and they will call the Chicago Transit Authority to see if the bidding specifications can be changed to allow the bid to go through.

Al Dellibovi, the Acting UMTA Administrator, should give this black entrepreneur a chance to build the 500 buses for Chicago and not disqualify the bid because of a regulation technicality which calls for the bids to be reopened. This move is worth taking in relation to the needs of the black community versus certain rigid regulations. Objections probably arose from the competition that wanted this bid but could not meet specifications.

Charlie Wilson (D-TX) played an amusing audio tape for me and Mickey Leland about a man who was trapped in a phone booth in Poughkeepsie, New York, by a mad dog. The fun part was his calling the Poughkeepsie Police Station for help. It was like an old radio comedy show, and I hope to get a copy of the tape. Sometimes we do things that are less than serious and have a little fun even in the Capitol.

The biggest news for me today was that the Congressional Budget Conference has concluded and apparently their report indicates more funds can be had for the transportation function. I may be able now to have additional funds for the Coast Guard.

Florida Whip Dan Mica called a meeting of the Florida members regarding President Reagan's upcoming trip to Melbourne, Florida, Democrat Bill Nelson's district. Nelson was invited to fly to Florida with the President and Dan called the meeting to discuss how Nelson should handle the matter so that a Republican

President would not capitalize on Nelson's popularity in his district. Nelson, however, jumped at the visit opportunity, and I believe he wants to be closely associated with the President. If the President wanted to come to my district I would have said, "Come ahead, but don't expect me to be a part of your entourage." I think Bill Nelson was conned into flying down to Florida with the President.

I had dinner with American Bus Association lobbyist Sue Perry, who wanted to thank me for the language our subcommittee put in the bill that said public mass transit properties could not compete with private enterprise. The language limited but did not totally prohibit public transportation from competing with private bus transit systems. Good people are on both sides of the issue as many of the elderly and disabled need public charter public bus service from time to time.

JUNE 19 FRIDAY

Allison Benjamin and I had breakfast together this morning. Allison is the daughter of Adam Benjamin, my predecessor as Chairman of the Transportation Subcommittee. In 1981, Joan and I traveled to Japan with Adam and Allison, and in September 1982 Adam died suddenly from an apparent heart attack one month after his 47th birthday. He was a very able and widely respected chairman and member from Indiana. For a few months after his death it was difficult filling his shoes. What compounded the situation for me was that not long after his death I had my cancer operation and recovery to deal with and, at the same time, I was coping with a new chairmanship for which I was not fully prepared.

9:00, I met with Mayor-Elect Tommy Hazouri from Jacksonville, who represents a large Lebanese community. It was a courtesy call to thank us for helping Jacksonville with the light rail people mover, and another transportation problem regarding a bridge to the port of Jacksonville. Admiral Yost, the Coast Guard Commandant, came in at 9:30 with his staff to complain about the shortfall in his AC&I (Acquisitions, Construction and Improvements) account. Our markup did not give the Coast Guard more than in the President's budget and the Conference Report was below the House-passed level, so he is pushing to increase AC&I by half a million. He is sometimes frustrated by the Coast Guard being within the Department of Transportation instead of the Department of Defense, where the pot is much larger.

I left at 4:45, headed back to Miami, with my Florida colleague Dante Fascell. Anna from the office met me at the airport with letters to sign, thanking those who were at the Black-Condo Leadership Brunch last Friday.

JUNE 20 SATURDAY

At the district office this morning, I met with Ruth Tinsman from my staff and Jill from the Select Committee on Children, Youth and Families, who had flown down a few days early to prepare for the hearing on Monday at Miami-Dade Community College. John Schelble and Nadine Berg from my Washington staff also flew down early for the hearing.

For dinner, Joan and I picked up Ohio Congressman Tom Sawyer and his wife, Joyce, at Turnberry, and drove to Williams Island. Our son Tom and his wife, Amy, joined us there. The dinner was rather expensive, but worth it for the credibility we derive among members that we invite down for our hearings. Tom is a new Democratic member on the select committee, and I was just happy to have him and Nancy Johnson (R-CT) who arrived too late for dinner, join me in Miami to make the hearing look more respectable, especially to the press and to the panelists.

The district office coordinated the logistics of bringing the members down and we provided complimentary rooms at Turnberry. I got the opportunity to know Tom better. Subsequent to this the only thing I knew about Tom was that he had a very fortunate name which everyone remembers. He was a State legislator and the Mayor of Akron before his election to Congress in 1986, and I believe he will move up quite smoothly in the House ranks.

JUNE 21 SUNDAY

Today, Joan and I went out to dinner with old friends - Van and Jane Myers. Still to come is their visit next month to Washington with their grandchildren, and the possibility of their grandchild becoming a page next year. In the district I am always dealing with the problem of being a "Congressman," and when I went to Williams Island last evening the security guard said I will let you in if you promise to keep voting against the Contras. This was something I did not expect to hear, as most people in Miami are pro-Contras.

JUNE 22 MONDAY

Before our hearing today on day care, Representatives Nancy Johnson, Tom Sawyer and I toured the day care center at the Miami- Dade Community College (MDCC) for two to five year old children of student, administration and faculty members. The center is very well managed, and the waiting list is so long that many of the women sign up for the service before their children are even born.

Following the visit, the hearing began at the north campus of MDCC with two panels of witnesses, all with reasons and case studies on the need for greater federal support for day care. Ray Goode, the previous Metro-Dade County Manager and now entrepreneur, testified as did several other business leaders in support of day care in the workplace. Florida State officials and child care experts from Tallahassee, Orlando, and Dade County provided testimony and statistics which indicated that only a paltry 90 businesses offer child care programs at the workplace, and that more than 25,000 Florida children whose parents cannot afford day care are on the State's child care assistance waiting list, with 5,000 more children added each year.

But the most compelling testimony by far was Detective Marva Preston's description of the events leading up to his discovery of the asphyxiated bodies of the two young children found in a washer/dryer as the result of their mother being unable to obtain day care while she worked in the school cafeteria. Both of the children had been on the waiting list for subsidized day care for over a year.

The witnesses were all excellent, including Phoebe Carpenter, Vice President of Community Coordinated Child Care for Central Florida, who said that lack of child care is the main obstacle keeping welfare mothers from getting jobs, and that "even the apes have figured out that if they go out to look for food, the children stay behind with one or two of the adults."

Following the hearing, TV and press people interviewed me

and Representatives Johnson and Sawyer. In the interviews I said that we spend a lot for military defense, but first we have to give children a life worth defending, and that I would be returning to Washington to lobby my colleagues to support a bill, of which I am a cosponsor, that would provide $600 million to the states for child care. Florida cannot grow economically without women in the job market, I said, and women cannot be in the job market without adequate child care.

The media stayed with us throughout the entire proceedings, including our tour of the day care center, and I think a story will be in the *Miami Herald* tomorrow and in the *Neighbors* section on Thursday. John Schelble did his job in getting good press coverage, and the staff was superb in putting it all together. In the afternoon after tennis I headed for the airport for my flight to Washington.

JUNE 23 TUESDAY

Great stories are in the papers today about our day care hearing in Miami. The *Miami Herald*, the *Fort Lauderdale News*, and the *Hollywood Sun-Sentinel* all repeated parts of the testimonies and relevant statistics in building our case for more federal funds and encouraging more employers to provide on-site day care. I told George Miller, chairman of the select committee, about the success of our hearing, and we are now thinking of writing legislation to mandate child care the same way we now mandate accessibility for the handicapped.

Miami Beach politicians Silvester Lukis, Bill Schokett, Bob Parkins and Dick Foesman came in at 10:00 to discuss their need for Florida Department of Transportation funds to conduct a feasibility study for a light rail system on Miami Beach. They also mentioned that perhaps later the light rail system could be linked to the downtown Metromover with the aid of federal funds. Then John Fitzgerald and Dean Wilkson, Greenpeace environmentalists, were in about the turtle problem with shrimp netting off the Louisiana coast. They wanted me to oppose the amendment being offered tomorrow by Louisiana Rep. Bob Livingston in the full Appropriations Committee eliminating the requirement that shrimpers have nets which permit the turtles to escape. Afterwards, the Florida Apartment Housing Association came in about their tax and fair housing legislation problems.

1:30, Tad Foote, President of the University of Miami, and my good friends and lobbyists, Marilyn Thompson and Art Roberts, came in. The University of Miami requested $1.3 million in Neal Smith's Appropriations Subcommittee on State, Justice and Commerce for a computer. The grant request is yet to be authorized by Dante Fascell's Foreign Affairs Committee. I have been working on this with Dante and with Neal since my meeting with Art Roberts and Tad Foote in January. If there is any additional, but unlikely, budgetary room in Neal's 1988 subcommittee appropriations bill maybe we can attach an amendment adding these funds when his bill comes to the full Appropriations Committee markup.

Later, I discussed the matter with Dante Fascell and he agreed to go with me to see Neal Smith and Neal's subcommittee staff person. After little debate, we worked out a deal whereby Neal would put money for the University of Miami's computer in the 1987 supplemental rather than try to find room or make cuts in the 1988 appropriations bill. This would have been impossible anyway since the only cuts we could possibly have made would have been from salaries and expenses.

At 2:30, Jay Morris, the new Administrator for the State Department's Agency for International Development (AID) came in. The "courtesy" visit from Morris was for assurance that I would help AID on population and other issues, including agriculture. He knows that I am not his opposition and that I will try to help him on these concerns. Harvey Cohen, Executive Vice President and General Manager of Channel 39 in Miami stopped by, but I really did not get a chance to talk with him as I was going back and forth to vote. I hope he comes back later.

I am getting calls from constituents who fish in the Bahamas complaining that they are getting abusive treatment from both Customs and the Coast Guard. One of the calls came from Paul Valentino, a neighbor of mine in Biscayne Park, who said he had an experience with Customs, and then another with the Coast Guard and that they treated him like a drug runner and not as a commercial fisherman. I think he is really just a normal short-tempered American.

Between votes, I took my Florida colleague Dan Mica to meet with the staff of the Appropriations Subcommittee on HUD and

Independent Agencies. The Veterans Administration has stopped funding nursing homes for veterans in Dan's Palm Beach County district, and we were hoping to work with the subcommittee to get funding restored. Dan spoke to Ed Boland of Massachusetts, Chairman of the VA Appropriations Subcommittee and Ed said to Dan, "Get away from me, don't talk to me. When you were on the Steering and Policy Committee you wouldn't support Joe Kennedy for a Ways and Means Committee assignment when I asked you, and now I don't want to have any conversation with you." Misunderstandings and antagonistic behavior can be as much a part of what goes on here as the friendships, the cooperative spirit, and the camaraderie.

Tom Boggs of the Patton, Boggs and Blow law firm, hosted a fundraiser reception this evening upstairs in my townhouse for Representative Bill Lowry of California. As enjoyable as it was, I left to attend Claude Pepper's stone crab feast held at the National Democratic Club. Claude's event was modeled after our fundraiser at the Folger, but it was not as good, as the stone crabs were not cracked ahead of time. He had a good crowd, though.

JUNE 24 WEDNESDAY

The full Appropriations Committee markup this morning was on the Commerce, State, and Justice Subcommittee Appropriations bill. There was hardly any conflict. On the Floor the Energy and Water Bill passed, first defeating the 1.7% across-the-board cut amendment, which rather surprised me.

I spoke to Public Works Subcommittee Chairman, Norman Mineta, about my thoughts on legislation to mandate child care, and he spoke to Jim Howard, Public Works and Transportation Chairman. Jim now wants to put legislation in the Public Works bill mandating that all future federally funded public works facilities have child care accommodations. Jim was once a high school principal and knows the child care need.

On the Floor I arranged a meeting with Republican Tom Lewis of central Florida and Democrat Tom Bevill of Alabama, Chair of the Subcommittee on Energy and Water, to help restore the Kissimmee River to its original riverbed. The Kissimmee River is now just an environmentally disastrous straight canal. Still on the Floor I spoke to Donald (Buz) Lukens from Cincinnati. I did not know Buz when he was first in Congress. He lost a re-election fifteen years ago and was re-elected last year; I believe he was in the Ohio Legislature on and off during that time. When Tom Sawyer was in Miami he told me that an Ohio colleague had a similar operation to mine. The colleague was Buz, and we commiserated on our post-operative problems. His difficulty is a lack of saliva more than control of his tongue. I have no problem with saliva but my tongue and the nerves in my lips on the right side are my handicaps. Buz also had chemotherapy, a treatment which I fortunately did not need. He seems okay but said he gets very tired. I sent him a six-pack of Ensure Plus which helped me when I needed strength.

Girl Scout Troop #433 from North Miami Beach in my district paid me a visit. The usual questions were asked, and then we had the usual photo session. Afterwards I took them to the Rayburn Cafeteria and let them buy whatever they wanted. This is the middle of the afternoon and they had come up to Washington by Amtrak and all of them looked tired.

I have a problem to work out with John Dingell about language in our transportation bill mandating 3-point seatbelts. The 3-point seatbelt is not advantageous to car manufacturers, but it is especially beneficial to rear seat children who need 3-point seatbelts.

Dingell complained to me on the House Floor, and I will try to work out something with him and his staff. I am right in this effort, but I do not want to make Dingell too unhappy. American auto manufacturers are ready to make this change but the conflict between John and me, and I am really fond of him, is that he is the "Congressman from General Motors," and I should have spoken to him before initiating this language. He had a legitimate complaint particularly about finding out second hand, and I guess I learned my lesson; but I could not back down now and told him so.

Dingell knows that the public would be unhappy with an attempt to strike my language from the bill considering the safety factor for children, and even though I suggested that he go to the Rules Committee in opposition to authorizing in appropriations, such a move would not be good for his image. John did help enormously with our bill last year when we tried to keep the highway trust fund from going off budget, and I owe him. In the future I will try to be more careful.

Don Edwards spoke to me about the problems he is having with the Bay Area linkage to the San Jose Guadalupe Corridor light rail. I will do everything I can for Don Edwards. He told me how much he and Edie are enjoying the croquet set I gave them for their summer cottage on the Chesapeake Bay. I am also working to accommodate Al Swift on the Belmont Washington Airport expansion. Many members wait until the last minute with their requests, when it would be a lot easier if they came in with witnesses to state their case in our hearings.

At the "Italian Extravaganza" reception this evening, hosted by California Congressman Vic Fazio at the Democratic Club, most of the California delegation was there, which made for a very good turnout. I also attended the Latin Builders Association reception at Dominiques, primarily because of my friendship with Armando Codina. The Latin builders are very ultra conservative Republicans, but I do have a good rapport with Armando. We like each other and I think he realizes that even though we disagree on Nicaragua, I have not given the Hispanic community problems on other issues. My mind won't change on Nicaragua, but I help their group especially on downtown development. I spent about thirty minutes talking with them and they appreciated my being there. When Senator Claude Pepper arrived he received their attention and this gave me a chance to leave.

I was unable to make Maryland Congressman Tom McMillen's "Summer Seafood Feast" at the historic Lewis House, nor was I able to attend the Michigan Sesquicentennial Celebration at the Sheraton Carlton. It is impossible to make all the receptions; not that I always want to go, it is just that I feel it is important to show support for my colleagues by attending their events.

JUNE 25 THURSDAY

In the full Appropriations Committee markup this morning on the VA/HUD and Independent Agencies Subcommittee, there was considerable discussion about overage in outlays which caused some difficulty for Ed Boland, chairman of the aforementioned subcommittee, but the bill did pass without further changes. Also this morning the House Democratic Caucus debated the Persian Gulf problem, but I never got to the caucus because of the full Appropriations Committee markup.

At noon, I escorted Jorge, winner of the Dade County High Schools Arts Competition, to the Cannon Caucus Room to have photos taken with movie actors Judd Nelson and Ally Sheedy, NBC's Willard Scott of the "Today" program, and Roger Smith of General Motors. The winners from all around the country were very excited, and Sherry Jones from our Miami office, who flew to Washington with Jorge, was also enjoying the event. Sherry was once the homecoming queen at Florida Memorial College.

Back at the office North Miami Council members Shelly Gassner and Bill Carr were in about the problem of toxic waste at the Munisport. They still want this property off the toxic waste list and are asking me to do this legislatively. It cannot be done by legislation and all North Miami can do is write letters to the EPA asking for an expeditious study of the site. The city of North Miami acquired the land in anticipation of the Interama locating there. Interama, a proposed theme park, fell through and North Miami leased the land for the dumping of waste, some toxic, and now the city cannot sell it until the toxic waste is cleaned up.

At 2:30, Dick Judy came in with the Airport Executives Council to talk about increasing in my bill the FAA's R&D funds to conduct a study on how to maximize airport traffic capacity.

Mike Espy, the new black member from Mississippi, hosted his reception this evening, and he had some of the best catfish I had ever eaten. The fish had been brought in for the reception by fish farmers who were all white. Afterwards, I went with Sue Stevens to the Turkish Embassy on 23rd Street Northwest for a seated dinner for about a dozen members. It was a beautiful affair, but North Carolina Congressman Charlie Rose's wife acted a little crazy. After the friendship toast by Turkey Ambassador Elekdag, Mrs. Rose started harassing him about the Turkish invasion of Cyprus and how the poor Greek Cypriots were brutalized by the vicious Turkish army. The Ambassador handled it well, and tension was released when I jokingly remarked that if white Mississippi farmers can honor a black Mississippi congressman then Cypriots, Turks and Greeks could get along. It put back a little life into the evening. It is always a pleasure to go to this Embassy, and I hope to visit Turkey sometime before the end of the year.

Bill Gray asked me on the House Floor yesterday if I wanted to go with him on a codel to London and Paris over the July 4th weekend. Bill said we could go to the Wimbledon tournament and also have meetings with the embassy officials in the economic sectors on the recent economic summit in Venice. The trip sounds great, and I wish I could go, but this is a crucial time for appropriations subcommittee chairmen who must be prepared for the markups and Floor action, and available for any problems that may arise.

JUNE 26 FRIDAY

We went into the full appropriations conference on the supplemental at 10:00, and my chapter came up about noon. I presented the report without my counterpart, Senator Lautenberg, being present. His staff aide, Pat McCassen, was there, and I just arranged for her to vouch for the Senator's approval as an indication to the full conference that we had resolved all our amendments in disagreement. The conference went very smoothly despite a problem involving the House Defense Subcommittee, which had receded in its mini-conference all the arms control issues to the Senate in order to prevent the supplemental bill from being vetoed.

Nine hundred thousand dollars was inserted into the State, Justice and Commerce chapter of the supplemental for the database funding at the University of Miami. It is a done deal and our office will put together a news release on it. I know that Tad Foote, President of the University of Miami is very pleased. I signed the Conference Report, although reluctantly, because I did not want to oppose Jamie Whitten who wanted to get the supplemental completed.

2:30, I took an Eastern flight back to Miami for the Florida Democratic Fundraiser being held this evening at the Fontainebleau Hotel. Speaker Jim Wright and the Florida Congressional Democrats are the honored guests. On this same flight were Jim Wright, Dan Mica, Bill Nelson, and Beryl Anthony of Arkansas (head of the D Triple C which raises campaign funds for House Democrats). Larry Smith and Claude Pepper are already in Miami. We landed at 4:30.

Joan and I arrived at the fundraiser too late for the cocktail party, but I did the welcome and the introductions. The fundraiser was for the three counties: Dade, Broward and Palm Beach. Richard Pettigrew, Chairman of the Dade County Democratic Party introduced me, and I introduced Mayor Ingram of Opa Locka who gave the invocation. Following the invocation Mr.

Rahming, a young black man, sang the National Anthem. I then led the group into the Pledge of Allegiance. Annie Ackerman was supposed to do this, and although she was there she was not well, so I did it for her. I then thanked and recognized my colleagues who helped cosponsor the program.

Introducing Bill Nelson, I said he was "a great candidate for Florida Governor." Speeches were also given by Larry Smith, Dan Mica, Dante Fascell and Claude Pepper; most were a little too long, especially Smith. Jim Wright gave a great speech and held his audience very well. The general opinion was that anyone who can speak that well should be our next Democratic candidate for president, and later I said these same words to Jim. He had asked me on the plane coming down what I thought was the best subject to talk on, and I said arms control. He did end his speech with a hopeful approach to arms control and peace for the future, and gave a benediction in Spanish which he translated to English. Jim speaks fluent Spanish which none of our presidents could do.

One thing strange was that Dick Gephardt, a bonafide Democratic presidential candidate, was there, but he was not recognized until after Jim Wright had spoken and everyone was on the way out. Gephardt made his speech, a nothing speech really, just a few silly stories. He would have been better off not speaking, as everyone was leaving.

It was a good Democratic turnout, with close to 900 people, but the event was sort of disorganized, and there was no television coverage even on Jim Wright's speech. Joan and I got home about 11:00.

JUNE 27 SATURDAY

This morning Dr. Groff, my E.N.T. specialist, examined me and everything is okay. I also picked up from him a campaign check from the Florida Medical PAC. Dante Fascell was also there to be examined, and I showed him today's story in the *Miami News* about how he, Senator Lawton Chiles and I had worked together in the supplemental conference to obtain a grant from the State Department for the University of Miami. There was also a story about last night's Democratic fundraiser.

Other than exerting myself at tennis this afternoon, the day was mostly relaxing. Joan and I went to the North Miami Beach

AMC Movie Theatre to see "Full Metal Jacket," a new Vietnam film. I knew we would not be able to get in without waiting in line, so I had Jeff call ahead to the theater manager. She was waiting to accommodate us when we arrived, and I gave her a couple of congressional-seal coffee cups. I don't often use my position in this manner, but when I do I always want to show my appreciation.

JUNE 28 SUNDAY

Jeff and I picked up Saul Simon this morning and went to the B'nai B'Rith Council at the Hallandale Jewish Center. When Hallandale was in my district, I was a frequent visitor to the Hallandale Jewish Center, but most of the people at the Center today were from the North Dade B'nai B'Rith and not South Broward.

Saul Simon was with us to make a request for volunteers for the Daily Bread Food Bank, especially among the condo Jewish community. The food bank needs volunteers to repackage food to redistribute to various nonprofit organizations, many of which are Jewish such as the Jewish Home for the Aged, the Hebrew schools, etc. Saul is working with me and the district office in putting together a collaborative black-Jewish group to serve once a week or even once a month as volunteers in the food bank, and our office will provide transportation for the groups or organizations assisting in this program. This was our first real step, and I think we made some progress in the 45 minutes that we were there. As a service organization, the B'nai B'Rith will be most helpful to us in this project.

My Eastern 5:30 p.m. flight to Washington was on time.

JUNE 29 MONDAY

Tom, Greg and Lucy met with me first thing this morning to review the bill report language that we will take to the full appropriations committee markup on Wednesday. I then went to the front office of appropriations to see if they had any new numbers for me on either outlays or budget authority. They did not. We were able, however, to get $200 million from the Congressional Budget Office credited to outlays from the sale of preference shares owned by the government, which is really indebtedness to the Federal government but in the form of preferred stock of certain railroads. Federal Railway Authority is going to sell about $700 million worth of the preference shares but our function will only be credited with about $200 million in outlays, mainly because the cash value of preference shares is nowhere near par since it is subsidized at a two-percent rate.

There are still minor problems regarding the language on charter bus operations by Long Beach, California's public operated buses that relate to the proposed new regulation that UMTA is to make later this year. Public Works and Transportation Committee Chairman, Jim Howard, also opposes the use of federally subsidized public transportation that competes with private sector charter services, and Jim and I are the two main members in surface transportation responsible for both appropriations and authorization. I will probably have to oppose Ed Roybal of California, who will make the amendment in the full committee tomorrow on behalf of Glenn Anderson of Long Beach.

We were able to satisfy Bob Carr and Larry Coughlin as to the report language in the bill that criticizes the Martin Marietta SEI (Systems Engineering Instrument) contract. In January 1984, the FAA and Martin Marietta entered into a ten-year, $684 million contract for systems engineering giving Martin Marietta full oversight authority for the $9 billion NAS (National Air Space) program. The contract is divided into three phases—a 5-year phase ending in January 1989, followed by two optional phases of 3 and 2 years. The report language contains criticism that Martin Marietta received over 80 percent of the available "performance award fee bonuses" despite delays, cost overruns, and acquisition problems related to the NAS plan's major systems. Questions were also raised about the independence of Martin Marietta's judgment and FAA's award fee process.

To satisfy Carr and Coughlin, who have been helped with campaign funds by Martin Marietta, we removed critical offensive language. However, Martin Marietta will still get the message that when the first option phase of the contract comes up for renewal in fiscal year 1989, our subcommittee will want a real definitive indication of accountability from them. The fault really is with the FAA which relinquished its authority to a contractual agent.

JUNE 30 TUESDAY

Our office has a new intern, the friend of appropriations staffer Mike Stevens's brother from Great Britain. Photos were taken on the Capitol Steps with him and the other interns in our office. It is a funny thing that no matter how many photos are taken with interns, they are never satisfied with less than two or three. These young people seem to be very vain about how they are photographed - the clothing, hair, pose, etc., all have to be just right. They are, however, a lot of fun and help to our office.

Chapter 7

JULY 1, 1987 - WEDNESDAY

In full appropriations committee this morning, I think I did fairly well in our transportation appropriations markup. We did not have to defeat many difficult amendments because the members cooperated. The bill was voted out with just one change, an amendment by Roybal of California on charter bus operations, but I offered a compromise substitute amendment which he accepted. Dick Durbin of Illinois offered an amendment expanding the smoking ban on airplanes, which lost. I was caught in the middle as I had personally supported Durbin's amendment in the subcommittee, but I could not support it in the full committee. In our subcommittee markup the members voted down Durbin's amendment, and I must support the subcommittee's position in full committee.

Following the markup, a *Miami Herald* reporter spoke to me about the passage of my transportation bill in the full committee, being more interested in the $20 million for Dade's Metromover than he was for the $10 billion in the bill for all other needs. In the Press Gallery I did a radio tape with Hal Cessna from WIOD, Miami, with Hal asking questions about the Persian Gulf, and also about the transportation bill we passed today. Later another *Miami Herald* reporter came to the office with questions for a followup story he was doing on our Miami hearing on day care funding by the federal government.

And, on the front page of today's *Washington Post*, my name was mentioned in a story on federal employees and the redistribution of leave time. The story told of the provision I had inserted into the continuing resolution for fiscal 1987 authorizing the leave sharing donations for Shannon and Joe Chiles and how this pilot legislation has now enabled the mother to continue in her job while going through a family crisis.

On the Floor, we debated Neal Smith's appropriations bill on Commerce, State and Justice. A two percent across-the-board cut amendment was passed, but I opposed it. I will try to stay and vote for final passage, but it may not be possible as I have an 8:00 flight to Miami this evening. Returning to the office, I picked up Barbara from my staff and we went to Congressman Bob Davis's office. Barbara's parents live in Davis's Michigan district, and the three of us had photos taken for her parents and for their hometown newspaper. Bob had constituents in his office from the 4H Club. Around his office walls were lots of photos of farm children. I have never had farm children to visit my office. Each district is so different.

My Eastern flight scheduled for 8:00 p.m. did not take off until 10:00. I spoke to Sister Jeanne O'Laughlin, President of Barry University, in Eastern's VIP Club and she told me about her experiences traveling on Eastern Airlines. She thinks it is now a battle between Charlie Bryant of the machinists union, and Eastern's President Frank Lorenzo, and that both want control of Eastern. The machinists are making it as tough as possible on travelers, she said, to get Lorenzo to negotiate with them, and Lorenzo was going to fix it so that one day when the machinists go to work they will find that Eastern no longer exists, and in its place will be Continental Airlines, which is nonunion. We finally arrived in Miami at 1:00, and Jeff was at the airport to meet me.

JULY 2 THURSDAY

Today I spent a few hours in the district office and then with Sharyn in the campaign office discussing a Miami fundraiser for late February of next year, if we can get a commitment from Speaker Jim Wright to come down. This year we have taken in over $100,000 and spent about $57,000. Most of the expenditures went toward the costs of the fundraiser in Washington, Sharyn's salary, and other miscellaneous expenses such as the $1,500 table the other night for the Jim Wright dinner by the Democratic parties of Dade, Broward and Palm Beach Counties.

JULY 3 FRIDAY

For the Fourth of July holiday, I will skip all the big parades and have a quiet weekend. Monday, John Smith of the North Dade Chamber of Commerce and I are to meet with the Dade County Public Housing Authority on the problems at Carol City Villas. It seems the Carol City Villas Community Center is not going to reopen, and the contribution I planned to make for the basketball court and the time we spent in this effort really do not mean anything now. I saw Al Moore of Little HUD at the Washington National Airport before I left for Miami, and he told me Carol City Villas should be sold because the condition of the housing there is beyond saving.

JULY 4 SATURDAY

Today's *Miami Herald* had an editorial on transportation and my role in securing funds for the Metromover in downtown Miami. The editorial was promoted by John Schelble in our office because the *Herald* did not run a news item on our subcommittee bill containing funds for Dade Metrorail.

JULY 5 SUNDAY

Jeff was with me this morning to pick up John Smith, who runs the Cloverleaf Bowling Lanes, which also serves as a political hangout, and the three of us went on to the Carol City Villas for our meeting with the Dade County Public Housing Authority and for another look at the community center. The Citicorp Corporation awarded $25,000 for summer job opportunities in the Carol City area near and around the center. I made a short speech in praise of the award, which was to provide jobs for young people between the ages of fourteen and seventeen to plant gardens, to clean up, and to beautify the area. Commissioner Clara Oesterle was there, and she keeps referring to me as the "best Congressman from Dade County" and the best Congressman that Dade County ever had, which sort of embarrasses me as Dante Fascell is a bigger name, especially in Washington. Clara says she sees what I have done, and refers to all the money I have brought into Dade County, but that is because I am on the transportation appropriations subcommittee and can direct funds to certain community projects.

JULY 6 MONDAY

At the district office I called Lucy at the Washington office and it was funny, as I had been trying to get in touch with Bill Taylor, the Washington liaison for the Florida State Department of Transportation. Telling Lucy that I wanted her to schedule Bill Taylor to meet with me, she said that "as we speak Bill is standing in front of me." Lucy put Bill on the phone, and I told him about Stan Whitman's problem involving the Bal Harbour Shops exits on Collins Avenue, which Stan is trying to keep. Bill agreed to call Whitman, and perhaps all will be solved before I get back to Washington.

JULY 7 TUESDAY

Back in Washington, I went at noon to the House Floor to file our bill's report to go before the Rules Committee. Then, in a meeting with Tom and Greg, I learned that we received a reallocation in budget authority and outlays from the full appropriations committee. We now have about $250 million more than we had prior to the full committee markup, and more than we now need because we do not want to go to the Floor and have room between what we have in our bill and the budgetary ceiling as members will try to add amendments for other projects. We also cannot tell those members whose projects we turned down because of the lack of funds in our bill that we now have available. Moreover, we don't want to increase the bill above last year's level because members, who usually want to reduce the appropriations bills, will try on the Floor to cut back to last year's level. Sometimes having too much money is as much a problem as not having enough, as it can open floodgates which are difficult to close.

At tennis with my House buddies and Judge Mikva, they talked about Robert Bork's appointment to the Supreme Court. Judge Mikva is a good friend of Bork's and does not seem concerned about him being too conservative. When they were in college together, Bork was a college liberal.

I am still getting the usual telephone calls from Jack Langer about his Amtrak problem. Also, Rep. Wayne Owens from Salt Lake City has come to me with a last minute effort for funds for a light rail project in his district. I like Wayne and will try to help him, but when the bill is ready to go to the Floor it is rather late to do anything. Some members do not go through the appropriations process but come in the last minute hoping to get funded. I cannot do it that way.

JULY 8 WEDNESDAY

First, was a meeting this morning with the subcommittee staff to figure out what to do with the excess funds. The money may disappear fast as the Congressional Budget Office may not allow funds from the preference shares sale to be counted for as much as we thought in the offset of outlays. Instead of a $265 million windfall, we may end up with only $40 or $50 million.

At 10:30, the Independent News Network came in to interview me about the federal leave sharing demonstration project that I initiated for the late Shannon Chiles and her husband, Joe.

JULY 9 THURSDAY

Today we marked up in the full appropriations committee the Treasury and Post Office Subcommittee appropriation bill, and the Military Construction Subcommittee appropriation bill. At 2:00, I went before the Rules Committee and got a "Rules Committee protection" on all unauthorized language in our bill. We received everything we wanted from the Rules Committee and Dick

Durbin, separately, received a rule protecting his right to offer on the Floor an amendment expanding the smoking ban on airplanes.

JULY 10 FRIDAY

The only appointment I had scheduled today was with Dr. C. Everett Koop, the U.S. Surgeon General, at his office in the Health and Human Resources Building. I primarily wanted a photo with him to use in our upcoming newsletter on AIDS, but we had a very interesting conversation, and the one thing he told me that I carried away with me was that as of now there is no solution for AIDS.

JULY 11 - 12 SATURDAY AND SUNDAY

Remaining in Washington over the weekend, I prepared for the Floor action Monday afternoon on our Transportation Appropriations Bill. I did play tennis with the Capitol Hill Tennis Club group, and visited my cousins Marx and Shirley Leva at their home in Bethesda. I took with me our cousin, Daniel Barton, who is serving as a House page.

JULY 13 MONDAY

Early this morning I met with Republican Rod Chandler from the State of Washington, who was leading the Republican effort to cut our bill's appropriations. Reportedly, this self-appointed group called itself the "budget task force." Out of customary courtesy, Chandler told me how their Floor plan was to work and what amendments would be offered. Later on the Floor it happened just as he said. [These are the days when we didn't blindside one another.]

11:30, we had an appropriations full committee meeting. Dave Obey offered an amendment to eliminate the present 302B allocation which limits subcommittee appropriations. The amendment passed, and that disturbed me because this meant that now I would have to go to the Floor in the afternoon without a 302B definite limitation; and, if members offered amendments to increase any part of our bill, I would be unable to make a point of order that adding the amendment would exceed the 302B limitation.

On the House Floor, debate on the rule for our Bill began at about 12:30, and was passed. Then began the general debate on the Transportation Bill. Two of the big funding agencies were the Coast Guard and the Federal Aviation Administration. The Coast Guard's overall allocation was $2.7 billion, with roughly $450 million earmarked for drug interdiction. The Federal Aviation Administration was allocated $6.3 billion, including $1.1 billion to increase the air traffic controllers to 15,900, an increase of 675 over the present number.

My concern that being without the 302B definitive limitation left me vulnerable was for naught, because no amendments were offered that exceeded the original 302B allocations except one Coast Guard amendment, which was defeated. We also defeated the amendment to cut funds for phasing out the flight service stations. Ohio's Jim Traficant was beaten badly on this, and I do not think he will bother us on this next year. The most clever thing I did was to ask for and get unanimous consent for the Washington Metro reduction amendment and the reduction amendment on public mass transit subsidy to be considered "in block." Either amendment may have prevailed independently, but with the two together these opposing amendments were defeated and the items were not cut. We also defeated the across-the-board cut exempting the FAA and another such amendment exempting the Coast Guard. I said that "all of God's children got shoes, and if these cuts were bad medicine for one it should be bad medicine for all the Department of Transportation agencies." It seemed to work as we also defeated the separate amendment to cut Amtrak subsidy.

Final passage on the transportation bill was at 10:30 p.m. Rod Chandler and his so-called "budget-cutting brigade," including members Phil Crane of Illinois and Alex McMillan of North Carolina offered amendments to cut many of the bill's proposed funding projects. In some instances, projects in their own districts would be severely cut. We defeated every amendment offered except the last amendment. In our meeting, Chandler had said that if all their amendments failed on the Floor, they would then offer an amendment cutting spending across the board. They first offered an across-the-board cut amendment of 3.3 percent, which we defeated. But then the group came back with a 2 percent cut across-the-board amendment, and it passed. Once you defeat one such amendment and it comes back reduced, then the members have a chance to vote a "fiscal responsibility" cut at a lower level.

Dick Durbin surprisingly won his expanded anti-smoking amendment, for which two hours of debate were set aside by the Rules Committee. I was in a tough position on this as I supported Durbin philosophically and hoped he would win; and yet because his amendment was defeated by two to one in the subcommittee and then two to one in the full committee, I had to oppose him. This was so ironic really, because I may be one of the House's staunchest opponents of smoking. This year alone I cosponsored bills to ban both smoking on all domestic flights, and the advertising and promotion of tobacco, in addition to a bill requiring that smoking in federal buildings be limited to designated areas. And, I will try to protect the House version of the anti-smoking amendment when it goes to conference.

It was a long session but we were victorious, and it was exciting with members constantly coming to me for advice on how to vote. This afternoon was the first time Kentucky's Bill Natcher, Chairman of the Appropriations Subcommittee on Labor, Health and Human Services and Education, came to me for advice. He was having a tough time deciding whether to vote for final passage because of Durbin's anti-smoking amendment. I told him to vote his district, which produces tobacco, and that I would not mind a bit if he voted against final passage, which he did. Bill is one of the real powers in the House and it was interesting that he would come to me before voting against final passage.

I was unable to transfer to Dave Obey's subcommittee the $100 million in outlays that he wanted as I was not sure about what would be needed at the Senate conference, and the $100 million would not have solved Dave's problem anyway. Following the session I gave an interview to the *Miami News*, and had a phone interview with the *Miami Herald*. A very busy day on the Floor, and I missed both lunch and dinner.

JULY 14 TUESDAY

In the cafeteria this morning, Jamie Whitten complimented me on the way I handled the bill yesterday. He did caution me, though, saying that I would need to find a different way to handle the Rules Committee because it gives me unsolicited waivers which can generate future problems. I told the chairman we would need to meet with members of the Rules Committee beforehand, to discourage any unwanted self-execution amendments which we do not want.

Before our bill's final passage yesterday, Marty Russo of Illinois rose quite suddenly and surprisingly spoke for an amendment to add $1.5 million to the National Transportation Safety Board. He sounded very passionate, but must have had too much to drink because fifteen minutes later he voted to cut $9 million from the Federal Aviation Administration. I told him today that his actions on the Floor did not make sense, and he said, "You know that I'm not consistent, but if you ever need me you can always count on me."

Bill Gray announced to me on the House Floor today that he was planning to run for chairman of the Democratic Caucus. Even though I told Gray I would help him, I want first to see who else is running.

I received a new copy on the report language in the Treasury, Postal Service and General Government Subcommittee's appropriation bill on the customs employees at Tamiami Airport, and the language is now resolved to the satisfaction of Dick Judy and Eli Feinberg. What pleased me was that by working with committee staffers Bill Smith and Tex Gunnels on this problem, it had not been necessary to involve other members.

Florida State Senator Jack Gordon called to request the $500 thousand grant to Florida International University (FIU) for Airway Science. We have wall-to-wall airway science programs in South Florida - Barry University, Florida Memorial, Miami-Dade Community College and now FIU, which is in Larry Smith's West Dade district, and Jack should have gone to Larry. I called Larry and told him that we would work with him on the FIU project, but he was upset that this University in his West Dade district continues to ignore him in their efforts to gain federal grants and programs. I like to tease Larry about the three powerful members of the South Florida delegation whom everyone talks about, and keeps leaving him out.

In the evening at a reception in the Capitol hosted by Senators Dole and DeConcini, neither senator was there, but I did see both Florida Senators Chiles and Graham. The reception was in honor of the former Cuban political prisoner, Armando Valladares, who authored the book, *Free the Eagle*. The reason I attended was to gather material to present to Armando Codina when I meet with him in the district Friday afternoon. Through Armando I hope to establish a better relationship with the Cuban American community.

Following the reception, I went to Bob Mrazek's fundraiser. Bob is a member on our transportation subcommittee, and I always thought of him as a little strange and somewhat like a loose cannon. His was the first fundraiser that I attended where the event was held in the member's own home. He has a beautiful home on Capitol Hill and seeing him in this setting made me think a little differently about him. I always liked him, but never knew that this young man was also in the antique business on Long Island and into real estate; he is apparently wealthy and has done a marvelous job of restoring this house, which shows much thought and creativity and a side of Bob Mrazek I did not know existed. The only other member there was Bob Carr.

JULY 15 WEDNESDAY

Oregon member Les AuCoin held his fundraiser breakfast this morning. The event was held at the LaColline restaurant on North Capitol Street, with a really good turnout and a great menu consisting of smoked Oregon salmon, omelets and delicious hazelnut pancakes. The "Guest of Honor" was Oregon Governor Neil Goldschmidt, who was Secretary of Transportation when I first came on the Transportation Subcommittee, and it was good to see him.

At the office, we had our weekly staff meeting and talked about problems with the proposed tax legislation on luxury items. I left to attend a meeting in the front office of appropriations with Chairman Whitten and all the appropriations subcommittee chairmen to see if we could reallocate outlays to Dave Obey, who is having a very difficult time meeting the commitments in his Foreign Operations Subcommittee. Jamie asked me to find $100 million in transportation outlays that we did not presently need, and I did. Other subcommittees came up with $300 million, which provided Obey with an additional $400 million in outlays to partially solve his problem but he was still short for many other programs such as UNICEF.

Bob Carr, who heads the Congressional Arts Caucus invited

me to his luncheon for a young writer by the pen name of Adam Smith. Smith does financial writing and complained that writers have a tax problem in that they cannot write off their research expenses until the book is published.

Dr. Carrie Walters has written to me about the experimentation on animals, following up a conversation we had during her visit to Washington a few months ago. Dr. Walters is now an Assistant Professor of Surgery at the University of Vermont, but when my daughter Kathy was diagnosed with brain cancer, Dr. Walters was one of her neurosurgeons at the National Institutes of Health in Washington, D.C. During her tenure at NIH, Dr. Walters experimented on chimpanzees, and now she is pushing the movement to reduce the experimentation on animals because, as she said, much of the experiments being done on animals can now be done on tissues or cadavers. I am arranging for her to come to Washington in August to meet with Mike Stevens and other staff on Appropriations Health and Human Services Subcommittee.

Taking a late afternoon Eastern Airlines flight, I arrived in Miami about 9:00. I have a very busy schedule in the district tomorrow and did not want to get into Miami at a late hour, but the plane was still two hours late.

JULY 16 THURSDAY

Lydia Gale, an activist in the Disabled Veterans and Veterans of Foreign Wars organizations, was at the office this morning, and had with her a young deaf man who lives in my district. Lydia has been taking lessons in sign language in order to communicate with him, and she does quite well. The young man, who is a post office employee, will start college in September at Gallaudet University in Washington, D.C., and will visit me when he is settled at school.

Afterwards, the office staff and I discussed problems and issues that need my attention in the district. I left the office for my 3:00 appointment with Armando Codina in his new bank building downtown on Flagler Street. Armando is a young, very wealthy Cuban American, and this meeting is at least a beginning to building better relations between me and the Cuban community. I already do a lot for the downtown Cuban community with transportation, but the present Cuban test is support for the

Contras in Nicaragua, and my opposition to the Contras has broken the ties I had to the Cuban community. I began the discussion by telling Armando of my willingness to meet with him and members of the Cuban community to discuss and work out our differences, and told him that with the aid of Mickey Leland of Texas I would push for the release of Cuban political prisoners by meeting with Fidel Castro in Cuba.

But the main thing Armando wanted to know about was the status of the extensions of the two new legs of the downtown Metromover. Presently, the decision is up to Metro-Dade Transit as to how they want to handle the full funding contract and the stipulation for the necessary dedicated local revenue. "If Metro-Dade Transit wants to delay full funding," I said, "then the need for dedicated local revenue could be eliminated." With the information that the environmental impact statement would be filed in the Federal Register in about a week and then hearings held in Miami in thirty days for any opposition witnesses, Armando seemed satisfied, and we ended with promises to continue working together.

JULY 17 FRIDAY

Today began with a Skylake-area condo leadership breakfast meeting at the Turnberry Garden Room. Jeff gave the welcome address, and Saul Simon did the invocation. In my speech I talked about problems regarding the new legislation which prevents doctors from prescribing prescriptive drugs for profit. I thought they would want the doctors to do the prescribing, but they overwhelmingly did not want to be dependent upon the doctors for their prescriptions, and would rather go to the pharmacists because their druggists are open all day or night and they can get their medication whenever needed. I really learned a thing or two about their views during the question and answer period. For my part, I did not care whether the doctors or pharmacists won out, I just wanted to make it as easy as possible on the consumers.

There were over one hundred guests at this event and after the program I circulated from table to table with a professional photographer, Al Kaplan, taking photographs at each table. Some older condo leaders have passed on and new people are now taking over. I will see about moving the voting precincts into the condo lobbies rather than have elderly people walk across the intersection to the mall, which is rather dangerous.

Back in the district office, I made phone calls and cleared my desk. At 11:30, I met with Mayor Howard Neu and a council member at North Miami City Hall to discuss the same old toxic waste problem at the Munisport. I told them I would try to expedite the EPA report so that the matter could be settled by February, and that with the cooperation of Senator Graham, we could have the EPA pay for the study instead of the City of North Miami.

Next, I went to see my lawyer on personal business and then on to Jackson Memorial Hospital to meet Dr. Margaret Fischl about the AIDS situation there. It was fascinating, but very sad. I had no idea AIDS was such a serious problem in Dade County, especially among heterosexuals and children. AIDS is a sexually transmitted disease and will be more and more transmitted sexually between heterosexuals. Education is only a temporary means to combat this disease. Eventually, in about ten years, maybe they will have some type of medicine to control it, but nothing is ready yet. Jackson Memorial is treating the disease with strong antibiotics on an outpatient basis, which they said prolongs the lives of their patients.

Leaving Jackson Memorial, I headed for the Hospice at North Shore Hospital to meet AIDS patients there. Some knew me and had voted for me. Hospice is now where the patients end up when they no longer respond to treatment at Jackson Memorial. North Shore Hospital tries to keep them comfortable, but the real need is more nursing home care for AIDS patients. A hospital wing is not the answer to treating a terminally ill AIDS patient, when what is needed is to be kept as pain free as possible and to have some type of support system from family or others. Right now there is no solution and the problem will get worse. We took photographs to include in our newsletter that we will mail to all the addresses and postal patrons in our district, along with Dr. Koop's pamphlet.

JULY 18 SATURDAY

With nothing scheduled for today, I went fishing, played tennis, and just relaxed.

JULY 19 SUNDAY

I am at the Miami airport working on my cover letter for the newsletter, as I wait for my plane back to Washington. I had planned to spend most of the flying time working on this cover letter, but, as usual, the plane is late, so I may have it finished before we even board.

JULY 20 MONDAY

This morning I devoted the first hour to Jane and Van Myers and their attractive ten and eleven year old grandchildren. I enjoyed being with these special old friends touring the Capitol, eating in the Members Dining Room, and then taking them on the House Floor.

At the office John and I went over the AIDS newsletter, and then talked to the subcommittee staff about how to deal with projects of those members who voted for the two percent across-the-board cut on our appropriations bill. We are calling those members the "two percent club." Members who had projects in our bill and voted for the two percent cut are going to lose, in conference, part of their project funding, as members cannot have it both ways. I have no quarrel with members who did not have projects in our bill and voted for the two percent cut, but those who asked for project funding, which we included, and then voted for the two percent cut cannot get away unscathed. They will know of our displeasure and will also realize that one cannot request projects and then vote to cut the bill.

Adele and I reviewed the foreign operations bill in preparation for the subcommittee's Democratic Caucus tomorrow. We did not have a Democratic Caucus on my transportation appropriations bill, but this foreign ops bill is apparently going to be very complex. Real problems exist because of the $300 million shortfall on foreign operations outlays, and maybe for the first time cuts will be made in the Israel and Egypt programs. I do not know what Chairman Dave Obey will do tomorrow, but he and his staff have been meeting all day to come up with solutions.

At 6:00, I stopped by the Longworth Cafeteria for the Jim Wright "Texas Style" Barbecue, and sat with Butler Derrick from South Carolina and his daughter. Butler is a special friend and used to tell me about the concerns he had with his children. Butler, his wife Suzanne, and Joan and I went on a codel to the Mideast and became good friends. Now the Butler's are divorced and, according to their daughter, the wife is doing family therapy work in a black community in Washington.

Following the barbecue I went to the Brasserie for dinner and read the rest of my newspapers.

JULY 21 TUESDAY

Today, although there was not a single vote on the House Floor, I was very busy, beginning at 8:30 with a breakfast meeting with Debra Benchoam's husband, George Rogers, who just got back from Spain, having left Debra there. George told me that he and Debra are moving to New York; he will be attending Columbia Law School and Debra will take courses at Columbia. When Debra returns from Europe, she is going to Argentina for about three weeks to give background information to a woman author who is to do a story on Debra's life. George said that when Debra is in Argentina, she would need to have her passport renewed, and this was cause for concern. Because of the legal action Debra took in the United States against the military in Argentina, which resulted in a jail sentence for several officers, the possibility exists that the military may make problems for her when she is in Argentina.

Debra's grandparents, who traveled with her in Spain, are concerned about her trip to Argentina and so is George. I am contacting our Justice and State Departments so that when she checks in at the American Embassy in Buenos Aires to have her visa renewed, maybe, as a courtesy to me, she will be able to alert the Ambassador's staff on any potential problems. I don't want her to go through the ordeal of being jailed again in Argentina, because all she has done is pursue the people responsible for the disappearance of her fiance and the execution of her brother, which occurred several years before I went to Argentina and found her in prison.

Friends of my son Bill, Mr. and Mrs. Bill Koppel, came in. Bill is a CPA from North Miami Beach, and he and his wife are in Washington attending CPA seminars. They live in Skylake in my district, and we had the usual photo opportunity. At 10:30, Lucy and I met with Ambassador Valdez, Manuel Diaz del Rio, Director of International Operations for the Spanish railway system, and Lorenzo Gonzalez, Commercial Minister from the Embassy of Spain. They want members of our subcommittee to visit Spain to ride the Spanish highspeed rail. Apparently the Spanish trains fit very well on the tracks of our northeast corridor rail system because of their low center of gravity, which causes them not to sway or have much movement, as opposed to the equipment which the Japanese and the French want to sell Amtrak. If I have a ten day window of time after we adjourn late this fall I could perhaps take a codel to Spain and observe the Spanish railroad.

At the Democratic Caucus in Dave Obey's office on Dave's foreign operations bill, preparations were made for the markup on Thursday or Friday. The subcommittee is short on outlays, which is of course a problem, but the matter has gotten even more complicated and more of a problem because Dave wants to take funds from Israel's allotment to fund other countries. I think this would be a bad precedent as Israel has been on a $3 billion plateau for about three years. A reason for the problem is that the Department of Treasury's Guaranteed Reserve Fund, to guarantee debt from other nations, is steadily being depleted, and about $500 million in our budget outlays are needed to rebuild the Fund, which goes to the federal financing bank to take care of the defaulting loans of countries such as Turkey and Egypt. I don't want to see Israel pay for the mistakes of other countries. I hope this can be resolved so that we do not have to score payments to the Guaranteed Reserve Fund as an outlay on our foreign operations appropriations subcommittee. As far as I am concerned, it also does not make sense for us to extend more foreign military sales to Greece, Spain, Jordan and other countries, as they already have more weapons than they need.

At the meeting I was the only member to raise the question of the Guaranteed Reserve Fund. I told them that I thought we had no alternative but to eliminate the Guaranteed Reserve Fund offsets from the bill in order to construct a workable foreign operations appropriations bill this year. This is a new problem with which other Democrats were not familiar, and I was glad to have been briefed the day before so that I could present my solution. In the meantime, AIPAC members Irv Katz and Esther Kurtz on AIPAC's Washington staff, had been in to see me concerned about the cuts on aid to Israel.

Herb Kelleher, Chairman of the Board and CEO of Southwest and Transtar Airlines, met with me at 2:00 about the re-regulation of airlines. Kelleher is afraid that Congress is concerned about poor service and will re-regulate, which would adversely affect him as he likes the idea of free enterprise and competing in an open market. I told him he did not have a problem with me especially since I thought the competition would soon work against those that gave poor service. The only problem is that unless you have competition you have no free market, and now in so many markets such as in St. Louis, TWA has about 90 percent of the market, and in Denver, Continental and United have about 95 percent of the market. Deregulation or re-regulation will not solve the problem, the problem is in the antitrust concept of the airline market. If we have no competition then we will have poor service.

In the evening I went to the Hunt Room, a part of Bull Feathers restaurant on Capitol Hill, for a reception for John Brademas, President of New York University and former House Democratic Whip before losing in re-election several terms ago. John was sort of my mentor during my first years in Washington, as we worked together about ten years ago when we both were on the Education and Labor Committee. At the reception John was signing his book that was just published by the University of Maryland National Press, entitled *The Politics of Education, Conflict and Consensus on Capitol Hill.* The event was very crowded and hot, but it was good to see John again. Former Speaker of the House Carl Albert was there. John was signing away on books and must have sold several hundred at this event. He had a large turnout of members, staffs, and old friends. I have not read the book, but I told John that one of the problems now in education politics is the difficulty of getting Democrats to serve on the Education and Labor Committee. For this session, House leadership had to temporarily assign Democrats to the Education and Labor Committee just to maintain a Democratic majority. Members no longer want to serve on this committee because funds are unavailable for new programs. In the old days of Adam Clayton Powell and Carl Perkins under Lyndon Johnson and Jimmy Carter, Education and Labor was a viable Committee with plenty of action.

Dan Glickman of Kansas was at the Brademas reception, and we went together to the dinner party for Secretary of State, George Schultz, at New York Congressman Jim and Emily Scheuer's home. It was an informal gathering for members, and spouses were not invited. Secretary Schultz spoke and then answered questions for a couple of hours, mostly about the Mideast and Soviet-American relations. He thinks that Gorbachev is doing the best job possible. Then Congressman Tom Lantos of California objected, bringing up the "evil empire" stuff on the Soviet Union, but other guests put him down. Mention was made of the Soviet increase from 1,000 last year to 10,000 this year in refugees to Israel, and Tom responded with, "But what about the 50,000 back in the late 1970's?" "Oh come on Tom, get off that soapbox," was the comment from one of the guests. Tom is very opinionated and was the only one disruptive. Schultz is an optimist, even about the Palestinian problem, and said he is still trying to move his Mideast peace process.

One of the things talked about before Schultz spoke was how some members use the television media in their districts. For instance, Dan Glickman from Wichita is the only member from his part of Kansas, so everything he does is TV worthy. On the other hand there is Martin Frost of Dallas competing on national issues with Speaker Jim Wright and ten other members from the metropolitan area, including Ft. Worth. It is almost impossible for Martin to do anything on national issues, but he uses innovative means to get television coverage, such as going out to toxic waste sites.

I spoke to Ed Fox, Schultz's aide, and made some progress regarding Israel's funds on the guaranteed reserve problem. Ed and I became friends while traveling together on a Select Committee on Narcotics codel about ten years ago to Afghanistan before its revolution. He will provide me with language that I can use instead of cutting Israel by $36 million, which will enable the foreign operations subcommittee to cut outlays in the Guaranteed Reserve Fund for that amount. This then generates for the foreign ops markup, $700 million in budget authority for appropriations to other nations for foreign military sales.

JULY 22 WEDNESDAY

This morning at breakfast with the Florida Institute of CPAs, I saw Bill Koppel, CPA of North Miami Beach, and his wife, with whom I met yesterday. I also met people from South Florida that I can possibly work with on future fundraisers. Andy Manatos came to the office at 9:30, and he, Adele and I discussed the 7 to 10 ratio for aid to Greece and Turkey in our foreign operations bill in relation to the Cyprus conflict. Afterwards Bill Draper, Administrator of the United Nations Development Programs (UNDP), came in to see if we could keep foreign operations cuts from hurting his program. I told him that from what I heard from Secretary Schultz last evening, the United States was far behind in payments to the United Nations. With all its faults, the United Nations is still the best instrument to bring peace to the world, especially in situations like the Iran-Iraq conflict. The United Nations is now bringing pressure on these two countries to stop the war.

At the office I met our new intern, Gabriella D'Alemberte, the daughter of Sandy D'Alemberte, Dean of Florida State University School of Law, and an old Miami friend of mine. Gabriella, a very beautiful young lady, is a senior at Coral Gables High School. Our office does not usually take high school students as interns, but Gabriella is very bright and will be staying with relatives in Washington. [As a student at the University of Iowa, a couple of years after Gabriella interned with us, she posed for *Playboy* magazine in its edition on coeds in Big 10 universities. I think she was angry with her parents for divorcing.]

Lucy and I talked about the difficulty in getting Tom Luken's subcommittee staff to call her back regarding the problem with City Gas and its hoped-for compensation from Amtrak. This is the same old case involving Jack Langer and the moving of his City Gas tank farm due to construction of the new Amtrak station. Lucy was finally able to converse with Luken's staff and the question now is whether we want Jack Langer to come to Washington and testify before Luken's Transportation Subcommittee of the Commerce and Energy Committee. Maybe compensating provisions will be in Luken's authorization bill, and Jack will not have to testify, which is better than going public with such special interest legislation. Our proposed language in Luken's bill, however, only requests that the Secretary investigate for possible damages that would entail justifiable compensation for anyone who has suffered because of the relocation of an Amtrak facility.

On the House Floor, I voted against the Jacobs amendment on catastrophic illness. I am on the wrong side of this issue because of longtime commitments and promises which I should not have made to condo groups in my district. Seeing Pat Schroeder on the Floor, I spoke to her about coming to Miami in September for the Forum Political Club. Pat is getting very busy with her presidential campaign, and she may go even further in the primary than many people think. Don Edwards was also on the Floor and I gave him a *Miami Herald* article about the cocaine labs in his district. I had two tickets for the Kennedy Center ballet, and leaving the Floor I went to see John Osthaus to give him the tickets. John is chief of staff on Appropriations State, Justice and Commerce Subcommittee, and he has always been helpful to me; I was glad to do this for him.

In our staff meeting today we discussed the catastrophic illness bill due on the Floor today and discussed Merchant Marine and Maritime Commission questions on allowing Canadian ships to do coastal shipping between American ports. I had to leave for a 2:30 meeting in the office of Sid Yates, the so-called Dean of the Jewish delegation, with the new Israeli Ambassador Moshe Arad, who served with the Embassy during the Nixon administration. Arad was in Mexico for a while and is now back. At today's meeting we laid the groundwork for a future meeting to discuss the Israeli part in arm sales to Iran.

Lee Hamilton was talking to me about his select committee that is handling the Iran-Contra investigation, and said that "Admiral Poindexter is the scariest person I have ever met in the federal government." Lee said the Admiral is a man who does not trust anyone - the CIA, Congress, or the Administration - and that he wants to run his own foreign policy and won't tell anybody anything. As I told Lee, the problem is that people like Poindexter don't believe in democracy or the democratic system.

JULY 23 THURSDAY

Sid Yates, Chairman of Appropriations Interior Subcommittee and a member on the Foreign Operations Subcommittee, has the understanding, as do I, that to prevent the $36 million cut for Israel, the Appropriations Committee would have to find some other available outlays. The Guaranteed Reserve Fund is no longer the issue. Sid and I discussed the possibility of his transferring outlays from the Interior Subcommittee and me doing the same from the Transportation Subcommittee and maybe we could come up with $36 million to transfer to Foreign Operations, which would create an additional $750 million in budget authority for aid to Israel and prevent a cut in budget authority for Israel in the same amount. Sid spoke to his subcommittee staff who told him not to make any additional cuts at this time because he may need the extra outlays in conference with the Senate. Sid and I were supposed to meet today at 3:00 with Dave Obey and the Democratic members of our foreign operations subcommittee, but it was called off. At that time I would have offered $18 million to Dave out of our subcommittee, subject to appropriations front office approval. That is the amount our subcommittee staff said would be safe to offer without threatening our own position in conference with the Senate.

Again, I met with Tom Luken about the City Gas problem. His Transportation Subcommittee of the Commerce and Energy Committee is holding hearings on rail safety legislation and Tom is now to include in the bill, language that would give City Gas the right to petition the Secretary for damages suffered by locating the Amtrak station next to its gas tanks, which forced City Gas to move. I think we have worked it out with Luken's chief of staff, John Arrington, who did not want City Gas to testify before their subcommittee, saying that he thought the case would appear too much like a special interest deal. I hope this works out for Sid and Jack Langer, as they have been fighting this battle for several years.

Fred Shockett, Editor and Publisher of the *Jewish Floridian*, called concerning problems with mail to his post office box being delayed, and that his news items and advertisements are coming in late and this was costing him circulation and money. Fred's office is in a rough neighborhood and does not use ordinary mail delivery to his building, and the Flagler Post Office he uses is really not servicing his post office box. I called my friend Woody Connors, the Miami area Postmaster, and Woody called Shockett and told him his problem was solved. Shockett could not get over the fast action I got for him. One of the things that seems to function best out of our office is the rapid service we deliver on problems of our district.

A problem I should have anticipated has come up concerning the report language on the Tamiami Airport in the Treasury, Post Office Subcommittee bill to transfer Customs personnel to Tamiami. I thought Dante Fascell, in whose district the airport is located, had signed off on this, but the Kendall Homeowners Association has sent Fascell a petition and he will have to oppose this transfer. I am waiting to hear from Eli Feinberg to discuss how we handle the homeowners' opposition.

Bill Nelson talked to me on the House Floor about his running for Florida governor, wanting to know if he should lead the fight for Television Marti to supplement Radio Marti. My advice to him was that he would not gain any Cuban voters and would lose credibility among the anglo, Jewish, and black communities. I suggested he speak to Sergio Bendixen and Mickey Leland who would know best if this was the right approach to take. Some Democratic members think they can get Cuban votes by going for Radio Marti. I also warned Nelson about the way Cubans always vote Republican in South Florida.

It is 5:20, and we have had people come in this afternoon requesting increase in student aid for Florida Memorial College, and for private technical training schools. Some student aid cutbacks have been really critical, and I tried to be as reassuring as possible.

That evening I had dinner with my old friend, Joan Godley. I knew Joan from when she worked for John Brademas on the Education and Labor Subcommittee; she is now on staff with the Select Committee on Children, Youth and Families, and brought me up to date on the direction and goals of the committee. Joan thinks that the select committee will run out of subject matter and that after this session George Miller, the committee chairman, will become chair of the Interior Committee. "After George Miller," she said, "no member will want to take over chairing the select committee." She may be right. [Pat Schroeder did, until Newt Gingrich eliminated the select committees.]

JULY 24 FRIDAY

This morning between the time of my 7:30 appointment at the Navy Yard Dental Clinic and the time I got out at 9:00 a.m., my car battery had died. A Navy submarine officer tried to get the car started, but couldn't, and gave me a ride back to the Rayburn Building. What was so special about his taking time to help me was that he missed his own appointment at the Navy Yard Clinic.

An idea I have to help resolve the impasse with the foreign operations' two percent across-the-board cut in foreign military sales is to find another $36 million in outlays. Another alternative is to transfer $18 million in outlays from our transportation bill which will create $175 million in budget authority and then do a one percent across-the-board cut on Israel, Egypt and Pakistan. I think we can do this without major reaction if we drop the cut from two to one percent. I will run this by Dave Obey for his reaction. If he likes the idea, I will get an ironclad commitment from him that this $18 million will only be used to resolve his outlay problem for foreign military sales. First, though, I need Jamie Whitten's approval to transfer those outlays from 302B in our transportation bill to 302B in foreign operations. I am philosophically opposed to foreign military sales going to Greece, Portugal, Turkey or other countries, but I am even more concerned that Israel maintain its $3 billion allocation; and for this I am willing to transfer funds from our transportation bill to the foreign operations bill.

John Arrington, Luken's chief of staff, told me that their subcommittee had put the City Gas language in Luken's rail safety bill. This gives City Gas the right to petition its grievance for the loss of relocating its tanks, and also eliminates City Gas having to testify before Luken's subcommittee.

JULY 25 SATURDAY

At breakfast in the Longworth Cafeteria, I spoke with Howard Coble of North Carolina about the new non-smoking law on airplanes. 2:00, I am to play tennis with Hill staff people at Haines Point.

JULY 26 SUNDAY

Joan and I went to the Jefferson Island Club for their "Crab Feast" picnic. The club is located at the mouth of the Potomac River and has been there for years - often used as a retreat by Franklin Roosevelt and Harry Truman. Last year we went by charter bus, and the bus was filled with members and their families, and defense lobbyists. This year the bus was rather empty and it was very hot. The only other member on the bus was Defense Subcommittee Chairman Bill Chappell, president of the Club. It was strange that this year Jefferson Island did not attract many people, even members who would ordinarily drive there. Membership is only $50 for members, but $500 for the private sector. It was an adventure, and Joan seemed to have a good time, but I don't think I want to go back soon. Members usually go but once.

JULY 27 MONDAY

The latest edition of *Politics in America* is out. This is a *Congressional Quarterly* publication, which comes out every other year, with "profiles on House and Senate members." My staff is pleased with this latest profile on me, and John Schelble is sending photocopies to the South Florida media. This profile is better than any of CQ's past editions, and mentioned the fundraisers I have every other year in my townhouse for Democratic members on my subcommittee. Now, however, I would like to change this to a weekend of fundraising in Miami for the subcommittee members, as most of them are no longer threatened by opposition and are re-election secure. A few, such as Bill Gray, Chairman of the Budget Committee, and Marty Sabo also on the Defense Subcommittee, have no problems raising money.

From 1:00-3:00, I played tennis with my friends Don Edwards, Judge Mikva, and Chaplain Ford. Don is seeing a lot better now and playing good tennis. Afterwards, I went to the office of Matt McHugh (D-New York) for a meeting with him and Charlie Wilson of Texas. The three of us are on appropriations foreign operations subcommittee and are trying to make sense of where we are on the Guaranteed Reserve Fund before going into the Democratic Caucus of the foreign operations subcommittee tomorrow morning at 10:00. We discussed three matters. The first concerned the proposed waiver on Pakistan nuclear proliferation, and how not to send aid if Pakistan fails to abandon its nuclear weapons program. As Charlie said, "They are going to build nuclear weapons anyhow." We are in a position now that if we don't hold Pakistan's feet to the fire on its nuclear weapons program, then our whole position on non-proliferation will go down the tubes. We need to put restraints on Pakistan, maybe by the temporary extension of a waiver subject to our President's certification that indeed the Pakistan government is not involved in the creation of nuclear weapons.

I called Lee Hamilton, a member on the foreign affairs authorization committee, as Lee is very sensible and feels as strongly as I do that we must protect our position on the proliferation of nuclear weapons. A nuclear arms treaty with the Soviet Union will not mean anything if we let all the third world countries make nuclear weapons, especially those in the Moslem world.

The second item discussed was the effect of a two percent across-the-board cut on Israel and how to get outlays from the Guaranteed Reserve Fund instead of taking the money from Israel to create the additional budget authority for foreign military sales to our base rights countries. I told Matt and Charlie of the possibility of getting $18 million from transportation outlays and transferring those funds to foreign operations outlays to take care of half the problem. I had already spoken to AIPAC officials about this, and of course they do not want to reduce any funds from Israel's appropriation. If we can find another $18 million in outlays somewhere other than the Guaranteed Reserve Fund, then we can let Obey keep the Fund intact.

The third item concerned the population control position and whether to put language in the foreign ops subcommittee bill overruling the "Mexico City proposal," as requested by the administration. The proposal maintains that we cannot send foreign aid to private nonprofit organizations that provide or encourage abortion or sterilization. It meant that even if we prohibited the use of U.S. funds for abortion and the organizations used non-U.S. funds for abortions, we still cannot appropriate grants to them. That is not the way we should provide aid, but this has been a very touchy political subject.

The way I see it, we have two choices. We can put this aid in the subcommittee bill where we pro-choice members have the majority, but I don't think this is the right plan because it gives the Right to Lifers opportunity to rearm with a substitute amendment in the full appropriations committee, which could probably pass. Or, we can just wait, leave it alone in the foreign ops subcommittee, and bring it to full committee markup with the administration's position on the Mexico City language in the bill. We can suggest to Dave Obey that he not speak out against the pro-choice amendment. John Porter from Illinois will offer the amendment in full committee, and it will probably pass on a roll call vote. Obey can even vote against the amendment, but not until everyone else has voted.

These were the three touchy subjects we covered. I think the three of us represent a cross section of the Democrats who will go along with us. My hope is that Budget Committee Chair Bill Gray, and Dave Obey, Chair of the Foreign Operations Subcommittee, come up with something on the Guaranteed Reserve Fund so we can resolve that problem. Things look better because Dave is back in town this evening, and he will meet with his committee staff to work out all the numbers before the Democratic Caucus tomorrow.

JULY 28 TUESDAY

This morning I had breakfast in the Rayburn Cafeteria with the very attractive Marcia Wiss, an attorney and lobbyist in Washington, and a helpful resource networker for me. Marcia and I met several years ago on an airplane coming back to Washington, and I thought her very knowledgeable on the developing world's problems. Today, she briefed me on the problems in Sri Lanka, her client, and told me that she was going to Zambia and would report back to me on the AIDS problem there.

We had the foreign operations Democratic Caucus and worked out the shortfall by taking money from Contra aid, so Israel will receive the full $3 billion. We still have the waiver problem for Pakistan on nuclear proliferation. I adamantly favor a nonrelaxation of our position for Pakistan before appropriating U.S. military and economic assistance. Pakistan is not a democracy yet, not by a long shot, and although there is some freedom of the press it is still a dictatorship. I am not happy with a Moslem country having nuclear weapons.

We agreed not to do anything with the population language in the subcommittee, but to wait and offer language in the full committee. I got the $5 million for Florida Power and Light for its utility electrification program in the Caribbean, and a $25 million appropriation over a period of five years for the Florida State

University Law School to codify the laws of the Caribbean nations. I was not able to help Al Moskovits's Phillips Company on the St. Kitts road contract bid because the work was now already underway. Dave Obey said he would write a letter to the State Department complaining about the way the bid was handled, and I think this will satisfy Al.

After lunch, there was a Democratic Caucus in Jamie Whitten's office with the subcommittee chairmen regarding reallocation of the 302Bs, and members are worried that they will lose control of the appropriations process to the budget process. A move is on to take away our authority because we do not always conform to budgetary limitations. Out of the meeting came a move to have Chairman Whitten of the Appropriations Committee bring in a task force of top members and staff to meet with the House leadership to make certain that appropriations are a part of the House-Senate conference on the bill for the increase in debt ceiling limitation. The conference is where leverage will be applied against Appropriations, and because the Ways and Means Committee will not raise taxes or cut entitlements like social security, all the pressure, burden and blame is dumped on the appropriations process. We appropriators are now in a survival situation.

The buffet dinner and screening, sponsored by Jack Valenti, President of the Motion Pictures Association of America, was held this evening, and I missed it. I was supposed to meet Maria Elena Torano at the event, but she called my office upon arriving in Washington and was told that I was still in markup, so we both missed it.

I went to the gym and then to the Brasserie for a quiet dinner and read my magazines. A party was being held at the Brasserie for Jim Howard and people from the party, Sue Perry, Regina Sullivan and her father Richard Sullivan, and Father George, legislative liaison from Georgetown, all kept coming by my table to talk to me. I really didn't get much chance to read, but I enjoyed the company.

It was a good day, though long, and the foreign operations markup went well. I was not happy with the language on Pakistan nuclear proliferation, but I think as to the January 15 extension we can live with that and then get certification from the President that Pakistan is conforming to the nuclear proliferation agreements.

JULY 29 WEDNESDAY

At 8:30, I was at the Dirksen Senate Office Building for a breakfast meeting concerning the public housing problem in Dade County. Senator Bob Graham headed the meeting, and present were Senator Lawton Chiles; Representatives Claude Pepper, Dante Fascell and Bill Nelson; Florida State legislator Carrie Meek; Metro-Dade Commissioner Clara Oesterle; Dade County Manager Sergio Pereira; Richard McEwen, former Chair of the Board of Burdines; and Marty Fine, head of the Task Force. A problem exists with Secretary Sam Pierce of the Department of Housing and Urban Development, who has misquoted dollar amounts in grants, and after the breakfast the group was scheduled to meet with Secretary Pierce at his office in the HUD building.

There is also a problem with technical corrections legislation relating to the tax bill, soon to come out of the Ways and Means Committee to the Rules Committee before going to the Floor. The technical corrections eliminate the ability of private concerns to invest or purchase public housing, even when that housing has totally deteriorated. Because the bill will first come before Chairman Pepper's Rules Committee, I suggested that Claude make what is known as a self-executing amendment that the Committee could write into the Ways and Means bill, allowing deteriorated public housing to be sold to private investors. Self-executing powers make the Rules Committee very, very powerful but must be used with great care.

"Senator" Pepper and Commissioner Oesterle liked my idea. The federal liaison person from Dade's Little HUD and myself went with Claude to his office to meet with his Chief of Staff, Tom Spulack. We then got in touch with Robert Leonard, Chief Counsel and Staff Director for the Ways and Means Committee. Pepper told Leonard what we wanted to do in the Rules Committee hopefully with consent of Ways and Means. Whether this takes place I do not know, but it is the only way we can get another $5 million for Dade County. I learned how to work this self-executing rule out of my experience with the Rules Committee when the Public Works Committee asked Rules to use self-execution language to take the federal highway trust fund off budget. Of course I opposed that amendment, but from that experience I learned the power of the Rules Committee and what it could do.

In today's staff meeting, we discussed the potential liability on nuclear plant disasters. I will stay on the environmental side of the issue, but I have spoken with representatives of Florida Power and Light to see which of the environmental protection amendments they find least objectionable. If they need one or two of my votes on these amendments, I told them that maybe I would be able to compromise a bit. My reason is not to sell out to FP&L, but the fact is we in Florida need more electric energy and I have not been anti-nuclear power, only anti-nuclear weapons. If Florida did not have nuclear plants, we would not be able to have our present comforts. A good part of energy in Florida comes from nuclear plants.

Berta Fondino from my district is in Washington with the Congressional Youth Leadership Council, and came to the office with members of her group around noon. Berta lives in the Belle Meade section of Miami, and I told her that Joan and I built our first house there at 7500 N.E. Eighth Avenue and she said, "That is where I now live!" It was quite a weird coincidence. I got Joan on the phone and they spoke, with Berta saying how much she liked the house. One day Joan and I will go by and see the house. It was our honeymoon cottage.

Lobbyist Art Roberts stopped by. I had spoken to his wife in the cafeteria a few days ago and told her about my plan to bring the subcommittee to Miami later this year. Art was very interested and had some ideas. We are tentatively planning to be in Miami the weekend of the Miami Dolphins football game, December 1. We also plan to take members on a Metrorail tour and then to Joe's Stone Crab restaurant to show them a good time. This kind of trip has already been done by our subcommittee to Houston and Los Angeles.

Peter Kyros, a former member from the State of Maine, was in about his HMO client in Miami. He wanted me to be sure his HMO was not being confused with another gone-bad HMO.

Charlie Wilson and I had lunch in the Rayburn cafeteria, and we always enjoy talking. Charlie is going to Korea and Japan in August. The trip is being sponsored by the Taiwan Chamber of Commerce to promote the Taiwanese economy. I was also invited to go. Charlie is feeling pretty good again, but with a heart problem his lifestyle is quite unhealthy. When he was hospitalized recently at Bethesda Naval Medical, I think I was the only member who went to see him.

In the evening I went to the National Democratic Club for a reception honoring Pat Schroeder. I talked to her two teenage children, and they are not very happy about their mother running for president. My neighbor Maurice Rosenblatt was at the reception, and said to me that Pat was the closest thing to a candidate that he had. I am gravitating toward her, although I have not made any decision yet. I saw Mary Rose Oakar from Ohio, and she reminded me that she had written me about supporting her for Chairman of the Democratic Caucus. I like Mary Rose, she is a gutsy lady and I may help her, but she did have some ethical staff payroll trouble. Her opposition is Bill Gray, an old friend and a member on the transportation appropriations subcommittee, and appropriators usually support each other. Gray, however, has been Budget Chair, and perhaps it is time to let someone else have the glory of leadership for a change.

I left to attend the wine tasting reception hosted by Roll Call and Douglas Bosco of California, to promote Sonoma County wine growers from his district. It was a much better selection of wine than last year's, but the place was crowded with interns. I talked to Doug and he will send me some good California dry wine. Afterwards, I stopped at LaColline's for a light dinner and got home about 10:00.

JULY 30 THURSDAY

My day started on the Senate side with a Florida delegation breakfast for Mayor Thomas Jazouri of Jacksonville. Mayor Jazouri had already met with me on Jacksonville transportation problems. Charlie Bennett and the two Florida Senators were there and everyone made a big fuss over me for all the appropriation help I gave Jacksonville for the Acosta Bridge and for the light rail transportation system. I got more credit than I deserved, and when they started pouring it on I said, "With a little help from Lawton Chiles," and that relaxed them a bit. I finally said that I had to leave while I was ahead and before they started finding things that I did not do so well. I made a little fun of the Mayor's heavy Southern accent with a lot of "y'alls." They let me know that they would be looking to me and my subcommittee for help on a road to the naval base in Mayport, Florida. I had not yet heard about this project, but I am sure to hear more in the future.

At 9:30 there was a full appropriations committee markup, and we voted out the Labor HHS Education appropriations bill very quickly, no one offering an amendment. It only took about fifteen minutes, and an extended exchange of compliments flowed among ranking Silvio Conte, Bill Natcher and Jamie Whitten, the old "Mossbacks."

Maria Elena Torano came in, and I called the Rules Committee to set up a meeting for her with chief of staff, Tom Spulack. When I spoke with Tom, he told me that the Rules Committee may add to the technical corrections tax bill a self-executing clause for $5 million, permitting a private sector investor to purchase distressed public housing and also to get tax benefits. This will be a big help to the public housing concerns in Miami, and I felt good that the suggestion had come from me. I'm getting to be a clever legislator.

I told Maria Elena about plans to bring our subcommittee members to Miami and she said she wanted to be "part of that action." She also had concerns about a client who had contracted for training air traffic controllers. Her client thought the contract was to terminate next year (1988), but it was actually not due to expire until 1990. In our committee bill, language this year did say that by the end of 1990 all in-house training should be done by the FAA and that present private contracts should be completed by the FAA. I will find out if her client's contract is to be phased out before 1990, and help her if I can. Before leaving, Maria Elena handed me a $500 check made out to the Dade Foundation for Joan's downtown sculpture. Joan will be pleased, as each contribution keeps the work in progress.

At noon I stopped by the Florida Army National Guard luncheon, but found that no one was there from the North Miami National Guard Armory or the Armory in Northwest Dade, so I did not stay and went back to the office. At 2:00 at a meeting of the Appropriations Committee's new task force, comprised mostly of the new young members who have a long career ahead of them in Congress and subcommittee chairmen, who were there as ex officio members, we dealt with the threat of the Appropriations Committee's authority being constricted by the Budget and Ways and Means Committees. Budgetary restraints are hard on the Appropriations Committee because Ways and Means does not help on the revenue side and with entitlements untouchable, the budget shortfall impacts only on discretionary appropriations.

The solutions to budget deficit reduction requirements are being squeezed out of Appropriations, and we will have to find ways to make each sequestration apply not only to appropriations but also to entitlements and to tax expenses, e.g., tax deductions on home mortgage interest. In the meeting younger members such as Vic Fazio of California, Ron Coleman of Texas, Marty Sabo of Minnesota and John Murtha of Pennsylvania are trying to come up with responses to basically educate House Democratic leadership on how to find deficit reduction solutions in other than just appropriations across-the-board cuts.

In the evening I attended the reception at the Sheraton Carlton's Crystal Room to congratulate Wayne Smithey on his retirement and to welcome Elliot Hall, his replacement as Vice President of Washington Affairs for the Ford Motor Company. I carried a letter from my son Bill regarding a meeting I had a number of months ago with Bob Howard of the Washington office of Ford, who had met with me and Jack Moore, a black executive who works for Bill, in regard to minority dealership opportunity. At the time, I thought that Bob Howard was the top person in the Ford Washington office, but now I find that he is just middle rank and that Wayne Smithey was the Vice President of Ford in charge of the Washington office. To pursue a Ford dealership for Jack Moore I gave Bill's letter to Hall. It turned out to be quite a reception. The new incoming Vice President, Elliot Hall, who is black, read the letter when I gave it to him, and said, "We can do something about this." When I saw Bob Howard a little later he said, "I thought you might be interested when you found out who Elliot Hall was." A lot of powerful black people were at the reception, but John Dingell, from Detroit, and I were the only members. Vernon Jordan from the National Urban League was there, and he may also be able to help. Bill does not want this for himself, but to provide Jack Moore this opportunity. He assures me that Jack will not be a black front for a white dealer.

Florida Power and Light exec Dick Sewell, who was at the reception, is very familiar with Ford's Washington office and may help as he always says nice things about my staff, like how Adele had worked and helped him get an appropriation for the FP&L electrification contract in the Caribbean.

In any case, I am very happy about the meeting with Elliot Hall, as I am sure Jack Moore and Bill will be. [But nothing materialized.]

JULY 31 FRIDAY

The papers were signed today with FRA Administrator John Riley for the Tri-County Commuter Rail for Dade, Broward and Palm Beach Counties. The signing took place at Riley's office in the Federal Railroad Administration building and unfortunately without enough time to alert the media. I am glad this is now done and Tri-County Rail will be in operation next year. Hopefully this commuter rail will take some of the traffic off I-95.

One other matter to be happy about is the Rabbi situation in the German Democratic Republic. Apparently Rabbi Neuman is on track to be in East Germany for the holidays in September. The question is whether I can be present for the ceremonies because during that time I need to be here for our appropriations continuing resolutions and to conference with the Senate Subcommittee. If I go it will be a fast trip flying back and forth across the Atlantic at night.

This afternoon Bill Gray, Chaplain Ford, Sonny Montgomery and I played tennis at the Army-Navy Club. This was my first time playing with Bill Gray, and it was fun. Perhaps I even earned some tennis respect from Bill, who, after losing with both the Chaplain and Sonny, played with me and won. A new layer of respect is built when you can go out and compete on the tennis court.

Lany Narot's daughter, Betsy Berg, who looks to me as a sort of father figure, works in Manhattan for a company which books celebrities into speaking engagements around the country. On my return to the office from tennis, Betsy called to ask if I could help get Senator Kennedy to speak at a reform synagogue in San Diego. I called the Senator, and then he called Betsy. She thought someone was kidding her on the phone and would not believe it was the Senator. Ted Kennedy called me back, and I thanked him for calling Betsy. Betsy also called, and when she goes home to visit her mother and friends she will have a nice story to tell them about her phone call from Ted Kennedy.

Bill Gray had asked me to sit in his box at the Sovran Bank Washington Tennis Tournament. I invited Kay Beall, Dr. Ommaya's office manager. Dr. Ommaya was the head neurosurgeon at NIH who took care of my daughter, Kathy, when she was being treated there. As we were watching the Boris Becker match, Sam Nunn came with his family, which amazed me, as I had heard about the Sam Nunn-Bill Gray Democratic ticket, but I had no idea they were personal and family friends.

Chapter 8

AUGUST 1, 1987 - SATURDAY

Joan Blakely of Opa Locka died, and I am in the office this morning writing a letter of condolence to her husband, Jack, one of my first supporters from way back in the days of the Dade County School Board elections.

AUGUST 2 SUNDAY

Mr. & Mrs. Mark Talisman and I went to a Dim Sum brunch at a Chinese restaurant called the Golden Palace. Mark heads the Washington office of the Council of Jewish Federation, and when administrative assistant to Ohio Congressman Charlie Vanik, he was known as the best AA on the Hill. He really knows Congress and all its players, who can get things done to who cannot. We have been good friends for a long time, and feel comfortable sharing our views on many issues. Mark takes a dim view of AIPAC and thinks it is hyperactive and overkills on the Israel issue, whereas he does more one-on-one soft sell type of lobbying. Mark also is an excellent speaker, making about a hundred speeches a year and, just back from Australia and Hawaii, he had some funny stories to tell about Dave Obey, with whom he is working on the Homeless Bill.

After the brunch I drove to Eastern Shore, Maryland, to visit Pete Stark and brought him the new edition of *Politics in America*, which he had not seen. He read his "profile," and was very happy with the writeup. Pete and I are in the same congressional class, sworn in together in 1973, and his political base in the San Francisco Bay area has remained very solid. He said he was raising money for Charlie Rangel to run for Mayor of New York and explained that if Rangel ran for Mayor and Rostenkowski retired, then he would become Chairman of the Ways and Means Committee. Pete has become important since his rise to Chairman of the Subcommittee on Health in the Ways and Means Committee, which has a $60 billion budget compared to the $11 billion that I have on transportation.

AUGUST 3 MONDAY

Florida members are trying to decide how to vote on Massachusetts member Ed Markey's amendment to the Nuclear Regulatory legislation. I told them I promised Dick Sewell of FP&L that I would vote against the legislation, and that I thought people in the Northeastern part of the country should not tell people in Florida how to vote, which is what Markey is trying to do with his amendment on nuclear energy plants. We do all right in Florida, so far, with our nuclear plants.

Dining alone at the Brasserie this evening, I was interrupted several times. First, Senator Lawton Chiles came by with his wife, Rhea, and cousin Joe Chiles, father-in-law of Shannon Chiles, for whom we initiated the leave sharing amendment. Lawton and I talked about the budget, and he agreed with me and Bill Gray that there would be no compromise debt ceiling limitation until Congress is back in September from the month long recess. Congress recesses at week's end, so there is not enough time to work out the many differences between the House and Senate versions of the debt ceiling legislation.

Then Barbara Boxer of San Francisco and Richard Durbin of Illinois stopped by, and the three of us walked over to the nearby American Cafe to meet up with Representatives John Rowland of Connecticut and Ted Weiss of New York. The talk, of course, was all about politics. I had the idea that one reason Marvin Leath of Texas dropped out of the race for Budget Committee Chair was because Barbara Boxer and other members who supported him for Armed Services Chair and lost were now supporting Leon Panetta of California. Barbara is concerned with dangers in the Persian Gulf, and I mentioned that I thought if resurgence of the Contras in Nicaragua gets to be a real civil war then what happens there will be as crucial for this country as the Persian Gulf, especially if the Soviets send the Sandinistas high-tech sophisticated weapons.

AUGUST 4 TUESDAY

B.B. Goldstein from Miami is in Washington and called me regarding a friend, Dan Heller, who is coming up for parole on an IRS violation. I told B.B. to draft a letter that I could show to Dante Fascell and Claude Pepper so that we might sign a joint letter requesting full consideration on Heller's parole. [The IRS dropped the case. Dan Heller was fired and wrote a book condemning the IRS.]

Our new intern, Josh Fuller, started work today and we had our photo taken in front of the Capitol. Josh is a former student of Dade County English teacher Carolyn Picard, my daughter Kathy's best friend in high school, so I will send Carolyn and Josh's parents a copy of the photo. Lil and Sam Leviten from Northeast Dade came in about catastrophic illness legislation. They are dissatisfied with outpatient coverage, but real answers to catastrophic health care are provided in the House version of the catastrophic illness bill. [My worst vote.]

1:30, I testified before the Post Office and Civil Service Subcommittee on Compensation and Employee Benefits. If House Resolution 2487 passes, it would extend leave sharing to all federal employees in a five-year pilot program stemming from legislation that I initiated last year in appropriations for Shannon and Joe Chiles. I told the committee of the happenstance of my involvement with Shannon and Joe, and related how their problem was particularly clear to me because I knew first-hand what they were going through from my own personal experience, which I shared with the committee. Just as Shannon had left two children upon her death at 35, my own daughter Kathy at 34 had left two children, and if not for extraordinary resources provided by a family back-up system, there would have been no way Kathy and her family could have handled her devastating and debilitating illness.

Joe Chiles, who has since transferred to the IRS office in Kentucky following the death of his wife, Shannon, also testified at today's hearing, as did Bill Bevill from the IRS office in Miami. Joe spoke courageously of the difference leave sharing made in his family's life while going through such a personal crisis, adding that testifying was his way of helping other federal employees who may be faced with a similar crisis.

I think we will get the authorizing bill passed this year, especially with William Pfeil, manager of the IRS Fort Lauderdale office and monitor of the leave sharing program for the Chiles's, testifying to the overwhelming success of the program. In less than a year, he said, $17,000 and over 6,000 hours of leave were donated to the Chiles's from IRS workers all over the Southeast.

Our office had a very nice farewell pizza party for the interns who worked the month of July. I gave each a briefcase and said something nice about each one. One really funny story was told when I asked the interns what were the best and worst things that happened to them while working on the Hill. Intern Gabriella D'Alemberte said that yesterday Barbara, our receptionist, asked her to take my shampoo to the gym to be put in locker 18. When she walked into the gym (even though on the door it said "For Members Only") and asked for locker 18, all these half-dressed men were running around and trying to shoo her out of there before she could get in any further. [Eventually she made a Playboy pictorial, coeds of the Big 10 universities, so she wasn't too naive.]

I am trying to get Dr. Jay Groff's relatives into the U.S. Embassy in Paris to obtain visas to the United States. Patty in the District Office called John Berg, my friend at the Embassy and I think he will solve the problem. I received a phone call from Eli Timoner who has opened a new airline called Challenger Air which flies from Miami to Central America. Eli is trying to prevent Eastern from coming in and wiping him out before he even gets started. I told him I would do what I could to protect his airline, as he has had enough problems now with his recent stroke that had partially paralyzed him.

On the Floor, members were talking about their travel plans for the recess and it seems they are going everywhere from China to Switzerland to Australia, and very few are going back to their districts. In the evening I attended a farewell party for Walter and Joan Mondale in the Rayburn Building. With such a great turnout of members, senators and lobbyists, it pleased me that Mondale so readily recognized me. We had worked together on the education reauthorization bill back in 1974 and I had helped him in South Florida in his 1984 campaign. The one thing Mondale said in his speech was that we did some good things in the Senate during the Carter administration and, taking a swipe at Reagan's "convenient" memory lapse in the Iran-Contra affair, he said, "and we remembered what we did." That statement brought down the house.

AUGUST 5 WEDNESDAY

Jim Taylor and his family are visiting in Washington. Jim is my son Bill's insurance agent for his auto dealerships in South Florida, and we did the usual breakfast in the Members Dining Room, a visit to the Speaker's Office, to the House Floor, and of course a photo opportunity in front of the Capitol. At 9:30, Donna Lenhoff, Associate Director of the Women's Legal Defense Fund, was in about support for the Family and Medical Leave Act. Then Theresa Woody of the Florida Sierra Club came in to thank me for my work on the Kissimmee River restoration in the Energy and Water appropriations bill, and to talk about the Clean Air Reauthorization Bill.

At our staff meeting, we discussed cosponsorship of bills, the Campaign Reform Act, and the textile trade bill. On the Floor today was the Labor, Health and Human Services appropriations bill. After a vote, I went to Tennessee's Jim Quillin's office. Jim is the ranking member on the Rules Committee and wanted to discuss the closing of a flight service station in his Bristol, Tennessee, district, which is included in our subcommittee bill. We will probably grant a one-year extension.

AUGUST 6 - 9 (THURSDAY-SUNDAY)

Congress is now in recess through the Labor Day holiday, and Bill Richardson of New Mexico has persuaded me to visit his district to meet with city, county and business leaders to discuss highway projects for New Mexico included in our transportation bill. I left Washington on a 9:15 flight this morning for New Mexico. Tomorrow, Friday, I am to meet with the Sante Fe Chamber of Commerce, and after that my schedule is pretty much free through Sunday. The New Mexico visit provided opportunity to see my eldest grandson Sean O'Connor, an intern at Los Alamos, and bring his brother Matt, so that I can spend a week with the two boys.

AUGUST 10 MONDAY

Today I met with the Director of the Los Alamos National Laboratories, Sig Hecker. We took photos and spent most of the afternoon touring the laboratories. Los Alamos is about 25 miles northwest of Sante Fe, and except for the Los Alamos National Laboratories and the tourist business in Santa Fe, New Mexico is a very poor state.

AUGUST 11 TUESDAY

At 7:30, Bill Richardson's staff picked me up at the Rancho Encantado in Santa Fe for a breakfast meeting at the LeFenda Hotel with GEM Nuclear Corporation officials (from whom I received a $1,000 honorarium); Santa Fe Mayor Sam Pickford; State senators and representatives; and various county commissioners. Santa Fe wants a better highway from Los Alamos to Santa Fe, but this group is very anxious to spend the first of the appropriations our bill provides them on a highway bypass around Santa Fe for hauling nuclear wastes from Los Alamos, even before the planned widening of the highway from Los Alamos.

At 10:00, we arrived at the Los Alamos County Chambers for a meeting with the county administrator who organized the event, and he presented me with a beautiful Indian pot. In Santa Fe I had received a nice plant. Los Alamos was interested in highway improvement as a means to economically revive the area. I suggested having rapid mass transit run down the median strip of the improved highway, and they liked the idea. There is no public transportation from Los Alamos to Santa Fe.

We went next to Taos for a beautiful outside luncheon hosted by the owner of the Sage Brush Hotel. Taos wants a better airport, and needs $25 million for its airport runway. At present the only way to come to Taos is by car. Taos is in dire need of airport funds in our bill, especially since closing the chemical plant has left many of its people out of work. This is a lovely city, and the audience of over a hundred people paying $10 each, was very responsive. At this event, I received another $1,000 honorarium.

My supportive remarks at all three stops were made to enhance Bill Richardson's prestige. Richardson's staff seemed to like me a lot, and I took this as an indication that I had done a good job. On the way back we stopped at the Santa Fe Opera and I paid for tickets to the evening performance for the boys and me.

Most of my work here is now done. I bought gifts in Santa Fe and Taos for my staff, and now till I leave on Saturday, I am free to ride horses, play tennis and take it easy.

AUGUST 12 WEDNESDAY

I spoke to a *Miami Herald* reporter who is running a feature story on Sunday, August 16, about the Miami Metromover. He also asked questions concerning problems with the FAA. The last 24 hours I have written thank you letters to people who have been so helpful and accommodating during this trip, especially those who hosted the events in Los Alamos, Santa Fe and Taos.

AUGUST 13 THURSDAY

Calling my Washington office, I gave Lucy permission to sign my name to a joint letter that Glenn Anderson of California has written to the Department of Transportation regarding UMTA's charter bus regulation and how it affects public transportation buses for charter service in his Long Beach, California, district. Anderson, ranking Democratic member on the Public Works and Transportation Committee, has made known both in our bill and on the House Floor his concern with UMTA's new charter bus regulation. As much as possible, I am trying to be cooperative and helpful to him.

AUGUST 14 FRIDAY

When I spoke on the phone today with Sandra Botwick of the *New York Times* regarding Rabbi Neuman's trip to East Germany, Sandra told me that the *Times* will now run the story because the American Jewish Committee has already issued a press release. I then called the district office to check the schedule, and my calendar looks clear through next Tuesday.

AUGUST 15 SATURDAY

At 11:20 Matt and I left Santa Fe for Miami and arrived home at 7:00.

AUGUST 16 SUNDAY

This evening Joan and I had a V.I.P. pass to the first exhibition game of the Miami Dolphins against the Chicago Bears at the new Joe Robbie Stadium. We were invited to Robbie's private party and I thought this strange because Robbie does not really like me ever since I helped engineer his removal as Chairman of the Dade County Democratic Party, to be replaced by Mike Abrams. Most of the South Florida politicians were invited, so I was in good company. Representative and Mrs. Clay Shaw of Broward were there, as were State Senators Jack Gordon and Elaine Bloom. I met Bob Floyd, Mayor of Miami thirty years ago, and saw Armando Codino and many old friends.

When we arrived home I went next door to see my neighbor, Mark Korvis, who is recovering from a ruptured appendix. Mark is the Barry University student who interned in our Washington office last semester.

AUGUST 17 MONDAY

Dick Capen, Publisher of the *Miami Herald*, is soon to leave for East Germany. I called and told him about an article that was in the August 15 *New York Times* about my and Rabbi Neuman's efforts in East Germany, and Dick will get a copy of the *Times* and take it with him to have all the information on hand.

AUGUST 18 TUESDAY

This afternoon I played tennis with Gardnar Mulloy and his friends at Fisher Island. Gardnar wants me to try to help him with Metro Commissioners on his Pet Rescue zoning facility problems.

AUGUST 19 WEDNESDAY

Most of the day was devoted to the Northside district office with Patrice. We talked to representatives from Florida International University, and Miami-Dade Community College about obtaining grants from FAA for teaching programs in air traffic control and aviation sciences. I told them they should work with Florida Memorial College which had the primary grant in South Florida, and to also include Barry University which has a grant from FAA for an aviation science building.

AUGUST 20 THURSDAY

At the district office this morning, Charlotte Greenbarg and her group were in about the Florida East Coast Railroad problems. They are making a big deal over the long freight trains, the toxic materials and the gate crossings. It was about 45 minutes of complaints that really had nothing to do with anything that I could do anything about, but I had to listen. They want to get the East Coast Railroad out of Northeast Dade County and we cannot do that, but they just don't seem able to understand the limitations in this matter. Joe Ploknik was there with Charlotte and did most of the talking. Ploknik is an obsessive nut about the East Coast Railroad, starting off with complaints about night whistle blowing at crossings; now he has all kinds of data on traffic and crossings that compare FEC to the CSX Railroad.

At noon, I went to downtown Flagler Street for a meeting with the Good Government PAC of Florida Power and Light, and received a nice warm reception from about fifty people who were there, including many of my old friends, such as Bill Klein. They asked questions about the Contras, the budget, and highway appropriations, and it was a very stimulating meeting.

AUGUST 21 FRIDAY

Mr. and Mrs. Gordon Rouse were at the district office this morning for a social visit. Gordon is one of the Florida Hillbilly Musicians from the old days, and has been a loyal supporter. Then a woman came in who had been arrested for telephone soliciting for a company which falsely advertised. She apparently is a grandmother and, as she has been in no previous trouble, I am trying to keep her from going to prison. This was a typical morning of constituents coming in with various problems. I left the office about 2:00, and took it easy the rest of the day.

AUGUST 22 SATURDAY

Joan and I had dinner this evening with a U.S. Air pilot and his wife. I wanted to talk to him about FAA air traffic problems, and I got some good information. Namely, that the air traffic controllers are doing a good job, and that about half of the pilots over 55 years of age should not be flying. Sixty years of age for mandatory retirement is too old. The pilot was not too familiar with the Microwave Landing System (MLS) vs. the Instrument Landing System (ILS), and said that many pilots that are supposed to make computer landings are instead doing hands-on which they don't want to give up. This information is useful when questioning the FAA at future hearings.

AUGUST 23 SUNDAY

Free day

AUGUST 24 MONDAY

Another free day except for an 8:00 meeting this morning with employees of the N. Miami Beach Social Security Administration Office.

AUGUST 25 TUESDAY

A few office appointments today, but not much else.

AUGUST 26 WEDNESDAY

This morning I went to the Cuban-American Democratic Club to speak with its members about the forthcoming political races. Ed Levy is President of the club, and I think he will be helpful in getting more Cuban Americans, especially in Hialeah, into the Democratic Party.

Next was a visit to one of the congregate living facilities in my district. These facilities are a growing part of Florida life, half condo/half nursing homes for elderly no longer totally able to care for themselves yet not so disabled as to need full-time nursing. When I visit such places in my district I usually see old friends living there whom I once knew as active in business and social life. Today at the Northeast Dade facility I met the sister of Harold Friedman, from whom I used to buy car radios when I sold used cars. His sister managed the operation, and now she is living in this semi-nursing home. Most of those occupying this facility were women, and they seemed happy to have me there.

Following the meeting last week with Charlotte Greenbarg, I arranged for the DOT Hazardous Waste Material staff to meet in the district office this afternoon with Charlotte and her disciples, including Joe Ploknik, concerning the Florida East Coast Railroad hauling hazardous materials through populated areas. The meeting lasted about an hour and half, which at least gave Charlotte and her community activist group the opportunity to express their apprehensions to the federal agency officials.

AUGUST 27 THURSDAY

Today's *Neighbors* section of the *Miami Herald* had a story about our meeting yesterday on the Florida East Coast Railroad. The article mentioned my name, but it mostly talked about Joe Ploknik trying to move the FEC from its present right of way, which is impossible. Joe is kind of weird and sort of *persona non grata* to responsible leaders in Northeast Dade. I accommodated him to keep him calm and off the back of our staff.

Customs personnel from Ft. Lauderdale and Miami were in for my first district office appointment this morning. They are very unhappy with the way Customs is being administered, regimenting some employees into certain job slots - not where the public really needs them - but simply as a means to prevent overtime pay. I will take the information they gave me back to Washington. If the Appropriations Subcommittee staff on Treasury and Post Office agrees to look into the problem, I will suggest to the Customs employees that they testify at a Treasury, Post Office Subcommittee hearing next spring. The group left very satisfied, and I am to get back to them.

Next in was the Army recruiting officer from the South Florida district. We talked about his problems and also about the improvements that have been made in the Department of the Army. He was very impressive, and we did not have any conflicts on the problems he was trying to solve. Army uniform personnel are no longer on food stamps, as I saw a few years back when visiting Ft. Carson in Colorado.

Afterwards, I had the staff get in touch with the Florida Insurance Commission to assist a lady who was having a problem with her All-State insurance premiums. I then went to North Miami Beach City Hall to see Councilman Jules Littman and Vice Mayor Jeff Mishoff about the Hot Meals Program North Miami Beach serves every day. We took photos with the Army colonel and people from the Hot Meals Program, so we will have a bunch of photos for a newsletter when I get back to Washington. I have already drafted the beginning and the wrap-up paragraphs for the newsletter and sent them to John Schelble for him to get started.

AUGUST 28 FRIDAY

At the INS office today I met with Director Perry Rivkind and staff from the Miami office of the Immigration Service. We did a photo opportunity and talked to the staff handling our office's immigration problems - especially concerning Haitians and other Caribbeans disembarking illegally up the Miami River. We also talked about the problems the INS had with young people coming into the United States with visas from Western Europe. Perry was born and raised in Miami and knows our area very well. Leaving the INS office, I stopped by the Episcopal Church in Biscayne Park and presented them with a U.S. flag which had been flown over the Capitol. When I see certain buildings with tattered flags, I get a new one for them before they ask me.

I then went to see Marjorie Deutsch. Marjorie (see March 22) has a brain tumor, and although she is surviving, her quality of life is not good, and now she has just had an accident and broken her hip. Marjorie is only about 28 or 29 years of age and I feel very bad for her. Today she reminded me more than ever of my daughter Kathy, as tomorrow is the anniversary of Kathy's death. Leaving Marjorie I stopped by the cemetery at Kathy's grave.

AUGUST 29 SATURDAY

Following a meeting with Jeff in the district office, I went to see Annie Ackerman in Point East. Annie though terminally ill is quite mentally active, and we talked politics and events and the future of the Democratic Party. As I was leaving in came State Senator Gwen Margolis, and we spoke briefly about her recent trip to Israel.

AUGUST 30 SUNDAY

Through funds appropriated by our Appropriations Transportation Subcommittee, Barry University was able to break ground recently for its new aviation building. In appreciation, the University held a very nice reception for me today in its Thompson Hall, and awarded me with a lovely and majestic plaque. Members of Barry's Board of Trustees were there including Mrs. Inez Andreas, Chair of the Board of Trustees. Afterwards, a rally was held at Barry on "One Peace at a Time." Many of the Dade County leadership were there such as Rabbi Lehrman, Alvah Chapman of the *Miami Herald*, the Chief of the Miccosukee Indians, President of Florida Power and Light and others. Everyone made a little speech. I made a speech citing Shakespeare's Antony saying of Brutus, "...his life was gentle..." and that gentle is the way we can have unity and peace in this community.

Because of the reception, I was late arriving at the Gateway Condo where Marty Harris's group was waiting patiently for me. During the question and answer segment, a question was raised that I had never heard before: Why do handicapped people who can't put gas in their own car have to pay full service price? Full service, of course, costs quite a bit more than self service, so I told them I would look into this and try to do something about it.

AUGUST 31 MONDAY

The *Miami Herald* had an article today about the "One Peace at a Time" rally at Barry University. My name was mentioned but they did not use my quotation from "Julius Caesar," which I was hoping they would.

At 10:00 a.m., I was at the Marco Polo Hotel for a meeting with the Sunny Isles Chamber of Commerce regarding the Sunny Isles beach restoration. Jeff Rose presided, and at the head table with me were State Senator Gwen Margolis and County Commissioner Harvey Ruvin, who also chairs the National Association of Counties. Bennett Lifter, owner of the Marco Polo Hotel, was also there, as were many residents of the Sunny Isles condo. A sign outside the hotel said, "Welcome Congressman Lehman," so after the meeting we gathered to take photos by the sign.

Chapter 9

SEPTEMBER 1, 1987 - TUESDAY

A good editorial appeared in today's *Miami Herald* about my position on the need to provide local dedicated revenue for the Metromover.

SEPTEMBER 2 WEDNESDAY

At noon I spoke at a Tiger Bay luncheon held at the Dupont Plaza Hotel on the necessity to proceed with the Metromover, with or without the one cent sales tax. Tiger Bay is only a vestige of what it used to be, but the luncheon produced the largest turnout that the club has had in the last few months. Even Ben Gilford, the Acting Director of Metro Transit, was there. In addition to the one cent sales tax, I also spoke about the problems of air safety and air traffic inconveniences and scheduling, telling them that existing problems are not due to insufficient spending of the FAA Trust Fund but that additional air traffic controllers have to be trained and new software developed to accommodate the new high-tech systems, and this all takes time. A *Miami News* reporter questioned me at length and perhaps there will be an article in the paper on the FAA. State Representative Elaine Bloom asked if we were going back from deregulation to regulation. "It would be like trying to put the toothpaste back into the tube," I told her.

The luncheon went well. People at these Tiger Bay meetings really want to socialize and have fun, and not be too serious. But it was good exposure, and I met one of the recipients of the Kathy Lehman Weiner FIU Scholarship Fund. I left the luncheon for my dental appointment with Dr. Schiff, and this evening Joan and I will be joining friends for dinner.

SEPTEMBER 3 THURSDAY

Dr. Casper from the Greynolds Nursing Home was my first appointment at the district office this morning, showing me the plaque that is to be presented to me later in September. Bernie Torra from my office will attend and accept the plaque on my behalf, as I will not be in Miami at the time of the ceremony. The award is in recognition of my help in dealing with the financial problem of Medicare payments to nursing homes. Florida nursing homes have a very high rejection rate from insurance companies that claim some people in nursing homes are not medically disabled and, therefore, are not under medical care but custodial care. Claims for custodial care are not allowed coverage, but most of the people I have seen in nursing homes appear critically ill.

The nursing home operators want a more flexible definition of medical care, and I will arrange a meeting in Washington and invite nursing home administrators to meet with me and Pete Stark, Chairman of the Ways and Means Health Subcommittee, who has jurisdiction over this type of legislation. This is a tough issue for nursing home operators and for families with relatives in these homes who are not receiving Medicare coverage and have to spend family savings to provide the necessary health care.

My son Tom came in next with a client who worked for the FBI before joining the Drug Enforcement Agency. Tom's client now wants to retire because the DEA is transferring him from Miami to Indianapolis, and he wants to work in the same geographical area as his wife, who also works for a government agency in Miami. If he is given credit for the time he worked for the FBI, he would meet the time served stipulation and qualify for retirement.

Afterwards, I met with Joe Moffit, the new Mayor of North Miami Beach. Joe wanted me to know how much he appreciated my nonendorsement of the incumbent mayor, Marge MacDonald, thereby aiding him in his Mayoral campaign. He spoke of the need for my help later in rehabilitating the inner-city section of North Miami Beach south of the 163rd Street shopping center, which happens to be unincorporated and not part of North Miami Beach.

Jeff and I then reviewed the case of an FBI couple who were fired from the FBI. The agents had visited a swingers sex club in South Dade, and upon exiting were attacked and had to shoot the assailants in self-defense. This incident led to their firing by Bill Wells, the new Director of the Miami FBI Office. Wells could not deal with the fact that FBI agents were in such a bizarre club. If the FBI couple had come out of a Seven Eleven and someone tried to rob them and the agents shot the attacker, they would be heroes. It was just a matter of being in the wrong place at the wrong time. Don Edwards is on the Judiciary Subcommittee which has jurisdiction over the FBI, and I will talk to Don to see what he thinks can be done. I do not have much sympathy for the agents though, because FBI agents should have more sense than to be in those types of places.

In the *Miami News* today there were two different stories about my speech at Tiger Bay yesterday. One was about my views on the Metromover and the other concerned my views on the FAA converting military airbases to relieve congestion at commercial airports.

Sharyn and I had lunch to discuss our future fundraiser. I suggested having the fundraiser on an Amtrak Station Train just to do something different, but Sharyn thinks this idea is too extreme. We want to do something different from the usual reception at Turnberry, where so many politicians hold their events. I always want our fundraiser to be a little more special.

SEPTEMBER 4 FRIDAY

This morning I went to the Carol City Villas to present the $1,000 in checks to light the basketball courts. There was a good neighborhood turnout along with county officials. Two very smart, talented young basketball players from Carol City Senior High School were there, and I feel these young men will go places in college beyond basketball. There was not much press coverage, only the community newspaper reporter and Channel 17. But, most important, the Community Center will be opened and additional money will be raised to light the basketball courts. With this beginning for the Center, hopefully other activities will follow.

At the Northside district office, Patrice had scheduled a meeting with Mrs. Henry Harris. Following Mrs. Harris's visit to Washington in June, I wrote to the Department of Justice in support of moving her husband Henry from an Alabama federal prison to a Miami halfway house; we are now awaiting their response. I want very much to help this family, as Henry is 60 years old, nonviolent, and will have a job when released. For the government to keep this man in prison for many years is really absurd. He may have been proven guilty of fraud and embezzlement, but he certainly is not dangerous.

I do not have any political activities over the next few days and on Monday, Labor Day, I head back to Washington.

SEPTEMBER 5 SATURDAY

I visited Williams Island today to see the possibility of having our fundraiser there next spring and it is perfect. I put in a call to Sharyn to have her look at it. Although this is Labor Day weekend, I am not participating in any events, not even Dante Fascell's picnic on Monday. I am taking the next couple of days to relax and to get ready for a busy week back in Washington.

SEPTEMBER 8 TUESDAY

Dante and Jean Marie Fascell were on my 11:00 flight out of

Miami. This morning my seat companion was David Rose, the son of an old friend from Tallahassee, and he wants to help in some way with our fundraiser. I told him that Sharyn would be in touch.

At 5:00 *Miami Herald* reporter, Ricardo Zaldivar, came in about the newsletter our office sent out with the Surgeon General's pamphlet on AIDS. Florida has the third largest concentration of AIDS patients in the country, and this was the first such newsletter by a Florida member. Obtaining the 238,000 copies of the pamphlet from the Department of Health and Human Services was a struggle, and I had to threaten to introduce legislation ordering the Department to provide the copies. I told Ricardo that some of the material was rather explicit and may offend certain people, but that I thought we had to take some risks as the situation just seemed to be such a potential time bomb and my responsibility is to do what I can to defuse that time bomb as it relates to the people I represent.

SEPTEMBER 9 WEDNESDAY

Ricardo Zaldivar's write-up on our AIDS newsletter was in the *Miami Herald* today. The article was very well written, really detailing the substance of our newsletter by explaining the complexities of AIDS and where we are now in combating this disease. On a more humorous note, he repeated my comment that there are not too many newsletters in which I get to put the words, "condom" and "prostitution."

1:30, I went to the Rules Committee office for Claude Pepper's surprise 87th birthday party, and Claude is "a piece of work." Not much is going on today, only two votes on the Floor and one was just procedural. Our subcommittee staff is preparing for the outside witness hearings next week on public charter bus operations vs. private enterprise. Other than that, our subcommittee is pretty well caught up.

SEPTEMBER 10 THURSDAY

At 8:00 I attended a breakfast meeting for Congressman Dave Obey from Wisconsin and his labor leadership people. The usual members and staff were there, i.e., Jim Moody from Wisconsin,

Pat Schroeder from Colorado, and Minnesotans Marty Sabo and Jim Oberstar. Dave was asked if he planned to run for the Senate. He said he did not know, adding that the Democrats do not have a sure victory in the Wisconsin Senate race, and that Republican James Sensenbrenner is going to be a very strong candidate, especially with the Indians. Jim Moody, who is just back from Moscow, may also run for the Senate seat. Jim was in Moscow viewing their nuclear weapons systems, and said the Soviets were very open and that much of their technology had been accessible to him.

Don Edwards said that we have to vote for the Mineta resolution to compensate the Japanese who were incarcerated during WWII; but the $20,000 compensation is really just a token payment. To my inquiry to the Majority Leader as to what would be happening from now till the end of Congress, apparently there will be a CR (continuing resolution) extending to just before Thanksgiving. After the House passes the CR, we recess for a week, come back after Thanksgiving, and then Congress will probably be in session till the 19th of December. The problem is in appearance and how the House will look during the week's recess if we give the Senate the whole CR package and leave. I think it would be more prudent to have the members remain in Washington until the Senate passes the CR, and then come to conference. Either way we lose as the President will beat up on the House if we are not doing anything even though we can't do anything until the Senate completes the process.

Pat Schroeder said that she sees a lot of concern among college students and young couples who already realize that after graduation it is going to take two full-time incomes for them to have a house, a new car, and daycare.

A number of members called me complaining about the service on American Airlines. Most people who do not fly often could not care less about the service, but congressional people in Washington are frequent fliers and are frustrated about the airlines' scheduling problems.

Back at the office the staff is watching television as the Pope lands in Miami. I went to see Tex Gunnels of Appropriations Treasury, Post Office, and General Government Subcommittee regarding Department of Treasury employees who visited my district office to complain about personnel scheduling in customs at Miami International Airport. I think Federal employees just love to gripe, but I have to follow through. Going back to the office I ran into Matt McHugh of New York, who will take over Dave Obey's position as Appropriations Foreign Operations Subcommittee Chairman if Dave runs for the Senate. I told Matt that I would talk to Dave and encourage him to run. Because Dave is not going any further in the House leadership, as he won't make Chairman of the Democratic Caucus, I think this is a good move for him.

I left McHugh to return to the office for my 10:30 appointment with Tim Hastings of Wackenhut concerning the polygraph amendment. Later I met with Elmer Johnson, the new Executive Vice President of General Motors, Harry Pearce, General Counsel, and Jim Johnston, Vice President of Government Affairs. They asked how my son Bill felt about General Motors, and I told them what Bill had so often communicated to me, that "General Motors will have to improve quality control to reduce its warranty problems." During our meeting, a former House colleague and Senator from Maine, Bill Hathaway, now a lobbyist for the textile manufacturers, called urging that I vote against the textile trade bill, and I had to tell him that I would have to support labor's position.

With me this evening at the Israeli Embassy is Rachel Bornstein, a friend of Jim Kukar's, my former district representative. Israeli Ambassador Arad was there, as were members Larry Smith, Ben Gilman, and Senator Inouye from Hawaii. I did not want to miss this reception because other commitments have kept me several times from attending Israeli Embassy receptions; also, I did not want to miss this opportunity to meet the Israeli Minister of Finance, Moshe Nissim.

SEPTEMBER 11 FRIDAY

This morning I went to the Navy Yard Dental Clinic. On the way back to the office I saw Bob Carr, and we went to Sherill's restaurant and had coffee. Bob had just come back from the Soviet Union with members Tom Downey and Jim Moody. They had visited the nuclear weapons facility in Siberia and, according to Bob, Russia really had not reached the U.S. development level in this technology. The Soviets may mothball the facility at its present level, which would be within the bounds of the U.S.-Soviet treaty. The present Soviet Union administration probably did not know that this facility was being built by the previous administration and was embarrassed and as concerned about it as the United States.

Bob did say he wants to support me on the letter I draft to keep the FAA on budget. He also said he was impressed with the National Transportation Safety Board during his onsite observation and inspection of the Northwest Airline crash in Detroit. Bob's district includes Pontiac, Michigan, and I told him that the Dade County School Superintendent, Joe Fernandez, had said the Pontiac Firebird automobile was causing high school dropouts in Miami. Bob said he would like to see all relevant information on this, so I am having Superintendent Fernandez write to me detailing the Firebird syndrome where students leave school to earn money to buy this car of choice. We will see if the Pontiac division will be able to do something.

After early afternoon tennis, I went back to the office to prepare for next week. The staff and I worked on an OpEd article to put in the *Washington Post* and perhaps the *New York Times* opposing the authorizing committee's attempt to have the FAA trust fund taken off budget. Most of my colleagues are very frustrated about air traffic control problems and think taking the FAA trust fund off budget is a "quick fix." The FAA cannot cure problems of the air transportation system by simply throwing money at it.

SEPTEMBER 12 SATURDAY

Debra Benchoam stopped by to tell me she is thinking about attending a university in Argentina next semester, and the credits she receives there can be transferred to Columbia University, where she is currently enrolled. In the evening, I entertained Representative Charlie Wilson and his friends at my townhouse.

SEPTEMBER 13 SUNDAY

I played tennis today with Cliff Madison, a lobbyist friend. Cliff told me I could expect from Norman Mineta's air transportation reauthorization bill, new additional language pertaining to consumer protection and the airlines' treatment of customers.

SEPTEMBER 14 MONDAY

Our newsletter on AIDS was received quite favorably, except for the mother of the AIDS patient we photographed at the Northside Hospice and featured. She was upset because she had told friends her son was dying from kidney failure, and said to me that we had no right to put his picture in our newsletter; but we did have the son's signature authorizing release of the photograph, so there is no legal problem. The real problem is the hostility between the mother and son, and she refuses to admit that her son is probably homosexual and that this may be how he contracted AIDS.

SEPTEMBER 15 TUESDAY

At 10:00, we had the transportation hearing on charter bus operations to determine whether to legislatively force UMTA to change the regulation prohibiting the public transportation systems subsidized by UMTA from competing with private charter bus operators.

The private charter bus operators testified that the new regulation did not provide sufficient protection for them and that public transit operators using federally funded equipment were forcing them out of business. The stickler, however, is that private charters won't serve the rural traffic, the very young, the very old, and the handicapped passengers, and UMTA's regulation prevents public transportation from serving these entities. The Department of Transportation needs to write a new regulation and undertake new administrative procedures to provide for those consumers adversely affected by this prohibition on public transportation.

We broke at 12:30, started again at 2:00 and went till 4:30. There were about twenty witnesses. The morning witnesses were from the private and public sectors, which included Congressman Glenn Anderson of California, who testified in support of the public bus charter interest of the Long Beach Transit Authority; and Susan Perry, Vice President of Legislative

Affairs of the American Bus Association, who testified in support of the independent, private bus operators. The afternoon session consisted of individuals and groups representing consumers as well as individual bus operators and individual public transit properties.

During the lunch break I attended a briefing on the House of Representatives Child Care Center. A number of congressmen were there, but my concern is that the center is preventing the children of part-time House employees from attending, even though the center is underutilized. I will be working on the problem with Debbie Dingell, wife of John Dingell, Chairman of the Energy Committee. Debbie is much involved with children's issues.

Dave Obey is withdrawing from the race for Chairman of the Democratic Caucus, and has also decided not to run for the Senate. He said he could not count on Jewish financial support and, with a son in college, he could ill afford to lose. If not for this he would run.

1:30, I met and was photographed with Daniel Kapp, a student from North Miami Beach Senior High School who had the winning experiment in the Space Science Student Involvement Program sponsored by the National Teacher's Association and NASA. At 1:45, Dr. Joel Sandberg from my district, and a friend of my son Bill, stopped by the office. Joel was in Washington for a Conference on Soviet Jewry. Afterwards, my cousin Harold Baer from Grand Rapids came to see me, and I hadn't seen him in thirty years. I took him to watch the continuation of our transportation hearing, and tomorrow we will have dinner together. After the hearing, I met with people from the International Council of Shopping Centers.

In addition to the transportation hearings and office appointments, I am also occupied with the task of making certain the Rules Committee next Tuesday does not make "in order" an amendment by Norman Mineta to take the FAA trust fund off budget. Today we have a letter going out to Washington newspapers, *Times* and *Post*, signed by me, Silvio Conte, Bob Carr and Larry Coughlin stating why it would be unwise to take the FAA Trust Fund off budget. The letter dwelled on the fact that technical problems and not funding were holding up the air traffic control computer modernization program now underway, and that with all the FAA complaints, the Federal aviation programs receive higher spending priority than most other domestic programs. If the whole FAA budget were paid for by user taxes, the aviation trust fund would soon go broke and there would have to be a user tax increase just to raise sufficient revenue to maintain current spending levels. The baggage, delay and other airline service problems brought on by deregulation and airline merger mania cannot be solved by more FAA spending. Deregulation and FAA spending are separate and distinct issues. Getting the airlines to provide better service is not a federal budget problem and emptying the trust fund is certainly no panacea.

I have also called Chairmen Dan Rostenkowski of Ways and Means, Bill Gray of Budget, and Jack Brooks of Judiciary to solicit their support in persuading the Speaker to disallow the "in order" amendment from being offered on the House Floor. If the amendment reaches the Floor, it would pit Democrats against Democrats, with the Public Works Committee Democrats going against the Budget Committee and the Appropriations Committee Democrats. The Republicans of course would enjoy this. My understanding with Tom Spulak, Claude Pepper's chief of staff on the Rules Committee, was that the "in order" amendment was not going to be made. But I do not want to be taken unaware in case this proves otherwise.

Dr. Cary Walters arrived in Washington today, and I took her to the Democratic Club for a reception honoring Congressman Ronald Coleman of Texas. We did not stay long although it was very nice with Southwestern cuisine and a live Mariachi band. I did see Bob Mrazak and told him that I would be in New York on September 25 (check-up at Memorial Sloan Kettering), and asked if he wanted me to view the Long Island transportation projects in his district. Leaving the Democratic Club, Dr. Walters and I went to a cocktail party honoring Norman Mineta at the Potomac Restaurant, where we saw many of the Public Works staff and members from the California delegation.

SEPTEMBER 16 WEDNESDAY

My schedule today has me very busy, beginning at 7:30 with a breakfast meeting at the Capitol Hill Club where the Air Force

Association honored the Florida Congressional Delegation. Sitting next to me was Charlie Bennett, Dean of the Florida delegation. The event gave me the opportunity to speak to the Miami members of the Air Force Association about opening up Homestead Air Force Base to commercial traffic. [Thanks to Hurricane Andrew this will be happening.]

Back in the office, my long-time friend Maria Elena Torano and I discussed my October meeting in Miami with her Cuban-American leaders. At 9:30, Dr. Carrie Walters, former NHI researcher, and I met with Mike Stephens, chief staff on Appropriations Labor, Health and Human Services-Education Subcommittee, to discuss the abuse of animals in medical research. Dr. Walters accused the subcommittee of being satisfied with whatever the medical researchers told them, and said that they were not being told the truth. I am putting together a newsletter on this issue to illustrate how alternatives other than animals may be used for the same research.

The meeting ran longer than anticipated, which prevented me from attending Sid Yates's annual reception for disabled Israeli war veterans, and to meet with Israeli Ambassador and Mrs. Moshe Arad. At 11:00, people from the Florida Association of Medical Equipment Dealers stopped by the office, but I was able to speak with them only briefly, as the Democratic Cloak Room had called for me to come to the Floor for the photograph of the entire House in session. This would be the first such photograph taken in about eight or nine years.

So much is going on today that I missed, regretfully, "A Celebration of Citizenship" with President Reagan and Chief Justice Warren E. Burger. At noon, I took Dr. Walters to the Members Dining Room for the luncheon Charlie Wilson was hosting for a Pakistan delegation. I shared with them that Dr. Walters' mentor, Dr. Ayub Ommaya, a native of Pakistan, was the neurosurgeon at the National Institutes of Health (NIH) who had operated on my daughter Kathy. Following the luncheon, Dr. Walters and I returned to the office for my meeting with Steve O'Toole of General Motors and Jack Moore from my son Bill's dealership. Last month I had spoken with Elliot Hall, the new Vice President of Ford Motors, about the opportunity for a black minority dealership, and the meeting today is a follow through on the meeting I had with Hall. Jack Moore, having arrived from Miami this morning to attend this meeting, is very anxious to have his own dealership, and both Bill and I are hoping we can help do this for him.

We voted today on the textile bill; I did not cosponsor the bill, but I did vote for final passage. Although I did not think it a good bill, I had put myself in a committed position with the textile labor people and also people in Miami's textile industry so I voted for it. I will be more careful to maintain my free trade position in the future.

Rabbi Neuman, I learned today, is finally established in East Berlin and has begun holding services. When Gene Dubow of the American Jewish Committee comes to Washington next week, we will bring photos taken to use in the newsletter to our Jewish community on the Rabbi in East Germany.

4:00, I attended the United Israel Appeal Refugee Program reception, and in the evening Dr. Walters, my cousin Harold Baer and I went to the American Medical Association/American Medical PAC reception in the Hart Building, where I met the head of the Washington AMA legislative team whose help I may need for a future fundraiser. The AMA contributed to my last campaign and will probably do so again.

We then went to the International Democratic Institute reception at the Georgetown home of Smith and Elizabeth Bagley. Walter Mondale was there with his sense of humor, as was Geraldine Ferraro and other Democratic party leaders. The International Democratic Institute is funded by the National Endowment for Democracy, one of Dante Fascell's major efforts. Primarily, when dictatorships change to democracy, as with the Philippines, Argentina, Portugal and Greece, all were totalitarian governments, which the United States supported because they were anti-communists; yet, these governments were overthrown by grass roots people without the help of the United States. Dante made a big speech about the International Democratic Institute and, yet, he votes for Contra aid; I do not see how he can be on both sides of the issue. Perhaps he knows more about the Contras than I do.

SEPTEMBER 17 THURSDAY

This morning, after taking our page David Aronberg and our

Barry University intern Eben Morales, to breakfast in the Members Dining Room, I headed to the full Appropriations Committee meeting to extend the continuing resolution for another 45 days. At the meeting Bob Carr and I agreed on how we would speak out against the move to take the FAA trust fund off budget. The problem is that we understand Speaker Jim Wright has instructed the Rules Committee to make "in order" the amendment to take the FAA trust fund off budget. If this happens, then the Highway Trust Fund will be next off budget, as this vote on the FAA trust fund will set a precedent.

1:00, I met with Penny Kahn, a friend of Peggy Gordon of Miami. Penny is an attorney looking for a job in Washington and I called a few law firms to recommend her. Penny should do well in Washington despite the multitude of lawyers in this city. Then Shirley Ybara, my best staff friend at the Department of Transportation, came to tell me she is leaving and going to Boston to work for a British company. I will miss Shirley and also miss having her support at the agency.

To develop a process for possible legislation on animal experimentation, we are setting up appointments in early October in Miami. Mike Stephens will also meet me in New York when I visit Sloan Kettering on Friday. Mike has arranged for us to visit Columbia or Rockefeller University for further enlightenment on animal experimentation and its alternatives.

Although involved with other matters, most of my day was spent trying to solve the FAA trust fund off budget problem. I asked Jim Wright's administrative aide, John Mack, to arrange a meeting with parties on both sides of the issue. On one side, Jim Howard, Public Works Chairman, and Norman Mineta, Public Works Subcommittee Chairman on Aviation, would be invited; on our side would be Budget Committee Chairman, Bill Gray; Government Operations Chairman, Jack Brooks; Bob Carr; Vic Fazio; and myself. Bob does not have his mind on the FAA problem since returning from the Soviet Union where he saw their radar stations; he is now into a CIA syndrome. As a kind of red herring, we will have our ally Dave Obey speak out in the Gramm-Rudman re-authorization budget conference on just how damaging it could be if members take other favorite programs off budget. We sent documentation to the media which maybe will appear and be of help to defuse these false claims that taking FAA off budget will improve air traffic. There was a piece in the *Miami News* this week stating my position, but the main quotations came from the opposing side, so the story did not lend much support to my position.

4:00 p.m., I left for the airport for my flight to Miami, and it was a mess. Eastern is so unreliable. These people like those now at Eastern that are very adept at takeovers don't know their ass from third base about running airlines, and moving FAA money around is not going to improve airline management. Finally I got on an 8:00 p.m. flight instead of the scheduled 4:40, and of course the 8:00 flight didn't leave until 9:00. I arrived in Miami around midnight.

SEPTEMBER 18 FRIDAY

Today was relatively easy, only an appointment with Dr. Schiff, my dentist.

SEPTEMBER 19 SATURDAY

Joan and I were on the dais at Turnberry this evening for the North Dade Forum's National Annual Awards Dinner. This year, Annie Ackerman and Marjorie Stoneman Douglas, a famous environmentalist, were being honored. Annie does not have much longer to live with her malignancy and Marjorie is 97 years old. Burton Young, President of the North Dade Forum, gave me an over-done introduction, mainly about the heart valve I smuggled into the Soviet Union and about Debra Benchoam whom I got out of an Argentine prison. I spoke briefly and then introduced Bill Nelson, giving him a big political plug to help with his campaign for governor in 1990, emphasizing that although his congressional district is less than nine percent Jewish, Bill voted to support Israel and against arms to Jordan and Saudi Arabia. I also praised his courage in joining the astronauts on the Columbia just ten days before the big Challenger explosion. This was a typical North Dade political occasion - lots of politicians and politicking.

SEPTEMBER 20 SUNDAY

Tomorrow our Transportation Subcommittee is holding hearings in Bill Gray's Philadelphia district at Temple University, and my flight to Philadelphia left today at 1:00 p.m. Airport officials and members from Gray's staff met me at the airport and escorted me to a special room for a quick briefing. Bob Carr (MI) had flown in from San Diego, and he was in the briefing room. The airport officials talked about the need for expanding the airport and for another runway, and then took us on a tour of the airport. We are staying at the Four Seasons Hotel, and Marty Fine from Miami was in Philadelphia and left word at the hotel for me to call him. Tom Kingfield and I met him for a drink at the Four Seasons bar and Philadelphia Eagles owner Norman Braman joined us for a short time. Marty spoke about having UMTA help Florida Power and Light with the Metro station that FP&L wants to build on its property in downtown Miami; he also mentioned the Metromover extensions. Our meeting with Marty had to be brief because we were joining the other members for dinner. He left, saying that he would see me tomorrow at the hearing. Temple University is Marty's alma mater. Tom and I then joined Bill Gray, Bob Carr, and several staffers at the Four Seasons dining room.

We had a good time talking politics. The Bill Gray/Sam Nunn presidential ticket was discussed. Gray had said that this was not a ticket because Nunn had too many "bad" votes to gain the Democratic nomination and said that Virginia Senator Charles Robb should be the next Democratic nominee. I assumed he favored a Robb/Gray ticket. Gray also spoke about his forthcoming campaign for Chairman of the Democratic Caucus when he is no longer Chairman of the Budget Committee. Mike Synar from Oklahoma and Mary Rose Oakar from Ohio are also running, but Gray mentioned that they did not have any real membership base. I suggested that he might have a problem jumping from a successful election to the House Budget Committee Chair and then running for the Democratic Caucus. Members who supported him for the House Budget Committee may feel that they had already paid their dues and may look at this as his being a bit power hungry and that some other Democratic members should have a chance for a prestigious House office. Gray, saying he realized this, asked what he should do. I advised him to build a base of supporters to draft him to run, and he agreed that this was a good way to proceed.

I was able to get more support this evening for the Tuesday meeting scheduled with Speaker Jim Wright to get him off his kick of taking the FAA trust fund off budget. If possible, we will try to prevent the Rules Committee making in order the amendment to take the FAA trust fund off budget. Too many members will vote for that amendment as a cure-all for the problems they have had with the airlines. The Rules Committee will probably not vote to make it in order because it doesn't want to see House Democrats fighting over jurisdiction. If we can neutralize the Speaker to not make this request to the Rules Committee, it will be a chance for us to pull out of confrontation with the Public Works Committee.

SEPTEMBER 21 MONDAY

At a breakfast meeting this morning with Philadelphia business leaders and transportation officials from the Philadelphia International Airport, problems regarding a runway extension were discussed. We also spent time on the difficulties surrounding the building of a new international terminal. Following the breakfast we went to the transportation field hearing at the Temple University auditorium. The hearing lasted until noon, establishing what we set out to do, which was to get on record the necessary team or group of officials to identify problems of the Southeastern Pennsylvania Transit Authority and its lack of safety precautions and high accident and injury rates.

Bill Gray, Bob Carr and I flew back to Washington in an Army helicopter - a really beautiful trip. Arriving at the Pentagon, Bob Carr used his portable phone to call the House Democratic Cloak Room and learned that a vote was in progress. He told them several members were coming in by van from the Pentagon and to hold the vote open till we got there in fifteen minutes. Calling again from the 14th Street Bridge, Bob was told only one minute remained but that the leadership would hold the vote open. That was the only vote today.

SEPTEMBER 22 TUESDAY

Representatives from the advisory council to CALTRAN, California Transportation, came in at 10:00 regarding the surface transportation re-authorization bill and its minority opportunity language which lumps women with Hispanics, blacks, and other minorities, and women want separate identity. It was an eight-member group, and I told them they had to first go back to the House Public Works Committee that wrote this crappy piece of legislation, and get it straightened out. Their fall-back position is to testify in 1988 before our subcommittee as outside witnesses. We can probably help them at that time, especially if they get "no objection" signoff from Norman Mineta and Glenn Anderson, Public Works subcommittee and committee chairmen.

I met at 11:00 with Bill Taylor and attorneys from the Florida Department of Transportation and representatives from the Interstate Commerce Commission. They were concerned about the transfer of $275 million of CSX right-of-way facilities between West Palm Beach and Homestead to Florida DOT. This transfer was to provide continuous right-of-way under the supervision of the State of Florida for not only the existing freight carriers but also for Amtrak over CSX tracks to help the new tri-rail commuter system to begin next year. I told all parties that my concern was that the Interstate Commerce Commission not throw a monkey wrench into this process, preventing the start of the new commuter rail, which would alleviate much of the congestion on I-95 from Palm Beach south into Miami. I think tri-rail will be a good operation because the State of Florida will own the right-of-way and CSX will have a contract to operate and manage.

At noon at a Democratic Congressional Arts Caucus luncheon featuring National Endowment for the Arts Chairman Frank Hodsoll, we discussed the future commitment of the Federal government to the general arts of this country, and how little the United States contributes to the arts on the federal level in comparison to Western European countries. Afterwards, I met with colleague Larry Smith; Edward Curran, Director of the FAA Office of Personnel and Technical Training; Virginia Krohn, Project Manager for the FAA Airway Science Program; and Tom Breslin from Florida International University, about a FAA airway science grant for Florida International University. When FIU first came to me I told them to see Larry Smith, as FIU is in his district. Larry was anxious to help but also angry that FIU did not come to him first, as most of Dade County has yet to realize that Larry is the West Dade Congressman. There are many institutions in Dade County trying for airway science grants. We have already provided grants to Florida Memorial College, Barry University, and also Miami-Dade Community College, and now I hear the University of Miami wants an airway science grant.

Jeffrey Miles, Chairman of the Federal Affairs Committee of the National Association of Life Underwriters, came in with Bill Flood, concerned about the Kennedy-Waxman bill mandating health care benefits. They want me to hold off support for this bill, and I assured them that I would not sign-on as cosponsor until I saw the final form the bill took and how it impacted on small businesses.

Charlotte Greenbarg of Miami came in next with members of the Dade County School Board and the Metro-Dade Engineering Department to meet with the Federal Highway Administrator, Ray Barnhart, regarding the Biscayne Boulevard, 203rd Street flyover. Charlotte, of course, is opposed to the overpass because it supposedly endangers the Highland Oaks school children, but I don't think that is the real problem. Where she gets all these ideas is puzzling to me, and she is always into some kind of community special interest group problem; that she is opposed to this project means nothing is going to get built on 203rd Street and Biscayne Boulevard for at least ten to twelve years. Her other ridiculous proposal is to have the Boulevard fly over 203rd Street, but that would not resolve the problem because the danger of the railroad crossing will remain. Barnhart was very polite but I do not think he is going to change the original Florida DOT plans. [Charlotte moved to north Florida but we still don't have the flyover.]

Jack Brooks of Texas, on the Floor, said to me that the Speaker clearly knows the right thing to do with the off budget problem, but he dearly loves the Public Works Committee on which he served for many years. I do not now know whether Wright will instruct the Rules Committee to make an in order amendment to take the FAA trust fund off budget or whether he will tell the Committee that he wants to be neutral and let Rules work its own will. The ball is really in Jim's court, and if he makes the amendment in order we will have to mobilize our people to defeat it on the Floor.

Speaking to Bill Grant, our new North Florida member, I told him not to bother coming to see me about a new highway demonstration project that he wants for his district. He asked, "Why?" and I showed him a letter that he had co-signed with Clay Shaw which implied that the airline crashes in Dallas and Detroit were caused by our subcommittee limiting money from the FAA trust fund. "You cannot ask me for things and then write something like this," I said. Grant was shocked. "That's not my signature," he said, "I never saw the letter." It was funny because earlier he had said he would be the last person to blame staff for anything and yet he now blames his staff. Clay Shaw had sent the letter to Grant's office, and a staff person had signed the letter because he thought it was what he was supposed to do. Now Grant has to apologize to me in writing, as well as study his position on taking the trust fund off budget, which is hard for him to do, being a member on the Public Works Committee; he is also a member on the Government Operations Committee which Jack Brooks chairs, and Jack is strongly opposed to taking the FAA trust fund off budget. So, on the one hand, Grant may be opposing Jim Howard, Chair of Public Works, but he may also be pleasing Jack Brooks, Chair of Government Operations.

In the evening I attended several receptions with Nancy Pollock who was in Washington to accompany me to the White House picnic, which was rained out today. Weather permitting, the picnic will be held tomorrow. At Alan Wheat's reception on New Jersey Avenue, we were treated to barbecue from one of Kansas City's famous restaurants. Leaving there, we went to the Longworth Building for Charlie Rose's (D-NC) reception for the Dalai Lama of Tibet. Nancy and I had our photo taken with the Dalai Lama, and I thought him a fascinating character. We then headed for a reception at the Florida House honoring Woody Kohrman and his wife Frances on their retirement from the General Telephone Company. Woody has been a loyal supporter in my fundraising efforts even though General Telephone does not serve my area but the west coast of Florida. It was the first time Nancy had been in the Florida House, and she got the opportunity to see many of the Florida members who were there.

Around 8:00 p.m., I held my nose and voted for legislation related to the Gramm-Rudman bill. When I asked Appropriations Chair Jamie Whitten how to vote from the standpoint of the Appropriations Committee, Jamie said the Committee needs all the friends it can get. But many Appropriations subcommittee chairmen did not vote for this conference report on the Gramm-Rudman budget extension because it also contained funding for the Contras in Nicaragua. However, Ways and Means Committee Chairman Dan Rostenkowski, who was managing this legislative conference report, went to bat for me yesterday on the FAA trust fund, and there was no way I was going to offend him after all he did for me on the off budget problem.

SEPTEMBER 23 WEDNESDAY

Gene Dubow of the American Jewish Committee is down from New York, and he, Adele and I met this morning for breakfast. Gene has recently returned from Germany and said that Rabbi Neuman is in very good shape, with a two-bedroom apartment, an automobile, a chauffeur, and a full-time maid and secretary. Everything seems to be working out, and I feel good knowing that we accomplished what we set out to do. There is still the possibility that I may visit East Germany during Hanukkah, the Feast of Lights. If so, I would hope to continue what we started regarding U.S. relations with East Germany, and to develop a working strategy to improve the trade situation between East Germany and the United States.

Tom Adams, Vice President of the Florida Institute of Technology, who had been Florida Secretary of State and Lieutenant Governor, was waiting for me in the office as I returned from the breakfast meeting. Tom is looking for federal airway science grants for his institution, but I could offer no encouragement because we are already over-committed in airway science funding for Florida universities. What I found interesting was his telling that he had a six-month-old baby boy and also a forty-seven-year-old daughter. The daughter was by his first wife.

Senior citizen members from my district are in Washington with Operation Close-Up. They came in at 10:00, and this was such a contrast from the high school students who usually are associated with Close-Up, but a good difference.

The word is now that Speaker Wright has asked the Rules Committee not to make in order the amendment to take the FAA trust fund off budget. At the White House Picnic this evening, I saw Butler Derrick of South Carolina, a member on the Rules Committee, and this also is his understanding of Wright's position. If this is true it is another victory for our subcommittee and peace for the House Democrats.

The picnic was interesting, although a smaller than usual crowd, with not quite as many celebrities. I did get to see Secretary of State Jim Baker again, and I spoke to Bill Miller, Chairman of the Office of Management and Budget, telling him how much I liked his editorial in the *Wall Street Journal*. Seeing Senator Dave Durenberger of Minnesota and his wife Penny, I wished them luck in the race against Humphrey. He is one of my favorite Republicans and Penny is a doll. Bill Grant was there and I told him I got his letter and that as far as I was concerned everything would be all right now in regard to taking care of his road project. It was a beautiful evening, with everyone in a good mood taking lots of photographs with the Reagan's.

SEPTEMBER 24 THURSDAY

Dr. Strong gave me a good health report at Memorial Sloan Kettering in New York this afternoon. He even used me as an example when describing to other physicians the operation he performed on me and how I accommodated and adjusted to a considerable handicap as a result of the operation. It was very flattering to be complimented on my health, particularly when Dr. Strong added that my recovery was due to my own motivation more than anything else.

In the evening I had a lot of fun taking my two grandsons, Bill's boys, to the Mets game at Shea Stadium, with seats right behind first base.

SEPTEMBER 25 FRIDAY

Still in New York City I met George Rogers and his wife, Debra Benchoam, for breakfast at the Regency Hotel where I was staying. Both are in school at Columbia University, and are still very much involved in South American human rights. Debra thinks she may later work with education for the handicapped instead of majoring in political affairs. At a nearby table, there was Bob Tisch, the Postmaster General, having breakfast with none other than Armando Codina of Miami. I told Tisch what a good job Woody Connors was doing as Miami Postmaster, and he said he would be seeing Woody in a few days in Miami and would share my comments with him. Codina told me that Vice President Bush had asked him if he wanted to be the new Secretary of Transportation to fill out the balance of Elizabeth Dole's term. (Elizabeth was leaving the Department of Transportation to take the top position with the American Red Cross.) Codina said that he would not be interested but he did not want me to tell anyone, and I didn't.

Lobbyist Liz Robbins had arranged a luncheon meeting for me at the offices of Goldman-Sachs, the investment banking firm on Wall Street. Goldman-Sachs does a lot of underwriting of bonds for airports and transportation systems, and I spent about two hours telling them about the airport trust fund on budget/off budget issue. Afterwards, Mike Stephens and I went to the Rockefeller University School of Medicine and met with Dr. Dennis Stark on the problems of animal experimentation. Rockefeller University is doing fewer animal experiments and more cell culture, *in vitro* instead of *in vita*. The fact that animals are so expensive and endangered, ultimately, will transform the overall mindset to the more preferable use of tissue culture, not only less expensive but also saving the use of many animals. Today we did see experiments still being done on mice, rats, rabbits, goats, and monkeys. Several years ago Mike and I visited the research department of Memorial Sloan Kettering after I had spent a month there as a patient. Now Mike is working with me to put together a newsletter on *in vitro* vs. *in vita*.

SEPTEMBER 26 SATURDAY

Back in Washington, at the Sheraton Hotel Tennis Club Bill Gray won in straight sets at tennis. We talked about his campaign for Chair of the Democratic Caucus, and I mentioned the *Wall Street Journal* article in Friday's paper on the surge of blacks toward leadership positions in the House, and Gray's statements regarding the increase in leverage that the Black Caucus has in the Congress. I told him that I thought it could adversely affect his candidacy because some members feel there are too many blacks in prominent House positions. Gray had not seen the article, but said he was interviewed for it about two weeks ago and now wishes he had not done the interview.

SEPTEMBER 27 SUNDAY

In addition to working for Babbitt in the Democratic Presidential Primary, and doing political counseling nationwide, Sergio Bendixen is now also doing the polling for the Miami mayoral race. This morning at breakfast we talked about Miami as well as national politics - good friends bumping ideas off each other.

At dinner Penny Farthing of Patton, Boggs and Blow, was doing a good job of lobbying me to support her efforts in the merger of US Air and Piedmont Airlines. I do not want to get involved but she asked if I could write or give a call to the Deputy Administrator for the FAA in the Secretary's Office. I will talk to Chairman John Dingell and Norman Mineta before I speak to the Administrator, Matt Cicosi. This is a touchy and sensitive matter, and I think one of the reasons DOT turned down this merger was because of expanding US Air, and probably also because DOT is being criticized for the mergers it has already permitted.

SEPTEMBER 28 MONDAY

Don Edwards, Bob Kastenmeier, Tom Kingfield and I had a good game of tennis this morning. It seems the word is out that Pat Schroeder is going to announce her departure from the Democratic primaries.

In the afternoon I met with Mike Stephens, Nadine and John from my staff, to go over the theme I had developed for our newsletter on the use of *in vitro* vs. *in vita* (test tube vs. live animal experimentation in labs). It will take another several weeks to produce the newsletter, which will also include a visit to the University of Miami School of Medicine for a South Florida relevancy viewpoint.

SEPTEMBER 29 TUESDAY

9:00 a.m., I was at the Capitol South Metro Station for a taping Sèlkirk Communications wanted to do on me as Chairman of Appropriations Transportation Subcommittee. I was photographed exiting the train, taking the escalator, and then going to my office, where we talked about my responsibilities as a subcommittee chairman. The taping will be shown on television stations in Miami and possibly in the Dade public school system. The young lady who directed the shot was Jennifer Shaw, the very able, professional and attractive young daughter of good friends Emilie and Clay Shaw, the Republican member from Ft. Lauderdale.

Today's *Washington Post* featured the letter Larry Coughlin and I sent to the *Post* on the need to keep the FAA trust fund on budget. As far as the media is concerned we are beginning to reverse their idea of releasing trust fund money as a way of solving the problems in the airway system.

Again, Frank Hodsoll, Chairman of the National Endowment for the Arts, is at our Congressional Arts Caucus luncheon. Today, most of the conversation centered on the need for private support for the arts and how we need tax changes to encourage more creativity and generosity. Arts Caucus Chairman Bob Carr hosted the meeting, and I went primarily in deference to Carr.

I do not have to appear in opposition before the Rules Committee at 2:00, as the Committee is not going to grant a rule making an in order amendment to take the FAA trust fund off budget. We now have to work to pass this rule on the House Floor, as I assume that those who wanted to make an in order amendment to take the trust fund off budget will now make an effort to defeat this rule. So, tomorrow we will have to man the Floor ever vigilantly to object if anyone makes a unanimous consent request for an in order, off budget amendment. A *Congressional Quarterly* reporter interviewed me at length about my role in changing the Speaker's position on this matter, and the story will appear in the next issue of CQ; I hope I didn't talk too much.

A number of people on the Floor complimented me on the *Washington Post* article which Larry Coughlin and I coauthored. That piece plus the *Post* editorial were very helpful in solidifying our position with the Rules Committee.

Back at the office Dr. Rosa Castro Feinberg, Dade County School Board member, made a courtesy visit, but she also asked for help on the proposed Ways and Means legislation that adversely affects the school board's bonding capabilities. My 3:00 appointment soon arrived, Olympian Bob Beamon, a resident of my district. Beamon is the [now former] long jump world record holder and an Olympic Spirit Award winner. I thought him a very fine man, a true Olympic hero, doing good works for the handicapped. Of course, a photo was taken.

In the evening at a reception for Senator Frank Lautenberg, hosted by Patton, Boggs and Blow on the second floor of my townhouse, Frank told me he had just marked up the Senate version of the Appropriations Transportation Subcommittee bill. We discussed the two-hour flight non-smoking rule be put in his markup, subject to a three-year time limitation, with funds earmarked for a feasibility study. Lautenberg moaned about the problems he anticipates on the Senate Floor because of the tobacco senators from Kentucky and the Carolinas. Apparently, he will have a tough race against Pete Dawkins, a Republican Rhodes Scholar and a West Point football hero, and he also is in the middle of a divorce. I had written Frank a condolence letter this week when learning of his mother's death.

SEPTEMBER 30 WEDNESDAY

A press conference was held this morning with the four originators of the Adoption Bill - Senator Orrin Hatch (R-UT), and members Pat Schroeder (D-CO), Frank Wolf (R-VA), and myself. Media was there from each of our areas, with Channel 7 in Miami covering my speech, while I held in my arms Alana, the daughter Adele Liskov adopted from Guatemala. Questions were put to Senator Hatch regarding Judge Bork's confirmation. Hatch is a member on the Senate Judiciary Committee. Pat Schroeder had to deal with questions regarding her recent announcement that she would not seek the Democratic nomination for president. I did say in my statement to watch out for Pat in 1992. I think the Adoption Bill is very worthwhile, placing tax benefits to those who adopt children on a more equal scale as families with natural born children.

At 11:00, Lucy and I met with Dr. Piedad Robertson, Vice President of Miami-Dade Community College, and spent about an hour discussing MDCC's joint pilot training venture with Eastern Airlines. The program offers not only pilot aviation training but also training in aviation industry support services, i.e., air traffic controllers, mechanics, etc. Her idea was that MDCC would be the umbrella for Florida Memorial and Barry University's aviation science programs for which funds have already been appropriated by our subcommittee, and schools such as Florida Institute of Technology in Melbourne and Embry-Riddle University in Daytona which had put in requests for funds. We suggested that she meet with Senator Lautenberg to have her requests included in the Senate version because our House bill had already been voted out and the only thing we can do is agree to whatever they put into the Senate bill. MDCC does not want funding this year, but they do want report language in this year's bill that will facilitate funding in future years. I also suggested that she include more institutions outside of Florida to get more broad base support.

Lucy continued the meeting with Dr. Robertson while I left to attend the farewell reception Bob Michel (R-IL) was hosting in the Capitol for Transportation Secretary Elizabeth Dole.

We took a whipping on the Floor today on the rule preventing an in order amendment to take the trust fund off budget. With only 180 votes, we lost the rule by about thirty votes. I made a speech in favor of the rule, but it didn't help. The Rules Committee is going to do a new rule to also make in order an amendment on the Floor to take the aviation trust fund off budget, and of course we will try to defeat the amendment. But this may be easier than trying to defeat the rule, as it will be a different kind of vote.

The primary reason we lost the rule is because Republicans voted three to one against; we also lost because we needed Jack Brooks, Chairman of Government Operations and Dan Rostenkowski, Chairman of Ways and Means, to speak favorably of the rule, and they were not on the Floor. Bob Carr, our main aviation person on the transportation subcommittee, also was not on the Floor; but all three will be there tomorrow.

At a reception this evening honoring Tony Coehlo (D-CA), our Democratic Whip, I saw Dan Rostenkowski who said he would speak against the amendment tomorrow and would turn around his Ways and Means Committee members who had voted the wrong way. With hard work I think we have a shot.

Later at La Brasserie, Sue Perry and Jim Howard were there and asked if I would like to join them. I was alone, but I said "No." Jim Howard led the opposition to defeat the rule yesterday, and won. I was still feeling a little miffed. A few minutes later the two of them joined me for coffee and Howard could not have been more gracious, saying that he was surprised about winning and thought he would lose by about a hundred votes. He also said a number of things were in his favor, namely that the Republicans automatically vote against a closed rule, and even that members on the Agriculture Committee mad at Dingell, for some reason thought that this rule was something Dingell wanted and they were out to get even with him for stopping the Agriculture Farm Credit Bill until it had been referred to Dingell's committee.

Today in the gym there was much talk about how the Dukakis people had sent the incriminating tapes of Senator Joseph Biden of Delaware to the media. It seems that Biden plagiarized language from a British politician's speech, and the proof was in the tapes. I saw Biden in the elevator this morning and he looked happy to be out of the primary. There are also lots of jokes now about Dukakis, and as Bob Mrazak said, "Here's a guy whose wife has been on amphetamines for eighteen years, and he didn't know it! What kind of person is he?" I thought of this because Lany Narot called me today to remind me that several weeks ago I had told her when Biden got in trouble that Dukakis would be next. She was sort of amused that the way I called it was the way it turned out. Lany is a real political junkie.

Chapter 10

OCTOBER 1, 1987 - THURSDAY

A strategy meeting was held this morning in my office with transportation subcommittee members and staff on how to defeat the amendment to take the FAA trust fund off budget. The amendment comes to the Floor this afternoon. Most subcommittee members were present, along with Buddy MacKay from the Budget Committee who offered to help. Afterwards, I headed for the Longworth Building for a meeting with Allan McArtor, the new FAA Administrator and his staff. I tried explaining to McArtor the adverse effects of taking the FAA trust fund off budget, but he does not understand or maybe does not want to, and thinks that taking the trust fund off budget would be beneficial to aviation. It is rather amazing that the administrator does not comprehend the full effect of sequestration on the FAA, which will happen when the trust fund is taken off budget.

The vote on the amendment is now over. We won, defeating the amendment 202 to 197, but it took a lot of work. I did not speak during the debate, but managed the opposition's Floor time and debate, and set the minutes for each of the members I wanted to speak against the amendment. Butler Derrick from Rules was a help, as was Dan Rostenkowski, Chair of Ways and Means. I was also able to get Bob Carr, aviation expert on our subcommittee and Jack Brooks, Chairman of the Government Operations Committee to speak. Those in our morning strategy meeting were able to turn a lot of people around that had voted against us yesterday on the rule, like Gerry Studds of Massachusetts whom we threatened by telling him we would eliminate funding for a radar tower at Nantucket Airport. He did not like the idea of a threat, but did vote "no" on the Howard amendment.

The vote was very close right up to the last minute. Jamie Whitten came up to me and said, "Boy, it is close." "What do you think I should do?" I asked. "Cross your fingers and hold your left nut," he said. I did, and we won. A great team effort of Buddy MacKay, Bill Gray, Budget and Ways and Means committee members all came together with Appropriations members who had worked very hard getting other members turned around to vote our way.

A number of members such as Sonny Montgomery, Jim Scheuer, Mickey Leland, and Sam Gejdenson among others asked me for direction on how to vote, and in the end those members voted the way I recommended even though they did not quite understand the issue.

Other members such as Pat Schroeder should have voted with us, and next time when she asks for Colorado transportation money we will remind her of her vote. Nonetheless, it was a good win for Appropriations and afterwards we celebrated in the committee room with Larry Coughlin, Marty Sabo, Bob Carr, and Silvio Conte. Afterwards, I went to the gym and then headed for the airport. Although successful, it was a very tiresome day and fortunately the plane left on time, arriving in Miami at 10:30. [Later when I retired, subcommittee staff said that what happened today was my best accomplishment during my tenure as chairman.]

OCTOBER 2 FRIDAY

At the district office this morning Arthur Pravda, a Biscayne Park neighbor, had a problem with Social Security. Apparently they thought Pravda had been working at his place of business even after retirement, which negates social security benefits, if true. After making a call to the claims office in New York, I directed our district office caseworker to follow through with a letter. I left the office and headed downtown to the New Horizons Mental Health Center where Rhonda Nixon presented me with an appreciation plaque for my support of their efforts to get the homeless and destitute off the streets.

Noon at the Miami Club, Maria Elena Torano hosted the luncheon for me with the Cuban-American leadership. I spoke of my role as transportation appropriations subcommittee chairman, and how this position had enabled me to help their families and community, and what I hoped to do for them in the future. The group addressed their frustrations and concerns that I, as their congressman, did not vote the way they wanted on aid to the Contras; but it was a more pleasant exchange than I anticipated, with no cross words, though this is a very emotional and volatile issue for them. I think we all realize the importance of working together especially in addressing the economic needs of our community, and I felt very encouraged by the reception I received.

Joan and I attended the Temple Israel Yom Kippur services this evening at the Dade County Auditorium, and I was invited to sit on the pulpit with past presidents and officials of the temple. The young Rabbi Rex Perlmeter spoke kindly of me, saying that it was a privilege to have me there and spoke of my work with inner-city projects and the homeless. He overrated my role in initiating legislation for the homeless, but it was a nice gesture and it was good to see old friends again.

OCTOBER 3 SATURDAY

Yom Kippur

OCTOBER 4 SUNDAY

This afternoon I went to the Blue Grass Festival hosted by the Ives Dairy Optimist Club and saw many of my old used car customers. The bandleader acknowledged my presence and said it was my birthday tomorrow, so I had many people coming up to wish me well. Mostly rednecks, they are the ones who sustained me in business for many years, and they are also the only group that I have been around still smoking cigarettes. It was like being back in the 1950's.

Afterwards, I went to the Jade Winds condo's ceremony and downshifted from the Blue Grass Festival to this entirely different group of primarily Jewish senior citizens. Hermione Spahn introduced me and Rabbi Simcha Friedman of Temple Adath Yeshum in North Miami Beach presided. The ceremony was in recognition of their successful fundraising drive for the third Mogen David Ambulance, a Hebrew Red Cross ambulance for Israel, and I congratulated them for the fine works they provide not only to Israel but to our Dade County community.

OCTOBER 5 MONDAY

At 10:00 a.m., I was in a meeting with airport director Dick Judy, civic leader Eli Feinberg, Metro Commissioner Clara Oesterle, Tex Gunnels of the Treasury and Post Office Subcommittee staff who had flown down for the meeting, and the Director of Miami's Customs Office regarding language in the Treasury Post Office appropriations bill which says that the Customs Office has to place the necessary number of customs agents at Tamiami Airport in South Dade to accommodate international flights coming in from the Caribbean and other areas. We reasoned that this action would redirect the number of overseas flights from Miami International Airport to Tamiami. This can work, but it will probably take a few months because the bill has not yet been enacted into law.

Following the meeting I caught the 11:15 flight to Washington where I will celebrate my 74th birthday today, October 5. The Washington staff has put together a celebration with three cakes - one from Amory Underhill of the

Florida Citrus Growers, another from Sears and Roebuck, and one from Operation Close-Up, which we will send to the House of Ruth, a Washington women's shelter. I received many cards and well wishes and later celebrated with Susan Perry from the American Bus Association, who took me to dinner at a nice restaurant on Connecticut Avenue. Afterwards, at a Patton, Boggs and Blow fundraiser reception for Montana Senator John Melcher held in the apartment above my townhouse, the jokes were all about problems of the Democratic presidential candidates. Tom Boggs mentioned that he was fundraising for Bob Dole and that for the first time he had very little trouble receiving contributions because agriculture is so supportive of Dole. He then said that Dole would not make a bad president, which is an unusual statement for Tom to make about a Republican, so maybe that tells us something.

OCTOBER 6 TUESDAY

This was a busy day, starting at 10:00 with Robert Strausz-Hupe, our 84 year old Ambassador to Turkey, who was accompanied by Townsend Friedman, whom I knew as political attache from the Embassy in Buenos Aires, and who was a big help in getting Debra Benchoam out of prison there. Townsend is now on the Turkish desk in the State Department. The two talked about problems providing sufficient funds to Turkey without putting prohibitions on the use of Turkish arms in Cyprus. I tend to sympathize with the Turks, as the problems in Cyprus were really initiated by the Greek junta who tried annexing Cyprus to Greece for their own expansion of power. The annexation did not work and I think the Cypriot Turks eventually would have been massacred if not for the Turkish Army which invaded Cyprus.

Townsend took Debra's phone number at Columbia University and said he would try to help her find a job in New York. Debra had called me last evening saying what a tough time she was having finding a job. She is on her own now in New York, a completely different world, and I think she is finally beginning to realize how difficult it can be in the United States without the connections or support system that she had in Washington with me and our staff.

My next appointment at 11:00 was with Charles Skinner, Wayne Merry's replacement on the German Democratic Republican desk at the State Department. (Wayne has been assigned to the U.S. Embassy in South Africa.) Skinner briefed me on matters in East Germany since my visit, and showed me a copy of Rabbi Neuman's cable from Germany which said that I was responsible for his being in East Germany in his present Rabbinical position, and that without me none of this would have taken place. Skinner also had German newspaper articles, all brimming with pictures and stories on the Rabbi's activities in East Germany.

He then told me that a congressional delegation was going to East Germany this weekend, and the information both gladdened and surprised me. Skinner said that Steny Hoyer, head of the Congressional Helsinki Commission, was taking a delegation to Geneva and then to Berlin and would be meeting with Rabbi Neuman and Klaus Gysi. I got busy trying to put together an itinerary to join this codel and wanted Terry Peel to join me, but Terry, who did want to go back, had some family conflicts. I had promised to return to East Germany when the Rabbi was installed and the opportunity is now perfect, as we are going into the Columbus Day weekend recess. I spoke with Joan and she did not mind if I went. The trip will be arduous for me, but I am sure the Helsinki staff will call Terry in the morning to see if he will go, and if he goes I go. I would like to get this trip over with, and although it is a hurry-up deal it will accomplish what I promised the Rabbi and Klaus Gysi before I left Germany. We will see what happens tomorrow.

After today's Congressional Automotive Caucus luncheon with guest speaker Robert Stempel, the new President of General Motors, I asked Stempel about minority black dealerships for South Florida and he said he would look into this. The Vice President of Pontiac was also at the luncheon, and I told him about the problems of "Firebird" dropouts in Dade County. As mentioned, the Firebird was one of the reasons the Dade County School Superintendent gave for the dropout rate as this particular automobile is a status symbol for male teenagers who drop out to work to afford this car.

Following the luncheon, I went to Matt McHugh's office to meet the President of Mozambique, who had with him the one Portuguese in his government left over from the Portuguese colony. The president, a very charismatic black leader, told of problems associated with Mozambique being caught between the two super powers and the threat of South Africa. Joan designs jewelry from semiprecious stones and has quite a collection from the overseas trips we have taken. I told the Mozambique president of Joan's interest in stones and of my hope to someday visit his country. He said he welcomed our coming and then proceeded to name for me the many precious and semiprecious stones indigenous to his country.

2:00, Jamie Whitten had all the Appropriations subcommittee chairmen in his office to discuss the next direction Appropriations should take. We just bounced ideas off each other, no real decisions. Dave Obey got everyone's attention and said that all the members should be grateful for the battle I waged and won in behalf of the appropriations process to keep the FAA trust fund on budget. I thought it grand of Dave to do this, and I thanked him.

Because of the meeting, I missed my 2:30 appointment with Peggy Hallock and Patty Pavelka of North Miami regarding the polygraph bill. I am opposed to polygraphing employees or potential employees because I do not think it works, and this basically is what I would have told them. At 3:00, Jim Wilding and Greg Wolfe from the Washington Metropolitan Area Airport Authority came in to give me a status report. Afterwards Kathleen L'Eculse from the California Vacaville paper interviewed me for an in-depth report her paper had sent her to Washington to do on Vic Fazio of California. Fazio is not only a friend, but a fine member and I gave her a highly complimentary profile on him.

Late afternoon I was lobbied on an amendment to take the airline flight scheduling advertising control from Jim Howard's Public Works Committee and put it with the Consumer Protection Agency under John Dingell's Commerce Committee. The amendment will be on the House Floor tomorrow, and although this removes some jurisdiction from my transportation appropriations I will support John Dingell and his committee since I cannot or will not support Jim Howard and Norman Mineta who have opposed our transportation subcommittee on every possible issue. In the House you have to stick with people who help and support you. Speaking to Steny Hoyer on the Floor, I told him I did want to go on the overseas trip, but that I was still having a problem getting a staff person that would be of help to me on the codel.

In the evening at a private showing of the 1988 General Motors cars and trucks at the Hyatt Regency, I had a photo opportunity with Roger Smith and Bob Stempel standing alongside Buick's new hot car, the "Regal." The food was a big disappointment, junk food and hot dogs, so unusually cheap for a GM event.

OCTOBER 7 WEDNESDAY

Dan Mica was honored this morning at the National Democratic Club. Terry Peel was there and finalized that we were not going to Germany tomorrow. Terry could not go, and I did not want to go without him.

10:00, Jayne Hart, Assistant Director for Congressional Relations for the American Medical Association, came to see me about Senate legislation encouraging the Feds to do something to contain the medical liability problem. She wanted me to cosponsor the legislation but the only Florida members to cosponsor were a couple of Republicans. I told her I would sign-on as a cosponsor if she could get several other Florida Democrats to do so, as changes are needed.

Leonard Levine, Minnesota Commissioner of Transportation, was my next appointment at 11:00, coming in with six other officials and business leaders from the Minnesota aviation community concerned with private sector aviation in Minnesota and the FAA reauthorization legislation on air traffic space. It seems Minnesotans fly a lot of antique, small planes that are incompatible with the modernized electronic systems. I informed the group that I would try to work out a compromise that would not impact adversely on their small planes and at the same time maintain the level of safety in air traffic control space. The Minnesota

Commissioner has friends in Miami and is a good Democrat.

Around noon Dr. Irene Runge came in. Dr. Runge, the Jewish community leader in the German Democratic Republic, is an associate professor in the history department at East Berlin's Humboldt University. She is in Washington as a representative of the East German Jewish community and as Goodwill Ambassador from East Germany to the United States. I met Dr. Runge during my visit to East Germany, and I thought then as I do now that she is unusual in that she is a German whose family migrated to America before WWII and became part of a New York Communist group that became active during the pre-war years in New York. After the war the Runge's were true believers in Communism so they migrated back to Germany and became part of the East German Communist Party. Besides being Jewish, she is a devout Communist. I would like her to come to Miami and meet with the Miami Jewish Committee and *Miami Herald* publisher Dick Capen, who was recently in East Germany. A press interview could be scheduled so that Irene could give a personal and close-up perspective on how well Rabbi Neuman is accepted in East Germany. I understand the East German Jewish community has already changed and so much has been accomplished since the arrival of Rabbi Neuman, even unprofessed Jews are now coming out and becoming active in the Jewish community.

2:00, Steve Rosenfeld with Governor Dukakis's presidential campaign in Florida came in seeking information on the nature and makeup of my congressional district. It seems Dukakis is still in the race though he has gotten his problemsome lumps from the ordeal surrounding the Biden tapes that his staff sent to the press. Apparently Dukakis survived the episode, at least for now. Just off the House Floor, I had a long conversation with *Miami News* reporter Joyce Jordan, who is doing a story on the Metromover extensions. My aim in speaking to her was to place the responsibility for funding the Metromover extensions on the need for a local dedicated source of revenue, which comes before the federal commitment to fund the two extensions on the Metromover. Hopefully I succeeded in putting this prerequisite back on the Metro-Dade Commission where it belongs.

I decided to cosponsor the TV-Marti bill, which is probably the first thing I have done in a long time to please the Cuban community in Miami. The big Floor vote today was to take the publishing control for the airline flight scheduling from DOT and put it under the Consumer Protection Agency, which moves it out of Jim Howard's committee jurisdiction to John Dingell's committee jurisdiction. This was a jurisdictional effort by Dingell for the protection of consumers. My own self-interest would have been to keep airline flight scheduling in DOT where I would have control over the appropriations part, but this case was different in that I had personally vowed to support Dingell who had supported me on the trust fund in opposition to Jim Howard. Personal relationships are important and most of the members on my subcommittee like Sabo and Coughlin also voted for Dingell's position out of loyalty to members on that committee who stayed with us in our jurisdictional battle with Howard on the FAA trust fund. Also a factor, but of less consideration in my decision, was the fact that I had written to Bob Butterworth, Florida's Attorney General, stating that I would support the consumer protection amendment in Dingell's legislation.

OCTOBER 8 THURSDAY

10:00 a.m., Sandy Murdock of the Heron, Burchette law firm; Bob Lambert, President of Aviall; and Bob Clark from Ryder Systems, Inc., came in regarding Caledonia Air, one of Aviall's companies that reconditions and overhauls airplane parts in Prestwick, Scotland. They were concerned with Ryder's exemption to continue overhauling engines of American airplanes offshore in Scotland. The problem with this was that I wanted assurance that the FAA had direct oversight responsibility so that the repair standards in Scotland would be on par with those in the United States. I assume the standards would be equal or better, but I do not want to set a precedent for opening overseas overhaul facilities in countries that do not have the kind of aircraft maintenance standards that we have in the United States.

11:00, Robbie Depietro and his group from the Dade Heritage Trust in Miami came to ask for my help with the

Appropriations Subcommittee on Interior for federal funding of historic preservation, especially in Miami. They are trying to preserve and maintain sites in Dade County such as Greynolds Park and the old Spanish Monastery. It was a very friendly meeting and we had a photo taken which will most likely appear in a Dade newspaper. It certainly will be in the *Miami Historic Magazine*.

I played tennis with buddies Don Edwards, Bob Kastenmeier and Sonny Montgomery at Haines Point, and it was a lot of fun even though I lost. It struck me as funny that I have a bad toe, Kastenmeier has a bad shoulder, Edwards has bad eyes and Sonny has a bad knee. We are a physical bunch of old wrecks, but we have a good time. Later, I stopped by the Capitol Physician's Office to have my toe examined and saw Tom Downey of New York who told me he had government officials from India in Room H131 and "I need some members and I can't find any. It's embarrassing." I guess he expected us to be in session today at 1:30 p.m., and we are not. Downey asked if I would come and I told him I did not even have a coat with me, and he said, "It's okay, just go there." Tom did a good job of rounding up other members, and we sat listening to the Indian Parliament leaders talk about nuclear weapons problems in Pakistan. Edie Wilkie from the World Peace Committee was there and we wished each other a happy birthday, as we were both born on October 5.

4:40, I was on a flight back to Miami. On arrival I saw a television crew stopping people and asking, I was sure, if they knew someone who had been on the plane. Curious, I asked one of the television crew whom they were looking for and the reply was "Congressman Lehman." (I might have been more readily recognizable had I been wearing a coat and tie.) "I'm Congressman Lehman," I said, and the reporters began to interview me about the loss of American helicopters in the Persian Gulf and my opinion on American forces there. "We should not be there," I said, "and the War Powers Act should be invoked to get the American troops out, because their presence there was only to protect the flow of oil to Japan and Western Europe."

OCTOBER 9 FRIDAY

Today was fairly easy at the district office. In the morning Adele Acosta and her mother, on their way to physical therapy, paid me a courtesy visit. Adele is nearly thirty years of age, and when she was about five I sponsored her at the Montenarri School for the Handicapped. She was born prematurely and partially blinded by the use of oxygen therapy, a once medically acceptable treatment before doctors realized oxygen could be harmful to premature infants. Although Adele has about 30 percent vision, she did drive but was in a really serious accident, and she now uses a walker. As Adele spoke, I noticed that something seemed strange with her eyes. I called my ophthalmologist, Dr. Henry Clayman, who said to send her over. I gave her $25 and instructions to Dr. Clayman's office and they left. Henry later called saying I had sent him a very bizarre patient as he had never seen anyone with such high glaucoma - 58, when the norm is about 15. What surprised him was that she did not have any pain even though she must have had this high pressure for a while. With a laser he punched holes to relieve the pressure and next week he will surgically remove the cataracts and begin treating her glaucoma. He also said that if Adele had not received prompt treatment, she would have been totally blind in a few days. I was amazed at my sensing something was wrong, having no knowledge about the eyes; but more than that, I was elated to have done something about it by calling Dr. Clayman.

OCTOBER 10 SATURDAY

I met my son Tom for lunch, and he is thinking about a career change, and perhaps he will join a large law firm instead of being on his own. The career move sounded prudent, and I so advised him. Ultimately, the decision is his to make.

Before leaving Washington, I had arranged for Dr. Runge to visit Miami as one of her U.S. stops. I met her at the Miami airport this afternoon and took her to my home in Biscayne Park. She liked the heat, the warm weather and the very green foliage in South Florida. We went to the *Miami*

Herald for our meeting with Richard Wallace on the editorial staff. Irene proved to be a good interviewee, and both she and Wallace were excellent in their one-on-one exchange. When Wallace asked Irene about my role in getting the Rabbi to East Germany, I left the room as I was feeling a little uncomfortable. I didn't go far, because Wallace was also to direct questions to me on how I became involved.

For dinner Joan, Irene and I met David Fleeman at Joe's Stone Crab restaurant in South Beach. Dave is a former president of the American Jewish Committee who helped sponsor the Rabbi in East Germany. Joan's friend Peggy Gordon also joined us. After dinner we all went to the home of Mike and Jo Ann Bander who gave a dessert party in Irene's honor. Mike, who is an immigration lawyer and activist in the American Jewish Committee, wanted Irene to meet members of the Miami AJC, and they were there waiting for us when we arrived.

OCTOBER 11 SUNDAY

It was an easy day today, no political events.

OCTOBER 13 TUESDAY

Back in Washington.

At 10:00 this morning, I met with Robert Parkins, City Manager of Miami Beach; Arnold Weiner, City Attorney; and Miami Beach lobbyist, Sylvester Lukis, regarding a light rail system for Miami Beach. When they left, the staff had me call the Miami *Jewish Tribune* regarding my position on the sale of arms to Saudi Arabia. After the call, the staff advised me that I needed to be more emphatically opposed than I sounded, because I have always opposed arms sales and believe it is in the best interest of our country to terminate this policy.

In the afternoon it was tennis with my friends Bob Kastenmeier and Judge Mikva, and then a relaxing evening with Kay Beale from Dr. Ommayo's medical staff, at the New York State Festival held at the Washington Hilton.

OCTOBER 14 WEDNESDAY

This morning Jorge Mas, Miami's number one anti-Castro Cuban American, and other Cuban American business leaders stopped by to thank me for cosponsoring TV Marti. My vote on this legislation has helped enormously in bridging the gap between me and the Cuban American community. At 11:00, John Lindstrom and members of the Miami Plumbers Local Union #519 came in to ask for my help on the coal slurry pipeline legislation. I was not ready to cosponsor this legislation, and told them that I would get back to them as the issue got closer to Floor action.

During lunch, most of the staff and I watched the tape that Dr. Runge had brought from East Germany on the Jewish holy days at synagogue services with the new Rabbi. It was quite fascinating and very moving.

At the Rachel Carson *Silent Spring's* reception this evening in honor of Joan Claybrook, the former Administrator of the National Highway Traffic Safety Administration, Joan made some very kind remarks about me to her colleagues there, especially mentioning my efforts on highway safety. It was a good gathering and I was very flattered, but I did not stay long, leaving soon after thanking Joan and purchasing Rachel Carson's book, *Silent Spring*, twenty-fifth edition.

OCTOBER 15 THURSDAY

Haitian leaders Gerard Georges, Katline Moise, Yves Auguste, and Carl Auguste came in at 9:00 this morning about the current political situation and problems in Haiti. The group spoke about the widespread human rights abuses and of an increase in government repression. They all seemed to have incidents to relate on how bad conditions were in Haiti. As a member on the Foreign Ops Subcommittee, I was fully aware of the atrocities. John tells me that Paul Anderson of the *Miami Herald* wants to interview me on the Haitian situation.

In our newsletter, I hope to include a section on infectious waste being dumped into the ocean by various hospitals. Articles have been written on toxic waste but none on infectious waste. Also interesting are Lee Hamilton's statements in the *Congressional Record* on the Social Security Trust Fund and what will happen when the baby boomers come on board in another ten or twenty years. Lee thinks it would be best to invest the social security funds in private enterprise and not U.S. Treasury bonds.

At 3:00, Drs. Jeff Raskin and Joseph Harris from the Florida Society of Internal Medicine came in regarding Medicare's unfair payment guidelines for internal medical diagnostic procedures. Doctors can only spend fifteen minutes with a patient, according to what Medicare allows as maximum charges, which is an insufficient amount of time for an internal diagnosis and is unfair to the patient. I let them know I would help when the bill comes to the Floor, and that I would check with Pete Stark, Chairman of the Health, Ways and Means Subcommittee, to find out if there is any way he can solve the problem.

I have spoken to both Neal Smith and Charlie Wilson about congressional delegation trips in November and December, but now I hear that all Air Force planes will be needed to shuttle Soviets back and forth for Gorbachev's visit to the United States.

Chrysler Corporation lobbyist Bob Griffin called wanting to do something about minority dealership opportunities, as I had spoken to him sometime ago about Jack Moore. The problem now is that Jack was fired a couple of days ago, which is sort of embarrassing. Bill does, however, have other minority employees in his organization for whom he wants to pursue dealership opportunities.

OCTOBER 16 FRIDAY

This evening I had dinner and talked politics with my cousins the Leva's. Marx was disappointed in his friend, Senator Howell Heflin of Alabama, for being such a buffoon in the whole Judge Thomas confirmation hearing.

OCTOBER 17 SATURDAY

Lobbyist friend Priscilla Perry and I joined Charlie

Wilson of Texas and his lady friend to see the New York City Ballet at the Kennedy Center this evening. Charlie is a member on the Kennedy Center Board, appointed by former Speaker Tip O'Neill, and has his own designated box right next to the President's box. Throughout the evening we talked politics and Charlie, I learned, is backing Richard Gephardt in the Democratic Primary.

OCTOBER 18 SUNDAY

At brunch today with former staffer Sergio Bendixen, we discussed the polling he is doing for Miami's Mayoral race. Sergio is also involved in the Venezuela presidential election.

OCTOBER 19 MONDAY

11:00 a.m., I interviewed with Miami's Channel 7 on the Persian Gulf, and was steadfast to my convictions that "the United States should not be there, and we should get out now."

My good friend Gardnar Mulloy, who was once on the tennis circuit and who is still well known and respected around the tennis world, called to inform me that he would soon be coming to Washington for a charity tennis tournament. Gardnar now heads the Racquet Club's tennis division on Fisher Island in Miami.

Bill Grant's fundraiser was held this evening at his home on New Jersey Avenue, where the talk was all about the stock market crash of 500 points. I enjoyed the event, a good ending to a quiet, relaxing day.

OCTOBER 20 TUESDAY

10:00 a.m., I had an appointment with some of Miami's black leadership, and was expecting Rev. Thedford Johnson, Pastor of the Baptist Church on Biscayne Boulevard where I have spoken on Saturday mornings before their Ministers' and Laymen's Political Action Group; T. Willard Fair, President of the Miami-Dade Urban League; State Representative Willie Logan from Opa Locka; and the Rev. Maurice Dawkins. They had asked to meet with me about peace and democracy in Angola, but they never showed or called.

10:45, Mickey Leland of Texas; John King, Chairman of Houston Transit; and lobbyist Sylvia DeLeon from the Bob Straus law firm came in attempting to work out a full-funding contract for the $2 billion federal share for Houston's proposed rapid mass transit system. I told them to start getting in line for the funds our subcommittee will be appropriating next year, and that the First Funding request should start small but hopefully grow in the out years. I suggested that they have subcommittee member Tom Delay invite our subcommittee to Houston.

Our office is working up a public relations story on Adele Acosta, giving credit to Dr. Clayman and to Sister Margaret of St. Francis Hospital, who has agreed to dispense with all hospital charges when Dr. Clayman performs the operation on Adele to remove the cataracts. The laser process relieving the pressure in Adele's eyes from the glaucoma is complete, and in several weeks Dr. Clayman will remove the cataracts.

2:00, the full Appropriations Committee met and passed the Rural Development, Agriculture, and Related Agencies Appropriations Bill. I just sat and read my newspapers while members offered amendments to report language. Agriculture jurisdiction except for food stamps, does not affect my district and I just stick with the agriculture subcommittee position.

On the House Floor today we voted on an amendment prohibiting the use of educational material for AIDS prevention in any manner that instructs homosexuals on safe sex. I think I was the only Florida member to vote against the amendment. I also voted against the amendment prohibiting Soviet occupation of the new Embassy in Washington, and against the amendment on sanctions against New Zealand for noncooperation with our nuclear arms programs by disallowing nuclear carriers into their waters. We had only the three votes today, and I voted against all three.

Solcoor, Inc., honored Bill Brock, U.S. Secretary of Labor, at a reception this evening in recognition of the second anniversary of the U.S.-Israeli Free Trade Area Agreement. Brock never appeared while I was there, but I did see Israeli

Embassy officials and lobbyists whom I knew. Afterwards, I attended another and rather large Patton, Boggs and Blow reception, this time for Mike Lowry who is running for the Washington State Senate in lieu of Senator Evans who announced that he was not running for reelection. Representative Al Swift may also run for this seat.

OCTOBER 21 WEDNESDAY

Phil Bakes, President of Eastern Airlines, and his legislative liaison, Philip McClure, came in at 11:00 to inform me of labor relations problems with which they have to deal to prevent the need to sell off Eastern's assets. The problem is with the Machinists Union and the fact that Eastern has workers such as aircraft cleaners making over $40,000 a year. Eastern cannot compete with other airlines which are paying about one-third for the same job, so Bakes wants to retrain those low skill workers who can be retrained for mechanic jobs. The possible loss of Eastern would be an economic disaster for the Miami area.

Dr. Cary Walters called from New York, and I let her know that in about two weeks I would see Dr. Barth Green, head of the Spinal Cord Research Center at the University of Miami, regarding the use of live animals in medical research. I also received my first Miami caller about the stock market crash who emphasized "no new taxes" and "cut back on government expenditures." I imagine I will be hearing a lot more from the fallout of this crash, especially regarding endangered pension funds.

In an interview today with a Houston TV station on Houston's requested proposed funding for rapid mass transit, I put in plugs for members Tom Delay, Mickey Leland and John King, head of the Transit Authority in Houston.

Many members and senators gathered this evening for the James Snyder retirement reception in the Senate Caucus Room. Snyder is retiring from the Transportation Union. I congratulated Snyder and then left to attend the Edward Roybal reception in celebration of his 25 years of service as a member in the House of Representatives. The reception was also to benefit the Edward Roybal Chair in Gerontology and Public Service at the California State University in Los Angeles. Don Edwards, Dean of the California delegation, was master of ceremonies.

OCTOBER 22 THURSDAY

Left Washington in the afternoon for Miami.

OCTOBER 23 FRIDAY

In Miami I met with *Jewish Floridian* reporter Ellen Stein, who is doing a long profile on me to appear in the October 29, 1987 edition of the newspaper.

OCTOBER 24 SATURDAY

This morning in the district office attorneys Leonard Kaminsky and Ira Kurzban came in concerning the new INS regulation on political asylum. They are concerned with the refugees and with the illegal immigrants, but also that their immigration law practice would be adversely affected by the I.N.S. regulation. Some immigration lawyers are like leeches on poor immigrants, and it is a shame because immigrants can go to any congressional office and get the same help gratis that lawyers provide for thousands of dollars. I told them I would write to the INS but only to inquire about the interpretation of this new regulation.

At tennis with Republican friends at Miami Shores, most were upset about the U.S. Senate turning down the confirmation of Judge Bork.

OCTOBER 25 SUNDAY

In a phone interview today with Bill Bayer of WINZ Radio, I was asked the usual budget and Metrorail questions, and the show will broadcast at 7:00 this evening. At 2:00 p.m., I caught an Eastern flight back to Washington.

OCTOBER 26 MONDAY

Adele Liskov and I are going over some of the itinerary for my trip to Turkey. Greg Dahlberg on our transportation subcommittee will be accompanying me on the codel. We plan to spend a few days in Paris, and then two other members will join us for our trip to Turkey on January 3. At my own expense, Joan and I are taking our grandsons Sean and Matt.

OCTOBER 27 TUESDAY

At a breakfast meeting this morning in the Humphrey Building, Social Security Administrator, Dorcas Hardy, held discussions on social security problems, stressing particularly the size of the surplus in the Social Security Trust Fund. With two other members present, the meeting was more formality than substance, but Hardy was the first social security administrator to reach out and be so readily accessible to the Congress. On Tuesday's and Thursday's, she comes down to Washington from the Baltimore Social Security Office to be available to House members and the senators.

Returning to the subcommittee office, I met with ranking Democrat Marty Sabo regarding the threatened amendment to make the Panama Canal a revolving fund, as some members have tried to do on the insistence of the Panama Canal Commission. To take the funds out of the appropriations process will adversely affect our 302B allocations if we ever need to transfer appropriated funds from the Panama Canal. I would like to keep the Commission in the 302B allocation process even though it is exempt from the Gramm-Rudman restrictions. This is a bookkeeping gimmick we have never used, but if we ever had to reduce the level of transportation appropriations it would be a way to save our 302B allocation without truly affecting the operation of the canal. Marty will be helpful.

The Coast Guard's Admiral Yost hosted a reception this evening and, as usual, he put on a big show for his legislative liaison staff. I soon left headed for the Cannon Caucus Room for the Barnett Bank reception. Barnett Bank is a Florida banking company and it surprised me that members were there from all over the country. I saw their lobbyist Howard Johnson and thanked him for his campaign help and also Charlie Rice, Barnett's Chief Executive Officer.

Afterwards, I went to the National Building Museum, a wonderful old building near Capitol Hill, for the 40th anniversary celebration of "Meet the Press." They showed lots of old clips from the program, even films dating from when Fidel Castro, Hubert Humphrey and Joe McCarthy were guests. It was all very enjoyable.

OCTOBER 28 WEDNESDAY

The full Appropriations Committee met today from 9:30 a.m. till about 2:00 p.m. working on the Defense Appropriations markup. Nothing was mentioned about reducing the Coast Guard's defense funds so I did not have to deal with that problem. Transportation has a little over $100 million in the Defense Bill, which is a big help to us.

When Carl Hongell with the Florida Rural Water Association came in about water problems in Florida, I took him to Dan Rostenkowski's Ways and Means Committee office, so that Hongell could tell the committee about the tax-free Rural Water Bond problem. When possible, I personally take constituents or Florida officials to the committee or to the member best able to help with a problem when the matter falls outside my jurisdiction. This way the person receiving the information feels he/she has been fully informed.

The Washington Advisory Council for UNICEF honored Jane Curtin, the 1987 National UNICEF Association Chairperson, at a reception this evening. I am a big supporter of UNICEF in our Foreign Operations Subcommittee, and I like Jane. She has testified before our Foreign Operations Appropriations Subcommittee. My next stop was to the Capitol City Yacht Club for cocktails and hors d'oeuvres. Much of the conversation was about the stockbroker who was killed in Miami by an unhappy customer. Monty Trainer, a Coconut Grove restaurant owner, hosted the reception on his very glamorous yacht with Claude Pepper, Dante Fascell and other Floridians, as guests.

OCTOBER 29 THURSDAY

We are again this morning in a full Appropriations Committee session on changes needed in the continuing resolution (CR) because on the Floor the rule on the CR to keep the government functioning after November 1st was voted down. The transportation portion of the CR was completed this afternoon. Four or five minor amendments were offered, all of which I accepted.

Back at the office several Dade officials were waiting for me - Clara Oesterle, the Dade County Commissioner and Chairman of the Commission's Transportation Subcommittee; Assistant Metro Manager Tony Ojeda; Ben Guilford of Metro-Dade Transit; staffer Rusty Roberts; and lobbyists Dennis Vierra and Syl Lukis. This group will be meeting with UMTA Administrator Dellibovi this afternoon, and had no strategy worked out, especially on the necessary local matching funds. We spent time mulling over the different ways Dade County could come up with the matching funds, and how best to present the proposals to Dellibovi.

About two months ago Northwest Airlines operating out of the Detroit area had a very bad plane crash. Bob Carr from Michigan and a member on our transportation subcommittee, has been working with me and our subcommittee staff putting together a hearing in his district on the crash. The hearing is scheduled for tomorrow, October 30, at the Detroit Airport Holiday Inn. So this evening, three hours late at 9:00, Bob Carr, our subcommittee staff and I departed from Washington National Airport on an FAA plane and headed for Detroit.

Arriving in Detroit at about 11:00 p.m., we went directly to the old Harry Bennett home(Henry Ford's old strongarm anti-union man), an imposing fortress-like structure, which is now the home of the CEO of a big Detroit company that deals with nuclear fusion. It was late and no one felt like eating dinner, but we went through the motions. Since it was now about 1:00 a.m., it was too late to tour the plant at the Detroit Metropolitan Airport, as scheduled, so we checked into the Airport Holiday Inn.

OCTOBER 30 FRIDAY

7:30 a.m., we went to the Detroit Metropolitan Airport and toured the facilities, including the control tower, to see what the problems were and if the need exists for a new tower. It was a good visit, but when you see one control tower you have seen them all. The problem is that Northwest Airlines has expanded service at the airport, producing an increase in traffic and a need for more runways and more control tower capacity.

Carr then took us on an inspection tour of the Northwest Airlines crash. We traced the crash step by step, from takeoff to the crash site to where various parts of the aircraft were found. We went over item by item, e.g., which light poles were downed, which buildings were hit, and which roadways were damaged with debris from the fallen aircraft.

After the tour, the hearing began at the Holiday Inn. We were joined by other subcommittee members, Larry Coughlin from Pennsylvania, Tom Delay from Texas, Richard Durbin from Illinois and Bob Mrazek from New York. Congressman John Conyers from Detroit, although not a subcommittee member, also sat on the dais with us. The press was there in full force. The hearing went from 9:30 to noon, when we recessed for lunch. In the morning session, the main witnesses were the CEO from Northwest Airlines and the Detroit Metro Airport Director. After lunch we heard testimony from other witnesses and were through by 2:00 p.m. The hearing revealed that apparently one of the flight attendants was on the flight deck talking to the crew, which might have distracted them. Bob Mrazek and I flew back commercial to Washington and I was back in the office by 6:00.

OCTOBER 31 SATURDAY

I am at the office today because the word is out that there will be votes. Apparently this is retaliation from the Republicans who are still angry about Jim Wright saying that "all time has expired" and then reversing the "time expired" so that Jim Chapman of Texas could change his vote. This is something former Speaker Tip O'Neill never would have done. The House went in session about 10:00 a.m., but a motion to adjourn at 10:05 a.m. was offered and carried, and the House is now out of session until Monday.

Some of my tennis buddies and I got together for a good match, and in the evening Ellen Kempler, her friend Tamara Lloyd, the wife of a White House NBC correspondent, my neighbor Maurice Rosenblatt and I went to the Kennedy Center and saw the play, "Breaking the Code."

Chapter 11

NOVEMBER 1, 1987 - SUNDAY

Representative Bob Mrazek and I played tennis today. Bob has vision only in one eye and has a hard time focusing on the ball, but we had a nice pleasant game. In the evening at the movie theater I saw Si Kinnen, the founder of AIPAC, whom I had not seen in a long time. Kinnen is now 82 years old. It was good to see him in such good health.

NOVEMBER 2 MONDAY

Sandy D'Alemberte, Law Dean at Florida State University, called this morning inquiring about the funds appropriated for FSU to create a uniform legal code for the Caribbean Islands. The legislation is going to the House Floor this week and will probably be enacted into law the following week. I told him I saw no reason for it not to go through.

Students from Highland Oaks Elementary School in my district are visiting in Washington as part of the Close-Up program. They were at the office this morning, and I took them to the subcommittee room and spoke to them on the usual topics, Congress, the passing of a bill, etc., and then the question and answer session. Afterwards, I took them to the Rayburn Cafeteria for soft drinks and cookies which had been set out for them. Metro-Dade Commissioner Sherman Winn's grandson was among the students and I said to him jokingly, "I have a message for your grandfather. Tell him I am trying to send him $180 million, and he won't take it." This was in reference to the *Miami Herald* article this past Saturday on the Metro-Dade Commissioners and their positions on whether to upgrade the present transit system before expanding the Metromover. Commissioners Winn, Redford, Schreiber and Valdes were against the expansion. Commissioners Oesterle, Phillips, and Ruvin were for the expansion, with Commissioners Carey and Clark undecided. Clark, however, was more pro-Metromover, so that left Barbara Carey with the key vote on a sharply divided Commission that must decide Tuesday whether to spend a quarter-billion dollars to expand downtown Miami's Metromover. The *Herald* quoted Carey as saying she was "leaning against the proposal," and that "deep down" she didn't want to support it. "Sometimes it's not good to take what's offered to you unless you can afford to have it," she said. If Carey sticks with that position, she will become the fifth vote on the nine-member Commission prohibiting further expansion of the Metromover. Maybe my message to Commissioner Winn will get to him through his grandson and change his support.

Gardnar Mulloy and his friend, Bunny Smith, arrived from Miami today. I picked them up at Washington National Airport, and we drove out to the Skyline Health and Racquet Club for the Sam Jones Celebrities Tennis Tournament. These political celebrity tournaments are put on every several months, and this tournament is sponsored by the New England Life Insurance Company to benefit one of the local colleges. Norman Dicks, a colleague from Washington state, is the chief organizer.

I was paired with Tom Gullikson, the former U.S. Open and Wimbledon doubles champion, and that was a lot of fun. Other participants included Congressmen Bob Kastenmeier of Wisconsin, Tom Bliley of Virginia, Bob Packard of California, Sid Morrison of

Washington state, and South Dakota Senator, Larry Pressler. It was a great evening, and I really enjoyed myself. Penny Durenberger, wife of Senator David Durenberger, also played. Penny is a lovely lady who raised David's four sons after his first wife died. David was out in Minnesota raising money for his re-election campaign.

NOVEMBER 3 TUESDAY

In the cafeteria this morning I teased Bob Walker, the Republican gadfly from Pennsylvania, about the fun he has "being outraged" at some of the goings-on recently, such as Speaker Jim Wright reopening the vote after all time had expired. He agreed he enjoyed being outraged.

The day has been slow, so I had time to help lobbyist Gary Hymel interest other members in joining us on our trip to Turkey. I spoke to members on Foreign Operations, and we may have Julian Dixon of California, John Porter of Illinois and Matt McHugh of New York. Dave Obey asked me to go on his codel, but it unfortunately coincides with our Turkey trip, so I had to turn him down. Toward the end of a busy and sometimes hectic year members begin looking for a kind of escape and contemplation of these trips is the perfect vehicle.

The Metro-Dade Commission today passed the Metromover extensions by 6 to 3. I was delighted. Clara Oesterle phoned to give me the news, and I understand that those who proposed the vote were very complimentary to me in my efforts to provide funding. Sherman Winn's grandson must have given him my message because Sherman reversed his previous position and voted for the Metromover, as did Barbara Carey and Steve Clark.

Speaker Jim Wright called for a meeting at 4:30 with Appropriations subcommittee chairmen asking that we move our bills individually and saying that he would like to send some of our appropriation bills to the White House so that the President would be unable to say that the Appropriations Committee was sitting on its hands. Jamie Whitten does not especially favor this, wanting instead to wrap all the appropriation bills into an omnibus bill. Whitten knows if he sends singularly the Labor HHS bill to the White House, the President will sign it and then we will not have the leverage of that bill to help other bills get through. Bill Natcher, who always prefers sending individual bills, wants to go with his

Labor HHS bill. A lot of convoluted politics is involved between the Congress and the White House.

Gerry Studds of Massachusetts is one of the two members of Congress to come out of the closet; Barney Frank, also from Massachusetts, being the second. Gerry told me today that he was in Miami last weekend and that the people there were very much with the movement of homosexual rights legislation. He was also sort of disgusted that there are many important members of the Miami community who won't come out of the closet, and he said that the gays were very happy with my "no" vote on the recent anti-gay rights amendment, especially since I was the only Florida member to vote for gay rights.

NOVEMBER 4 WEDNESDAY

The House went into session this morning at 10:00, and I was on the Floor to ask for unanimous consent for my subcommittee to go to conference and for the Speaker to appoint conferees. Bob Walker on the Republican side had reserved the right to object, but he and I had been having some friendly morning fun in the cafeteria, and I soon overcame his concerns and he withdrew his objection. I will try to work with Walker in the near future to have a conference report that can be passed by both Houses and signed into law so that we won't have to wait for a continuing resolution. Members have been speaking to me on the Floor concerned about the vote amendment banning smoking on airplanes.

Lately I have been too busy to attend many receptions, but today I did go to the National Conference on Soviet Jewry with Bob Carr, and it was enjoyable meeting and talking to attorney Keith Braun and his wife, Svetlana, who had just recently received permission to emigrate from the Soviet Union. Afterwards, I attended a book-signing reception for Congressman Claude Pepper, hosted by Dick Sewell of Florida Power and Light, and then went to Bob Mrazek's house for a Dukakis campaign reception.

NOVEMBER 5 THURSDAY

At 1:00, Pat Schroeder and Steve Neal hosted a baby shower to welcome Kelly Josephine Rose. The proud adoptive parents are Charlie and Jane Rose. Around 5:00, I was headed back to Miami.

NOVEMBER 6 FRIDAY

8:00 a.m., I attended the North Dade Chamber of Commerce Business Roundtable. The discussion was on the new immigration law pertaining to employers, and our office caseworker Bernie Torra and our immigration specialist Patty Diaz were with me to learn of any new information and to provide whatever insight they had into the new law. 11:00, Jeff and I went to the University of Miami Animal Research Center to meet with Dr. Norman Altman on abuses in laboratory animal experimentation.

NOVEMBER 7 SATURDAY

The Florida Democratic Party Convention was held today at the Fontainebleau Hilton Hotel, and I spent most of the day there. I did manage to get in some late afternoon tennis with Judge Nancy Pollock.

NOVEMBER 9 MONDAY

Back in Washington.

I was concerned about rounding up other members for our trip to Turkey, but when I spoke to Gary Hymel today he said that even if no one else went, he still wanted me to go. I would go, but I would rather have other members along.

Judge Mikva and I played tennis today, and I learned a few things about the President's appointments to the Supreme Court. Anthony M. Kennedy was all set to be appointed and then at the last minute Reagan switched to Judge David Souter from Vermont.

Back at the office, a *Ft. Lauderdale News Sun Tattler* reporter called and asked if I ever smoked marijuana. "Yes," I replied, "and that is all I am going to say because I have to draw the line somewhere on these personal questions." I then asked the reporter if he had ever smoked marijuana and he said, "Yes." Apparently he is polling the Florida delegation.

My North Florida colleague, Buddy MacKay, came in. I had told Buddy to run for Governor in 1986, but he did not take my advice; now he says he has formed an *ad hoc* campaign group and is going to run in 1990, and this time I advised against it. I have been helping Bill Nelson and I hope Buddy does not run, as both are friends. Besides, by 1992 at the latest, a seat will open up for Buddy on the Ways and Means Committee or also on the Appropriations Committee, and then in 1994, he could run for Budget Committee Chairman. Buddy really belongs in Washington although at present his committee assignments are lousy. He is good, but I do not think he can beat Bill Nelson. Part of his problem is his wife who has to remain in Florida to take care of both their 82 year old mothers.

Last weekend at the North Dade County Chamber of Commerce Roundtable, Maria Elena Torano told me that when she is next in Washington she would buy me dinner. She arrived today, but before dinner we went to the combined celebration of Congressman Silvio Conte's 66th birthday party and his and Corinne's 40th wedding anniversary. The event was held at the U.S. Botanical Gardens among a huge gathering of members and friends, but members had to soon leave because beginning at 7:00 p.m., there were seven or eight votes on the House Floor. I spoke to members of the Florida delegation about the question, "Have you ever smoked marijuana?" Not one South Florida member admitted ever having tried it and they were very nervous about the question. I told them I had admitted it and that I felt telling the truth about smoking marijuana was more important. The only other Florida Delegation members to admit to it were conservative Republican Connie Mack and moderate Democrat Senator Lawton Chiles.

The last vote over, Maria Elena and I went to dinner. Maria's consulting firm "Meta" is now doing over $1 million annually, and although she is a minority Hispanic woman, giving her a leg-up on the competition, she fully earns her way and really knows how to go after these contracts - putting in many business hours. We have been friends for a long time, since when she was first in Washington during the Carter Administration, and I admire her for the career advancements she has made.

NOVEMBER 10 TUESDAY

Jeff Donnelly, a Close-Up participant from the Miami Country Day School, was given the school assignment of "shadowing" me and reporting on what a working day is like for a member of

Congress. His assignment started this morning.

Today's *Ft. Lauderdale Sun Tattler* reported that I had smoked pot. I saw Connie Mack on the House Floor and we teased each other about being two of the only Florida members besides Lawton Chiles to admit ever smoking marijuana. Connie said, "Well, we are in good company."

Graham Claytor, the President, and Tim Gillespie of Amtrak came to the office asking for my support on curtailing the number of free passes for Amtrak's Board of Directors and their families, especially retired Directors. These unrestricted free passes diminish Amtrak revenues, and I assured them that I would do anything to help in this effort. Graham and I are friends and have worked very well together on Amtrak problems; we will probably go to Spain next year to look at equipment for Amtrak.

Around noon, seven of Jeff Donnelly's Close-Up classmates joined us in the Transportation Appropriations Subcommittee room. One student's father, Harvey Abramson, is very conservative and writes me highly critical letters about once a month. I do answer all his letters, but I was glad to have this opportunity to be responsive to his son. One student wants to be a page and I briefed her on the process. We then went to lunch in the Rayburn Cafeteria, where I told them to order whatever they wanted.

John Myers of Indiana said he and his wife Carol are definitely going with us to Turkey in January. They have been with us on other trips, and we enjoy traveling with them. Politically it is better to travel at the expense of a foundation than at taxpayers' expense, even though these codels involve far more work than the public realizes. These overseas trips are not all fun and games as the overwhelming population seems to think.

Speaking to Charlie Wilson on the Floor, I told him I could not go on his trip. I think he really needs me because he does not have anyone really dependable to go on his codel. I also spoke on the Floor to Vic Fazio. Vic is having a hard time both financially and emotionally with his daughter who is ill with leukemia and who recently had an expensive bone marrow transplant. I offered to help with an honorarium in Miami but he was maxed out on honorariums for this year. I certainly would like to help Vic, and maybe I can get him an honorarium in December, which can be made payable in January of next year. [Sadly, his daughter later died.]

At the office, environmentalist David Ferrari of Jacksonville came in to thank me for my support of the Arctic National Wilderness Refuge bill. Afterwards Bill Holaytor from the Machinist Union came in to discuss his problem with airlines doing maintenance work overseas. I recommended that he propose language to be included in the Senate bill or perhaps have the authorizing Public Works Committee offer a suspension bill to restrict overseas repairs. The problem is we cannot react or do anything until the Department of Transportation comes out with this new regulation, which the machinists oppose. And apparently DOT is withholding the measure until it is too late to legislate against it.

3:30, I met with Esther Kurtz and Doug Bloomfield of AIPAC. They want me to introduce legislation for the restructuring of Israel's debt, and are having problems with Foreign Ops chairman, Dave Obey. The way it could work is that Israel pays off the present debt to the United States at 14% interest and then borrows, with U.S. guarantee, at a commercial rate of 8%, which saves about $150 million a year. Therefore, U.S. economic aid to Israel, which is $1.2 billion a year, would be $150 million more than necessary to pay the present interest rate, which becomes an economic windfall to Israel. Dave Obey has trouble with this, but we will try to bring him around. Israel has never been late or defaulted on its indebtedness.

At the airport for my flight to Miami, I saw Maria Elena, and because she had once worked for Eastern Airlines she was able to upgrade my ticket to first class although she remained in economy. Earlier, Jay Kislak, a friend from Miami who has his own jet, came to the office wanting to fly me back to Miami. He wanted to leave at 5:00, the same time as my commercial flight, but he could not get a take-off slot at Washington National Airport due to heavy congestion. He said if I came with him my being a Congressman would enable him to get a slot before 7:00. When I checked with subcommittee staff, they advised against any intervention, saying if I requested and received a slot for Jay the tower would probably leak to the media that "Congressman Lehman on a flight in a private plane preempted a commercial jet of 150-200 passengers." That is not the type of publicity I need. If the commercial flight had been cancelled I would have gotten back to Jay, but even if I flew with him I would have to pay him the equivalent of a first-class ticket, so I would not have saved any money. I will call Jay tomorrow and explain what happened.

NOVEMBER 11 WEDNESDAY

It is good to be back in Miami, the weather is beautiful! It had started snowing when I left Washington. I am not going to any Veterans Day events today, not even the one in North Miami Beach. I am, however, meeting Jeff at the district office this morning to go over papers that I brought down from Washington. First, though, I called Jay Kislak and explained why I took the commercial flight out. He understood also that I would have had to pay full fare to him because many members have run into problems accepting free flights on corporate jets, and I did not want to make the same mistake.

Jeff and I spent about an hour discussing his concern about the fallout from my admission to the press that I had smoked marijuana. He wanted to know what to say if asked about it. I told him to tell anyone who asked that he thought I was bragging, or something to that effect, or that maybe I was not telling the truth because I did not want to seem like a "square."

NOVEMBER 12 THURSDAY

This morning Mayor Mike Colodny of North Miami was at the district office concerned about his daughter's admission to Ithaca College. I called my New York colleague Matt McHugh, but he was out. Mike's daughter is somewhat disabled with a deformed jaw and needs a great deal of corrective surgery, so I want to help her for her own sake and not because of her father's political influence. Mike can, however, help both Matt McHugh and me. In fact, this Sunday he is hosting a fundraiser for Bill Nelson's campaign for governor. Mike was Nelson's roommate at the University of Florida, and is a potent political force in South Florida; his wife Lou Anne is Chair of the Board of Trustees of the North Miami Art Center.

Then Cheryl Hendrick, Scott Johnston and Dick Baker from the Underground Contractors Association came in with a campaign contribution, which I turned over to Sharyn. I suggested that they think about legislation for diversification in the investment of the Social Security Trust Fund, which will soon amount to billions of dollars before the baby boomers start to draw down on it. This surplus money in the Social Security Trust Fund should be invested in state and municipal bonds which could in turn be reinvested in the infrastructure improvements that states and cities need. It would also create the jobs and contracts that the underground contractors are interested in.

I soon left the office going to South Miami to do a public announcement radio tape warning people to take precautionary measures against lightning during thunderstorms. Florida is number one in lightning injuries and deaths. I thought I did a good job, and the tape did not indicate any speech problems, which always concerns me.

In Miami Shores I played tennis with Stan Whitman, business leader and owner of the Bal Harbour Shops. "If we do have a depression," Stan said, "you can blame it on the media, because the media keeps talking about a depression just on the horizon." He feels if the media keeps putting fear in the hearts of people, the people are going to act accordingly. That is his particular observation, and I do not know whether I agree with him or not.

I then went to Channel 17 at the Dade County School Board Administration Building and did a short television take. Janet McAliley and I were the guests for this twelve-minute segment hosted by Maria Elena Torano. Janet is on the Dade County School Board. The topic was "Children at Risk," and I used the term "throwaway children" (unwanted or abandoned children, especially children born with AIDS or drug addiction). [This became a term of the late 1980's and 1990's.]

In the evening I attended the North Dade Democratic Club at the McDonald Center. When the club's president, Bill Farber, introduced me, to show vigor I hopped energetically upon the stage, and said greetings to the group of about 200 of my condo constituents. Annie Ackerman, Evelyn Schuengrund and many people from Northeast Dade were there. Usually only about seventy-five people show up, but tonight a free meal was to be had and many more attended. I felt like a real celebrity with so many wanting to shake my hand and telling me how young I looked compared to how I look on television. Everyone seemed happy to see me. These people revere elected officials, especially Congressmen, as they have not become cynical about government and are always very impressed when I show up. State Senator Gwen Margolis and her challenger for the Senate seat, David Young [now Judge Young and out of the closet] were among the guests. But the fact that I am a U.S. Congressman was so much more important to this group. I received most of the attention and enjoyed every minute of it.

NOVEMBER 13 FRIDAY

The North Dade Forum holds a monthly luncheon the second Friday of each month. This Friday the luncheon was held at the Miami Shores Country Club, and I sat at the dais and said a few words. Burton Young, President of the Forum, was rather ill at ease and tense because his son, David, as mentioned, is running for the State Senate challenging Gwen Margolis. The featured speaker was Arthur Tietelbaum, Director of the Miami Anti-Defamation League. Most of his speech was about Nazi war criminals in the United States and how his office had helped the Office of Special Investigations of the Department of Justice find, investigate and deport Nazi war criminals that had relocated in South Florida. When he finished, I had the urge to stand and speak on the subject as Tietelbaum gave no credit to the fact that the Office of Special Investigations did not just suddenly appear on the horizon. Former member Elizabeth Holtzman, who came to Congress with me in 1973, and is now a district attorney in Brooklyn, initiated the authorizing legislation establishing the Department of Justice's Office of Special Investigations. Tietelbaum never mentioned Elizabeth or Alan Ryan, who conceptualized the idea of an OSI.

Working with Elizabeth and Alan, I legislated appropriation funding through the Appropriations Subcommittee on Commerce, Justice, State, and the Judiciary, for a $300 thousand annual budget for the OSI agency. And, when in Moscow, I went to the Soviet Department of Interior to inquire about the evidence and whether it was solid enough to hold up in U.S. courts. I really felt slighted by Tietelbaum, but I also realized he did not know the history of OSI's establishment and the role that Alan, Elizabeth, and I played in its conception, authorization and funding. Perhaps I will write him a letter. Staff directors of these non-profits have to show their own and their institution's importance to gain financial support.

After the speeches, I worked the tables as usual, speaking to my many constituents and also Burton Young's wife, Sheila. Sheila has cancer, and I had arranged for her to have treatments at the National

Institutes of Health in Washington, and at Memorial Sloan Kettering in New York. She said she was fine now, and she looked really well.

Later, Joan and I attended the party of her interior designer friend, Tom Luyk, at his home in Coral Gables. Ruth Shack, the former Dade County Commissioner, was there and we spoke about the problems of Dade County. Ruth now heads the Dade Foundation, and will be coming to Washington soon with her husband, Dick, to hopefully procure funding for the North Miami Arts Museum. The museum receives no public assistance, and I offered to help Dick in this funding effort. [The museum has since been renamed The Museum of Contemporary Art.]

NOVEMBER 14 SATURDAY

At Larry Smith's fundraiser this afternoon held at the Diplomat Hotel in Hollywood, about 900 people attended. Twelve hundred tickets were sold at $200 each, a huge affair. Joan and I sat at the dais. I did notice that no complimentary tickets were extended, other than to elected officials. None of the Broward County condo people that I knew, like Leo Coslow and Arnold Lanner, were there. This was strictly a "fundraiser," and I guess Larry does not have to cultivate his condo people with "comps" as much as I do. I saw many labor leaders and AIPAC's Mike Adler, but some condo people were quite conspicuous by their absence. I have always given condo leaders complimentary tickets to my fundraisers, and people now expect them. Larry's fundraiser cost about $65,000, and he made about $150,000. Bernie Friedman, Larry's former administrative aide, put the fundraiser together, and what a job he did. But, the total effect was not in good taste, effective but without class.

NOVEMBER 15 SUNDAY

1:30 p.m. I left for the airport for my flight back to Washington. The Eastern flight was on time and Maria Elena had arranged for an upgrade of my ticket to first class. Dante Fascell was also on the plane. Arriving in Washington, Dante was met by ABC television reporters for an interview on the new Contra Investigation Report. After the interview, Dante and I rode back to the Rayburn Building together. Every day more and more information is leaked on the

Contra investigation, and the leaks are what the press wants to hear about now.

Speaking of the press, there was one final item last week in the *Washington Post* on how members had responded to the marijuana question, and the reference to the Florida Delegation was that "Three Florida congressional members had admitted to smoking marijuana - conservative Republican Connie Mack, liberally moderate Democrat Lawton Chiles, and liberal Democrat William Lehman." This indicated that there was no ideological tie-in among members of the delegation on whether they had smoked or even tried marijuana. I think it is time to put this issue to rest and I do not think we will hear any more about it. Let's hope. At least they did not change the name of the William Lehman Causeway, which I had warned Joan might happen.

NOVEMBER 16 MONDAY

Dick Durbin called this morning to say he and Senator Lautenberg had worked out compromise, legislative language on the nonsmoking amendment. The language called for a two-year trial period on two-hour flights. I told him I personally favored the compromise language, but that he would also need supportive votes from subcommittee members and other appropriations subcommittee chairmen, as this may come up in the continuing resolution conference and that Bill Gray would probably be one of the key votes.

In the afternoon I met with Kaye Henderson, Florida Secretary of Transportation, Deputy Nick Serianni, and Bill Taylor, Florida's DOT representative in Washington. They were concerned about legislation to exempt the Florida Turnpike from the 55 mph speed limit restriction. Presently the only exception to the 55 mph rule is in rural areas of interstates, and the Florida Turnpike, in the way it was built, is equivalent to an interstate highway. The argument was that people who want to drive over 55 mph will not use the Florida Turnpike, therefore causing the turnpike to lose revenue. I am certainly no ally as I did not like raising the speed limit even on rural interstates. In any case, the legislation first had to be authorized, and I did not want to do authorizing legislation in the appropriation process, and even then I would not do it without the approval of Jim Howard, the Public Works Committee Chairman. If Jim gave the go ahead, I would reevaluate my position, but I do not think this is likely as this matter is not top priority as far as Jim Howard is concerned and what he is trying to accomplish in his highway safety position as Chairman of the Committee on Public Works.

Dr. Ayub Ommayo came in later with cost data on head injuries due to vehicular accidents. Ayub is the physician who took care of my daughter at NIH during her illness, and we have remained friends. I told him I would try to help with the $25,000 needed, and called Johns Hopkins University, one of five institutions the National Highway Traffic Safety Administration (NHTSA) had designated this past January to research and study the problems of injury control. NHTSA and I have been working together for the prevention and rehabilitation of head injuries for a number of years, and the funds necessary to set up these injury prevention research centers were appropriated by our Transportation Subcommittee. Additionally, our subcommittee provided $10 million over the past few years to the Center for Disease Control in Atlanta, for the total trauma epidemic problem. This year the House appropriated $10 million, but the Senate did not. I think we will have more difficulty keeping the $10 million in the conference than we have had previously, and we may have to drop down to $7 million to prevent the Senate conferees from taking this item back in disagreement.

Gary Hymel and I spoke about the trip to Turkey, and everything is progressing satisfactorily. I also spoke to Charlie Wilson and reconfirmed that I would not be going with him to Pakistan. Charlie's codel is going to Morocco, Pakistan and Turkey, leaving the end of this week, when we recess, and coming back on the Monday after Thanksgiving. A problem with me is that as Chairman of an appropriations subcommittee I have all these balls up in the air before the conference and so much other unfinished business that I am reluctant to go overseas and be so far removed from any problem that might come up. Traveling will be much more flexible and relaxing for me during the December/January holidays when there is nothing hanging over my head as there is now.

That evening I attended the Hughes Corporation reception honoring John Winkel, who is retiring, and welcomed William Merritt as the new incoming Vice President of Government Relations. The event was held at the Willard Hotel and it was quite a lovely party. Many colleagues on the Armed Services Committee and on the Appropriations Subcommittee for Defense were there, as were many lobbyists involved in defense contracting. I spoke to Hughes's new CEO and to their liaison executive on FAA concerns (Hughes has various FAA contracts), alerting them that I would be in London in late December and may call on their London office to obtain hard-to-get theater tickets. The Hughes Corporation got me tickets for "Phantom of the Opera" in London last April, when no one else could.

NOVEMBER 17 TUESDAY

In the Members Dining Room this morning with Diane Steed and George Reagle from the National Highway Transportation Safety Administration, we talked about the problems of passenger restraints and airbags and the fact that dealers are having difficulty accepting them. I offered to contact several dealer associations to find out how the dealers intend to handle the new mandated airbags and passenger restraints. We also spoke about the Jackson Memorial Trauma Center, and George has agreed to make an onsite visit to the center. I will call Dr. Ommayo to let him know that this too is being done.

Back at the office, Jack Gilstrap and Chip Bishop from the American Public Transportation Association (APTA) came in to talk about the charter bus regulations, asking me to insist on House protection to keep in conference the report language we have in the House version of the legislation and not the version in the Senate report language. This is twice in two days that someone has asked me to initiate or change report language. I gave them my patented answer, which was that for bill language they had to get the okay from Public Works Chairman Jim Howard and, in this case, ranking minority member John Paul Hammerschmidt, as I was not going to do bill language in the continuing resolution conference report without their approval. I put the ball back in APTA's court and warned Jack that he should be aware of possible reductions in Section Nine transportation subsidies because under Gramm-Rudman our subcommittee will have to deal with this budget problem.

Afterwards, a former Georgia colleague, Billy Lee Evans, came in. Billy Lee represents the tobacco industry and needed help with the proposed legislation prohibiting smoking on airplanes. I told him I could not personally help him, but I did give him the names of swing-vote members on our subcommittee. When he left, I called Gary Hymel and gave him the news that Congressman John Porter of Illinois may also be interested in going to Turkey. Gary was very pleased.

I got a lot done on the House Floor today. I spoke to Pete Stark about the rejection of nonskilled nursing home claims in my district, and showed him the letter from his office which indicated he had written the letter, but that he personally had not signed it. Pete was pissed at his staff for not taking care of this matter, saying they should have done more. He then said he would take care of it, so now I will not have to bring to Washington the nursing care people from my district to deal with the problem.

Don Edwards approached me about the light rail in the San Jose Guadelupe Corridor, and in conference he wants me to hold firm for the House language versus the Senate language in order to protect the funds earmarked for San Jose. I also spoke to Foreign Ops members Bob Mrazek, Sid Yates and Matt McHugh about restructuring the Israeli debt. We agreed to meet with AIPAC leaders in Mrazek's office on Thursday to work on a position statement drawn up by AIPAC, which will pacify Chairman Dave Obey. Obey is opposed to the Israeli debt restructuring, and AIPAC has launched an adversary campaign against Obey intimating that he is hostile to Israel. Obey in indignation has threatened to do a "special order" against AIPAC on the House Floor, but hopefully our conciliatory gesture will prevent him from doing so.

Though reluctant, I voted to make the Veterans Affairs Administration a Cabinet position. I did this solely to please several veteran organizations in my district. Perhaps I should have voted my conviction, but sometimes it isn't worth the effort when the vote raises so much flack and accomplishes nothing. Only about fifteen members voted against it, and the majority who voted favorably probably think along the same lines as I do.

In the evening I went to the Florida House reception honoring the "substantial contributors to the Florida House," and from there to the Cannon Caucus Room for the Jefferson Island Club's Hunters' reception. Once a year the club serves wild game. This year there were bear, alligator, duck, geese, rattlesnake and oysters. I enjoyed the food and stayed till about 8:30.

NOVEMBER 18 WEDNESDAY

At Dave Obey's monthly conference this morning, his friends from the labor community were there, as were the usual House members - Pat Schroeder (CO), Marty Sabo (MN), Jim Oberstar (MN) and Pat Williams (MT). Williams is on the Budget Conference Committee, which is trying to package taxes and budget cuts to reestablish confidence in the world financial markets by showing the determination of the United States to reduce our deficit. His predictions were not optimistic, the main reason being that no one wants to deal with the social security cost-of-living adjustments (COLA). As Obey said, the only way to resolve this is to get President Reagan and Congressman Pepper (Rules Committee) together and let them come up with solutions that both can live with. As long as we are all playing politics with the social security cost-of-living increases we are not going to gain any substantial ground in dealing with our budget deficit. To me, at my income level, I think it is ridiculous to receive a cost-of-living increase on my social security payments because I do not need it and many thousands like me don't need it. Many people are willing to cut the COLA in half to balance the budget, and having the equivalent of ten people working to pay taxes for my social security benefits is a bit crazy.

I returned to the office to meet with the Washington Director of the Cuban-American National Foundation regarding the immigration policy on reunification of families. The Foundation is having trouble with this immigration policy, and the director has offered to help me set up a meeting next Tuesday in Miami with Armando Codino, a leader of Miami's Cuban-American National Foundation.

On the House Floor Dave Obey handed me his list of the necessary domestic budget cuts we must take in the Appropriations Committee. Jamie Whitten and appropriations subcommittee chairmen will have to decide very soon which cuts to make. Pat Williams also gave me a list of the days we will be in session during the first quarter of next year. Congress reconvenes on January 20, but will not be doing any business until the 16th of February. I just remembered that I was to stop by the press conference announcing the observance of a National Day of Prayer for Haiti. It is now 1:00, and the press conference was at noon.

I will have to apologize to Congressman Fauntroy and Archbishop McCarthy of Miami.

A *Miami Herald* reporter is to call me this afternoon, or perhaps I am to call him, on the report just out from the Iran-Contra Investigative Committee. From reading the report, apparently a secret government existed within our government which was more a threat to the freedom of our country than any threat from other countries. I will convey this to the reporter, but first I will clear my statement with Representative Lee Hamilton who chairs this investigative committee.

I spoke to Charlie Hayes from Illinois about the trip to Turkey, and he seems interested. I now have to get details and exact information on the trip, as Gary has yet to get a definite financial commitment from Turkey to pay our expenses from Washington to London to Turkey.

At 3:15, representatives from the North Dade Chapter of the National Council of Jewish Women came in. This six-woman group included Nan Rich, who had run for the Dade County School Board, and Anna Mae Ross, who had run for the State Legislature. Both lost, and I doubt if they will run again. They checked me out, querying me on my position on specific legislation, most of which had nothing to do with Jewish issues but with children, especially day care centers, shelters for abused children and educational programs. The National Council of Jewish Women does much good work on peace programs, but mainly it deals with women and children's issues such as the family leave legislation. I had already cosponsored all the legislation they favored and we had a happy half hour together. Afterwards, I gave the States News Service statements on my reaction to the Iran-Contra Report. The States News Service works with the *Miami Herald*, so I am anxious to see how it reads in tomorrow's paper, if it appears at all.

Rabbi Neuman is back visiting in the States, and is in Washington with his son Mark. At dinner this evening with Mark, Adele Liskov, and the escort officer who had been in East Germany with us, the Rabbi told of the main problem he is encountering with his congregation. It seems the old group of religious Jews, those holding Orthodox views and who had been the hard core Jews in East Germany, are reluctant to admit Jews into their congregation who have been disassociated from the Jewish religion for almost a generation. Dealing with this has been frustrating for the Rabbi as his primary mission in East Germany is to reignite the Jewish faith to those who have been disaffiliated for so many years, and unless he can accomplish this, his job in Berlin, he feels, is not going to be very productive.

The Rabbi also spoke of his frustration with the East German government and the fact that millions of dollars had been spent on the restoration of buildings, but that practically nothing had been done to restore the old Jewish buildings such as the synagogues and community centers that were such a prominent part of Berlin before the war. On a more positive note, he and Klaus Gysi, East Germany's Secretary for Church Affairs, have a good relationship and are working well together. Though his mission was heavily challenging, Rabbi Neuman said he was looking forward to returning to East Germany, and promised to send me a copy of his Hanukkah sermon on East Berlin Jewry.

NOVEMBER 19 THURSDAY

The *Miami Herald* had only a one-line statement on my reaction to the Iran-Contra Report, saying simply that I thought the report was too soft on the President and that the President had lied. The main story was on Dante Fascell as Vice Chairman of the Iran-Contra Investigative Committee.

Boeing and McDonnell Douglas sponsored a breakfast this morning with the Congressional Aviation Forum, which I found quite interesting, revealing that there exists a problem in competition from European governments who subsidize their aviation manufacturers. Representative Dan Glickman of Kansas presided, with Bob Carr and many other colleagues there.

Afterwards, in the office with Dick Shack, Miami's "mover and shaker" for the North Miami Arts Museum, and Neil Sigmon from appropriations' interior subcommittee staff, we committed to helping Dick with museum funding by arranging appointments for him with officials of the National Endowment for the Arts. There is a problem, however, in that the museum does not have its own collection. It is a small museum, but does a lot culturally for the North Dade area.

Then Pat Cregan, Chrysler Corporation's representative, formerly on the staff of the Senate Appropriations Transportation Subcommittee, came in with longtime Chrysler lobbyist, Bob

Connors, about the House version of the continuing resolution which opposes the purchase of long range aircraft for the FAA, replacing the old aircraft that the FAA has now. We will work together to get the Senate to accept the House language. Chrysler, which owns Gulfstream, wants to sell a corporate jet to the FAA.

I spoke to Greg and Lucy about Les AuCoin (OR) who wants my help for a trailer train truck company in his area that manufactures rail "truck" cars. Les wants me to write asking the Interstate Commerce Commission to waive extension of the antitrust exemption for this particular type of railcar. Greg, Lucy and I agreed that this would put me in the uncomfortable position of being opposed to antitrust and not being able to explain why. I must turn down Les's request.

11:30, Billy Cypress, Chairman and legislative liaison for the Miccosukee Indians, came in with a request for economic development funds for the Miccosukee tribe comparable to the type of economic development now available in Broward County for the Seminoles. At noon I attended the Greater Miami Chamber of Commerce luncheon meeting to discuss the Caribbean basin and its importance to Florida's international trade.

Mississippi member Mike Espy and the Mayor of Greenwood, Mississippi, came in regarding the industrial foundation of Greenwood. Later, Rosemary Chalif of the Florida Chapter of the National Association of Social Workers came in to discuss welfare reform and the consumer freedom of choice provision within the Kennedy/Waxman Minimal Health Benefit legislation.

That evening I failed to attend a reception for Mary Rose Oakar, my colleague from Ohio who is running for the Democratic Caucus Chair. Also running are Bill Gray (PA) and Mike Synar from Oklahoma. I have to support Bill Gray as he is the ranking Democrat on our subcommittee. I think, however, that Mike will win because Bill Gray, as mentioned, has already been Chairman of Budget and members won't vote him another high ranking position, and Mary Rose has been involved in a congressional office payroll scandal.

NOVEMBER 20 FRIDAY

Congress is now in a ten-day recess through Sunday, November 29, and I caught an early afternoon flight to Miami. On the plane my seatmate was Archbishop McCarthy from the Catholic Diocese of Miami, but we really did not have much of a conversation. I was sorry to miss the press conference and prayer luncheon for the Haitians with Walter Fauntroy, the D.C. Representative in the House, and I apologized to the Archbishop for not showing up after promising to be there.

NOVEMBER 21 SATURDAY

At 4:45, I went to the Fontainebleau Hilton for the Jewish Federation Convention. My good friend Mark Talisman, Director of the Federation's Washington office, was moderator of the panel which consisted of Dante Fascell, Larry Smith and myself. Dante spoke about the Iran-Contra investigation and, as Vice Chairman, was very authoritative on the subject. Larry Smith has been fascinated with the budget process and did okay speaking on the Budget Summit Conference. I talked about what I had done in East Germany and what I was trying to do with refugee funding and resettlement for Israel and the problems now involved in the debt restructuring for Israel. I cautioned the Federation Council members and the 700 people in the audience to stop the adverse publicity and negative stories on Senator Lawton Chiles and Dave Obey, Chair of our Foreign Ops Subcommittee, questioning their support for the State of Israel. I then told them about the meeting on Thursday afternoon in Bob Mrazek's office with Tom Dine and Doug Bloomfield from AIPAC, together with Matt McHugh, Charlie Wilson, Sid Yates and myself, alerting AIPAC that attacking Dave Obey was not productive. I said I thought we came out of the meeting committed to reevaluating Obey's position as it relates to holding Israel exempt-free from the two-percent cut that was at one time considered a way to provide additional budget authority for other foreign aid programs. How well this was accepted I could not judge, but I felt it needed to be said.

In Thursday's meeting, we had also discussed the fact that because Israel spends the money so quickly a small cut for Israel and Egypt would result in fifteen times that much budget authority for countries that did not spend outlays as expeditiously as Israel. I think we five members gave AIPAC a good lesson in dealing with Obey and the problems of its adversarial positions.

NOVEMBER 22 SUNDAY

At the Miami Shores Country Club with members of the North Dade Taiwanese community, I raised $3,000 in campaign funds. I had no idea such a community existed in North Dade, and I was most impressed with the quality of people at our meeting, about fifteen couples - all very aggressive and interesting. I enjoyed the luncheon and the chance to know them. Dr. Robert Chen, a University of Miami professor, and the designated leader of the Taiwan community here, called for the meeting. I met Dr. Chen a couple of years ago when one of my friends that he also knew, Eva Brock, told him to get in touch with me regarding his work status permit at the University of Miami. Dr. Chen brought in his immigration papers, and our office was able to work successfully with the INS to get the documents approved, which allowed him to stay in the United States to continue his high-level math studies at the University.

After the meeting I went to the Cotillion Hall on 164th Street for a luncheon with Lorri Kellogg, founder of adoption agency Universal Aid for Children. The organization was honoring Frank Perrili of the INS whom I had met several times. There were close to two hundred people there and children from many different countries. I had helped Lorri with her Single Parent Adoption Bill many years ago, and it was wonderful to see how people have helped those less fortunate children from other parts of the world.

NOVEMBER 23 MONDAY

George Berlin was in the district office this morning. George is in charge of the South Florida Transportation Task Force, and wanted to know about future transportation funding for South Florida. He has problems not only with future mass transit funding but also with funding for highways in Northeast Dade, especially the overpass at 203rd Street and Ives Dairy Road and Biscayne Boulevard. George is a good friend and we have worked together on several transportation-related projects for Dade County. He saw a copy of my letter to Charlotte Greenbarg and understands that I want the overpass to run east and west, which does not endanger the school children. The decision, however, is not mine to make, and will be decided at the State level.

Following the meeting, I headed for the Marco Polo Hotel for a work-session luncheon with the Concerned Citizens of Northeast Dade. I spoke to about 200 people in the auditorium on catastrophic illness legislation and was asked about the new Cuban influx and the impact it would have on our social system in Dade County. They also asked about the beach restoration project which should be completed sometime around the middle of 1988. "The check is in the mail," I answered, and they were happy about that. I then went downstairs where our campaign fund had sponsored several tables, each table sitting ten people, and Dave Sampson, the leader of this group, took control making sure I had a photo taken with guests at each table. I did not get to eat lunch, as so often happens when I am trying to touch base with as many people as possible, and this was a very important political coalition group. The cost to us of $2,500 was a good investment as a political maintenance system, devised to prevent potential candidates from making political inroads or becoming serious threats to run against us in the Democratic primary.

NOVEMBER 24 TUESDAY

Dewey Knight, the Acting Dade County Manager, and people from the homeowners association near Joe Robbie Stadium [now Pro Player] met with me this morning regarding problems with the Lennar Development Corporation. This is an association at war with the Lennar developers, and fans at the stadium who use their home sites for parking lots which causes trash all around. I advised them that the matter with Lennar could possibly be resolved by just having the HUD office in Jacksonville investigate whether Lennar developers have violated any of the federally subsidized housing laws in their treatment of the purchasers of this subsidized housing. Our office will work with them to help initiate this action.

Afterwards, I went to Temple Israel for the memorial service for my very dear friend, Lany Narot, who died suddenly last Sunday morning following surgery. As an elected official I was part of the memorial service for Lany at the Temple where her husband was once the Rabbi and I was a board member. There was a large audience of our mutual friends. I think I did an eloquent enough job speaking about Lany, as I did not want to be intimate in telling how I felt about her, and at the same time I did not want to appear hypocritical about our relationship by just saying how bad I felt about her death.

Joan and I had dinner at Gatti's Restaurant on Miami Beach with old friends Henry and Zelma Wolff. I have been working on a case for Henry and his son-in-law and they may come to Washington next week to deal with the problem of a mutual fund that they want to have approved by the Securities and Exchange Commission. While there I saw Dr. Manny Papper, former Dean of the University of Miami Medical School, who told me he was coming to Washington in May with his wife, Pat, for a meeting of international anesthesiologists. I will arrange for a meeting room in the Capitol for him and his group. Going to Gatti's means seeing a lot of old friends from old families who have been around for a long time.

NOVEMBER 25 WEDNESDAY

I had several district office appointments this morning. Phil Hammersmith and his wife Jackie Basha were in to speak about the proposed school bond issue and how I could possibly help. I was one of three cosigners endorsing the school bond, the other two were a Hispanic banker and a black state senator. I advised them to get a fourth signature, someone from the WASP community, so that all possible bases were covered before the vote next week on the bond referendum, and they agreed.

Bernie Fagen was in. Bernie used to be a rather important figure in Sunny Isles politics but has antagonized a number of people and is no longer effective. He was seeking an intern position for his granddaughter who is doing a semester this spring at George Washington University. I told him "yes," she could have a job in my office, and "yes," I would try to get her a staff position on the Select Committee on Children, Youth and Families. But my "yes" responses were not getting through to him as he continued the litany on why she should have the job. Bernie has had so much opposition that he did not realize I had immediately acquiesced to his requests. It took a while, but he finally got the message.

Sam Bloom, an old friend in the air-conditioning business,

came in complaining about the reverse discrimination used against him in his business because he is not a minority. He resents the preference shown to blacks and especially to Hispanic contractors. We are also working to resolve a case for him with the Social Security Administration. Sam had his own business, and when he retired he turned the business over to family members. SSA is saying that Sam did not adequately separate himself from the business, accusing him of having worked at the business after his retirement. Sam has good documentation, and we can probably resolve this for him.

When I went to a massage therapist to have my sore neck massaged, one of the masseuses, also a postal worker, told me that she wanted to take a year's leave of absence to obtain a master's degree, but she had been refused the year's leave. I think I can prevail on our local Postmaster, Woody Connors, to grant her the leave.

Jeff and I visited Annie Ackerman at her apartment in Point East. Annie is doing well considering the severity of her illness. She does have difficulty getting out of bed, but the cancer seems to be in remission. Leaving Annie's, we went to the Point East Wednesday night discussion group, hosted by Charlotte Weinberg. Before her illness, Annie headed this group. Charlotte does not have the know-how and informed background that Annie has, but she did an adequate job. The questions dealt primarily with extended health care for catastrophic illness and the usual hostile questions, e.g., "What are we going to do about the rioting Cubans in the Atlanta and Louisiana jails?" and "How are we going to handle the influx of new Cubans (about 20,000) arriving in South Florida over the next few years?" "Before the Cubans are allowed to enter the United States," I said, "they first have to meet the criteria of 'reunification of families.'" This is a nonarguable reason to permit immigration. Referring to the immigration law that allows 500,000 immigrants to come to the United States, 20,000 from any one country, I reminded them that this same law also applied to the Jews in Iran or Soviet Jews who may want to immigrate to the United States.

As to the prison riots, I told them I had no patience for the prisoners' cause. They were here on parole and should have thought about their expulsion back to Cuba before committing violent acts of crime and dealing in drug trafficking, which placed them in our penitentiaries to begin with. The microphone system was not very good and I was tired, so I made this my last event for the evening.

NOVEMBER 26 THURSDAY (THANKSGIVING DAY)

Today, nothing political, just enjoyed Thanksgiving dinner with the family.

NOVEMBER 27 FRIDAY

My grandson Matthew and I were at the Federal Building today in the U.S. Passport Office to secure his passport for the trip to Turkey. We had forgotten Matthew's birth certificate but Mrs. Siebert, Chief of the Passport Office, very kindly prepared the passport anyway. Patty Diaz from our office was there, and will bring the birth certificate to Mrs. Siebert on Monday when picking up the passport. Patty will send it to Washington to have the visa for Turkey stamped into the passport.

NOVEMBER 28 SATURDAY

I called Rabbi Neuman today to discuss last Wednesday's *Wall Street Journal* article about the new attitude of eventual elimination of the Berlin Wall and the death of 79 year old Helmut Aris, President of the Association of Jewish Communities of the GDR. Strangely, and according to the Rabbi, Aris was buried today, Sabbath, which is contrary to old Jewish customs.

NOVEMBER 29 SUNDAY

It's 7:00 p.m., and I am back at my Washington townhouse. I would have been here sooner, but the plane was hovering over Virginia for about an hour waiting until the President's helicopter landed.

NOVEMBER 30 MONDAY

Meeting with Tom, Greg, and Lucy, we still do not know the precise cut our appropriations subcommittee will be subjected to in the transportation portion of the Budget Summit Conference. It could be anywhere from zero to $300 million depending on how cuts are allocated and how the Congressional Budget Office scores the sale of preference Federal Railroad Administration shares which we hope to use as an outlay reduction in our bill. The Senate, of course, does not use such a sale in the same way in their bill. We have a lot to work out, but we have to wait until Jamie Whitten calls together all the subcommittee chairs and tells us if the cuts will be taken evenly across the board or based on some other criteria.

In the afternoon after tennis with my House buddies, Gerald Greenfield came in with teamster members to discuss problems with the Rico racketeering law and how it could possibly adversely affect the teamsters. They handed me a letter addressed to the Department of Justice with approximately 180 of my colleagues' signatures, and wanted me to also sign. I did not particularly want to sign, but since most of my member friends had signed I asked Nadine and Marsha, two of my legislative assistants, to check the matter thoroughly, and if there is nothing woefully objectionable, I will sign.

Irma Rochlan of Hallandale, Florida, called to ask for my endorsement of her reelection to the Florida State Legislature. I had endorsed her in previous elections, and did so again without hesitation.

Chapter 12

DECEMBER 1, 1987 - TUESDAY

Much media attention have been given to the Cuban detainees held in the Atlanta Federal prison, and this morning South Florida Cubans, including representatives from the Florida State House of Representatives, came in to inquire about the situation. I said to them that in terms of the immigration section of the proposed agreement between the United States and Cuba, I have no problem with the "reunification of families" program, enabling people coming in from Cuba and even Cubans from third world countries to join their families in the United States. And, as to those in jail or others on parole status, I indicated my strong advocacy for due process before deportation. They seemed satisfied after hearing this, but this is a no-win situation. Many of the detainees had in Cuba committed violent acts of crime and although most have paid their debts to society, there is no place to release them to unless we send them back to Cuba or a possible third world country that may or may not want them. They also wanted to know if I could get for them the original list of Cubans whose names are in the proposed agreement, to have on hand in the event the agreement went through. I doubt if I can get the list, but I told them I would make inquiries through the Justice Department.

That evening I went to the Kennedy Center where NBC did a live broadcast on "America's Future, a Presidential Forum" featuring the Democratic and Republican candidates for the President of the United States. None of the candidates on either side was particularly impressive, but I did think George Bush did best; Dukakis was unexceptional.

DECEMBER 2 WEDNESDAY

Jeb Bush from Miami, our Vice President's son, hosted a breakfast meeting this morning that included the Florida Congressional Delegation, staff from the Florida Department of Commerce, heads of the State Universities Systems projects, and Presidents Criser of the University of Florida and Brown of the University of South Florida. I stayed long enough to hear Jeb's speech on the development of Florida's high-tech industry, and then left for a meeting in my office with former colleague, Teno Roncalio. Teno is now a public relations lobbyist, and was in to discuss the Canadian free trade agreement and its adverse effects on his uranium mining clients in Wyoming. I am a free trader, but when Teno was a member, he was one of my favorite colleagues, a liberal Democrat from a conservative state, and I will do what I can to help him. He understands though that if the trade bill vote is close, I will vote for the trade agreement.

Jamie Whitten called a meeting of the appropriations subcommittee chairmen to discuss the rule on the Continuing Resolution, and we all agreed to oppose any authorizing legislation made "in order" by the Rules Committee because of the difficulty this would pose to the passage of the Appropriations Continuing Resolution. After the meeting, Machinists Union members approached me about adding language to the CR prohibiting a Department of Transportation regulation which permits American Airlines to do certain overhaul procedures overseas. Authorizing committee chairman Norman Mineta also asked me to do this, but I told them all that I would stick with Jamie and keep authorizing legislation out of the Continuing Resolution.

The problem fast approaching is how to deal with the transportation portion of the total domestic cuts in outlays, to be worked out in the Senate-House Conference on the Continuing Resolution. From our share it looks as though we may have to cut about $300 million in our transportation bill. On the House Floor, I saw members whom I had not seen since before Thanksgiving. Charlie Wilson had a good trip and said the Turks were looking forward to my visit.

A Dade Christian School student, Troy Williams, came to the office and we had a photo opportunity. Troy is part of the Congressional Youth Leadership Council and is applying to the West Point Academy. An overachieving, old-fashioned 1950's kid with a crew cut, a "back to the future" type, I got him on the phone with Patrice and I think we can help him with an appointment to West Point. As he's captain of the baseball, soccer, and football teams, and president of the student body, West Point could do worse.

DECEMBER 3 THURSDAY

Gary Hymel came in this morning representing the tobacco industry, lobbying for the new R.J. Reynolds cigarette that does not give off any tobacco smoke. Apparently the cigarette has a smoking element by which flavor passes through the tobacco and contains no tobacco element that burns. R.J. Reynolds is promoting this newfangled cigarette as something that could possibly be smoked on airplanes. I told him if this cuts down the harm from tobacco I would not have a problem, but I would first have to see how it did in real life.

We had many votes on the Floor today, and at 6:15 p.m., I am in the office waiting for the bells to ring for our next vote. Voting was supposed to go until 9:00 p.m., but we will be out in a half hour because of a threatening snowstorm. There is nothing like a snowstorm to get legislation moving much faster. Similar, accelerated action is going to happen later, on the Continuing Resolution, when some members opposed to the CR will vote for it as that is the only way they will get out before

Christmas and avoid having to come back after the holiday to complete the Continuing Resolution conference.

I am now involved with an airport in Ft. Walton Beach, Florida, where DOD is kicking commercial and general aviation out of Eglin Air Force Base. Lobbyist Eli Feinberg and I are working together to keep it there.

DECEMBER 4 FRIDAY

Dr. Hubert Rosomoff and his wife Rene, from the University of Miami's Medical School Pain Center are in town, and we met today with staff head Mike Stephens of the Health and Human Services Appropriations Subcommittee office for clarification and assurance that the Rosomoff's out-patient pain clinic is medically verifiable and therefore can be accorded the same consideration as any other medical service in the handling of Medicare payments. Mike Stephens was very helpful, and had the Rosomoff's leave written questions with him that he could have his subcommittee chairman ask the Social Security Administration when the Director comes before the subcommittee next March. Staffer Bettilou on the subcommittee was there, and told of recurring pain that she had in her neck and back. Mrs. Rosomoff showed Bettilou how to relieve her pain by using pressure points and manipulation and even in the way she handled her body. Afterwards I spoke briefly in the corridor with Dade County Manager Sergio Pereira, who was in Washington meeting with South Florida members about potential problems of a new wave of Cuban immigrants.

1:45 p.m., lobbyist Stu Eizenstat came in with Moroccan Ambassador Bargach about earmarking funds for Morocco in the Continuing Resolution. The Senate has already earmarked and Morocco wants the House to do the same. This will put Morocco in the same league as Israel, Egypt and other countries that have earmarks. I did not promise anything but Morocco has been a good friend to the United States and one of the least harmful nations to Israel in the Arab world.

2:15, Neville Lamdan from the Israeli Embassy came in regarding Israeli debt restructuring, which is also coming up in the Continuing Resolution. The money Israel owes on arm sales, the United States should have sent to them as a grant, as is now done, and not as a military credit sale. So now Israel owes over $5 billion for these past years in military credit sales and the United States, to make up for this, should help Israel. Next week I will be meeting with staffer Bill Schuerch on Appropriations Foreign Ops subcommittee, and I'll also get with other Foreign Ops subcommittee members to try to bring Israel some relief on these interests cost and the resulting financial burden.

My next appointment at 3:00 was with Mike Finkelstein and directors of the injury prevention research centers involved in the joint injury prevention program of the National Highway Transportation Safety Administration and the Center for Disease Control. Dr. and Mrs. Rosomoff were there. Injury is epidemic, especially in relation to highway traffic accidents, and should be treated as a disease. The trauma treatment people there expressed appreciation for the transportation money we appropriated for the CDC for epidemic research on trauma, which now qualifies as an epidemic at the Center for Disease Control.

This evening at the reception honoring the new Secretary of Transportation, Jim Burnley, and the new Deputy Secretary of Transportation, Mimi Dawson, I told Jim that among the Department of Transportation Secretaries I've worked with, he was my favorite tiger and also my favorite pussycat. He laughed, as he knew what I meant. At the reception I then looked for Allan McArtor, FAA's new Administrator, as I had information to give him from Eli Feinberg regarding the new Emerald Coast airport in the Florida panhandle that Eli's clients want to construct. Eli wants and needs the FAA's support because officials at Eglin Field Air Force Base are opposed to this new private airport. My problem is that there may be others trying to build airports in other locations in the panhandle and I do not want to be caught up in panhandle politics.

DECEMBER 5 SATURDAY

Quiet day.

DECEMBER 6 SUNDAY

Today I took Joan on the Washington Metro with Adele, Wynne, and Karen, the three young female Jewish staffers in our office, to participate in the March for Soviet Jewry. There must have been two hundred thousand people at the March, but we managed to find Floridians: Senator Lawton Chiles, Congressman Bill Nelson, State Representative Elaine Bloom, and activist Miriam Wolfe. Marching with them for a while, we found other South Florida delegation members and joined them. We also saw and spoke with George Berlin, President of North Miami Beach Temple Sinai, and reporters from the Hollywood/Ft. Lauderdale papers and from the *Miami Herald*. While looking for other Florida members, I missed the opportunity to get up in the V.I.P. section for the ceremony.

In the evening Joan and I will go to the Kennedy Center Gala, and in the morning Joan leaves for Miami.

DECEMBER 7 MONDAY

Greg, Lucy, and I met this morning to discuss the problems we may face in next week's conference on the transportation section of the Continuing Resolution. Because the Budget Summit Conference added $500 million to Foreign Operations, the other twelve appropriations subcommittees will have to reduce by $3.1 billion, instead of the $2.6 billion as originally thought. Our transportation function will therefore be cut by $300 million, and this is in addition to the two percent across-the-board cut we already took on the House Floor. Transportation Secretary Jim Burnley called during the meeting, imploring me to exempt the reduction for appropriations to the FAA as the FAA wants to add more traffic controllers. I made no commitment, but told him he should speak to my subcommittee colleague Bob Carr if he wanted FAA allies.

It is 3:00 p.m., and the big news today is that Senator Lawton Chiles has decided not to run for reelection. This is a shock, but I think part of the reason for his decision is that the Senate keeps such crazy working hours, plus the fact that it has such a terrible system. I do not think Lawton wants to spend six more years meeting the Senate's scheduling terms. He called personally to thank me for my friendship, and I told him how much he had meant to me; we have not always agreed but we do have a community of spirit. Traveling to China together and the fact that we both had serious illnesses within the last five years I guess gave us a common bond. The *Miami Herald* called asking for my interpretation of why Lawton was retiring. My response was that "Lawton must have had a kind of spiritual revelation that said it is time to quit." It will be interesting to see if the *Herald* prints my comment.

In the evening at the Airbus Industries of North America reception, it was good to see and speak with my old Florida friend Alan Boyd, the former Secretary of Transportation, who is now the legislative liaison for Airbus. The event was held at the Corcoran Gallery of Art, and it was a great party - musically and culturally entertaining with excellent food, including Russian caviar.

DECEMBER 8 TUESDAY

Gorbachev has been in Washington for a few days and for several hours each day the House goes into recess while some members, mostly of the House leadership, go to the White House to meet with him. Thankfully this gives me the time I need to catch up on details and settle any loose ends before the CR conference.

Bill Schuerch and Adele are in a working-lunch session with me today on debt restructuring for Israel and perhaps for other countries. We tried for a solution to prevent Dave Obey from asking for a separate Floor vote on the issue or from taking out "special orders" to oppose this debt restructuring. Any break in the high interest rates that Israel, or Egypt or Turkey is hoping for is going to be reflected in increased congressional budget authority scoring and perhaps also in larger outlay numbers. Obey does not mind reducing Israel's debt service cost, but he does not want to break congressional budget restrictions to do so. This is more a matter of bookkeeping than anything else. The money Israel uses to service the debt comes from U.S. foreign aid funds for economic security (FES); the same to Egypt and other countries.

During the meeting Miami Haitian Jacques Despinossa

arrived early for his appointment. Not wanting to leave the meeting I had my secretary Wynne tell Jacques to come back at 2:00, the time originally scheduled for his appointment. Despinossa said he would come back, but he never showed. I was also to meet with Mary Rose Oakar to discuss her race for Democratic Caucus Chair, but I had to call to ask her to postpone the meeting until early 1988, and she agreed.

After Bill and Adele, most of the remaining afternoon was spent with Lucy, Greg and Tom going over the amendments in disagreement we have with the Senate version of our transportation bill. This is hard, detailed work, splitting the differences or receding to the Senate, or asking the Senate to recede to us or receding with a compromise amendment. This is part of the job that I do. Thursday I will meet with my counterpart, Frank Lautenberg, Chair of Appropriations Senate Subcommittee on Transportation, to see if we can resolve most of the differences before going into conference.

Many holiday parties are being held. Typically the parties will go on until Congress adjourns for the year, but I have managed to skip most of them. I did get to Boeing's party this evening at the Hyatt Regency. Boeing has been supportive of my position in siding with DOT against the Machinists Union which wants me to prevent DOT from changing regulations permitting American air carriers to have their planes serviced overseas. This country services more foreign aircraft here with our union labor than we will ever have serviced overseas. I need to get information and evidence from Boeing officials to support my position.

DECEMBER 9 WEDNESDAY

9:00 a.m., the Florida Congressional Delegation had its meeting on the medical malpractice problems in our State, and also received a briefing on the recent events with Eastern Airlines. Charlie Bennett, the Dean of our delegation, chaired the meeting. Bill Bryant from Governor Martinez's legal office, and Don Gifford and David Nye on the State's Academic Task Force assigned to study the medical malpractice problem gave a review of their findings. I primarily wanted to find out what we should do to relieve the malpractice liability that has been a stumbling block for the implementation of shock trauma centers. We have gotten money for shock trauma from the National Highway Traffic Safety Administration to help support trauma hospitals in Dade County, but the original second level trauma centers have now closed, and for two reasons: Too much indigent care, and the trauma surgeons' exposure to malpractice. I made these points to the governor's malpractice task force, but there is really nothing that can be done on the federal level other than to be supportive of the State's effort.

Then Phil Bakes, CEO from Eastern Airlines, briefed us on the problem with a Labor Department mediator renegotiating a labor contract for the Machinists Union with Eastern. If the machinists and unskilled laborers of the Machinists Union, like baggage handlers, do not renegotiate their level of pay, which Bakes says is way out of line, $40,000 a year for a baggage handler, then Eastern will probably shrink its operations in Miami to practically nothing, and we will lose one of our biggest and best employers in South Florida.

Eastern has for years been the largest private employer in Greater Miami. I have a good relationship with Bakes but I have to stay out of these negotiations between labor and Eastern management. Speaking about this to a *Miami News* reporter, I told her that we will try to do what we can to get the Labor Department mediator moving before Eastern, which is financially hemorrhaging with its present cost structure, is no longer able to function. I took the reporter to meet with staffer Bob Kingsley on Appropriations Labor, Health, and Human Services Subcommittee, who briefed her on the mediation process and the critical time factor.

Back at the office Ken McKay, President of Local 29 of the Miami Transit Workers, and Art Luby, Washington representative of the Union, were waiting for me to discuss the failure of the Department of Transportation PEP Grant in Miami. The PEP Grant provided for ninety-one buses from UMTA, half to be used by private-sector contractors and the other half to be used by the Metro-Dade Transit Authority to compare efficiency of private versus public sector operations. The main problem is that Dade County's budget is shy of the necessary funds to pay the operating costs of these ninety buses, which came free from UMTA. Miami's bus fleet is decreasing because Dade does not have a dedicated source of revenue to operate its transit system. What Dade County promised in order to get this grant is not what they are now able to deliver. I spoke to Commissioner Clara Oesterle at great length today about the failure of Dade County's administration to live up to its commitment. It is all very complicated but the gist of it is, expectations were greater than the funds Dade County could make available for these new additional buses. In truth, public versus private was a gimmick to get these badly needed buses for Metro-Dade.

The Democratic members on Appropriations Foreign Ops Subcommittee met this morning with Chairman Dave Obey. Nothing much was decided on debt restructuring except an agreement that Dave would tell lobbyists such as AIPAC for Israel and others for Egypt and Turkey that we would not make any commitment for any plan to restructure the debt, whether it was a "buy down" by lowering the interest rate, or allowing countries to prepay present debt loans through private sector banks with a ninety percent guarantee by the United States. Dave will not do anything that will increase either Congressional budget authority or budget outlays. I think we may have a way out by just lowering the present interest rate or going through private banks and then the United States compensate the first year by cutting back foreign military sales (FMS) to Israel and extending a grant for the same amount. This would not increase our outlays, as the loss of interest income will be offset by the decrease in foreign military sales, at least for the first year. The negative aspect is that this will be reflected in budget authority increase in the out years. This is all an accounting charade to make the budget look better.

Mid-afternoon we had our office Christmas party. My former personal/appointment secretary, Ida Levin, was back, as was Maggie Schneider, our former receptionist. Maggie now has a job in the private sector, and Ida seems happy in retirement. It was like old home week and very nice. I went to a flop of a party, however, in the Senate Dirksen Building with Maggie and Wynne. Twentieth Century Fox and Berkeley Books held the affair in the Rayburn Building in recognition of the author of *Wall Street*, a book made into a movie starring Michael Douglas. The party was prologue to the private screening of the movie.

After the party everyone it seems, but me, went to the Circle Avalon Theater on Connecticut Avenue for the private showing. Later I was sorry I did not go, as Michael Douglas was there, and I thought that I would have enjoyed meeting him.

DECEMBER 10 THURSDAY

This morning I learned that the House would be in session Friday and there would be votes on the Endangered Species Bill, so I cancelled my Friday trip to St. Louis on the funding request for bi-state transit. I do not have what I consider a good environmental voting record, and feel I need to be here to vote. Besides, I will probably need to be here tomorrow to follow through on the results of my afternoon meeting today with Senator Lautenberg, in preparation for the CR conference Monday. We are hoping to work out the differences in the transportation appropriations bill between the Senate and House versions on fifty or sixty amendments, perhaps more.

At 10:00, lobbyist Hector Alcalde came in about the problem of access roads for trucks, especially in New Jersey. The trucking company he represents wants to expand the use of heavy duty trucks now on certain restricted roads in the Northeast. 10:30, Julian Garcia came in with Ambassador Valdez, a former AID official at the State Department. Julian, who is Chairman of both RENFE, the Spanish Government Railway Company, and the joint venture of RENFE/TALGO, invited me to Spain. At this time, however, I do not want to take on any overseas trips. When I told him of my busy schedule, he said they may bring over a high-speed train as a demonstration project to see how it runs on our tracks. Maybe with RENFE's low center of gravity Amtrak can do a higher speed on the same roadbeds it has now.

Afterwards Congressman Lindsay Thomas of Savannah, Bill Sprague, President of Savannah Foods, and the Vice President Joel Williams, came in asking for help with legislation in our Foreign Operations bill which would increase sugar imports, to be refined in Savannah and then sent back to Caribbean countries and the Philippines. Everything they said sounded okay, but I understood that the Clewiston, Florida, sugar people had some problems and I knew that my good friend, Atwood

Dunwody, represented them. I called Atwood and he was most appreciative saying that he would look into the matter and call me back.

Eli Feinberg, Lloyd Blue, and Larry Anchor were in at 1:30 to discuss the proposed regional airport on the Emerald Coast (Florida panhandle). Working with Congressman Earl Hutto, we hope to convince the FAA to recommend an airport in that area. Undoubtedly the need exists for another airport in that region, but the Air Force has presented a problem in that it has closed Eglin Field and the adjacent airspace to commercial aviation. I will support the effort to get the airport started, but I won't work against Earl Hutto to do so, as the location is in his district.

Senator Lautenberg and I went into our meeting at 2:00, and we were able to come to terms on many of the amendments in disagreement, especially on the highway demonstration projects. There were only two Senate demonstration projects and eight House projects. The Senate receded to the House on the House projects, and the House receded to the Senate on the Senate projects except that Lautenberg wanted House members with more than one project to give something back. So, I had to go to Bob Carr to have him give up one of his demonstration projects in order to keep the House funds for the new airplane that he wants bought for the FAA. And, I had to see Marty Sabo about his FAA language Senator Lautenberg wants dropped. Marty was willing to drop the language to preserve his demonstration project. I also spoke to Steny Hoyer from Maryland because Lautenberg wants the House to recede to the Senate on the Washington-Metro figures, which is $19 million below the House. If the House does this, Lautenberg will recede on Hoyer's demonstration project. We will probably split the Washington-Metro two-thirds of the way down and try to preserve most of Hoyer's demonstration project. This took some back and forth negotiating.

Budget Committee Chair Bill Gray did not put the $240 million from the sale of preference shares in the House-Senate Budget Conference. I told Gray that this would threaten his two projects at Temple University and the Broad Street Station in Philadelphia. He will try to recover the projects, but said it may already be out of his control. If it is, then he will lose his two projects.

The main thing now is cutting about $400 million out of our final bill which is about a four-percent cut across the board, and Lautenberg wants to cut only two percent in FAA operations because of his public position on air traffic safety, and cut five percent on everything else. I am reluctant to do this because there are other programs in our bill that deal with safety besides air traffic. Coast Guard Search and Rescue, Federal Highways, National Highway Traffic Safety, Railway Safety are but a few, so I will see what can be done that will be less adverse to these essential programs.

On the House Floor the talk was about Florida Senator Lawton Chiles not running for reelection. My House colleagues Larry Smith and Dan Mica are all pepped. Former Democratic Florida Governor Reubin Askew is said to be interested in running, but Larry Smith and Dan Mica both feel they can beat him. I think they are both delusional.

DECEMBER 11 FRIDAY

My first meeting this morning with Ed Stimpson and General Tallman, President of Embry-Riddle Aeronautical University in Daytona, Florida, was an effort on their part to secure $2-3 million in our transportation bill for the airway science program at Embry-Riddle. Unfortunately there just is not that kind of money available, and I said to them that it looked as though they would end up with about $200 thousand. Afterwards, Admiral Yost and Guy Goodwin of the Coast Guard came in primarily to emphasize the dire problems of reducing the Coast Guard funding, but they also spoke about their ongoing frustration with the appropriations process. The Coast Guard would like to have a steady appropriation instead of each year waiting to see what Appropriations Transportation and Defense Subcommittees will provide.

The CR conference begins next week, and it is going to be very painful, as we may have to cut even more than $400 million. Not only did the Budget Conference take money out of transportation to put into foreign operations, but it reprogrammed funds for the IRS and the Treasury Department as well. Now, on the Floor, we are awaiting one more vote on the reconciliation bill so that conferees can be appointed. While waiting, everyone has been "hitting me up" on the House Floor. Members want me to protect, in the rule, the amendment prohibiting the FAA from closing down flight service stations. Also now instead of a ninety-day period, Bob Carr wants a year's extension on the time charter airlines now have to revise fire prevention materials inside airplanes. And, Richard Durbin wants me to write a letter to be made part of the CR conference report language about OMB's misrepresentation of the costs to enforce his legislation on the nonsmoking ban on airplanes. In the midst of this, Dave Obey asked if I would do a fundraiser in Miami for him in January. I agreed to the fundraiser, but told Obey I would have to do it in the Spring, after my own fundraiser.

The National Aeronautics Association put on its black-tie dinner affair this evening at the Omni-Shoreham Hotel on Calvert Street. I went especially to hear the keynote speaker Lee Iacocco. Invited to sit on the dais, I declined since Joan was not with me and chose instead to sit at a table with Maria Elena Torano, with whom I came, and with people from the Chrysler Corporation. Tom Kingfield from my subcommittee staff sat at a nearby table with other Chrysler people. Chrysler wanted the FAA to buy its Gulfstream Jet because the FAA's own major aircraft is twenty-five years old and is costing the FAA $3 million a year to maintain. We have $18 million earmarked in the House bill for the purchase of a new aircraft for the FAA, but Lautenberg in the Senate has not yet agreed to this. I think the purchase of this aircraft is to everyone's advantage. The evening wore on too long, and I was tired, so I did not stay for Iacocco's speech. I did speak to him, however, saying jokingly that my son Bill was a Dodge dealer, and if he would write Bill telling him to convince me to buy Chrysler's Gulfstream Jet, then that is what I would do. "You've got a deal," responded Iacocco.

Admiral Yost was at the event, as was FAA Administrator Allan McArtor. McArtor is worried that he is going to lose some air traffic controllers due to cutbacks. Although I left before the speeches began, I felt I made points with the Chrysler Corporation.

DECEMBER 12 SATURDAY

Today I took it easy and will do the same tomorrow and catch up on my reading.

DECEMBER 13 SUNDAY

I had brunch today with Bob Carr and his girlfriend who works for Michigan Senator Don Reagle, and Diane Blatman who works for Carr on Appropriations. Still full from breakfast, I ordered a Bloody Mary and a cappuccino while they had the brunch. We were at Julio's, a new restaurant on Pennsylvania Avenue, and it was fun talking about what was to happen next week when trying to wrap up the Continuing Resolution.

Later, Bill Bayer from WINZ Radio in Miami called to interview me on the PEP Grant. Expressing my total disappointment in the way the private vs. public bus demonstration project was handled, I said that the PEP plan had not come up to the anticipation or projection from when it was first conceived, and I placed blame on the Dade County administration, where it rightfully belonged. The interview will be aired this evening in Miami.

DECEMBER 14 MONDAY

Arizona member Mo Udall, Interior and Insular Affairs Committee Chairman, had a book-signing reception this evening, and I took Theresa Williams, with whom I play tennis, and Jo Deutch, her roommate. I bought copies of Udall's new book, "*Too Funny to be President,*" one for each of us, and eventually I will ask Mo to sign them for us.

DECEMBER 15 TUESDAY

Gary Hymel came in this morning with the Turkish Ambassador Sukru Elekdag. I need to spend more time with them, but the appropriations CR process has kept me constantly on the move and in negotiations. Also, twice I was invited to dinner at the French Embassy, and both times I just did not have a chance to go. But this evening I am looking forward to attending my friend and colleague Pete Stark's annual Christmas party.

Each year Pete hosts a dinner party at his home on the same day as the White House Congressional Black-Tie Christmas Ball. Members first attend Pete's party, and then go on to the White House Ball. Pete's parties are always delightful, full of congenial atmosphere, and this year he added a harpist, which I thoroughly enjoyed. As mentioned, Pete and I came to Congress together in 1973, and we have many mutual friends, namely Don Edwards from California, Bob and Dorothy Kastenmeier from Wisconsin, Judge Abner Mikva and his wife, Zoe, and James and Pat Schroeder from Colorado, who also came in with me in 1973. They were all there, as was Barbara Boxer, George Miller, and other San Francisco Bay area members. George Miller was telling some funny stories. George bought a house on the Hill for his family but his wife moved back to San Francisco, so he now shares the house with three other members - Leon Panetta also from California, Marty Russo from Illinois, and Chuck Schumer from New York. The stories were all about the house and the antics of these four weekday bachelors living there. California member Howard Berman's wife is doing a television sitcom based on the house and it is funny how she changes the characters around. Instead of having four males she will probably have one black female in the bunch. I took Alice Rivlin with me and many of the people there were her old friends as well.

We then went to the White House Christmas Ball. It was beautiful and Alice was very impressed. Alice and I thought the President might have left the Ball by the time we arrived, but he was still there and we got to greet him. I had been to this gala several times since coming to Congress, and after an hour it was pretty old; we left about 9:30, and I was home by 10:00 pm.

DECEMBER 16 WEDNESDAY

This evening I took Wynne Frank to the Turkish Embassy but had to leave early to get back to Appropriations' foreign operations conference. We did stop by my neighbor Maurice Rosenblatt's party, but I had to miss Bob Kastenmeier's and Don Edwards's Christmas parties, also held this evening.

DECEMBER 17 THURSDAY

This has been one busy week trying to put provisions of my transportation appropriations bill into the Continuing Resolution package. It's meant several meetings with my counterpart on the Senate side, Frank Lautenberg, to work out the seventy-five amendments in disagreement; working with Tom, Greg, and Lucy on the details; and then meetings with the Democratic members on our subcommittee and with ranking minority member Larry Coughlin to bring him up-to-speed on the changes.

We now have the problem of fitting into the bill the amendments that the Senate wants. The authorizing Public Works and Transportation Committee Chair Jim Howard does not want any authorizing language in the conference report. I thought we had it wrapped up yesterday, but finally this afternoon the Senate and House conferees worked out all the differences and I sent Jim Howard the message that we will have to authorize when necessary. It was one tough deal because I was being tugged back and forth. The staff did not want to do anything for members who had voted on the Floor for the two-percent cut in our bill. I was caught between Jim Howard and the appropriations process, and I was caught between what the Senate and what the House wanted. It was a four-day tug of war and my purpose was to have a transportation bill we could include in the Continuing Resolution that would not have amendments in disagreement between us and the Senate, which would make the entire transportation section of the bill open to amendments when the conference report came to the House Floor.

Besides my own bill, I have also been deeply involved with the foreign operations bill. The full conference worked until 11:00 last night, and we wrapped up the foreign ops portion by solving the main issue, which was debt restructuring for Israel and some of the other poorer debtor nations.

At this point it is difficult to recall people I have been in touch with during the week. I have been hammered on the Floor by members who wanted projects in the bill but asked too late for my help. Others wanted assurance that I do not recede to the Senate on things in our bill that they had wanted. Up to now we have been able to deal with what colleagues requested and still make the cuts that we had to. We have not, however, been credited for the $240 million from the sale of the FRA redeemable preference shares, so now we yet have to cut a little over $400 million from our bill. If we could get the preference shares scored in our favor this year, the cut could be reduced to a little over $140 million.

The Coast Guard is upset more than most of our agencies, but others also are not very happy. On the other hand, I am relatively satisfied, as I think Senator Lautenberg and I did the best we could. The members on our subcommittee were very helpful and did not cave in to Jim Howard's attack on the authorizing language. Senator Alphonse D'Amato (R-NY) was very sharp on the Senate side and the Senate staff, Pat McCann and Jerry Bonham, were easy to work with. In fact, right now the Senate staff and our staff are working in our subcommittee room to find out where we really are in this bill before taking it to full conference tomorrow.

I missed the ceremony today at the Urban Mass Transit Administration for Al DelliBovi who was sworn in as the new Administrator. I like Al, and wanted to be there for him, but I was very busy and could not make it. I also had to miss the opening celebration of the new Cineplex Odeon, which featured a champagne buffet and private screening of the film "The Last Emperor." The CR has really kept me tied up, and this has been a very tough week.

DECEMBER 18 FRIDAY

Last night was a dreary session. To summarize the events, around 5:00 p.m., we reported our subcommittee conference agreements to the full conference. Lautenberg and I had resolved our differences and had no amendments in disagreement. Senator D'Amato and Coughlin, the ranking minority members, also agreed. In full conference I moved to close our chapter and our portion is now done, thank God. Then the full conference adjourned until 7:00 p.m.

When we went back into session, it became a little chaotic because Mississippi Senator John Stennis, who was chairing the conference at his age of 86, was very tired, and could not hear or see well enough to recognize members who wanted to be recognized. About 9:30 p.m., the conference again recessed because now we could not agree on a television "fairness doctrine" provision or on compromise language for humanitarian aid to the Contras in Nicaragua. These two items still need to be resolved for us to have a conference report agreement that the President will sign. The House leadership, plus Foreign Ops chair Dave Obey, and Senator Ted Stevens, ranking minority on the Senate Defense Subcommittee, are meeting to resolve these issues to bring an end to the conference. Everybody is anxious to get back to their home districts for the holidays.

I went to the Brasserie and had a late dinner with Bill Gray, Marty Sabo, and Matt McHugh, three of my favorite members on Appropriations. Bill Gray was kind to pay the check, and it was a real pickup after a dreary evening.

Today I had to go back to the Senate for a transportation subcommittee mini-conference dealing with amendments which Public Works Chairman Jim Howard wanted us to put in from his committee's not-yet-passed technical corrections bill. Lautenberg and I agreed to take some Senate authorizing language and some House authorizing language. We took the $1 billion, which we had taken from the airport and airway trust fund for FAA operations, and put it back into the trust fund. We did put some Jim Howard demo projects in our bill, as we cannot get his support otherwise. But Jim did not think we did enough for him compared to what we did with Senate authorizing language, and he was unhappy.

We had to compromise on the 65 mph speed limit. On roads equivalent in character to the interstates, we agreed on a demonstration of 65 mph for four years, for the first twenty states that apply. That made Howard, Lautenberg, and myself unhappy, because we do not want to see the speed limit raised on any road any place. But, we needed votes from rural state senators. Finally, we hammered out the agreement. I had trouble with our own staff people. Apparently they had made commitments to the Public Works Committee staff to which our members did not want to adhere, as they did not know what was in the Public Works amendments. I said to the staff that we had to go with what we had because we had to satisfy our own members first, and if Jim Howard did not want it or did not like it there was not much he could do about it this year. Even if he voted against the Continuing Resolution we have the votes to pass it.

What I did not want to do was to take anything back to the House in disagreement, as to do so would open up our whole bill on the House Floor. That is why I accepted the compromise amendment on 65 mph from Senator Don Nickles of Oklahoma, although it made staffer Greg Dahlberg on our transportation subcommittee, and Lucy Hand, very unhappy. Finishing our section of the conference, we had to wait for the call of the full conference Chair.

The good thing is that, other than the disagreement on Contra funding, the conference really is about done. The problem with Contra aid is that unless the House passes a solution or compromises on a voice vote, I am afraid the House will not concur with the Senate. Too many House appropriation members in this conference are not only members of the Foreign Operations Committee but are also committed anti-Contra senior appropriators. We are not through yet.

A luncheon is scheduled in Miami Monday with our nominees to the Service Academies, but I am not sure I can make it. I will call Jeff and have him cancel the luncheon, as I think I will still be here in Washington Monday and Tuesday.

DECEMBER 19 SATURDAY

Today was good as I had nothing to do but just hang around. I had breakfast in the Longworth Cafeteria with my colleague friends Sonny Montgomery, Ed Boland, and Bill Natcher. At noon, Dante Fascell and I had lunch in the Members Dining Room; later, I played tennis at the Army-Navy Club with Sonny Montgomery, Bob Kastenmeier and Susie Hamrack, a court reporter on the House Floor.

Members are just hanging loose and making the best of things under stressful circumstances. Since getting through my part of the Continuing Resolution, I am more or less a spectator, even as far as foreign operations is concerned. We have all the Israel problems resolved. On the Contras, I am opposed, but I told Dave Obey that I would accept any compromise that he could work out, and to "just get us a bill which will be signed by the President."

DECEMBER 20 SUNDAY

At noon the House went into session and we adjourned at 5:00 p.m., after passing a one-day extension of the Continuing Resolution. The conference is to begin again tomorrow morning at 10:00. I hope next year we do not have to do a Continuing Resolution like this, as it is an awful way to legislate.

DECEMBER 21 MONDAY

We went back to conference this morning at 10:00 on the Continuing Resolution and passed the Contra compromise on a voice vote, so no one had to be recorded. The disagreement now is on the broadcasting fairness doctrine, and although this is not part of the appropriations Continuing Resolution, it is still part of the package. The conference recessed until the call of the Chair, which will probably be late this afternoon, and perhaps later this evening we can vote and then go home.

At 3:00, a meeting was held with Appropriations Chair Jamie Whitten, the subcommittee chairmen who support the Continuing Resolution, and Majority Whip Tony Coelho. Earlier I went to a leadership task force meeting, and between the task force and the subcommittee chairmen, we are trying to get enough votes to pass the Continuing Resolution. The problem now is that approximately only ninety Democrats and seventy-eight Republicans favor the Continuing Resolution. My job was to turn members around who were against the CR and who owe me because of what I had put in for them in the transportation bill. I did manage to turn six or seven members around whom I had helped. I put them on notice that they had to vote for the Continuing Resolution if they want subcommittee help in the future.

At the Capitol Physician's Office the lady surgeon on duty told me that she could remove the lump on the back of my shoulder right there in the office under local anesthetic. I told her I would prefer going to Dr. Elliot Strong who had operated on my neck at Memorial Sloan Kettering in New York. She had trained under Dr. Strong, and readily offered to schedule an appointment for me with him. So, on December 23, I am to be in New York to have the lump removed. I have to be careful because of my "big

C" problem, and I get excellent service from the Capitol Physician's Office, for which I am very grateful.

This New York trip means that I will not be returning to Miami as planned. Also, we will probably not be finished with the CR until Christmas, and I am now concerned about whether we will be finished by Sunday, December 28, when Joan and I plan to leave for England with our grandsons, Sean and Matt, and Wynne from my office staff. It is 7:15 p.m., and we are still waiting on a call from the Chair of the House.

The Associated Press called today about the conference and the $8 million earmarked for the school in France for French Jewish refugees. I told the reporter that the funds were earmarked at the request of Senator Inouye of Hawaii, and the reason Inouye had made the request was because his good friend (Zev Wolfson) had asked him to, and Inouye promised him that he would. I did not give the Associated Press the name of Zev Wolfson, as I thought that would have to come from Senator Inouye.

DECEMBER 22 TUESDAY

We went last evening until about 2:30 this morning, and the House passed the Continuing Resolution by one vote. It was an interesting session. I let certain members off the hook so that they could vote against the Continuing Resolution. Some members would have voted with us if I had needed them. The Whip's office complimented me for the job I did in turning members around. And yet, though I accept the credit, I think in the final analysis members really voted for the Continuing Resolution just to get out for Christmas.

Today we are just waiting for the President to sign the package. We will go into session at 1:00 p.m., and I believe an announcement on the President signing the CR will be made at that time. Many members have already left. My tennis buddies have all gone home so if I play tennis today it will be with Judge Mikva.

It was a dreary day with my friends gone, but I had to stay around to go up to New York tomorrow for the minor surgery. Radio reporter Harold Cessna came in. Cessna is with the Cox News Service which broadcasts over WIOD in Miami, and he taped me on the year's wrapup. I also did a tape late last evening with Bill Bayer of WINZ Radio and gave basically the same information that I gave to Cessna on what we had or had not accomplished during the year.

DECEMBER 23 WEDNESDAY

In New York today, Dr. Strong removed the lump on my shoulder. I was there and back the same day, and even for those few hours, I was eager to leave Washington and have the change of scenery. Dr. Strong is to call tomorrow with the results.

It is 5:00 p.m., and quiet in the office, even in the Rayburn Building corridors. The computers, the phones, the typewriters and the chatter have all just about shut down. Around 7:30 p.m., I called Irwin Witt, Miami's new Democratic Club President, and spoke to his group on a long distance, public address hookup. The call was very successful, and I enjoyed doing it. Those on the receiving end thought it took a good deal of time and technology to set this up, but it only took about an hour. They had wanted me there in person, but at least this effort showed I was involved with them. After a brief statement, I answered their questions on social security, aid to Israel, and beach restoration. It was good politics, and a big hit with my basic community support system in Miami.

DECEMBER 24 THURSDAY

This Christmas Eve morning, the good news is from Dr. Strong. The biopsy from the lump on my shoulder showed no signs of any cancer cells. I am fine and can now relax and not worry about future surgery.

I am waiting now in the office for the plane tickets to come from the Turkish Embassy.

DECEMBER 25 CHRISTMAS

From now until we leave on our trip to Turkey, I will be making preparations for the trip.

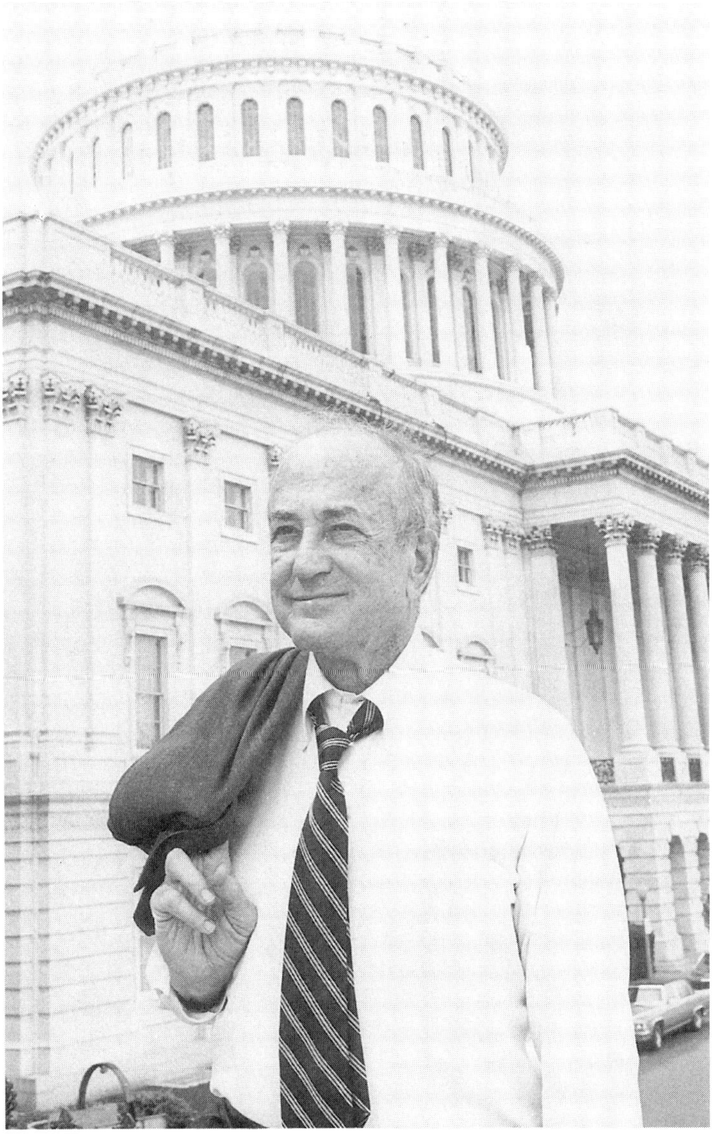

William Lehman at the capital

The Miami

76 PAGES

WEDNESDAY, OCTOBER 19, 1988

Lehman wins release of 3 from Cuban jails

By IVAN ROMAN and RODRIGO LAZO

Three of Cuba's long-term political prisoners — men who spent more than 20 years in jail for opposing the Cuban government — arrived in Miami Tuesday with U.S. Rep. William Lehman to a warm reception ...

... release of the men.

"I'm breathing liberty for the first time in 23 years," said Alberto Jose Padron, 49, turning to his 83-year-old mother.

"You're so beautiful ..."

Local

Metromover payment clears hurdle

Veto of crime funds upsets Opa-locka officials

Congress responds with calls for president to take command

WASHINGTON — Miami Congressman Dante Fascell, chairman of the House Foreign Affairs Committee and a member of the select committee investigating the Iran-contra affair, praised the Tower Commission's work and said it would help the congressional committees probing the scandal.

Fascell agreed with the commission that the person responsible for the conduct of foreign policy should be the president. He also agreed that the fault lay with individuals, not with the system.

"As a result, the president doesn't look good, unfortunately," ...

Rep. Fascell | Sen. Chiles | Rep. Lehman | Sen. Graham

Among the lessons of the affair, Graham said, is: "When you deal with terrorists, that only prompts more terrorism."

... ranking Republican on the House Foreign Affairs Committee.

Woman's story reminds us to appreciate freedoms

Tom Fiedler

Media coverage of my endeavors.

The "F. P. and L." Fascell, Pepper and Lehman. Speaker Tip O' Neil said Miami-Dade had the most effective delegation in the House.

In the Roosevelt Room the "Gipper" tries to sell the house appropriators on aide to the contras.

Codal Dole in Southeast Asia

At an annual subcommittee hearing, the chairman hears testimony from Secretary Dole on the needs of the Transportation Department for the next fiscal year.

Prime Minister Shamir calls on a foreign aid appropriator on U.S. support for Israel.

Chapter 13

JANUARY 3, 1988 - SUNDAY

For several days now I have done nothing in a political way. We flew very early December 28 from Washington to New York, transferred to Pan Am and landed in London about 10:00 p.m. With me are Joan, our two grandsons Sean and Matt, and Wynne Frank from our office staff. Fran Karp, an Embassy VIP liaison, met us at Heathrow Airport and was very helpful; we did not impose further on the Embassy because its staff was shorthanded over the holidays. The press is aware of our visit, and since we were in London on holiday, we did not want any "bad junket" publicity.

I had hoped to take Sean and Matt to see the Parliament in session, but it was closed for the holidays. We had a good time, though, staying in London and spending New Year's Day in Cambridge. The following day, January 2, we departed London for Paris, where we stayed overnight in an airport hotel. The next morning we met the rest of the group at the Charles

DeGaulle Airport for our flight to Turkey. Including myself, there are five Congressmen and spouses on this trip - Dan Akaka (D-HI), Richard Durbin (D-IL), Mickey Edwards (R-OK), and John Porter (R-IL). Others include our staff aides and of course Gary Hymel and others from the public relations firm of Hill & Knowlton, under contract with the Turkish government. All of the congressmen are members of the Appropriations Committee, and Joan and I have traveled previously with them and their wives, so it was like being with old friends.

We arrived in Ankara, the capital of Turkey, late afternoon Sunday, January 3. Ankara is an uninviting, muddy, provincial capital. We will be in Turkey seven nights.

JANUARY 4 MONDAY

At 10:00 a.m., we were at the Embassy for a lengthy meeting with the Turkish Minister of Foreign Affairs. The message is getting across to us that Turkey wants more economic aid and that they do not want to pull their troops out of Cyprus. As we end the Cold War with Russia, Turkey worries we will no longer need bases in Turkey, where we spend approximately $500 million a year in military and economic aid.

At noon the Turkish Undersecretary for Bilateral Political Affairs held a luncheon at a private-estate guest house. The Secretary is very pompous and talked about Turkey giving more to the United States than they are getting from us. They do not care about our own budget restraints. Next on the agenda was a meeting with the President of the Turkish Parliament and with members of the Foreign Affairs Committee to discuss the various problems in appropriating for Turkey. The Turks are very good with English and did not need an interpreter, as many have spent years in the United States. Later, we attended a reception at the home of Bill Rope, the Chargé d'affaires, and afterwards we had dinner at a small restaurant with the Durbin's and the two boys to get away from the crowd.

JANUARY 5 TUESDAY

This morning we visited the Hittite Museum and then drove

forty miles to the factory where F16's are assembled. It is costing $20 million to build an F16 in Turkey, when the United States could send it over for $16 million, but Turkey needs the symbol for their own aerospace industry. It was a huge installation, and very interesting to see the F16's assembled by the Turks. They were very helpful and informative, and provided us with an excellent lunch.

Being very busy this afternoon, I tried to get out of meeting with Turkish Defense Minister Ercan Vuralhan but there was no one else to represent our group and the Chargé d'affaires and Gary Hymel prevailed on me to go. I was glad I did, as the Defense Minister was very impressive as he spoke about Turkey's military needs. 4:30, I met with the Turkish Prime Minister Turgut Ozal, a nice elderly man who had a good grasp of the issues, but is just a grandfather figure.

I find myself as senior member, on what I thought would be somewhat a holiday, in effect a codel leader, giving all the ceremonial toasts and all the diplomatic responses, introducing the members of our delegation and working like back in Washington. But it has been very interesting and I have learned a great deal, especially about Turkish relationships, not only to the United States but to its unique group of neighbors such as Syria, Bulgaria, Greece, the Soviet Union, and Iran. They have the most unusual common borders of any country in the Mideast and yet they have been a force for stability.

I feel good about the job I am doing here, keeping the meetings flowing and preventing the strong pro-Armenian, pro-Greek factions in our delegation, such as John Porter, from disrupting the meetings or causing problems. I make a conscious effort to share the spotlight and keep matters on a casual basis. Gary Hymel and our Ambassador have told me several times that I have been "right on target" in managing our side of the meetings.

At 9:00 p.m., we took the plane from Ankara to Izmir.

JANUARY 6 WEDNESDAY

In Izmir, we went to Ephesus in Western Turkey and spent most of the day sightseeing the Greek and Roman ruins. It was a wonderful way to view ancient history. We got back to the hotel at 5:00, just in time to dress and leave for the reception at the American Consulate. The reception was sponsored by the Board of Governors of the Turkish Businessmen's Association in honor of the U.S. Consulate General and Mr. and Mrs. Albert Williams, and it was very crowded. I met a friend there who lives part-time in Hallandale and was a contributor to my campaign. He is a big Turkish cotton grower and dye producer, and was actually the host of the post-reception dinner. The dinner was held in a private dining room among approximately fifty guests, featuring a belly dancer for entertainment. I sat at the head table where I again had to give the toast and make a speech. The guests included some very wealthy Turkish-Americans, and it surprised me the number of prominent Jewish-American Turkish businessmen there. I learned that the Jews had been in Turkey since 1492, and in four years there will be a big 500-year anniversary celebration marking the time that the Turkish ships brought the Jews from Spain into Turkey to save their lives. For 500 years the Jews have lived under a number of different regimes and governments in Turkey, the whole time without any persecution.

JANUARY 7 THURSDAY

Gary Hymel met me at the hotel this morning, and told me that last night he received a phone call from his Washington office about a very recent news article in the *Miami News* concerning the Turkish Ambassador. It seems that Jeff in our district office, who is also President of the North Dade Forum, a political club in Northeast Dade County, had booked the Ambassador Elekdag to speak at the Miami Shores Country Club. Meanwhile, Jeff had a standing invitation out to any of the presidential candidates who happen to be in the Miami area. Learning that the only presidential candidate to be in the area was the Greek-American Michael Dukakis, Ambassador Elekdag backed out; the Forum program subsequently fell apart as relations between the Greeks and Turks, both U.S. allies in the North Atlantic Treaty Organization, are strained and tension-filled with longstanding territorial and political disputes.

Having no prior knowledge of any of this, I was very disappointed in hearing that the Ambassador had accepted and then cancelled his speaking engagement, as he would have had some interesting stories to tell. The Forum has a strong Jewish membership and he would have told them that Turkey was the second country after the United States to recognize Israel. He would have also told them about the 500th anniversary of the Jews coming to Turkey in 1492 from Spain. Jeff should have been more aware of the dissension between Greece and Turkey, especially since there had been media coverage about Greek Prime Minister Andreas Papandreou and the Turkish Prime Minister Turgut Ozal meeting together in Switzerland in the very near future to try to resolve the Cyprus problem. When Dukakis accepted, Jeff told reporters he was so excited that he "didn't even think about the deep political background," and that it did not occur to him to tell the Dukakis people about the Ambassador. I called John at our Washington office, Jeff in the Miami office, and then the Turkish Ambassador to explain the mixup. I also told the Ambassador how gratifying it would be to me personally to welcome him in Miami, and how meaningful I thought it would be, especially to the Jewish community, to hear him speak about the Jewish history in Turkey. I ended by telling him that when I returned to the States we would write to reinvite him to Miami, and that I hoped he would accept.

After the phone calls, I went to a NATO briefing at the Southeast NATO Headquarters where we heard the same old bullshit, that the Warsaw-bloc countries are equipped three to one over the Turks. The only comment I made was that there is one of the Turkish armies on the borders of Syria and Iraq, which I thought ridiculous. It was like the United States paying to have one of our armed forces on the Mexican border to keep the Sandinistas from invading the United States. I have listened to NATO briefings in Belgium, Norway and elsewhere, and in all of the military operation briefings I have listened to, it is always the other side which has three to one firepower advantage over our side. I just wonder if the Warsaw-pact generals are telling their governments the very same thing: that the Western powers have a three to one advantage.

By the time I got back to the hotel there was no time for lunch as I had to go to the airport to get the plane to Istanbul. We departed Izmir at 2:00, and I am now at the Hilton Hotel in Istanbul. Joan is still in Izmir. The flight departure time was advanced one hour while Joan was sightseeing and therefore unaware of the change. She will be arriving in Istanbul about 10:00, and has cabled that she is okay.

At the Turkish Industrial and Business dinner this evening, I was the co-emcee with Omer, one of the business leaders. I told anecdotes about talking out of one side of my mouth - both as a politician and literally, because of my recent throat surgery. This went over very well, with laughs all around, especially when I added that I was also a former used car dealer. Prior to the dinner we had a small problem as Matt and Sean were told they could go to the dinner, and at the last minute were told they could not go. We got it straightened out, but not before I had the head man for the organization who had uninvited them, call them in their room and apologize; Gary Hymel also apologized. Nevertheless, everything is going okay, and I am getting comfortable in the role as the stabilizing factor among the members. They will not have a meeting without me because I seem to be able to keep the members balanced, not going excessively either anti- or pro-Turkish in their statements.

Joan has yet to arrive in Istanbul. Dick Durbin had lost his clothes on Air France and I told him, "You may have lost your clothes on Air France, but I lost my wife on Turkish Airlines." When I got back to the hotel, I happily greeted my wife.

JANUARY 8 FRIDAY

At breakfast this morning with the President of the Turkish Cypriots, the President was very emotional about the fact that he cannot get the Greek Cypriots to talk to him. All I could tell him to do was to be patient and things will come around. I used the example of the blacks in Mississippi and how things have changed there. It was a good breakfast. Later I had lunch with the Mayor, who talked about the horrendous mass transit problems in Istanbul. He is thinking about a light rail system, but gets no help from the central government.

Back at the hotel I took a genuine Turkish bath and will get ready for this evening's event, a fancy dinner given by the Naga's at the Renaissance Restaurant. Tomorrow morning our group will hold a press conference. So far on such occasions I have called on the other members to respond and they all do a good job, especially Dick Durbin, the least senior member, who wraps it all up very humorously and to the point. Mickey Edwards also does a good job. Danny Akaka, though good, goes on too long.

JANUARY 9 SATURDAY

Rep. Porter left Friday morning and Rep. Edwards left this morning. There are only three members now - Durbin, Akaka, and myself. I thought the three of us did a good job at the press conference this morning. Seyfi Tashaw, who heads the private-sector agency that funds the programs for the Turkish Institute for Foreign Policy, and who, incidentally, is sponsoring our trip, told me my statements to the press were his own feelings. One of the things I said at the press conference was that I thought if the IMF Treaty that Gorbachev and Reagan were speaking of at the Summit had to be confirmed by both the Turkish Parliament and the U.S. Senate, then the Treaty would not be ratified. The Turks are more fearful of the Soviet Union than we are. Seyfi said that we do a good job at press conferences, but I did have to clarity Danny Akaka when he said that the Greeks and the Turks had to settle the Cyprus question. He should have said that the Greek Cypriots and Turkish Cypriots had to settle it. This could have been a real blunder.

This afternoon we toured the Bosporus Strait (the waterway which connects the Mediterranean to the Black Sea) and on board I spent most of the time writing thank you letters. In the evening we went to the synagogue and will return there tomorrow for a photo opportunity, as it was very impressive. The synagogue, damaged by terrorists, has been rebuilt with private Turkish money. The Shamus, a young boy, was there. The former Shamus was killed in the recent attack. We saw photos of the damages, but it has all been rebuilt. The Jewish community in Istanbul is now about 15,000.

We had dinner at the Galata Tower Restaurant, located atop a 1500 year old tower built as a defense against invasion. After dinner there was a floor show and, again, a belly dancer was featured. Dick Durbin, who was sitting with his wife Loretta at the end of the table next to the stage, was invited to dance with the belly dancer. Dick, who only wanted to be a good sport, agreed to go up on the stage. She took off Dick's coat and he did a belly dance with her, all while flash bulbs were popping off. About an hour later we learned that one of the pictures taken was by a newspaper affiliate; fortunately, our Turkish hosts were able to discourage the printing of the photo.

JANUARY 10 SUNDAY

Today we went back to the synagogue and Durbin went with us. I let him do most of the talking to reporters so that he would have a good photo opportunity. There are no Sunday papers, but the Monday paper in Istanbul should carry the Saturday morning press conference as well as the story and photos taken at the synagogue. Gary Hymel said that the synagogue will be a "must" stop for all future delegations he brings here. We then went to a seaside resort for a late lunch hosted by the Hatat family; the meal was delicious, with the usual goodwill toasts between countries. The Hatat's are into everything, from manufacturing to agriculture, and were very gracious hosts. A common complaint is that Turkey espouses torture as a necessary part of its judiciary system. The Hatat's do not apologize, believing that captured terrorists should be tortured, if necessary, and then executed. Many Turks still have the old unyielding attitude which has been part of their culture for centuries.

At 6:00 p.m., we boarded the plane for Paris. Our grandsons left earlier this morning for the United States. Wynne also went back to Washington with the rest of the group, as she did not want our office to pay for Paris expenses. It was an easy trip from Istanbul to Paris and our U.S. Embassy friend, John Berg, sped us through DeGaulle Airport and got us to the hotel. John was his usual efficient self and I do not know what we would do in Paris without him. Gary Hymel and the rest of the group were very impressed with John. He was even able to find Dick Durbin's missing luggage which never arrived in Ankara; it was in the Air France luggage storeroom.

Hopefully we will have two quiet days in Paris and then Wednesday morning depart for Washington. At the departure lounge in Istanbul the American Consulate officer had brought all his notes for me to review and correct. The notes were on our Ankara interviews with government officials, and these documents will probably be in Washington at the Turkish desk sometime next week. Townsend Friedman is now the officer in charge of the Turkish desk in Washington; he is also the same officer who helped me six years ago get Debra Benchoam out of Argentina. At that time Townsend was a political officer at the American Embassy in Buenos Aires, and I have been in touch with him ever since.

JANUARY 13 WEDNESDAY

Paris was fun, but also quite expensive - everytime we had a meal it cost about $100. We did, however, get a break on the hotel. We had planned to stay at the Crillon, but learning that we had one free night at the Meridian in Montparnasse, we checked in there. It is not as nice as the Crillon, but it served our purpose and saved us money, costing $140 for two nights instead of $240 a night for three nights. Don and Beverly Massey of the Washington office of Hill and Knowlton, the public affairs office to the Turkish Embassy, are the only ones to remain in Paris with us on this leg of the trip. Mickey Edwards was there when we arrived but we never saw him, as he left early the next morning for the States. The Massey's stayed the first night at our hotel, but the next morning they moved to a smaller hotel, returning this morning to be picked up with us by John Berg to go to the airport. At the airport, the only incident was that the Massey's had a toy gun they were bringing back for a child, causing the airport security to detain us for about fifteen minutes. It was an inconvenience but also reassuring to me that the French are that careful at their airports. We made the plane just in time.

We did have a nice lunch with John Berg before we left. He told us all about his experiences during the war when he was underground in and around Berlin with his mother, and how they survived. John has enough material for a book.

Our plane landed in Washington around 2:30 in the afternoon. Seeing that everything was okay at the townhouse, I went to the office to go over what had accumulated on my desk. This was about 4:30, and there was a lot of work to be done. I read most of the press releases and there is a big hassle and a lot of negative publicity about the $8 million that the Foreign Operations Subcommittee earmarked in the Appropriations Bill under the Refugee Assistance Program for construction of a school for North African Jews settled in Paris. The bill classified the group as refugees even though, reportedly, many had lived in Paris for a decade or more and had prospered. There was no vote on this, as the funds were contained in the $600 billion Appropriations Bill that President Reagan signed into law before Christmas. The matter was negotiated between the House Foreign Ops Chairman Dave Obey and Senator Daniel Inouye (D-HI), Chairman of the Senate Appropriations Foreign Ops Subcommittee. Inouye promoted the project at the request of a New York real estate developer. Members just voted on the total foreign operations chapter in the appropriations conference. Inouye, a greatly respected Senator and war hero, with best intentions really blew it here and we just went along.

As a member of the House-Senate conference committee who voted to fund the project, primarily because of Inouye's urging, I anticipate reporters coming at me with questions and I will need to be ready with acceptable answers.

JANUARY 14 THURSDAY

Today I met with Wynne, John and Adele to go over the Turkish trip material for a possible newsletter to the South Florida Jewish community. For me, one of the trip's most meaningful events was visiting the restored synagogue, and my idea for the newsletter is to put primary emphasis on the synagogue, using some of the excellent pictures taken by Wynne and Dick Durbin. We also decided to do an interview with the *Miami-Jewish Tribune,* and then reprint the interview as part of the newsletter.

In a call to Patrice at the district office, we discussed the status of the Black Ministers meeting to be held sometime in February; the luncheon for the nominees to the service academies; and the Black Leadership luncheon in May. Afterwards,

I walked over to the transportation subcommittee office to speak with Tom and Greg, and the consensus is that we are going to have a rough fiscal year, especially with the Coast Guard starting to close bases. Moreover, the FAA is going to ask for considerably more money and with our 302B allocation only up two percent, we will have difficulty giving the FAA everything that it wants in F&E (facilities and equipment), which is where the FAA wants large increases.

Adele reminded me to get in touch with Steny Hoyer, House Chairman of the Helsinki Commission, about the forthcoming adverse human rights report that is coming out on Turkey. Steny was very aware of the probable fallout from the report, and promised to call Townsend Friedman on the Turkish desk as Steny is meeting with the Turkish Ambassador on Friday. He guaranteed me that there would be no factual errors in the report. As he said to me, if you only bash the Warsaw-pact countries then his commission would not be doing its job. He and I both know that although torture has been greatly reduced in Turkey, it still exists, but there will be no "erroneous" accounts of torture in the report. The report has been screened and rescreened for six months now. Turkey is not the Netherlands nor Denmark, but, except for Israel, compared to the rest of the Mideast countries it is a shining light on human rights. They have just had free elections and are moving toward a democratic process as fast as a country like that can move.

At the office, Carolyn and I got together to sort out and distribute the presents I brought back. Returning from these overseas trips, there is so much work and so much catching up to do, and I am trying to get as much done as I can before Joan and I leave Washington tomorrow for Miami. Congress continues to be in adjournment until the President's State of the Union Address, Monday, January 25. I will, therefore, have a ten-day stay in Miami, and I am looking forward to the rest and the warm weather.

JANUARY 16 SATURDAY

Back in Miami, Sharyn and I met this morning in the campaign office for over an hour going over the fundraiser list.

The campaign office, necessarily separate, is located in a spacious room above our district office in our nonfederal building on 163rd Street in North Miami Beach, which makes it very convenient for me to walk up or down to our congressional suite. Leaving Sharyn, I walked down to our congressional office to meet with Patrice on the appointments for the service academies. We will see the applicants later this week at our annual luncheon.

JANUARY 17 SUNDAY

Another restful day.

JANUARY 18 MONDAY

Today is Martin Luther King Day and as Co-chair of the school bond issue, I opted not to participate in the parade so that I could attend a meeting with the condo leadership, the Superintendent of the Dade County Schools, and members of the school board to initiate condo-area support for the county-wide school bond referendum. With the passing of the referendum we hope to build new schools totaling over a billion dollars. This is going to be a tough sell, however, because most of the condo people in my area no longer have children in school. Using congressional politics to influence local issues is something I do not often do but schools are too important not to become involved.

JANUARY 19 TUESDAY

Signing hundreds of postscripts on my fundraiser letters, which have to go out this week, has kept me quite busy. To those I know personally, I often add that if you cannot pay $500 just pay whatever you can. Many more letters still need to be signed, not only for Miami but also Washington, Houston and even New York. I have also been busy with constituents and with the press. George Dooley of Channel 2 public television was in first about a conflict in the use of their facilities. Channel 2 has a separate "for profit" entity set up to generate money to support the public broadcasting system (PBS), which competes with the private sector. It is the only way to raise money locally to support PBS, but when PBS uses a public subsidy to compete with private enterprise in producing electronic media, it makes for a difficult situation. The staff on the Appropriations Subcommittee on Health, Education and Human Services will be helpful with advice and guidance, so I asked Channel 2 to leave the documentation with me and either I or the subcommittee staff will get back to them.

Next was Dr. Barry Silverman, who came with Paul Cejas, Chairman of the Dade County School Board. Dr. Silverman's organization purchased the old Miami General Hospital which was the HMO that Mike Recarey owned before it went bankrupt. [In 1994 the hospital sold for $60 million.] Barry and Paul are tying to reorganize and need help with their cash flow. I told them I would have staff on Pete Stark's health subcommittee look into the matter and get back to them. Then Councilman Jules Littman from North Miami Beach came in with Soviet Jewish refugees who had settled in Colombia and now want to immigrate to the United States. We may have to do a private bill because they are retired and cannot come in under a labor certification permit. First, however, we need to get an extension on their temporary visa and then help them with permanent status.

Eli Feinberg was in regarding the ongoing Emerald Coast airport problem. I need to speak with Rep. Earl Hutto to possibly reduce his opposition to this airport in the Florida Panhandle district. The problem is that Eglin Field does not want to release any of its airspace to commercial aviation. It really is the FAA versus the Department of Defense. All along I have advocated the use of military facilities for commercial aviation, but the Department of Defense seldom wants to give up anything.

I soon left for the tennis court, where I was interviewed by a writer for the Florida Tennis Association regarding an article which appeared last week in the Fred Tasker column of the *Miami Herald*. The article said that People's Bank president Arthur Hill was not able to beat me in a tennis match. The Tasker column is trivia, a sort of gossip column, but many people read it, and this writer was hoping to expand on the article.

Back at the office I spoke to *Miami News* reporter Ellis Berger, who wanted more information on my relationship with Pat Tornillo, President of the Florida Federation of Teachers. After the interview, I invited Ellis to the school board luncheon we are having for the condo leaders in our district. I also spoke to reporters from the Houston newspapers on what effect their referendum last week will have on the future funding of their mass transit plan approved by sixty percent of the voters, who had already approved the one cent sales tax. There can be public support for mass transit, as evidenced in Houston. The Metro-Dade commission should not be so timid about a referendum for local dedicated transit funding.

Andy Ryan, a Washington reporter for the *Miami News,* called regarding ratings, as I had the highest Democratic party rating of any Florida member and the lowest Reagan administration support rating of any South Florida member. I also had a 97% attendance voting record. That was the one I felt the proudest of as it indicated that my health was good. I told the reporter that I did not vote because of party or administration position, but that I vote my way.

JANUARY 20 WEDNESDAY

This morning my appointments began with Marie Pettit, the widow of Don Pettit, a former aide to Senator Claude Pepper. Marie works for Eli Feinberg, and came in regarding a federal prison case of an eighteen year old woman in our district whose mother shot her father. The mother is now in prison. Searching the premises, the police found explosives in the backyard and charged the daughter, taking her to jail. We are going to request that the federal prison system hold a hearing for the eighteen year old. I do not think my help will amount to anything because congressional dealings with the federal prison system only seem to make situations more complicated. People come to us for help on judicial matters, and we cannot refuse. But the judiciary branch does not allow any interference from the legislative branch, making any effort on our part counterproductive. We may write to the federal prison authorities with a request, but such requests are given a perfunctory response, and then probably disregarded.

Then a member from the Israeli Consulate for Political Affairs in Miami came in wanting my help on the trade agreement legislation, and I told him I would help in any way I could. Taiwan native Dr. Robert Chen of the University of Miami came in next for help in getting visas for his relatives. I turned the cases over to Patty Diaz, our immigration specialist, telling Chen that Patty would follow through on the cases and would stay in touch with him at each development.

At 2:30, I left the office to attend the "Annie Ackerman Boulevard" dedication. Annie was in a wheelchair, and it was sad to see her like that. Ernie Samuels, the master of ceremonies, and all the politicians were there for her. I said a few words regarding my relationship with Annie, and how the Annie Ackerman Boulevard intersects with the William Lehman Causeway. And while the Causeway comes to a stop there, like a political career in its last term of office, the Annie Ackerman Boulevard goes on into the distance like its namesake whose involvement in the private sector goes on forever. People, I hope, understood what I meant.

Later, a *Wall Street Journal* reporter interviewed me on the effect that the condominium vote will have on the Super Tuesday Primary. Most of our condo leaders already support Reubin Askew for Senator Chiles's Senate seat, and that will help me solve the problem I have with Dan Mica. Mica is also planning to run for Lawton's seat, and next week in Washington I will tell him of my support for Askew. I will also inform Askew and Bob Traurig, Askew's senior law partner. The *Wall Street Journal* interview was followed by an interview with old friends Bernie and Ruth Fuller's daughter-in-law, a Channel 4 television reporter. She handled it very well, and I liked her.

JANUARY 21 THURSDAY

At the campaign office this morning, Sharyn and I wrapped up some side issues on the fundraiser. I have signed all the letters and written all the postscripts, so this part of the fundraiser effort is complete.

At noon I was at Aventura for the luncheon with our twelve nominees to the Service Academies. Their guidance counselors were there, as were members of our review board committee, which included Mary Alice Brown, David Sampson, and Angel Menendez. Only ten of the twelve nominees can be selected, and our appointments will be announced in April. Channel 7 television and the *Community News* reporters were there, and interviewed me and several of the candidates. The luncheon lasted about an hour and half and it went off very well.

The *Miami News* ran a good story today about the voting record of the South Florida Delegation. I was the only member quoted as to why my voting record was lowest in support of the Reagan administration and highest in support of the Democratic leadership. I had jokingly said to the reporter, "This time, the party was right on the issues. They were with me." In the article, the reporter included the comments along with the quote, "I don't really consider positions in relation to the administration or party when I vote. I just vote the way I want."

JANUARY 22 FRIDAY

Jeff picked me up at 9:30, and we went to the James L. Knight International Center for the first Transportation Summit ever sponsored by the Greater Miami Chamber of Commerce. The purpose of the gathering was for a deep examination of what Dade's priorities should be under the State's $40 billion statewide strategic transportation plan introduced by Governor Bob Martinez in November. From 10:00 to noon, I sat on the panel with Metro-Dade officials and we took questions from the several hundred people in the audience. A comment was made about Tamiami Airport and I replied that there is legislation now to place officials at Tamiami to relieve congestion at Miami International. I also mentioned that John King, head of the Houston Transit, was able to promote a successful tax referendum in Houston and that Dade County could do the same. By the end of the summit, we endorsed a one-cent county sales tax, higher gasoline taxes and vehicle registration fees, additional expressway tolls, and taxes on new construction as ways to raise the $492 million a year needed to support transportation. None of this will ever happen with this Metro Commission.

At noon I was the guest of honor at the summit luncheon, which included my South Florida colleagues and the Governor, and was given more awards. At least 300 people were there, including my two sons, and it was very emotional. Afterwards, I was interviewed by the *Miami Herald* and the *Miami News*, but my problem with some of the questions was that the reporters wanted me to comment on issues the Metro-Dade County Commission had not yet decided.

Following the luncheon, I went to the *Jewish Tribune* to talk about the Jewish community in Turkey. I told how well the Jewish community was integrated into the Turkish society and the story will appear in the *Jewish Tribune* next week.

JANUARY 23 SATURDAY

On the front page of the *Miami Herald*, I was quoted as saying that federal Metromover construction funds came out of a different pot than the bus money and would not adversely affect federal funding for more buses. The statement was made in answer to the reporter's question regarding the 30 or so Transit Workers Union members who picketed the summit in opposition to the proposed $240 million expansion of the Metromover.

I went to see Annie Ackerman for about thirty minutes. I see her every few months and we talk about many things - personal, political, whatever is on our minds. Today we discussed how all the public affection we both seem to be getting at this time of our lives is wonderful, but how it can also be a very heavy burden and, at times, very fatiguing.

Tonight Joan and I will be going to dinner with old friends, Al Green and his wife Esther, and tomorrow I return to Washington.

JANUARY 24 SUNDAY

Left Miami for Washington late afternoon.

JANUARY 25 MONDAY

At the State of the Union Address, I sat next to Vic Fazio (D-CA). From where I sat I could see, for the first time, the Reagan side of the teleprompter. To me the most interesting thing that happened was when Reagan mentioned his intermediate range nuclear weapons treaty with Gorbachev and the Democrats stood up and cheered. With this reaction from the Democrats, the Republicans had to do the same. After the speech I went to the Press Gallery and gave an interview to Harold Cessna from WIOD. I then called the *Miami News* and WINZ and did a tape for them, saying that Reagan was talking about an idealistic America that existed in Norman Rockwell paintings, which was not American reality. The reality, I said, are the street people, unwed teenage mothers, AIDS, etc.

Coast Guard's Admiral Yost called to inform me that he is eliminating 48 bases to meet the $100 million cut from the budget summit agreement. I know that those base cuts will be politically hurtful, and I expect colleagues to want to restore them. There is also going to be an effort to reprogram from transit or from other places in the Department of Transportation budget. Yost is upset and wants to restore his cuts anyway he can, either through politics or through using the administration to take monies from other programs.

The president of the FEC Railroad called about a problem he has with the elimination of piggyback trucks using flatbed trailer train transportation. Apparently this has something to do with the manufacture of flatbed trailer train cars. I asked him to put the information in writing to me, and I would see what could be done. He laughed and said at least this time he wasn't calling me about the whistle blowing along the FEC tracks in the condominium area in Northeast Dade.

JANUARY 26 TUESDAY

This morning I had breakfast in the upstairs apartment over my townhouse, which the firm of Patton, Boggs and Blow rents. Penny Farthing was the host, in behalf of Mayor Pena from Denver, Colorado, and other Denver officials. The Denver group wanted mass transit funds and funds for the new regional airport they are trying to develop. I gave them a lead on how to pursue their goals by suggesting that they talk to Bob Carr, a licensed pilot, and a member on our transportation subcommittee.

Bill Gray spoke to me yesterday about a problem in SEPTA (South Eastern Pennsylvania Transportation Authority). He wants me to call for an investigation, but I do not want to get involved between Larry Coughlin and Bill Gray. They are both my friends and, as one is the ranking Republican, the other is the ranking Democrat on my committee. I do, however, want to find out if the alleged corruption is in procurement, as Bill Gray suggests.

I spoke to subcommittee members about a response letter to the Coast Guard's request to restore funds reduced by the budget summit agreement. I also spoke to Bill Natcher about doing our bills this year on an individual subcommittee basis instead of waiting for the Continuing Resolution. Natcher said the only way to do it is to get the Budget Committee to get us our 302B budget allocations in time to move our markups. When I spoke to Appropriations Chair Jamie Whitten about expediting hearings in our subcommittee, he said to express my concerns to John Mack, the administrative aide to Speaker Jim Wright. The longer we wait the worse the economic figures may be, and with the economy falling what we will have are larger cuts in appropriations to keep the budget deficit at the numbers that we must maintain. We have to move the appropriations bill as rapidly as possible.

It has been a fairly slow day, but I could not get my tennis buddies for a game. At the office, John is working on an outline for the animal experimentation newsletter. In the afternoon I met with two representatives from the Beer Distributors Association, one from my area in Ft. Lauderdale and one from Washington, and they presented to me a $500 check from their political action committee (PAC).

At the meeting that members had yesterday with the Israeli Ambassador, they mostly told him what he expected to hear, a very negative reaction to some statements - especially the idea of Israeli leaders publicly talking about breaking Arab bones. This publicity makes our job in Congress to provide funds to Israel much harder.

JANUARY 27 WEDNESDAY

At 8:15, I had breakfast with the Reserve Officers Association of Florida. I went mainly because I am very fond of Charlie Bennett, a retired reserve officer and Dean of our Florida Delegation. Also present was Bob Sikes, who was Dean of our delegation when I arrived in Congress and is still a factor in the reserve officers organization, and a political factor in Northwest Florida. At 10:00, I met with Close-Up students from a Dade County senior high school. Amie Green, the daughter of friends of mine from Miami, was with the group, and I greeted her personally. I took them to our subcommittee office and there we had a question and answer period, and then a photo opportunity.

I met next with Neal Katz and Richard Strauss on the United Israel Agency Refugee Program, and they talked about the number of refugees coming in to Israel from the Soviet Union, Iran, Romania, North Africa and the Falasha Jews from Ethiopia. They also spoke about naming a refugee center in Israel after me, and I will be going to Israel later this year if that were to happen. If I do go, I said, I would like to see a visible indication of the success of the refugee program, including some Falasha Jews making it in the private sector and contributing to society, paying his or her own way, and as a family being absorbed in productive activities. They said they would try to provide that.

John Schelble and I have been discussing the problem of handling the Coast Guard cuts, which will now be public information, and the Dan Mica/Reubin Askew problem and how to graciously withdraw my support for Mica in favor of Askew. An idea of how to do this, if Askew shows up at my fundraiser, is to introduce him as the next Senator from Florida. Dante Fascell's office is just across the corridor from my office. I walked over and explained to Dante my position on Askew and Mica, and he agreed with me that I should tell Mica personally and up front that I intend to support Askew. I then went to Mica's office for a second time, and he still had not returned.

Marwin Cassell had sent a letter which I received too late to help him obtain some legal work from the home loan credit bank. In the letter he had asked me to contact the agency in support of his application, but by the time his letter reached me, the decision had already been made. I made the call anyway, just in case something might have fallen through on the decision. Marwin was Chairman of the Democratic Party in Dade County, and has been one of my loyal supporters for many years.

In the evening I went to the Massachusetts Farmers Reception, called "A Taste of Massachusetts." The Massachusetts Food and Agricultural Department sponsored the event, and it was the best food I have had at a reception in a long time. It was a beautiful, wonderful spread of food - crepes filled with bean sprouts, tofu with mustard sauce, capers, turkey, apple strudel, and all kinds of cheese. But it was pathetic because only four or five members were there and only one member from Massachusetts. Unfortunately it is very cold in Washington, and with no business on the House Floor, most of the members went home and did not stay for the reception.

I was invited to speak to a small dinner group of the Shipbuilders Association, an organization of American shipbuilders struggling to survive. The primary reason they asked me was that they need Coast Guard funds for two ice breakers to be built in this country, earmarked in the 1989 transportation bill, which would help them considerably. Their main problem is that they need a level playing field to meet foreign competition. Even our present cruise ships are made in Germany and ninety percent of American cargo is exported on foreign ships. I do not know how much good I can do, but I did tell them that if they wanted Congress to subsidize American merchant shipbuilding they would have to find a revenue source to do it.

JANUARY 28 THURSDAY

This morning I took an 8:00 flight to Miami. At the district office Jeff and I reviewed several constituent cases and discussed some personnel matters. I spent time with Sharyn in the campaign office on the fundraiser. The money is coming in fairly consistently and by the middle of next week Sharyn will get on the telephone, as this is the last week we mail out letters.

JANUARY 29 FRIDAY

Calling the Washington office this morning, I had Lucy on the phone for a long time discussing the Coast Guard problems and what we will run into when I get back to Washington next week. I hear from colleagues that the Coast Guard is threatening to close bases in certain key districts. Tuesday in Washington we will call for a meeting of our subcommittee members to get a united front against changes in the Appropriations 1988 Bill. We had to cut over $220 million from our bill between the time the House passed our conference report and the time the budget summit told us we had to reduce our total outlays by over $300 million dollars. We did that by cutting three percent from the FAA, four percent from Coast Guard operations, and five percent from everything else. The Coast Guard is mounting a public relations campaign just like AIPAC does in foreign operations. The Coast Guard and AIPAC think that they are in a different category from everything and everyone else when cutbacks are necessary.

Meeting Ruth Jacobs at the Dade County School Board studio, we taped a ten minute segment for educational television on the school board bond issue forthcoming in March, explaining why we need it. Ruth is an old friend from my school board days. I then went to the S&S Diner where I met by chance some old friends and constituents, and we had a good time talking and reminiscing.

JANUARY 30 SATURDAY

At the campaign office, Sharyn informed me that the contributions are now up to $24,000, which is more than we expected for the first week, many contributions coming from people I least expected. It is very satisfactory so far, and I hope it continues.

JANUARY 31 SUNDAY

Yesterday I visited my son Bill at his automobile dealership and this morning my younger son Tom came to visit with his son, little Tommy. The weekend has been quiet and a time for getting together with my family.

The *Miami Herald* ran a story today about the most influential people in Miami. The article was primarily about the private sector, but, with my picture attached, I was named one of the five most important elected public officials in South Florida.

Chapter 14

FEBRUARY 1, 1988 - MONDAY

In Washington the day has been slow other than a meeting with Rep. Bill Richardson [now United Nations Ambassador] of New Mexico and FAA Administrator Allan McArtor, regarding improvements at the Taos, New Mexico, airport to include accommodations for Boeing 727's. This project evolved from my visit last August to New Mexico on behalf of Bill Richardson, and he is reiterating how essential this project is to the Taos community - providing jobs and an increase in tourism. With the assurance that I would make every effort to safeguard the funds in our bill for this project, Richardson and McArtor soon left.

FEBRUARY 2 TUESDAY

A busy day, starting with the Tampa Sierra Club, an environmental organization that came in specifically to thank me for helping with the national wildlife bill. At 10:00, some of us

Jewish members met with an Arab resident of Israel who is mayor of a West Bank city. The mayor spoke to us from the Arab standpoint, saying that there are emerging leadership groups in Gaza and the West Bank which are disillusioned with the PLO as much as they are with Jordan and Israel. "This is a new phenomenon and a different ballgame," said the mayor.

People in the West Bank and Gaza are indigenous to their area and are forming their own leadership - opposed to both the PLO and to Jordan as alternatives to Israel. They are impatient for solutions and answers to their problems, but until we solve the Gaza problem which has most of the camps, most of the poverty, and most of the fundamentalism, we will not be able to solve the West Bank problems. Moreover, the Gaza problem cannot be solved alone because the Palestinians consider Gaza and the West Bank as a unit.

After the meeting I went to the Select Committee on Children, Youth and Families and voted to adopt the committee budget. The biggest budget question was travel expenses, but we quickly resolved this rather nit-picking issue. Once I had thought about relinquishing my membership on this committee, but as the committee's ranking Democrat, I will probably remain.

At 11:00, Army Corps Colonel Robert Herndon, District Engineer, and his public relations assistant, Juan Carone, were in to inform me of the time schedule for the Sunny Isles beach restoration. The sand will be coming from Florida offshore and not from the Bahamas, and hopefully before the hurricane season Sunny Isles will have a 150-foot-wide beach.

Spokesmen from the Federation for the Blind came in next to discuss the problems they are having with the FAA. We covered this issue extensively in our last year's hearing, and I feel strongly that the disabled should receive the same consideration as other passengers on commercial aircraft. I told the group that I would try to help by putting language in our bill this year to protect the blind from being discriminated against on airplanes. Transportation Secretary Jim Burnley came in next to ask for my help in solving the Coast Guard's budget shortfall. I listened, but made no commitment.

I then walked over to my subcommittee office where members of the subcommittee had gathered to discuss the Coast

Guard's threat to shut down bases. The consensus I got from the members was that they are willing to take from the Coast Guard the adverse publicity because, as they so rightfully said, our subcommittee is not to blame for the Coast Guard's budget shortfall. The shortfall really stems from the Gramm-Rudman cuts that we had to accept, after having worked out our conference report with Senator Lautenberg and the Senate transportation subcommittee. I did, however, want the DOT to know how I felt. The administration got the Department of Transportation into this situation, and it is up to the administration to get them out of it.

Rosa Feinberg and others from the Dade County School Board are in Washington, and we met for almost an hour discussing school problems, family leave, and the need for refugee assistance. They left when my next appointment, Rep. Lindsey Thomas of Georgia, arrived. Lindsey has a problem with the mandated study called for in our bill on smoking on airplanes, legislation initiated by Rep. Dick Durbin. I told Lindsey I would give him the opportunity to sit with our subcommittee and direct questions to McArtor, the FAA Administrator. This pleased him, especially the idea that there would be a photo or media opportunity.

12:30, Tony Costa from the Cuban-American Foundation came in to lobby me on tomorrow's Contra vote. Tony is very personable and a good friend, and it is hard to say no to him, but I have to maintain my position as opposed to Contra aid.

Florida member and Defense Appropriations Subcommittee Chairman Bill Chappell held his fundraiser this evening at the Sheraton Grand Hotel. Many defense industry executives were among the guests, including big-time lobbyist Bill Cable and others who said to me that they may come to my Miami fundraiser. My good friend Kay Thomas, a former legislative representative of Dade Metrorail who now works for Chappell, was there and offered to provide names for our fundraiser list. Kay is most liberal and Chappell conservative but it's a symbiotic relationship that works.

FEBRUARY 3 WEDNESDAY

On the House Floor today, I voted against the House joint

resolution to approve President Reagan's request for continued military aid to the Contras, an anti-government guerrilla fighting force in Nicaragua. The resolution was defeated, 219-211, in what was considered a victory for the House leadership and defeat for the administration. Except for Republican Bill McCollum, who I thought courageous in his vote against the administration's position, and Democrats Dan Mica and myself, the remaining Florida delegation voted to approve the President's package. My opposing vote will displease many if not most of the Cuban-Americans and Nicaraguans in Dade County but, after giving much thought to this issue, reasoning that a vote to rearm the Contras meant an end to any possible talk of a peace negotiation between the Sandinista government and the Contras, I decided to vote my conscience, on the side of peace, and take whatever fallout or criticism resulted.

Seeing John Dingell on the Floor, I asked him about an environmental letter that Nadine and Adele want me to sign. The Health and Environment Subcommittee falls under Dingell's oversight Committee on Energy and Commerce. Dingell advised me not to sign the letter, and I told him that before I did I would let him know. But I am totally committed to environmental issues, and Dingell's objections in this case have not convinced me that I should not sign the letter. But Dingell supported me on the Trust Fund vote.

We had a good legislative staff meeting this afternoon discussing the letter John Dingell did not want me to sign, and the North Miami Munisport toxic waste site which is still on the superfund list. A favorable report from the EPA study has been released, and we hope now to get this off the toxic waste list so that the City of North Miami can sell the land for development.

FEBRUARY 4 THURSDAY

Today was slow, so I left on an early afternoon flight to Miami.

FEBRUARY 5 FRIDAY

At the campaign office Sharyn and I worked on the fundraiser. I signed more "thank you" letters and a few last minute invitations. The fundraiser is only a month away on March 6, and we have sent out almost 1,000 invitations.

FEBRUARY 6 SATURDAY

My Miami schedule was pretty much free, so I got together with Hurley Ridgeway and some old friends for tennis at the Sans Souci Tennis Club, where I spoke with Dr. Leo Blauh, the tennis writer who again said he was doing a write-up on me. A Sans Souci resident heard I was going to be at the club and stopped by to thank me for my vote on the Contras. It is reassuring to know that there is quiet support out there for my position.

FEBRUARY 7 SUNDAY

Groundbreaking for the Aventura Synagogue was held this morning with Rabbi Salzman, and it was a long and very dusty ceremony. There was a good turnout, however, with speeches from Commissioner Barry Schreiber, Miami Mayor Steve Clark, and Mayor Neu of North Miami. I also made a rather brief speech.

FEBRUARY 8 MONDAY

Free day.

FEBRUARY 9 TUESDAY

Guillermo Martinez had an editorial in today's *Miami Herald* about my vote on the Contras. The editorial headlined: "Lehman Angers Cubans," and I am now in the process of writing an opposition piece in response to the editorial. Martinez missed the whole idea of what representative democracy is all about. I do not have to answer to a voting bloc on such issues. As a U.S. Congressman, I am responsible to the 245 million people in this country. Many people told me they wanted to write to the *Herald* in support of my position, and that is fine with me; but I am writing my own letter. The editorial really got me a lot of publicity, mostly favorable.

The North Miami Beach Senior High School has invited me

to speak to their debate team. I went this morning with Bernie Torra on our staff, and it was the first high school I have been to in a while. The students had assembled in the auditorium, and they were very bright and asked some tough questions. It was a good practice run on answering questions about Nicaragua and other situations such as Gaza and Israel. We left the debate team and went to Nancy Moldonado's literature class. Nancy was a recipient of the FIU Kathy Lehman-Weiner Memorial Scholarship. As a former high school English teacher, I spoke to the class about the poems of John Donne and about *Huck Finn*, and thoroughly enjoyed this brief return to the classroom.

It has been years since I have been to the Buckley Towers condominium, and the residents there this evening were the oldest group of people to whom I have spoken. There were some intelligent questions but the fun part was when one person would ask a question and then before I could answer, someone from the audience would answer in his or her own way. It was really amusing. Afterwards Joan and I headed for what I thought was the Miami Film Festival "Reception" at the Intercontinental Hotel, but what turned out to be a nightclub where some film festival patrons had come to see a jazz show. It was a waste of my time, but I did see Rep. Larry Smith there.

FEBRUARY 10 WEDNESDAY

After phone calls to Reubin Askew about his senate campaign and to Senator Graham about the Coast Guard problems, I just relaxed for the rest of the day. Joan and I visited Marjorie Deutsch at her home. Marjorie is not doing well. She is very brave but the situation is very sad.

That evening I attended the meeting of the new Democratic Club held at the McDonald Center in North Miami Beach. The North Dade condo leaders seemed happy to see me, as we are all good friends. They are like aging tigers and if anyone opposed me in the election, they would bust their behinds to turn out the vote. I felt secure in the knowledge of these warm and protective people, as though I had nothing to fear from any opposition.

FEBRUARY 11 THURSDAY

This morning I spoke about the politics of cancer research at the Cancer Symposium held at the University of Miami Medical School. Steering the meeting was Dr. Bernard Fogel, the medical school dean. Other participants included Dr. McDougal from the National Cancer Institute, President Tad Foote from the University of Miami, and State Senator Jack Gordon. For lunch I met with Elaine Friedman to discuss an appropriate memorial to Lany Narot. Saturday I had received some of Lany's books of poetry which her good friend, Len Rappaport, had mailed to me. I miss Lany, she was a good friend, and I plan to read her poetry on the plane back to Washington.

Adele Liskov is down from Washington for our meeting today with Lorri Kellogg, owner of an overseas adoption agency, and Perry Rivkind, Director of the Miami INS office. The meeting was held in Rivkind's office on 79th Street, and along with Adele, Lorri and myself, were Bernie Torra and Patty Diaz from our district staff, and several sets of parents wanting to adopt children from the Caribbean area. The purpose of the meeting was to see how we could get around a new regulation preventing children, whom these prospective parents want to adopt, from coming to the United States. This inhibiting regulation applies to children who still maintain contact with their fathers, even though the children are in foster homes. I think we made some progress with Rivkind, but we now plan to meet in Washington with INS Director Nelson to request that an exemption be made so that these children can be placed in good homes in the United States.

After the meeting I went to the Miami Shores Country Club and played several sets of tennis. I heard that Ellis Rubin may be running against me, but I am not overly concerned. Ellis is an attorney, and I believe he just wants the publicity - as he sometimes does. It really would not surprise me if maybe two or three others expressed interest in running. I have had it easy for a long time.

FEBRUARY 12 FRIDAY

Early this morning a school bus loaded with about 25 condo

leaders met me at North Miami Beach City Hall for our trip to a North Miami Beach elementary school to show the condo and Northeast leadership the overcrowding conditions in our elementary schools. As co-chair with State Senator Carrie Meek on the school board bond issue, we are anxious to gain the support of this group. The visit was a real experience for both the elderly and the children. *Miami News* reporter Ellis Berger covered the story, and the children put on a good show, as did the principal and faculty who were super. This fantastic morning went from 10:00 through noon, which prevented me from attending the luncheon of the North Dade Forum, the political club with which Jeff is affiliated. Ruth Tinsman from our office attended, and returned with the information that the Martinez column was the main topic of conversation and that Burton Young, President of the Forum, was adamant in his support of me and in his criticism of the column. I have to write Burton to thank him for the kind words and also to Raul Martinez, the main speaker. Raul Martinez, who is actually a friend of Guillermo Martinez (no relation), said he was offended by the criticism of me for doing what my conscience said was correct.

Today's Fred Tasker column in the *Miami Herald* mentioned that out of the first hundred phone calls received on the Guillermo Martinez column only three supported Martinez and ninety-seven were outraged by his criticism of me. Completing my response to the column, I ran it by Judge Abner Mikva in Washington for his comments, and then sent it to Jim Hampton of the *Miami Herald.* I sent a copy to the *Jewish Floridian,* which also wants to publish it. Sharyn called and informed me that she has made about five hundred phone calls. I am hoping for $75,000 by the first of March and perhaps $100,000 by the time we close the books.

Early afternoon at our Liberty City district office, Patrice has scheduled several appointments for me. Preston Marshall, who was in charge of the Martin Luther King Day Parade, was the first appointment, and I handed him a $200 check to help underwrite the parade. I was not available to participate in the parade this year, but I am sure he was happy to get the funds. I have just about eliminated my participation in parades as they take a lot of energy and are not worth the effort.

Next was Mr. Timmons who runs a steel fabricating plant in

Northeast Dade. He wanted me to be aware of senate legislation which adversely affects steel imports from Venezuela. This legislation will make for new regulations on the importing of raw materials and the finished products of Venezuela. Although Timmons does not live in my district, he was quick to point out that he employs approximately fifty people who do. I told him I would see if I could help and this pleased him.

Then Walter Fauntroy, the Representative for the District of Columbia, and his brother Roy, a Miami resident, came in concerning federal funds which they thought had been misappropriated. These funds were expected six years ago during the Carter Administration to help in the reconstruction and renewal of the Liberty City area which was ravaged and burned following the judicial verdict on the McDuffie case. Arthur McDuffie was a young black man who, while on a motorcycle, was chased, shot and killed in Liberty City by several white police officers, who were eventually acquitted by the court. The entire episode got huge media attention and many well-meaning promises were made by the administration.

The funds, although promised, were never appropriated, and unfortunately the black community was led by unrealistic expectations as the money was never really available to begin with. In Liberty City black businesses are failing and cannot compete because the black consumers with easy access to transportation can go into better shopping areas. The area is very depreciated and is like a wasteland as far as commercial enterprise is concerned.

Maria Elena Torano came in with a group which wants Dick Judy's permission to use the old vacant National/Pan American Building to train air traffic controllers. I did not see a problem with this, and I said to them that I would call Dick Judy in support of their request. In all there were about a dozen visitors, including two officers of the federal savings and loan institution in North Miami. They now live in Broward County but grew up in Dade and are friends of my children. They told me that Andy Cuomo (Mario's son) from New York and his group forced them out of the bank in a hostile takeover. I do not know who is right but I would like to see savings institutions survive in our district. I instructed them to write down the information in a letter to me, showing the possible illegality of the takeover, and I would talk to the staff on the House banking committee.

I am now lobbying for Lillian Liberti for the new Metro-Dade Transit Administrator position. I spoke to Metro Commissioner Clara Oesterle to see if she could get the Metro Search Committee to consider Lillian as a candidate. I think Lillian would be perfect in this position, and when the opportunity arises I will speak to the *Miami Herald* about her candidacy.

My son Tom and I had dinner at the Miami Shores Country Club, and Seal Oxford was there. Back in the 1960's, Seal had a political base in Miami Shores. He tried to maintain racial status quo at the white Miami Edison High School, and the all black Northwestern High School at a time when the Dade County School Board under court order was trying to desegregate. Demographic forces took over and Edison in a few years became a largely black school.

FEBRUARY 13 SATURDAY

Today was our Black Ministers Luncheon on which Patrice has worked so diligently. Only about twelve showed out of almost twenty ministers who accepted our invitation. There was a time when I attended black churches at least once a month, but I have not been now for several years. The meeting was interesting, as the ministers were enlightened and much more concerned about foreign affairs than I anticipated. Adding further to the program was Sherry Jones from our office who sang the Lord's Prayer in a most beautiful soprano. After the luncheon several ministers extended invitations to attend their churches and to meet with their youth groups, and I readily accepted as I have always had good relations with the black religious community.

One of the things I do when in Miami over an extended period is to have the Washington office send me the mail in a federal orange mailbag. The orange bags are treated as first-class mail by the postal service. When a bag had not arrived by Friday, I asked Sherry to pick it up at the North Miami Beach Post Office and bring it to me at the Black Ministers luncheon. Somehow the mailbag did not contain the incoming Washington mail but my outgoing mail to Washington. I do not know what happened to the mail from Washington which will probably arrive Tuesday as Monday is a holiday, and any action on that mail will now have to wait until I get back to Miami next Thursday.

Joan and I drove to Fort Pierce for a family birthday celebration. I thought it would be nonpolitical but my brother-in-law started off with the Fort Pierce Airport expansion problem. He and his group want me to have the FAA prevent the runway extension because of the additional air traffic over their residential areas. I listened, but I told them they would have to contact Tom Lewis, the Fort Pierce Representative.

FEBRUARY 14 SUNDAY

After tennis this morning with Judge Phil Bloom at a Miami Beach mansion, and lunch at the Ham and Eggery with owner Lori Angin, who lobbied me about how bad the increased minimum wage would be for small businesses, I went to see Annie Ackerman, and we talked politics. Even bedridden, Annie is a political factor in the Northeast section.

In today's *Miami News*, reporter Ellis Berger wrote a long story about the School Board bond issue which told about our visit to the North Miami Beach Elementary School. The article named all the condo participants and included their comments. Joe Plotnik, a resident at Del Prado Condo on Biscayne Boulevard, was a participant, and the article featured both his comments and his photo, which Joe will just love.

FEBRUARY 15 MONDAY

Barry University has dedicated a William Lehman Room at the University to house my Congressional papers when I leave the Congress. Meanwhile, I am working with Barry University Professor Mike Melody recording events from when I first came to the Congress in 1973 (93rd Congress). Today I wrapped up the taping on how I got on the Appropriations Committee; how the Dade Metrorail funding started in Washington; the rescue of Debra Benchoam from prison in Argentina; and my involvement with the Haitian Refugee Program. Professor Melody has about fifty pages of transcript, going through the 95th Congress, which now have to be edited.

Although today is President's Day, a federal holiday, it does not stop the phone calls. Bernie Wall, an old friend, called about the toll road on Venetian Causeway and whether there is a prohibition on the use of federal monies for toll roads. I know this is now prohibited but I will get back to Bernie about possible exceptions or exemptions being made by the FHWA.

At 1:30, Joan and I flew to Washington, where I was to join twenty other House members at the State Department for a meeting with Secretary of State George Schultz. Schultz's Deputy Assistant, Richard Murphy, was there and I remember Richard from when I first went to the Philippines about ten years ago. At that time, he was Ambassador to the Philippines, and met Joan and me at the airport and put tropical leis around our necks. Schultz discussed his new plan for Mideast negotiations and he is making a real effort in the Middle East, though it is difficult. We must set principles that will put in place a formal procedure which will then lead to negotiations. It sounds like a lot of semantics but rather than steamroll, we have to ease into negotiations because Israel, Syria and other Mideast countries will say there is nothing about which to negotiate. Each country has leadership which would topple if appearing the least bit weak. The only thing going for the Mideast is that *no one* is happy with the situation as it is. Schultz emphasized that there can be no negotiation without a strong Israel, and with the help the United States has been able to provide, Israel's economy and military now is much stronger and viable than it was three years ago.

Joan and I dined at the Primo Piatti Restaurant on Pennsylvania Avenue. Senator Lautenberg was there with a friend and asked about the Coast Guard shortfall situation. It seems Senator Graham has been calling Lautenberg, as he has been calling me, about the Coast Guard matter. To the information that we would probably reprogram $60 million from other sources, which is less than the Coast Guard is requesting, Lautenberg had no objectionable comments. A good friend, Harry McPherson, was also at the restaurant, along with his new wife. Harry was a top aide to President Lyndon Johnson and is a very good lawyer and writer. I had tried to help him adopt an offshore child, but he happily managed to adopt a child within the United States.

FEBRUARY 16 TUESDAY

At the office this morning, I am updating myself on the story on the $8 million line item for the Jewish School in France that was put in the Foreign Operations Bill as part of last year's Continuing Resolution. Early this month there was a vote in the House and in the Senate to rescind the French school's funds from the CR. Senator Inouye's effort succumbed to scrutiny by the press. Even his personal popularity did not prevail.

Last night on the plane from Miami to Washington I saw Congressman Sikorski of Michigan, who was wearing a badge with a photo of Eastern Airlines President Frank Lorenzo. The badge had a cross running through it, and Sikorski said he received it from Machinists Union members at the AFL/CIO Convention in Bal Harbour, where he was a guest speaker, along with Joe Moakley of Massachusetts.

The *Miami Herald* today printed my letter to the Editor in response to the Martinez article, with the headline: "Lehman's Contra vote not 'casually dismissed.'" The letter reads, in full text:

> **To The Editor:**
>
> Guillermo Martinez's February 9 Viewpoints Page column taking issue with my position on aid to the Nicaraguan *contras,* though understandable in some respects, was both disturbing and misleading in others.
>
> First, there was certainly no attempt at any time to 'casually dismiss' or otherwise trivialize this important issue or the community's feelings about it. As I said after the vote and as was reported in *The Miami News*, 'I'm sure that the way I voted displeased a large number of Cuban Americans who live in my district and South Florida, and I can certainly understand how they feel so strongly about the Communist problem in Central America. I just don't think the solution to it

is a military one.'

The heart of the matter, though, is a basic misunderstanding of the responsibilities of my office.

Martinez writes that `a vote against *contra* aid from a congressman in Dade County who has at least 30,544 Hispanic voters in a district that includes North Hialeah and Hialeah-Miami Lakes is intolerable,' as if that alone commands a `yes' vote. Well, the job requires a lot more than just counting heads.

I am a representative in the United States Congress, not merely a delegate from a part of Dade County. I was elected from the entire 17th Congressional District — which contains some 560,000 people of many differing interests and viewpoints — but I also have an obligation to the entire nation on issues of national security.

Every congressman takes an oath to `support and defend the Constitution of the United States against all enemies, foreign and domestic.' Especially on matters of great national importance, that commitment must take precedence over more-practical concerns.

I cast my vote in accordance with what, in my judgment, is in the best interests of our country. If I did any differently, I would be violating my oath. I trust that those with opposing viewpoints will respect my decision, as I do theirs, even as we disagree. This is a basic tenet of democracy.

The analogy of the *contra*-aid vote to a vote on aid to Israel is most unfortunate. Israel is a sovereign nation and a key democratic ally of the United States, strategically crucial to the containment of Soviet influence, and the only democracy in the Middle East. I have been a strong supporter of aid to Israel because I think this is in the best interests of the United States. That is the same standard that I apply to my votes on other foreign-aid issues.

There have been circumstances under which I have supported military aid to Central American

> countries. This year alone, as a member of the Foreign Operations Appropriations Subcommittee, I supported over $130 million in military aid, $440 million in economic-support funds, and $153 million in humanitarian aid to Central American nations. I did so because I feel that these expenditures for those governments are in our best interests here at home and of peace in the region.
>
> In my judgment, the 47,000 casualties so far in the seven-year *contra* war are enough. Let's now give peace a chance.
>
> That has to be good for America."

Several other letters were published alongside my letter, all in support of my position. This response may or may not make a difference to those I angered by opposing Contra military aid, but I do feel better now with this rebuttal to Martinez's editorial.

The big news at tennis today with Judge Mikva, Kastenmeier and Edwards was the New Hampshire primary. Everyone thought Bob Dole would do better but it looks as though the Republicans will be fighting each other and this will be a tough year for them. The fact that Republicans cannot get good, moderate candidates to run was a major part of our discussion.

On the school board bond issue, I am completing a letter to be mailed to approximately 30,000 condo residents. I saw Joe Early of Massachusetts and relayed to him that as a participant in the Cancer Symposium at the University of Miami Medical School I had informed the audience that Joe was the number one appropriator for NIH and medical research. He smiled and said he had been in Miami for the AFL/CIO Convention and drove over the Lehman Causeway.

FEBRUARY 17 WEDNESDAY

Tom Kingfield came in this morning to talk about the administration's transportation budget. The report came out today, and it's tough on some transportation properties. Basically, the FAA is up about $600 million and the Coast Guard is up about $400 million, but the administration "zeroed out" Amtrak as usual and just about zeroed out all subsidy for mass transit. The entire budget as far as transportation is concerned, instead of being plus two percent for 1988, is fifteen percent under the 1987 budget, with some funds going to other areas in the appropriations process.

Colorado member David Skaggs was in about the new Denver Airport and highways in his area. Denver really needs a regional jetport, and Skaggs is talking about a Denver trip for members of our subcommittee for an onsite view of the problems. Then, Chief Billy Cypress of the Miccosukee Indian Tribe came in with his group to discuss problems in education. As he got up to leave, he promised me a Miccosukee Indian jacket and said he would be at my fundraiser.

FEBRUARY 18 THURSDAY

Jack Gilstrap, the Executive Vice President of the American Public Transportation Association (APTC), was in this morning with Reba Malone, Chairman of the board, and I had to tell them the hard truth regarding the difficulties in federal funding for mass transit. Along with advising them to lobby our subcommittee members I told them to seek support from the elderly organizations, like AARP, that especially need public transportation to visit their health services.

Miami Herald reporter Ricardo Zaldivar stopped by to discuss my appointees to the academies. I am proud of the group we nominated, and I told Ricardo that one of the real pleasures of this job is being in the position to nominate such worthy young people to the service academies. This is true, not only in relation to the nominees to the service academies, but also in regard to the people you help in so many big and little ways who could not find help otherwise. Regardless of whatever else it is deemed, this can be a very rewarding and gratifying profession.

It is 4:45, and Joan and I are at the Washington airport in the "VIP" Ionosphere Club waiting for our flight to Miami. We wondered if we would leave today, as it looks as though Eastern is cancelling some flights. Rep. Claude Pepper is also here. Larry Smith and his wife Sheila have decided to forego the 5:00 flight and leave at 8:00. Larry is threatening to hold a press conference about Eastern Airlines and to ask Frank Lorenzo to resign. I am choosing to remain neutral, as I do not want to get in the crossfire between the labor unions and Eastern, which is bleeding to death financially. Fort Pierce member Tom Lewis is also in the club. I took the opportunity to mention the runway extension problem that my brother-in-law in Fort Pierce had spoken to me about, and Tom was well aware of the issue.

FEBRUARY 19 FRIDAY

At 10:00, I hosted our condo leadership brunch at the Turnberry Garden Room. I had invited the Hallandale Postmaster to join us, and he told the group about the new post office opening in their area. The residents have to travel some distance to the post office presently serving their area, and upon hearing that a more conveniently located branch was in the works, they clapped and cheerfully showed their appreciation. The Postmaster was a big hit. Janet McAliley from the Dade County School Board made a pitch for the school bond drive, and then the president of the condo association introduced me. The condo residents are very receptive to any information on Israel and were particularly responsive when I told them about my Wednesday evening meeting with Secretary of State Schultz and what he had said about a strong Israel being necessary in the peace process and how he was going to establish the procedures to permit the negotiations to take place.

Back at the district office was Wally Pesetsky, the former Mayor of North Miami Beach, who wanted to know which of the presidential candidates he should support and if he should back Bill Nelson for the Senate. I am still uncommitted in the presidential race, but I told him Nelson would not be a problem. Following my meeting with Wally was Evelyn Scheungrund, who came in with several black ladies to talk about daycare problems, especially the lack of daycare facilities. Evelyn is a real activist in the North Dade Democratic Club, and an amazing woman for eighty years of age. Next in was Seymour Fishman, who had with him a colleague from the Hebrew University in Jerusalem. I think next year the Hebrew University wants to have a fundraiser in Miami for the William Lehman Scholarship Fund established there. I view it as another occasion to use people like me to encourage others to give money to a cause in Israel.

A *Wall Street Journal* reporter called today wanting to know about money we appropriated a couple of years ago for the Aviation Science Building at Barry University. I think he was trying to tie in the coincidence of the building funds for Barry University with Bob Dole, who has an apartment at Dwayne Andreas's Seaview Hotel. Inez Andreas is Barry's Chair of the Board of Trustees. He also wanted to explore Tip O'Neill's connection with Barry. I gave him answers that I hope were satisfactory, telling him that the only reason I did not take the original initiative on the Barry appropriation was because I had already marked up funds for Florida Memorial for aviation science and I did not want to appear overly opportunistic to my subcommittee members by appropriating for two universities in the same congressional district. It will be interesting to see how the article reads. At the Miami Shores Country Club tennis courts, Dr. Leo Blauh showed me the article he had written about me for his tennis magazine.

FEBRUARY 20 SATURDAY

Dante Fascell represents the 19th congressional district, and this afternoon he and I went to the Dade County Cultural Center for the 17th and 19th Congressional Districts Art Winners Award ceremony. This is in conjunction with the Burdines Scholastic Arts Awards and the turnout was much larger than last year's event at the North Miami Museum. Our office awarded first, second and third prizes. The first prize was a trip to Washington and the second and third were gift certificates for art supplies. At the campaign office, Sharyn said she had $70,000 on hand and she had not even been to the post office today, which means that we should eventually have about $100,000 or more.

Jerry Berlin is president of a Florida committee that raises money for Democratic senators and for this purpose, he and his wife, Gwen, were hosts this evening to a big, elaborate Democratic Senatorial Campaign Committee Dinner, which included Senators Frank Lautenberg (NJ), Bob Graham (FL), Lawton Chiles (FL), Tom Daschle (SD), Barbara Mikulsky (MD), and Rep. Claude Pepper and a number of other congressmen from other states. I admire the Berlin's. They put considerable effort into these political affairs, all seemingly for the benefit of helping a cause that they believe in. They have also raised money for Joan's sculpture. I saw Askew and Mica, and both lobbied me for support in their Senate races. What I will probably end up doing is announcing for Askew sometime in April. State Senator Joey Gersten wants my help with the condo leaders against Jim Redford for County Commissioner. I am willing to do that as I like Joey; he is not special, but at least we can work together. I do not feel this is the case with Redford. Harvey Ruvin from the Metro-Dade Commission was there and I lobbied him on Lillian Liberti for Metrorail Administrator. I have to get back with Lillian because I think she has a real shot at getting this position.

Joan and I stayed through the announcements, standing when our names were called, but by 10:30 dinner had not been served, so we left. Having appeared at so many of these political affairs, Joan and I have now lost some motivation to attend these functions, and when we do it is often an early exit for us. Jeff and Sharyn occasionally represent me at political events in the district, but Jeff is ill and Sharyn has been working very long hours on the fundraiser.

FEBRUARY 21 SUNDAY

At the campaign office, I see that we have received contributions from people that I have not heard from in years. Frank Smathers, a retired banker, whom I worked with on the Dade County School Board and whom I have not heard from in seventeen years, sent a contribution. I have always sent Frank letters but he never responded, and this time he sent $500.

FEBRUARY 22 MONDAY

Charles Gerson from Memphis is in Miami putting together a presidential primary effort for Al Gore. He and my son Tom had worked together on the ESM bankruptcy case, and this morning at breakfast he was very complimentary about Tom. Jeff is setting up a meeting with Gerson and condo leader Bill Farber. Most of our condo leaders are for Dukakis, which means that Al

Gore has his work cut out for him if he wants to move into this area.

I have to be careful not to offend any of the Dukakis supporters. Farber and Gerson will work together with Jeff and at least try to get an appearance for Gore. We need to broaden the political base of the condo groups and not have them locked into just one candidate. What I hope to do is convince the condo leaders that it would be good to have someone from the Concerned Citizens or the North Dade Democratic Club involved with other presidential campaigns, so that they would have an "in" to the Democratic nominee, whoever it might be.

Taking a late morning flight, I arrived in Washington around 2:00. My back has been bothering me, and before going to the office I stopped by the Capitol Physician's office. Examining my back, the physician said I had a cyst. He applied medication and a dressing over the cyst, and said that he did not think it was anything to be alarmed about. Bill Norris, Senior Vice President of Thrifty-Rent-A-Car, was waiting for me when I got to the office. Norris was seeking airport access for his rental car company, and complained that most rental car companies have facilities at the airport and with this advantage his company could not possibly compete. I will see what I can do to help, as I would like to see his company have a level playing field.

FEBRUARY 23 TUESDAY

I met with Tom, Greg, and Lucy to go over questions for tomorrow's hearing with Transportation Secretary Jim Burnley. Afterwards, I returned to the Capitol Physician's Office to have the dressing over my cyst changed, but found the physicians very busy administering to the many State Governors who had become ill. The governors are in Washington this week attending the State Governors Conference, and when some of them became ill, apparently from some virus, the Capitol physicians were asked to exam them.

In the afternoon Representative John Porter from Illinois came in about the Coast Guard phasing out the helicopter station on Lake Michigan. I invited him to sit on the panel in two weeks when the Coast Guard would be testifying at our transportation hearing and, at that time, ask questions directly to the Coast

Guard; he said he would. Dukakis called to ask for my endorsement, and I told him I was not ready to endorse anyone for the Democratic primary. It was a pleasant conversation, as Dukakis knew that Jeff had my consent to operate on his behalf in the North Dade area. I was keeping Jeff on a very long leash, and letting him do whatever he wanted for Dukakis.

The day was mostly quiet, and it was nice for a change. In the evening I went to a birthday reception for New York Republican Bill Green, a member on Appropriations. Afterwards I attended a very impressive fundraiser dinner for Jamie Whitten given by the University of Mississippi to raise funds to establish a Chair of Law and Government in Whitten's honor at the University. The dinner was held in the Department of Agriculture's auditorium, and I took Katherine Karpoff, a good friend and an employee on Norman Mineta's staff. We sat at table 1, right by the stage, and my favorite caterer prepared the meal. What I enjoyed best were the congenial people at our table: Hughes Corporation executives, my good friend Charlie Wilson and his girlfriend, Ana Lise, and Joe McDade, ranking Republican on Defense Appropriations. The program was good and Miss Mississippi, who looked like a young Lena Horne, sang and she was just beautiful. It was a lovely evening.

FEBRUARY 24 WEDNESDAY

The National Council on Public Works Improvement held a working breakfast this morning regarding problems with our country's infrastructure. Hanna Hunt, who does some fundraising for this group and who also manages my townhouse, had called expressly to invite me. I was glad I went as only a few people were there which was unfortunate considering the vast problems the United States has with its infrastructure.

Norman Mineta and I later met with members of the Metropolitan Washington Airport Authority. Mineta and I are on the Congressional Airport Review Board, which was authorized by Congress just last year. We listened to their presentation on future plans for Dulles and the Washington National Airports, and they seemed to have anticipated the questions we might ask, as they answered each question in detailed and somewhat overlong responses. I missed my 9:30 meeting with Steve

Stephens of the Florida Apartment Association, but I was able to reach him by phone.

11:00, Diane Pickett from the Greater Orlando Chamber of Commerce came in, and I assured her of my participation in the Florida Congressional Partnership Weekend in April. This proposed event is similar to the Congressional Weekend held last May in Miami by the Greater Miami Chamber of Commerce, which was a huge success and a lot of fun. At noon I attended the Congressional Arts Caucus luncheon where Frank Hodsoll, Chairman of the National Endowment for the Arts, was guest speaker. I usually go to the National Endowment for the Arts events because about ten years ago I tried to get together David Lloyd Kreeger, Chairman of the Board of Trustees of the Corcoran Museum, Jack Blakely, Chairman of Armed Services, and Military Construction Subcommittee member Bo Ginn to see if fine art shows could be included on military bases. I have seen that military bases in our country are culturally deprived, having no art whatsoever. There is bowling, skeet shooting, weight lifting, and everything but art. Some bases may have an old Flying Tiger airplane mounted on a stand or a piece of WWII equipment. Although nothing really resulted from my efforts of ten years ago, I am still very much interested in bringing this about. I left before the luncheon ended to join Penny Farthing for a second luncheon in the Cannon Caucus Room. Penny, as president of Women in Government Relations, was hosting the luncheon. Other personal friends were there, including Charlie Wilson who had at his side, Ana Lise, a lobbyist. They seem to be everywhere together lately.

At 2:00, we began our transportation hearing with Transportation Secretary Jim Burnley. Last year Elizabeth Dole was the DOT Secretary, while Burnley was General Counsel and Deputy Secretary. All the subcommittee members were present and on the panel, but we were delayed by two roll call votes on the Floor. The hearing ended at 5:30, and midway through I played good cop to Bob Carr's bad cop in a heated exchange with Jim Burnley, who blamed our subcommittee for FAA problems which he said resulted from our reduction of the NAS Plan by over $200 million. This was a cheap shot by Burnley. The FAA procurement process is so flawed that there was no point in appropriating additional funds, and even now the FAA has not obligated what we have already appropriated.

The biggest problem in commercial aviation is the lack of airport facilities, and I said to Burnley that I wanted to explore with him the further use of military bases to include commercial aviation. He mentioned that Dick Cheney, the newly appointed Secretary to the Department of Defense, had to close some bases to live within the Defense budget restrictions, and that this might help in the conversion.

I always enjoy going to Bob Mrazek's big house on Constitution Avenue, and I went there this evening for Bob's fundraiser. It was great, as usual, with wonderfully delicious food catered by Design Cuisine. Trent Lott's annual Mississippi Gumbo Festival was also held this evening, and this was the first time I could not make it. I had promised Rosemary Murray of Pan American Airlines that I would come to the Sixth Annual Tourism Industry Unity Dinner at the Grand Hyatt Hotel. I usually go to the receptions and skip the dinners, but Rosemary and I have been good friends for a long time and she has been so supportive that I promised her I would come and sit at the Pan Am table. I only stayed for the soup and then left. I was home by 8:00, after a long day from early morning.

FEBRUARY 25 THURSDAY

The Select Committee on Children, Youth and Families held its hearing this morning on "Children and Families in Poverty." The hearing room was very crowded, as the hearing had received much public and media attention due largely to a very recent, popular book entitled, *Rachel and Her Children.* It was an impressive hearing with some interesting testimony, especially from a young indigent white woman from Kentucky, and I may do a newsletter on poverty. In the 17th District in Dade County, one mile west of Biscayne Bay, in Little Haiti, is our own American third world country.

I spoke to several members this morning on various issues. I first saw Earl Hutto and spoke to him about Eli Feinberg and others who are anxious about Hutto delaying the expansion on the Emerald Coast Airport near Destin in North Florida. Hutto said he was waiting for the Defense Department's report due out April 1, so I will get back to Eli and his Ft. Walton Beach client to relay this information. To Matt McHugh I pointed out how important it would be for him to go to Turkey, and he promised to call Gary Hymel. And then to John Dingell I spoke about import limits on Suzuki vehicles. The United States has been counting Suzuki's as trucks to avoid passenger car quotas. If the United States eliminated Suzuki's from the truck category this would adversely affect the number of Suzuki's brought into the United States. I told Dingell that my son Bill, who has a Suzuki dealership and was concerned about the proposed import limits, wanted to know how hard he was going to push to change this. Dingell said he is now just asking questions to the Customs Office to see how Customs was going to score Suzuki's.

We were to vote today on a humanitarian aid package to the Contras, but the vote was postponed until next week. Also postponed until after the decision handed down on an appeal was the expulsion vote on New York member Mario Biaggi, who was convicted this past September on charges related to accepting an illegal gratuity. Wisely, the vote was postponed. If the House votes to expel Mario and the appellate court overrules the lower court, we would look silly. In 1974 Mario and I traveled to Israel together and I got to know him pretty well. He has been a good friend.

At lunch with the Florida Bankers Association, they are in pursuit of broadening their banking business into insurance and other activities. I do not have a problem with this, especially with banks in the underwriting business, but I told them that a problem exists between the Banking Committee Chairman Freddy St. Germaine and the Commerce Committee Chairman John Dingell, who has said the banking industry had better be careful in its request to move certain banking committee jurisdiction in the House from him to St. Germaine, as this would mean possible other troubles for banking if Dingell were to lose this jurisdiction.

Dick Warden from the United Automobile Workers spoke with me about the upcoming vote on the civil rights bill. He wanted assurance that I would be voting "correctly" on the bill, and I told him that I vote on civil rights legislation the same as Don Edwards. "That would be fine," he said. Edwards is one of the most liberal members in the House.

FEBRUARY 26 FRIDAY

Two representatives of transit labor, Bob Molofsky and Art Luby, came in this morning to discuss two problems. One concerned the Metro-Dade PEP Agreement in which organized labor in Miami is running an experimental bus system in comparison with a private sector effort. Their second and primary problem was with the President's budget which eliminates general funds for the Section Nine subsidy for mass transit for both capital and operating costs. Mass transit will have to take a cut this year and is hoping that the cut is not too great. I suggested that they appear on this year's public witness portion of the hearings and that they work the members of our transportation subcommittee as well as members of other appropriation subcommittees to have funds shifted into transit, as transit's 15% cut is larger than other appropriation cuts.

I have been busy setting up the program for the meeting in Miami Friday regarding the Metro-Dade trauma network's announcement of the trauma report. When I phoned Metro Commissioner Sherman Winn, he said he would be at the program. John in our office sees this as a media opportunity, and has been busy orchestrating the event. The report, produced with a $250 thousand grant that our subcommittee appropriated for trauma research, was approved by the House on the condition that Metro-Dade create a trauma agency and advisory committee. Conditions were put in place because of the earlier flawed trauma network which Dade set up in 1985 to get severely injured people to designated hospitals where a special team of doctors and nurses could help them. By 1987, however, only Jackson Memorial Hospital was left in the network and according to a recent task force study, the lack of a sufficient trauma network led to a significant increase in the number of preventable deaths. In the *Miami Herald*'s announcement of the grant's approval, I was quoted saying, "The conditions echo recommendations that a trauma task force delivered earlier this year. I hope this will encourage Dade County ... to get the show on the road."

Dick Judy of Miami International Airport called to tell me he would be able to bring his people to my fundraiser and that he would also have a private small fundraiser for me later in the year. I said, fine, and then questioned him on the concerns that Treasury Subcommittee staffer Tex Gunnels had on the Tamiami Airport. Judy said that Tamiami and Opa Locka Airports would serve both passengers and cargo, and that the information that Tamiami would serve only passengers and Opa Locka only cargo is false. I will get this message to Tex, as he and I have discussed his coming to Miami during the first week in April to meet with Dick Judy and Customs officials.

Tom Kingfield came in to discuss the possibility of our office sponsoring his daughter as a page next spring. Tom said he is up for retirement at any time if he wants to take it, and that he may not even be here next spring if he has a good job offer. I said, "Don't you leave before I leave," and he laughed. I would hate to lose Tom as he is a very valuable part of our operation. 1:00, Marilyn Marsh came by and we had lunch. Marilyn and I have been friends since before I came to Congress. I helped her get a job on the Education and Labor Committee staff about thirteen years ago, and she moved her family here from Florida. We frequently get together for breakfast or lunch and talk about old times.

Charlie Wilson, who is a good friend, of playwright Larry King, has invited me to join him this evening to see the new play, "The Night Hank Williams Died."

FEBRUARY 27 SATURDAY

It is too cold to play tennis outdoors so I will just take it easy today. Tonight we had our office party at Windows Restaurant in Rosslyn, VA. Everyone enjoyed it, and this office get-together has now become an annual tradition.

FEBRUARY 28 SUNDAY

At a reception at the Ritz Carlton Hotel this evening, I spoke to members of the Dallas, Texas, Jewish Federation, telling them that they should be meeting with members they really need such as Dave Obey, who really matters when it comes to funding for Israel. I also mentioned the importance of Julian Dixon, another member on Foreign Ops, and asked if they had any black congressional members who were close to the Federation, and they said no. "The Black Caucus is getting stronger," I said, and suggested that they open some lines of communication there. Texas member Marty Frost was there, having put the reception together, and Steve Bartlett, a Republican from the Dallas suburbs, who only told them what they want to hear. I hope to arrange appointments for the Jewish Federation members with Dave Obey and Julian Dixon. I do not know if the meetings will come to anything, but I think it is worth the effort.

FEBRUARY 29 MONDAY

Trying now to convince some members to join me and lobbyist Gary Hymel on a trip to Turkey, I spoke to New York members Matt McHugh and Frank Horton, and they will get back to me. I also spoke to John Dingell, Chairman of the Energy and Commerce Committee, about our hearing on Wednesday with the Interstate Commerce Commission (ICC). Dingell said he would give me a few questions to ask. He wants more regulations on railroads, and he is especially concerned about captive shipping railroads and the labor protection problems involving ICC and the railroads. He doesn't like the ICC, and said, "They are bastards, but they are our bastards."

I saw Republican member Bill Gradison from Ohio, a senior member on Ways and Means and the husband of Heather Gradison who will be testifying as Chair of the ICC. Bill tells me that the conference on the trade bill is coming together and will probably be on the Floor soon. I will not be as protectionist as are most of the Democrats.

Returning to the office, I got Sharyn on the phone and she, rather anxiously, told me that a mysterious phone call had come in on our unlisted number in the district office, and the caller had asked for her and said to advise the congressman not to use his congressional office to plan his fundraisers. Sharyn was not in the district office, of course, and I do not think there is any consequence to the call, as we have been very meticulous in keeping her out of our congressional office and keeping her operation separate, having her phone calls go to her home or to our campaign office. We also have a post office box for contributions and campaign-related mail.

About six months ago I mentioned to the Speaker's staff that

I would like to have Jim Wright as guest of honor for my Miami fundraiser this year. His staff said they would get back to me with a date, and yesterday his aide called to say they had a June date. Once I had decided not to have the Speaker, I should have gotten back to his staff, but I didn't. So this afternoon at the Speaker's office, I thanked his staff and, as a semi-gracious way out of never getting back to them, I said that I really did not have a tough election and that I would rather have the Speaker use his time to help others who may have tough opposition and needed his presence in their districts. Frankly, I did not get back to his staff because I never thought they took my request seriously. The fact that they are just getting back to me after six months may have contributed to this train of thought. Nonetheless, during those six months I asked former Speaker Tip O'Neill to be our honored guest, and he accepted. Tip is an even greater presence than the present Speaker, although Wright did make a stirring speech in Miami last year at the dinner held in his honor by the Democratic Parties of Dade, Broward and Palm Beach Counties.

Chapter 15

MARCH 1, 1988 - TUESDAY

Our office continues to get complaints about the Customs service in Miami. Now Jerry Isan, owner of the Don Carter Bowling Lanes in Miami and a good supporter, has written to complain about the service. I took his letter to the Treasury, Post Office Subcommittee staff for them to make the necessary inquiries. Commissioner Sherman Winn called about one of his relatives who is trying to immigrate from Yugoslavia, but is having trouble because the relative does not have strong enough family ties for the Consulate in Yugoslavia to issue him a visa. So, I spoke with John Osthaus from the subcommittee staff on Commerce, Justice, State and Judiciary, and he is to get back to me. By 9:30 I was back in my office meeting with personnel from Metro-Dade's Family Health Center about medical problems in Miami. They tell me how I should vote, though I continually tell them that I have always voted for the health center's position on issues.

At 10:00, Larry Salci, President of the Bombardier Corporation, a consultant Myles Mitchell, and Barry Crickmer who represents Bombardier in Washington, came in to discuss high speed rail passenger safety issues. Bombardier is the last company to build train cars in North America. The group spoke about its equipment in comparison to that of Europe and Japan which have only half the Bombardier's crash worthiness, and I suggested that they submit rail safety questions our subcommittee should ask when the Federal Railroad Authority (FRA), the National Transportation Safety Board (NTSB), and Amtrak come before our subcommittee. With that they seemed satisfied and said they would get back to me with the questions.

Rabbi Neuman is back again in the States. He and Gene Dubow of the New York American Jewish Committee came in for about an hour this morning. The Rabbi, who has been settled in East Germany for several months now, said that his time there though interesting has been frustrating. Klaus Gysi continues to be cooperative, but some of the Jewish community is still more Communist than Jewish. The facilities, he said, are still cramped and his Friday evening services are jammed full of people. He will probably last the rest of this year and then retire. I understand the Rabbi has a German girlfriend.

I am meeting with people from the National Federation of Federal Employees and then the National Treasury Employees Union. Both groups have the same concerns: shared leave, and equal pay with those in the private sector. Considering all the fringe benefits federal employees receive, the salary difference is compensated for in job security and in retirement benefits. These two groups might find more support for their concerns if more federal employees were quitting for the private sector, but this is not the case. Federal employees usually serve about twenty years or more and then retire; in many cases, retired federal employees on pension go on to work an additional five to ten years in the private or public sector.

In preparation for the luncheon and press conference Friday in Miami on the new shock trauma report, task force members Chief Perez of the Dade County Fire Department, Tom Sheib of NHTSA, and personnel from Dade hospitals flew up from Miami to discuss with me the findings and recommendations in the report. As mentioned, the shock trauma network established in

1985 has just about disappeared in Dade County except for Jackson Memorial Hospital, which is a county facility. And there a real problem exists because Jackson has taken on so much neurosurgery from trauma that elected neurosurgery such as brain tumors, for instance, has to be done elsewhere. With this new plan, Mt. Sinai and Baptist Hospitals can become second level trauma centers.

Leaving them in the office talking to John and Lucy, I went to the Capitol Physician's Office. My knee is starting to act up from playing tennis yesterday. The knee is swollen, and the doctors want me to come back later to make sure there is no infection. When I got back to the office the Miami trauma group had left and Milton Toppel and his wife were there. The Toppel's own the huge X-Tra Supermarket located across US 441 from my son's Lehman Land dealerships in Miami, and we discussed their concerns about the minimum wage, family leave and compulsory insurance. I tried to be reassuring, but business people are concerned with the current minimum wage legislation now before the House Education and Labor Committee, which would raise the minimum wage to $5.05 an hour over the next four years from the current $3.35 an hour. The mandated health insurance legislation is now before the same committee.

As an added attraction to our fundraiser, I have invited Rep. Joe Kennedy as an honored guest. This morning his staff called to say that the congressman did not feel comfortable staying at Turnberry because it was too high class for his image. We put him, instead, at the Seaview on the ocean where Tip O'Neill is staying. Speaking of fundraising, Dave Obey wants me to raise money for him in Miami at an April 25 event. I have to get back with his campaign staffer Mary Schecklehoff to discuss what I can do for him on that day.

The Israeli Embassy called proposing a luncheon with Prime Minister Shamir on March 15 at the Sheraton Grand. I spoke to Sid Yates and he said a luncheon with the Prime Minister in the middle of the day when the House is in session is ridiculous, as no one would be there. Yates suggested that they schedule an evening event or hold the luncheon in a room in the Capitol to avoid our having to leave the Hill. I called the Embassy and repeated Yates's suggestions, and now they are to get back to me.

I walked through the connecting underground corridor from

the Rayburn Building to the Longworth Building to where the combined reception of the National Association of Convenience Stores, the National Wholesale Grocers Association and the Food Marketing Institute was being held. I had told McCarthy from the Tom Thumb Stores who stopped by my office yesterday that I would meet him at the reception. I also looked for the Toppel's, but they were not there. Speaking to my longtime friend and supporter, Glen Woodward, from the Winn Dixie Stores, I noticed for the first time that Glen did not look well. We talked about the fundraiser, and Glen said he would have someone there from Winn Dixie. I had hoped that Glen might be able to come.

WEDNESDAY MARCH 2

At 10:00 we began the Interstate Commerce Commission (ICC) hearing with ICC Chair Heather Gradison. The hearing went well, nothing unusual, and Heather was a good witness. Last year, a big issue with the ICC was the administration's proposed sun setting of this agency. From Heather's response to my question as to how far along they were in resolving this matter, it was clear that they are no farther ahead than they were last year. Legislation is no longer pending in Congress that would provide for the sunset. This legislation is part of the trade bill and the ICC sunset portion of that bill has now been tabled. According to Heather, the administration is presently working on a new sunset bill, but she believes no sunset legislation was going to happen this year.

After lunch I went to the Foreign Operations hearing where witnesses testified on concerns regarding Israeli security and the comparative military power of Israel and its potential enemies. The Iran/Iraq conflict was also discussed. The Foreign Ops Subcommittee information is optimistic about the ability of Israel to win another war, but Israel would suffer many casualties because of the increased military capability of both Syria and Egypt.

Everyone has been lobbying me on tomorrow's vote for humanitarian aid to the Nicaraguan contras. Because I tell them that I have not decided, I get a lot of attention from colleagues and the peace lobbyists.

My good friend and colleague, Marty Sabo from Minnesota, is celebrating his 50th birthday this evening. There with his own little band was Dave Obey, and it was wonderful food and really fun.

MARCH 3 THURSDAY

The Florida Congressional Delegation held a breakfast meeting this morning with Dr. Ken Tefertiller, Vice President of Agricultural Affairs of the University of Florida. Israel is heavily involved in the further development of irrigation projects in third world countries. I wanted to know from Dr. Tefertiller what kind of joint endeavors were being made with Israel on these projects. Dr. Tefertiller said that Israel was the frontrunner in developing irrigation projects, and that the University of Florida had joined with Israel in working in Nepal, Zaire and Haiti on the proper use of irrigation. Earl Hutto and I were the only House members, the others were staffers. I will start delegating some of the Florida issues and meetings to my staff as other members do.

Yesterday our subcommittee's ICC hearing was very productive as was this morning's hearing with the Inspector General. We learned that the Inspector General has a lot of doubts about the efficiency of the Department of Transportation, especially within the Coast Guard and the FAA. He has information that will be helpful to me when questioning the FAA, Coast Guard, Mass Transit and other agencies as they come before us.

The *Wall Street Journal* had a front page story today on Annie Ackerman, which included my statement that "Annie has been wooed by more Democrats running for President than any other woman in America," which is true. Florida Democratic party chairman, Charles Whitehead, said, "Annie wields more power than any one private citizen in the state of Florida," which is also true. The article referred to "Annie's Army," a group of her friends who, among other things, provide "palm cards" to those headed for the polls which list all of Annie's choices. "We'll even breathe for our people," she said. An essential member of "Annie's Army" is Mollye Lovinger Fox, who was described in the article as Annie's "nuts and bolts person," and as a "4-foot-10-inch New Yorker who once climbed to a condo roof to talk down a suicidal retiree." It was a very long article, very complimentary, and included Annie's picture wearing the ever-present hat, for which she is noted. This was a well-done, well-deserved tribute to Annie.

Members of the Catholic Dominican Sisters political network came in about the vote today on humanitarian aid to Nicaragua, wanting assurance that I intended to vote the Democratic position. They were so serious, and I could not resist the urge to have some fun with them. When I said that I had to vote the Democratic position, they asked "Why?" "If the Democratic position does not pass, we will be in session three more hours," I said, "and I will miss my 8:00 p.m. flight to Miami." They laughed. I then spoke about "filibusters" in Central America in the mid-nineteenth century and they had never heard of this. I told them we have been interfering in Nicaragua since 1850, so why should we stop now. I was being very facetious and showing off my knowledge of history but they were enjoying the conversation. The *Congressional Quarterly* reported that the issue divided both liberal and church groups and that several groups backed the Democratic leadership's plan, including the Presbyterian Church and the Friends Committee on National Legislation. According to the CQ, the two groups said in a joint letter to the House leadership, that "Our political judgment is that Congress is likely to approve some sort of contra-aid package, and our moral judgment is that the House leadership proposal is preferable to any alternative that would include military aid." Reportedly, there were other groups who sent letters voicing just the opposite opinion and urging the defeat of contra aid.

Later on the House Floor, I voted on the joint resolution amendment for humanitarian aid for the Nicaraguan contras, and it passed. I also remained to vote for final passage of the bill because my colleague friends were "warning" me that if final passage failed, the President would send back a military aid package which could possibly pass. Unfortunately the resolution was defeated in final passage, which now means that the whole day was meaningless as the President will presumably now send the package to Congress as a military aid program for the contras. It is very frustrating, especially for the Speaker to blow this deal, forcing the Democrats to make a tough but futile vote. Jim Wright just could not bring the votes on final passage.

Arriving at the Washington National Airport at 7:30, I learned that the 8:00 p.m. flight was delayed. It will be midnight when I arrive in Miami. I hate this because it is so tiring, but then it goes with the territory.

FRIDAY MARCH 4

The shock trauma network luncheon and press conference are being held today. I got to the district office early to meet with constituents and left around 11:30 headed for Florida International University for the luncheon Mt. Sinai and Parkway General Hospitals had put together for the trauma task force members. Diane Steed, Administrator of the National Highway Traffic Safety Administration was there, as were many people from Dade County's Fire Department and Public Service Division, as the task force was composed of local firefighters, doctors, hospital administrators and lawyers.

Following the awarding of appreciation plaques to the task force members, we walked outside on FIU's beautiful campus down by the bay for the press conference. John from my Washington office is in Miami, having arrived on Wednesday. At the press conference, the report was officially handed to me by Chief Perez, head of the task force, and I in turn handed it to Commissioner Sherman Winn. We all made short speeches, including Diane Steed. As the conference ended, I was interviewed by Channels 4, 7, and 10 and by the *Miami Herald*, and I think we are off to a good start. If this works, Dade County will be a model program for other areas of the country that wish to establish a trauma network. It will cost Dade County about $300,000 a year to operate an advisory board and a trauma agency, but that is probably less than what it would cost the county to support an indigent suffering from improper treatment of a severe accidental injury.

MARCH 5 SATURDAY

This morning's *Miami Herald* carried the story on the funds for the shock trauma network, with an account of yesterday's event. The article included my statement that "It is like nailing

Jell-O to the wall to try to build from the top down." This was said in reference to the failure of the first trauma network which proved that you cannot build a system by importing experts, as was done in 1985 when the system was based on advice from experts from around the country. Diane Steed was quoted on the problems of uninsured drivers and soaring malpractice insurance as obstacles facing Dade's trauma network. The task force report called for stronger enforcement of mandatory car insurance laws, and the establishment of a trauma agency. The county commissioners working together with the county manager will need to decide soon on how to go about creating the trauma agency.

At 8:30 a.m., John Schelble and Bernie from the district office picked me up at home and we drove to the Miami Regional Air Traffic Control Center for the dedication of the new IBM air traffic system. We saw the new building and the very impressive new Host Computer System for the expansion of air traffic over South Florida, which is more complex and a much larger computer system than the one used by air traffic controllers at the Miami International Airport. The program was very effective, with short speeches from Regional FAA Administrator Cas Castleberry, Representative Clay Shaw, and Mayor Steve Clark. I also said a few words, and was later interviewed by Channel 6 and the *Miami Herald.*

In the afternoon I assisted in the dedication of the reconstructed Arch Creek Park Bridge, a pedestrian walkway over a 40-50-foot section of Arch Creek. The original bridge, which collapsed in 1973, was once used by the Tequesta Indians dating back to 500 B.C. Paddy Cunningham, supervisor of the 14-acre park, who spoke, said that the creek linked the Indians to both Biscayne Bay and the Everglades, and "the road we are standing on right now is the first road ever built in Dade County." This is the second consecutive day that I have sat out in the sun bareheaded for a program in the middle of the day. I'm glad it is not summer. Rev. Chuck Eastman, who formerly pastured a church in North Miami and is one of my favorite liberal clergymen, was master of ceremony. Ninety-seven-year-old Marjory Stoneman Douglas, a great writer and environmentalist, was on the program, and paid homage to the late Alice Cohen and Jessie Freeling who initiated this bridge restoration project. I was last on the program, and just as I was unveiling the plaque a train came by and cut my speech short, but it was a very nice ceremony.

MARCH 6 SUNDAY

At the Asthma Walk-A-Thon at Haulover Park this morning I made a short speech, as did other politicians such as State Senator Gwen Margolis, State Representative Mike Friedman, and North Miami Councilman Fuchs. This annual event is put together by Ruth Rosen, and it has two things going - raising money for the Denver Asthma Immunization Center, and promoting Sea World's anti-graffiti effort. The *Miami Herald* and Channel 6 TV were there and held interviews.

Miami Herald reporter Richard Wallace had a story this morning on the Arch Creek dedication, describing Arch Creek Park as a "compact oasis of water and subtropical greenery surrounded by concrete, asphalt and railroad tracks." I was mentioned in reference to bringing my grandchildren to the park and that I had mixed feelings about it. "In a way it is one of the best kept secrets in Dade County," I said. "A person who wants to go to Greynolds Park goes to Greynolds Park. A person who wants to go to Crandon Park goes to Crandon Park. People pass by this park a thousand times and never take the time to stop." I did not now want the park to be overrun by everybody stopping even though they should know about it and appreciate that the park is here. It was a good article, and even my rather possessive, ambivalent feelings about the park read okay in print.

Our fundraiser reception was held this evening in the Garden Room at Turnberry. Of those present, about two-thirds were contributors and the rest were "comp'ed" political office holders, condo leaders and County and State officials. Annie Ackerman and Marjorie Deutsch came in wheelchairs. Two photographers were there for the many guests who wanted a photo taken with Tip O'Neill and Joe Kennedy - especially with Joe Kennedy. Jack Gordon and his wife, Myra McPherson, a *Washington Post* writer, were there, and Myra gravitated right over to Tip O'Neill, as she is a Tip addict. Many of my old friends from Miami Shores came so it was rather like a reunion.

I introduced Sharyn, Joan and the family and then I introduced Joe Kennedy as a future President and Tip O'Neill as a great leader. I thought I was through but Billy Cypress, Chief of the Miccosukee Indians, came up and presented me with a gorgeous Indian jacket. Senator Bob Graham spoke very flatteringly about not only my efforts in behalf of Dade County but for the State, which pleased me. The food was great, with plenty to drink, and a harpist which added just the right ambience. Everyone seemed to have had a good time. It was really more a love-in than a fundraiser. Katherine Karpoff from Norman Mineta's office said she had been to a lot of fundraisers but never to one this special. From the points of view of Joan and her sister Emily, the hit of the show was Joe Kennedy with his charm, vitality, sexuality and intelligence. His and Tip's presence was impressive, as you have to appear capable of delivering influential and prominent people, as well as raising money. And in these regards, the party was a huge success. We raised, I think, about $109 thousand going in and about $15 thousand at the gate. Sharyn did a fantastic job of coordinating the entire event, with all the pieces coming together with a lot of good volunteers.

MARCH 7 MONDAY

In today's *Miami News* there is a story about Metro Commissioner Beverly Phillips being arrested a few blocks away from Turnberry after leaving the party last evening. She ran into another car and was charged with driving under the influence of alcohol. This was most unfortunate. There was no mention of my party, however. We did serve alcohol, but I did not notice anyone drinking too much, and it did not seem that Bev was.

My 11:30 flight out of Miami arrived in Washington around 2:00. Admiral Yost of the Coast Guard came in about the Coast Guard hearing tomorrow. We are both in the same predicament, and neither really knows what to do. He asked me to reprogram about $60 million from other parts of the transportation budget, but this request needed the recommendation of the Secretary of Transportation and the Office of Management and Budget. Tom Kingfield, Lucy and I then went over questions for tomorrow's hearing. I do not expect many of our members to be at the hearing because there are no votes on the House Floor tomorrow, which means that they can remain in their districts.

MARCH 8 TUESDAY

The *Miami Herald* came out today with its report on Metro Commissioner Beverly Phillips's auto accident, and the article did mention that she drank a vodka martini while attending my fund- raiser, but that was all in connection to the gathering. Beverly expressed disappointment in herself more than anything else, saying that the public did not expect this from a public official and that nobody expected it of her. Even though this is not the kind of situation and publicity you want to have happen, I am sure she will ride this out okay. Beverly is well respected and appreciated for the job she does as county commissioner.

The Coast Guard hearing began and ended today, and it was the first time we have ever finished it in one day. The hearing went from 10:00 to noon, breaking for lunch, and then from 2:00 to 5:30. Admiral Yost and I were both a little tired. Nonetheless, it was a good hearing, very informative as to the needs and performance of the Coast Guard. In his request for a supplemental $60 million, Admiral Yost talked about more base closings and a reduction in Coast Guard services, such as drug interdiction, if this $60 million was not appropriated. Apparently, though, the Admiral wants to be very cooperative in working with us this year on the shortfall problems, and hopefully we will be able to get some help in 302B allocations from discretionary funds of other appropriation subcommittees. The Coast Guard's inventory shrinkage problem has made little improvement, if any, since our last year's hearing. Admiral Yost, in answer to inquiries by ranking minority member, Larry Coughlin, indicated that he would look further into inventory management, getting rid of obsolete equipment, and agreed that this could produce big dollars saved. But the Inspector General, who testified at yesterday's hearing, probably hit the nail on the head when he said, "You can tinker with the system but I'm not sure how much better it will be."

Back at my office I returned a few phone calls. Billy Cypress has another $2,000 to send us, and I received $500 in the mail from Ellen and Ken Rosen. The only visitor today was Sam

Rabin from Miami about insurance legislation. I called Jerry Berlin about raising money for Dave Obey in Miami in April. Berlin told me he is no longer president of the Florida committee that raises money for members of Congress who support Israel, and that Mike Adler is now the president. I will call Mike tomorrow to see if he can do anything.

Bell South had its party this evening, but Joan and I arrived when the party was pretty much over. Everyone is surprised about the Super-Tuesday Primary and how badly Gephardt lost, and how well Al Gore did.

MARCH 9 WEDNESDAY

I stopped by the National Continental Shelf Study Planning Conference this morning, and California member Melvin Levine was talking to the group when I arrived. Spokesmen from the Florida Sierra Club and other Florida activists were there. I let them know of my support and told them that I enjoyed sport fishing too much to let it be damaged by offshore drilling. Together with my son Tom and his son, Little Tommy, I often go fishing, one of my truly relaxing activities.

The Children, Youth and Families hearing was held this morning, but I was unable to attend as it conflicted with my National Transportation Safety Board hearing at 10:00. The NTSB hearing went to noon, and during the lunch break I met with non-union employees from Eastern Airlines who wanted assurance that I would remain neutral in the battle between union and management. I assured them that I am trying to do this, and that I am staying off the concurrent resolution offered by Norman Mineta and drafted by the Machinists Union, which asks the Department of Transportation to investigate the management of Eastern and Continental. Both labor and management have enough faults and I do not want to be in the middle. If I have to say anything I would quote from Shakespeare's Mercutio, "A pox óre both your Houses." I do, however, want to help to maintain an Eastern presence in the Miami area.

The National Transportation Safety Board hearing went off without anything unusual. We ended about 4:00 after covering every mode of transportation safety from airplanes to bicycles to elevators. As the hearing wound down, I made the observation to NTSB Chairman Jim Burnett, somewhat for my own amusement, that it had always puzzled me that the safest form of transportation was the elevator. "What is it about elevators that makes them safe?" I asked. Jim, quite seriously, said that they had eliminated the human element. This answer came quite readily to him, as it should have, since he had just completed hours of drilling from the panel concerning the number of accidents in major modes of transportation caused by inexperienced pilots and overworked controllers, fatigued truck drivers and the failure of motor carriers to oversee the mechanical aspects of the vehicles, serious drug and alcohol use of train engineers - and the list goes on.

On the House Floor I spoke to Dick Durbin about our trip next Thursday to Chicago. I also talked to Silvio Conte of Massachusetts in the gym and he will attend the FRA hearing tomorrow because of difficult railroad right-of-way situations adjacent to his district in Massachusetts. Members do a lot of business in the gym. Speaking about Eddie Boland, his Massachusetts colleague retiring, Silvio said that Eddie did not file election papers as he is seventy-five years old and will probably drop out this year to spend more time with his young children.

Stopping by the Shipbuilders Council reception, I felt bad because we have not been able to appropriate any Coast Guard funds for an ice breaker and they need ice breaker construction for the shipbuilding industry. I suggested that they testify at the outside witnesses portion of our hearings, and they will prepare for this. There were Apalachicola oysters at a Hill reception for the first time and they were very good.

Pete Stark held a reception this evening at his home in honor of John Burton, who is running for the California State Senate. John was a colleague, but retired, and Barbara Boxer was elected to his seat. Barbara asked me to help her with the Coast Guard to reduce activity on their shooting range which causes a noise disturbance problem for homeowners adjacent to the shooting range in her district. I said, "There is no way I can help you." Barbara asked, "Why?" And I said because you keep voting to take the trust funds off budget. She said to give her a little more time, and I said "No." She finally went to George Miller and he more or less said the same thing. She came back to me and said if I helped her with the Coast Guard problem she would never vote against me again. Now I have to deliver for her on the Coast Guard disturbance matter.

Joan and I left to visit Bob Mrazek and his wife Kathy at their home on Constitution Avenue, one of my favorite homes in Washington. Joan enjoyed the antiques and the style in which their home was decorated. We stayed about an hour, and they invited us back on Tuesday evening for dinner with guests of honor, actors Burt Lancaster and Jimmy Stewart. The Mrazek's are very special friends, and it was a lovely evening.

MARCH 10 THURSDAY

At 10:00, we began our hearing on the Federal Railroad Administration (FRA), with Administrator John Riley. Many members were present as Riley testified on the FRA rail safety programs and ongoing initiatives to improve rail safety. At yesterday's hearing, the National Transportation Safety Board, indicating that their agency had written to Riley three times over a period of a year-and-a-half trying to get a response to their grade-crossing recommendations, and that the FRA had not responded, accused the FRA of being unresponsive to their recommendations. So before general questions began, I asked Riley about this and he said that he had "heard through the grapevine" that NTSB yesterday had accused them of being an unresponsive agency. He produced a NTSB analysis chart and passed it up to the committee saying that the analysis concluded that the FRA was the most responsive of all the "modal" agencies. I reminded Riley that it was the grade- crossing recommendations which seemed to be NTSB's concern, and told him that I would like to have for the record his responses on the five NTSB recommendations on grade-crossings.

To say that there is friction between the two agencies may be putting it somewhat mildly. Riley testified that he thought NTSB would be significantly more effective if they became part of the solution and not just part of the identification process. He cited several examples of the FRA offering to discuss with NTSB several points that they had raised and NTSB's response was always "no," that they identify problems and were not part of the solution. John felt that if NTSB did not want to be a part of the solution, then they shouldn't criticize. I thought his point had real merit, but I did not pursue this further at the time.

We broke for lunch at noon, and did not get started on the general questions until 2:00. During the break, I met with Congressman Buddy MacKay and former colleague, Bill Gunter, who is now the Insurance Commissioner of Florida. I spoke to Gunter about the mandatory liability insurance for Florida and the lack of enforcement of it. If the State of Florida does not enforce liability insurance then we cannot have a trauma network in Miami because a large percentage of shock trauma costs must be covered by liability insurance. Florida will have to mandate enforcement to implement shock trauma treatment. Gunter and I have agreed to meet in Miami in April with the Dade County Shock Trauma Task Force to do something about this. Buddy MacKay will help with the Florida legislature.

I took Joan to the Senate Dining Room for lunch because I thought the dining room would not be too crowded since the Senate was not in session. It wasn't, but the new hostess did not recognize me and said they did not have any room. When another member of the House came in and got a seat, I questioned why he was able to get seated and she immediately got us a table.

At 3:30 I left the FRA hearing to meet with Chuck Ordahl, Vice President of McDonald Douglas Aeronautics and Chris Rosander who works with Rosalee Roberts in the Legislative Affairs Office of McDonald Douglas Military Defense. They had not heard about the problems regarding the full Appropriations Committee's response to the President's budget requests. I photocopied and gave to them information which summarized where we were in the President's budget requests. As Eddie Boland said in our full Appropriations Committee meeting on Thursday, it was going to be tough meeting the President's request for increases in funds for NASA. The material which I had given to them was a reaffirmation of that fact.

After the hearing, I returned a phone call to Joe Fernandez, Superintendent of Dade County Public Schools. Joe said that without my support the school bond issue in Miami would not have passed, and that he was going to tell the *Miami News* and

Herald that the letters of support I sent to the condo leaders and residents in my district made the difference. I believe that is true. I sent out thousands of letters to condo residents in my district asking for their support, and it did make a difference.

Norman Mineta asked if I was signing the resolution condemning Eastern Airlines for unfair labor practices. I said "no" and he seemed a little disappointed, but I told him I would talk to him later about it.

MARCH 11 FRIDAY

In the *Wall Street Journal* today, I was mentioned in a very positive article on my vote against Contra aid, which said that the Republicans will target Democrats in Spanish-speaking areas, such as "Florida Rep. Lehman." In fact, I was the only member mentioned as being targeted because of my vote against Contra military aid, and if I had had this article when sending out my fundraiser letter, I could have probably raised an additional $20,000. It was the second time this month that my name appeared on the front page of the *Wall Street Journal*. This is unique for me. The other appearance was in the Annie Ackerman story.

I hear Jim Howard may be doing another off-budget amendment again this year to take the FAA Trust Fund off budget. I wonder if it will be part of the Public Works Committee technical corrections bill. When I voted against Contra military aid, I did so because I thought it was the right thing to do. But my vote was also supportive of the Democratic leadership's position. I told Jim Wright that if I was willing to take the heat to help him against the Contras, then I want the leadership to help protect me against another off-budget battle. I spoke to Marty Frost (Texas) about the article in the *Wall Street Journal*. Marty, who is close to the Speaker, said he would bring the matter to Jim's attention. But the Speaker has long ties to Public Works Committee members and wants to help.

Miami Beach City Manager Bob Parkins, and lobbyists, Sylvester Lukis and Ernie Weiner were in the office to discuss the possibility of a light rail system for Miami Beach. On my suggestion, they will submit for the subcommittee record later this year plans for the light rail system. Then Yvonne Reagan,

Chief Executive Officer and the new Director of the YMCA of Greater Miami came in to inquire about federal programs available for her institution. Offhand, I did not know of any available programs, and asked my legislative assistant, Marsha Runningen, in Yvonne's presence, to make inquiries and get back to Yvonne. While waiting for the House photographer to arrive for a photo opportunity, I presented Yvonne with a YMCA donation of $100. Growing up in Selma, Alabama, I lived across the street from the YMCA, and it served as a second home during my early teens. During this era, the "Y" was much the focal point of the community and, for me, it is always the one constant in my flashback of good memories - especially remembering people like Paul Grist, who served as the YMCA secretary and whom I wrote about in an earlier document. Paul was an amazing man, and all the "Y" boys wanted his approval and support. Although he was married, he had no children of his own, and he gladly served as a second father for a great many of us. Along with my father, Paul had a very strong, positive impact on my early development.

I left the office at 10:00 for tennis with my buddies and Susan Hanrack, court reporter on the House Floor. Sonny Montgomery said that it looked like his pal George Bush has the Republican nomination wrapped up and that George is going to surprise everyone as to how liberal and how humanitarian he is going to be if he becomes President. [He did turn out to be extremely likable and friendly, but was afraid to be too liberal, as on abortion.]

Colleague Jim Scheuer from New York had asked to meet with me, together with a group which is trying to do fish farming in a joint venture with Israel, Jordan and Egypt. Meeting this afternoon, they showed me the program's brochure, and it looks fascinating. The project is already underway. This would help the mutual relationships and also provide for the protein shortage that is prevalent in Egypt and often third world countries. The problem is that the funds the State Department's AID agency had for this venture are now earmarked for something else. As a senior member on Foreign Ops, they want me to free up this money so that it would be available for this program. I am interested in helping and Adele, who was also at the meeting, will make some inquiries.

WMATA General Manager Carmen Turner and former member Bill Ratchford came to talk about funding for Washington Metro this year. Carmen and I are good friends, and I asked her somewhat jokingly to come to Miami and be our County Manager. I am flattered, she said. I told her I was pushing for a woman in that position and that I was seriously pressing for Lillian Liberti, whom she knew. I don't know how seriously Carmen took my offer, if she considered it at all, but she would be an excellent candidate, the ablest Black woman bureaucrat I've seen in action.

We are getting calls in the district regarding the widening of Miami Gardens Drive through the area around Skylake. This not being a federal issue, Dade County has full responsibility in the decision making. We are dealing with the same problem on Ives Dairy Road with the flyover. The whole community around Skylake is opposed to the widening which would bring on more traffic. I will not take an official position as it will set a bad precedent. State legislators Gwen Margolis and Mike Abrams may want me to take some of their heat but I will try to avoid it as much as possible. Working with the State's Department of Transportation on a daily basis, I do not want to get boxed into a hostile position with the State because there are times when I need them and they need me.

Coast Guard Liaison, Lt. Goodwin, stopped by to let me know that he had called Barbara Boxer regarding the noise disturbance problem on the Coast Guard firing range. Barbara was not available when he called, so he was waiting to hear back from her. He is a good friend.

In the evening Joan and I went to the home of Mr. & Mrs. Dave Brody for their 45th wedding anniversary. Dave heads the Anti-Defamation League in Washington, and also now works closely with Republican Senator Steve Symms from Idaho. I happily had helped Dave make this connection. The Brody's have one of Joan's sculptures in their home.

MARCH 12 SATURDAY

We have been invited to the Kennedy Center this evening with David Bockney and his wife, Jill, to see a musical. Dave was a very effective White House lobbyist on the House side, and now has his own law firm. He told me about one of his clients who has a problem in Jamaica. I thought about Julian Dixon (California) who is interested in Jamaica, and told Dave that it might be good for him to speak with Julian. He thought this was a good idea, and I offered to call Julian to arrange a meeting. Terry Peel on the Foreign Ops Subcommittee staff was at the Kennedy Center for the musical production, and I will include him in whatever meeting I am able to arrange with Julian. We saw Susan Blumenthal, the young, beautiful and blond psychiatrist friend and future wife of Congressman Ed Markey (Massachusetts).

MARCH 13 SUNDAY

A good afternoon of tennis and in the evening a reception at the Marriott Hotel. The reception sponsored by the American Public Transportation Association (APTA) included public transportation officials from all around the country. There must have been at least 500 people, and I do believe Joan and I met most of them. Clara Oesterle took us around. I was the only Congressman there, and my hand is sore from shaking so many hands. Joan felt good, as she was able to meet with three key Miami officials - Dick Judy, Clara Oesterle and Ben Gilford, head of Metro Transit - on her sculpture location problem. Afterwards, Joan and I went across the street to the Occidental Restaurant and had dinner with lobbyist Dennis Vierra and his wife Alice.

MARCH 14 MONDAY

At the Capitol Physician's Office this morning with Joan, they told her that her foot had become infected. On the way back, I met Speaker Jim Wright in the corridor and he said we are going to have trouble with the Public Works Committee again attempting to take the FAA Trust Fund off budget. I asked if he could help me, and he said he would try. I told him that I was being targeted now by the Republicans, according to a *Wall Street Journal* article on Friday, because of my Contra vote. If Jim Howard proposes taking the FAA Trust Fund off budget in one of the technical corrections bills coming out of Public

Works this year, there is not much the Speaker can do to stop it, especially since he is an old buddy of Chairman Jim Howard and served with him on Public Works before becoming Speaker. If not victorious in the House election for Speaker, Wright would have become Chairman of the Public Works Committee instead of Howard. Howard's support was very instrumental in Wright's victory, but of course Howard had his own motive to move Wright up and out of his way to chairmanship.

I am exploring the possibility of converting military Air Force bases, scheduled for phase-out, to regional jetport bases. I spoke with Don Richberg, Chief of Staff on the Defense Appropriations Subcommittee, and he recommended that I speak with Jack Edwards, who is heading the base phase-out task force. Jack is a former colleague from Alabama and was also on our Transportation Subcommittee and knows the defense problems from when he was a ranking Republican on the Defense Subcommittee. He is a great guy and someone I can talk to, so maybe we can start the ball rolling. I think the only solution to the eventual problem of adequate airport space is to convert to commercial use these military bases such as Peterson Field in Colorado, Warner Robbins in Georgia and perhaps Homestead in Florida.

John, Lucy and I spent considerable time today going over shock trauma in Miami. The Metro Commission will conduct a hearing Wednesday on the Task Force recommendations and John will go to Miami for the hearing. I will also have someone from the National Transportation Safety Board testify that it will put in about $150,000 if Dade County will put in about $50,000 and the State about $100,000 for an advisory board and a trauma agency. I called Sue Samuels, a lawyer in Miami who is Chair of the Health Trust, to find out if there were any elected public officials in Miami on the Health Trust. She said no, and advised me to stay away from county officials and employees because they have their own narrow view of what their own interests are. The best thing to do is to have a broad base of people and to separate the advisory board by eliminating from the membership, as much as possible, the bureaucracy of the county. The advisory board is to be created by the task force.

As to problems related to insurance liability, I am to meet

in April with Bill Gunter's staff. If we do not have in place State enforced liability insurance, and considering the many indigent trauma patients, we will never get the shock trauma system off the ground. Hopefully by providing Federal government seed funding, the county will move on the shock trauma network. Arrangements can be made for additional funds from the National Highway Traffic Safety Board and together with the county's $50,000, almost $300,000 can be generated in grants to finance the system. When you get right down to it, Metro-Dade really has no choice because elective neurosurgery is now almost wiped out at Jackson Memorial.

Tom Boggs of the law firm Patton, Boggs and Blow and a Director on Eastern's board, called today about an emergency they are having at Eastern. Norman Mineta's resolution calls for the Department of Transportation to investigate Eastern Airlines. If the resolution passes, a side effect will be travel agencies cancelling or changing reservations from Eastern to other airlines. This in effect would force Lorenzo, who controls Continental and Eastern, into bankruptcy with Eastern, thereby forcing the airline to sell off its assets. There would be no more Eastern and this would be a disaster for Miami's many Eastern employees. I quickly arranged for a 3:00 meeting today with Tom Boggs in Norman Mineta's office. They didn't exactly resolve anything, but Tom may be able to buy some time before Norman introduces his resolution. I think labor wants just to destroy Eastern Airlines and Lorenzo. What Mineta should do is get Charlie Bryant, head of the Machinist Union, and Lorenzo in the same room and tell them to get together and resolve their differences or he will introduce the resolution and they both will be up shit creek.

When I arrived at the Hilton Hotel for a gala dessert reception by the young leadership of the United Jewish Appeal, security forces were out in the hundreds. Joan and I were led into a large banquet hall which held several thousand people, and I was very disappointed because all we saw was some sort of Mideast floor show and no one from Miami. We soon left. On my schedule for tomorrow is a visit from a group of these young members of UJA.

MARCH 15 TUESDAY

The morning began with a breakfast meeting of the Air Transport Association. A number of issues were discussed, like the budget, the FAA and mandatory drug testing, which they favor. But mainly I spoke about getting help for converting some of the military air bases to commercial use. We will work with the Department of Defense and see how this develops.

Around 11:00, the UJA Young Leadership group from Dade came in, many from my own district. They thanked me for my support of Israel and asked if there was any erosion of support for Israel among the House members. I told them there had to be because for the first time some of the Jewish members were openly criticizing Israel. I asked if any of them knew who Dave Obey was, and they said, "No." I told the group that Obey was the most important player in the House on aid to Israel, and then I explained to them the appropriation process.

When they left I again placed a call to Mike Adler to discuss the fundraiser in Miami for Obey's PAC. I felt it was imperative, if I am ever to have any influence with Dave Obey who, as chairman, marks up the Foreign Ops bills, that Mike get back in touch with me to do this.

At 1:30, colleague Julian Dixon, staffer Terry Peel of Foreign Ops, and Adele from my staff gathered in the office to meet with David Bockney. Dave talked about a development his client is trying to put together in Jamaica and wants U.S.-AID money, about $15 million, to build roads into this area. The client will spend about $125 million and bring in 4,000 jobs. I do not have a real feel for this but I am a good friend of both Julian Dixon and Dave Bockney and if I can bring the two together and help Jamaica as well, then I have served a purpose. Dave said if I ever need help, he would hold an office fundraiser for me in Washington. I would have helped him regardless.

On my way to a meeting at Sid Yates's office I met Dave Obey. Dave told me he saw Mike Adler at another meeting and Mike told him that he would be seeing him in Miami. It looks as though Mike will be setting up the Miami meeting. Sid had called a meeting at 2:30 with all the Jewish members to plan our strategy this evening with our meeting with Prime Minister Shamir. I said that we should not have the meeting as it was like writing a letter and then tearing it up. The only thing that can come out of this meeting was that either we backed Shamir one hundred percent, which was wrong, or we criticized him, which was also wrong. "Either way," I continued, "it is a no-win deal. Members will say what you are doing is fine, the hard language we understand, and we will support you, but you must also understand that what you are doing is not really best for Israel's support in the Congress and throughout the country. Our aid to Israel is not set in concrete." Some members agreed saying that this is something Israel must be more aware of as time goes on. Most Americans, however, don't even know about the $3 billion that go every year to Israel.

The meeting lasted for about an hour, and I returned to the office to meet with Tom Bulger and representatives from the San Francisco Metropolitan area concerning funding for their expanded San Francisco Bay Rail System. The problem is getting every Bay area member in agreement, such as Tom Lantos, who has yet to get together, and having a common ground for us to support. They brought me a couple of bottles of Cake Bread Wine from the Napa Valley Vineyards, which I had visited a couple of years ago.

I met at 4:00 with Florida DOT Secretary Kaye Henderson and Bill Taylor, their representative in Washington, and they informed me that the new commuter rail will go all the way to the Miami International Airport. This was welcomed news, as I had been seeking confirmation on this. I then went to the gym and had some of the stiffness worked out and got relief from my tension headache. I had tried to relax during lunch but Alan Wulkin, who now runs the Phoenix, Arizona, metro transit system, spent time talking to me as I ate about transit problems throughout the country. Alan was an Assistant Manager with the Metro-Dade Transit System before taking the position in Phoenix. He asked if I would come out to Phoenix, but I do not want to go unless I am invited by a member. He then suggested John Dyer for the County Manager position in Miami. Dyer is Alan's former boss and the initiator of the Dade County Metro Mass Transit. My primary choice for this position is Lillian Liberti, but I can see that there are also other very attractive candidates.

This is the evening of the dinner party at the home of Bob

Mrazek honoring Jimmy Stewart and Burt Lancaster. A number of movie directors were there as well. Jimmy Stewart made a little speech; he is a bit dotty now and his speech wandered all over. Burt Lancaster, on the other hand, made a marvelous speech. The main issue concerned legislation to prevent the colorization of classic old movies such as "High Noon," "Casablanca," and "The Maltese Falcon." Most impressive was Director Fred Zimmerman who did "High Noon." The film rights are owned by Ted Turner Television, which feels it can do whatever it wants with these classics. But these are real works of art and should not be tampered with. I would support the position of the artists. Dave Obey and other colleagues were there. Dave said to me, "Whose house is Bob Mrazek using?" I said, "It is his house." Dave said all this time I have been feeling sorry for him and he has this super-expensive house.

Joan and I left the party about 8:30 p.m., and went to the reception in honor of Prime Minister Shamir. The reception was just about over when we arrived and it wasn't long before the Jewish members of Congress were called into a private meeting with the Prime Minister. My old friend Moisha Arens the Defense Minister and former Ambassador to the United States was at the meeting. We gave the Prime Minister our ideas on what he should be aware of because apparently he is not getting this input directly from his own people. There are things he has to know about public opinion in the United States. The $3 billion annually that Israel has received since the 1977 War is not automatic but is an amount we vote on each year. About ten of us spoke. I told the Prime Minister that not only does he have a constituency that he has to deal with in Israel, he also has a constituency in this country that he needs to recognize, and to measure his actions and statements in such a way as to not upset this constituency. If the U.S. constituency begins to form a negative outlook on Israel, then this would be translated to the representative congressional members and right into adverse votes in the House on Israel. Most of the members thought the meeting was very worthwhile, but I have my doubts. The two members who always have an opinion and could have spoken but did not, which was surprising, were Larry Smith and Steve Solarz. I have to find out why they did not speak as they usually have something to say about everything.

The meeting was like a family get-together with almost everyone voicing his or her own opinion. Shamir was not as hard line as most members expected, and came across as wanting to follow the Camp David Accord. If Shamir could get the Palestinians to the table and if Jordan agreed to a three-year autonomy West Bank trial period and then, with these conditions in place, move to a self-determination status, the peace movement could get started which would help to stop these violent outbreaks. There was no press at this private meeting and that was good. The press, no doubt, would have reported that either the Prime Minister argued with Jewish members or the Prime Minister is supported by the Jewish members.

MARCH 16 WEDNESDAY

At 9:30 this morning, Alan Woods, U.S.-AID Administrator, stopped by the office. He was really just paying me a courtesy call. I took the occasion to mention the fish farming projects using Israeli technology and the Administrator, who seemed very interested, said he would do something with it. He may have to transfer funds from student aid, but he was very positive about fish farming in the Mideast.

At 10:00 we had our transportation hearing on the Panama Canal Commission. Recent political disturbances have been occurring in Panama, so there was television coverage. The two primary witnesses were William Gianelli, Secretary of Defense Representative for Panama Canal Affairs, and Dennis McAuliffe, PCC Administrator.

News of the political situation in Panama has been aired on television and in the papers for weeks. There was hardly any mention of the disturbances in their testimonies, except a brief sentence by McAuliffe who said, in effect, that the disturbances occurring in Panama had not affected the operations of the Canal. Their presentations were so positive that I said to them, "You are both so upbeat compared to what we see on television and read about in the papers as to what is happening in Panama, that one would think the Panama Canal was in Switzerland instead of Panama." When we asked them to bring us up-to-date on the current situation in Panama, Gianelli talked about the rapidly changing political scenario, and agreed that they had been extremely fortunate so far in their ability to continue operating the Canal apart from the on- going political problems. When Gianelli mentioned some sort of a coup is perhaps underway right now, rather facetiously I asked him if we should adjourn the hearing so that he could go back there and find out.

It seemed strange that the Canal had not been affected when the dock workers and government employees were striking, and even some of the major ports were closed due to the striking Panamanian port employees, but apparently this was indeed the case.

At 1:30 I went to the Capitol for a briefing by Foreign Ops staff on the Annual Child Survival Report, and spoke briefly about the Child Survival Fund. Several years ago I was instrumental in appropriating in the Foreign Operations Subcommittee the original funds for Child Survival. This line item is now $65 million a year. The money was primarily allocated for oral rehydration for children around the world suffering from malnutrition, dysentery and diarrhea, with strong emphasis on immunization and nutritional programs. Adele said my statement was right on target as it stressed not only child survival but also adult well-being. In most cases, children suffering from these types of ailments sadly become very dependent and non-productive adults.

Larry Coughlin began presiding at our 2:00 hearing on the St. Lawrence Seaway Development Corporation, as I was delayed at the briefing. I returned in time to begin the question and answer session with Administrator James Emery, who reported an increase in seaway tonnage and attributed this to an increase in the export of grain and iron ore, grain being the primary commodity. The hearing lasted only forty-five minutes, the shortest agency hearing we have ever had.

I received the reprogramming request from the Office of Management and Budget on the additional $60 million needed by the Coast Guard, outlining where the funds could be located in the transportation 302B allocation. Except for about $30 million of the suggestions, I told Tom and Lucy that I did not see too much in the outline that I wanted to do. I will probably fund about half of the money, but I won't take funds from Amtrak, mass transit or cancel out Charlie Wilson's bus project or Vic Fazio's highway project. We might be able to find

Panama Canal funds that have not yet been obligated. I think between the highways and other unobligated funds we may be able to get about $30-$40 million of the $60 million needed. We don't have to do anything now until after the April recess and I want to see what effect transfers would have on Amtrak and urban mass transit funding. I told the *Miami Herald* reporter when he called that the problem with the reprogramming of urban mass transit was that much of the funds had already been obligated by urban mass transit properties from all around the country. Cutting two percent across the board for operating substance for urban mass transit will all come out of the cities that had not yet received their formula funds, and that would be grossly unfair. As to Amtrak, the Office of Management and Budget wants to take all of the two percent from capital. Financially Amtrak is in dire straits, and if the corporation does not or cannot obtain new locomotives and better equipment, service will continue to deteriorate.

Late this afternoon I met with representatives from the fishing and boating industries. It was a non-scheduled appointment and they spent time talking about the boating safety fund and the amount needed to support sport fishing. The boating safety fund comes from a trust funded by a sales tax on fishing equipment. These funds unfortunately have always been used to help the Coast Guard, which makes for a very complicated appropriation process, the end results not making too many people happy.

On the House Floor today I told Dave Obey that I had called Mike Adler and the April 25 date is good. Mike had asked how much was to be raised and I said between $5,000 and $10,000, and Mike said he would get back to me with the exact time and place for the event.

Tip O'Neill was in the Capitol Physician's Office and he talked about the good time he had at the Miami fundraiser. I told him how much I appreciated his being there for me. I assumed he was in town for the black-tie Democratic Congressional Dinner this evening. Usually I attend this event, but I am not going this year even though Gerald Cassidy, who has purchased a table, extended an invitation to me.

I spoke with Norman Mineta, and he told me he has put his resolution on hold. Still, with this threat, we might be able to convince the machinists and Eastern Airlines to come together to try to resolve their differences. If this should happen, Mineta would have no reason to throw his resolution in the hopper. Eastern's President, Phil Bakes, appreciated my not getting on this resolution as did Harry McPherson, a lawyer friend of mine who represents Continental Airlines. I asked Dante Fascell who also is not on this resolution to speak with me if or before he decided to sign, as I thought it would be ill-advised for him to do so. If this resolution passes the House, I believe Eastern Airlines is then finished in Miami and that is my big concern.

MARCH 17 THURSDAY

Gary Hymel came up to me in the Rayburn Cafeteria this morning and asked if I would help get Julian Dixon to take a trip to Turkey in April. I told Gary I would try by getting in touch with Americo Miconi (Migo), Dixon's chief of staff on the District of Columbia Subcommittee and the most influential in reaching Julian.

As to the Democratic Convention, I learned how the regional congressional delegates are selected. Apparently 80% of the Democratic members from the House will be chosen as regional delegates and 20% chosen "at large" by the leadership and the regional caucuses who meet the middle of April. If I wanted to be a delegate, it could be done on a seniority basis and arranged by Ronnie Flippo of Alabama, our regional member on the Steering and Policy Committee.

Dick Durbin has invited our Transportation Subcommittee to Chicago to conduct a hearing. Durbin represents a central Illinois area around Springfield, and has become the activist for his State's delegation on appropriation issues. Today, Marty Sabo (D-MN), Tom Delay (R-TX), Bob Carr (D-MI) and I left Washington and arrived at O'Hare Airport in Chicago at 6:00 p.m. We had forty-five minutes to get ready to meet the bus taking us downtown. After checking into the hotel, I took a quick shower, and was ready on time. The bus was a super luxurious Greyhound with three stewardesses aboard to welcome the five subcommittee members, Delay, Carr, Sabo, Durbin and myself, along with Tom Kingfield.

We went to the supremely elegant Sears Towers and rode the elevator up to the swank Executive Club on the top floor. Waiting for us were some of Chicago's top business executives and hierarchy - members of the Chicago Ambassadors - which included the President and CEO of the Harris Bank, President of the University of Illinois, and Bill Farley, head of Farley Industries which make everything from automobile parts to Fruit of the Loom underwear. Bill is a fascinating character. What was impressive were these business executives coming out on a St. Patrick's Day night to meet with us when almost everyone in Chicago makes a big deal of this festival. The Chicago Ambassadors is a group of high-profile business leaders that reach out to the governmental agencies to solicit government cooperation in the Chicago area, and do a very effective job. One idea they tried to convince us on was building the "super collider" near Chicago. Our group was impressed. One of the main speakers for the super collider was Nobel physicist Leon Lederman from the University of Illinois. He looks like a scientist out of central casting, a fascinating man. Dick Durbin in his introduction made some very kind statements about me and the used car aspect of my background.

This is the largest subcommittee delegation we have ever taken to an outside Washington hearing. I mentioned in my statement that the way we turned out in numbers for this hearing in Chicago was a direct tribute to Richard Durbin by his colleagues. Congresswoman Lynn Martin, a Republican from Rockford was also at the gathering and told some really funny stories. It was a good evening and Joan would have enjoyed it had she been here, as she went to school in the Chicago area on Clark and West Streets. Before leaving downtown Chicago, we stopped at Harry Carey's Bar where a big St. Patrick's Day celebration was going on. Harry is a sports broadcaster for the Chicago Cubs. Sabo and I went back to the hotel but left Bob Carr and Tom Delay, the younger and more vigorous members, at Harry's Bar.

MARCH 18 FRIDAY

We met at 7:45 a.m. in the lobby of the Airport Hilton and walked across to the air traffic control operations at the takeoff and landing section of O'Hare Airport. I spoke to some air traffic controllers who complained about the amount of overtime. One controller said he had put in sixty-five straight six-day weeks. Heavy stress can be detrimental not only to the controllers but with the density of air traffic they have to control the likelihood of mistakes increases. They were really moving the airplanes around early this morning when we were there. I admire controllers for the job they do. It is not easy. We soon boarded a bus which took us to the United Airlines maintenance facilities to view multi-billion dollars worth of new state-of-the-art maintenance equipment. A United Airlines official said the equipment costs about $2 billion. We left and rode across the access roads and runways for a panoramic view of the airport. This is one of the few airports that has runways crossing the middle of the airport, adding another burden to the air traffic controllers.

At 9:30, the hearing began and all five members were on the panel. The two playboys, Carr and Delay, were hung over and looked a little beat up from too much celebration last night, but made it to the hearing on time. Everyone seemed to be in good shape and happy that Dick Durbin had such a good turnout in his state. We broke for a lunch sponsored by the Chicago Department of Aviation headed by Earl Herd who was the first to testify this morning. Maps depicting future plans and changes for O'Hare were handed out and discussed.

The hearing resumed at 1:00. Testifying in front of a congressional committee was obviously a new experience for some of the witnesses. Instead of summarizing their statements and submitting the full documents to the committee, they read from nine- or ten-page statements which took about twenty minutes. It was Durbin's party, though, and we wanted to make him look good in his state, and we did. He received a lot of media coverage, and even I was interviewed by the local CBS station. Bob Carr, missing his flight out of Chicago, came back to the hearing and took over for me at 2:00 for the last panel, which was the FAA. I left to catch my flight to Miami.

At O'Hare I am waiting for my plane and writing thank you's to our Chicago hosts. On my arrival at Miami International at 7:00 p.m., Jeff was there waiting for me with my schedule and letters to sign.

MARCH 19 SATURDAY

At the campaign office this morning I dropped off the signed thank you's which Jeff had given me and which Sharyn had typed on Friday. We are now at about $130,000 and are sure we will get to $140,000. Our total cost was $15,000 and we will probably net about $125,000 not counting Sharyn's salary. I hurried to pick up my grandson Sean at the airport, who was coming in from Denver, and Sean and I rode to Coral Gables to pick up my other grandson Matt. We will spend the day together, and then with Joan go out to dinner.

MARCH 20 SUNDAY

The Milt Littman Memorial Foundation Breakfast was held this morning at the Turnberry Garden Room. This annual event is promoted by North Miami Beach Councilman Jules Littman for student scholarships. Approximately 300 people were gathered, and of the funds raised, ten/fifteen percent goes toward scholarships, the rest goes toward the cost of the breakfast. This is sort of a Jules Littman campaign event, and about one-third of the people present were elected officials and public relations people directly related to politics. People are more or less mandated to come, because not to come will antagonize the Littman's. I seized the occasion to lobby Commissioner Sherman Winn on the trauma shock network. Winn is very supportive, but said he had to work on Clara Oesterle and Beverly Phillips to get their support for Dade County's $50,000 share to match the Federal and State funds for shock trauma. This is once again like nailing Jell-O to the wall. I did not stay long, and was home by 11:00.

In the afternoon I took Sean and Matt to visit the en-route flight control FAA facility on Northwest 58th Street and the Palmetto Bypass. I had asked Cas Castleberry, Regional Director of the FAA in Atlanta, to consider Matt for an intern position at this FAA facility. Cas said he would think about it, so I wanted Matt to see where he may be working this summer. Sean said it reminded him a lot of Los Alamos with all the computer technology. The boys were interested but not too fascinated.

At 5:00 we had photos taken for our family holiday card. This is the sixteenth year we have done this. Today Matt, Sean and little Tommy were photographed with Joan and me.

Later we will have photos taken with Billy's two boys and his daughter Deborah. There will be two poses this year for the Hanukkah/Christmas holiday card. This is a tradition we started and is now very difficult to stop. Our number of cards is at about 5,000, but people tell me they save them and many write letters thanking me for remembering them on the holidays. It is another way of solidifying your base.

MARCH 21 MONDAY

10:30 a.m., I said goodbye to Joan and headed for the airport for an 11:30 Eastern flight back to Washington. Once there, I learned that the 11:30 was postponed to 1:30. Every time I go to the airport I tell my driver to wait a few minutes to be sure the flight is on time. I don't call the airline ahead because the information given by phone is not reliable. This time, however, I did not tell Jeff to wait and the flight was two hours late. I didn't mind too much as it was a nice day so I sat out in the fresh air and read the paper and relaxed. Arriving in Washington at 4:00 p.m., I went straight to the House gym in the Rayburn Building to meet Pete Stark, Bob Kastenmeier and Jerry Elliott on Stark's staff for tennis at the Haines Point Bubble.

Having played for an hour and a half, I returned to the office and relaxed for a while before dressing for New York member Jim Scheuer and wife Emily's 40th wedding anniversary at the Congressional Club. It was a great party with lots of interesting people there from the art world such as Roger Stevens from the Kennedy Center and art collector David Lloyd Kreeger. Many senators were there, including New York Senators D'Amato and Moynihan. Moynihan was a little drunk but managed okay as Master of Ceremonies. Jim and Emily made short sentimental speeches. Jim said, with forty years with Emily he had had it all. They have had their ups and downs but have survived as a couple and are good with each other. Jim is better accepted today among his colleagues than he was a few years ago. He had seemed very arrogant, and he was the only chairman with a select committee (on population) to be defunded in the second term that he would have chaired it. All the other select committees managed to survive such as Mickey Leland with Hunger, George Miller with Children, Youth and Families, and Claude Pepper's Aging. Scheuer never put together a coalition base to keep his select committee going. As a ranking Democrat on the Energy and Commerce Committee, Scheuer has never chaired a decent subcommittee. Somehow he has antagonized members on Energy and Commerce, especially its Chairman, John Dingell, and he has never been able to achieve any status on that committee. What was interesting about the party also was not who was there but who wasn't. There were no other members from the New York City delegation other than Charlie Rangel. But the party was lots of fun, and I was glad I went.

MARCH 22 TUESDAY

9:00 a.m., North Miami Mayor Howard Neu came in with City Manager Bill Carr and several North Miami Councilmen, including John Hagerty. We talked about the Munisport problem which seems is finally to be resolved. The EPA report will be out by the first of April favoring the City of North Miami and we will then talk about the question of who pays for the study. Hopefully the land will come off the toxic waste site list and the City of North Miami will be able to sell the land and pay off the bonds which were used to buy the land.

10:00 a.m., we began the transportation hearing on the Research and Special Programs Administration, with Administrator Cindy Douglass. Last year our subcommittee had concerns about the disorganization in the agency's handling of the transport of toxic materials. The Federal guidance provided by RSPA to the state and local agencies was often ignored, causing inconsistent and diverse regulations. I reminded the Administrator of last year's critical report by the Office of Technology Assessment on the transport of hazardous materials, and the fact that the agency did not have accurate or reliable data on which to base its regulatory decisions or enforcement priorities.

Douglass was more prepared for our questions than last year; perhaps the fact that I told her I wanted better answers this year was a factor. In any case, rather than just talking about the problems, this year she talked about solutions to the problems, which is what we wanted to hear. A number of corrective measures have been put in place, she said, sounding enthusiastic about the development of "user-friendly software" for a joint data base with RSPA, the Coast Guard, and the EPA. The data base would contain information which the State and local agencies could access in addressing regulatory problems, thereby eliminating the State and local agencies from issuing hazardous materials regulations with little or no understanding of the problems they were trying to address. She spoke of "rule-making and an enforcement program" already underway, and acknowledged that enforcement of regulations was still a problem.

The only members on the subcommittee panel were Larry Coughlin and myself. Knowing that Coughlin had a heavy concentration of petrochemical manufacturers around his Philadelphia area, I turned the presiding chair over to him for questions. We broke for a vote at 12:30, which shortened the hearing by half an hour.

While on the House Floor I promised Charlie Wilson I would attend his luncheon for the Egyptian Minister of Defense. The Egyptian Ambassador was also there. It was a sit-down affair with name tags at the plates, and catered by Design Cuisine, one of the best caterers in town. My attending was a show of Charlie's and my friendship, and I do believe I was the only Jewish member there among the Texas members and members from Foreign Operations and Defense Committees. The talk generally was about politics in the Mideast. None of the members had been to Alexandria and the Defense Minister extended an invitation and expressed a desire for us to visit.

At 4:00 members of the Florida Education Association came in to talk about the usual things for which I am always supportive. Many of these people come in taking fifteen minutes to a half hour urging me to vote on issues that I never oppose. I guess when they make a trip to Washington they have to put in their reports that they visited a certain number of congressmen.

MARCH 23 WEDNESDAY

Tunisian Ambassador Habib Ben Yahia was in this morning for his annual visit. We spoke about problems in the Foreign Operations Subcommittee bill regarding funds earmarked for Tunisia, and talked about the possibility of my going to Tunisia. I told Habib that Joan and I would love to visit Jerba, where the oldest Jewish synagogue in the world is located, and that I would give his invitation serious thought.

The Washington Metro Area Transit Authority (WMATA) hearing started at 10:00. The two visiting North Miami Beach Council members wanted to attend the hearing, so I escorted them personally into the hearing. Hearings with WMATA are usually very crowded, and this was no exception. Carmen Turner, WMATA General Manager, and UMTA Administrator Al Dellibovi, were to testify. The hearing took about two hours. We would have finished in less time but when Virginia member Frank Wolf and Maryland member Steny Hoyer came in with questions, and with questions from the other members who were there, the hearing was prolonged. Exchanges between the two witnesses Carmen and Dellibovi were noticeably more amicable than relations last year between Carmen and Ralph Stanley, Dellibovi's predecessor. Coughlin mentioned this fact in the beginning of his questioning session, reiterating for their confirmation that WMATA and UMTA were only in disagreement over how many transit cars to acquire in completing the 89.5 mile system.

It seems the biggest problem WMATA has is the lack of parking spaces in the suburbs as now they fill up around 7:00 a.m., and then no one can park and ride on the rapid transit system. In regard to this, Carmen said that she thought the demand for parking would always be greater than they are able to supply, for parking with every major mode of public transportation is a problem. It was a good hearing. Both Carmen and Dellibovi were excellent witnesses, not missing a beat on any of the questions. We were through by 12:30.

From my office I returned phone calls, one to Carl Hiaasen of the *Miami Herald* who called to thank me for writing him a congratulatory note on his column in the *Herald* opposing the deployment of troops to Honduras. In the column he had written that not only should we not send troops to Honduras, but that we should tell the people in South Florida who want us to send aid to go to Nicaragua and fight themselves. This took courage, and I told him so. Hiaasen said to me that he would be honored to have the aforementioned column appear in the *Congressional Record*. I said I would do so gladly, and with a complimentary heading.

3:00 p.m., I met with the American Jewish Joint Distribution Committee in Sid Yates's interior subcommittee office. This committee is trying to get funds through AID for their private non-profit agency that does agricultural, irrigation and other programs in third world countries with the aid of Israeli technology. The only place the committee is working now is Ethiopia, and doing a good job. The problem is that countries want AID funds to go directly to their government and unless there is major corruption, like in Haiti, we usually do that. Adele is already working on this with the joint distribution staff, so we fully understand the committee's problem, and we will see what can be done to help with the funds needed to carry on this very productive and necessary work. The woman at the meeting who heads this agency is part of the family that owns the Hasbro Toy Company. Sid Yates said she is probably one of the wealthiest women he has ever known. The jewelry she was wearing today could probably finance most of the projects in these countries.

4:00 p.m., I met with Dr. Julian Groff and another Florida physician regarding their concerns with the Professional Oversight Group (P.R.O.) that subcontracts with HICFA, the monitoring agency for Medicare. They related to me a case in which a physician had tried to have a patient hospitalized whom he had diagnosed as hemorrhaging. The problem was the Professional Oversight Group did not recognize this condition as requiring hospitalization, so the hospital did not admit him. The patient returned home where he continued to hemorrhage. A few days later he was rushed to the hospital for major surgery. If the individual had been admitted to the hospital and received treatment at the time the physician requested, the cost factor would have been far less. But because the attending physician could not reach a P.R.O. physician to explain the situation, the patient was turned away. At the time, only a registered nurse was available, and the registered nurse was not really qualified to fully determine whether the patient should be hospitalized. There are so many of these kinds of cases, and it is difficult to break through the red tape to obtain any meaningful policy change. Our district office is inundated with such cases, which means that HICFA too is probably overwhelmed with requests to investigate such matters. The only present recourse seems to be to continue writing to HICFA, as I will do in this case.

Dave Johnson of the Florida Governor's Office in Washington dropped by to tell me that Interior Department Secretary Odell has eliminated the Florida Keys from offshore drilling. He was very pleased and the environmentalists and Keys fishermen will also be happy with this decision.

MARCH 24 THURSDAY

I saw Jim Howard in the cafeteria this morning and he was all dressed up in this bright, wild golf outfit, very colorful, I hardly recognized him. He was all excited about going out and playing his first day of golf "on this beautiful spring day." Jim, as mentioned, has been my adversary on maintaining the trust fund on budget but we are good friends.

Running into John Warner of Virginia on the Senate side, I was thanked for the letter I wrote him regarding his leg injury in a golf cart accident. I also saw Jesse Helms of North Carolina, who told me that his wife was just operated on for colon cancer, and said that his work in the Senate was secondary right now. He complained that he also had back problems.

Before reaching my office, I learned that Jim Howard had a severe heart attack on the first tee and had not gained consciousness. By the time I was leaving the office to go home, Jim had died.

MARCH 25 FRIDAY

Dade County Commissioner Barbara Carey is in Washington with the Transit Workers Union leadership. When I met with them this morning, Barbara reiterated the fact that she wants to get Metro out of the PEP Grant but yet not have to give back the $7.5 million that Dade County received for the grant. She does not want the labor unions to have to compete with the private sector under the terms of the contract, and wants my help on this. I told her that Metro received the funds, bought fifty-one new buses, and that Metro had to either give back the money or live up to the contract. She wants to change the arrangements. They left my office to meet with Dellibovi at UMTA.

Barbara just does not seem to understand the meaning of a contractual relationship and says there was misrepresentation, although she signed the agreement as a Metro Commissioner. She is getting a lot of pressure from both labor and her community about bus service problems. I expect I'll be part of the mediation process, which could take months to resolve.

MARCH 26 SATURDAY and MARCH 27 SUNDAY

This has been a quiet weekend with no political or social activities.

MARCH 28 MONDAY

Barbara Carey called me from Miami this morning and said that she was treated very rudely last week by Al Dellibovi. Al was very adamant, giving them two weeks to come up with an acceptable compromise or UMTA was going to take the $7.5 million out of their Section Nine grant money this year. Apparently, Al came flat out and said Metro had to honor the contract or turn back the funds. He wasn't very happy about Barbara wanting to welsh on the contract.

MARCH 29 TUESDAY

Three busloads of members boarded the plane this morning at Andrews Air Force Base going to New Jersey for Jim Howard's funeral. We arrived in New Jersey at McGuire Air Force Base and then boarded a bus which took us to Jim's hometown of Spring Lake for the funeral service at St. Catherine's Roman Catholic Church. After the service and leaving the church, conversation among the members was very subdued; but by the time we boarded the plane back to Washington everyone was chattering up a storm, no visible signs of sadness. When members travel together like this it is good bonding, even if it is for such a sad occasion.

We arrived in Washington around 2:00 p.m. There were no hearings or votes today because of the funeral. Back at the office my son Bill and granddaughter Deborah were waiting for me. We lunched in the Rayburn Cafeteria and then I took them on the House Floor. Bill had an opportunity to talk to John Dingell about the Suzuki problems before he left for Middleburg, Virginia, to buy a pony for Deborah.

Pete Shields, Chairman of Handgun Control, stopped by the office at 4:00. Pete is very optimistic about his group being able to counteract the National Rifle Association, especially because of pending legislation to control the proliferation of handguns and the call for a waiting period on handgun purchases. About fifteen years ago his son was killed in a tragic gun crime incident. His wife is working with Sarah Brady (Jim's wife) in this effort.

At the National Academy of Sciences' impressive reception this evening, I was sort of the honoree in recognition of the funds our transportation subcommittee provided to the Academy to undertake the report, *Injury in America*, a study on trauma injury as a disease of epidemic proportion. NTHSA Administrator Diane Steed was there, as were people from various medical schools all around the country. I told them that I appreciated all that the National Academy had done in bringing trauma injury awareness to the forefront of the American public, but that the real problem was not so much medical or scientific as it was political and financial. The fact that we cannot get hospitals to handle trauma patients because of the number of indigent patients, I said, and the inability of physicians in certain areas to work on the injured because of medical liability costs are primary factors to overcome in combating this disease.

Later I stopped by Bull Feathers for a drink. I saw Wendell Belew, former Chief Council of the Budget Committee when I served on that committee with Chairman Bob Giamo. Wendell is now a lawyer in Washington and a very sharp young man. He was the youngest chief council of any major House committee. I also met a young woman who works for the Seafarers Union; she informed me that the head of Boating USA was unhappy with me because I had not responded to his letter. I will call him in the morning and apologize, but there really is not much I can do for this industry because funds for this enterprise are all tied up with the Coast Guard.

MARCH 30 WEDNESDAY

This morning Michigan members David Bonior and Bob Carr came in regarding FAA problems in Michigan. Bonior has a problem with the Selfridge Military Air Force Base in his district. It seems Carr has put language in the Continuing Resolution calling for a study on shared commercial use of airspace at Selfridge. Bonior did not know about the CR language and felt blindsided, but it was just a lack of communication between staffs. When staffs screw up, members sometimes get in trouble with each other. Military people, though, are paranoid about sharing space with commercial airlines, yet it works pretty well in other places I have visited such as O'Hare Airport in Chicago. Bonior is now in trouble in his district as he found out when attending a meeting where approximately 2,000 military people "beat up" on him because of language in the Continuing Resolution, and he is trying to re-establish his credibility. My feeling is that the Air Force bases no longer being used to full capacity should be shared and used for commercial airspace as needed. There are members on our subcommittee pushing for commercial use of military bases, including me.

I met Ambassador Allan Flanigan several years ago in Lisbon. Flanigan is now special U.S. negotiator for the Greece base rights agreement, and when I met with him this morning he had concerns about the push to get American bases out of Greece. U.S. bases in Spain have already been phased out. These overseas military bases are expensive, useless wastes but the brass loves them. This year in our Foreign Ops Subcommittee we are giving Greece the same $300 million level in outright military grants that were formerly credit sales. My problem is with Greek Prime Minister Papandreou who is such an asshole. Papandreou won't establish diplomatic relations with Israel, so I don't feel like helping him in any way. I will have to go along with the subcommittee but I hope Papandreou gets the message.

At 1:00 all the chairmen of the appropriation subcommittees met in Chairman Jamie Whitten's office. We expected to find out how much of the 302B discretionary allocation each subcommittee would receive, but Jamie was not telling us anything. He got us all together for a less than zero result. Wanting the chairman and the other subcommittee chairmen to know what I was up against, I told them that the problem is the summit freeze and that for transportation the administration wants $1.2 billion more for the Coast Guard and the FAA. If I have what now is a freeze, I said, and yet have to find $1.2 billion more for the Coast Guard and the FAA, this means $1.2 billion has to come out of highways, Amtrak and other transportation services. This will include projects in many of the subcommittee chairmen's districts.

Bill Natcher has a similar problem because for political reasons the administration added increases for AIDS research and education. As Vic Fazio said to me, what we really need is a tax increase. I will have to seek funds for the Coast Guard from the Defense Appropriations Subcommittee, but I did not want to mention this because Defense Subcommittee Chairman Bill Chappell was not there. Over the past few years the Coast Guard has been getting $250 million from Defense and now the Defense Appropriations Subcommittee is short of funds. It won't be so easy to get funds from them this year. I am trying to get my transportation 302B allocation increased by $250 million and Defense decreased by the same amount and use that for the Coast Guard increases. If I cannot get it worked out among the subcommittee chairmen, I may have to offer this as an amendment in the full committee and hope it passes. Without these funds, the message I was trying to get across was that I would not be able to fund demonstration projects for members of the Appropriations Committee or other members.

I saw Steny Hoyer and Ed Roybal and wanted to be sure they supported increased funding in their Health and Human Services appropriation for the Centers for Disease Control and Prevention in Atlanta. This relates to the meeting I had at the National Academy of Sciences encouraging me to lobby Hoyer and Roybal.

Members have invited me to go on two congressional trips over the Easter recess, but I cannot go on either one. Steny Hoyer asked me to join him on a trip to the Soviet Union with the Helsinki Commission and make a stopover in Poland, and Sonny Montgomery wanted me to go on his trip to Southeast Asia, China and Tibet. I have too heavy a schedule back in the district.

The Florida State Society held its reception this evening in the Montpelier Room of the Library of Congress. This annual event is held primarily to introduce various members of the Florida delegation to Florida lobbyists and business execs in Washington. I made the rounds, speaking to lobbyist George Patton and his wife Janet and lobbyists for the CSX Railroad. I also spoke with Larry Adams from FP&L who said he wanted expressly to tell me how much the Miami Chamber of Commerce appreciated my work. Dorothy Weaver from the Chamber called me yesterday about the problem Commissioner Barbara Carey has created for Metro transit by coming to Washington and antagonizing Al Dellibovi on the PEP Grant. Al was going to take the $7.5 million out of Dade's federal transportation subsidies, and I suggested to Dorothy that she call Al and tell him that Barbara is not really representing the Dade County position. Barbara is just a captive of the labor unions, and I hope that the remaining Metro Commissioners have enough sense to help her back off and resolve this.

There was a great deal of talk in the House about Jesse Jackson's candidacy for President. John Dingell, for instance, who has worked very hard for Gephardt, is very discouraged and unhappy with Jackson, as well as with Dukakis.

MARCH 31 THURSDAY

This morning Jim Wilding of the Metropolitan Washington Airport Authority came in to brief me on the new master plan for the Washington National Airport. The plan seems fine and everything should come together okay, but it means five long years of the worst possible road congestion.

We finished our Amtrak hearing today at 4:00, and I caught the 5:00 flight to Miami. I did correspondence on the plane and tried to catch up on other paperwork, especially a letter to *Miami Herald* Publisher Richard Capen regarding my involvement in the shock trauma network, telling him where we are now in putting it all together.

On the plane, I remembered my conversation yesterday with colleague Jim Jontz of Indiana. Jim wants a highway demonstration project in his district and asked, "What should I do?" I told him the first thing to do was "Pray, because we don't have any money."

Chapter 16

APRIL 1, 1988 - FRIDAY THRU APRIL 10 - SUNDAY

For these past ten days in Miami, it has been busy either meeting with constituents, or city, state and county officials, or with elected officials like North Dade State Representative Mike Abrams, the probable heir apparent to my congressional seat, if and when. There is much concern in the Jewish community about the Jesse Jackson presidential candidacy and this, in particular, is what Mike and I spent time discussing. Indeed, on several occasions, such as an appearance before the New Horizons Condo Men's Club, comprised of mostly elderly Jewish members though still sharp and politically astute, their disapproval of Jackson was quite adamant. And Annie Ackerman, whom I visited after her recent return from the hospital, wanted to discuss Jackson's candidacy.

I decided to call my colleague Mickey Leland in Houston, knowing that Mickey was a close confidant of Jackson's, and suggested to Mickey that he get the message to Jackson's campaign that a way to reduce the barrier between Jackson and the Jewish community was for Jackson to announce that if he were elected President he would appoint a Jew to the first vacancy on the Supreme Court to fill the old "Brandeis-Cardoza" seat. Mickey listened but had no comment other than that he would get the message to Jackson's campaign. We spoke on other issues for a few minutes before hanging up, saying that we would see each other back in Washington.

There was also concern about the status of support for Israel in the House, which brought to the office Michael Bander, chairman of the local chapter of the American Jewish Committee and Bill Guralnick, the director. Upon my assertion that this year Israel would be getting $3 billion but that I saw a possible gradual reduction in funds for Israel in the out years, they asked what the AJC should do. I advised them, as lobbying is still effective, to have their American Jewish Committee members in North Florida schedule appointments with Florida Congressmen Charlie Bennett, Buddy MacKay, and Sam Gibbons.

The William Lehman Aviation Center is to open soon at Florida Memorial College, and Patrice had scheduled a meeting at the Northside district office with F.M.C. President, Dr. Willie Robinson, to discuss the opening. Dr. Robinson also wanted to know if there was anything I could do to provide endowments for student assistance. There is not much I can do on the federal level, but I told him I would help with a fundraiser and make a contribution to the endowment fund.

Other meetings at the Northside district office included Patrice's brother, Dr. George Koonce, Principal at Northwestern Senior High School. Dr. Koonce spoke about drop out prevention among the Hispanics and blacks. Hispanics drop out into jobs and blacks drop out into the streets. Then there was Newell Daughtery who operates an office supply story, a black minority enterprise. Newell asked for my help in getting government contracts. He also wanted to thank me for the conference we held in Miami on government contracts, especially the 8A awards for minority contractors. When I first ran for Congress, Newell supported my opponent Lee Weissenborn, but we have worked well together since then. We ended talking about old times and politics.

When I spoke to my neighbor Mark Karvas about his application for air traffic controller, Mark told me that he received a score of 88, but to be assured of his acceptance as a trainee, he needs a score of 90 or above. Mark worked as an intern in our Washington office while a student at Barry University, and I would like to help him as he is a good and very bright young man. A much more selfish reason for wanting to help him has to do with his working evenings as a chef. When he arrives home from his job, his car lights shine into my bedroom window and wake me up. If I can get him into Oklahoma City with this job I can be assured of a good night's sleep.

I received several community service awards. One from Jacques Despinossa, representing the Haitian Democratic Club, who asked that the Appropriations Foreign Ops Subcommittee discontinue its funding policy for the present government of Haiti. Jacques and I are good friends and with him often acting as liaison for the Haitian community, our office has been successful in providing needful assistance to the Haitian community.

The National Association of Railroad Passengers (NARP) presented me with its "George Falcon Golden Spike Award" (given in recognition of one's contribution to rail passenger transportation). In my case, the awarding was "in recognition of the role [I] played in maintaining and improving Amtrak and mass transit service around the nation." The ceremony was held at the Miami Amtrak station on N.W. 37th Avenue. Ross Capon, Executive Director of NARP, whom I have known for many years on Capitol Hill, was the emcee, giving me high praise for "exceptional efforts to keep Amtrak alive in the face of relentless efforts by the Reagan administration to kill Amtrak and dramatically cut transit funding." But the surprise at the presentation was philanthropist Mickey Wolfson. Mickey is the son of the Wometco founder, and inherited about a hundred million dollars. He has his own private railcar, and told me that I could use his railroad car anytime I wanted when traveling to Washington. Commissioner Clara Oesterle introduced me with some very flattering comments. I told Clara that I should transfer $25 million to Amtrak from the Coast Guard because Amtrak interdicts more cocaine on its trains than does the Coast Guard on the high seas. Amtrak uses trained dogs to sniff for drugs on trains on the Miami to New York run.

And, an award for which I am exceedingly proud was presented in recognition of my efforts toward the development of the Opa Locka community. The merchants are now trying to get federal aid to rebuild Opa Locka to give their businesses the original Arabian Nights type of appearance. There have been many changes in Opa Locka and there is fresh hope. The residents are basically poor, but a lot more businesses have opened and debris that could be seen scattered throughout the area is gradually disappearing. Lawton Chiles's nephew Thorn Grafton is the architect of the new development. The award and a book on the history of Opa Locka were presented to me at the Community Development Week ceremony. State Senator Carrie Meek, former Mayor Riley and current Opa Locka Mayor Ingram, and other officials were there. It was a strenuous three hours out in the sun, but it was worth it for me to show how healthy I am. There had been much media coverage, and the event was televised during the evening news.

I also had the occasion to present an award. The recipient was Maria Fernandez, a postal worker at the Palm Village Branch of the Hialeah Post Office. While on her route, Maria had rescued a man from a burning house, and the framed *Congressional Record* statement which I presented to her told of her heroic rescue. It was a small ceremony held at the Palm Village Post Office. Woody Connors, Postmaster for this area, and Alonso Jimenez, Postmaster for the Palm Village Branch, and some of Maria's co-workers were at the presentation. Maria was a bit awed by all the attention. She has a great smile, and it felt good being there in recognition of such a brave young lady. I surprised Woody Connors with a souvenir of the first two-tone airmail stamp, a six-cent stamp from the 1930's.

The Israeli Bond organization wants to honor me at their annual dinner later in the year, which in effect means that they want to use my name to raise money. I guess I have to do it, but I told Howard Klein who approached me that I would not want them to plan the dinner at a time when I may be traveling overseas. They will work around my schedule and I am to get back with them around the middle of July when I know better what my plans will be.

Meeting with Eastern's Machinists Union leaders concerning Norman Mineta's resolution, I found they are now even more hostile toward Eastern. They hate Lorenzo but, as I told them, my concern was for the preservation of an Eastern Airlines entity here in Miami and I did not want to be in the crossfire between the unions and Eastern Airlines. I have not changed my position on this, but the union is nothing if not persistent.

Besides Eastern and the Machinists Union, the two major local problems are the Florida liability insurance law and the Metro PEP Grant. For several days the Miami newspapers ran front page stories on the problems of liability insurance in Florida, leading up to our April 4 meeting with Insurance Commissioner Bill Gunter and the Dade Shock Trauma Task Force. The meeting was held at the Airport Hilton with extensive media and press coverage. To relax the crowd I said if I had known there would be five TV stations for the occasion, I would have announced my candidacy for the Democratic presidential nomination. I went on to point out the overwhelming number of drivers who do not carry liability insurance coverage, emphasizing the fact that unless this coverage is enforced there was no way a shock trauma network could exist in South Florida. I told them about Jackson Memorial and how it could not possibly continue to absorb most of the costs of trauma patients, which took away from the elective surgery that Jackson needs to maintain certification as a neurosurgical teaching institution as part of the University of Miami School of Medicine. The meeting went well, with Gunter very flexible and open to suggestions, and I found this encouraging. This is not something that can be settled in a day, but it was a good start.

Even more problematical is the Metro PEP Grant. Commissioner Barbara Carey's threat to renege on the PEP contract has really gotten things in an uproar. I spoke to those I thought might have some influence with her, even to Lester Freeman, former Chairman of the Greater Miami Chamber of Commerce, who said he would talk to her. Dorothy Weaver, President of the Greater Miami Chamber of Commerce, called wanting to know if Dellibovi was indeed serious about taking the funds back if the PEP Grant contract was broken. I told Dorothy that Al was not bluffing and if the contract was not honored, he could deduct the amount from Dade

County's other UMTA funds. A day or so later I heard from Metro Commission members that they had received a harsh letter from Dellibovi about the threat to cancel the PEP Grant.

If the bus experiment is dropped, as Commissioner Carey wants, the government would charge the 51 buses against future federal bus funds for Metro-Dade Transit, and this means that in the future Dade County would have fewer much needed new buses on the street. Working with me to save the PEP Grant is Clara Oesterle, but Barbara is managing to make inroads with other commissioners.

As I head back to Washington tomorrow, these problems are still unresolved, although in some cases I feel considerable progress has been made, especially with Florida Insurance Commissioner Bill Gunter on the problem of liability insurance. I am less optimistic about Eastern, as the friction and discord between management and labor seems insurmountable. This extended stay at home wasn't all work, though. The fun part was having a steady dose of family and friends - like having Seder at my son Bill's house, and going fishing for a day with my two sons, Bill and Tom, and just us hanging out together. Many evenings Joan and I went out alone to dinner and perhaps to a movie. On one occasion, we went to Fisher Island, a very upscale development, with our friends the Al Green's, and the Joe Davis's, and then one evening we spent with Ellen Kempler and her husband, Ken Rosen.

APRIL 11 MONDAY

Now on the plane to Washington, I realize more and more how wise a decision it was to forego any overseas trip at this time, not only because so much is happening in the district, but to conserve energy for the remaining transportation hearings in Washington. Dade County Commissioners are up for re-election in September and Jeff, who manages our district office, spoke to me about $20,000 that he stands to gain between now and September working for four candidates for the County Commission. Two are running against Beverly Phillips and the third and fourth are Clara Oesterle and Mayor Steve Clark. For him to work for Mayor Clark and Commissioner Oesterle would be acceptable to me, but I would not approve of his working after hours for the opponents of good incumbents. I cannot okay his working for someone I would not support myself. I did advise him, though, to get the entire $20,000 from the two incumbents and not to sell himself too cheaply.

Jonathan Slade, a lobbyist for the Cuban American Foundation, was on the plane. Jonathan also works with Mike Adler and AIPAC. The Jewish Federation has its own studios to tape a daily television program, hosted by Mike. Last week I did a thirty-minute interview segment with Mike covering a number of issues. Mike was very professional, and I felt satisfied with my performance, as I feel this form of communication is one of my strong points. Telling Jonathan about my appearance on the program, I mentioned that I was able to solidify with Mike the visit of Dave Obey to Miami on April 25. By the time our plane landed in Washington, Jonathan and I had finalized plans for Dave to meet not only with the AIPAC group but also with the Cuban American Foundation.

At the Washington office Tom and Lucy were preparing to go over questions with me for the FAA hearing. First, however, they criticized me for inviting the Eastern Airlines machinists in Miami to testify at the public witnesses portion of our hearings. They thought by my extending an invitation to the machinists, this would be perceived as taking sides; but I do not have a problem as I only informed the union members of the public portion of the hearing process, as I would have done for any individual or group.

APRIL 12 TUESDAY

The morning began with Wendy Yanis and a small group from the Association of Floral Importers, big business at Miami International Airport. It seems at MIA there is not a sufficient number of customs people available to process floral arrangements through customs. They had a problem as well with shipment of potted flowers due to agricultural restrictions. I told them we could meet with Matt McHugh on the Agricultural Appropriations Subcommittee and Steny Hoyer on Appropriations Treasury, Post Office Subcommittee to get help with these problems.

Next was Pat Moody whose daughter had suffered a severe head injury in a boating accident. The daughter had been standing up in the boat as it went under a low bridge. Although the daughter survived the injury, she never fully recovered. Pat has been to see me several times in connection with her involvement with the National Head Injury Foundation.

At 10:00 the FAA hearing began and, as usual, we first heard the General Accounting Office (GAO) report on the FAA. What was amusing was when I asked the GAO if he would give a grade such as "A," "B," "C," or "D" on the NAS Plan. He said they wouldn't as a matter of policy, give a grade. First they criticized the FAA and then said how well the FAA was doing. I said the grade was getting better the more the GAO talked. I often interject such humor to keep the hearings free of tension and the people relaxed; and, for the first time this year I imposed a five-minute rule so that all the subcommittee members would have a chance to ask questions before the lunch break, and the members praised this ruling.

We recessed at noon and during this break Mimi Dawson, the new Deputy Secretary of the Department of Transportation, paid me a courtesy visit in anticipation of her testimony later this week for the Office of the Secretary. She seemed nervous, as this will be her first time to testify before a House committee. After our meeting, I headed for the House Floor to ask for a unanimous consent request to withdraw my cosponsorship of a bill that contained a clause moving the Coast Guard out of the jurisdiction of the Department of Transportation to the Department of Treasury. It was an anti-drug bill and the objectionable clause apparently got by the staff when they agreed to my sponsoring the bill. When Lucy found out about it, she was pushed all out of shape. Arriving on the House Floor, Norman Mineta was managing a suspension bill, and he was most gracious in letting me do the unanimous consent request. Tom Luken was on the Floor and told me he was still hanging tough in the conference on rail safety legislation language to take care of the City Gas Company problem.

When I saw Representative Ron Flippo in the Capitol, he told me he would be convening all the Democratic members from the Southeast Region - Louisiana, Mississippi, Alabama, Georgia and Florida - to pick the fifteen super delegates to the

Democratic Convention. Everyone who wanted to go will be able to because some members like Sonny Montgomery, Charlie Bennett and Sam Gibbons, opted not to go. Jamie Whitten would not commit himself but was listed as going anyway. Jamie never says yes or no to anything, but that is part of his character. I am not too happy to be a delegate now with the Jackson and Dukakis problems, and if there is a contested convention my vote will make part of my constituency unhappy no matter which way I vote. In an interview with *Miami News* reporter Bud Newman, who wanted to know if I was committed to any candidate, I most emphatically answered, "No." I will probably go to the convention still undecided. Our hearing resumed at 1:30 and ended at 4:15 p.m., having gone through twenty-four of the twenty-six pages of questions despite all the interruptions. We will continue the FAA hearing tomorrow morning at 10:00.

At the office for their 4:30 appointment were representatives of the American Association of Airport Executives - Linda Daschle and Chip Barclay. They basically went through the motions of asking me to support more airport improvement funds. In return, I asked them to help on shared commercial use of military airports. The very beautiful and very smart Linda Daschle is the wife of South Dakota Senator Tom Daschle, who went to the Senate from the House of Representatives. A former "Miss Kansas," Linda married Tom after his election to the House.

In the evening the Society of American Florists passed out beautiful floral arrangements at their reception. Taking mine with me, I went on to the National Grocers Association reception. The NGA had said that they would send a bag of groceries to any charity named, so I designated the Camillus House in Miami and the NGA will arrange to have someone meet me in Miami for delivery of the groceries and a photo opportunity.

APRIL 13 WEDNESDAY

The Washington-Metropolitan Airports Authority Board of Review held a meeting in the Capitol. Homeowners who live near Washington National Airport are not very happy about airplane noise, and in the meeting I essentially told the people complaining to "cut the bullshit," because there was no way to eliminate that noise. They had either built or bought homes knowing that the airport was near and airport noise will continue for many years until there is a new generation of quiet planes. Anyone who told them differently was just misleading them, I said, as there is little that can be done to change the flight patterns of planes taking off or arriving. Afterwards, I went by the Florida Congressional Delegation meeting and listened to the Florida Building Trades group complain about jobs going overseas and the fact that Japan is cutting Florida out of exports to that country.

The second and final day of FAA hearings began at 10:00. The hearing went for five hours yesterday and I expect another five hours today. When our FAA hearing broke for lunch, I rather hurriedly left the room to attend a reception my colleague George Miller was hosting with Group W Television in honor of "Americans who have shared the gift of time with young people." Commander Bill Johnson from the Metro-Dade Police Department was one of the honorees, and I especially wanted him to know that I cared and appreciated him enough to be there.

After a photo opportunity with Commander Johnson, I headed for my office where the FAA was preparing to brief me prior to resuming the hearing, on fining Eastern Airlines $823,000 in penalties for certain safety violations. What they briefed me on was essentially what I expected to hear, that the FAA is adding extra inspectors to keep a sharp eye on Eastern to be sure that financial problems and labor management conflicts do not affect the safety of passengers. These are operational inspections, so-called "ramp inspections," and aircraft will be inspected at airports when they arrive and before they take off. I am expecting a call from the press as the FAA put out a press release on this; if and when the call comes, I will tell of my support for the FAA in what they are doing, emphasizing that Eastern will be the safest airline on which to fly because of all the attention from the Federal Aviation Administration. The long-term problems are that Eastern has to resolve the labor conflict and substantially improve its financial situation.

Going back into the FAA hearing at 2:00, we finished at 4:30. During a break in the hearing for a vote, Glenn Anderson

(D-CA) spoke to me on the Floor saying that he would try to get more highway authorization funds for me so that I can get him a larger appropriation for highway demonstration projects in his district. Glenn is the new Chairman of Public Works. I saw Charlie Wilson on the Floor and gave him the *New Yorker* article on Afghanistan and he was pleased. After the hearing, Congressman John Rowland of Connecticut came to see me about the Coast Guard station closing at Block Island in Long Island Sound. There is very little we can do, but Rowland will try to work with Earl Hutto who serves on the Armed Services Committee with him. Hutto is also Chairman of the Maritime Commission Coast Guard Subcommittee.

Sid Yates called to tell me about Illinois's need for $20 million in interstate transfers, which are unobligated allotments to certain states, and I am expecting letters on this same subject from Vic Fazio of California and Bill Green of New York in regard to their states. I told Sid I would do what I can but first our subcommittee needs an increased 302B allocation. This will be my patented answer to all such inquiries, including those from Fazio and Green. Joe Hall, the Congressional Army Liaison officer, was waiting in the office. Joe has been trying to help me get a compassionate leave for one of my black constituent servicemen in Germany whose father is dying. We are working on a way for him to get home.

I was invited this evening to the opening night's performance of *Cats* at the National Theater in downtown Washington. I stayed through the first act; it was all I could take. I saw my friend Harry Teeter there who often gets me complimentary tickets to the National Theater.

APRIL 14 THURSDAY

Larry Wheeler and Blaine Shull, President of the Ground Systems Group in Fullerton, California, and Bill Merritt, Vice President of Government Operations for Hughes Corporation, came in as my first appointment this morning. Lobbyist Wheeler is the person from Hughes who so successfully got me front row balcony seats for *Phantom of the Opera* when I was in London. Hughes is now competing with I.B.M. on an advanced automation system for a $5 billion contract, which is part of

FAA's NAS plan. Hughes is also part of General Motors and kidding with them, I asked, "If you get the FAA contract, will it help my son Bill get more Buicks?" They wondered whether I was serious or not.

A large group of South Florida physicians dealing with problems of child care is in Washington, and following my meeting with Hughes executives, Dr. Robert Grayson came in. Dr. Grayson is a representative for the American Academy of Pediatrics, who took care of our children when they were young. Also, my granddaughter's physician, Dr. Gary Bong, came by the office. We hope to set up a hearing in Miami with our Select Committee on Children, Youth and Families on the problem of AIDS babies at Jackson Memorial Hospital. Most of these babies are abandoned by their mothers and funds are needed for foster care rather than have them remain in hospitals.

I then left the office for the hearing on the Office of the Secretary, which went from 10:00 to noon. It was an easy hearing after two long days of FAA hearings and Mimi Dawson, the Deputy Secretary of Transportation, did quite well. I thought she was particularly effective in the question and answer session when most of the panel members directed questions to her on passenger safety and FAA safety standards. Mimi answered "yes" to the question as to whether Eastern Airlines was safe, but she did, however, say this in conjunction with her approval of measures the FAA is taking to assure the safety of Eastern Airlines. At 11:30, I turned the chair over to Larry Coughlin and left the hearing to attend the Annual National Commemoration of the "Days of Remembrance," when Holocaust survivors were freed by U.S. troops.

Wynne from my office, whose father was a Holocaust survivor, accompanied me to the commemoration ceremony. All that mattered was that I was there. I lit a candle with my particular designate, whose name was Gertrude Getz from California, a survivor from Vienna. A woman from my district, Rosita Kornisberg, was there and told me the story of what happened to her family in Germany on Crystal Night. Her father was the Shamus at the synagogue. The ceremony was very moving, especially the Armed Services portion, as each contingent represented an Army division that liberated a concentration camp.

Back at the office Marsha, Adele, and I went over the overseas adoption problems. Three families in my district are waiting to adopt children from the Dominican Republic, but a road block has been placed on these adoptions because of the INS interpretation of the Barney Frank Amendment which says that on domestic adoptions the mother cannot put a child up for adoption without the father's consent. This has prevented the four children that are in institutions in Santo Domingo from coming to the United States for adoption. After our office's deliberation with Barney Frank, Barney will write to Judiciary Subcommittee Chair Romano (Rom) Mazzoli of Kentucky stating that the intent of the Frank amendment did not apply to offshore adoptions. If we can get Mazzoli, who is often very wary about doing anything, to call and convince the INS to remove these barriers, then the three Miami couples can move forward on the adoptions.

Following the meeting with Marsha and Adele, I left for Jamie Whitten's office for an emergency meeting with Whitten and the subcommittee chairmen regarding a section in the Armed Services bill that would prevent any authorizing on a continuing resolution. If the bill reaches the House Floor and passes, it will eliminate considerable power of the Appropriations Committee because appropriators have always authorized on continuing resolutions. We are trying to get this changed by the leadership in the Rules Committee and, if not, make an amendment "in order" on the Floor to strike this section of the bill. I think we can defeat the bill on the Floor but some subcommittee chairmen are not so optimistic. Bill Chappell called for the meeting, as it will first affect his Defense Subcommittee and then the other subcommittees as well. It is the same old battle for power between the appropriating and authorizing processes. As long as we can authorize in appropriations there is less urgency and less leverage for authorizing bills to move through the legislative process. Authorizers want to reduce the power of appropriations in that process.

In the evening Joan and I went to the beautiful home of Pamela Harriman in Georgetown for a fundraiser Pamela was co-hosting with Robert Strauss for former Florida Governor Reubin Askew. At $1,000 a person Joan and I had complimentary tickets. I told Bob Strauss I intended to help Askew in his campaign for the Senate and that in Miami on May 14 at my condo leadership breakfast, I would formally announce my endorsement. Art and Rosalie Roberts were there as was Sam Gibbons who has already indicated his support for Askew. Bob Traurig from Miami, a law partner of Askew's, came up and told me about his conversation with Joan and how he and Eli Feinberg are raising money for Joan's sculpture. It was a good evening with a lot of good friends.

APRIL 15 FRIDAY

Scott Fulton, an intern in Senator Chiles's office, did not show for his 9:00 a.m. appointment. His mother, Marcia Fulton, interned in my Washington office about ten years ago and although Marcia still teaches in my district, the family has moved to Kendall in South Dade.

It was not long, however, before my next scheduled appointment arrived: Edward Forbes of the American Shipbuilding Company in Tampa, Florida. Forbes and the company's Washington legislative representative came with the same sad story, that we are building fewer ships in this country and they needed government contracts to remain in business. Coast Guard cutters and icebreakers are the only ships for which I have any direct influence. Other than to co-sign a letter with the Florida Delegation to the Department of Navy in their behalf, I could offer little encouragement for their immediate needs. They left saying how much they appreciated this gesture and that they would stay in touch.

Afterwards Eli Feinberg and his client Lloyd Blue from the Florida Panhandle came in to discuss their continued interest in building an airport in Destin, Florida. I want to help as this is the first opportunity in the past fifteen years to build a new Florida commercial jetport. The Department of Defense is hindering the effort because of Air Force airspace in that region. The FAA does not want to take on the Department of Defense, and Earl Hutto, that district's Representative who will not oppose the Defense Department, is a legislative rubber stamp for the DOD. I thought the first thing to do was to have them touch base with Bob Carr. I called and spoke to Mark Miller, Carr's appropriations staff person, who told me to send them right over and he would meet with them and see that they got together with Carr. Later at a luncheon in the Florida House hosted by Adele and Senator Bob Graham, I again saw Eli and Lloyd who said that Mark Miller was very helpful and Eli especially was very pleased that I had arranged for him to meet with Carr.

Wynne, who had never been to the Florida House, accompanied me to the luncheon. This was the ideal occasion for her visit because the luncheon was quite elegantly done and Wynne was very impressed. We then went to the Golden State luncheon, an event which California holds every year, featuring California foods and beverages. Wynne was not able to get in, but I brought out a basket containing fruits, vegetables, breads and other foods for her and the office staff. Later, playing tennis with Bob Kastenmeier at Haines Point, it was great fun being out in the fresh spring air. Washington is very beautiful in the spring when the air is clear and the cherry blossoms are in full bloom, and the sweltering humidity is yet to arrive.

Barbara Burris in Dante Fascell's office reminded me about a phone call I received a while back from a partner in Arquitectonica, a Miami architectural company, who had been selected the architect for the new Embassy in Lima, Peru. It is good to see someone from Miami get this award, and I had helped by asking John Osthaus on the appropriations subcommittee staff of Commerce, Justice, State, to call the State Department to let them know of my recommendation of the Miami firm.

Bernie in the district office called about two immigration cases on which we are working. One case concerns Judith Kreeger (the attorney who drew up my will), who is helping a Haitian get his 10-year-old son out of Haiti. It may mean my going directly to the head of the Miami INS Office. And last week in Miami I spoke to my old friend Arnold Rubin about getting a green card for one of his relatives. Arnold has called the district office for a follow-up appointment with me, and I am to see him on my next visit to Miami.

Harry McPherson called to inform me that Norman Mineta was indeed going to introduce the resolution condemning Eastern Airlines. Harry thinks this is "piling on," and with the FAA investigating, this probably means the end of Eastern. I advised Harry to call Bob Carr who had also refused to go on the Mineta resolution. Harry then suggested that the Florida delegation sign a letter asking Mineta and the Speaker to prevent this resolution from coming to the Floor. Machinists Union president Charlie Bryan, a loose cannon, created this resolution idea, and several members of the Florida delegation, such as Larry Smith and Claude Pepper, are taking orders from organized labor. I told Harry that I thought enlisting Bob Carr was the best way; he said okay, that he would get in touch with Carr and get back to me.

Adele and Marsha showed me a request "wish" list from the University of Miami for State Department appropriations plus one for Energy appropriations. I will ask Dante Fascell who chairs the Committee on Foreign Affairs to go with me to speak with Hunter Spillings, Chief Council on the Energy and Water Subcommittee and also John Osthaus, Chief Council on State, Justice and Commerce Subcommittee. Dante's committee authorizes for the State Department and I hope, by Dante accompanying me, this diminishes the appearance of me alone pressuring the subcommittee staffs with my many projects.

Learning that the machinists would not be testifying next week on our public witnesses portion of the hearings, I called attorney Harry McPherson to give him this bit of information. Lucy and Tom had been upset about the machinists testifying because of the possible implication that I am taking sides in the Eastern problem. Now I have the benefit of having invited them but they, for whatever reason, chose not to testify. So often things worried about ahead of time are not a problem after all.

Then Marvin Rauzin from Miami called to tell me that the "Transition" organization which he heads wants to honor me at their annual dinner. Transition is an organization that works with soon-to-be-released prisoners to help them make the adjustment back into society. Marvin is a good friend and supporter, and I really admire everything that his organization represents. But this and the Israeli Bond dinner where I am also being honored are both coming at the same time. I told Marvin I was already honored just to be asked, and that I would have to get back to him when I knew more about my travel plans.

APRIL 16 SATURDAY

Sergio Bendixen and I met for breakfast this morning. Sergio has done very well for himself since leaving my office. He now has his own political consulting and polling firm in Washington and is very close to the political center of things. When I asked Sergio what he thought of the coming election, he said Jesse Jackson was running an amazing campaign but would not get the nomination. He did say, however, that Jackson may become Secretary of State and that he also wants to be Ambassador to the United Nations. Personally I worry that after the campaign Jackson probably won't even be as diplomatic to the Jews as he is now, and for the next twenty years he will be a very big player in the Democratic Party. Sergio continued, saying that Jackson would have veto power on whomever is nominated for Vice President and that Jackson would not accept Gore but would probably accept Floridian Bob Graham. Graham, he said, will be the Democratic Vice Presidential nominee as the nominee will come from the South and the states with large electoral votes are Texas and Florida.

He also spoke about Jeff in the district office working after hours and getting paid for it by three of the Dade County Commission candidates: Steve Clark, Clara Oesterle and Joe Gersten. I reminded Sergio that he did the same thing when he was working for me, and he said, "It wasn't right then and it isn't right now, and you can expect some adverse publicity." I said that I would handle it the best way I could, as Jeff needs the money and I cannot control what he does after five o'clock. Besides, none of the candidates for whom he is working is an embarrassment to me.

APRIL 17 SUNDAY

This Sunday evening around 5:00, I bumped into my friend Pete Stark who asked what I had planned for dinner. "Nothing," I said, and we ended up at Pete's house till 7:00 when we went to La Brasserie for dinner. This was really good as I was able to discuss with him Bob Brin's problems with tax returns. Bob is a head accountant in the Miami firm of Coopers and Lybrand. Pete said he would be happy to meet with Bob if and when he comes to Washington, but that it would be better for Bob to meet with members on the Ways and Means Committee who were on the committee on taxation, and offered to give me their names. We also talked about the House leadership, our colleagues in the House, Jesse Jackson, and where the Democratic party is headed. It was a nice evening for me.

APRIL 18 MONDAY

At 10:00 a.m. our hearing began with National Highway Transportation Safety Administrator, Diane Steed. There were no votes today, so we went straight through until 1:00, with no interruptions on a rather routine NHTSA hearing and ended with a photo opportunity. I returned to the office to place a congratulatory call to one of our black female nominees who had been accepted to the West Point Academy.

1:30, John Snyder and Vince Carr from the Marine Industry Association of South Florida came in hoping to obtain more direct funds for boating safety, and complained about how all such funds now go to the Coast Guard. This is true and I want to help, but with the Coast Guard threatening to close down base stations due to lack of funds, I certainly could make them no promises.

At the Restaurant Association reception this evening in the Cannon Building most of the members there were Republicans. Heading the association is Ron Sarasin, a former Republican member from Connecticut who came to Washington the same time I did in 1973. I also saw Harry Johnson who is running for Dan Mica's Palm Beach seat. Harry has an appointment with me tomorrow to get my endorsement. I told him to save his time as I will give him my endorsement, and to just send me the blanks. He will probably come by anyway.

Leaving the Cannon Building, I went to a New York Wine Tasting Party honoring Congressman Matt McHugh at the home of Ron and Susan Platt. Matt was there with his wife Alana and we recalled a trip we had taken together to Jordan. The military officer on the trip with us was at the party. He had taken Joan and me in the King's helicopter to Petra to see the ancient ruins near the Dead Sea. We also met with the King of Nepal and Indira Gandhi on that trip.

Apparently Jeff wants to work from 9:00 to 3:00, but I find objectionable his leaving early to go out and politic for other candidates. I want him to work 8:00-3:00, but preferably 9:00-4:00. If he puts in one less hour, it will be in effect giving him a raise, and I do not need the criticism for giving him a raise at taxpayers' expense so he can politic for local candidates.

APRIL 19 TUESDAY

Stanley Tate, a contributor and a big real estate developer in my district, came in today. Stanley is doing work with the State of Florida providing educational insurance policies to families with children, designed to cover the costs of a college education by the time the child is ready to enter college. Nadine has all the information and I may be able to help him with a ruling to prevent taxation on the interest accrued on this educational insurance fund because the interest will be earned by the State of Florida and not the parents. This is a new undertaking, and Stanley is very enthusiastic about it. He is doing this for the public good, deriving no profit for himself, having already made his money and, as he said, now wanting to do something for the young people in the State. When he gives me the word, I am ready to go ahead with my effort to change the ruling.

Afterwards, a group from the Joint Action Committee for Political Affairs, a Jewish women's PAC, came in to present me with a PAC check for $250. We basically discussed the problems of and the support for Israel in the Congress.

At the outside witnesses portion of our subcommittee's hearing today there were ten groups in the morning and ten this afternoon. At the afternoon session we heard from emergency medical service and trauma witnesses who flattered and at the same time rather embarrassed me with all the praise and credit they gave me for providing trauma funding. After the hearing I saw Charlie Wilson who told me that the Richard Barnett article I gave him on Afghanistan published in the *New Yorker* was very well written but that Barnett was absolutely wrong on some parts of the story. Charlie wants to meet with Barnett, whom I know personally, so I have written to Barnett suggesting that the three of us get together. I saw Dan Mica and told him that I will support his opponent Reubin Askew, and that I would be making the announcement sometime in May. He sort of anticipated this on my part.

At the Coast Guard reception this evening in the Senate Russell Building, Admiral Yost said to me he has announced that the Coast Guard does not want to be transferred to the Department of Treasury but wishes to remain in the Department of Transportation. I told him that we received word yesterday that other branches of the uniformed services unlike the Coast Guard were not adversely affected by the summit agreement. Admiral Yost is adverse to our subcommittee's position as he wants to transfer money from other parts of our budget to the Coast Guard, and I am definitely opposed to this. I attended the reception primarily to show my appreciation to Guy Goodman, the Coast Guard legislative liaison who always looks out for me and who has been very helpful in practically every constituent problem that I have presented to him. It was through Goodman's constituent intervention that the claim of a Miami architect was resolved regarding money the Coast Guard owed on the design of a new building on MacArthur Causeway. Also, he had been successful in resolving my colleague Barbara Boxer's noise problem the Coast Guard was causing at the air base in her district.

Staying only a short while at the reception, I returned home to attend a party being held in the upper floors of my townhouse hosted by Tom Boggs and Penny Farthing for Joe Lieberman, the Democrat running against Connecticut Senator Lowell Weicker. Tom Boggs suggested to me that I get Eastern machinists leader Charlie Bryan together with Eastern's Chairman Frank Lorenzo to save that airline. I said I really did not know Bryan or Lorenzo well but that I did know Charlie Kurtz, the local machinists union head, and Phil Bakes, President of Eastern, and maybe I could get those two together to work out something. I am willing to try almost anything within reason to save Eastern Airlines before it self- destructs, but I told Tom in a situation like this there was no point in my getting Kurtz and Bakes together unless I had some leverage that would be adverse to both if they did not work out their differences. Harry McPherson was at the reception, and I related to him the conversation I had with Tom Boggs. Harry is extremely dedicated to and constantly in pursuit of saving Eastern and is appreciative of any help he can get toward this end. I still have a feeling of Doomsday for Eastern like it has passed the point of no return.

APRIL 20 WEDNESDAY

Fred Herter, President of the American University of Beirut and Bill Hoffman, their Washington representative, came in first thing this morning. Last year in our Foreign Ops Subcommittee, we appropriated $40 million for the American Schools and Hospitals Abroad Program, of which the University of Beirut received $6 million. This year they are asking for $6.5 million, and Herter and Hoffman want to get the total line item up from $40 to $50 million. I told them I would not lead the charge but would offer no opposition to such an increase. I am for American schools abroad but not so much for the Beirut school, as it is too tilted toward the Arab position. On the whole, however, ASHA is too Mideast involved.

Richard Barnett of the *New Yorker* magazine called just as I was leaving for the subcommittee hearing for our second day of outside witnesses. He wants very much to meet with Charlie Wilson and me on the Afghanistan article, and we set a tentative date for next week.

Witnesses for the morning session included Governor Donald Schaefer of Maryland, Congressman John Lewis of Georgia, Chairman Bob Kiley of the New York transit system, and other chairmen and/or top officials of our major "rail modernization" cities. There was considerable media coverage for Governor Schaefer, the first to testify. Member Steny Hoyer of Maryland introduced the Governor, reminding us that Schaefer had testified several times as a Mayor before our subcommittee, but that this was his first time to testify as Governor. After Steny's long and flattering commentary, Governor Schaefer thanked him and with laughter said, "I just hope the television got all of that." The Governor finished his testimony and left, taking most of the press with him. "I can't imagine why all the cameras are leaving when I come up," said our next witness Congressman Dave McCurdy, Chairman of the Subcommittee on Transportation, Aviation and Materials of the Committee on Science, Space and Technology. The outside witnesses portion of the hearings is very relaxed and much more informal than the agency hearings. Plus, Governor Schaefer had left us with his own particular brand of humor, which set the stage for others to follow.

At 1:15 we broke for a forty-five minute lunch, and as I was having lunch in my office Stu Eizenstat came in about the Export/Import Bank. He also brought up the earmarking for aid to Morocco. I had no problem with the request but, in a very serious face, I said that I did have a problem with not being invited to dinner at the Moroccan Embassy for about five years now, and that if he wanted me to help him he would have to see that I got one of those good Moroccan Embassy meals again. Of course I was kidding.

At 2:00, we began the afternoon session with Metro-Dade Commissioner Clara Oesterle, who requested federal funding to complete the final two legs of the Metromover. One leg would connect the Metromover with the Brickell financial district and the second would connect with the Omni retail and hotel complex - both legs vital to the growth of Miami's downtown business district. Clara performed well for Miami, and following the question and answer session, Larry Coughlin commented very favorably about me to Clara and Alan Dimond, who was there as a witness in behalf of an ill Dorothy Weaver, Chairman of the Greater Miami Chamber of Commerce. With Coughlin saying that "Miami was very fortunate to be represented by the `distinguished Chairman of this Subcommittee,' and that he is not only respected, but beloved in the Congress," Clara responded with, "You just don't know how much." It's nice to hear both your constituent and your colleague speak about you in such flattering terms.

Following testimony from several witnesses from other states, Mayor Kathy Whitmire of Houston testified. Whitmire does not read from script and is very articulate. She had people from Houston with her including Tom Delay on our subcommittee and former Houston Transportation Board Chairman John King. King now manages the system and together with Mayor Whitmire, they exhibited maps and other illustrations on phase II of Houston's regional transportation system, and were nothing short of excellent in their presentation. Earlier, I had suggested to Clara Oesterle and Alan Dimond that they remain at the hearing to hear the testimony from Houston. They did so and Clara said to me later, "Next year I will know how to do it."

Richard Alterman, who lives in my district and owns with his father and brothers the Alterman Transport Line, Inc., also testified at the afternoon session and did a good job for the American Trucking Association. He requested our subcommittee to appropriate the full $44.2 million to the Interstate Commerce Commission to ensure that the agency is able to carry out its mandated responsibilities, some of which are data collection and reporting, and the enforcement of regulations intended to protect motor carriers and the public from unsafe, unlawful and unfair practices. About 4:00, as the hearing was winding down, Miami attorney Marty Fine presented the proposal for Florida Power and Light for a Metrorail station on its new riverfront development. The main reason FP&L testified was to start a hearing record on its proposal which is still a few years off. It has already received $250,000 from UMTA for a feasibility study.

Earlier on the House Floor I voted for the Immigration Reform Bill and spoke to the bill's manager, Rom Mazzoli, about getting the four children out of Santo Domingo to Miami. I gave him another copy of Barney Frank's letter, and it seems Mazzoli's staff has not kept him informed as he had not seen the letter. I told Mazzoli that he and I must work this out as it was important to me and to the families in my district who have been waiting seven months now for the release of these four orphans from institutions in Santo Domingo. The delay by Mazzoli's staff in interpreting the Frank amendment is preventing us from getting this accomplished, when all Mazzoli has to do is send a message to the INS and they will let the children come in. Mazzoli said he would get back to me.

Keith Mainland, former chief clerk and staff director on the Appropriations Committee, received a special award this evening at a reception in his honor. Keith was very well liked and respected when he headed the committee staff; he was not only the professional staff head but also its sort of "guru" as well.

Lucy told me yesterday that Tom Kingfield was embarrassed because he thought I was discussing campaign fundraising when I spoke to Lloyd Blue and Eli Feinberg about their airport problem. I told Lucy that when Eli and I spoke about funds it was in regard to money he was raising for the Dade Foundation. When

I mentioned this to Greg Dahlberg at the Keith Mainland party, as Tom had already left, Greg said that Tom had felt a little uncomfortable. I told Greg that the conversation between me and Eli was not about my fundraising but about paying for art in public places in Dade County, and how any other interpretation was derived, I could not figure out.

In any case, the Memorial Day recess is coming up and I am looking forward to going on one of several possible trips. Jack Brooks and Charlie Wilson are planning a possible NATO trip, and they want me to go. The trip itinerary sounds interesting, and I hope they can put something together.

I heard today that Bill Chappell had won over the leadership to his side on the problem caused by the Armed Services Authorizing Bill, an attempt to curtail defense appropriation authority which could severely hamper all the appropriations subcommittees. It is a victory for the appropriation process overcoming authorizing obstacles.

APRIL 21 THURSDAY

9:00 a.m., I met with Mayor Tom Bradley of Los Angeles and his entourage about funds needed for the Los Angeles Metrorail (MTA). Los Angeles wants $170 million but at $100 million, it would be doing pretty well. I told them that I would do my best for Los Angeles and they assured me that they knew this. During the photo opportunity, I joked with Tom about running for Vice President on the Democratic ticket. Tom said he just wanted to go back to Los Angeles and get re-elected.

Seeing Mazzoli on the House Floor, I told him that I still had not heard from his staff. Mazzoli said he would straighten it out and "not to worry." About ten minutes later Adele received a call from Rom's staffer who was madder than hell because her boss had "come down" on her. But if she had done her job the way she was supposed to there would have been no problem. Dave Obey spoke to me on the Floor about his plans in Miami, and I spoke to Charlie Wilson about the meeting next week with Richard Barnett of the *New Yorker*.

As I left the House Floor to return to our subcommittee hearing, North Carolina member Bill Heffner, a member on the Appropriations Committee, came up and said that he heard I had criticized Tim Valentine, his North Carolina colleague in the House, when he appeared yesterday before our subcommittee as an outside witness. Heffner was apparently pleased with the way I handled Valentine, who had requested funds for small community general aviation airports in and around his North Carolina district. I had asked Valentine how he could vote last year for across-the-board cuts in our transportation bill and then expect us to earmark additional money for his airports. He obviously was not expecting the question and seemed embarrassed, saying that he realized he could not have it both ways. Later I learned that the Raleigh, North Carolina, *News and Observer* had run the dialogue between Valentine and me in its April 21 edition, headlined: "Airport funding request gets Valentine a lecture." Following the headline, the article read: "Tim Valentine got a brief lecture ... on the old congressional admonition, 'to get along, go along.'"

On this our third and last day of hearings with outside witnesses, Clara Oesterle was back with Miami Beach City Manager Bob Parkins to provide additional information about the light rail transit planned for the MacArthur Causeway. I reminded them that first there must be matching local funds in order for them to receive federal funds for this project. Not much time was spent discussing the project, as a feasibility study has yet to be done. Ranking member Larry Coughlin did extend congratulations to Clara and Parkins for doing such a good job in putting the project together privately and locally with no federal funds. Nearing the end of our hearing, the sister-in-law of Bob Strauss, Mayor Annette Strauss of Dallas, Texas, testified, requesting $15 million for a new rapid rail system to run along the South Oak Cliff corridor, located in Texas member Marty Frost's district. Frost was first to testify in support of the funding and then Mayor Strauss, with both affirming that there was no real community opposition to their project. Our hearings for fiscal >89 are now ended, and the subcommittee members and staff celebrated with a small office party.

Denis Neill was my last scheduled office appointment. He wanted to go over problems regarding the Export/Import Bank, and by the time we finished and I cleared my desk I was not able to keep a dinner appointment with Art Roberts and still make my flight to Miami. The dinner meeting was important, as I wanted to promote Joan's possible sculpture project in Dallas. Art said he would arrange a "dog and pony" show in Dallas so that I could speak to people there about their transportation system, and perhaps Joan would also like to come.

On the plane on my way to Miami, I thought about the meeting today with the appropriations subcommittee chairmen regarding the 302B allocations. Unhappy because my allocation had not been changed to take care of the loss of funds we were not getting from the Defense Appropriations Subcommittee, I told Whitten and the subcommittee chairmen that in previous years we had gotten Defense Subcommittee funds of $350 million and this year we are getting zero, which means we will have to transfer funds from Amtrak and Interstate Mass Transit. I will offer this as an amendment in the full committee, and told them that I hope the subcommittee chairmen will support the amendment. When members approach me about highway projects, I now say you have to help us with the 302B allocations. I arrived in Miami about midnight, feeling a little tired, but also a bit excited about the commitments I had in the district this weekend with Dave Obey and in Orlando with the Florida Congressional Partnership.

APRIL 22 FRIDAY

Up and out early, I met Patrice for our visit to Myrtle Grove Elementary School on Miami Gardens Drive. In February, our office received about 300 letters from Myrtle Grove students for a new flag that had been flown over the Capitol, as a replacement for the worn and tattered flag at the school. In answer to their letters, I said I would not just send them a flag but would deliver it to them. They had an hour's ceremony planned, with the students proudly adorned in handmade red, white and blue hats in the shape of the American flag. Upon my arrival, the Northwestern High School ROTC students paraded, and afterwards the students sang patriotic songs. As they sang the National Anthem, I helped to raise the new flag. "The flag is but a symbol, a wonderful symbol," I said to the students, "and you are the ones who will make this country worthwhile." The mistress of ceremonies was a remarkable fifth grader by the name of Evelyn Terrero, who introduced and presented me with a Myrtle Grove Eagles jacket. She was so impressive in her presentation on the significance of the American flag that I invited her to visit me in Washington in June to see Congress in action. Following the ceremony a reception was held in the school library. This was a most wonderful event for the students, but everyone seemed to enjoy it, including Dade Superintendent of Schools, Joe Fernandez, who took part in the ceremony. The event drew media coverage from Channel 4 and the *Miami Herald Neighbors*.

2:00 p.m., I met at the Miami-Dade Chamber of Commerce in Edison Center with Dorothy Baker, President of this black Chamber of Commerce, and approximately twenty-five other people assembled regarding the problem of access and exit roads on I-95 to relieve traffic jams in the 62nd Street Edison Center area. Dorothy and I are friends, and I have worked to help her group in the past. Now the new access road that runs from 54th to 62nd Street is almost completed and will help the traffic. Staff from the Florida DOT were there and showed maps depicting the access roads. I can relate very well to this area, as this is where I had my original used car lot. After the meeting and riding to the Northside office with Patrice, I observed that the area had improved greatly. The Northside shopping center is again completely rented.

My fifteen-year-old grandson Matthew was waiting for me at the North Miami Beach office with his father and our special family friend, Ellen Kempler. Ira Clark, President of Jackson Memorial Hospital and of the Metro-Dade Health Trust, came as a favor to me to meet Matt and possibly find him a summer job at Jackson working with one of their computer programs. He was wonderful to Matt and gracious to Don and Ellen, a teacher, and this could be a great opportunity for Matt to not only learn but also to use his computer skills. At the campaign office, Sharyn told me she has arranged for two breakfast fundraisers in Washington during June.

Later around 4:15, I played tennis with Al Moskovits and then went to Dr. Groff's office to try on a hearing aid. A sample aid was very helpful, but at the cost of $500 I will check with the Capitol Physician's Office to make sure that is a fair price.

APRIL 23 SATURDAY

The *Miami News* had interviewed Admiral Yost while he was in Miami and, among other things, he told them that there should be a referendum in Miami to see, first, whether South Florida wanted drug interdiction before subsidizing public mass transit. This was an outrageous statement for Yost to make, and his aide called me to apologize; but Yost did it quite calculatingly.

As mentioned, the Greater Orlando Chamber of Commerce is sponsoring the Florida Congressional Partnership Weekend in Orlando. The event is being held at the Peabody Orlando Hotel. Last year the event was sponsored by the Greater Miami Chamber and held in Miami. The conference began yesterday, Friday, with state elected officials, key business leaders, and economic experts such as John Naisbitt, author of the best-selling book, *Magatrends*. Naisbitt spoke at the conference luncheon on Friday, and I wanted to be there, but because of my schedule in the district I was only able to get away this morning, arriving in Orlando at 7:30 a.m., on a one-hour flight out of Miami. Having breakfast at the Peabody Hotel, I noticed that the only Congressional delegation members absent were Sam Gibbons and Larry Smith, and I understand that Gibbons is on a retreat in Tennessee for members of the Ways and Means Committee, having indicated beforehand that he would not be able to attend this conference. Following breakfast, we all assembled at 9:00 for a meeting on "The Growing Needs and Concerns of the Fastest Growing State in the Union." Transportation was the number one growth problem on the agenda. Fred Leonhardt, a partner in Orlando's Holland and Knight law firm, was moderator of the discussion, with panelists David Blumberg of Miami, an advocate for highspeed rail; Bob Martin of the Florida Transportation Building Association; a staffer from the Florida Department of Environmental Impact; and George Carpenter from Proctor and Gamble.

The session focused on the federal highway bill and tax law changes to implement the highspeed rail. Individual panel members made their statements, and then Leonhardt called on me.

"On Tuesday," I said, "our transportation subcommittee will be `marking up´ the supplemental appropriations because the `dumb´ summit conference had made across-the-board cuts and our transportation subcommittee had to reduce the appropriation for the Coast Guard and now the Coast Guard cannot perform its missions and will have to close bases. The administration in asking us to transfer to the Coast Guard funds which will adversely affect Amtrak, mass transit subsidy, and highway funds, puts the subcommittee in the position of either drug interdiction or federal subsidies for transportation." This conference was about a "partnership" among the local, state, and federal governments and that meant funds, which will be increasingly more difficult to come by on the federal level. I laid the facts out there and told it just as it was. I did know my subject and what the problem was, and I was not the least bit hesitant to offer the hard truths.

After the discussion, members then boarded a fleet of about eight helicopters for a thirty-five minute tour over Orlando. Bob Martin, Chairman and CEO of the Martin component of Martin Marietta, directed this particular operation. People were still gathered at the conference when I left for the Orlando airport at 1:30 to catch my flight back to Miami.

APRIL 24 SUNDAY

Jonathan Slade had met Dave Obey at the Miami airport, so Dave was already at the home of Tony Costa when I arrived at 5:30 for the meeting with members of the Cuban National Foundation. The group is strictly anti-Castro, right-wing Cubans. Tony Costa is very charming and has a beautiful home. Some Cuban-Americans there had just gotten back from Angola and were very much concerned about the Cuban troops in Angola. Dave told them there is no way the United States could ally itself on the side of South Africa in the Angola situation. They didn't necessarily want to hear that but understood it. I think Dave received $2,000 in honoraria and hopefully there will be another $2,000 forthcoming in a campaign fund contribution.

Afterwards, I took Dave and his aide Mary Schecklehoff and Jonathan Slade and his secretary Marilyn to meet with our two sons and their wives for dinner at Joe's Stone Crab. Obey is one of my favorite people and one of the most capable members we have in the House. He too prefers the honest approach and tells it like it is. Dave is also a gifted storyteller, and my sons enjoyed hearing him tell about his two meetings with Arafat.

APRIL 25 MONDAY

I saw Dave again at the AIPAC gathering this morning, the event for which he had originally come to Miami. As he is Chairman of the Subcommittee on Foreign Ops that provides aid to Israel, AIPAC is going to raise funds for Dave. The event was held at the new and very impressive Adler Building on Brickell Avenue, with Mike Adler as host. Mike introduced me and I introduced Dave, who spoke very encouragingly of his continued support for Israel in the House, getting a good reception from the AIPAC members. Muriel Russell who funded construction of the Michael-Ann Russell facility at the Jewish Community Center was there. My son Bill was very active at one time with the Jewish Community Center but he has not been as active or able to contribute lately because of expanding business commitments. When Bill's name came up, I explained this to Muriel and to Harvey Friedman of the Jewish Federation.

Joan and Sharyn had accompanied me to the AIPAC meeting. Dropping Joan off at home, Sharyn and I went to the Miami International Airport to meet with Dick Judy and Tex Gunnels, staff head of the subcommittee that appropriates for the Department of Treasury. This meeting was all about locating customs personnel at the new general aviation facilities at Tamiami Airport. Dick Judy also wants additional FAA funds earmarked for runway extensions and taxi facilities at the Miami International Airport and additional funds for the Opa Locka General Aviation Airport. It is necessary to have general aviation alternative airports to Miami International as we do not want to "Loganize" Miami International as has happened at Boston's Logan Airport, overloaded with general aviation. South Florida really needs more airports.

I got Tom Kingfield on the phone for Dick Judy to find out exactly what the FAA was doing about the Miami International Airport problems. One problem is that Judy is spending money in advance of appropriations and needs a letter of intent from the

FAA that the money will be refunded in the 1989 budget. This is not the usual practice but the FAA did this for the Washington National Airport, and I hope it does the same for Miami airports. Lorri Kellogg and Lee Klein stopped by Judy's office while the meeting was going on, and I excused myself to have a photo opportunity with them. Lee Klein lives in my district and had won the Kathryn Lehman-Weiner Award for her service to children.

5:30, I boarded the plane for my flight back to Washington.

APRIL 26 TUESDAY

10:00 a.m., Tom, Greg, and Lucy were in to discuss the administration's proposal for the supplemental appropriations bill to provide $60 million for the Coast Guard. The three of them have been working on this while I was in Miami, and have managed to come up with what I think is a very workable alternative proposal. Instead of the administration's proposal which cuts Amtrak, mass transit and highways, they have found unobligated appropriated funds that can be used, or funds that were about to lapse in programs such as in the Panama Canal appropriations. And most important is that half of the needed $60 million will come out of the Coast Guard's own capital expenditure account, which we are transferring into operating funds. Tomorrow afternoon I will be meeting with the full transportation subcommittee and, hopefully, I can get this proposal included in the supplemental. The administration was using the needed increase in the Coast Guard drug interdiction program as reason to reduce funds for Amtrak, mass transit and highways. Now we can present this alternative and prevent the funding reduction in surface transportation programs.

Dick Judy is in the Washington office this morning, having come to Washington for a gathering of the Airport Operators International Council. He spoke to Tom and Lucy about the Tamiami Airport in Dante Fascell's district and the Opa Locka Airport in my district, assuring them that Dante was on board regarding the Tamiami Airport and that he (Dante) had no problem with the thousand-foot proposed extension of the Tamiami runway. Judy reiterated the need for a letter of intent from the FAA Airport Improvement Program, for without it the FAA could deduct in its next year's budget the money that Dade County airports will spend this year, which amounts to a couple million dollars. Ordinarily airports cannot get money back if they use local funds in advance, so the letter of intent will assure Judy that Miami can advance the funds for improvements at Tamiami and then apply for and receive a refund. We also talked about the problems of Eastern. Judy said he would try to find out if there was any particular role I could play between labor and management that could help Eastern to survive.

The people I had met in Los Alamos came in and gave me some very nice Indian pottery, and asked that I continue to work with Bill Richardson of New Mexico to help with the highway between Los Alamos and Santa Fe. I hope to visit New Mexico again soon with Joan, and also stay at the same ranch I stayed previously.

Marvin Rauzin of Transition called and we are looking at a date in late October for their dinner. Betsy Berg called from New York and I got her in touch with Elizabeth Dole's staff. Betsy still works for the company that schedules celebrity speakers, and she is hoping to arrange for Mrs. Dole to speak at an event. And then Massachusetts member Ed Markey called. Markey wants me to work out with Bob Carr a reconciliation on general aviation regulation changes at Logan Airport. Markey is trying to limit general aviation at Logan and Bob Carr has a problem with restrictions on general aviation and with the new schedule of landing fees. I will try to get Markey and Carr together to resolve their differences.

Jim O'Hara from Patton, Boggs and Blow came in about the Wayne County Metro Detroit Airport, reporting on improvements at the airport since I was last out there with Bob Carr for our subcommittee hearing. This visit was really a "dog and pony" show for Jim's clients who were with him and who happen to be the airport authority officials seeking improvement money for runways. Then Hector Alcalde and Don O'Bannon came in to try to convince me to change my cosponsorship on the carbon fluoride bill, saying the bill would adversely affect Jim Walters, a supporter of mine with a business in South Florida. The main focus of the bill is to take the United States out of the carbon fluoride business, though fluoride is still being made by many other countries. I had cosponsored the legislation because my good friend Pete Stark had asked me to, but more important I had cosponsored because of the bill's relevance to the environment and to saving the ozone, of which I am highly supportive. But now learning that the bill will put a particular Florida industry out of business which will, of course, affect many employees, disturbs me. If a public relations firm finds that legislation is being introduced which concerns South Florida, it should let me know in a more timely manner so that I can take this into account before cosponsoring. Charlie Bennett, Dean of our delegation, is in the same position having also cosponsored the bill. Removing cosponsorship is not easy.

Minnesota member Bruce Vento called to gain my support for his amendment to put a limitation on the highway fund in the supplemental appropriations bill, as he wants to restrict expenditures for highways around Manassas Park in Virginia to preserve the national park area. His amendment, however, has no business in the supplemental, which is only to deal with Coast Guard funds. Bob Mrazek, a Civil War buff, also wants to preserve the historical battlefield.

In the afternoon I went to the Budget Conference in the Cannon Building to talk to Bill Gray about the Panama Canal's revolving fund. The Senate bill has a revolving fund as a discretionary item and the House bill has it as a mandatory item. I wanted to make clear to Gray that if his Budget Committee recedes to the Senate in the budget conference on the $400 million for the Panama Canal, this will mean a cut in the House in our 1989 Transportation Appropriations Bill. Gray said he understood and would talk to Vic Fazio and Dick Durbin, members on the Budget Committee. I will follow this closely.

When I spoke with Dick Judy this evening at a reception of the Airport Operators International Council, he reaffirmed the commitment he had made to the Dade Community Foundation. He is raising $3,000 for Joan's sculpture, and the money will go to the Foundation to be used for art in public places. I saw Bob Graham and asked if his wife Adele had moved to Washington; he said no, that they were still looking for a home. Graham, who can be quite circumspect, had no response when I commented that perhaps he should wait as he may be moving to the Vice President's home next year. He did ask me about the Coast Guard problems in the Persian Gulf, but I do not think he wants to take a position on that issue. When the *Miami Herald* interviewed me recently about the President sending the Coast Guard into the Persian Gulf, I told them that the cost will reduce resources and equipment for drug interdiction, and this I thought was wrong.

APRIL 27 WEDNESDAY

The Foreign Operations Subcommittee held its hearing today with outside witnesses. I was there with Adele, and Representative Mickey Leland was testifying on world hunger. Obey's assistant Mary Schecklehoff was at the hearing and told me that the Miami meeting was very good, particularly so because AIPAC execs Mike Adler and Harvey Friedman have now a good relationship with Dave Obey. Dave had handled the event like a business meeting and that is the style that Miami group understands. I believe the barrier has been broken now between the Miami Jewish leadership and Dave, allowing for a meaningful relationship - no more sparring with each other and both parties able to deal with problems on a mutually beneficial and competent basis. What was interesting was that Dave's meetings with the Jewish leadership last Monday morning and the Cuban leadership the previous day were both arranged by Jonathan Slade formerly of Dave's staff. The two groups of young people were so much alike, and even though one group was Hispanic and the other Jewish, they were both upwardly mobile, very dynamic and energetic, and very committed to their own concerns. The Hispanics concerned with freeing Cuba from Castro and the Jews for preservation of security for the State of Israel. Both groups have the same type of self-assurance, dedication and awareness of the political aspect of their causes.

I returned to the office for my 11:15 meeting with Larry Coughlin to go over the supplemental bill we are marking up in the transportation subcommittee this afternoon at 2:00. We hope to resolve all the problems, including Washington's Union Station financing and preservation of the Manassas Battlefield. Of course the big problem is finding the $60 million for Coast Guard operations, and I hope the solution Tom, Greg and Lucy came up with will be acceptable to our subcommittee members. The government is buying Union Station from the CSX Railroad for $10 million - $6 million to come from the District of Columbia interstate highway funds and $4 million from Amtrak. I spoke to John Snow, President of the CSX Railroad, and he said he would call me back next week and let me know about the final negotiations with the State of Florida and the right-of-way of the Tri-County South Florida commuter rail. We hope to have that in operation by the end of the year or early next year.

Seeing Charlie Rose of North Carolina and Jack Brooks of Texas on the Floor, I reconfirmed that I definitely wanted to go on the trip to Madeira Islands. Also on the Floor was Les Aspin, Chairman of the Armed Services Committee, who told me that the Defense authorization bill will authorize $250 million for the Coast Guard. This is something I needed to know before the appropriations committee chairman decides on the final 302B allocations. Now I no longer need to offer an amendment in full committee to transfer $250 million from the Department of Defense to the Department of Transportation.

Meanwhile, our subcommittee is preparing to markup the supplemental. I have been talking with staff about offering an amendment in full committee to prevent the Defense Department from using its funds to send the Coast Guard to the Persian Gulf. It would be making foreign policy in the Transportation Department. I am reluctant to push this too hard though, as we continue to need funds from Defense appropriations. If we prevent the Coast Guard from fulfilling the Department of Defense's orders, the Defense Subcommittee may not in the future provide funds for the Coast Guard. But, if we are going to lose Department of Defense funds anyway, then I can at least try to stop Defense from using the Coast Guard in the Gulf. Some Coast Guard officers are telling me that sending the Guard to the Persian Gulf is a mistake as it is neither equipped, nor armed, nor trained for that type of operation.

At 2:00 p.m., we had the transportation segment of the supplemental markup for the $60 million of program transfers for the Coast Guard. With the unobligated funds that the staff found to cover the Coast Guard request, we were able to protect mass transit subsidy and also Amtrak and interstate highway funds. We also worked out the deal for the government to buy Union Station from CSX Railroad. I kept pressure on the members to keep the agenda moving, which prevented too much trivial conversation, and we were able to successfully grind out all the legislation.

The markup took about two hours, so it was around 4:00 when the Indian River Citrus people came to the office. There was nothing specific that they wanted, other than for me to "look out" for their export business. Having owned part of an orange grove for several years, I told them that I was very familiar with their concerns and that, yes, I would be on the alert for anything affecting their business.

People from the Hertz Corporation came in about airport-user fees and the competition with Alamo which has off-airport privileges and perhaps does not pay its fair share of airport costs. Although I am a cosponsor of the "Alamo Bill," I told them that I was not locked in, and if nothing happens this year the bill is dead as is my cosponsorship. I assured them that before I cosponsored again, I would get in touch with them.

A reception honoring my good friend and California colleague Don Edwards was held this evening at the National Democratic Club. It was your typical California reception, including California Delegation members like my friends Vic Fazio and Richard Lehman. People were there from the Arab American League who had testified the day before at our Foreign Ops Subcommittee. I spoke to Pete Shields from the National Handgun Association and he was pleased about the new plastic handguns legislation that he hopes will pass, saying that this legislation would be the most positive step that he has seen in the past fourteen years that he has headed the Handgun Control Caucus's public relations effort. Pete got involved with handgun control fourteen years ago after his son was gunned down during a robbery attempt. At the time, Pete was working as an executive at DuPont. He quit his job not long after his son was killed because DuPont had been making ammunition and he did not want to be a part of any such company. I had seen Jim and Sarah Brady at the hearing on plastic handguns. Sarah works with Pete Shields and is a terrific lady. Jim, on the other hand, is so sad and helpless and seems very depressed.

I left this California reception to attend the reception of George Miller, another California member. George's reception was also held at the National Democratic Club, but it was a bit more lively. George has lots of friends, including his housemates, Leon Panetta and Marty Russo, who were there, and members of his Children, Youth and Families Select Committee. Lobbyist Liz Robbins from New York invited me to visit her new home in the Hamptons on Long Island. I stayed about thirty minutes, and enjoyed both receptions.

APRIL 28 THURSDAY

This morning I met with Adele regarding a list of amendments and some report language I want included in the Foreign Ops markup next week to increase funds for refugee resettlement. Afterwards I called Jeff who is back in the office from his "vacation," and stressed the need for him to keep a log of his district activities for as long as he worked on campaigns for Mayor Clark and Commissioners Clara Oesterle and Joe Gersten. I am becoming a bit more apprehensive about Jeff taking on these campaigns, although technically he is doing nothing unethical.

There was a short article in today's *Miami Herald* with my comments about the Coast Guard in the Persian Gulf. Channel 7 came in to do a tape regarding the $60 million we provided the Coast Guard yesterday in our supplemental. I don't know whether it will air or not, as many of these tapes are never shown.

Lynn Prusin, who once lived in Coral Gables but now resides with her family in Atlanta, Georgia, is in Washington and paid me a visit. Lynn was one of my daughter's closest friends. Her son Todd and my grandson Sean were good friends when they were young children. We talked about old times and brought each other up-to-date on our families. I took her to see Atlanta member John Lewis, her Congressman whom she knew, and also Pat Schroeder, a friend of Lynn's mother who lives in Denver. We all had a photo taken together on the Capitol steps. On the way back to the office I ran into Bill Gray who told me that he had taken care of the Panama Canal problem that I discussed with him recently, so now in conference we can recede to the Senate on the Panama Canal's revolving fund and still be protected against any discretionary funding cutbacks.

New York member Bob Mrazek has approached me and several other members and non-members about a deal to purchase

Pierre Island in the Bahamas. Good friends and colleagues such as Richard Durbin, Matt McHugh, Tom Downey, Tom McMillan, and Al Gore are members Mrazek has asked to go in on the deal. The non-members are House Sergeant-at-Arms Jack Russ and multi-millionaire Arnold Picker, who bought United Artists from Mary Pickford and Buddy Rogers years ago. Meeting in Mrazek's office this afternoon to discuss the matter, everyone was having a good time talking about the island which will be used partly for a retreat, but mainly for investment. Mrazek is a genius at putting this deal together, and I am delighted to be a part of it. Mrazek said the biggest problem he has is explaining to other friends why he did not include them. Each member has to put up $12,500 as an initial deposit, and then $3,000 a year over three years. We hope to make money, but you never can tell about the Bahamas. We have some trepidation about how the press will handle the idea of members going in together to buy an island in the Bahamas, especially with the drug traffic problem there.

Later I met with students from North Miami Beach Senior High School and after a photo opportunity, I took them to the Members Dining Room for snacks and cold drinks. I know the students appreciated it, but I am not so sure that the dining room waiters were particularly appreciative. Fortunately the dining room was not too busy as it was past the usual rush for lunch. I stayed with the group awhile, giving the students a chance to quiet down as they do become restless.

With the group settled, I left them in the dining room and returned to the office to meet Dave Bockorney, who was waiting for me with his clients who have an interest in a Jamaican project. Our meeting was scheduled with Julian Dixon in his office. At the meeting, Julian suggested combining old AID funds that Jamaica had accumulated, but not spent, with new U.S.-AID funds to build the infrastructure for the project that Bockorney's clients want to build there. If we can have some success in bringing this project about, it would be a helpful boost to Jamaica's dire economic problems; and with Julian so interested in the welfare of Jamaica, Bockorney and his clients have a good ally.

I saw Jamie Whitten and he talked about a transportation project he has in Mississippi. He was supposed to be at our subcommittee supplemental markup yesterday but didn't show, and we don't have the language he wanted. Nonetheless, Whitten is chairman of our full committee, so we will have to take his language and run it by the subcommittee members for approval so that next week the language will be in our bill when it comes to the full committee. Such is the special privilege of the Dean of the House.

APRIL 29 FRIDAY

Channel 7's interview with me yesterday was televised on the 6:00 news last evening, and Admiral Yost complimented me in a news story yesterday. Transportation Secretary Jim Burnley called to thank me for finding the $60 million for the Coast Guard. Jim said he is going to Miami tomorrow to visit Coast Guard facilities there, and during his press conference he intends to say a few words about me. In the markup I had helped not only the Coast Guard but also the FAA, and the Secretary of Transportation knew this.

The House did a lot of work this week on the Armed Services Defense Authorization Bill. There was an amendment almost every ten minutes, which had me running back and forth to the Floor to vote. During one of the Floor votes, Charlie Wilson invited me to a dinner party next Tuesday at his home.

APRIL 30 SATURDAY

Dante Fascell and I were both in our offices this Saturday morning. We talked about the trip to the Madeira Islands and to Ireland and I called my grandson Sean, who is touring in France, to see if he could leave France for a few days to meet us in Ireland. He was not sure, but said he would try.

John Bryant (D-TX) told me on the Floor yesterday that the funds request by Dallas Mayor Annette Strauss at the outside witnesses hearing is a long way from having wide support in Dallas and that the project for mass transit is in trouble locally. Texas member Marty Frost had testified and then introduced Mayor Strauss at the hearing in support of the funding request, and in answer to inquiries about local support, they said there was no major problem within the community. It will now be a big problem if the community is not united in this effort, as there is no point in appropriating funds for a project without the community's approval. Art Roberts, a friend and lobbyist for Dallas transit, is putting the word out that I am for what the community wants.

When I spoke to Lucy during the week about Logan Airport in Boston, we agreed that I will need to tell Bob Carr that I have to support the Logan Airport position on general aviation regulations. We are trying to bring Carr around on the Logan problem. Massachusetts member Joe Moakley, with seniority on the Rules Committee, knows that I am working on Carr to dissuade him from offering an amendment to eliminate funding for the Massport because Massport has raised the general aviation fee. Ed Markey is also working on Bob Carr as is Norman Mineta. Even if Carr gets his way in the Appropriations Committee, Joe Moakley can eliminate Carr's amendment in the Rules Committee.

It has been a busy week and I am thankful that today is slow. I called my tennis buddies and we got together for a good match. Joan is in town this weekend and later we are going out to dinner and a movie. Representative Don Bosco from Sonoma County sent me, as promised, three bottles of white wine.

Chapter 17

MAY 1, 1988 - SUNDAY

Joan and I had a very nice time today at John and Karen Riley's azalea party in the yard of their home in suburban Virginia. They have this very beautiful party every year when the flowers are in full bloom. As Administrator of the Federal Railroad Administration, John had lots of congressional members and government officials there, including Admiral Yost who again thanked me for the additional $60 million for Coast Guard operations.

MAY 2 MONDAY

Dante Fascell and I at breakfast in the Rayburn Cafeteria ruminated over the story in today's *Washington Post* on Roy Dyson of Maryland. His administrative aide allegedly committed suicide and the story implies homosexual activities in Roy's office. The *Washington Post* has a huge staff of investigative reporters and, as Dante said, if the *Post* wanted to go after any of us, it could literally destroy your career in one day.

Our office is still working to get the four children whose ages range from 16 months to 9 years out of Santo Domingo. It has been two weeks since Barney Frank wrote to Rom Mazzoli, Chair of Judiciary's Subcommittee on International Law, Immigration and Refugees, clarifying the interpretation of his adoption amendment, and I have yet to see any results. Rom was to write to the INS the moment he received Barney's letter and to send me a copy of the INS letter that he wrote. Seeing both Barney and Rom on the House Floor today, I let them know of my disappointment in the progress so far, and reminded Rom that I had not received, as promised, a copy of the letter he supposedly sent to the INS. Barney's amendment dealt specifically with U.S. servicemen adopting sons and daughters born out of wedlock in Southeast Asia, and Rom only has to make the necessary distinction. It is a constant struggle, and I have to keep pushing on this so that both Frank and Mazzoli will get moving on the problem.

And when I spoke with Les AuCoin of Oregon, he said he is going to offer an "add-on" amendment in the Defense Subcommittee on Wednesday for the Coast Guard. As another approach Charlie Bennett tells me he will offer a Floor amendment to reduce the SDI "Star Wars" by $600 million and, our subcommittee can then offer an amendment to the amendment to take $250 million of the $600 million reduction for the Coast Guard for drug interdiction. So much is going on with the Coast Guard. Dennis Eckart from Ohio, for instance, is unhappy about the Coast Guard base closing on Lake Erie in his district. I cannot help him in the 1988 supplemental, and I really do not think that the base will reopen in 1989. I told Dennis that I would see if there was any backdoor way we could help and also avoid opening up the floodgates of other requests from members such as Chicago's John Porter and Baltimore's Steny Hoyer, and for a base closed in New Jersey in the late Jim Howard's district.

Perhaps because of my bout with cancer, people sometimes bring me their medical problems. Sid Yates told me that his wife, Addie, is having a difficult time with the blood transfusions so necessary in treating her cancer. Apparently her veins are worn thin. Sid is also worried because he is to go in for a biopsy and does not want Addie to know. And Bob Carr in the gym showed me the lump on his arm that was scheduled for a CAT scan. Carr was dreading the intake of dye used to distinguish the lump under scanning, saying that the dye made him feel bad. "You don't need a CAT scan for that," I said, "but a needle biopsy." Carr was pleased to hear this, and is now going to the Capitol Physician's Office to see if he can have the needle biopsy instead. [He followed my advice, and everything was okay, as the cyst was benign.]

MAY 3 TUESDAY

We had a Democratic Caucus in Dave Obey's office this morning on our Foreign Operations markup, a preliminary to the actual markup on Thursday. After the caucus, Adele spoke to me about funds for refugee resettlement in Israel, saying that as long as the subcommittee staff puts it in fiscal 1988, "Why don't we ask for the $5 million increase instead of compromising at $2.5 million." I went back and presented this proposal to Dave Obey, who said he did not mind if we made the $5 million request for 1988. We also talked about the language that Larry Smith wants included to prevent our aid recipient countries from buying sugar from Cuba. I told Dave that I personally was not for punishing the people of Cuba or of other Communist countries but would go with whatever made it easier for him to pass the bill, and that he could let me know.

After lunch, the Tunisian Ambassador came in to discuss the problems caused by plaguing locusts in his country and the resulting bad crops. When I informed the Ambassador that I would help by putting in our markup report language directing AID to give top priority to their agricultural problem, he thanked me and then cautioned me about other problems in Tunisia following the assassination there last month of a PLO leader. He also boasted a bit about the good transition Tunisia had made from the late to the present president. Afterwards, lobbyist Andy Manatos came in to talk about Cyprus problems in the Foreign Operations bill scheduled for markup on Thursday regarding aid to Greece and Turkey.

On the House Floor for a vote, I saw Charlie Wilson and he assured me that we are going to do the trip to Madeira. With the trip now confirmed, I went to see Terry Peel to ask if he would be able to accompany me. But before I could put the question to him, Terry said, "I have a deal for you on increasing the refugee assistance for Israel from $25 million to $27.5 million," and that I should wait and offer the $2.5 million increase in the full committee tomorrow in the supplemental markup for 1988 instead of in the 1989 bill. On my reporting this to Adele, she was not very happy, so it was back again to Terry Peel in the subcommittee office.

At 4:30, Charlie Wilson, Richard Barnett and I met in Charlie's office to discuss Barnett's *New Yorker* article about Afghanistan. After introducing Barnett to Charlie, I soon left, as the meeting was beyond my understanding of the problems in Afghanistan, on which Charlie is an authority.

Back on the House Floor for a vote, I spoke with John Bryant about the trouble in Dallas with DART - Dallas Area Rapid Transit. John said that when he appeared before our subcommittee he did not realize that forty percent of DART was going to be in his district, and now he has told DART that the people in his district had to be satisfied on the route or he would oppose the request. Apparently DART is trying to satisfy Bryant but if it fails to do so, I do not think Marty Frost is going to make a request this year for the $15 million that Dallas wants. Joe Moakley, who is anxious about funds for Massport (Massachusetts Port Authority), said to me in not so subtle terms, that "Massport is very important to me and to your subcommittee," intimating that we have authorizing language in our subcommittee bill that has to be protected by the Rules Committee. Bob Carr in our transportation markup is going to present the biggest problem for Massport. Carr, a small plane buff, argues that the Massport plan, raising landing fees for small planes, is discriminatory to their pilots. So I must reconcile Moakley's and Carr's positions to prevent a Rules Committee problem.

In the evening at Dave Obey's fundraiser held at the National Democratic Club, I spent time talking to Dave's wife Joan, and his aide Mary Schecklehoff. Dave and I are still working for earmarked refugee assistance funds to Israel. I am not going to request the $5 million in the supplemental, but try for the $2.5 million in the 1989 bill so that I won't have to offer in full committee a $2.5 million increase to the 1988 supplemental bill. Leaving the Obey's, I went to Bob Carr's fundraiser reception at the historic Edward Simon Lewis House, and then to Charlie Wilson's party, at his condo, for the Japanese parliamentarians. We waited for Appropriations Defense Subcommittee Chairman, Bill Chappell, to arrive. Chappell never called but did come after dinner when, unfortunately, the Japanese had already left. It was a nice party, with good food, and all the proper toasts were made. As usual at Charlie's, attractive young women were seated on each side of me, which made the evening quite pleasant.

MAY 4 WEDNESDAY

The House Democrats caucused this morning with Jesse Jackson, and I think it was good that he spoke. I am guessing that he was there to pick up any super delegates that he could, but I do not think he changed anyone's position, although he did receive a couple of ovations. Later in the morning, at the Foreign Operations Democratic Caucus in Dave Obey's office, everything seemed to be coming together pretty well. Adele tells me that in Israel the new housing for the Ethiopian Jewish refugee resettlement will be named after me or any member of my family, and I want it to be named after my late daughter Kathryn Lehman Weiner. David Bockerney called about language in the Foreign Ops bill to aid the Jamaican project. Julian Dixon had evidently heard that I would go with him to Jamaica to look at the project, and perhaps in late June or July we will make the trip.

Tony Costa in Miami called urging me to support Larry Smith's amendment. Larry had spoken to me on the Floor about this amendment that he and Tony want me to offer in the Foreign Ops markup, prohibiting countries that receive U.S. foreign assistance from buying sugar from Communist countries, especially sugar from Cuba. I have already informed Larry, who put this language in last year's authorizing bill, that I did not feel one way or the other, and if Dave Obey wants me to support the amendment, I will. Regarding Egypt buying sugar from Cuba, Dante Fascell, Chairman of the authorizing Foreign Affairs Committee, does not want authorizing language in the appropriation bill language because it would weaken the chances for his authorization bill being passed this year. We could, of course, offer the language later in Appropriations if his authorization bill is passed. I informed Tony Costa on all of the ramifications, and he understands now that at present the language will not be in either authorization or appropriations.

I have definitely backed off trying for the $5 million in the 1988 supplemental for refugee assistance, and we will settle for the $2.5 million in the 1989 bill. Dave Obey told me and Matt McHugh (D-NY) that the White House will sign his Foreign Operations bill as it is now drawn, and he could probably get it signed into law as a free-standing bill and not as part of the Continuing Resolution. This was pretty good maneuvering on Dave's part. He offered me the $5 million add-on in the supplemental next week for additional refugee assistance, but as I really do not need the political benefit, I will let Bob Mrazek offer the amendment for Israeli resettlement funds.

This afternoon with California member Leon Panetta and Florida member Andy Ireland, we tried to unify the coastal states' position for a moratorium extension on offshore oil drilling and to have a joint letter to Sid Yates for his Interior Subcommittee markup so that Yates would know that the congressional delegations from Oregon, Washington, California and Florida, as well as Massachusetts, favor continuing the moratorium on offshore drilling. This is doubly important to Dante Fascell because most of the endangered coastal Florida area is just north of his Florida Keys district.

I spoke to Charlie Wilson on the Floor, and he thought his party last night was "all right"; he was not as unhappy that Bill Chappell came late as I thought he would be. Florida member Charlie Bennett's SDI reduction amendment passed on the Floor today, which will provide $600 million for the Department of Defense to the ACI (Acquisition, Construction and Improvement) account of the Coast Guard. Armed Services Committee Chair, Les Aspin, also has an amendment planned that would transfer Department of Defense funds back to the Coast Guard. These Department of Defense funds are in accounts that are already funded up to the President's request. The problem is that although $350 million is provided for the Coast Guard, Aspin is itemizing the amendment language to the kinds of line items not needed by the Coast Guard, such as for helicopters and other equipment not included in the President's budget. When Aspin's amendment comes up again for debate, I plan a colloquy on the Floor with him so that he can explain for the record that the funds in his amendment can be utilized by the Coast Guard where it sees best. When Aspin goes to conference with his committee counterpart in the Senate, he could state that the amendment obligates the funds not just to the ACI account but also to Coast Guard operations. I spoke to Aspin about this and to his staff person, who told me that the reason Aspin is offering the amendment was to enable members to vote for "drug wars" instead of "star wars."

MAY 5 THURSDAY

This morning on the Floor I did my colloquy with Les Aspin on the Coast Guard amendment. The colloquy was just to request that Aspin, in conference, keep the Department of Defense funds for the Coast Guard flexible, and not lock the funds into any specific programs. Unfortunately, Michelle on Les's staff had called the Coast Guard asking for a "shopping list" on where to spend this money without even checking with our subcommittee or the Maritime authorizing committee. She just included what the Coast Guard asked her to include, and that is not the way Les or his staff should have dealt with this. As a result, the matter was handled very carelessly.

At the Foreign Ops markup today, I increased the $25 million earmarked for Israeli refugee resettlement. The administration had requested $10 million, the Chairman earmarked $25 million, and I got it up to $27.5 million. It was a good markup, not too many surprises, and I was happily successful in putting in bill language for all of the other items on my agenda, i.e., Florida State University for the Caribbean island countries legal codification unification; Florida Power and Light to be the electric energy consultant in the Caribbean; a Jamaican project which David Bockerny brought to my attention; and Larry Smith's project regarding Nova University in Broward County, enabling Nova to have satellite broadcasting of educational programs in the Caribbean.

Jerry Lewis of California, second ranking minority member on the Foreign Ops Subcommittee, asked me at the markup about including in my transportation bill money for an airport in his district. Members know when I am marking up and often ask, "Is my item in your bill?" not realizing, of course, how little money there is to spread around.

At the end of the Foreign Ops session, we all saluted ranking minority member Jack Kemp, who is leaving the Congress after finishing his presidential effort. Jack has served on the Foreign Operations Subcommittee ever since I have been a member, and we all appreciate his efforts. He said that ever since he was a young boy he wanted to run for president in the worst way, "and I did," he said, "in the worst way."

Bill Gray, passing me in a Capitol Building corridor, said smilingly, "I am jealous of you," referring to his seeing me with Katherine Karpoff at a reception. Everyone likes Katherine. I also saw Judge Mikva and told him that Janet Studley asked about him, and he was pleased. When I told him that Janet had broken up with Senator George Mitchell, he said, "Well tell her to call me," but he was kidding. At the office, colleague Frederick Boucher, a young Democrat from Virginia, came in as he needs help on southwest Virginia airports. I will put language in our bill requesting the FAA in their AIP Program to give his airports priority, but I may have problems as the subcommittee staff does not want to earmark airports in this manner. Tom and Greg have complained that they also frequently get such requests from the members.

In the evening I wined and dined on the excellent food at the East German Embassy at its reception hosted by the East German Ambassador and Mrs. Gerhard Herder in honor of Hermann Axen, member of the Political Bureau and Secretary of the Central Committee of the Socialist Unity Party of Germany and Chairman of the Committee of Foreign Relations of the People's Chamber of the GDR. Axen is the equivalent of the Foreign Minister but more powerful. A recent article had appeared in the *New York Times* about Rabbi Neuman leaving East Germany, and that the Jewish community in East Germany is trying for a younger Rabbi. Chairman Axen and I talked about this, and my commitment to find another and younger Rabbi to serve the East German Jewish community. Axen is quite an impressive political figure. The diplomatic corps at the reception from the socialist bloc countries was also impressive.

MAY 6 FRIDAY

Washington lawyer Maury Markowitz met with me at breakfast in the Rayburn Cafeteria this morning. Maury is a sophisticated, bright Washington "hustler," in the kindest sense, whose speciality is entrepreneurial law. He had worked for Norman Braman in Miami and for Congressman Hamilton Fish, and he also did some work for former Florida Senator Paula Hawkins. We had an interesting conversation about the automobile business. He came back to the office with me and I got my son Bill on the phone for them to talk. I met Maury several nights ago at the Bob Carr reception; he and Bob are old friends, and I really enjoyed our visit together.

There wasn't much happening in the office today. I placed a call to Southeastern Medical Center, an osteopathic hospital in North Miami Beach, where I was heard over a PA system in the medical center's auditorium congratulating the Dean and his group on receiving a $2.1 million award for their health education centers in the rural areas of Central Florida. Through my connection with the Appropriations Subcommittee staff on Labor, Health and Human Services, I was partly instrumental in obtaining this grant. The original plans were for me to be there in person, but I didn't go to Miami this weekend. It was a three-minute remote conversation, which Jeff arranged, and it worked out just fine.

Joan arrived from Miami this afternoon, and in the evening we went to see *The Merchant of Venice* at the Folger Theatre.

MAY 7 SATURDAY

Jeff called to say that Reubin Askew dropped out of the Senate race. A few minutes later, I received a call from Dan Mica saying, "Okay, you said if Askew dropped out you would help me, so I'm asking you to keep your word." "I did say that," I told Mica, "and put me down as an endorsement." I do not think I will be too active in the campaign right now because it sounds like my friend Buddy MacKay is also running, and between Dan and Buddy, who is sure to ask for my endorsement. I don't care who wins. Buddy has been shopping around for a statewide political office for which to run, and has not been consistent. Dan is more consistent of the two, but I think Buddy would make the better Senator.

MAY 8 SUNDAY

Thinking today about the withdrawal of Reubin Askew from the Senate race and my promise to Dan Mica that if Reubin got out I would back him, I have no choice but to tell Buddy MacKay that I cannot support anyone except Mica. I will, however, do this very low key. Also, I will go ahead with our planned Miami meeting Friday morning with the condo leaders, even though Askew will now cancel his appearance. If I cannot get someone like Senator Graham, we will probably just not have a special guest.

MAY 9 MONDAY

Today was one of my easiest on the Hill. In the morning lobbyist Hector Alcalde came in regarding a bridge to an island in the St. John's River at Jacksonville. Last year for this our subcommittee earmarked $5 million, and now funds are needed to continue the project.

In the evening Joan and I attended a reception for Elliott Abrams, the Assistant Secretary of State for Inter-American Affairs, hosted by David Rockefeller, Chairman of the Council of the Americas. I think I was the only member of Congress there. Abrams is really a loathsome person and on the side of the dictators in Central America. It was, however, a good party, and we had our photo taken with David Rockefeller. The affair was held in the beautiful Benjamin Franklin Room at the Department of State, and the view from the top of the State Department is spectacular. There we met by accident our friend from the American Embassy in Paris, John Berg, and his wife Francoise, who were in the downstairs lobby. Joan and I took them up to the reception and they were thrilled. John and Francoise had just been vacationing in Florida and will be returning to Paris on Saturday.

MAY 10 TUESDAY

8:00 a.m., at a breakfast hosted by the Florida Electrical

Power coordinating group, Dick Sewell of FP&L was there to discuss the electric utilities position on acid rain legislation. The three oldest members in the delegation, Claude Pepper, Charlie Bennett and myself, were the only members to show up. I did not stay to eat, but went to the Rayburn Cafeteria instead. My eating habits have changed. When I first came to Washington and my office was on the fourth floor of the Cannon Building, I used to go to the Members Dining Room in the Capitol for lunch; then I found there was a special dining room in the Capitol with a Democratic table "for members only," and I would go there and catch up on things. I learned about the legislative process by listening to then-icons on the Hill like Phil Burton and Wayne Hayes, who sat around the table talking about what was happening in the House. It was an education. I no longer go there but to the Rayburn Building Cafeteria, as it is right below my office; we moved from the Cannon to the Rayburn Building during either my third or fourth term in office. Many of the Rayburn Cafeteria employees now come to me with their various problems while I am eating in the cafeteria, which has become a distraction. Recently I do mostly carry out from the Rayburn Cafeteria or brown bag from my house and eat most of my lunches in the office.

Reubin Askew called to thank me for supporting him and to explain why he got out of the Senate race, saying that it was the high cost of running for office and he did not want to raise the necessary $5 million. I told Reubin that I did not blame him, and that I had been happy to support him and understood his reasons for getting out. He will be at the North Dade Forum luncheon in Miami Friday to speak about election reform, but has cancelled his appearance at the condo leaders brunch where I was to officially endorse him.

At the Congressional Arts Caucus luncheon, actress Kelly McGillis from the *Merchant of Venice* production now at the Folger was the honored guest. McGillis was very down-to-earth and unpretentious, which perhaps accounts for my telling her that I thought the actor for Bassanio was too immature and the actor for Antonio too macho. She was still gracious enough to have a photo opportunity with me.

Mid-afternoon we had ten suspension votes, which took about two hours. Between votes I spoke to members on several issues, including Mazzoli, who again promised he would have the letter on the adoption problem. With the last vote I headed for home to pick up Joan for our trip to Dumbarton Oaks in Northwest Washington, D.C., for Harvard University's annual cocktail party given for Members of Congress who are Harvard alumni. President Derek Bok and his wife Sissela were there, as were Massachusetts members and some of my colleagues who attended Harvard such as Pat Schroeder, Mel Levine and Ham Fish. I think I am invited mistakenly, as my son Bill, also named William, graduated from Harvard Business School and Harvard thinks that he is the Member of Congress. But every year I get the invitation, and every year I attend. We stayed only for the reception, but before leaving a most interesting thing happened. While I was talking to a professor and his fifty-something wife, a member of the British Parliament, she suddenly looked very familiar. I asked her with what party she was affiliated, and her answer was the Socialist Democratic Party. I then asked if she knew Shirley Williams. She looked up at me and said, "I am Shirley Williams." How funny! I reminded her that we were together in Iran about 12-14 years ago at Persepolis. She too remembered, as Joan and I had arrived a day early and were already settled at the hotel in Isfahan when Shirley and the rest of the group arrived. Shirley was not feeling well and spent the afternoon in our hotel room while someone took care of checking her in at the hotel. She was the Margaret Thatcher of the Labor Party and if Labor had won, Shirley would be the Prime Minister today. I asked this very intelligent, funny lady how Margaret Thatcher was doing, and she said, "Unfortunately, too well."

We left Dumbarton Oaks and headed for the Moroccan Embassy for a dinner by Ambassador and Mrs. M'hamed Bargach in honor of New York Congressman and Mrs. Stephen Solarz. Some days before I was lobbied by Denis Neill and Stu Eisenstat to earmark $20 million in the economic security fund for Morocco. At that time I told them that I was not going to help because I had not been invited to the Moroccan Embassy in over five years. I was joking, of course, but out of it came this invitation. The dinner was fantastic, with lots of diplomats, press, and Jewish community leaders there from New York and Washington. The food, however, was the main attraction and everyone was in good spirit.

MAY 11 WEDNESDAY

The morning began with a Florida Delegation breakfast in one of the special dining rooms in the Rayburn Building. Our host was the Florida League of Financial Institutions. Bill Walker, Vice Chairman of the Board and Corporate Secretary of AmeriFirst Bank in Miami introduced me, and I spoke about current legislation of interest to their group. Bill is an old friend from Miami Shores and I have known the family for many years. I nominated Bill's son to the Naval Academy and he was accepted, but because of a head injury the Academy wanted to review him again. In so doing, they jerked him around so much that he decided to go to Pepperdine in California.

After the breakfast, I walked over to the Members Dining Room in the Capitol to meet Ruby Steiner, his wife Gladys, and some of their friends. Ruby is the condo leader from Aventura. I first took them on a short tour onto the House Floor and then out on the East front of the Capitol for a photo opportunity. We went back to the Members Dining Room where they ordered breakfast, and I left them there while I went to the Rayburn Building for the full Appropriations Committee markup of the Energy and Water bill. In the meantime, I had asked Barbara in my office to meet Ruby and his group in the dining room and bring them to the markup after they finished eating. They were there in good time to see how the appropriation process worked at the committee level, and afterwards commented on how interesting it all was.

At the office I met with constituents June Pruitt and her husband. June is a survivor of alternative cancer treatment therapy, and comes to see me every year. She also went through the "standard" cancer treatment program, and ended up weighing 85 pounds and having no hair. Now, looking at June, she seems to be in amazing health and as well as anyone. I left the office to meet with Florida executives of the National Association of Realtors, who were waiting for me in the Health and Human Services Subcommittee office. Gerri Fontanella from Miami Lakes in my district headed the group. I spoke to them for about fifteen minutes, addressing their concerns about banks going into the real estate business, and promised that I would try to make their reception this evening.

Mike Lemov and Don Randall of the National Glass Association, an auto service industry, came in at noon to discuss reworking state automobile inspections on a national basis. Their gimmick on automobile inspections would provide more safety, they said, although I have always thought that the biggest danger with automobiles was the condition of the driver and not the automobile. Many people depend on old junkers to get back and forth to work, and tougher inspection requirements may prevent some from doing so. As I shared these thoughts, they agreed, but were obviously committed to their ideas. Afterwards, the legislative representative from Delta Airlines in Washington and two top officials from Atlanta came in to discuss the need for additional funding for instrument landing systems in Orlando and Cincinnati, especially Orlando, as one control tower does not really serve both runways and a similar problem exists in Cincinnati.

I took a break and went for lunch on the Senate side for a change. On my return Linda Davis and Dave Johnson from Governor Martinez's Florida office were in to go over the offshore drilling studies. I merely restated my position as very much opposed to any offshore drilling that would create pollution or interfere with the environment.

4:00 p.m., the Greater Miami Chamber of Commerce people came in with Bill Cullom, Dorothy Weaver and Jim Batten. They talked about the kinds of protection legislation needed for Miami against the cost of another influx of refugees, perhaps this time from Central America. South Florida does not have the votes in Congress to take care of what is considered a local problem. I told them if Claude Pepper, Chair of the Rules Committee, would put a self-executing clause in one of the rules, which is germane to a refugee bill or a health bill or whatever would provide federal assistance, this would be a way to incorporate a rule into the legislation. I cannot do anything on this in Foreign Ops because our subcommittee funds $300 million in assistance for refugees that only go to other countries, like those from Afghanistan, for instance, that go to Pakistan. We also appropriate for Israeli refugee assistance. But in our bill we do not give assistance to refugees after they find their way into the United States. That assistance, I told them, would need to come from the Appropriations Subcommittee on Labor, Education and Health.

Next was Lou Gerber from the Communication Workers of America. AT&T laid off many of its employees and, according to Lou, it was now hiring people off the street and people laid off by the Baby Bell systems. He wants to force AT&T to first rehire its own ex-employees, but I do not want to get caught between labor and the management at AT&T. AT&T now is competing with other companies, and if it paid its workers more money it would make AT&T noncompetitive.

We had a lot of votes today on the Armed Services bill. Something quite out of the ordinary for me, I voted for final passage on the Armed Services authorization bill, but only because the bill had designated $350 million for the Department of Transportation for the Coast Guard. When the House Appropriations Defense Subcommittee goes to conference with the Senate Defense Subcommittee, I want the Coast Guard language protected, and I did not see how I could ask for that protection without voting for final passage of the bill. The bill passed by 100 votes anyway. I just hate to see $300 billion for defense expenditures when there are cuts in domestic spending.

At the Unisys Corporation reception this evening, I went primarily to see Mike Blumenthal, Unisys CEO. I knew Mike when he was Secretary of the Treasury under President Jimmy Carter, and we became friends. I also met someone there who had worked for Burroughs (now a part of Unisys) in Miami, back when I was using the Burroughs seisomatic bookkeeping machine in my used cars business. It was a nice event, featuring Apalachicola oysters from Florida, which are my favorite.

Later at the Brasserie for a light supper, I ran into Pete Stark and his daughter Sarah and we talked for a while about his coming to Miami to speak to my condo leaders and to the Miami health care leadership. I offered to get him an honorarium, but he is already over the honorarium limit for this year. As Chairman of the Subcommittee on Health of the Ways and Means Committee, Pete probably receives and accepts many speaking requests, which usually come with an honorarium. He said he would like to come to Miami, particularly if it would help me, and if he were to receive an honorarium it could be made out to a charity. We will try to work out a visit in late June or early July. Our conversation then turned to the presidential election, with Pete asking whom I wanted for vice president. I said Rep. Lee

Hamilton, and Pete thought Lee would be a marvelous vice president. I named George Brown of California as my second choice, and Pete agreed that George was a good choice, especially if he were to lose about ten pounds.

Home by 9:30 p.m., Joan was still out with Wynne at the Kennedy Center to see the Alvin Ailey ballet. I did not want to go.

MAY 12 THURSDAY

At the Appropriations full committee markup this morning, we voted out legislation for the military construction appropriation bill. I spoke to Labor, Health and Human Services, and Education Subcommittee Chairman Bill Natcher about funds in his subcommittee appropriation bill for the Centers for Disease Control for trauma study, and Natcher said maybe $10 or $20 million had been appropriated. One reason Natcher provided for the Centers was that he wants a new bridge over the Ohio River at Owensboro, which is earmarked in our transportation bill. I saw Republican Florida member Clay Shaw, and he understands that I cannot make a commitment to him about a tunnel in Ft. Lauderdale. If we have the money, and if he would come around to our side and not support off budget for the highway trust fund, then I may try to appropriate for his Ft. Lauderdale tunnel.

Tom Luken told me that his Energy and Commerce Subcommittee on Transportation and Hazardous Waste did have the authorization language in place in the rail safety bill's conference report, enabling the City Gas Company to reapply to the Department of Transportation for the cost of moving its gas tanks away from the Amtrak station in Miami. This project has been ongoing for several years, and maybe now Sid Langer is satisfied. I also saw Barney Frank on the Floor and told him that I still had not received the INS letter that Mazzoli keeps promising.

In response to our subcommittee requesting a report from the FAA on the joint use of military airports, Quinton Taylor, the FAA Deputy Administrator for Airports, came in this afternoon to discuss the issue. Staff members from the offices of Bob Carr and Dick Durbin were also at the meeting, and I think we now have people in the administration giving this matter serious attention.

The Florida U.S. Senate race is cause for some excitement among Miami residents. Jay Weiss from Miami, one of my main supporters, called to ask whom I was supporting, and I told him I would not be active in any campaign, but that I was voting for Dan Mica. Jay said he too was voting for Mica. At 5:00 p.m., I took an Eastern flight to Miami, and John Smith, a lawyer with Steel, Hector and Davis, was on the plane and asked the same question. When I told him that I was voting for Dan Mica, Smith said he was voting for Buddy MacKay. Sitting next to John was Dr. Willie Robinson, President of Florida Memorial College, who confirmed that next month the dedication of the William Lehman Aviation Science Building at Florida Memorial would take place.

MAY 13 FRIDAY

Our condo leaders brunch was held this morning at Turnberry, and rather than go without a guest speaker, we decided to invite Frank Mann, campaigning for the Democratic nomination for Florida Secretary of State against Jim Smith. Frank seemed to be well liked and got a good reception at the brunch, but he talked too long. Clara Oesterle was there, as was Florida State Senator Gwen Margolis. I am, of course, endorsing Clara in her reelection for Metro Commissioner, but not Gwen. Gwen is an effective legislator but I am supporting David Young, a friend of mine campaigning for Gwen's seat, whom I feel I could work with very well in the State legislature. Needless to say, Gwen was a little annoyed with me.

Annie Ackerman was there, as was Joe Plotnick. I still see Joe as eccentric, but he does have a constituency at the Century 21 condo and controls a batch of votes. Joe works many causes, one being to help free Anne and Jay Pollard, the latter sentenced in 1986 to life in prison on charges of spying for Israel while working as a civilian analyst for U.S. Naval Intelligence. Anne Pollard was convicted on charges of conspiracy and accessory after the fact, receiving five years on each count to run concurrently. I told Joe I would try to help on a humanitarian basis as apparently the wife, Anne, is quite ill, suffering from a chronic stomach ailment. My usual policy, however, in dealing with judicial matters is basically "hands off," and in this particular case, I am sure any attempted intervention would only fall on deaf ears.

One other cause for Joe is, of course, his commitment to doing something about the Florida East Coast Railway and the whistles that blow at railroad crossings, seeking to move the FEC roadbed somewhere else.

Tomorrow is our Black Leadership Brunch at Turnberry, and Patrice has already been to the airport to pick up our honored guest, Atlanta member John Lewis, and taken him to get settled before our dinner tonight at Williams Island. Stocky and chubby, John exudes a lot of self-confidence. At dinner John told us about his experiences in the 1960's with Rev. Martin Luther King and the civil rights movement, about Selma Sheriff Jim Clark, and about his marching on the Pettus Bridge and being arrested. John was also in the hotel in Los Angeles with Bobby Kennedy when he was shot and talked about how devastating it was. It was fascinating to hear him talk about Bobby Kennedy and what might have been had he lived.

MAY 14 SATURDAY

The turnout for the Black Leadership Brunch was the best we have ever had. Sherry from our staff sang the Lord's Prayer. I introduced John and he spoke about his many experiences, both during and after the civil rights movement. He went over very well, very interesting, and afterwards there was a question and answer period. Miami businessman Al Dotson, one of John's friends from Morehouse College in Atlanta was there, and we took all the usual photographs. It was a really good event.

The wedding of attorney Marty Fine's son was held this evening at Temple Israel. Failing to note that the invitation read "Black Tie," I went down in a white sport coat and then had to double back home to put on a tuxedo for the dinner. I sat at a table that included many of my supporters, and met Leonard Miller of Lennar Corporation, whose company is the largest in Florida home building. Perhaps I have gained another supporter.

MAY 15 SUNDAY

In the morning before my afternoon flight back to Washington, I spoke before a group of about 150 men and women at the Temple Adath Yashuran Men's Club. Al Entin, a former campaign opponent, gave me a great introduction, and my remarks seemed to go over well with the audience. Before leaving I spoke to Rabbi Simcha Friedman and invited him to Washington to again give the invocation in the House of Representatives. The Rabbi had done this several years ago at my invitation. Today he seemed interested, but said he would let me know.

MAY 16 MONDAY

Tom, Lucy and I went over our markup scheduled for next week. The subcommittee members all have their wish lists in, and we do not need to have a Democratic caucus on our transportation bill before marking up. Some things we agreed on were to put approximately $100 million into highway demonstration projects this year, and try not to take on too many transit new starts that are lightly front loaded but heavily committed in the out years. It sounds easy enough, but we will see.

Later in the day I went to a couple of receptions because of supporters and constituents who are in town and expect to see me there. At the telecommunications reception, I saw Representative John Lewis who reiterated how much he enjoyed his trip to Miami. Dave Walker of Bell South was there and introduced me to many of the other Bell South directors. I had seen Dave earlier when he stopped by my office. Mark Hollis of Publix Supermarkets and other business leaders from the South were there. At the American International Automobile Association reception, I met up with Jim Evans representing his Mercedes dealership and Frank Bolton representing his Toyota dealership - both from my area - in addition there was Irv Lebow of Burt Kahn's Toyota dealership.

MAY 17 TUESDAY

Transportation Secretary Jim Burnley came in this morning with Larry Coughlin to talk about the joint use of military airports, and we pretty much agreed that we are all working toward the same goal to make this happen. Jim thanked me for helping with the $60 million supplemental appropriation for the Coast

Guard and said that he hoped this money in the supplemental would not be earmarked other than for how it was now designated and, more specifically, that the funds were not to be earmarked to reopen the Coast Guard bases closed in places like Ohio and Chicago, for instance.

I went over our bill with Lucy to sort out the way in which we are to use the contract authority rescission to relieve restrictions on our budget authority. Everything is up in the air right now in trying to stay within the subcommittee's 302B allocation, but I do have a better understanding of how we are manipulating this money to increase funds for the Coast Guard and the FAA without adversely impacting Amtrak and mass transit. I do not think we will have too much trouble with this in our subcommittee or in full committee, but on the Floor members on the authorizing Public Works Committee might object to the game we are playing with trust fund contract authority limitations. Though the highway and aviation funds will remain in the trust account, reducing the limitations will relieve pressure on budget outlays for Amtrak and mass transit.

At 4:30, AIPAC members arrived. Among them was Bill Ullman, the son of the Bill Ullman who was my son Bill's good friend when they went to Temple Israel together. The son attends Williams College in Massachusetts and is a big supporter of Israel, telling me that he is going there soon. Occasionally, it is hard for me to keep family generations in order, as I thought *he* was my son Bill's friend at Temple Israel. "No," he said, "that was my father." Time goes by quickly. Muriel Russell was also in the group, and mentioned again how much she appreciates what my son Bill has done for the Michael-Ann Russell Center, her daughter's memorial at the Jewish Community Center in North Dade. A woman with Muriel who lives in North Dade at the Palm Bay Club reminded me that I had helped her when she was searching for an attorney to handle her divorce.

With this an election year and Joan wanting to remain at home, I have decided to forego the trip to Ireland and Madeira. I have already told the committee staff putting the trip together, and they were all disappointed but not too surprised. Members often bow out of these trips for one reason or another, and I suspect the committee staffs are used to it.

Dan Mica in the gym asked me to tell Jeff to be low key on

Bill Gunter, for whom Jeff is working, because he thinks Gunter is going to get blown out of the water by the press. I will tell Jeff to be careful.

The newsletter that went out on the use of animal medical experimentation is getting good response, especially from animal lovers. I had been eagerly awaiting the response because of the controversy surrounding the issue, and I was a little apprehensive about sending the newsletter. I have to tell John to mail a copy to Dr. Carrie Walters in Arizona, as she will be interested in how the newsletter turned out. It was largely her concern that got me interested and started on the subject.

No evening events for me because at some point during the day I developed a bad case of laryngitis, hardly able to speak above a whisper.

MAY 18 WEDNESDAY

Les AuCoin and Marty Sabo have done all they can as members on Appropriations Defense Subcommittee to make the funds from the Department of Defense to the Department of Transportation for the Coast Guard more flexible. They had some problems, and they were not able to keep the funds as discretionary as they had wanted, but at least Transportation got $300 million and perhaps we can work around some of the imposed restrictions.

Sid Yates on the Floor asked for my help with Florida Senator Lawton Chiles on the environmental clean-coal legislation. "There is no way I can deal with Lawton," I said to Sid, "as far as I know he listens to no one." Lawton, who chairs the Senate Budget Committee, is also having a problem with House Budget Committee Chairman Bill Gray.

For lunch I met Larry Smith, Tony Costa, Jorge Mas, and Jonathan Slade in the Members Dining Room to discuss TV Marti. I offered to help providing there was no opposition from Neal Smith, Chairman of Appropriations Subcommittee on Commerce, Justice, State, and the Judiciary, that funds Voice of America and the Marti programs. Tony Costa and Jorge Mas were also pushing for language in our Foreign Ops bill that would cut funds to Egypt for buying sugar from Cuba. I told them I would not even attempt to submit the language unless they got

Dave Obey to support the effort, and that I would not bring it up in the full committee.

After lunch and still suffering with laryngitis, I stopped by the Capitol Physician's Office and felt better after some medication they administered to my throat. At the office I met with Dan O'Connell from Ryder Systems, who came in with Don Smith from Cassidy Associates and Dr. Martin Moore-Ede, a Washington consultant for the Institute for Human Alertness. They had testified at our Transportation Subcommittee hearing as outside witnesses for $3.5 million to come from the Secretary's office to create a simulated airplane cockpit and a simulated truck cab to test people for alertness and ability when operating at night with loss of sleep. This would be a $3.5 million windfall for their institute, matching the funds that the private sector is contributing.

Dorothy Wilkin from Palm Beach County, a candidate for the 14th Congressional District running for Dan Mica's seat, came in knowing that I am endorsing her opponent Harry Johnson. She wanted me to co-endorse, and I will not do that. I have known Harry Johnson for many years, and when he asked for my endorsement, I just said flat out, "Yes." Sometimes, though, the first to ask for support is the one you go with. I've known Dorothy for a long time as well, and if she had asked before Harry, she would probably be the one with my endorsement. When Dorothy left I called the new chairman of the American Jewish Committee to solicit his help in finding another Rabbi to serve in East Germany. Rabbi Neuman is definitely leaving, taking with him his new East German bride. I feel we must go forward on this and not waste time. The AJC chairman has certain reservations and thinks the East German government is using the Rabbi situation for its own benefit. Though I think the East German Jewish community needs a religious leader, what I hope to also come out of this are reparations from the East German government to the Jews who lost property there and to establish U.S.-East German trade relations that would help both the farmers in the United States and the East German industry. This then is more than just a Jewish religious effort, although the main priority is to have a Rabbi in place to help keep the community together and to bring nonpracticing Jews back into the East German Jewish community.

MAY 19 THURSDAY

Primarily because of the budget restrictions, Dave Obey's Foreign Operations Subcommittee markup took only about an hour this morning, the fastest we have ever gotten Foreign Operations reported out and ready for the full committee. The main contribution I made was the refugee resettlement assistance of $27.5 million that I arranged to have earmarked for Israel. I was involved in several other pieces of the legislation but that particular part was my priority. At the office was Len Williams of Bethlehem Steel who wanted to be sure of language in our bill for the Coast Guard's Great Lakes icebreaker (Mackinaw), to clear the way for iron ore shipments in the spring through the Great Lakes. With assurance that the language was in place, we talked about other matters. Len is an old friend, and one of the few black executives in the steel industry.

11:45, FAA Administrator Allan McArtor and Marty Pozesky, FAA Deputy Associate Administrator for Development and Logistics, came in to talk about the FAA's advanced automation system (AAS) and its funding needs. The air traffic computer contract award is coming up soon between Hughes and IBM. I am fairly certain that IBM will get the award, as the FAA and IBM have worked closely together over many years. It is too bad about Hughes. McArtor said both are very good and either would do a good job.

A kind of kooky black man from Houston named Ian Knight came in. Knight presents himself as chairman of the citizens advisory board to the Houston-Metropolitan Transit Authority, but is in reality a self-appointed ad hoc transportation person who really does not represent anyone. Even Houston member Mickey Leland warned me against him, as he had met Knight. I just listened him out.

With the Legislative Appropriations Bill on the Floor today, members were constantly going back and forth to the Floor to vote. There are always many amendments, primarily by Republicans, when it comes to legislative appropriations, as they want to eliminate congressional perks, like the House Beauty Shop, with the self-serving idea that it makes good propaganda broadcast over C-SPAN for them.

Bob Foster, staff chief of the Agriculture Appropriations

Subcommittee, told me he could arrange to have a top Department of Agriculture official come to Miami to talk to the rare tropical fruit people regarding a funding extension for the Agricultural Department property at Chapman Field, an experimental agriculture station. I forwarded the information to Stan Whitman, Dr. Bob McNaughton, and to Frank Smathers, the brother of former Senator George Smathers - all tropical fruit growers, but are mostly in Dante Fascell's district as is Chapman Field.

Joe Moakley is still riding my tail about funds for a University of Massachusetts program for Massport. Massport did not apply for a grant to the Department of Transportation and that may be a problem, but I will try to help Joe, even though it is not our fault. Our subcommittee staff does not like to help members who do not hold up their end of responsibility. I think I can work it out, but I will need support from our Democratic members. I have spoken to the subcommittee members and told them the situation with Massport and that I may have to finagle Joe Moakley $1.5 million though it is a lousy program. Moakley is ranking Democrat on the Rules Committee, and we cannot afford to make him too unhappy.

Calling the office of Dade County School Superintendent Joe Fernandez, I informed them that with laryngitis I was not feeling well and, unhappily, would not be able to co-host the reception this evening for the American Trauma Society. The reception is being held in the Rayburn Building at 6:00 p.m., but I am eager to get home to Miami and had my 8:00 p.m. flight reservation changed to 5:00 p.m. Dante Fascell, Larry Smith, Clay Shaw and other South Florida members were on the plane, so I do not think there were many present at the reception. The word should get out not to plan Thursday evening receptions as on Thursdays most members go back to their districts. I got home about 8:00, and went right to bed.

MAY 20 FRIDAY

In the morning at a Biscayne Boulevard area condo brunch at Turnberry, well over 100 people were there, including Annie Ackerman. It was really a love-in, as these are my people and my base, and I felt good because even with laryngitis I spoke well and did not appear to be ill. After a brief stint at the office, I went to the Intercontinental Hotel for lunch with Richard Friedman, who has been my antagonist on Metrorail issues. We are friendly personally and he makes a good case, but what bothered me at the lunch was that he asked a hotel employee to take a photo of us together. I don't think, however, that he will use it politically.

At 2:15, I went to the Immigration Naturalization Office to meet with Frank Parodi about the Arnold Rubin immigration case. Arnold has some relatives in Brazil that he is trying to get into the United States on permanent visa status. They can, of course, come on tourist visas, but not on permanent visas. They went from Europe to Brazil because no other country would take them at the time, and because Rubin is only a cousin we will have difficulty getting them to the United States from Brazil on permanent status. This means a great deal to Arnold, and I want to show him that I am giving it my best effort.

Perry Rivkind, head of the Miami Immigration Center, was next on my agenda in regard to the children from Santo Domingo. I am to meet with INS Commissioner Nelson next week in Washington about the children; in the meantime, I am trying to hit as many bases and solicit as much help as I can to apply pressure on INS. Rivkind said he would speak with the INS Commissioner, if he could get through to him in Washington. Afterwards, I headed for the Camillus House on 1st Avenue, arriving just before a huge semi-refrigerated truck-trailer with tons of high-quality groceries pulled up. Brother Paul Johnson runs Camillus House, a facility for the homeless, and does a great job of feeding and housing these people in downtown Miami. Television crews were there, and I was captured helping to unload the van. The groceries were provided by my good friend and supporter John Hart, President of Associates Groceries, whose son I had helped to obtain a "hardship" discharge from the Navy for reasons concerning his family's health. I was feeling very glad that I took the time to attend the American Grocers reception in Washington last month to bring all this about.

MAY 21 SATURDAY

Today began with a nostalgic brunch in Hialeah at the Miami

Lakes Country Club with about fifty of my old friends and used car customers from Hialeah. They have helped me in previous races and are friends of staffer Anna Thaxton who put this together; but I am not going to get a whole lot of votes out of Hialeah, as most do vote Republican. Then lunch at the Epworth Village, a Methodist retirement home in Hialeah, where many widows there were those of the husbands I knew when they were an important part of Miami, like the widow of George Holt, once a prominent judge, and Judge Herring's brother also resides there. Jerry Derbish does an excellent job in operating the home, and I was very happy to take part in celebrating its 40th anniversary. I had also put a statement in the *Congressional Record* in commemoration of the occasion.

MAY 22 SUNDAY

On the flight back to Washington today I was moved up to first class and I think it was because I was wearing an "I Love Eastern" button more than the fact that I am a frequent traveler. In Washington I met Sue Perry from the American Bus Association for dinner at the Brasserie and we discussed the problem she is having with the Long Beach, California, public transit. Sue represents private buses and Long Beach wants to rent its public buses for private charter. It is a complex situation made even more so by the problem existing between Public Works Committee Chairman, Glenn Anderson, who represents Long Beach, and the American Bus Association that does not want unfair competition from the public sector. Also APTA (American Public Transportation Association) wants public buses to compete in the private sector. I understand that UMTA is coming out with a regulation which limits public transit companies receiving UMTA funds to only compete in certain areas with the private bus sector, mainly with the handicapped or for charity events.

MAY 23 MONDAY

Pete Stark told me at tennis this morning that he is having problems with Congressman Claude Pepper's longterm health care bill. Apparently Pepper's bill provides longterm home health care without figuring out how to pay for it.

Seeing Lee Hamilton in the gym, I spoke to him about the possibility of his receiving the nomination for Vice President. "I would like to be Vice President," Lee said. When I first started talking about Lee as a Vice Presidential nominee, I thought I was the only one and maybe I was, but today in the weekly *Congressional Quarterly,* Lee was written up as the new top person for the second place on the ticket. My problem is that I have to support Bob Graham as a favorite son, and if I wrote to Dukakis in favor of Lee Hamilton I would have to have Bob Graham sign off first. Graham has already told me that he would not campaign for the position, but if it comes he would take it. Graham also knows of my strong opinion of Lee Hamilton for the position. I need to find out from Graham just how interested he really is, as I can't be with Lee if an old Florida friend like Bob Graham wants the nomination.

From 1:30 until 7:00 p.m., Tom, Greg, Lucy and I were in the subcommittee office going through our bill line item by line item in preparation for our markup tomorrow. We made lots of changes, some of which included increases to mass transit funds for Dallas and for Baltimore, and cutting back on some of Joe Moakley's requests. It was a long, drawn out process, but through juggling figures around, the major part of the bill I think will be acceptable to the subcommittee members, hopefully avoiding too much hassle during tomorrow's markup. Norman Dicks (D-WA) wants earmarked in our bill $1 million for Seattle to put transit tracks into one of the lanes in a Seattle highway tunnel. We will do it, and Norm can take the credit. I will let him know that it is done when we finish the markup and Norm will now help us on the Department of Defense funds for the Coast Guard.

At the Capitol Physician's Office, the doctor told me the chest x-rays that I took revealed no evidence of a tumor, but he did arrange an appointment for me at Bethesda Naval Hospital to have the cardiac surgeon examine my carotid artery for a problem I am having as a result of the radiation administered six years ago on my tumor area.

Bill Allen, a banking friend in Miami, called the office at 8:00 p.m., and was surprised that I was there to answer the phone. Bill is now CEO of Pan American Bank, and he wanted our staff to help locate one of his former college classmates from upstate New York for a reunion. We get all manner of calls in Washington.

MAY 24 TUESDAY

Ranking minority member Larry Coughlin and I met for a couple of hours this morning to go over the markup notes. Larry is easy to work with and we got everything done. Before Larry left, Norman Mineta, authorizing Chairman of the Aviation Subcommittee, called and was unhappy that we offset $250 million of budget authority by making a rescission in FAA's appropriation that had been authorized, but trapped by the trust fund obligation ceiling limitation. Around $400 million from previous years was so authorized but unavailable because our subcommittee had put the FAA Trust Fund obligation ceiling below the authorized obligated ceiling level. We rescinded that difference to have extra outlays to make an increase in FAA's appropriation in the facilities and equipment account. Although the money stayed in the same FAA pot, Mineta did not like the idea of infringing on his authorizing process. This is something we must protect in the Rules Committee, and our chances of doing so look good. If we lose, it means across-the-board cuts, which threaten projects of members on the Rules Committee, some of which include airports, highway demonstration projects, and the like.

Our markup began at 1:30 p.m., and it was probably the most difficult I have ever had. It was hard to keep some members under control - especially those who wanted to go off on tangents and put authorizing legislation in our bill. Bob Carr and Bob Mrazek wanted huge authorizing for highway projects, and Dick Durbin wanted to exempt Illinois from the first fiscal quarter limitation on highway expenditures because of the Ryan Expressway Project problems in Chicago. Bob Carr wanted to practically close down the Boston Logan Airport because it was overcharging general aviation during peak hours. Everyone was sort of angry. There were problems concerning the Coast Guard and Marty Sabo who, as a member on the Defense Subcommittee, did not like the reprogramming we did for the Coast Guard, which changed from the way the Defense Subcommittee had reported out the measure that transferred from Defense to Transportation. Marty was, however, very helpful in stopping Bob Carr with his schemes on Logan Airport.

We prevented Bill Gray from using UMTA money for a trauma center in Philadelphia, but we figured out another way to help him. Bill Gray was helpful in curtailing some authorizing that members were trying to do. I was able to hold together the basic items of the discretionary funds in Section Three, mass transit. The main change was by Texas member Tom Delay who took $5 million out of Los Angeles for Houston. We also had the problem with new regulations on charter buses, and Carr wanted to write language permitting all public transportation to compete with private charter buses. The lobbyists outside in the corridor were sending in messages, especially to Carr and Mrazek, to offer outrageous changes. I managed to hold it together and got a fairly decent bill within the 302B allocation.

I planned to attend a few receptions tonight, but I was too tired, and went instead to the gym for a shower and sauna before dinner, and then home.

MAY 25 WEDNESDAY

This morning Eddie Boland (D-MA), retiring at the end of this 100th Congress, presented his last bill in a HUD and Independent Agencies full Appropriations Committee markup. I was there, but I am still trying to recover from the rough markup yesterday. Part of the reason for the difficulty was that we have a new Chairman of Public Works to deal with, Glenn Anderson, and also the fact that our subcommittee had cuts on the 302B allocation larger than other subcommittees.

At noon I attended a luncheon meeting in the Capitol that my secretary Wynne set up for Dr. Manny Papper for the American Society of Anesthesiologists and for principal officers of the World Federation Society of Anesthesiologists. I sat at a table next to the father of Mark Willis, a young man from England who interned in our office a few years ago and is now, said the father, attending Harvard Business School. Pat and Manny Papper are good friends from Miami, going back many years. Even before Joan and I were married, I played tennis on Pat's family court in the Bayshore section of Miami, and that was over fifty years ago.

Dave Obey brought his Foreign Ops bill to the Floor today and it passed without amendments. The amendment that was supposed to be offered was for ten and five percent across-the-board cuts by Ohio member Jim Traficant, and Dave didn't know whether to offer two percent in the form of a substitute. I told Dave to follow his own instincts. He said he was going to take them head on, and I told him that I thought that was the right thing to do. When we got to the section of the bill where Traficant was to offer his amendment, Traficant was off the Floor. Later, he could not get unanimous consent to go back to that section of the bill where he needed to offer his amendment. He is sometimes such a crazy nut, but he is dearly loved in Youngstown, Ohio, and it was probably the best thing that happened.

Our staff meeting in the afternoon was very laid back, with everyone having some issues to talk about. It was good just to sit around and chat for forty-five minutes, as we have not had a staff meeting in a while with all that has been going on. Adele is bothered that INS Commissioner Nelson is trying to worm out of meeting with us Thursday, as promised, concerning the children in Santo Domingo. For such a worthy endeavor, the delays and reluctance to act on this by authority figures are mindboggling. One would think we were asking for something wholly detrimental when just the opposite is true.

In an interview with the *Congressional Quarterly*, the reporter asked for comments about the appropriation bill our subcommittee passed yesterday. Strangely, there were items in the bill pertinent to where some of my relatives live. An instrument landing system is in the bill for Selma, and I have cousins in Selma who like to fly. I have a cousin in Kentucky, and we earmarked funds for a bridge across the Ohio River at Owensboro. For Miami we put in an additional $16 million for the Metromover and $250 thousand for the Shock Trauma Network.

We had students from Miami in Washington on the Closeup Program. Three of the students were on a new pilot program, "The Program for New Americans." Two Nicaraguan students and one Mariel student from Hialeah were all strongly anticommunist, but mostly their concern was about getting assistance for college. I put them in touch with my staff in Miami to see what federal aid or grants may be available.

MAY 26 THURSDAY

At 7:30 a.m., I left the townhouse for my morning appointment at Bethesda Naval Hospital. At Bethesda, a Dr. Rodriguez in cardiology examined me, but the Doppler ultrasound equipment used for examining the carotid artery was unavailable, so this rendered the trip rather useless. Arriving back on Capitol Hill before 10:00 a.m., and before the first vote, I still have not missed a vote this year. I did, however, miss the full Appropriations Committee markup on the Agricultural Appropriations Bill, but I was back in time for Neal Smith's Commerce, Justice, State and the Judiciary Subcommittee markup. Tony Costa wanted me to offer an amendment to provide funding for TV Marti, and I told him if Neal Smith agreed to accept the amendment, then I would offer it. During the markup, the bells rang for a roll call vote on the Floor.

While on the Floor, Larry Smith, Dante Fascell, Neal Smith and I got into a discussion about TV Marti and decided to approach the Speaker about whether to offer an amendment. Wright, who was sitting in his Speaker's chair, asked Neal to accept the amendment, but Neal said, "I am not going to do it unless it is authorized. If you, Mr. Speaker, get it authorized, I will put it in." Neal was stubborn, but he was right, as there were chances for authorizing this amendment a couple of weeks ago when the State Department authorization bill was on the Floor, but they slipped by. I kept my word by being supportive and willing to offer the amendment, and Tony Costa knew that unless Neal Smith agreed to accept it, I could not offer the amendment. Everything in Neal's bill was authorized, unlike my bill in which so much is unauthorized that we had to go to the Rules Committee for protection of the unauthorized parts.

I stopped by the Capitol Physician's Office to let them know that the Doppler ultrasound was not available at Bethesda, and the physician got on the phone and called Dr. Strong in New York at Memorial Sloan Kettering. I now have an appointment at the facility in New York, and Dr. Strong will review the results. This worked out well, as I would rather have Dr. Strong involved in following every aspect of my case since he did the original surgery.

Billy Cypress, the Miccosukee Indian Tribe leader, came by

the office after his meeting with Joe Kennedy, whom Billy had first met in Miami at my fundraiser. Later, I saw Joe on the Floor and he said that Billy had given him a list of things that he wanted, but that he also measured him for an Indian jacket. Joe seemed very pleased about the jacket.

INS Commissioner Nelson did not show for our 2:15 appointment today, and did not bother cancelling. Lorri Kellogg is in Washington, having come specifically to attend the meeting and bringing with her members of the families who hope to adopt the four Dominican Republic children. When the Commissioner failed to call or show for the appointment, we kept the pressure on the INS staff, and at 5:00 p.m., we got a call from them saying that the adoption exemption we had asked for was granted. We were all excited. I spoke to a future mother whose husband is head of the Psychiatric Department at the University of Miami School of Medicine, and she was thrilled, as was Lorri. This outcome happily negates all the frustration I have felt in dealing with Mazzoli's staff and the legislative liaison at INS who have been obstructing this case by being too legalistic when more humanitarianism was called for. I am just happy it is over, and perhaps we can introduce these children to our community through a newsletter.

Many members have spoken to me on the Floor about their line item requests in my bill. Bill Richardson of New Mexico wanted to know why he did not get two highway demonstration projects, and I told him that no one got two. Henry Hyde of Illinois offered an amendment on the Floor to remove the restrictions placed on the CIA for aid to the Contras. Buddy MacKay and I were the only Florida members to vote against the Hyde amendment. The budget conference report finally was on the Floor, and because it threw everything out of proportion on the already passed appropriations bills, I voted against it. The bill did pass, however, but I had no choice but to vote against it because with this budget proposal my bill is suddenly $138 million above both outlays and budget authority, as in the conference report. It seems nonsensical to me to go back and have to change my bill in full committee just because the two Budget Committees could not complete a conference report before my bill was reported out.

The House adjourned before 4:00 p.m., in time for me to ride to the airport with Lorri Kellogg and her group for the 5:00 flight to Miami.

MAY 27 FRIDAY

At the district office my first appointment was with Rabbi Ronnie Kahani, who is hoping to replace Rabbi Neuman in East Germany. I found the Rabbi not too impressive, but eager. I was more impressed with Rabbi Neuman, and that did not work out. Now, perhaps it is best not to be too impressed and then be pleasantly surprised when the person turns out better than expected. When the opportunity arrives I will introduce Rabbi Kahani to Klaus Gysi, the East German Minister of Cultural Affairs.

I met next with the National Association of Retired Federal Employees, who were concerned about the catastrophic health care bill. I told them that they would not receive fewer benefits nor would they have to pay twice. Jeff usually meets with this group at their evening meetings, and he arranged this morning appointment because I am not available to meet with them during the week. They are a good voting group, but like most special interest groups they have one interest and, in this case, it is to get the best retirement protection that they can. They do a good lobbying job as the federal pensions are the best in the country, and the retirees want to keep it that way.

Members of the North Dade Chamber of Commerce came in, led by Milton Hornstein and Ted Krawitz, to discuss a possible site for a new airport in North Dade. The proposed site was actually in Larry Smith's district in extreme northwest Dade County. They really were thinking more to the future, say ten years down the road when Miami International will be even more congested and overcrowded. They have a long way to go, and the project does not look too promising to me. Before they left, I shared with them the information that we were trying to get joint use of Homestead Air Force Base. Afterwards Patrice and I went to the Sofitel Hotel for a luncheon meeting with the National Black Coalition of Federal Aviation Employees. Ron Jennings, a former used car customer, introduced me, and I spoke about the recently passed transportation bill and the additions we put in for the FAA. One other guest speaker was Cas Castleberry, the FAA Regional Director.

As Patrice drove us back to the office, I wrote a note to Ira Clark, President of Jackson Memorial. Ira had offered my grandson Matt a job at Jackson, but Matt had gone with his father to meet with Brian Gunther, the Director of Operations at the airport, and was offered and accepted a job for the summer there. I just wanted Ira to know of my appreciation for all he had done to help Matt.

Bernie Wall, an old friend who lives on the Venetian Causeway Islands, continues to call about the inability to use federal funds to improve the causeway road if residents keep the toll on the Venetian to maintain their privacy. I have told Bernie so often that they have to get rid of the toll if they want federal money to repair those bridges, but he keeps coming back trying to figure out a way to keep both their privacy and to get federal money. Feeling a little exasperated, I finally told Bernie to get in touch with Congressman Pepper as the matter was in his district, not mine and maybe Claude could figure out a solution.

An item in the paper yesterday stated that I was going to appropriate $4 million in the Labor, Health and Human Services Subcommittee for a trauma center building. This was a misstatement, as I am not on that subcommittee and therefore cannot appropriate out of that subcommittee. I will, however, speak to the Subcommittee Chairman Bill Natcher when I get back to Washington next week to see if he can help on funds for the building.

MAY 28 SATURDAY

Today was restful. I met some friends at the Neighbors Restaurant, then tennis with Stan Whitman, and then a movie. In the evening Joan and I took our grandson Matt to dinner for his sixteenth birthday.

MAY 29 SUNDAY

My son Tom came by the house this morning, and we sat for a while discussing the possibility of his running for office. Presently Tom is thinking about running for the Miami Shores Council, and I am very optimistic about his chances and think he can win. We went to Neighbors for breakfast and he met John

Stembridge, the former Mayor of North Miami, and that may be of some later help to Tom. Tom has the potential to eventually run for my seat, but first he will need to run for the State legislature. He is young and has time and is going in the right direction.

And then our other son Bill, in the evening, took his mother and me out for a belated Mother's Day dinner at The Palm Restaurant. We saw there Victor Potamkin, one of my good supporters, who was at the restaurant with his family doctor. Victor's wife has Alzheimer's, and we spoke about his coming to Washington and talking to the staff of Health and Human Services to get more information on the disease.

MAY 30 MONDAY

Today, on the way to the American Legion Post on West Dixie Highway, Jeff and I spoke about fundraising for Frank Mann, who apparently is not doing too well in his campaign for what I believe is a meaningless job: Florida Secretary of State. The fact that Frank is not well known is his major problem. At the American Legion Post, I presented to the veterans group a flag flown over the Capitol. The ceremony was very nice, and Channel 4 was there. I am a little uneasy taking part in veteran ceremonies, as I was not in the military service. I was a civilian employee on contract to the Air Force, but that is not like uniform military. Listening to *Taps* being played, I recalled many of my friends that I grew up with who were killed in WWII, and it is sad that they had to lose their lives so young.

My flight to Washington left two hours late. Before I went to the airport, Jeff drove me by to see the "Queen of the Condos," Annie Ackerman. Annie is still active, although not well, and we talked about the fact that no new condo leaders are emerging. Art and Rosalie Roberts were at the airport waiting to take my same flight, so the time spent there was not all wasted as I got a chance to talk to Art about Joan's sculpture project and the plans for Dallas transit that he represents.

MAY 31 TUESDAY

8:00 a.m., I took an Eastern shuttle to New York for my

appointment at Memorial Sloan Kettering. My friends Marvelle Colby and her husband, Selig, met me in New York, and took me to Sloan Kettering to have the Doppler ultrasound done. After the procedure, I waited for the results across the street in Dr. Strong's office. After I had waited about an hour, Dr. Strong called me in with the preliminary report before him, and said that I did very well on everything. This was great news, and I thanked him and left with Marvelle and Selig to have lunch at the Harvard Club; afterwards, I grabbed a cab to go visit my two teenage grandsons, Bill's boys, who live in New York with their mother, Bill's first wife.

Taking the 7:00 p.m. shuttle to Washington, I was back in the office before 9:00 p.m. The *Congressional Quarterly* that came out yesterday about the transportation appropriations bill was on my desk. The only thing I did not like was a quote by me about the changes made by Glenn Anderson, the new Public Works Committee Chairman. Instead of the item saying, "Subcommittee Chairman Lehman says," it read: "Subcommittee Chairman Lehman *complained that*," which I thought made me sound like a crybaby.

Chapter 18

JUNE 1, 1988 - WEDNESDAY

We have a new intern in our office, Rachael Timoner, the daughter of my good friend Eli Timoner. I remember when Rachael visited Washington with her parents about twelve years ago, and we had lunch in the Members Dining Room. At the time she was a small child and now she is a student at Yale University. A good student, she'll make a good intern.

Playing tennis today with Judge Mikva, Sonny Montgomery and Bob Kastenmeier, I thought because I had played well in Miami I would do well here but it was about the worst I have played and lost two sets; but I had fun. After tennis, a Mr. Ortiz, President of Miami Research Institute, a consulting firm, came in to discuss his ideas on bringing the 1996 World's Fair to Miami, indicating Interama land in North Dade County as a proposed site on which to hold the event. I asked if he had made inquiries with the condominium leadership in and around Interama, because if they don't want a World's Fair in their area then there is not going to be one. When he acknowledged that he had not spoken with any of the condo leaders, I told him in that case he should hold off raising funds until he did so and advised him to speak to them soon so that if they are opposed to the use of Interama land, then his group could start thinking about another location, perhaps the area around Opa Locka Airport.

Next was Redding Stevenson who came in with Richard Davenport of the Florida High Speed Rail Corporation about a proposed private enterprise regional airport in Palm Beach County. In seeking federal funding for this project, they first will need to make a legislative record. To go about doing this, they should appear, I advised, as outside witnesses before our subcommittee next spring.

Ambassador Keith Johnson of Jamaica came in about a problem concerning a parcel of land in Jamaica that belongs to a constituent in Charlie Wilson's district. Charlie had discussed this in our Foreign Ops meeting, saying that the land is being wrongfully confiscated from his constituent. Dave Obey has proposed a special hearing to resolve the matter because the dispute could hold up AID funds to Jamaica. Dave, as chairmen do, respects such committee members' concerns when constituents are involved. As I told Ambassador Johnson, I will wait for the hearing before making any comment either way.

The bells rang and I left the office to vote. On the Floor Nancy Pelosi of San Francisco spoke to me about her bus project that we excluded from our subcommittee report language. I asked if she could support our subcommittee the next time the House voted on taking the trust fund off budget, and Nancy said that she would. With this indication of support, I told her that I would help on her bus project. I also spoke to Tom Downey, Matt McHugh and Dick Durbin about the Bahamas Island project, which is still a few months away from closing on the purchase. My son Tom had given me some good advice which I passed on to them regarding a business plan which would enable this project to take care of itself. Joe Moakley came up to me about a Coast Guard problem and I suggested he speak to Earl Hutto of the Coast Guard Subcommittee. If Earl cannot help you, I said, then feel free to come back to me. I left the Floor to attend a meeting with Jamie Whitten and the appropriations subcommittee chairmen on how to meet the limitations imposed on the Appropriations Committee by the Budget Committee. It seems we will probably have to make a one percent cut in full committee in the transportation appropriation bill that we already passed in our subcommittee.

In the evening I attended a reception honoring the editors and publishers of Cox Newspapers, held at the Decatur House and Museum on H Street, Northwest. The *Miami News* and WIOD are affiliates of the Cox newspaper and radio chain. David Krasner, publisher of the *Miami News* was there, and we spoke about the problems of the *El Herald*, the Spanish edition of the *Miami Herald*, with Krasner saying that the Miami-Cuban subscribers ridicule the Spanish edition of the *Miami Herald*. I circulated around the room speaking to people like Larry Lipman, a Cox News reporter in Washington who often interviews me. I did not go to dinner afterwards because of all the delicious food I consumed, catered by my favorite, Design Cuisine.

JUNE 2 THURSDAY

In the Rayburn Cafeteria this morning Jack Edwards (R-AL) was talking to Bill Chappell, chairman of Appropriations Defense Subcommittee. Jack is chairman of the base-closing commission set up to dispose of surplus military installations, and I said to him in front of Bill Chappell that we really need to have some military air bases converted to civilian use. Bill laughed and said, "Didn't we give your subcommittee enough for the Coast Guard? Now you want to take all my air bases too?" We laughed, but much has been reported in the newspapers about the overcrowded commercial traffic airports and no one is talking about a solution. These surplus military air installations are already constructed and the people living around these facilities already know about airport noise, so noise would not be a problem.

Later in the morning at the full Appropriations Committee meeting, the bill on treasury and postal service and the defense appropriations bill passed fairly easily. The biggest discussion concerned the 302B allocation reductions and how to hold harmless the military construction appropriations and foreign operations appropriations. Holding these two subcommittees harmless from any of the cuts means that to bring the whole 302B appropriation allocation in line, the other ten subcommittees will have to cut more. Many of the subcommittee chairmen concerned with domestic programs do not want to see only foreign ops and military construction held harmless in these budget reduction situations, and they presented very valid arguments. Chairman Whitten, I think, will need to call another meeting with the subcommittee chairmen to deal with this.

On the Floor Butler Derrick asked me what happened in my bill to his airport in South Carolina. There are so many of these projects that I don't even try to keep them all in my head. We went to the Members Cloak Room so that I could put him on the phone with Tom Kingfield. After speaking with Tom, Butler turned to me and said that he was very pleased with all we had done for him by including in our bill the runway extension that he had asked for as well as provisions made for other requested improvements at the airport. Butler has been helpful to us in past years in our effort to keep the trust fund on budget, and I do not think we will ever have a problem keeping him on our side. He asked about Sharyn, my fundraiser, and wanted to know when she would be coming to Washington, as he likes her. Not really knowing Butler, Sharyn is a bit apprehensive. Rather jokingly, but also serious, I said to Sharyn that there were many women on Capitol Hill who would kill for a chance to go out with Butler Derrick.

Seeing Henry Neill, subcommittee chief of staff on Health and Human Services Appropriations, I told him that I hoped the one percent cut to meet the Health and Human Services 302B allocation would not adversely affect the money his subcommittee allocated to the Centers for Disease Control and Prevention in Atlanta. Henry said the funds earmarked for the Centers were not so large as to draw the necessary reduction from that allocation. The cut is not a one percent across the board, but just a one percent cut that can come from any part of a bill. Our subcommittee of course is working on the same one percent in our transportation bill to bring it back in line with the necessary 302B budget allocation, and when I go before the full committee I will offer a "mini" amendment to reduce the bill by one percent. I also saw Bob Foster, staff on Appropriations Agriculture subcommittee, who told me that he thought the problem with the Department of Agriculture's rare fruit station in South Florida was now taken care of.

Evelyn Terreros and her fifth grade teacher from Myrtle Grove Elementary School are in Washington, having arrived this morning. Evelyn is the student who so impressed me as the mistress of ceremonies at her school's recent flag presentation, prompting me to invite her and her teacher to Washington. After several photo opportunities, we met for lunch in the Members Dining Room and from there went to the Speaker's office where the Speaker spoke to them for about ten minutes. From the Speaker's office, I took them to the Visitors Gallery so that they could watch the Floor action. Eventually, John Schelble took them sightseeing to the Supreme Court, and then back to the airport.

Miami lawyer Don Slesnick brought a group of government supervisors in to see me - all members of the Government Supervisors Association from the local, county and state levels of government in Miami. Following a group photo opportunity, a separate photo was taken with the North Dade supervisor from my district. The *Miami Times* is now using a lot of the photographs we send of our black constituents, which is very helpful. Then, Doug Dennison and Jim Gall, owners of an auction firm dealing in real estate, came in to discuss the possibility of contracting with the government to auction government property obtained through Resolution Trust FAIC foreclosures. Their credentials are good, and we will write the usual "bread and butter" letter to the Resolution Trust. George Patton, a lobbyist who formerly worked for Senator Chiles, called to see if I was ready to endorse Dukakis. I told George that I was not going to endorse anyone and was going to stay uncommitted. Perhaps I sounded a bit irritated because he said he was not trying to bother me, but was just trying to get a count.

At Memorial Sloan Kettering last week I had indicated to Dr. Strong that I would assist the hospital with some of its grant problems. Today I got a call from someone in their grants division about information that would be mailed to me regarding the new national health legislation now in Henry Waxman's authorizing subcommittee. I welcome this opportunity to help Sloan Kettering and Dr. Strong for all they have done for me, and I will follow up with Waxman and with the Appropriations Subcommittee on Health and Human Services.

Many of my colleagues congratulated me today on the favorable results of my examination in New York last week, and I was wondering how they knew. Sonny Montgomery, I was to learn, had made the announcement at a prayer breakfast this morning, and now I will have to go to the next prayer breakfast and thank them. This outpouring of concern by my colleagues was very heartwarming. Naturally, Jewish members are rare at prayer breakfasts.

The airline pilots and airport operators are anxious about the FAA's new move to tighten antiterrorism restrictions on access in and out of airports. The FAA may indeed be overreacting, and I will write to the agency pointing out some of the pilots' and airport operators' concerns. It is important, though, that I am careful with my wording, as I do not want to appear soft on terrorism.

Maurice Rosenblatt held a reception this evening at his home honoring Congressman David Skaggs of Colorado. At the event, Maurice told me he is to receive $4,000 from a motion picture company for the use of his house located two doors from mine. He seemed really excited about it. The movie was "Chances Are" starring Ryan O'Neil.

JUNE 3 FRIDAY

Although close to 100 members were absent this Friday, we still had votes. At the office there was some confusion, as Adele did not know about our fundraiser that Zel Lipsen is sponsoring with David Bockorney's cooperation. Adele has been putting together a Jamaican trip to look at the project David's clients are asking our Foreign Ops subcommittee to help fund. Her concern is that the fundraiser gives the appearance of quid pro quo, and I agree. We may reschedule the Jamaican trip for later this year, after Foreign Ops has reported out its bill, as I do not want the trip to coincide with a fundraiser activity in Washington. In any case, the situation with Charlie Wilson concerning the confiscation of his constituent's land in Jamaica has prompted a money freeze on any new projects for Jamaica, so there is really no point to push this funding effort. I am committed to helping David, though, because for several years as a White House legislative liaison under Reagan, he was a big help to me and the only one I could go to when I needed to do White House business.

Mickey Leland says that we can now get some Cuban prisoners released because of a new connection he has at the Cuban Interest section in Washington, who told Mickey he wanted to help in any way he could. The staff at the Cuban Interest section also knows me, and I am very much interested in helping to free these political prisoners and bringing them to Miami. The problem is that many of the Cubans in Miami do not like to acquiesce to anything that could place Castro in a more favorable light to the American public.

Jim Quirk, Vice President for Government Affairs at Memorial Sloan Kettering, has written to me at the suggestion of Dr. Strong, and I am working with Mike Stephens on the Subcommittee for Health and Human Services to see about changes in the conference report on the Health Care Reauthorization Bill for research hospitals.

In Georgetown shopping for a gift for my administrative assistant Carolyn's son, who is graduating from high school, I vowed to make this my last time in Georgetown on a Friday evening when thousands of suburban high school kids are on the loose.

JUNE 4 SATURDAY

Sonny Montgomery was in the Longworth Cafeteria this morning, and we talked about an hour and just enjoyed each other's company.

In the afternoon, I visited my cousin Marx Leva on his estate in Bethesda, Maryland, a suburb of Washington. Marx, who served on board the USS LST-386 (tank landing ship) as navigating officer and later executive officer during World War II, has had a couple of articles published in the *U.S. Naval History,* and when he sends me copies I will put one or two in the *Congressional Record.* I always enjoy my visits with Marx. We grew up together in Selma, attending the same junior and senior high schools and then the University of Alabama. Marx went on to graduate from Harvard Law School, served as clerk to Justice Hugo Black, and after the war, Special Counsel and Special Assistant to Secretary of Navy Forrestal. He has been for some time now a senior partner in a prominent law firm in Washington, and we talked of old friends, family and politics.

JUNE 5 SUNDAY

Today Sonny Montgomery, Bob Kastenmeier, Pete Stark, Dick Conlin (the Director of the Democratic Study Group - active liberal Democrats), and I joined Don Edwards at his home on Chesapeake Bay for a very relaxing day of tennis and croquet, lunch, and more tennis and croquet. It was a really good outing.

JUNE 6 MONDAY

This morning another breakfast meeting with Maury Markowitz who deals in automobile sales, and then tennis with my colleagues. On my return from tennis the subcommittee staff got with me to prepare for our full committee markup Wednesday. We were interrupted so that I could take a live, on-the-air interview with a Selma, Alabama, radio station reporter on the priorities I put in the subcommittee markup for Selma Airport and for several other airports in which our bill provides instrument landing systems and runway lighting. During the interview I wondered if any of my old friends in Selma would be listening and if I would receive any feedback from Selma in the mail or by phone. It was rather nostalgic.

3:00 p.m., Mike Stephens brought over staff from Henry Waxman's authorizing health subcommittee to go over the requests I had received from Jim Quirk, the liaison for Memorial Sloan Kettering. Quirk wanted changes to the Reauthorization of the National Cancer Act just recently drafted, and we succeeded in resolving all of the problems except increasing the three-year extension to a five-year extension. The senior staff does the legislation because most members don't want to be involved in details.

Bob Duncan, who served as Chairman of the Transportation Subcommittee when I first came on that subcommittee, was in today. Bob is a dear friend but unfortunately he wasn't paying much attention to his district and lost in the Democratic primary in the early 1980's. Actually I still wish he were chairman; I'd have a lot of fun with him as the ranking Democrat on the committee, and also a lot less responsibility, and he would have included all my requests in his chairman's markup. I left the office headed for the Capitol Physician's Office to have precancerous blemishes removed from my face. It is funny, but on Monday, when this Office is not busy, all of us old members are here. Older members don't go home to their districts every weekend. Today, I saw 72-year-old Sam Stratton from New York, 75-year-old Walter B. Jones from North Carolina, and 88-year-old Claude Pepper from Florida. The attending physicians take good care of us.

This coming Monday is the groundbreaking ceremonial luncheon in Miami for the beach restoration on Sunny Isles, which we finally accomplished on appropriations after a twelve-year effort. When I spoke to Bernie Torra in the district office, he said the dredge had broken down, so now I am wondering if we should have the newspaper and television media there, as I had planned for television to show how the sand is pumped onto the beach from offshore.

JUNE 7 TUESDAY

Starting at 10:00, our subcommittee staff and I began going over the reductions we had to make for the $53 million cut, the level in our subcommittee markup funding, and I will offer the cut in full committee as an amendment. Bob Carr and I will meet to discuss his concerns about certain items now in the bill, such as the public charter bus problem and the Massport Airport problem in Boston. I need to meet with Budget Committee Chairman Bill Gray today to have him define outlay figures that deal with budget score keeping on the $15 million rent the Department of Transportation pays to the General Services Administration (GSA). Also, there is the matter of the offset against outlays from the federal railroad preferred stock sales in our bill. Last year we tried this maneuver in the Continuing Resolution but the Budget Committee said we could not count this sale as offset. I want Bill, as Chairman of the Budget Committee, to know about this and to help us eliminate some of these extra problems for our subcommittee that his Budget Committee continues to cause. He is a member of our subcommittee and will best understand both sides of the case.

The ranking Republican member on the Public Works Committee, Bud Shuster from Pennsylvania, sent me a letter complaining about our subcommittee putting authorizing legislation in our bill. Shuster complained just like the late Jim Howard used to do. But the situation is different now with the new Public Works Chairman, Glenn Anderson, who needs and wants us to include authorizing legislation to protect his public-owned charter buses in Long Beach. In a call to Butler Derrick, I let him know that I would get back to him if any problems are anticipated with the Rules Committee in protecting the unauthorized projects in our bill. Butler is the ranking Democratic member on the Rules Committee and, of course, he is concerned about his unauthorized projects in our bill.

I lunched with Priscilla Perry and lawyer lobbyist Gerald Cassidy. They are after a transportation grant for Miami Beach's Mount Sinai Hospital. Priscilla works for Gerald, and the main thing they now need is a better working relationship with the staff on the Transportation Subcommittee. Like some lobbyists they antagonize staff because they only want to talk to members, when they should really go to staff first. Lobbyists Gary Hymel and Denis Neill first talk directly to staff and get a lot more done. After lunch I went to the American Trucking Association and the International Brotherhood of Teamsters joint reception in the Rayburn Building. Some of their staff people were there like Joe Rosso, their ATA legislative liaison, also consultant Bill Cable with whom I spoke regarding Claude Pepper's elderly health care bill coming up tomorrow. Members know it is a bad bill but are afraid to vote against it during an election year. As I told Cable, it is the wrong way to do the right kind of thing. Claude wants to do it as the Pepper Bill instead of going through the Commerce or the Ways and Means Committee, as traditionally done. If it goes through the Commerce Committee it would be a Waxman Bill, or through the Ways and Means Committee it would be a Pete Stark Bill. I don't think Claude Pepper wants it to be anything but a Claude Pepper Bill. I saw Sid Yates in his office and persuaded him to put language in his bill to mandate seatbelts for the national park roads so that those roads will be under the same rules as the states.

Kaye Henderson, Secretary of the Florida Department of Transportation, called from Tallahassee saying he needed in our bill, language for the Acosta Bridge in Jacksonville. He wants UMTA to put money into highway bridge funds for an extra lane to accommodate future light rail mass transit on the Acosta Bridge. As this is a local issue in Bill Chappell's district, we wrote language for Chappell to offer in the full committee markup. The language was actually offered by another Florida member, Bill Young, because Chappell was out of town. The language was accepted in full committee and there will be funds for the extra lane on the Acosta Bridge.

Around 4:00 I met with Bill Gray to get a better deal on the scoring on the sale of preference shares and on the way the rent is paid to GSA by the Department of Transportation. Bill said he would not oppose us and would do what he could to help, and that is the best I could get from him. I hope he can help, as we need these offsets to prevent an across-the-board cut. In the evening at a Pamela Harriman fundraiser reception for Hubert Humphrey, III, I was the only House member present among a few Senators who were there, including Paul Simon. I felt a little strange being there because I am very fond of Republican Senator David Durenberger, against whom Humphrey was campaigning. Walter Mondale introduced Humphrey, and I must say that "Skip" Humphrey is nothing like his father. He is an attractive man but very dull, very boring, and I think he is a loser unless Durenberger does something outlandish.

JUNE 8 WEDNESDAY

At 9:30 a.m., Bob Carr and I got together on the Massport Logan Airport problem. I had hoped to reach a compromise with Bob, but the meeting ended with nothing settled and he still wants to cut funds because of what he perceives is discrimination against general aviation. On the Floor, I got Joe Kennedy to sign two books written about his father, Robert, which I will give to Sergio Bendixen. Joe did this very graciously and wrote his own words in Spanish.

11:00 a.m., I met with ranking minority member Larry Coughlin to go over the reductions to meet the new level of funding. We have to reduce $53 million in budget authority and $30 million in outlays from the bill as originally passed in our subcommittee because the Budget Committee's conference report reduced us by that amount. I wanted Larry to see the amendment I was to make at the full committee markup to be sure he was in line with me, and he was.

2:00 p.m., the full committee markup began. I offered my committee amendment and it passed on a voice vote. Again Bob Carr wanted to offer authorizing language for $160 million in highway projects. I had told Carr that I would have to oppose him, and I was hoping that he would not offer the authorizing language; but he did, with support from his Michigan colleague Dave Bonior, who is also on the Rules Committee, and was beaten badly on the vote. The reason it was important to defeat Carr was because even though he could with Bonior on Rules protect this authorizing language in the Rules Committee, we could lose the vote on the rule that brings the bill to the Floor and a lot of members' projects would be lost.

JUNE 9 THURSDAY

This is the morning of my fundraiser/breakfast at the Phoenix Park Hotel hosted by Zel Lipsen and Dave Bockorney. At the breakfast I told Dave and Julian Dixon that I wanted to support Dave's project because it would bring employment to the northern coast of Jamaica, but that I did not think the trip to Jamaica would be appropriate so close to this fundraiser; they agreed, and we will now wait a few months before going. Sharyn was in Washington for the event, and I had called Butler Derrick to let him know. Butler called Sharyn and they have a luncheon date scheduled.

Back in time for the full Appropriations Committee reconvening, everything worked out well. All of the amendments I opposed were defeated, but I think I made one mistake by offering the amendment on the charter buses. Bob Carr had asked me to offer the charter bus amendment, and I agreed, but I did so because he had played fair with me and told me what he was doing on his authorizing amendment for highways. Also, I could have told Carr to have someone else offer the amendment, but I did not want to oppose a Glenn Anderson request when I need Anderson to help me on the Floor. The only problem is I sort of messed things up for Sue Perry of the American Bus Association who was counting on me to oppose this charter change. Lucy tried to call Sue last night when she knew I would go with the amendment, but could not get her. I am sure Sue is upset with me and I feel bad about it, but maybe the Senate will keep the status quo in its version and then in conference I could recede to the Senate.

In a letter to Jim Quirk of Memorial Sloan Kettering, I explained that we were able to work out some changes in the House version of the authorizing bill for the National Cancer Institute (NCI), and that these changes would be to the liking of Memorial Sloan Kettering. Quirk and his people at MSK had preferred the Senate version, but Henry Waxman and his staff provided language with which Quirk will be happy.

The one-year oil drilling and leasing moratorium is another pressing issue. This afternoon I attended a meeting in Dante Fascell's office with Dave Johnson from the State of Florida's Washington Office and Brian Ballard, Governor Martinez's chief of operations, to discuss the matter. I assured them that I would do what I could in the full committee to keep the prohibition against oil drilling intact in Yates's appropriations interior subcommittee bill, to be marked up next week. All members of the Florida delegation have signed a letter backing the one-year moratorium, except Tampa Democrat Sam Gibbons, and by all accounts, Interior Department officials are really "scrambling" during this Reagan administration to prevent the one-year moratorium. It has also been reported that ranking minority member Ralph Regula (OH) on the interior subcommittee is planning to offer a compromise amendment to postpone drilling and new leasing for six months instead of for one year. I don't think the environmental questions that must be answered can be answered in six months, and I believe most members would agree with me. Later, in another meeting of the subcommittee chairmen about the new 302B allocation, I learned that I do not have to make any more changes.

Yesterday was not so good for Claude Pepper when he lost his rule on the "Pepper" bill on aging legislation on the House Floor. Dante Fascell said that when the chairman of the Rules Committee is defeated by 70 or more votes on such an important bill, it is bad news. Apparently, no one ever took a count and Pepper assumed that everyone was going to roll over for the chairman of the Rules Committee and for the "aging" lobby, but the members did not. I voted with Pepper as it was a well-intentioned bill, but it was not brought to the Floor in the traditional manner for reasons that appeared too self-serving on Pepper's part.

Our transportation subcommittee is to fly out to Houston on the 23rd of June for a hearing in Tom Delay's district. When I called the FAA Administrator Allan McArtor about a plane to accommodate our group, McArtor said the largest plane he could get was a six-passenger. A six-passenger is not large enough to seat the subcommittee members and staff who will be going, but I told McArtor to hold onto it until we could get a larger plane. Returning to the Floor, I saw the lobbyist for the State of Massachusetts, who told me not to worry about the Logan Airport because the Conte amendment took care of the federal funding restriction as tied to the judge's forthcoming decision on July 4. When I asked how he could be so certain, he explained that the judge in the ruling was his father's college roommate, and he got his information from the judge.

JUNE 10 FRIDAY

Rules Committee staffer Terri Dean wanted to know what she could do to stop the nonsmoking amendment offered in the full committee by Dick Durbin (D-IL). I asked staffer Sue Burlew on Bill Natcher's Labor, HHS, and Education Subcommittee, and Sue said not to worry, that the legislation would be knocked out on point-of-order on the Floor. I doubt if Durbin will offer the amendment in the full committee, but he may go to the Rules Committee and request that it be made "in order" on the House Floor. Sometimes I am stuck having to unoppose other appropriations subcommittee chairmen like Natcher as they stick with me. It is difficult to oppose subcommittee chairmen yet maintain control over your own bill in full committee.

The full Appropriation Committee markup today on Labor, Health and Human Services and Education went through okay. Interior Subcommittee Chairman Sid Yates tried to put in an amendment to equalize the staff pay at the National Cancer Institute with that of the Veterans Administration's medical staff, but Natcher, as Chairman of the Labor, HHS, and Education Subcommittee, would not accept his amendment, as he did not want legislation in his bill. I told Sid to offer the amendment on the Floor; no one may object on point of order, and it might pass.

I am glad to be going home to Miami this weekend. Bill Nelson, who was also on the plane, said he was going to Miami to attend a few meetings in relation to his campaign for governor. Nelson is to meet tomorrow with some of the black leadership and asked about Garth Reaves, Editor of the *Miami Times*. Garth has been a little hostile toward whites and especially Jews lately, and I advised Nelson to be careful with Garth but that attorney Jessie McCreary would be more amicable.

JUNE 11 SATURDAY

It was a very laid back day - tennis with Nancy Pollock and in the evening Joan and I went to dinner with Bill and Betty Seidle.

JUNE 12 SUNDAY

A brunch in honor of Michael Gonzalez as Administrative Assistant to Robert Renick of the school board was held today at the Turnberry Garden Room. Mike is thinking about running for the school board, and whereas he is a very good administrative assistant, I have my doubts about his being the right political material for a school board campaign.

JUNE 13 MONDAY

This morning I attended a meeting at the Marco Polo Hotel with state officials regarding boating speed restrictions on the intracoastal waterway. We discussed the need to control the waterway traffic to slow the speedboats and the reckless drivers of these boats, which are very hazardous on the heavy Indian Creek Canal congestion. Following the meeting there was the Sunny Isles Beach Restoration celebration at the hotel. The Sunny Isles Beach Restoration is the culmination of twelve years of work to get the Appropriations Subcommittee on Energy and Water to do a line item in its appropriations bill to provide funds to restore the beaches in the Sunny Isles area. I just hope the beach sand stays for a while before washing away. In the afternoon Patrice, Jeff and I took a tour of the Navy and Marine Corps Reserve Training Center in Northwest Dade, and at 6:00 p.m., I was on an Eastern flight back to Washington.

JUNE 14 TUESDAY

I had a breakfast meeting with members of the Cuban-American National Foundation concerned about TV Marti. I think TV Marti is a waste of funds, but I would never say that to this group, as they can make a lot of political noise and I want to keep them calm about opposing me. Alan Reuther was one of my afternoon appointments. Alan is Associate General Counsel for the United Automobile Workers and his father, Walter Reuther, was the number one labor leader during the Depression and the one most responsible for organizing the sit-down strike at General Motors, changing the whole automobile industry. Alan and I had a great deal to talk about, and he seemed pleased to know that I knew this history about his father.

The evening was filled with one reception after another. First, a very beautiful garden party in honor of soon-to-be-retired Massachusetts member Edward Boland, hosted by the Secretary and the Board of Regents of the Smithsonian Institution. Then a reception for Martin Lancaster of North Carolina held at Eastern Market, where I do my Saturday grocery shopping. Afterwards, a reception hosted by the Commissioners of the New York/New Jersey Port Authority held at the Sheraton Grand Hotel, where my friend, Commissioner Lillian Liberti, had been expecting me.

JUNE 15 WEDNESDAY

The morning began with breakfast with the Executive Board of the Congressional Arts Caucus, and then a Florida Congressional Delegation meeting about the shipbuilding industry in Tampa and the need to get a Coast Guard shipbuilding contract for Tampa shipyards. At noon I went to the Senate side to meet with Senator Alfonse D'Amato from New York. Senator D'Amato is the ranking Republican on the Senate Appropriations Transportation Subcommittee, and I like to maintain contact with him. Also, I just like D'Amato.

At 2:00 I met with Ken Waters, Assistant Vice President of Government Relations and Bob Cromwell, Vice President of Government Affairs of the General Telephone Company of Florida on the west coast of Florida. They have always been supportive of me in my campaign efforts.

Before coming to the Congress I thought of receptions as mostly evening affairs, but on the Hill "receptions" are going on from early morning to late evening. At an early afternoon reception today honoring Texas member Kiki de la Garza and Missouri Republican member Bill Emerson hosted by the Independent Bakers Association, I helped myself to loads of fresh bread from their featured Bread Sample Table and took it back to the office staff.

JUNE 16 THURSDAY

I stopped by the Congressional Prayer Breakfast this morning primarily to show my appreciation for the concern for my health expressed by the members who generally attend this breakfast and because of my friendship with Sonny Montgomery.

Very few office appointments today - Harry Freeman, Executive Vice President of the American Express Company, came in regarding the U.S. and Canada Free Trade Agreement. And then Coast Guard Commandant Admiral Yost came in to discuss the Coast Guard funding in our transportation bill.

JUNE 17 FRIDAY

Today was very easy, and I had time to catch up on mail and to clear my desk.

JUNE 18 SATURDAY

On the flight to Miami I sat next to Walter Fauntroy, the congressional delegate from Washington, D.C., who was going to Miami to speak to a black accountants' group; I had also spoken before this local chapter. Walter and I have been good friends. Later in Miami I played tennis with my grandson Sean who came in from Europe yesterday.

JUNE 19 SUNDAY

I met Belle Meade leaders this morning at the Neighbors Restaurant and they are doing a good job upgrading the 79th Street, Biscayne Boulevard area. I will try to help with federal grant funds to further the upgrade of this area.

The four children from the Dominican Republic arrived today - Father's Day - and for the new parents the timing could not be more perfect. My friend Mike Burns, the Customs Inspector, opened the gate for me to go through to greet the children as they came off the plane. The media covered the children's arrival and it was very touching and very moving, with some of the families in tears.

JUNE 20 MONDAY

Both the *Miami Herald* and the *Miami News* had stories on the children's arrival from Santo Domingo. The *Miami News* included my picture with the caption: "Lehman Brightens Trio's Dad's Day." The articles spoke about the events leading up to the children's arrival, including details on the eight months of frustration it took to get them here. But what really matters is that they are here and out of the foster homes in the Dominican Republic, and their new parents will now give them the love and individual attention that they need.

On the plane back to Washington, I thought about how rewarding it was to have been a part of bringing this all about.

JUNE 21 TUESDAY

Dr. Steve Rudd, the son of a Turnberry condo leader in my district, met me for breakfast this morning. Rudd is a young physician doing his residency at Walter Reed Army Hospital in Washington. He is practicing to be a pediatrician, and serving in the Army is his way of paying back his student loan at Emory University.

At the office, Bob Parkins, the City Manager of Miami Beach and Syl Lukis, the City of Miami Beach's Washington representative, were in to see me about funds for a light rail to Miami Beach over the MacArthur Causeway. We can try to get funds maybe next year to do a feasibility study, since the State of Florida has now dropped its original opposition to state funding a light rail system. Metro-Dade's Metrorail would be granted federal funding for the extension. Parkins is gung ho for the Dade County one-cent sales tax dedicated source of revenue, which is what we really need to expand rapid mass transit. He also has Priscilla Perry working with him as a consultant.

In preparation for the Rules Committee tomorrow, I spoke to members on the House Floor urging them to talk to the Rules Committee members to convince them not to concede to Anderson who is going before the Committee tomorrow to ask that the highway projects in our bill go unprotected. Anderson, however, has gotten himself in a box by telling members he will take care of them later in his highway reauthorization bill and not to worry about their unauthorized highway projects in our bill. If the Rules Committee fails to protect our highway projects, this also means that Anderson's charter bus language will go unprotected. I spoke to important appropriation members such as Natcher and Bevill and they are upset at the way Anderson is behaving, and I hope they can convince him to pull back. Tony Coehlo, the Democratic Whip, asked what was happening and I told him what we were up against and that the only thing to do was to tell people like Natcher to send letters to encourage the Rules Committee in our favor. A big problem is that Anderson's own Public Works Committee members are pushing him to take us head on.

I made a careless vote today on a suspension bill to take the Post Office subsidy off budget. Because of my opposition on principle to off budget, I should have been paying more attention. Meeting with Marty Sabo this afternoon, I asked him to vote in his Defense Subcommittee to protect the $400 million in the defense appropriations conference for the Coast Guard, and reminded him that Armed Services Chairman Les Aspin and I had a colloquy about giving the Coast Guard more flexibility on how the funds are to be spent, rather than have it all go to the acquisitions and construction improvement account. Marty can be just the help we need, and perhaps I can reach other members to gain their support in the defense appropriations conference.

Florida Governor Bob Martinez came in to thank me for my help last week in the full appropriations committee on the environmental problem regarding oil drilling and leasing in the Gulf of Mexico. This show of appreciation by the Governor had to do with a phone call that I made to him in Tallahassee last week before our full appropriations committee was to meet and vote on the measure. Two days before our committee meeting, Governor Martinez had agreed with the Interior Department to a six-month delay of lease sales, but for no prohibition on oil drilling 25 miles north of Key West. Fearful that this was being translated as the governor opposing the moratorium, I called Martinez about an hour before our committee was to meet urging him to send a letter stating unequivocally that he favored the one-year moratorium. His faxed letter arrived just as the meeting began, and I used it in argument against Ohio Republican Ralph Regula's compromise amendment to delay further lease sales off the Florida coast for one year. The Regula amendment was defeated 27-19. The drilling ban and the phone call episode were highly dramatized by the press, with *Miami News* reporter Larry Lipman headlining: "Martinez's Letter Helped Oil-Drilling Moratorium." Hopefully the outcome will be as favorable when the measure comes before stiff Senate opposition later this summer. The *Miami Herald* reported that a tougher challenge will be in the Senate and that Senator Bennett Johnson (D- LA), Chairman of the Senate Energy and Natural Resources Committee, is expected to lead a Floor fight against the moratorium.

With the governor gone, I phoned Korean veteran and former POW Tibor Rubin to let him know about the private bill I sponsored to do away with the statute of limitation so that he could receive a Congressional Medal of Honor for his bravery in the Korean War. Tibor, who is Hungarian by birth, is also a survivor of a Nazi death camp. He had begun a new life in America when he volunteered for the U.S. Army and was shipped out to Korea, where he spent two and a half years in POW camps, risking his life night after night to provide medicine and food to his fellow prisoners. When I talked to him about the private bill, he was so grateful on the phone. Then Janet Studley came in about electronic data processing that her client needed in our bill. It was too late to add the language to our bill and Janet knew this. She is a good lawyer and knows her way around, so she will probably try to have the language added to the Senate bill. If she is successful, I will help her in the conference proceedings.

Joan is in from Miami and will accompany me to Houston on Thursday. We attended Norman Mineta's fundraiser this evening at the American Institute of Architects and that is where I will have my next fundraiser. It was a sushi party, great food, and a good turnout of lobbyists, congressional members and friends. We went next to the Netherlands Embassy residence for an "International Evening" hosted by the American Council of Young Political Leaders. There were five choices as to where you could have dinner, and we chose the Dutch Embassy residence, a beautiful home situated across the street from the Woodrow Wilson House off of Embassy Row. The place was filled with paintings of Dutch masters. We then went to the home of Mr. and Mrs. Roger Stevens, Kennedy Center Administrator, to honor the African Elephant, but arrived too late for the cocktail and buffet.

JUNE 22 WEDNESDAY

This morning I met with Tom and Lucy in further preparation

for the Rules Committee today. I spoke to Amo Houghton, a Republican member from upstate New York, about doing a colloquy on the Floor on the highway project he is building in his district. Amo of Corning Glass is the wealthiest member in the House.

At noon we went before the Rules Committee and I think we succeeded in having all of our highway projects protected. But one nonhighway exception may be for Massport. Anderson, by the way, had a hard time in front of the Rules Committee. A *Congressional Quarterly* reporter who saw me later and said he was in the Rules Committee hearing, questioned me about the highway demonstration projects in our bill. Around 1:00 we had a very enjoyable crab feast in the full committee. Governor Schaefer of Maryland had sent two bushels of the best of Maryland steamed crabs to our subcommittee in appreciation of our support for projects in his State.

In the evening Joan and I drove to the home of Elizabeth and George Stevens, Chairman of the Board of the Kennedy Center for a cocktail reception honoring Louise Slaughter (D-NY). The event was hosted by the Women's Campaign Fund and the actress/comedian Lily Tomlin. We had a nice time, but we missed seeing Lily Tomlin who had already left for her stage play by the time we arrived. Dining later at the Prima Piatti Restaurant, we saw Senator Lautenberg, who said he was having trouble with Senator Chiles on the Senate version of our transportation bill. We will find out more about it when we go to conference, but apparently there is much conflict in the Senate Appropriations Committee.

JUNE 23 THURSDAY

On the Floor today I spoke to several members about different problems, including Dave Bonior who may need help on the rule he will manage. Majority Whip Tony Coehlo told me he is trying to calm Glenn Anderson so that he won't oppose the rule. Bonior said if he is going to have a problem with Anderson, then he will need all the help he can get from Appropriations Committee members.

4:45 p.m., Marty Sabo (D-MN), Frank Wolf (R-VA), Tom Delay (R-TX) and I, along with Joan and subcommittee staff, boarded a bus at the Rayburn horseshoe entrance and headed for

Dulles Airport to catch our flight to Houston. Our transportation subcommittee is conducting a field hearing in Tom Delay's district tomorrow. We had first class accommodations on Continental Airlines and received red carpet treatment. In Houston, Joan met with a representative from the Houston Transit Authority and then left to pick up Elizabeth Burgower, her old friend, and would meet us later at Bob Lanier's house for the big party for our delegation. The rest of us boarded a huge helicopter for a trip over the Houston freeway and transit construction projects being developed, and landed atop the transit authority garage. We all got in cars and went to the beautiful home of Bob Lanier, Chairman of the Houston Transit Authority. Many of Houston's VIP's were there, including Mayor Kathy Whitmire and Dr. Lamagre, head of the M.D. Anderson Medical Center. We had a very good time and Houston really put on its "dog and pony" show for us.

JUNE 24 FRIDAY

Our hearing began at 8:00 a.m., at the downtown Four Seasons Hotel and lasted until noon. It went off very well. I told Tom DeLay that he outdid Dick Durbin who had put on a very big deal for us when we were in Chicago for a hearing. After the hearing Tom and I did a press conference, at which I praised Houston for its dedicated source of transit funding in the penny sales tax and offered encouragement for federal funding for their transit program. Following the press conference, we joined others already seated at a luncheon sponsored by the Houston Chamber of Commerce, and both Tom and I made speeches.

After lunch I was driven to the airport for my flight to Dallas. Dallas Mayor Annette Strauss, her staff, and Art Roberts were at the airport to meet me; Joan had taken an earlier flight to Dallas. Again I was interviewed by newspaper, radio and television reporters, and I gave the pitch to "vote for the bond issue in support of the Dallas transit system." My primary reason for being in Dallas is to push for the passage of their bond issue transit plan, but we are very worried now that it may not pass. The election is tomorrow.

At a dinner which included Mayor Strauss and some leadership people of the Dallas community, there were about three tables of ten each and they all seemed very happy that I was there, especially John and Marianne Tatum, our hosts for the evening.

JUNE 25 SATURDAY

1:00 p.m., Art and Rosalie Roberts picked us up for our visit with Ray Nasser at his home. Nasser is a big builder and supporter of the Department of Transportation and a big-time art collector. We hope Nasser can play a part in the Art in Public Places program.

4:30, our flight left for Washington. It was a good trip to Dallas to view the transportation system, I have learned a great deal about the transportation problems in both Houston and Dallas, and I hope Dallas passes its public transit bond issue today. We arrived back at the Washington townhouse about 8:45 p.m. I went to the office about 10:00 p.m. and called the Dallas newspaper and learned that the bond issue failed by three to two. I guess the trip to Dallas was sort of futile.

JUNE 26 SUNDAY

Free day

JUNE 27 MONDAY

The subcommittee staff and I met this morning to go over my Floor statement for tomorrow. Now that we have prevailed in the Rules Committee to protect the authorizing language in our bill, we have to get the rule passed on the Floor. Dennis Eckart of Ohio has spoken to me about his proposed amendment to add about $5 million for his Coast Guard stations on Lake Erie to keep them open. Calling Eckart this morning, I told him that I would accept his amendment if he would help me on the Floor on the rule, and he said he would call his colleagues that co-signed his "Dear Colleague" letter and ask them to support the rule. If we pass the rule, I will accept Eckart's amendment on the Floor.

In the evening Joan and I were guests of the Wolftrap Board of Trustees at a performance by flutist James Galway. We sat in a box with Jim Oberstar (D-MN) and other members. During intermission I spoke to Oberstar about the rule on the transportation bill and asked him what was to happen. He understood that the Republicans were going to oppose the rule because of the Rules Committee's adding a self-executing clause into the bill on labor protection, adding that Glenn Anderson and John Paul Hammerschmidt (R-AR) would definitely be in opposition. I expected this, and told Oberstar to tell Anderson that if he defeats the rule that the next rule would not contain protection for his Long Beach charter bus language.

JUNE 28 TUESDAY

Larry Coughlin surprised me in the cafeteria this morning by telling me that he also thought he would have to oppose the rule, saying that his reasons were based on the labor protection agreement. I got Dave Bonior on the phone and asked him to mobilize his Rules people and sent over a list of members' projects that we have protected by the rule in our bill. I also called Tom Bevill (D-AL), Bill Natcher (D-KY), and Joe McDade (R-PA); maybe McDade, as a Republican, can dissuade his fellow Republican, Coughlin, from opposing the rule, considering that we are protecting one of his projects in the rule. I do not want to overreact, but I don't want to take for granted that the rule will pass.

At a breakfast reception hosted by Doug Walgren (D-PA) and Apple Computer, Inc., a winning club from Samuel Scheck Hillel Community Day School in North Miami Beach in my district was being honored. Eighth grader Diane Kasher, the daughter of Robert Kasher, a friend of my son Bill, was the winner. Diane was there with her teacher Jill Weber, and after the reception we all had a photo opportunity. 11:00, I went to "An Artistic Discovery" program - a national exhibition of winning entries from high school art competitions. Our district winner, Anthony Acosta, had come to Washington today with Sherry from our district office. Channel 7 interviewed us in front of Anthony's exhibit and then we had a photo opportunity with General Motors officials and a couple of movie stars, one of whom was Judd Nelson. Anthony was very tickled about having his photo taken with the actor Nelson.

Tom Delay sent me the clippings from the *Houston Chronicle* about our trip, which included photos of me and Tom. The articles, which boasted of our subcommittee's approval of Houston's efforts in mass transit, were very flattering and especially significant for

Tom and Houston's Mass Transit Authority. Neither Tom nor their MTA could have asked for a better endorsement of what they were bringing to the Houston community.

Our bill did not move today as anticipated. The District of Columbia bill took until almost 5:00 p.m. Afterwards, we did the rule on our transportation appropriation bill and surprisingly carried the rule by over a hundred votes. We then went into general debate on our bill without any problem. But about 7:00 p.m., there was a big huddle on the Floor with Minority Leader Bob Michel, Speaker Jim Wright and Majority Leader Tom Foley. It seems the Republicans were having a big campaign dinner downtown this evening, and did not want to miss any votes on the Floor or to cancel their meeting. A compromise was made by unanimous consent to put the Durbin nonsmoking amendment, which required a vote, at the end of the bill, and then proceed with anything else in the bill that did not require a recorded vote.

We did all the general debate and all the projects in the bill that were not protected on points-of-order made by the Republicans. I accepted amendments on the Coast Guard for a drug-free work place, and colloquied with members. We got by the Massport language, but toward the end with the bill almost finished, I moved the members to rise. This caused a commotion because the motion was made before Florida minority member Clay Shaw had a chance to offer his amendment, and he thought I had set him up. It wasn't true of course, but Shaw was very upset. Nonetheless, the motion to rise protected the Massport provision which I had promised to Joe Kennedy, and I was very glad that the motion worked. Joan had been in the Family Gallery for about an hour watching the debate, and at dinner at LaColline we talked about all that had occurred on the Floor.

JUNE 29 WEDNESDAY

Republican Clay Shaw offered the same amendment today when we resumed to finish our bill, and although I opposed the amendment, I did not make a point-of-order against it. I do not think the parliamentarian wanted to rule on that point-of-order, and when Shaw moved his amendment I rallied a loud voice vote against it and he then asked for a division. After the division went against him, he did not ask for a recorded vote. We got by Shaw, and he is now not too unhappy after last night when he thought I had pulled the rug out from under him. Really, it had been Shaw who rallied his side on the points-of-order, and if not for him I think we could have even gotten by without some Republicans making points-of-order. They were all very unhappy about Glenn Anderson not being on the Floor and, as Chairman of the Public Works Committee, Anderson lost a lot of credibility by not even showing up for passage of the Appropriations Transportation Bill.

Today went a lot smoother than yesterday. I had to oppose the Durbin nonsmoking amendment and it was defeated by four to one. After that amendment we went to final passage and were finished by noon. Everyone congratulated me and it was a good way to wrap up the $10.8 billion transportation budget for 1989. For my district, the bill included another $15.5 million installment payment on the proposed Omni and Brickell Avenue legs of the downtown Miami Metromover, to be added to the $140 million which I have been instrumental in appropriating over the past several years. Dade's trauma network was earmarked for $250,000, but only on the condition that the county agrees to follow the task force plan to establish a special agency to run the trauma system. Funding for the Coast Guard was increased to include over $400 million for drug interdiction, much needed funding for the Coast Guard with reports that the Miami-based 7th Coast Guard District, the largest in the United States, is also the busiest in terms of drug interdiction and search and rescue missions.

Back at the office, Carol Jane Gotfried from Miami was waiting for me to discuss a letter that she wanted me to sign to John Dingell. The letter was on environmental issues, and I have been holding off signing it. And again I put it off. I have to be careful with Dingell as he just helped me on the Floor. I missed a meeting this morning with Elliott Silverstein and Larry Chernakoff of the Directors Guild regarding the colorization of films. I wanted to be there, but I was on the Floor at the time. I spoke with Lee Hamilton in the cafeteria line, and Lee said that the Dukakis people are still talking to him about the Vice Presidency even though Senator John Glenn will most likely receive the nomination.

The House was in a late session today, but I managed to make several receptions away from the Capitol building before returning for a final vote. One reception was in honor of Joe Kennedy at the National Democratic Club located to the rear of my townhouse. It was a good party, and I sat and talked with Ed Boland, Dan Rostenkowski and Joe Early. The second was a fundraiser reception for Dante Fascell at the Florida House, which had only charged Dante $1,000. At that price I can have my next fundraiser there. Dante had shrimp flown in from Florida, and plenty of it. And last, I attended an Open House that lawyer Tim Furlong had for his new offices at 555 New Jersey, N.W., which included a beautiful view overlooking the Capitol. Tim and I talked about his maybe doing a fundraiser for me in July. After the Furlong party I went back to the Capitol for the final vote, and I believe I have a 100% voting record to date.

JUNE 30 THURSDAY

This morning I did a radio taping for the Children's Defense Fund with Alice Rivlin's son Doug. Then lobbyist Hector Alcalde came in about the upcoming appropriations transportation conference and what he would like me to do as far as receding to the Senate language. I told him my actions would depend on the kinds of tradeoffs I receive from the Senate. As he was leaving, he complimented me on the personal notes that I put on the invitations and thank you letters for my fundraisers.

This is Rachael Timoner's last day working as our office intern, and we had a farewell party for her in the office. Just when you are getting to know the interns, their four weeks are up. We are finished voting for the day and this afternoon I will be leaving for Miami. Reading today's *Congressional Record*, I see our transportation bill apparently had the lowest "no votes" on final passage of any of the appropriations bills so far this year. Energy and Water also had a low number, which indicates that the more colleague projects in appropriations bills the fewer negative votes there are. Also, we learned last night that Glenn Anderson, who was not on the Floor to oppose the rule and had everyone wondering about his absence, had undergone open-heart surgery. If Glenn had announced that he was going to have this surgery, he probably would have gotten fifty or more sympathy votes against the rule.

Charlie Wilson told me on the Floor yesterday that Speaker Jim Wright's wife, Betty, is very depressed about what is happening to Jim. Jim, on the other hand, seems to be weathering the storm pretty well. The House Ethics Committee voted this month to open investigation on several allegations against Jim, one of which concerns a book deal for which he is accused of receiving "unusually" high royalties and that his book, *Reflections of a Public Man*, was published by a longtime associate with a criminal record who had been paid large sums of money from Jim's campaign committee. The investigation will focus on whether House rules were violated by the channeling of campaign funds to Jim's personal use. Along with the other allegations against Jim, Betty may be right, this could be cause for alarm.

Clay Shaw is now happy. He said we both had a good write-up in the Broward edition of the *Miami Herald* (on the transportation bill). I also had a good write-up in the *Miami News*.

Hector Alcalde was in again, this time to show me some language he had requested in the Senate transportation bill that he wanted me to recede on. I told him we recede to the Senate only when we get something in return, and that's the way the game is played in conference.

I flew to Miami this afternoon, and Larry Smith and Dante Fascell were on the same flight. I arrived home in time to get out for a good game of tennis with my grandson Sean, before dressing for the Metro-Dade County reception and dinner this evening at the Doral Hotel. It was a nice party with lots of media coverage. Senator Graham was there, as were most of the State officeholders; probably half of the people there were either in office or seeking office. Senator Nunn was a special guest and when he spoke he recognized Smith and Fascell, but forgot to mention me. It does not matter, as Nunn doesn't mean anything in my district. I stayed till 9:45 p.m., through most of the speeches, but left before the dinner started.

Chapter 19

JULY 1, 1988 WEDNESDAY

I will be in Miami through Monday, and my schedule is light except for some office appointments today. Rosita Korningberg, a Holocaust survivor, was one of the appointments. I first met Rosita several months ago in Washington at the annual National Commemoration ceremony of the "Days of Remembrance." The ceremony had taken place in the Cannon Building with Holocaust survivors there from all around the country. It was at this occasion that Rosita told me the story of what happened to her family in Germany on Crystal Night. Last month I had inserted into the *Congressional Record* an article on the Holocaust, and today I showed Rosita that copy of the *Congressional Record.* She was very pleased, saying that she would show the article to her father.

Others on the schedule included Pepe Colada and Jimmy Jones of the carpenters union concerned about the number of jobs available to union members in the construction of the Metromover extensions. As much as possible I tried to reassure them that union members would be well represented in construction of the Metromover. Truly Burton and other members from the Home Builders Association came in regarding FHA loan restrictions. I told them I would arrange for a meeting with Appropriations housing subcommittee staff to see about help, if not for this year then next year.

The CEO of North American Biological was in. This company does a lot of blood plasma business, but the lack of free trade agreements causes a real problem. Though free trade is a hardship for some American businesses, it helps this business, as surprisingly one of Florida's biggest exports is blood plasma.

JULY 2 SATURDAY

This morning I went to see Patrice at the Northside district office. We talked about the general run of her office and several constituent cases she had pending. At 4:00, I was to play tennis with Bill Rogers in Miami Shores, but it started to rain. This was the fourth time we had to call off our game because of rain. Into each life a little rain must fall.

JULY 3 SUNDAY

The Haitian-American Democratic Club of Greater Miami held its reception/dinner this evening at the Dupont Plaza Hotel. Jacques Despinossa is the leader of this group and does a lot for the Haitian community. Jacques and I communicate pretty well, as he understands that I too am working to help the Haitian community. All the politicians were at the event for this time of the election year, with almost as many people running for office there as there were Haitian-Americans. I left before the dinner began, but was there for an interview with Bob Mayer of Channel 4, who wanted my reaction to the Iranian commercial jetliner which was recently shot down by an American Navy cruiser in the Persian Gulf. "This was a tragedy that had been waiting to happen," I said. I have received word from John Schelble that the *Miami News* is also trying to reach me regarding this tragic incident.

JULY 4 MONDAY

My picture was on the front page of today's *Miami News* in a story in which I said that Americans were "trigger happy." The article repeated my comments that protecting oil going to Western Europe and Japan was not in the United States's best interest. So far there have been no repercussions or derogatory remarks about my comments, although I do expect that there will be. Last evening a lot of people saw and heard me on television saying that we were in the wrong place at the wrong time for the wrong reason, so people are very much aware of my feelings concerning our country's military presence in the Persian Gulf. My position is certainly not a popular one. Most of the other members interviewed were much more conciliatory and less critical of the American position and did not seem overly concerned about the loss of Iranian lives, which included sixty children who were lost in the shootdown.

JULY 5 TUESDAY

When I arrived back in Washington today, the staff had placed on my desk the *Wall Street Journal* article mentioning Tom and Greg, the two key staff people on our Appropriations Transportation Subcommittee. In the article, Transportation Secretary Jim Burnley complained that Tom and Greg were the ones actually running the Department of Transportation and not him. This criticism by the DOT has been ongoing for a long time, but the problem is that Tom has been staff chief of Appropriations Transportation Subcommittee under ten different DOT Secretaries, and he knows far more about the Department than any of them. This bothers some of the DOT officials, I am sure, but I view it as both the administration and Congress benefiting from Tom's expertise.

An accident happened with me and Katherine Karpoff this evening following dinner at the restaurant Two Quail's on Massachusetts Avenue. Katherine was the driver, waiting in the pedestrian walk to make a right turn when a young woman on a bicycle came barreling off the sidewalk and into the right side of my car. I think the young woman wants me to take care of her medical bill as her finger may be broken. Fortunately it seems to be nothing more serious than that.

JULY 6 WEDNESDAY

Our new interns for the month of July are here, and this morning I took them for the traditional intern breakfast in the Members Dining Room and then the photo opportunity. Afterwards I met with Ambassador William Boddy of the European Bureau of the State Department. Boddy's present rank is Deputy Assistant Secretary of the Department of State, and he had with him an official from the East German Desk. We discussed the recruitment of the next Rabbi for East Germany, but the meeting primarily concerned the Jewish reparation due from the East German government. I was all for helping Boddy and the State Department's foreign bureau to push the GDR on this issue, as West Germany had already paid property reparations to the West German Jews who had survived. We agreed that this would be a coordinated effort with my friend Peter McPherson, also at the State Department. I am to call McPherson, outlining what I want the agency to do, and then get back with Ambassador Boddy. Boddy said he would send me a list of possible Jewish recipients, as some may now live in my district. If there are those who live in my district, I plan to bring them together to let them know what I am trying to do.

In the meantime I spoke to Rosita Korningberg in Miami and she said that her father saw his picture in the Holocaust booklet that I had given to her. Rosita's father had been liberated from one of the Nazi concentration camps and, together with other survivors, he had been photographed as the American troops liberated the camp. I hope to interest Fred Tasker at the *Miami Herald* in doing a story on the celebration of the 60th anniversary of Crystal Night, and in the article include the account of Rosita's father seeing the Holocaust booklet for the first time and being surprised at seeing his picture there. Background information would not be a problem, as Rosita's father is still in touch with some of those who were in the concentration camp with him.

My son Bill is in Washington to meet with Suzuki officials about the Suzuki rollover problem, as cited in the *Consumer Report*. We are to have dinner together this evening, and I am happily looking forward to it.

The Capitol police came in to examine my car. There is a sizable dent in the right front fender where the bicycle made contact, and the car will have to be repaired. Although immobile while waiting to make a right turn, we were wrongfully in the crosswalk.

Meanwhile, John has brought to my attention that the Veterans Administration is closing a drug halfway house in my district. The facility is scheduled to close on July 13, apparently due to the lack of funds to continue operating. This leaves us with little time to try and save the facility. We got Tom Dougherty, head of the VA Hospital in Miami, on the phone, and Tom said he would try to help. I then called Dick Malow, staff chief on Appropriations VA, HUD and Independent Agencies Subcommittee, who said he thought this could be worked out internally with the Veterans Administration, without going through any supplemental appropriation legislative action. Sonny Montgomery, Chairman of the Veterans Affairs Committee, has also agreed to help.

On the editorial page of the *Miami Herald* today, I was described as "Indefatigable Bill Lehman," followed with "...has come through again, securing a $250,000 federal grant to help breathe life into Dade's all but vanquished trauma network." The funding of course is conditional and dependent on how successful Dade County is in complying with the recommendations set forth by the trauma network task force. To this end, the *Herald* writeup was invaluable as it supported the task force's recommendations, saying that Dade County commissioners now had a "well-marked chart ... to save the county's faltering trauma program." Obviously I was very pleased. Not only did the writeup put me in a good light, but it was a big boost in the effort to keep the funding alive for our Metro-Dade County Trauma Network.

Surprisingly we have not had much criticism on my "trigger happy" comment about the Navy, although we did have one irate phone caller who said I should go and join the Ayatollah. It was amazing the number of people who saw the telecast on Sunday evening, and I think most agreed with my position, judging from the more positive comments I received.

There was only one vote on the Floor today, so I was able to get away early to have dinner with Bill. We had a very nice time, and I miss this contact with my sons when I am away from Miami.

JULY 7 THURSDAY

People from Electronic Data Systems met with me this morning.

This Texas-based corporation is owned by General Motors, having been purchased from Ross Perot back in 1984. EDS designs, builds and operates computer systems, and is seeking the FAA contract to computerize the FAA's data base. Presently the Senate subcommittee has $20 million for this in their DOT appropriations bill. We do not have anything for this in our bill. I told them to keep their options open and perhaps we could work something out for a one-year appropriation, without any commitment for future years. But we have to be very careful when appropriating a few million dollars for a project that may become a multi-year $700 million expenditure. Janet Studley, my special friend and a lobbyist for EDS, was also at the meeting. It is not easy being professional and business-like with a very attractive lobbyist that I have taken out to dinner a few times. I am, though, as careful and objective as possible, and I am sure Janet understands that.

Word has just reached me that the VA drug rehabilitation center will remain operative until the first of August. Dick Malow is working with the head of the VA Hospital in Miami, and has managed to obtain the necessary funds to keep the facility open, at least temporarily. At my request, Malow is now working to find funds to extend the August 1 closing date to October 1, the beginning of the new fiscal year when new funding for the facility can be authorized.

The young lady that ran into my car with her bicycle called to inquire about my insurance company, as "my little finger will never be the same," she said. The official accident report determining who was at fault will be issued in three or four days. She was a bit hysterical, but agreed to wait for the report.

On the House Floor Bill Nelson asked me whether he should hire Sergio Bendixen to help with his 1990 campaign for Florida governor. Sergio is one of the best pollsters that I know, and I assured Nelson that he could not go wrong with Sergio.

Dade County Commissioner Clara Oesterle called to find out whether Metro-Dade needed to lobby the Senate before we go to conference because the Senate had no funds for Dade Transit in its bill. I assured Clara that this was one of those routine items that the Senate leaves out and then recedes to the House in conference, and promised to touch base with her if my assessment of the situation proved otherwise.

JULY 8 FRIDAY

Good news from Dick Malow. Funds are now available through the remaining fiscal year to maintain the VA drug rehabilitation center in Miami. This means everything to the twenty-nine Vietnam veterans housed at the facility, and I must go by personally to thank Dick Malow. Now I have to work on keeping the facility open beyond the October 1 deadline. My first step will be to put in a request to the VA authorizing committee, and for this I will speak again to Sonny Montgomery.

JULY 9 SATURDAY

It was a usual Saturday in Washington - tennis, a movie, and back home to catch up on some reading.

JULY 10 SUNDAY

Easy relaxing day.

JULY 11 MONDAY

I spoke to Florida Senator Lawton Chiles about appropriating $20 million for the Center for Disease Control Injury Research, as Lawton is chairman of the Senate Appropriations Labor, Health and Human Services Subcommittee. If he can help in his subcommittee with this appropriation, I will help him with funds for the control tower he wants at the Orlando Airport. Lawton only agreed to look into it, but at least he did not say no and that was encouraging.

I was speaking with Senator D'Amato, the ranking Republican on Senate Transportation Appropriations, and he said it would be another day or so before the transportation appropriations bill is on the Senate Floor. He believes we can work out our differences in conference, but there are a number of items in our bill that the Senate definitely does not like. D'Amato did not go into specifics, but I have an idea the "differences" he referred to concern the outlay offsets that we counted from the sale of the preference shares in our bill.

While exercising in the gym Lee Hamilton told me he thinks he is still on the list of vice presidential possibilities, although no one has made him a firm offer. Lee has had numerous meetings with Mike Dukakis, and his office receives fifty phone calls a day from Dukakis's campaign headquarters wanting more information. Also, the local newspapers have been interviewing Lee's family and friends in Indiana.

Back at the office Frank Lautenberg called all bent out of shape about Senator Graham, who is proposing to offer on the Senate Floor a $60 million add-on amendment for Coast Guard operations. It really won't do any good for Senator Graham to do this, because the Coast Guard is in the final months of the fiscal year and we are taking care of the Coast Guard in the supplemental which comes out this week. Graham could be doing this for drug-war publicity, but his actions could embarrass Lautenberg. I have a call in to Senator Graham to ask him to withhold his amendment, and our relationship is such that I could ask him to do this and he probably would.

JULY 12 TUESDAY

The morning began with a breakfast meeting with Paula Berg, whom I knew from a trip to Ecuador. Paula is now an Executive Secretary in the Foreign Service division of the State Department. She had left the private sector a few years ago and joined the Foreign Service because she wanted to travel. This very adventurous middle-aged woman has now served in several different countries, and leads a seemingly very exciting and fulfilled life.

In today's editorial page of the *Miami Herald* there is an article about what I did to keep the VA halfway house open. It was a good article, telling of the success of the halfway house and how, of the 136 veterans who have stayed there for the 30 to 90 day period, 107 had been discharged and about half of those had jobs. I even know some of the people that have been treated and helped by the facility. I saw Sonny Montgomery on the Floor and thanked him for his help, and showed him a copy of the article. The *Herald* also ran the story of my being one of the "players" in the effort to push East Germany to pay some of the Jewish war claims. This is beginning to take hold, and where the idea seemed initially somewhat surrealistic it now has the feel of reality about it.

At noon the Greater Miami Chamber of Commerce hosted a luncheon with the Florida Congressional Delegation to discuss the plight of Eastern Airlines and what the shutdown of Eastern will mean to the Miami community. Miami produced a good turnout, and I sat next to Dick Capen, *Miami Herald* publisher. There are both pro- and anti-Eastern members among our delegation, and I thought that whatever action our delegation took it should be done as a whole and not be splintered. So I suggested that *all* members of our delegation sign a letter to the mediation people, advising them to set a deadline for the mediation, so that they could get on with the cooling-off period and get something resolved before Eastern went bellyup. The delegation members liked the idea and agreed to a letter being sent to the Eastern mediators signed by every member of the Florida delegation.

Leaving the luncheon, I headed for Jamie Whitten's office for a meeting with Whitten and all the subcommittee chairmen concerning the appropriations supplemental bill that Whitten wants to bring to the Floor, without going through the full appropriations committee. I left the meeting satisfied, as the legislation takes care of the $60 million that I had reprogrammed to the Coast Guard operations for the remainder of 1988. The other subcommittee chairmen, however, were not as happy, as the supplemental does not take care of their wishes.

Students from Nova University came in, and I spent time talking to them about educational issues and taking them to the full committee room for a photo opportunity. One of their primary concerns was the proposed "ABC" Education Program legislation that they want to see moved by Congress. I told them that any education legislation this year will most likely be in the appropriations process, and suggested other members that they might meet with to further their cause. They were a good, well-informed group.

Senator Graham sent some people to meet with me about a new product called Lojack. Lojack is a beeper instrument that can be attached to automobiles, and in the event the car is stolen it can be traced. This innovation seemed to me long overdue; I told them I would help by contacting the National Highway Traffic Safety Administration and, since the FTC has the broadcast band for this type of beeper, perhaps Appropriations Subcommittee on HUD and Independent Agencies, which has the responsibility for funding the FTC.

When I called Senator Graham, he told me that he and Senator Lautenberg had already discussed Graham's amendment for the $60 million in the 1989 bill for the Coast Guard operations. Senator Graham's aide called me at home last night to inform me that Graham had decided against offering the amendment and agreed instead to colloquy with Lautenberg on the Senate Floor, which worked out very well for both of them. With the passing of the transportation appropriations bill in the House, and a Senate version of the bill which has now also been passed, we will go to conference some time after the Democratic convention, which kicks off next week in Atlanta.

Dewey Knight, the Acting Dade County Manager, is meeting today with all the essential people involved with establishing the shock trauma network in Miami. I called Dewey and stressed the importance of convincing all parties involved to approve the recommendations set forth by the trauma task force. The *Miami Herald,* in its editorial today on my interceding to save, for now, the VA halfway house, also alluded to the $250,000 federal grant I had "snagged" for the trauma network, which should help to push the commissioners to approve the task force recommendations.

Lt. Goodwin, the Coast Guard liaison in the House, is leaving for a new assignment, and a farewell reception was held for him this evening. I went especially to let him know how much I will miss him, and I will. He has been a good friend and helped with a lot of Coast Guard cases. He was also the escort officer when we visited the bases on Nantucket last May to dedicate lighthouse restoration that our subcommittee had funded at Senator Kennedy's request.

Afterwards I went to the Jim Wright party in the Longworth Building. It was his yearly Texas-style barbecue party with civic leaders there from his Fort Worth district. A Mariachi band could be heard as you entered the room, and I enjoyed it. Staying only a few minutes, as Jim was not there, I went on to a reception at the National Democratic Club for Florida's Speaker of the House designate, Tom Gustafson. The reception, I think, was more a fundraiser for his leadership council and to help get his friends reelected, as much as it was to help in his campaign for Speaker, which would put him in a position in charge of redistricting Florida in 1992 more favorably to congressional Democratic members. It was an enjoyable reception, as I saw many people there from Florida that I knew.

Leaving the National Democratic Club, I went for a brief stay at the reception/fundraiser for Florida Republican member Michael Bilirakis of Tarpon Springs, hosted by Larry Coughlin at his home. Afterwards, I attended a dinner party hosted by the Ambassador of Morocco for visiting delegates from the Moroccan Chamber of Deputies. At the dinner I was seated with several Moroccans who did not speak any English, and I didn't speak French. Diplomats from many of the developing nations speak French, and no English. Representative Bill Chappell was also at my table, and I hoped his French was better than mine. I got home a little after 11:00 p.m., as the dinner turned out to be really drawn out, with too many long toasts.

JULY 13 WEDNESDAY

Democratic Presidential candidate Mike Dukakis has chosen Senator Lloyd Bentsen of Texas as his Vice Presidential running mate, and this morning the House Democratic Caucus honored both Dukakis and Bentsen. Senator Bentsen by all accounts is a good choice for a running mate, but I would have put my money on Lee Hamilton. Both candidates' wives were there who also made speeches.

At the conclusion of the caucus I went back to the office to meet with representatives from the Florida Tobacco Association concerned with the ban on cigarettes in Coast Guard facilities. I am a cosponsor of this legislation, but I will rethink my position before cosponsoring next year. If any adults are stupid enough to smoke, you really cannot protect them from themselves. However, the effects of second-hand smoke on nonsmokers is really becoming a big issue.

For lunch I met Florida members, Democrat Sam Gibbons and Republican Bill Young in the Members Dining Room. They wanted to talk about future rapid transit for the central and west coasts of Florida, and how to make the approach for federal funding for this endeavor. After the Democratic Convention, I will arrange for a meeting with UMTA Administrator Dellibovi and his staff, along with Gibbons and Young to discuss the problem. Public transportation between Tampa and St. Petersburg is now very difficult.

Students from the Adath Yeshurn Temple in North Miami Beach are visiting Washington. They came to the office, and I took them over to the subcommittee room where I spoke to them on my responsibilities as a member of Congress and about my two major subcommittees - transportation and foreign operations. They had some questions, but not many, and afterwards we went to the cafeteria and then had a photo opportunity. I enjoy meeting with the students, as it is a good change of pace for me from what goes on in my daily activities in the Congress.

I went to a reception for presidential and vice presidential hopefuls Mike Dukakis and Texas Senator Lloyd Bentsen. The reception was hosted by Congressman John Bryant of Texas in the Appropriations Committee room with about forty members. Several speeches were made and everyone got a chance to congratulate Senator Bentsen and his wife Beryl Ann. Anticipation of the Democratic Convention permeates the Hill, and as a convention delegate, I too am finding myself caught up in the excitement.

In the evening I went to a reception for Steve Pruitt who is leaving to work in the private sector. Pruitt is the staff director for Bill Gray, but he will soon be working for a law firm as a lobbyist.

JULY 14 THURSDAY

Mary Schekelhoff called this morning to tell me that she would be leaving Dave Obey's office to work in a law firm, also as a lobbyist. Penny Farthing called wanting to know if I could help her get an invitation for a client to the Delta Airlines reception. The client was Mayor Pena of Denver. Lobbyists can keep you pretty busy.

I was speaking to Michigan member John Conyers, and he was so pleased that I was able to get him the Tom Fiedler article in last Sunday's *Miami Herald*. Fiedler gives John a lot of credit for coming out statesmanlike on the impeachment issue of Judge Alcee Hastings.

There also is a brief mention of me in today's *Miami Herald* about the Eastern Airlines mediation letter. That some mention of the letter should appear in the *Herald* did not surprise me since publisher Dick Capen had been at our delegation meeting with the Greater Miami Chamber of Commerce. If I was surprised at all it was that more had not been written up about our meeting. If Eastern is saved, it will be a miracle.

On my late afternoon flight to Miami today, I had a first class seat next to Richard Waxenberg, an old friend who made out right there on the plane a check for $100 to my re-election campaign.

Labor lawyer Tom McAliley was also on the plane and said that I would not have any opposition by noon tomorrow, the filing deadline, and that his wife Janet, Dade County School Board member, was putting out that information.

JULY 15 FRIDAY

My morning was spent at the district office in meetings with Evelyn Scheungrund and Dr. George McCulla on aging and health care programs, and with Steven Westein and his group from Amnesty International on a bunch of issues which I will take up with my staff in Washington. Also Louis Davis was in to talk about reparation from the Germans for the loss of his family property in Germany during WWII.

A group from an American Legion post came in to present me with a lovely appreciation plaque. I had asked Rosita Korningberg to come in to be photographed so that we could include her picture alongside the story in our newsletter on the Holocaust. She and her father have been very cooperative in working with us, providing material for our newsletter, and I am very appreciative. For some survivors the Holocaust is too painful to remember, much less talk about; for others, it helps that they are able to remember and to talk about it.

JULY 16 SATURDAY

My son Tom and two of my grandsons and I went fishing today in the Florida Keys. It was a dual purpose fishing trip, pleasure and politics, as I had arranged to meet up with Michael Byrne from the Florida environmental research group, known nationally as (SPRRG). Byrne worked with our Washington office on my opposition to the Regula amendment offered in the full appropriations committee which would have, if passed, enabled ocean areas to be leased for oil drilling on the western coast of Florida and in the Keys. Today Byrne and I had photos taken of areas that would be adversely affected by oil spillage from the offshore drilling to include in a newsletter I am putting together on the need to protect our fragile environment in Florida.

Joan and I at dinner with Ruth and Richard Shack, discussed Joan's "Art in Public Places" exhibition, as Ruth is head of the

Dade County Community Foundation spearheading the fundraising drive for the project. Ruth is quite an interesting woman, having run for mayor against Steve Clark and having served on the Metro Commission for eight years. Richard is active in show business events. They are good company.

JULY 17 SUNDAY

I arrived in Atlanta this afternoon, checking into the Double Tree Hotel where the Florida delegates are booked throughout the Democratic Convention. Looking around the hotel I saw a few congressional members, including Senator Graham, and hordes of Florida media. My good friend Al Green's granddaughter, Pam Druckerman, is working at the convention and has called wanting to see me, but I do not think I will have the opportunity. I do not plan to stay to the convention's end, as I need to get back to Miami on Tuesday to attend the Metro Commission meeting determining the outcome of the trauma task force recommendations. Jeff, Sharyn, and Katherine Karpoff have accompanied me to Atlanta and we are all staying at the same hotel, with Sharyn and Katherine rooming together.

JULY 18 MONDAY

The four of us - Jeff, Sharyn, Katherine and myself - had breakfast together in my hotel room, and afterwards we went to the 9:00 a.m. Florida Caucus, where I made every effort to be as visible as possible. I saw all the Dade County delegation and most of the other Florida congressional members. I shook hands with all who were on the dais and worked the area as much as possible to keep a high visibility because I knew I most likely would not be here the next couple of days and I wanted to leave the impression that I was there.

10:00 a.m., we picked up our delegate credentials and as I saw many of my Florida colleagues coming up to get their credentials, it reminded me of a Washington scene suddenly transposed to Atlanta. The delegates took a General Motors shuttle bus to Buckhead to a hotel near the Governor's mansion, where General Motors was honoring senior Michigan member John Dingell. Katherine Karpoff joined us there later. I had to return to our hotel to meet Greg Dahlberg from our subcommittee staff, who was in Atlanta as a guest of MARTA, Atlanta's transit agency, and also for me for the Centers for Disease Control and Prevention which receives funds from NHTSA for the study of highway trauma. At 2:30 Greg and I were picked up at the hotel by Dr. Houke of Atlanta's Centers for Disease Control and taken to his offices at the CDC. Dr. Houke works specifically with the injury control program at the CDC and in my meeting with him and his staff, a great deal of information was provided to me that I can use Tuesday when I go before the Metro-Dade Commission at its meeting on the trauma network.

Leaving the CDC, I went back to the hotel where my entourage of Jeff, Katherine and Sharyn were waiting for me to attend a party being held by Larry Johnson and his law firm. The party was in honor of Vice Presidential nominee Lloyd Bentsen and his wife. Once again I was reminded of a Washington gathering, as all the members, lobbyists, and staff were there that one would see on Capitol Hill. We soon left to attend a party at the Atlanta Art Museum honoring Speaker Jim Wright, and as everyone evidently had the same invitation, we saw most of the people that were at Larry Johnson's affair.

Jeff and I left Katherine and Sharyn at the museum party, and went back to the convention hall to find the Florida delegation. I stayed over an hour talking to members before going back to the hotel. Transportation was excellent to and from the different events and everything went very well - a real smooth operation, and one of the best organized conventions that I had ever attended. Of course it helped to have staff along, as Katherine, Jeff and Sharyn did a fine job in seeing to my tickets and arranging ground transportation.

JULY 19 TUESDAY

I flew out of Atlanta this morning for Miami, cutting my time short at the convention, in time for the Metro-Dade Commission meeting today, but now that I am here I really do not think it was necessary for me to leave the convention early to come back for this meeting. The commissioners had already made up their minds, and approved without a dissenting vote the task force's shock trauma recommendations. They also voted for the resolution to establish a trauma task force agency and voted for the ordinance to support the task force advisory board.

John, who is in from Washington, and Bernie Torra of our district staff, had met me at the airport to drive me to the Metro Commission meeting. There I was asked to make a brief statement, which I did, based on my visit to the injury control center in Atlanta, telling them that the best way to prevent human suffering was to approve the recommendations of the trauma task force and that costs in the long run would be considerably lessened if Dade County had a shock trauma network. In my statement I said that $180 million would be needed, when I should have said $180 thousand. At the time I did not realize my error, and it is easy to make this mistake for in Washington I am almost always talking in millions. Jay Weiss was there from the Health Trust as was Ira Clark, President of Jackson Memorial Hospital. But it was a doctor, unknown to me, who later called my attention to the mistake and said he wanted to know "what the hell is going on." He thought I was trying to put all the doctors out of business. (This was the only person to give me any indication that I had made this blunder.)

Miami attorney Marty Fine came up after the meeting and invited me to lunch at his office. It was raining so it was easier for us to take the Metromover and avoid the traffic. This was the first time I had taken without pomp and ceremony the Metromover as just a rider, and I found it very convenient to get from the Government Center to the Centrust Building. Marty wanted to talk about two things: the next step in establishing a new station in the Metrorail system where it passes over the Florida Power and Light riverfront property; and the housing project he has in Allapattah. For the new station in the Metrorail system, I am hoping to arrange $250 thousand from UMTA for a feasibility study which could start a tremendous redevelopment along the river in downtown Miami. As soon as the feasibility study is completed Metro-Dade would then prepare a proposal for UMTA for around $10 million in federal money to match the local effort to build the station necessary for the accessibility and development of this riverfront property.

Concerning the housing project in Allapattah, Marty said he may want my help with the Ways and Means Committee to get an interpretation of the tax law regarding private corporation noninterest loans for low-income housing buyers so that the amount of money that would be deducted by the buyer for the interest payment on his house could also be deducted by the corporation that is making the noninterest bearing loan. This would not be a tax loss to the government, Marty said, but an incentive to stimulate corporate funds for low income buyers by giving both the lender and the borrower a tax break. The gathering Marty had invited me to was his Tuesday afternoon partnership luncheon. About a dozen partners were there and all had questions, which I had no problem in answering.

In the evening with the rain having stopped, Joan and I joined Nancy Pollock and other friends for dinner at the Miami Shores Country Club, where Nancy announced to us that she is running for a judgeship.

JULY 20 WEDNESDAY

Today was rather quiet. The morning was spent in my district office meeting with constituents and going through mail. I phoned Appropriations Committee chief staffer Ed Powers about a possible trip to Africa. And, I was able to help Nancy Pollock by getting her some plastic shopping bags to hand out, with her name imprinted on the bags. She is very naive about this campaign and thinks it can be run on $5,000; but I said to her that whatever she thinks she will need to run a viable campaign, she should multiply by ten.

JULY 21 THURSDAY

People from Palm Beach County came in about building a cultural center in West Palm Beach. Their congressman is Dan Mica, so I got them on the phone with him in Washington. Dan's campaign for the Senate is now in full swing. Raman Katz was with the group, as he has an interest in the proposed cultural center. Raman is a very wealthy Israeli who owns beachfront property in Sunny Isles, and I had first met him at the Marco Polo Hotel a few weeks ago during the big celebration of the Sunny Isles beach restoration.

Later I went to the Southwest Dade bus maintenance facility to see the work being done on Joan's metal arches that make up her sculpture. It is quite a job that this Quiet Nacelle Company is doing

- about $25,000 worth of labor. I stopped by the cemetery at my daughter Kathy's grave. I was thinking that she would be in Atlanta now if she were alive. Of all my children, Kathy was the most political. No one seems to notice that I am not in Atlanta and part of me is glad that I am not there to vote for either Jackson or Dukakis. If I had voted for Dukakis I would have offended some of my black supporters, and if I had voted for Jackson I would have offended my Jewish supporters and a great deal of my other supporters. It is probably best that I returned for the Metro-Dade Commission meeting, to be there as they voted out the ordinance for the shock trauma network.

JULY 22 FRIDAY

At the office by 9:30 a.m., I made a few phone calls and talked to the staff about things I wanted them to take care of. It is vacation time and things are very quiet in Washington and in the district office.

JULY 23 SATURDAY

Sharyn and I spoke about the Democratic Convention and about a mini-fundraiser next Tuesday in Jim Furlong's office in Washington. Apparently Nancy Pollock got a good "slot" in which to run, and I will continue to help her. This quiet time is good for me, but it does not look as though Joan will have her sculpture in shape so that she can go on any trip in August; perhaps I will go somewhere alone. Dan O'Connor of Ryder Corporation has just sent a $500 check for Joan's sculpture fund, as contributions continually arrive at the Dade Foundation for the project. Joan is very encouraged by all the support, as am I.

In the afternoon I played tennis with Al Cardenas, State Committee member of the Republican party and Chairman of the Task Force on Transportation of the Greater Miami Chamber of Commerce. We talked about the next step, following the election, in moving forward on the Metromover extensions. He is a nice fellow and I like him. I introduced him to Stan Whitman, another conservative Republican, and they talked about how I was their good friend even though I am a "liberal" Democrat.

JULY 24 SUNDAY

Nancy Pollock was in the district office to discuss how Jeff and I could best help with her campaign for judgeship. I called Dave Samson, Ruby Steiner and Annie Ackerman for her, and I think her chances to win are good. With Nancy gone, Jeff and I turned our attention to plans for a unification brunch with Dukakis in August which will cost about $5,000 at Turnberry. We are also thinking about a brunch in August for the North Miami Beach condo leaders.

JULY 25 MONDAY

I arrived back in Washington at 4:00 p.m. today, took a shuttle bus and picked up a rental car from Alamo. Since the accident I have not had the use of my car, which is being repaired. Alamo has offered the car to me at no charge, but I will pay for the rental because Alamo has report language in our bill and to not pay could bring on allegations of conflict of interest.

At the office Nadine had a problem with the Interior re-authorization bill regarding a switch of public land from Arizona to Florida and other public lands from Florida to Arizona. The land switch can permit the sale of public lands in Arizona to be used to buy Everglades land from the Collier estate in Florida, which is a good deal for Florida but upsetting to Sid Yates, Chairman of Appropriations Interior Subcommittee. Dante Fascell is on one side of the issue and Sid on the other. I need to find out what it is all about. The legislation has yet to come to the Floor, but the rule for the bill has already been passed.

Tom Kingfield's father died in New Jersey and it looks as though our conference might be delayed a few days. I just hope we have the conference before the Republican Convention so that the President can't veto our bill because of low FAA and Coast Guard funding in the bill.

JULY 26 TUESDAY

Bob Brin of Miami's Coopers and Lybrand firm is in Washington with his family, and we had breakfast together in the Members Dining Room. Several months ago I had spoken to Pete Stark of Ways and Means about meeting with Bob Brin, and Pete had recommended that Bob speak with a member on the tax subcommittee. So, I introduced him to Sam Gibbons on the Ways and Means Committee, so that Bob could talk about the tax bill and how difficult it is to fill out the new tax forms. Bob does both my personal and campaign tax returns, and my son Bill's business and personal taxes, and has done so for years. He is a senior partner in the Miami accounting firm, and we have a great deal of confidence in him.

In a meeting with Bill Taylor and Nick Serianni of the Florida Department of Transportation there was talk about the highway funds for mass transit in Jacksonville and also about a much needed bridge that they propose to build from Dodge Island to the mainland in Miami.

Afterwards, when I met with airlines union officials, i.e., Robert McGlotten, Director of the Legislative Department of the AFL/CIO, Paul Hallisay of the Airline Pilots Association, Bill Holaytor of the Machinists Union and Dave Mallino of the Industrial Union Department of the AFL/CIO, they were concerned with the problems of Eastern Airlines and the fact that Eastern is laying off more workers and that Continental Airlines, which controls Eastern, really wants to do away with the airline. Primarily, though, they were concerned that in conference our House bill will have a labor protection agreement, self-executed by the Rules Committee, that gives airline labor issues to the Department of Labor, thereby taking these issues out of the domain of the Department of Transportation. There is no such language in the Senate version, and labor does not want us to recede to the Senate.

I called Ruth Shack to ask her advice on how to handle the in-kind contribution from the Quiet Nacelle Company that is doing so much work on Joan's sculpture. She said to have the company send a bill or letter estimating their work on the sculpture and that the Dade Foundation would send the company a letter in return thanking them for their in-kind contribution. To my question about handling the conflict between Joan's nonunion and Metro Transit's union people that work at the bus garage, Ruth's advice was to keep Joan's exposure as low as possible.

Dr. Hatem Abu Ghazala, Chairman of the Society for the Care of Handicapped Children in the Gaza Strip, and A State Department official on Israel and Arab Affairs, came in about funds for hospital care in the Gaza Strip, and also about redirecting AID funds designated for the West Bank and Gaza. The way AID funds are presently directed, they go through Jordan first and Dr. Ghazala's complaint was that Jordan has created too much bureaucracy in the distribution of these funds to the West Bank.

At 1:30, the Appropriations Committee met on the dire supplemental appropriations, and the bill was passed. Transportation funds were approved in the bill for $60 million for the Coast Guard operations.

JULY 27 WEDNESDAY

The vote on the Arizona/Florida public land exchange was on the Floor this morning, and on final passage I voted for the outright swap. It is a good swap for Florida but I think it is a bad swap for U.S. taxpayers because the land in Phoenix is worth a lot more to the Collier family than the land they are giving up in Florida.

Then a meeting and photo opportunity with students from the Congressional Youth Leadership Council from my district before stopping by a luncheon reception hosted by Addie Yates, Sid's wife. The luncheon was in honor of Dutch immigrants who had sheltered and hid a number of Jews during the Holocaust. I wasn't able to stay very long, but I was glad to see Addie looking so well.

I spoke to Marty Sabo, Richard Durbin and Bob Mrazek on the Floor about not having a fundraiser this year for the Democratic members of our subcommittee, as I have done for every session of Congress since becoming subcommittee chairman. Instead, I am proposing to have a party in Miami in January where members can participate in the Super Bowl Weekend - play golf or fish or just relax - and perhaps pick up $2,000 each in honorarium. They all seemed to like this a lot better than the usual fundraiser that I have for them at my townhouse. None of the subcommittee members are really threatened by opposition and they all have plenty of campaign funds. The reason I like the idea of doing this in Miami is because this can be done on a bipartisan basis and the Republican members can be included. I try to keep a bipartisan subcommittee, and ranking minority member Larry Coughlin is as big a help to me as the Democrats.

There were a few receptions in the early evening, all held at the National Democratic Club, one honoring my colleague Pat Schroeder, another honoring Congressman Bob Wise (W.VA), and then another honoring Florida State Representative Jon Mills. Professor Terry Anderson of the University of Miami, who is a friend of my son Tom, was at Mills's reception and spoke to me about the impeachment process for Alcee Hastings. I had spoken to members concerned about Hastings, such as Don Edwards and John Conyers, and they say he is "guilty as hell" and that he should be impeached. At the moment, "ambivalent" best describes my feeling on the issue, but I will continue to give the matter much thought before the vote to impeach him, as Judge Hastings is well respected among many of my constituents.

Joan arrived in Washington this afternoon and we are making plans for dinner. It is a quiet time of year, with almost everyone on vacation.

JULY 28 THURSDAY **and JULY 29** FRIDAY

We had an enjoyable farewell bagel breakfast for our interns, and my schedule remains very light.

JULY 30 - SATURDAY

After breakfast at Eastern Market, Joan and I stopped by the office and found Lucy packing and moving boxes as the Rayburn Building superintendent will be installing new carpet. Later I played tennis at Haines Point with Sonny Montgomery and members of the Capitol Hill Tennis Club. In the evening Joan and I went to dinner with Dante Fascell and his wife Jean Marie at the Windows Restaurant. It was a very nice evening, good food and good company.

JULY 31 SUNDAY

The day has been very restful - with me and Joan going out for a movie in the evening.

Chapter 20

AUGUST 1, 1988 MONDAY

I learned today that our transportation subcommittee will probably not go to conference this week because we don't want to get too far ahead of Appropriations defense subcommittee and have our numbers revealed for fear of criticism over the low budget amount in our bill for the Coast Guard. Later, the anticipated windfall from the defense subcommittee will make up the difference in the reduced amount for the Coast Guard in our bill.

AUGUST 2 TUESDAY

The August recess begins in two weeks, and Charlie Wilson has asked me if I would be interested in going on a trip to Australia with him and the Speaker during the break. The occasion would be to join in the 200th anniversary celebration of the independence of Australia. I would like traveling with Charlie and the Speaker but, again, Joan is tied up with her sculpture and would not be able to make the trip, and I would not want to go without her. I have, however, spoken to Greg on our subcommittee staff about traveling out west to Utah and Arizona to view some transportation properties that later may need my subcommittee help.

In the meantime Jamie Whitten, in a meeting with the subcommittee chairmen regarding our conferences with the Senate on the 302B allocations, has advised us to stick together and not to make separate deals with the Senate subcommittees without letting him know how we are compromising. We won't go to conference until the House is back in session after the August recess.

AUGUST 3 WEDNESDAY

On the House Floor I moved to request the appointment of conferees, but the main event today was the vote on the House Resolution for the impeachment of Judge Alcee Hastings of the U.S. District Court for the Southern District of Florida. The House voted 413-3 (I wasn't one of the 3) to adopt the resolution calling for Judge Hastings' impeachment, and the matter now goes before the Senate, which acts as jury in impeachment proceedings. In this case, Judge Hastings would go on trial before the Senate for "high crimes and misdemeanors," and with a two-thirds vote he would be removed from the Federal bench. Following the vote, Channel 10 did an interview with me in front of the Capitol on my reaction to the House's overwhelming vote to impeach Judge Hastings. I have also spoken to Channel 7, and Bill Bayer of WIOD radio has a call in to me.

Back at the office Channel 4 did a video with me regarding the impeachment, which I regard more with sadness than anger. I returned the call to Bill Bayer of WIOD radio, but his inquiry was not about the impeachment; Bayer was interested in the new HOV regulations that will affect the highways of I-95 in South Florida, increasing the passenger minimum from two to three, of which I am supportive.

Eastern's President Phil Bakes called regarding the labor protection agreement. He wants me to put language in the conference report of my bill to prevent possible retroactive action for labor protection on any merger or consolidation of two or more airlines approved by the Department of Transportation. This would mean that a merger between Eastern and Continental Airlines would not be subjected to the labor protection agreement, and it also appears that this issue may be a difficult part of our transportation conference. This issue as of now is outside the scope of the conference.

At 4:00, Florida colleagues Mike Bilirakis, Sam Gibbons and Bill Young joined me in a meeting with UMTA Administrator Al Dellibovi. This is the meeting I had promised Gibbons and Young last week I would set up with Dellibovi to discuss the horrendous traffic problems in the Tampa Bay area. It was a good meeting with suggestions all around as to what might be done to correct the traffic problems. Dellibovi said he would give the matter further study and get back to us next week. I will probably have to make a visit to the Tampa area.

AUGUST 4 THURSDAY

Not much was happening on the Hill today when Joan and I left for the airport. We had a 4:30 p.m. flight to Miami scheduled to arrive at 6:30, but the flight was two hours late.

AUGUST 5 FRIDAY

Joan and I went to the photographer this morning with my son Bill, his wife Shirley and their three children, Mickey, John and Deborah, and had our Christmas photos made. Later at the district office I went over some constituent cases with the staff. Elaine Gordon of North Miami called and I gave her my endorsement for re-election as Florida State Representative. I also cosigned an endorsement letter with Joan for Nancy Pollock for the Dade County District Court Judge.

AUGUST 6 SATURDAY

Relaxed today, just tennis in the afternoon.

AUGUST 7 SUNDAY

Bill Bayer of WIOD radio did a taping with me today, which will be aired on August 15.

AUGUST 8 MONDAY

Arriving back in Washington today at 2:00, it was quiet so I played tennis with my buddies. It is good to be able to take it easy.

AUGUST 9 TUESDAY

The Metropolitan Washington Airports Authority Board of Review held its meeting in the Capitol this morning. The main issue was the proposal to open the Dulles Airport access road to all traffic, and the Congressional Review Board has a veto right on this proposal. As a member of the review board I have no problem with this, but other members want to prevent the measure and keep the access road open only to Dulles Airport traffic. Not having a quorum at this morning's meeting, we adjourned till 4:00. I intend to offer a six-month compromise proposal of the airport authority resolution, which may be acceptable. Earlier, Republican Representative Frank Wolf of Northern Virginia came to my office and we discussed this compromise proposal. Frank, of course, is hoping to have the access road opened to all traffic for the benefit of his constituency during peak rush hours.

Between votes back and forth on the Floor Robert Anderson, the Florida State President of the Fraternal Order of Police, came in with members of the FOP organization to lobby for the seven-day cooling off period for the purchase of handguns. The legislation is to come to the Floor soon, and I let Anderson know that I intended to support the measure.

At 4:00, the Congressional Review Board of the Washington Metropolitan Airport Authority resumed its meeting. We now had enough members to make up a quorum, consisting of chairman Norman Mineta, and members Senator Fritz Hollings of South Carolina, Dan Rostenkowski of Illinois, John Hammerschmidt of Arkansas, and myself. Introducing my compromise proposal, I then moved for a six-month demonstration to test the adversity on the flow of traffic leading to the Dulles Airport. But, I was the only member to vote for the compromise, and the measure to open the Dulles access road to all traffic was vetoed. Another issue resolved was the noise factor, and we agreed to extend the present landing and takeoff curfews beyond the 7:00 a.m. to 10:00 p.m. restriction.

On the House Floor Richard Lehman (D-CA) told me about a trip to Africa that he and his wife Patty are taking during the August recess, with plans to visit Botswana and Mozambique. Members are either thinking about, talking about, and/or planning overseas trips that they will take during the break. I have spoken again to Joan, and such a trip at this time is definitely out. I stayed late at the office this evening going over the environmental newsletter, especially as it relates to oil drilling on the west coast of Florida and the Keys. Several of the pictures we took in the Keys, including one of me with the environmentalist, will be in the newsletter; I am happy with the way it is coming together, and I think it will be both informative and good for our position on environmental issues, particularly the need to protect our oceans.

For dinner Maria Elena and I went to Prima Piatti. Maria Elena has done an excellent job with META, her public relations firm, and she has offered to help with the Super Bowl event in Miami that I am planning for my subcommittee members.

AUGUST 10 WEDNESDAY

Today's *Washington Post* had the story about the Congressional Review Board's veto on opening the Dulles access road to all traffic, and I was not mentioned. I wish I had been more vocal in recording a "no" vote on the veto, but calling particular attention to my vote would have probably antagonized Norman Mineta and that I would not want since I have to work with Norman on a daily basis. I have already made a little unhappy senior Michigan member John Dingell by signing the Bruce Vento (D-MN) auto emissions letter.

Jesse Jackson is in town and was honored this morning at a breakfast hosted by Speaker Jim Wright. Jesse and I had a photo taken together, which will most likely appear in the *Miami Times*, a black-owned newspaper in my district. What he said at this morning's gathering was not particularly new, but he was tough on the Palestinian rights issue and on apartheid in South Africa, and an amazing amount of press was there to hear him. Jake Pickle of Texas asked me about providing him with material on the airport trust fund and the money that seems to accumulate in that fund. Jake is having a Ways and Means hearing tomorrow on the airport trust fund, so I had sent over to his office a copy of our 1989 Bill Report which explains what appears to be unspent surplus in the airport trust fund, but what is really not surplus but funds held in abeyance for future costs of the new air traffic system and the FAA's NAS Plan. The real problem is the political inability to build more airport capability in this country, and everyone's "not in my backyard" attitude.

Some very bright Nicaraguan and Honduras students visiting in Washington came to the office, and during our question and answer session, they voted about three to one in favor of the Contras. Their trip was being sponsored by the Washington International Center, and I was helped at the meeting by Maria Elena who acted as interpreter. Afterwards, Maria Elena and I got Al Cardenas on the phone to discuss the subcommittee's trip to Miami. Cardenas heads the Transportation Task Force for the Greater Miami Chamber of Commerce and, together with Joaquin Avino, the new Dade County Manager, I am hoping that suitable arrangements can be worked out for both our subcommittee members and the subcommittee staff.

Following our phone call to Cardenas I had to leave the office for the Democratic Caucus on the House Floor for discussions on member participation during the fall presidential campaign. Dukakis's campaign manager Susan Estrich was there, as was Kirk O'Donnell, senior advisor to the campaign. I spoke about the unity breakfast I was proposing to put on for Dukakis in Miami in October. Beryl Anthony, Chair of the Democratic Congressional Campaign Committee (DCCC), the fundraising organization for the Democrats in Congress, has asked member Democrats to send some of their surplus campaign funds to the Democratic National Party for the Dukakis campaign. In answer to his request, I told Beryl that I was sending $5,000.

Bob Carr spoke to me after the caucus about the Speaker's letter concerning the labor protection provision. The Speaker has asked that we accept the Senate version transferring labor protection jurisdiction to the Labor Department from the Transportation Department. Bob and I both think the labor protection agreement will be detrimental to Eastern and Pan American Airlines because it threatens Eastern's merger with Continental and makes Pan American with seniority protection an undesirable merger, or buyout. No one will want to purchase Pan American with a protected unionized seniority. We see labor protection as an instrument that will cause Pan American to go bankrupt rather than survive, but labor leaders sometimes seem more concerned with the labor union philosophy than the reality of what is best for the rank and file, especially when it comes to airlines.

Heading back to the office I saw Bill Gray, and he is interested in buying a condominium in South Florida, particularly in the Naples or Boca Raton area. I suggested Turnberry, of which he had never heard, and I told him I would have some materials on Turnberry mailed to him. Concerning Bill Gray, I heard that the leadership is pushing for Mary Rose Oakar of Ohio in the race for Chairman of the Democratic Caucus. The thinking is if Bill Gray should become chairman of the Caucus he could, in future years, be a threat to the Majority Leader or Speaker, if he wanted to make a move in that direction. At the office, Southern Bell representative Dave Walker was in. Dave asked me to cosponsor a bill granting Southern Bell the right to compete with AT&T in the manufacture of electrical equipment. Viewing this as only fair that Southern Bell should have the opportunity to compete on an equal basis with AT&T, I readily agreed to cosponsor the legislation.

That evening I attended the Annual House Gymnasium Membership Supper in the Longworth Cafeteria. Vice President George Bush came in with Sonny Montgomery (D-MS), and we all stood in line to shake the Vice President's hand. He is the nicest man, and having heard about my operation, he asked how I was feeling. I thought he came across as a very warm and caring person, and if that personality came through on television he would be a very formidable candidate. But somehow it does not, and that is too bad, as I believe Bush would make a decent president, especially if the right people are around him. Nicholas Brady was there, and he too was impressive. Brady is the former senator from New Jersey and an investment banker, and Reagan has just recently named him to replace Jim Baker as Secretary of the Treasury. Baker is leaving the Cabinet post to run Bush's presidential campaign. Many retired members attended the gym party. I shared a table with Sid Yates (D-IL) and Butler Derrick (D-SC), and it was quite an evening.

AUGUST 11 THURSDAY

This morning I attended the Congressional Prayer Breakfast. I had enjoyed my first experience at the breakfast several weeks ago, finding that I like the people who attend this gathering. Since that first visit, they have continuously asked me to come back, and I have wanted to because it reminds me of my old YMCA days back in Selma and the same kind of small-town people. The members make you feel very comfortable, and it does not hurt to maintain contact. I am not bothered by references to Christianity, but I won't make a weekly habit of it. At the breakfast I had a chance to speak with Jake Pickle of Texas concerning his hearing today on the FAA trust fund and the tax program. The Ways and Means Committee is in charge of collecting the tax on airline tickets and Jake has a problem with the backlog of the FAA trust fund money being appropriated too slowly.

Back at the office I met with Dade County Manager Joaquin Avino, and Syl Lukis, his lobbyist. I enjoyed talking to Joaquin and he seems ready to go all out when our subcommittee is in Miami. We agreed to meet again in Miami to firm up the details for the Super Bowl weekend. He also spoke about the full-funding contract for the Metromover and how Dade needs to accept new language that UMTA requires. Joaquin said he is now looking for a good administrator for the Dade County Public Transportation system. I told him that the next time he comes to Washington I would set up an appointment for him with Carmen Turner, the successful Director of the Washington Metro Transit, so that he could talk to her about the kind of person he is looking for to help improve the Dade County transit system.

AUGUST 12 FRIDAY

The House is now in recess through Labor Day, and I headed for Miami.

AUGUST 13 SATURDAY

At the district office, I left messages for staff, and signed mail.

AUGUST 14 SUNDAY

Today the Sunny Isles Resort Association honored me and Gwen Margolis, candidate for reelection to the State Senate, at a brunch in recognition of our work on the Sunny Isles Beach Restoration project. Chuck Rosen who manages the Marco Polo Hotel where the event was held, also funded the brunch. Many politicians were there, including Mayor Steve Clark and Dade County State Attorney Janet Reno. I made a speech, received two lovely plaques, which I will take back to the office, and worked the tables and tried to shake hands with everyone.

Before going to the brunch I had stopped at Neighbors Restaurant for breakfast and the owner would not let me pay for my breakfast. After the brunch I stopped at the Poppy Seed Bagel Restaurant for bagels and cream cheese and the owner there would not let me pay. I felt like the police officer who gets free meals and drinks at restaurants.

AUGUST 15 MONDAY

At the district office I called Adele in Washington about a possible trip to Israel, and spoke to John about the trip to Phoenix and to Salt Lake City later this month. I then rang the staff on the Foreign Operations Subcommittee to get help on a visa for someone in Guatemala. For lunch I met lobbyist Priscilla Perry and we talked about problems related to my subcommittee's visit to Miami during the Super Bowl. I hope the new County Manager follows through, as this is going to be a big deal if it works out.

AUGUST 16 TUESDAY

Wendy Yanis from the Association of Floral Importers was to meet me at the district office this morning, but she had to cancel and sent a beautiful floral arrangement with her apology. This gift could not have come at a better time, as today is Joan and my 49th wedding anniversary. I must thank Wendy and tell her of this happenstance, as she did not know this was our anniversary. Dr. Gidian Stock, a dentist and an old conservative friend, came in and handed me a $1,000 check from the Dental PAC. We are friends from way back when his father had a market on 79th Street, near where I had a used car lot on 71st Street.

Dukakis's office called, and Dukakis wants to meet with me Thursday. I also am scheduled to attend the Milt Littman Memorial Bridge ribbon cutting ceremony on Thursday, so I called Jules Littman, the surviving brother, and told him I would be a little late and explained why. Jules said he understood and would stall the program as best he could. Leaving the district office I went to the Oak Grove Elementary School that runs an afterschool daycare program.

Photos were taken, but the message I wanted to convey was that school activities with computers, sports, etc., are among the best resources we have to offer children.

AUGUST 17 WEDNESDAY

This morning I went to the ribbon cutting ceremony for the I-95 access road that the State Highway Department opened today. This access road runs from Northwest 62nd Street to Northwest 54th Street, parallel to the west of I-95, and I was instrumental in getting federal approval to open up this road. The road will help to unblock traffic jams at Edison Center, facilitating the accessibility of the Edison Center merchants and bring in more customers to their businesses. Several officials of the Florida Department of Transportation were there, as was an Edison Center civic action group. I saw community activist Wally McCall, who has done a fine job in the area. Wally asked me about Nancy Pollock and whether he should support her, and said that he would if I gave the word. I, of course, told him "yes," so this is another boost for Nancy in the black community. The *Miami Herald* and *Miami Times* reporters were there and a couple of radio and television station reporters.

I then went to the Miami Club to meet Atwood Dunwody and his partner John Armstrong, senior law partners with Evans, Mischon and Sawyer. They had problems with legislation pending in the Congress permitting Indian tribes on reservations to operate parimutuel facilities, such as dog tracks, and still be exempt from State laws on parimutuel betting. Atwood wanted a three-year moratorium before changing the rules, which would put the Indian parimutuel operations on a level playing field with other parimutuels. Arizona member Mo Udall, Chairman of the authorizing Committee on Interior and Insular Affairs, has a large Indian constituency and is for the Indians. Democratic Whip Tony Coehlo, however, is for the parimutuel operators. I got Nadine in my Washington office on the phone to find out where we were on the legislation, and according to her several Seminole chiefs had been to the office and said that I had told them I would be supportive on Indian reservation casino gambling. But I did not mean that to include parimutuel gambling; I had said I would not mind continuing the bingo and other types of gambling, but not parimutuel. I told Nadine to get back to them and find out exactly what they had understood, and then to get back to me.

The legislation is expected to reach the House Floor and voted out this year. In the previous Congress, legislation to regulate high-stakes gambling on Indian reservations failed in the Senate but passed the House.

Whenever I have lunch with prominent lawyer Atwood Dunwody there is always an issue that he wants to discuss, whether it is the sugar industry, the parimutuel operations or what have you. My son Tom stopped by and sat with us a few minutes. A few years ago Evans, Mischon, and Sawyer gave Tom his first job out of law school. I always see familiar faces at the Miami Club, and today I saw Lee Spiegleman who ran against me about ten years ago and is now doing very well as a developer; Dr. Phil Frost who founded Key Pharmaceuticals; Dan Paul, a controversial lawyer in Miami and a good friend of Hamilton Fish, my colleague in Washington; and Bill Allen, a bank president friend.

Joan and I spent the evening in Coral Gables with our grandson Matt, and his father and stepmother. Matt, at sixteen years old, spent this summer working at Miami International Airport, and had some interesting information. A wire fence is going up around Eastern Airlines repair facilities in preparation for a strike. The fence will serve as a barrier to separate the strikers from those who continue to work. This suggests that Eastern will indeed go on strike. Talking about Pan American, which is in deep financial trouble, Matt said Pan Am will probably go out of business at Miami International Airport. "Out of the mouths of babes" you get some revealing information.

AUGUST 18 THURSDAY

Jeff picked me up at Neighbors Restaurant this morning for our trip to the airport to meet Democratic Presidential nominee Mike Dukakis. We waited for him in a small office at the airport. Before Dukakis arrived *Miami Times* owner, Garth Reeves, discussed with me the possibility of building public housing on the corner of Northwest 74th Street and 12th Avenue, which is near where my used car lot used to be. Garth said he wanted to name the project the "William Lehman Public Housing." I'm sure he is naming it such just to gain my support in receiving a grant for the project, but I would like to see more good public housing. Garth will get in touch with Patrice at our Northside office, and I suggested to him that he appear at the public hearings for the appropriations subcommittee on housing next year so that language for Miami could be in HUD appropriations for the 1990 housing bill.

Dukakis's private plane arrived at the rear of the airport away from the main terminal. His first meeting was with a group of black leaders - State Representative Carrie Meek, Jim Burke, and others. He next met with me, Dante Fascell, and Larry Smith, three South Florida Members of Congress. Dukakis was very upbeat. Larry spoke to him mostly about the drug problem, especially as it relates to Panama. Dante did not have much to say. I mentioned the fact that we should put more emphasis on drug prevention in this country and stressed the need for more after-school programs as a good place to start. I reminded him that I was Chairman of the Appropriations Transportation Subcommittee, and that I would want to be part of his transition team to have some input as to the choice of the next Secretary of the Department of Transportation, as I felt it was important to have someone in that position who would work well with me. To this Dukakis said he would be his own Secretary of Transportation as he is really into public transportation, especially mass transit. "I personally use public transportation in Boston and I would use it in Washington," he said unrealistically.

With the meeting over I went back to the office. Unfortunately I was unable to attend the Milt Littman Memorial Bridge dedication as the meeting with Dukakis preempted my attendance. Being listed on the program I felt bad that I was not there, and called Jules Littman and explained the situation to him. He again understood. Fletcher Sessons and members of the Association of General Contractors soon came in, with a $1,000 campaign contribution. This group has always been supportive, and Sessons of the architectural firm of Sessons and Grice, has built several of my son Bill's automobile dealerships.

Afterwards members of the Underground Contractors Association came in, and they also had a $1,000 contribution. They are concerned with the highway department building roads without first putting in sewers. I told them to give me questions to ask the Federal Highway Administrator when he comes before my subcommittee next year, and we can include in the bill regulations stipulating that before federal monies go into highway programs certain preliminary engineering conditions must be met pertaining to drainage and sewage to prevent highways from being torn up later.

AUGUST 19 FRIDAY

Most of the day was spent with my young grandson Tommy. We went to the MacArthur Causeway helicopter pad and Bill Ter Hurst gave us a free ride in his helicopter. We really had fun. Ter Hurst had been to my office in Washington about six months ago with an FAA regulatory problem and I am not sure whether I was able to help him, but he appreciated my attention and offered to take me for a ride anytime. Today I used that invitation.

AUGUST 20 SATURDAY

I went to see Annie Ackerman, spending about an hour with her, and she did not want me to leave. I may have created an opportunity for Jeff by talking to Annie about Point East management. Ernie Samuels has run Point East condo association for almost twenty years and is getting up in age where the responsibility may soon be too much for him. I think it is the type of job that would suit Jeff very well, and before going back to Washington I will talk to Ernie about training Jeff.

AUGUST 21 SUNDAY

Today I went to Turnberry for a breakfast that Florida Senatorial candidate Dan Mica put on with the condo leaders in North Dade. The same people were there that usually attend all the North Dade condo brunches, i.e., Bill Farber, Marty Kahn, Annie Ackerman, etc. It was a good turnout and he will need the support, as Florida Insurance Commissioner Bill Gunter has also announced that he is running for the senate seat.

AUGUST 22 MONDAY

For dinner Joan and I went to the Sea Shanty with our two grandchildren. Just being a congressman can attract people, and we had about four groups of people come to our table to talk to us, including Mickey Weinkle. Mickey, a practicing dentist, is a former Mayor of Hallandale, and was my campaign chairman in 1974; he was also the Master of Ceremonies at our campaign dinner at the Doral Country

Club when I had Tip O'Neill as guest. His daughter Tracy, who was once our summer intern, now has two children of her own. Another who stopped at our table was Bill Landa, a good supporter and contributor, who shared with us that he is now constructing a high-rise executive building adjacent to the William Lehman Causeway.

AUGUST 23 TUESDAY

Joan and I left this morning at 9:30 on a TWA flight for Salt Lake City, Utah. Our flight was made more pleasant by a customer service representative who upgraded our tickets to first class. On our arrival in Salt Lake City, Alan Wulkan, the former assistant manager for Metro-Dade Transit, met us at the airport. Alan is now Deputy Area Manager of the engineering firm of Parsons Brinckerhoff Quade and Douglas. With Alan at the airport was John Pingree from the Salt Lake City Transit Authority and engineer Mike Snyder, Vice President of Parsons Brinckerhoff Quade and Douglas. When I was in Honolulu some years ago, Parsons Brinckerhoff was doing the HOV-3 road that our subcommittee legislated as a demonstration project. Tomorrow there will be a helicopter ride, just as in Honolulu, to show me the traffic problems. I think I have seen more traffic jams from helicopters than anyone else in the country, at least it feels that way.

We did a short sightseeing tour by car when we arrived, just to see what the city and surrounding hills area were like. They wanted to show where the Salt Lake City light rail would go, on 16 miles of abandoned Union Pacific Railroad right-of-way, should Salt Lake City get the federal funding and the local support needed. There is already a quarter percent sales tax as a dedicated source of revenue and another quarter percent is to be obligated by the State in the next legislative session. After the tour they dropped Joan and me at the Marriott Hotel, where we are staying, and said they would be back to pick us up for an honorarium dinner for me this evening at the University Club. The dinner turned out to be a long, drawn-out affair, ending sometime after 10:00 p.m., with the guests consisting of business leaders, managers of the transit system, Alan Wulkan, and engineer Mike Snyder. The service was slow and the food was fair, but the people were exceptionally nice.

AUGUST 24 WEDNESDAY

Alan Wulkan and Mike Snyder met me for breakfast at the Marriott and at 8:00 a.m., we met Utah Senator Jake Garn and the manager of the Salt Lake City Transit system for a helicopter flight over the general area. We also flew over the ski resort area to where, eventually, a light rail will be constructed. At this time, however, a light rail to a ski resort is only a pipe dream. Salt Lake City had better stick to what it can get accomplished.

At noon a luncheon had been arranged by Congressman Wayne Owens of Utah. Joan joined us, and then someone took her for an automobile trip through the Canyon. The luncheon focused on efforts to provide local matching funds to show UMTA there is local support. Wayne Owens and Utah's Transit Authority Chairman John Pingree escorted me to the Federal Building for a press conference, which was all on Utah's light rail transit plans.

Afterwards I played doubles tennis with former Utah Governor Scott Mathiason, a Department of Transportation intern, and a tennis pro from one of the local tennis clubs. We had a good workout, the air was thin and the tennis balls just sailed. I like Mathiason very much, and he intends to run for Senator Garn's seat if Garn does not run for reelection in 1992. Jake lives in Salt Lake City and commutes to Washington four or five days each week. He told me this morning that he is really tired of Washington and much prefers staying in Utah.

One of John Pingree's interns chauffeured Joan and me to a restaurant up in the Canyon where the two of us had a quiet and very delightful dinner. The restaurant was quite beautiful, with a lovely view, and it was good of the Utah Transit Authority to provide us with a chauffeur for the evening.

AUGUST 25 THURSDAY

8:00 a.m., Alan Wulkan picked us up at our hotel for a 9:30 flight to Phoenix. Arriving in Phoenix, we took Joan to check in at the Hyatt Regency, and I went with Alan to his office to make a phone call to Washington, as John had left a message to call him. When I got John on the phone, he said there were some misunderstandings concerning several of my endorsements. Rosa Castro Feinberg, for one, had thought that I was endorsing her for the Dade

County School Board, but I had committed to Mike Gonzalez. I called Rosa and was able to clear up the misunderstanding. I also got a letter off to Rosa stating that my endorsement of Mike was in no way adverse to her, it was just that Mike has been a longtime helpful friend. Also some of the condo people and old friend, Dr. Sy Sarasohn, are not very happy about my endorsement of Nancy Pollock; Nancy is running an ad in the paper with Joan and me endorsing her. With each endorsement there are bound to be people made unhappy by my choice. The people I have endorsed this time are Elaine Gordon for State Representative, Mike Gonzalez for the Dade County School Board and Nancy Pollock for Dade County District Court Judge.

Joan went shopping with Alan's secretary while Alan and I met with the Regional Public Transportation Authority, which includes several cities such as Glendale, Tempe, and Scottsdale. We drove around and viewed the traffic problems and sites for future transit stations, and the airport where the hope is to build a rail system. A half-cent sales tax dedicated to the construction of more freeways has already passed, but next spring an effort will be made to pass another half-cent sales tax dedicated to rapid rail mass transit, which will probably be about twenty-five miles of overhead rail. Over the next three years Phoenix will be asking for a $200 million program which will be 80% federally funded. Because bus- way funds, unlike rail mass transit, have never yet been earmarked by our subcommittee, I cautioned them that this would be very difficult.

At 3:00 in Tempe, we met in the Mayor's office. The news media was present, and I repeated my comments on the problem of getting bus funds earmarked, saying that it may be the wrong way to get started. Former House Minority Leader John Rhodes of Arizona was at the meeting, as were staff members from Mo Udall's and Arizona Senator DeConcini's offices. I tried to give them good advice on mass as well as rapid mass transit. I let them know that there were obstacles to overcome as I did not want to leave them with the impression that "the check was in the mail."

7:00 p.m., Alan and his wife met Joan and me at our hotel to take us to dinner at a private club called The Mansion, where we were joined by transportation and local government officials and business leaders. They thanked me for coming out to their part of the country to view their transportation projects, and I reiterated my offer to do what I could to help. It was a good evening.

AUGUST 26 FRIDAY

This trip has been very easy, very relaxing, and Joan and I have enjoyed it. For dinner this evening the Parsons Brinckerhoff people took Joan and me to the Hyatt Regency, and tomorrow we head back to Miami.

AUGUST 27 SATURDAY

Joan and I checked out of the hotel at 7:00 and left on an 8:30 a.m. flight, arriving in Miami at 5:30 p.m.. On the flight I wrote thank you letters to the people in Utah and Arizona, taken from the list of names and addresses Alan Wulkan had given me; by the time our plane reached Miami I had completed all the correspondence.

AUGUST 28 SUNDAY

Jeff met me at the district office, and we went over all the thank you letters and discussed the problems of moving Patrice, who manages the Northside office, into Bernie Torra's position in the main district office. Bernie has taken a position in the private sector. Neither Patrice nor Jeff thought it a good idea to have Patrice leave the Northside Office, so for now we are going to leave things as they are. After the election Jeff will spend more time in the district office and then we will hire another case worker. If we can get our Barry University intern now in Washington to work in the district office this would be a solution. With this semester completed, he will have finished college and could be a good addition to our staff. I am also exploring the possibility of installing computers in the district office. Dante Fascell's office already has his cases on computer, and Jeff feels our system could also be better managed on computer.

AUGUST 29 MONDAY

Spending the morning and part of the afternoon at the district office, I left at 2:00 to visit Arnold Picker, a big time operator in the Democratic party. Arnold formerly was part owner of the United

Artists Film Company and has always been one of my big supporters. I have not seen him in a long time, and he and his wife Ruth are not in the best of health. When we do see each other, we very much enjoy each other's company, and today was no exception. I know if I need Arnold's help he would come through for me; he is a very concerned Democrat. Back at the district office, I returned phone calls, and arranged some possible details for my trip to Israel in October for the dedication of the Absorption Center there named for our daughter Kathy. Adele is also working to put this trip together.

AUGUST 30 TUESDAY

Arriving at the district office this morning, I first made a series of phone calls - one to a former West Point appointee, another to Nadine in Washington to help clarify some proposed Miccosukee legislation, and to Adele who filled me in on further details concerning the trip to Israel. Hanging up from Adele, I called staffer Terry Peel on Appropriations Foreign Ops to have him help coordinate the Israeli trip, as well as to see whether he could accompany me. Terry took down all the information we had so far, and then told me about a trip with Neal Smith's appropriations subcommittee in November for twelve days to Rome and three capitol cities in the East Bloc, coming back through Copenhagen. I was very noncommittal about this trip in November, but I will see what Joan thinks about it. I then phoned Dr. Henry Clayman about a possible news story on Adele Acosta, whom we both have helped with her eyes, and also about dealing with the public relations person at St. Francis Hospital regarding Adele. John Schelble will touch base with PR person at the hospital to perhaps push the story.

I spoke to Lucy about Janet Studley's request. Janet wants me to write to Ira Clark, head of Jackson Memorial Hospital, recommending Janet's law firm of Holland and Knight to represent Jackson Memorial on the problem it has with the Social Security Administration. The problem relates to Jackson's failure to deduct social security taxes from the salaries of interns and resident physicians. Lucy and I are in the draft stages of the letter to Jackson, and we both agree that I have to be careful in recommending Holland and Knight, as it is really unjustifiable for me to lobby for a lobbyist, and neither Janet nor I want Jackson to perceive me as being overly partial to any law firm.

Between phone calls Rae Abrams, one of our elderly lady constituents, came in to bring me some health food. It was a busy morning with people stopping in or calling for future appointments. Sharyn and I have begun making plans for my next fundraiser. For several reasons, I have decided not to have any elaborate 75th birthday party in Washington. For one, I do not want to advertise that I am seventy-five (in October) and, two, the timing is wrong, as my birthday falls during the busy portion of getting our transit bill through the House and through conference. A party would be too much.

Mid-afternoon I left the office to meet Tom Fiedler of the *Miami Herald* for tennis at the Miami Shores Country Club. Tom is the *Herald's* political editor and has been a good friend ever since I have been in office. One thing I hoped to accomplish by playing tennis with Tom was to show that I am in good physical condition, and it is important to reassure the media that I am not getting old and decrepit. We talked a little about the senate race and the time he had spent in Washington.

Joan and I went to dinner with friends Charlie Goldstein and his wife Elaine Silverstein. Charlie has been a steady contributor to my campaign, and we talked some politics. Elaine is very involved in the Dukakis campaign but is very concerned that Dukakis cannot get his campaign off the ground. She runs the Beber Silverstein Advertising Agency.

AUGUST 31 WEDNESDAY

At noon, lobbyist Priscilla Perry and I met with Dade County Manager Joaquin Avino. Priscilla is helping me to coordinate the Super Bowl weekend, and she is also heavily involved in the Metromover extensions. We talked about the full-funding contract which should be in place by the end of October, and it is up to me to maintain the annual funding appropriation for the Metromover extensions. Avino says he sees light rail transit on Miami Beach and will be supporting the City Manager of Miami Beach when that referendum comes on the Miami Beach ballot in November. Our attention then turned to problems related to my bringing the subcommittee to Miami in January for the Super Bowl. Avino will try to work through the Beacon Council, a downtown business leadership group, to pick up the tab and also to have the

Council use its influence with the National Football League to obtain Super Bowl tickets for the subcommittee members. I think it will all work out but there are some hurdles to overcome. For seed money, in case he needed it, I gave Avino $5,000 from my campaign fund.

During our meeting, Mickey Leland called to let me know that he had received the six names I sent him of the prisoners in Cuba that we hope to get released. The names were provided to me by the Cuban-American Foundation (CAF) leader Tony Costa, and Mickey said that the prisoners were all hardline political prisoners. He said that we would have to arrange for our own plane to fly to Havana and back, and that he was leaving tomorrow for Vietnam and would like to go on this Cuban prisoner refugee mission when he gets back the weekend after Labor Day, after we have a chance to go over all the details in Washington. I called Tony Costa, and gave him the information Mickey had relayed to me. Tony said he would figure out how to get us a plane, but that he personally was very uneasy about us going, especially two liberal Democrats as me and Mickey. Cuban-Americans would prefer to see George Bush get the prisoners out of Cuba and not myself and Mickey Leland. "Absolutely not" was his response when I asked Tony if he would like to come with us. When I mentioned all this to Avino, he did not seem to care one way or the other; I will run the matter by Maria Elena Torano to get her reaction.

Telling Joan about the twelve-day trip that Terry Peel had mentioned to me, visiting Rome and three Capitol cities in the East Bloc, it did not appeal to her very much. I settled in at my desk at home and wrote a few letters, one to an Air Force Academy appointee who was turned down because of bad dental alignment, which he is going to have fixed. He would have been an excellent appointee, and I just wrote him a letter of encouragement.

Chapter 21

SEPTEMBER 1, 1988 THURSDAY

I met Maria Elena Torano at the Holiday Inn in South Miami for a breakfast meeting with her women's group, the Business Network. About twelve people were there when I arrived, none of whom I knew personally, but I did know of their companies that made up the network. I spoke mostly about transit problems and then opened the meeting for questions. The meeting lasted about an hour, long enough for them to get to know a little more of me and my position on issues that they care about. I will follow up with a letter to each from the list of names and addresses Maria Elena left with me, and also add them to my Christmas card and fundraiser lists.

After the meeting Maria Elena and I sat for a while longer as I filled her in on the Cuban prisoners refugee mission. She was quite interested and said that she would get in touch with Tony Costa, who has yet to call me back. I headed for the Northside district office where Patrice had scheduled several appointments. This was around 10:00 a.m., and the traffic was heavy because of construction of the new commuter rail station next to the Metrorail station on 79th Street and 36th Avenue. On the way, I stopped by the cemetery at Kathy's grave.

As I arrived a few minutes late at the Northside office, several of my appointments were already there. First, however, I called Adele in my Washington office to get a progress report on the Cuban mission. Adele said she had passed the project by the Foreign Ops staff and also by the State Department and the Immigration & Naturalization Service. The big question was how we go about getting the prisoners released. If we are really the reason they are being freed, it is one thing, but if these prisoners are already in the pipeline and are being released anyway, it is silly for us to go to Cuba just to take credit for their release.

Following the phone call to Adele, Patrice had George Hepburn of the New Center Development Corporation come in. George and I have known one another since my school board days, and he is now trying to develop the Liberty City Poinciana area as an industrial center. That area is ten blocks due west of N.W. 7th Avenue and 71st Street where I had my used car lot, and it does have possibilities for what George is hoping to do. We agreed that George would come to Washington sometime in February for a meeting with HUD, the Department of Transportation, and Health Department officials regarding funding for development of that area. Gail Williams came in next with her group of community activists, and they basically had the same request for the Liberty City area as George, but they want to use some of the leftover UMTA Urban Initiative funds to provide the infrastructure for development in that neighborhood. Dade County has about $1.5 million from the Urban Initiative Grant (which I had earmarked in a previous appropriations bill) that has not been spent, and Gail and her group are well aware of that fact. We will work together on this and other ongoing problems concerning the black community, and hopefully we can see positive results from our combined efforts.

Art Hill, President of Peoples Bank, was in about his problems with Metro-Dade County. Dade County advanced his bank $3 million guaranteed by Southeast Bank, and now the county wants its money regardless of the guarantee by Southeast Bank. I think Art will be able to work this out, even though it is a problem with which he would rather not have to deal. He also wanted help in his effort to gain deposit funds from the U.S. Bureau of Customs, and I agreed to help in any way I could. While in New Orleans, Art had learned that many of the black-owned banks there had received federal government deposits, coming especially from the Customs Office. Art may come to Washington to testify to the need for more black minority opportunities on highway projects, as his bank will be doing business with some black-owned asphalt businesses which have contracts on the Florida highway projects. The Florida Department of Transportation sets aside ten percent of highway funds for minority enterprise but that seems to redivide into one tenth to black minority companies and nine tenths to Hispanic minority companies.

Then Dr. Michael Melody from Barry University came in about the dedication next year of the Aviation Science Building at Barry. He also wanted to get better organized on some of the material I have been sending to Barry, such as my papers and the oral history I have been recording.

Eugene Mann, lobbyist Priscilla Perry's husband, spoke to me about helping him get a grant to do additional Alzheimer's study in Israel. I am to go to the Israeli Embassy soon after returning to Washington, and when I do I will take with me documentation from Eugene to leave with the Embassy officials; hopefully they will be interested enough to help see about the grant.

That evening Joan and I went to Eastern Shores in North Miami Beach for the opening of the North Dade office of the Dukakis campaign. Mike Dukakis's staff was there as were approximately one hundred people, some political, such as State Senator Gwen Margolis and State Representative Mike Abrams, but mostly those gathered were from the condos. Jeff made sure I greeted all the condo leaders, and soon I was called on to make a speech. Keeping it short, I encouraged all to work hard for Dukakis, because "we do have a chance to carry Florida in this election." It was a good rally for Dukakis, and everyone there seemed to be very optimistic about his chances of winning the election. Afterwards Joan and I stopped next door at a restaurant called Shooters, which is sort of the new "in place" in town. It was nice, and we met there the grandson of Red Harris, one of my old used car dealer friends.

SEPTEMBER 2 FRIDAY

Patrice and I were at the Miami Postal Headquarters this morning for a community meeting with Miami Postmaster Woody Connors and his staff concerning postal service problems in the Miami area, which is everything south of Vero Beach and across to Ft. Myers. Several community activists and organizations had been invited to air their complaints. Ruby Steiner, President of a Northeast Dade condo community organization, was there, as was Charlotte Greenbarg, among others. The condo problem with the postal service is that these residents have to go several miles west of where they live and into a different neighborhood to pick up special delivery mailings and packages if they are not at home when these mailings are delivered; also, they have to travel that distance to do special mailings. Consequently, they have been trying for a nearby post office that would serve the 33180 zip code. After several people in the group had voiced their complaints, Woody suggested what I thought was the perfect solution: to use the old Hallandale Post Office near Northeast Dade, once the new Hallandale Post Office is completed. The facility would be available to them to pick up packages and to do special mailings, and Woody's suggestion got the approval of the group.

Not everything they wanted was accomplished, however, as those homeowners in the area where Charlotte Greenbarg lives still have to go west to the Norland Post Office to get packages and special mail. The *Miami Herald* covered the meeting, and Postmaster Woody Connors was very cooperative as usual, but I really think this a big deal about nothing because there probably are not a dozen pieces of mail that have to be picked up in any given day, and meetings such as this are all a waste of energy.

Patrice and I then went to the Veterans Administration Hospital to meet with Administrator Tom Dougherty. I try to meet at least once a year with Tom and this morning, his concern was with funding for the VA rehabilitation halfway house that services primarily Vietnam veterans suffering from drug and alcohol abuse. This is the facility that had been close to shutting down a few months ago, but emergency funding from Appropriations Subcommittee on the VA, HUD, and Independent Agencies has allowed it to remain open until the end of the fiscal year, October

1. Now, according to Tom, the Veterans Administration does not have any idea what funding it will have after the October 1 deadline. I told Tom that I would get what information I could and get back to him. In the meantime, I have been talking to my colleague and tennis buddy Sonny Montgomery, Chairman of the Veterans Affairs Committee, about this veterans rehab facility, and hopefully I can finalize something when I get back to Washington. Judy Gordon, a Veterans Administration social worker and an old family friend, came in to the meeting to see me. Judy's specialty is spinal cord rehabilitation, and I was happy to see her.

At the district office when I arrived was an old friend, Milton Wallace. When I first ran for the Dade County School Board, Milton was the lawyer representing the Dade County Teachers Union. Today Milton spoke about the critical need of homecare for dialysis patients. HICFA in Atlanta said it is going to cut down on the differential in payments for home dialysis in relation to institutional dialysis. Calling Blue Cross/Blue Shield, I wanted to see if I could delay that decision until a study could be done to show that, in the long run, home dialysis would save money and, not only that, it would be much more humane to give dialysis to a patient at home, especially the elderly. BC/BS is to get back to me, and I am hopeful that this will be a beginning to help patients on dialysis so that they do not have to be taken to institutions to have this treatment.

I called Tony Costa and then Adele about the Cuban prisoners mission. The more we talk about this the more mind boggling it becomes. Now it seems the real reason Mickey Leland and I are able to get the prisoners released is because the United Nations is sending its human rights staff into Cuba to see the political prisoners, and Castro, perhaps, wants the prisoners released before the human rights people arrive. I do not want to be used that way, but if just by going, I am able to get prisoners released that otherwise would not be, then I will go to Cuba to do with Mickey Leland what needs to be done.

At the tennis court, local public television Channel 2 was there doing a program on tennis prodigies and their potential for joining the professional ranks. The reporter asked if I would hit balls to one of the twelve-year-old prodigies, and I did. I understand that this will be shown in November on public television.

SEPTEMBER 3 SATURDAY

Today I worked on several newsletters, but drafting the newsletter on the VA Hospital and its rehabilitation halfway house was my first priority. The newsletter will develop around the premise of redeploying our resources on the drug war to the demand side and, if necessary, take from the supply side like Coast Guard interdiction. If we are to be successful in fighting this war on drugs, this measure seems most practical, although in some quarters this is not the thinking. Using the old Hallandale Post Office when the new Hallandale Post Office is completed will be of particular interest to those in the Aventura zip code area, and I have just about completed the newsletter draft on that issue. A newsletter on what we did to reduce speeding on the intracoastal waterway should also be of interest. This intracoastal waterway problem was brought to my attention by Golden Beach Mayor Arnold Picker and George Berlin of Aventura, and together we were successful in getting a speed reduction on the intracoastal. I will wait until I am back in Washington to start the draft on what we did to upgrade the Poinciana Park/Liberty City area and on the new economic development in the Northside shopping facility. I don't know if we will do all these newsletters, probably just the ones that develop the best.

SEPTEMBER 4 SUNDAY

State Senator Ken Jenne of Ft. Lauderdale, running for Florida Insurance Commissioner, had an early campaign brunch today at the Marco Polo Hotel. This was to be the last of the campaign breakfasts in Northeast Dade before the primary, and it was a real mob scene. I knew Jenne from when he first worked for Claude Pepper, and speaking briefly to the crowd of his enthusiastic supporters, I thought he had a very good chance of winning. Before today, I was not so optimistic about his chances, and hopefully this feeling remains true and I am not just caught up in the moment. The present Insurance Commissioner, Democrat Bill Gunter, in the Florida primary, is in a very competitive race against Congressmen Buddy MacKay and Dan Mica for the senate seat soon to be vacated by Lawton Chiles.

For lunch Joan and I met Sergio Bendixen and Sharyn Fallick

at the Grand Bay Hotel in Coconut Grove. The rest of the afternoon I just took it easy and worked a bit on the newsletters.

SEPTEMBER 5 MONDAY

Today, Labor Day, I just rested, as tomorrow I return to Washington following this three week August recess.

SEPTEMBER 6 TUESDAY

Taking an 11:00 a.m. Eastern flight, I was at my Washington office by 2:00 and at tennis by 3:00 with my House buddies Don Edwards, Sonny Montgomery, and Bob Kastenmeier. Together talking politics, they think Dukakis has to get going or he will lose.

In the evening, I went to the Israeli Embassy reception honoring Toval Herzl, the departing Embassy legislative liaison. Herzl introduced me to the incoming Embassy legislative liaison, Judith Varnai-Dranger, but Judith and I had met several years ago in Israel; she remembered me, and I certainly had no problem remembering her. She is a very attractive and gracious lady. Neville and Susan Lamdan were the party's hosts. I gave Neville the information on Eugene Mann to see if he could help Eugene with a medical school grant in Israel for research on Alzheimer's. Neville took a cursory glance at the document, and said that he would call universities in Israel to inquire about getting Eugene into one of their medical schools.

Regarding the Florida elections today, some of the people I endorsed did not win. Clara Oesterle, my transportation person on the Metro Commission, lost, and that may be a problem for Dade Transit and for me, and a really tough loss for Clara who has been on the Dade County Commission since 1974. Michael Gonzalez, whom I endorsed, lost in the Dade County School Board election to incumbent Rosa Castro Feinberg. Nancy Pollock in the Judicial race got 45 percent of the vote, but will have a runoff in November. I also endorsed Elaine Gordon for State Representative, and she won. Bill Gunter won over Buddy MacKay and Dan Mica, but with not a large enough margin to avoid a runoff in October with Buddy MacKay. State Senator Ken Jenne in a race for Florida Insurance Commissioner also faces a Democratic runoff in October.

The condo vote was not as strong as in the past, and the leaders are not getting their people out to vote in the large numbers as previously. The condo residents may be getting too old, and the new condo leaders, who sometimes pompously pretend to have power, are not able to turn out the vote as did the old leadership.

SEPTEMBER 7 WEDNESDAY

Washington attorney Harry Teeter, head of the National Theater in Washington, came in at 10:00 this morning. Harry is also Executive Director of the American Trauma Society and wanted to see me about trauma funding for the Centers for Disease Control and Prevention in Atlanta. Several other people came in, but the main thing I did today was to meet with Tom, Greg, and Lucy to go over the conference notes. I needed to know which of the 150 amendments in disagreement we could recede on, or compromise with the Senate on, and on which we will have to insist on the House position, and on which the Senate will probably recede to us. We spent most of the afternoon doing this.

Mickey Leland called about our trip to Cuba, and we are to meet tomorrow. I also spoke to Rom Mazzoli about the offshore adoption problem, as he is still holding up legislation that could get around the Frank Amendment. The problem is that Neal Smith, Appropriations Subcommittee Chairman on Commerce, Justice, State, and the Judiciary, won't in conference recede to the Senate language in his subcommittee bill until he gets Mazzoli to sign off. The Senate language in his bill would clear up the interpretation by the Immigration & Naturalization Service, and I cannot understand Rom's delay in signing off on this measure. Our own Transportation subcommittee will have some interesting times when we go through the conference process this week, but the Democrats on our subcommittee don't feel that we need to caucus before the conference.

On the Floor, some members approached me about my bill - Bud Shuster about the highways in his Pennsylvania area, Bill Alexander about the Arkansas airport, and before this is over, many more will approach me about projects for their districts.

SEPTEMBER 8 THURSDAY

At 9:15 a.m., Sisters Nancy Silvester, Aleli Jose, and Dominican Sisters from the Philippines came in regarding human rights in the Philippines. The Dominican Sisters are wonderful and very much into human rights. I have learned a great deal about the Philippine situation from the Sisters, whom I first knew through Sister Marie Carol Hurley who was my teacher at Barry University and later my campaign chairperson, and then later an intern in our Washington office. Afterwards, representatives from the Florida Independent Automobile Dealers Association were in about the Internal Revenue Act which hurts small dealers that do their own financing, as I used to when I was in the used car business. The new tax law forces dealers who do their own financing to pay a tax on the finance charges before they are earned. One of the benefits I had was to defer the future profit, both on the car sale and the financing, until it was collected and earned. This is a tough situation for these dealers.

Senator Lautenberg and I met at 11:00 a.m. in my committee office to go through the notes on the transportation section of the Continuing Resolution conference. The meeting, which included both of our committee staffs, lasted until 3:00 p.m., and we worked out most of our differences, the biggest problem being to come up with a bill that the President will sign. The "labor protection provisions (LPPs)" in the bill, requiring airlines to pay benefits to employees hurt by mergers, were added by the House Rules Committee, and the administration is opposed to the LPPs, labeling the measure a "breach of free-market principles." The bill, as reported out of the subcommittee, had no "labor protection" language, so the language was added by the Rules Committee at the request of the Speaker because of pressure from organized labor. We had to go to the House Floor and to conference with a bill containing a provision not of our subcommittee. And, we have distinct messages from the White House that unless the House in conference recedes to the Senate, which has no labor protection plan in its bill, the President will veto the Conference Report Bill. This means all the "new stuff" in our fiscal 1989 Bill will be lost because we would have only the bill from the last fiscal year in the form of a Continuing Resolution.

Four members on our subcommittee - Durbin, Mrazek, Conte,

and Wolf, two Democrats and two Republicans - have already carelessly given word to organized labor that they would support the labor protection provisions. What I needed was six of our eleven subcommittee members to vote to recede so that we could go with our well-crafted 1989 Appropriations Bill. Lautenberg and I are willing to drop the LPPs if we can be assured that the bill will be signed. The rest of the items are being worked out very well, even though we do have some small problems with the appropriated funding levels and with some general provisions put in the Senate bill. Tomorrow morning we start at 9:00 with a pre-conference meeting with our own transportation subcommittee, then with the Senate subcommittee at 10:00, and hopefully finish by 5:00 p.m. Following the meeting with Lautenberg, I had to go over the same conference notes with ranking minority member Larry Coughlin, and he was most agreeable with my positions.

Having completed the newsletter on the Northeast Dade Post Office problem, John is ready to send it to the printer. Lots of phone calls have come in from members about their provisions in my bill: Steve Neal regarding highways in North Carolina, Bill Chappell on the bridge over the St. John's River, and Joe McDade on the airport in Scranton, as well as Pennsylvania highways. Marty Frost is unhappy because of the cutbacks on the Dallas DART transit program, but the Dallas leadership did a poor job working with the subcommittee and sent the wrong signals as to their level of need. Neither Marty Frost nor Mayor Strauss of Dallas knew how to handle the Dallas referendum vote, and now there is only a $5 million appropriation for DART in both bills. Public Works Committee Chairman Glenn Anderson called to ask for my help with the public transit charter buses in Long Beach, which I probably won't give. My first reaction is that I just don't want to help him and, second, Lautenberg needs the public charter bus prohibition for New Jersey to prevent competition from the subsidized local public bus service. Glenn also wanted help to recover highway funds held back by FHWA because the 55 mph speed limit is not enforced in California. I told him that Jim Howard, his predecessor as Public Works Chairman, would turn over in his grave if he thought that Anderson was trying to circumvent the 55 mph penalty laws to states that would not enforce the 55 mph speed limit.

I have also been busy going about speaking to members on my

subcommittee to convince them to recede to the Senate in conference on the labor protection provisions. Dick Durbin was willing to reconsider, but both he and Marty Sabo want to talk to the machinists union first. I also spoke to Republican members on my subcommittee, such as Frank Wolf of Northern Virginia, because I do not want to ask the Democrats to change unless the Republicans can change as well, and Wolf won't vote to recede to the Senate. For Wolf, with his large constituency of unionized airport workers based at Dulles and National Airports, this would be difficult. In a call to Transportation Secretary Jim Burnley, I told him where we were and that I needed a letter from him saying that "only if we drop the labor protection section in conference would we have a bill that the President would sign." When Burnley's letter reaches me, I will call Dick Durbin so that he can get in touch with the machinists union. In the meantime, I have asked Larry Coughlin to try and convince Frank Wolf to change his position. I feel that I have now done everything I can to produce this bill, and if the majority of members on my subcommittee are still in opposition to receding to the Senate there is not much more that I can do.

Because of the projects in the bill, politically they would be in a worse position with a Continuing Resolution, than they would be by offending the machinists and airline pilots unions. If the bill is vetoed, Congress would probably have to fold it into a "catch all" continuing resolution that included spending for other segments of the government, which means that their own projects in the bill would end up in an end-of-the-year measure that would be more vulnerable to across-the-board spending cuts.

SEPTEMBER 12 MONDAY

I am thinking about joining Neal Smith's codel to the Soviet Union. Initially I had thought about joining the Armed Services Committee on their trip to Siberia, but I am not so sure I want to go with such a mob scene. The Armed Services staff told me that about thirty-three members on their committee had signed up to go on the trip, which makes the Neal Smith codel even more appealing.

SEPTEMBER 13 TUESDAY

When I brought Marty Sabo up-to-speed on the labor protection provisions, Marty said he wanted to meet with the machinists before making a commitment. Larry Coughlin has not been able to turn Frank Wolf around, but I should be receiving Jim Burnley's letter soon stating that the President would sign the bill only if we dropped the language pertaining to the labor protection provisions. I saw Burnley in the evening at a Department of Transportation reception, but we did not talk business. I also saw there Najeep Halaby, the former head of the FAA, who is also the father of the Queen of Jordan. UMTA Administrator Dellibovi was there and asked, now that the Dade County election is over, if the County now had people in place that would sign its full-funding contract; "I sure hope so," I said.

I then went to the National Democratic Club for Texas member Ronald Coleman's fundraiser. Some of the Airline Pilots Union leaders were there, and told me they were not happy with my position on the labor protection provisions. Jerry Baker, head of the Airline Pilots Association, in particular gave me a bit of a hard time for not standing up to the President on the bill. My response was, "I have to do what I have to do, and you have to do what you have to do." And, "I have to send the president a bill that will be enacted into law."

Leaving the NDC, I went next to the annual Florida House reception and dinner. I was amazed at how few members showed up, but it may have been because the event was held on the night before Congress reconvenes and many members were still out of town. Lawyer/lobbyist Janet Studley was there and thanked me for earmarking funds in my bill for the Electronic Data Systems Corporation FAA computer program. Later, I saw Susan Perry at the Brasserie, and she seemed satisfied with the legislation limiting public transit charter buses in Long Beach, California.

SEPTEMBER 14 WEDNESDAY

Hill and Knowlton lobbyist Gary Hymel came in this morning with the Turkey Ambassador Sukru Elekdag. They wanted me in the Foreign Ops conference to vote to recede to the Senate position on aid to Turkey. The Ambassador filled me in on the latest on Cyprus, and I told him I saw him playing tennis at the Army/Navy Club, and that I would play him for double or nothing on aid to Turkey. Sometimes I have a lot of fun.

Then, in a long meeting with Ron Hauck of the Homestead, Florida-based International Aircraft Inc., concerning problems with civil aviation, I listened as Ron told me about his ideas to solve some of the problems. Admittedly, I thought a lot of his ideas were good but, unfortunately, I could not do a whole lot, if anything, about most of them. I will, however, be able to work with him on appropriating for Essential Air Services legislation. Ron is trying to get commuter airlines to use imported planes that he is bringing in from Great Britain and refitting in this country to help preserve commuter service to small towns, which is now being phased out. He is also working to get the State Department to open up additional flights to Havana, Cuba, and the Soviet Union. This, he said, would reduce some of the Cold War barriers.

A delegation from the Cuban-American Foundation, which included Jorge Mas, Jonathan Slade, and Tony Costa, came in to go over the plans for the Cuban prisoners mission. We agreed that they would get a letter from former Bay of Pigs war prisoners, now living in America, requesting that I take this mission. Having such a letter will clear my position so that I will not affront the Miami Cuban community, even though I am going to Cuba with the Foundation's support to bring back political prisoners. They also encouraged me to ask Neal Smith to support in conference TV Marti, which I have been doing and will continue to do.

I had called for a meeting at 2:00 with our transportation subcommittee members to see if we could get six votes to recede to the Senate on the conference report. Marty Sabo offered the suggestion that we give the airline pilots a week to change their position, and meet again next Thursday. Marty would sign to recede to the Senate, which had no LPPs in its bill, if the airline pilots had not convinced the White House to accept the labor protection provisions by that time. The outcome of this meeting was that five members promised they would sign to recede when we meet again next Thursday, and, by then, if the President has not agreed to sign with the labor protection provisions language in the bill, we would still have the votes to recede to the Senate. We bought time, but we have put labor leaders in a critical position. What I really want is a 7 to 4 instead of a 6 to 5 vote, so that "labor" could not blame any one of our subcommittee members for a one-vote loss.

There were a couple of interviews today, one with the *Congressional Quarterly* about the present impasse on our bill, and the other was for a Philadelphia paper concerning POW Korean war veteran Tibor Rubin and my efforts to get the Armed Services Committee to include in their bill a waiver of the statute of limitations so that a Congressional Medal of Honor could be awarded to Tibor for his bravery in the Korean War.

The Patton, Boggs and Blow law firm held a party this evening in honor of Evan Bayh who is running for Governor of Indiana. Birch Bayh, Evan's father, was there. Birch was Chairman of the Senate Subcommittee on Transportation when I first was on the House subcommittee, and we got to know each other pretty well. Evan, I understand, is now leading in the Indiana Governor's race.

SEPTEMBER 15 THURSDAY

This morning I went to the Sierra Club's presentation of awards ceremony, held on the steps of the Capitol. Awards were presented to each of the cosigners, myself included, of the Bruce Vento-Bill Green letter for the Clean Air Legislation Action Now. Afterwards, Adele and I spent time going over the amendments to the Foreign Ops subcommittee bill, with me mainly trying to reduce the military aid to Pakistan. During our meeting, Senator Chiles called and asked that I use my influence to get Neal Smith's help on the shortage of federal judges in South Florida by earmarking in his appropriations bill funds for additional South Florida federal judges.

President of the Southeast Bank in Miami came to the office around noon to discuss problems with a proposed banking bill that, he said, adversely affects banks as to insurance and real estate companies invading banking territory. I have had lobbying from both sides of the issue - banking and the real estate and insurance companies - and, as before, when these lobbyists have approached me, I just tell them that I will continue to keep abreast of the situation, as I need more time to review the legislation. Southeast Bank in Miami, though, has been good for Dade County, but even though people from the bank have supported me in the past and I have good friends from Southeast Bank like Mac Wolfe, now retired, I really cannot let these things be a factor in my decision-making.

Later, in a conversation on the Floor with Speaker Jim Wright, I filled him in on where we were with my bill. Wright wanted to know if he could help, and I said I did not think so because of his commitment to the labor protection provisions. "Even though I am in favor of the LPPs," Wright said, "I consider it more important to get your bill out as a free-standing transportation appropriations bill." And, he again asked how he could help. Naming several members that he could talk to like Mrazek, Durbin and Carr to turn them around, I said we could then recede to the Senate. But Jim seemed a bit distracted, as he had other things on his mind like the House Ethics Committee, before which he had been testifying for a couple of days. I then went to the Appropriations front office and spoke to Dennis, one of the head staffers, who in turn spoke to John Mack, the Speaker's Administrative Aide, who said to Dennis that at the first opportunity he would mention my LPPs problem to the Speaker.

The White House Congressional Picnic was this evening, and the food was very good. Secretary of Defense Frank Carlucci was there, and I complimented him on his dancing at last year's White House Christmas Ball. "I am not worried about a Secretary of Defense going to war if he loves to dance like you do," I said to Carlucci. I sat with Senator Graham and other congressional people, and everyone seemed to be having a good time.

SEPTEMBER 16 FRIDAY

On the Floor during the vote on the *Journal,* I spoke again to the Speaker, this time telling him that I had an LPPs Suspension Bill to bring to the Floor and that we could do that next Tuesday. If the bill passed the House and then the Senate, I said, it would be sent to the President and thus would give the airline pilots and labor people the expected Presidential veto to use against the President. The Speaker thought it a good idea, but I reminded him that the Texas-based Continental Airlines did not benefit from the labor protection provisions. He said he would see if Norman Mineta (D-CA), Chairman of the Public Works Subcommittee on Aviation, would offer the LPPs suspension, rather than have me do it. It may not work, but it is worth a try. In the meantime, I have spoken to Jim Jontz (Indiana) and he will talk to Dick Durbin about voting to recede to protect Jim's project, and I will be in touch with the Speaker's staff to keep this moving.

Teachers and the principal from Miami Shores Elementary School in my district are in Washington to meet with President Reagan at a ceremony in the White House Rose Garden. The school was selected by the U.S. Department of Education as one of the top elementary schools in the country. At 11:00 this morning, they stopped by my office before going to the White House, and I took them on a tour of the Capitol.

When I got back to the office Bill Gunter was calling, urging me to stay away from the Buddy MacKay appearances in Dade County. The Democratic runoff election between Gunter and MacKay is just a little over two weeks away, on October 4, and the race between these two has really heated up. In answer to Gunter's urging, I said to him that if Buddy should come to Dade County with my colleague Mel Levine of California, and if he agreed to sign a position paper that in the future he would not vote against arms sales to Israel, I would not oppose Buddy MacKay. I am doing this not because I think Buddy deserves it, but if by some chance Buddy is elected, I don't want him to be unreachable for me on issues concerning the Middle East or elsewhere. But regardless of which candidate wins in the Democratic runoff, he will have a tough time in November with his Republican opponent, Representative Connie Mack, III, who easily won the Republican nomination in Tuesday's election. The *Miami Herald* reported that analysts give Florida Republicans a good chance of winning the U.S. Senate seat.

In the afternoon I continued to pursue the possibility of having Norman Mineta offer a free-standing LPPs suspension bill next week, and then we could recede to the Senate without a problem. Mineta, who had already passed in the House two bills on LPPs, which died in the Senate, said to me that the only way the LPPs could get through would be by way of a transportation appropriations bill. The Speaker wants to get the bill enacted, but, as his aide John Mack said, "The Speaker wants *you* to do it, but he can't ask *you* to do it." I also have to speak again to Jim Jontz of Indiana about Durbin's need to protect Jim's project in the bill. The pressure is now on the members who want to have it both ways, their highway projects in this bill and also protecting labor unions.

When I arrived in Miami at 5:30, Anna from my office was at the airport and told me we had been getting a lot of phone calls in the district office from union members about the LPPs. When I got to the office, Buddy MacKay's administrative assistant Greg Farmer, called about the Buddy MacKay meeting next week in Miami, saying that Buddy would like me to make an appearance on his behalf. George Berlin, I believe, is the organizer for this meeting.

SEPTEMBER 17 SATURDAY

First thing at the district office this morning I called George Berlin and then Buddy's administrative aide Greg Farmer, about the meeting Monday at 11:00 a.m., at the Turnberry Yacht Club. The meeting was to be an effort to reach an understanding on the Jewish/Israeli issue in the Senate race between Buddy MacKay and Bill Gunter. The "misunderstanding" revolves around Buddy's vote on a bill introduced by Congressman Mel Levine of Southern California banning arms sales to Saudi Arabia in 1986. To his discredit, Buddy voted against the bill, and now the Gunter campaign is using that vote as Buddy being anti-Israel, which is not true; he is neither anti-Semitic nor anti-Israel, and I think we should do what we can to downplay the matter; that may not be so easy, however, since only this morning the story appeared on the front page of the *Miami Herald.*

Jeff and I met at 10:15 a.m. for the "Send-off to Washington Brunch" with the North Dade Chamber of Commerce. Elaine Adler hosted the event at the Jockey Club, which had the usual North Dade politicians, i.e., State Representatives Ron Silver and Elaine Gordon, North Miami Mayor Howard Neu, and Nancy Pollock, in a runoff election for a Dade County judge position. I received an honorary cowboy hat and was asked to say a few words. When questioned about the furor surrounding the Gunter/MacKay campaigns, I told them how unfortunate I thought it was, that MacKay had made a "wrong" vote, but that neither candidate was anti-Semitic nor anti-Israel, and that either one would work well with Israel and the Jewish community. Thinking about it later, I focused too many of my remarks toward the Jewish audience when there were a lot of non-Jewish people there who probably did not understand what I was talking about.

SEPTEMBER 18 SUNDAY

Meeting Anna at the district office this morning, we went to the Biscayne Boulevard Groundbreaking Ceremony in celebration of a beautification project by the Northeast Dade Coalition, the Florida Highway Department, and the Dade County Department of Parks. Joe Plotnick ran the show, and I was part of the program. During my brief speech, I said that "Joe Plotnick was the 'Lady Bird Johnson' of Northeast Dade County," and that got a laugh. It was hot and muggy but the people turned out anyway. Channel 6 interviewed me, asking about Haiti and the military coup there. On the platform with me was Congressman Mel Levine, Barry Kutun and State Representative Mike Friedman. Nancy Pollock was there, and also her opponent Robert Jones, whom I thought very impressive. It is going to be a close race for the judge position. Metro Commissioner Beverly Phillips and I had a photo together. Beverly also is in a runoff election, and she really seemed to appreciate my having a photo with her.

SEPTEMBER 19 MONDAY

The Buddy MacKay brunch was held today at the Turnberry Yacht Club, with a lot of media coverage. When it came time for me to speak, I said, "This issue of Buddy being anti-Semitic or anti-Israel does not serve Israel or the Jewish community well, and the campaign should not escalate on the issue of Buddy's one vote being pro-Israel or anti-Israel." As both are very capable of serving as Senator, I said, I have not endorsed either candidate, but I did want it known that I have no reservations in being here and appearing on Buddy MacKay's behalf. Buddy has some good people backing him like State Representative Mike Friedman, and my colleague Mel Levine of California, who made some good comments to the group about Buddy, saying that Buddy was a true friend of Israel despite the split on the arms sales measure which Levine had introduced, and added that Buddy had "fought to sustain America's $3 billion in foreign aid to Israel." It was a good meeting and a good move on Buddy's part to have Levine campaign with him in Dade County, since it was Levine's bill that he opposed. Certainly I tried to do what I could to help Buddy through the dilemma, and I don't anticipate any fallout in the district for having supported him. Afterwards we all gave television interviews.

I now have a copy of President Reagan's September 16 letter to Appropriations Chairman Jamie Whitten, which says, in effect, that he will veto the transportation bill should the LPPs be included in the bill. Now the other subcommittee members will have to give in or lose the funds in the present bill for their projects.

SEPTEMBER 20 TUESDAY

The *Miami Herald* had a story today on Buddy MacKay and it was not too bad, quite similar to the story in the *Miami News* yesterday, with comments on my supportive statement. State Senator Jack Gordon, who supports Gunter for the Democratic nomination, was quoted in the *Herald* article as saying, "It's really a very simple issue, which is: If somebody agrees to sell weapons to my enemy, he's really not my friend." But the article also said that even Gordon and other of Gunter's supporters "concede" that the issue has grown all out of proportion. Hopefully this issue can now be laid to rest, and the senate campaign can get on with other issues before the October 4 runoff.

In a meeting today with North Miami Beach Councilman Harry Cohen, we talked about the property around the North Miami Beach Mall, with Harry saying that he wanted to explore the possibility of federal funds to expand the adjacent library, or other means to improve the area. Later, Jeff and I went to see the property, and it definitely does have possibilities for expansion. Patrice will look into what grants might be available and whether the grants could come directly to North Miami Beach or through Metro-Dade. Harry, who will be running soon for Mayor of North Miami Beach, used to own a gasoline station on 163rd Street when I was in the Buick business across the street, so we are old friends.

At Temple Israel for Yom Kippur this evening, I sat on the pulpit between two friends, Eli Timoner and Henry Wolff. Rabbi Perlmeter acknowledged my presence on the pulpit, while my two sons, Bill and Tom, sat with their mother in the audience. It was a very nice evening, and the people in the congregation really seemed to appreciate having a member of Congress join in their service.

SEPTEMBER 21 WEDNESDAY

Leaving Miami, I arrived in Washington at 1:30 p.m., and Adele greeted me at the office with the information that there was to be a Democratic Caucus of the Foreign Ops Subcommittee this afternoon. She and I went immediately to work on issues to bring up in the caucus. My meeting tomorrow with the Speaker has been changed to 2:30. We were originally scheduled for 10:00 a.m., but Jim is to meet with Senate Majority Leader Robert Byrd to see if Byrd can move in the Senate the existing bill on labor protection. If Byrd can indeed move the bill along in the Senate, this would remove the reason forcing us to put the labor protection provisions in the Transportation Appropriations Bill. There is also a meeting at 1:45 tomorrow in the Speaker's Office with all the Democratic subcommittee members, and after that, at 3:00 p.m., we go into conference on the Foreign Ops bill.

At the Foreign Ops Democratic Caucus this afternoon with Dave Obey, Charlie Wilson, Matt McHugh and Julian Dixon to go over Dave's bill, I am getting most of what I was concerned about in this Foreign Ops bill, namely refugee assistance. There is a big difference in being just a member on a subcommittee, therefore not having direct responsibility as chairman for getting a bill out. As far as the Foreign Ops bill is concerned, I am almost like a spectator. Adele is my appropriations staff person on Foreign Ops and works closely with this subcommittee while I devote most of my time to transportation matters. She is with me at the caucus to point out certain items in the bill that I should be particularly aware of, especially in regard to Pakistan arms issues.

Maria Elena Torano and I at dinner talked about politics in Miami. Maria Elena is doing all right with her lobbying efforts, and has agreed to help Nancy Pollock in her runoff election.

SEPTEMBER 22 THURSDAY

Jack Murtha (D-PA) in the cafeteria this morning told me that the latest he had heard when Congress might adjourn was October 22. How this will conflict with my trip to Cuba is unclear, as it is now pretty much certain that I will go to Havana Saturday, October 15, and meet there my colleague Mickey Leland. Adele has told me that we would have the letter from the Cuban-American group sanctioning the mission. I have to see Dante Fascell to be sure he signs off on this undertaking, so that the trip is not presumptuous on my part and would not be damaging to Dante in his own relationship with the Miami Cuban community.

I took a draft of a letter to Tom Spulak, Chief Council to Rules Committee Chairman Claude Pepper, regarding money that the U. S. District Attorney had confiscated from drug dealers in Dade County. The letter is to go to the Metro-Dade Police Department under either Spulak's or Pepper's signature, and they can change the letter anyway they want, but I want $100 thousand of the money that was confiscated to go directly to the City of Opa Locka, which has severe drug problems. Then stopping at the front office of the Appropriations Committee, I picked up a copy of the letter Speaker Wright had written to Senator Byrd, urging Byrd to move the labor protection provisions in the Senate. I have already spoken to Jerry Baker of the Airline Pilots Association, telling him that I had nothing against LPPs but that I had too many good things in the bill that I could not afford to jeopardize with the labor protection language, and Jerry said he understood.

Dick Malow, chief staff on Appropriations Subcommittee on the VA, HUD and Independent Agencies, who has worked with me from the beginning to save the Dade County VA rehabilitation facility, said he spoke to the Veterans Administrator and was assured that there would be sufficient funds for the V.A. rehabilitation halfway house in Miami for the fiscal year 1989.

11:30 a.m., I met with Norman Mineta, Chairman of the authorizing Aviation Subcommittee, and the FAA Administrator Allan McArtor, regarding funds for the Melbourne, Florida, and the Jonesboro, Arkansas, Airports. City officials from both of those areas have come to Washington, and the meeting with Mineta and McArtor was to help get authorizing bill language for the airports.

Tony Costa from the Cuban-American Foundation has brought me the letter from the Foundation sanctioning our mission to Havana to pick up the Cuban political prisoners. I took a copy of the letter to Mickey Leland, and then checked it out with Dante Fascell, who said there was no problem and that he appreciated my talking to him about it. I leave for Havana Saturday, October 15, meeting Mickey in Havana, and together we will meet with Castro. The plan is to get the prisoners out and to Miami the following

Monday, and this would be the first time that I have been to Cuba in thirty years.

One rather distressing experience I had today was with Jim Wright, who was so spaced out over his problems with the Intelligence Committee and with the press about the statement he made concerning the CIA and Nicaragua, that he was hardly focusing on what I was advising him to do in relation to his meeting with Senator Byrd today on the labor protection provisions. It is a very good thing that John Mack on his staff will be with him when he speaks to Byrd so that Byrd can get a clear message as to what we want done.

Reconvening my subcommittee at 3:30 p.m., and again at 7:30 p.m., I was able to get seven members to agree to recede to the Senate on the LPPs agreement. Marty Sabo was the first to change his vote; then Bob Carr made it 6 to 5, and Bill Gray, after some arm twisting, was our 7th and "cushion" vote. Receeding to the Senate brought the conference to a close.

The Foreign Ops conference reconvened at 8:30 p.m. It was a strange conference, with no votes, and all the members seemed to want to do was argue. Adele gets me all prepped up for these conferences on foreign operations, and I just sit there like a potted plant. The only thing I spoke out on today was in opposition to the earmarking of $50 million in emergency refugee assistance for Afghanistan. But I may have made an impression, as I said, "How can we now earmark 100% of these emergency funds when we don't know what the other emergencies are going to be? We don't know what is going to happen in Nicaragua, Soviet Jewry, Iran, or other potentially explosive places." The members did pay attention. The House side insisted that we not earmark, and the Senate will probably recede to the House. I sat next to Charlie Wilson and Matt McHugh, and we spent a good bit of time swapping stories. During a break in the conference, lobbyist Denis Neill took me downstairs to where he had some beer stashed, and we had a quick beer.

The Foreign Ops conference was still going on when I left at midnight, and I only left then because all the things I wanted done had been accomplished. It was a long hectic day, but mainly and happily I had finished my transportation bill.

SEPTEMBER 23 FRIDAY

A fundraiser was held this morning for Democratic Presidential nominee Michael Dukakis. Tom Boggs held the event in the law firm's office at the upper level of my townhouse. Ways and Means Chairman Dan Rostenkowski was there, as were some very big Washington campaign money people. Lobbyist Andy Manatos had called me the other day about his own fundraiser for the Dukakis campaign. To each fund raiser I gave $1,000.

Since I had not heard from Dr. Granville of the Veterans Administration on the 1989 funding for the VA halfway house, I went again to see Dick Malow. Dick said he heard that the facility would be funded at 85% of the 1988 level for 1989, which allows the facility to remain open. With this information, we can complete our newsletter on the VA rehabilitation facility, and also issue a press release.

At 3:15 I took an Eastern flight to Miami.

SEPTEMBER 24 SATURDAY

I met Jeff at Neighbors Restaurant this morning, and we headed for Haulover Beach Park to meet with people from the Center for Environmental Education for Ocean Clean-Up. Once there, we joined in the walk along the beach picking up plastics and other debris. The press took photographs, and one in particular was of a woman who found a medical syringe. We were there for about an hour, and I am thinking about doing a newsletter on this event. Leaving the beach, Jeff and I went to the Hallandale Post Office. Photos were to be taken with Postmaster Woody Connors and especially with Ruby Steiner, head of the Aventura condo group, as it was Ruby who initiated the effort to change the Hallandale zip code to solve the postal service problem in the Aventura area. Today, however, Ruby was out of town. Having photos with Charlotte Greenbarg and Joe Plotnick, I felt bad that Ruby was left out. If I put out a newsletter on this, I certainly will want a Ruby photo included.

SEPTEMBER 25 SUNDAY

Today there was nothing scheduled. Al Moskovits and I got together for tennis in the afternoon.

SEPTEMBER 26 MONDAY

9:30 a.m., Jeff picked me up at home for our trip to the North Campus of the Miami-Dade Community College for the conference on the homeless, entitled: "Federal Initiatives for the Homeless." Officials from HUD offices in Jacksonville were there, as were local housing officials and the media. In my remarks, which opened up the conference, I spoke about the many rooming and boarding houses which used to be in both the black and white communities to take in the then-homeless, and the fact that today those facilities no longer exist.

At noon I had to be at Florida Memorial College for a dedication ceremony for the new William Lehman Aviation Science Building. Over the past several years, I had been successful in getting funds from transportation appropriations, which enabled Florida Memorial to construct this building. First, there was a luncheon, then a tour, and I felt very honored to have my name on this new and very impressive aviation science building. When we went outside to begin the ceremony, F-16 jets flew over the building, which was quite thrilling. Dade County Manager Ray Goode, who is on the Board of Trustees for Miami-Dade Community College, was the emcee, and said that I was a "superb Congressman." I know Ray from the days of the Dade Coalition, a citizens group way back in the 1960's. Joan, our sons, and good friends like Ellen Kempler were at the dedication and full of cheers as I was presented with a very lovely plaque.

Leaving the Florida Memorial campus, I was just able to make my 4:15 Eastern flight to Washington. When I arrived at the office, the staff told me I had missed a vote, my first miss of the year, but I did make the second vote of the day.

SEPTEMBER 27 TUESDAY

This morning I have been busy rearranging my evening calendar, as Joan will be in Washington this week. Tom, Greg, Lucy and I spent about an hour getting ready for the conference report that I am taking to the House Floor at noon today. Hopefully we won't have too many colloquies or a motion to recommit with instructions.

At noon I took the conference report to the Floor and, on

passage, we had only thirteen votes in opposition, which is the lowest number of opposition votes of any appropriations conference reports this year. All the amendments were approved except for two in disagreement, which we sent back to the Senate: on DOT regional representatives, and on a Coast Guard cutter appropriation and where the cutter would be built. I anticipate that the Senate will recede on the DOT amendment, and send back the Coast Guard cutter amendment for us to recede on in behalf of Senator Hollings of South Carolina. It was almost two hours of hard work on the Floor, but very satisfying. Just outside the House Floor were constituents from the North Dade Chamber of Commerce. I had left instruction with the staff to have them meet me there for a photo on the Capitol steps. It was a group of thirteen people, and after the photo session, we walked back to my office in the Rayburn Building for a discussion meeting on the Metromover and other issues affecting Dade County. After the meeting, I had a courtesy visit from a couple who live in North Miami, good friends of Irene Faugno, who so effectively ran my first school board campaign. Irene had told them to be sure and call on me when they got to Washington.

In the evening at the Barnett Bank reception in the Cannon Caucus Room, I spoke briefly to Janet Studley from the Holland and Knight law firm, and circulated among the guests talking to Barnett Bank officials about banking legislation and also about my son Bill and his business with Barnett. Then Janet took me to dinner at the Prima Piatti Restaurant, and we had a lot of catching up to do on things that had been happening with us, as we had not seen each other for a while.

SEPTEMBER 28 WEDNESDAY

10:00 a.m., I was at the retirement ceremony for Joe Hall, my favorite Army legislative liaison officer. Joe is leaving the military to join the Melbourne, Florida-based Harris Corporation as its legislative representative in Washington; when I walked in, Joe gave me a very hearty welcome, as did the other military personnel there, and they really seemed to appreciate my being there. Members hate to lose the military personnel with whom they have worked so well over the years, and I will surely miss Joe.

As I had predicted, on the Floor today we got the amendment

back from the Senate on the Coast Guard cutter. On my request for unanimous consent to recede to the Senate's position, there was no objection, and that finalized the Transportation Bill. Now the bill is being documented to send to the President for his signature. After working so long for several months every day for the sole purpose of producing a transportation bill, the goal that had been the engine that drove me, now that it is finished, it is sort of a let-down not having a real top-level, important priority pushing me. However, I will be busy for a good while yet.

I was talking on the Floor to my colleague Olympia Snowe from Maine, and she said that the debate on October 5 between Republican Vice-Presidential nominee Dan Quayle and the Democratic Vice-Presidential nominee Lloyd Bentsen is more important than the other two debates because Quayle will either prove himself or not, and this will bear heavily on establishing Bush's credibility. Olympia may be right. But late in the afternoon at the gym, most of the Democrats I talked to are not too hopeful about Dukakis. They seem to think that the Dukakis campaign is slipping fast, but I don't see that as yet and am still a bit more optimistic. It certainly won't be the kind of landslide there was in the Carter/Mondale campaign, as Dukakis will carry a lot more States than they did. It is still pretty much even in California, but it will be difficult for Dukakis to carry the southern states, and that will hurt him.

In today's *Miami Herald* there was a small item about the passage of the conference report, and also an article in the Durham, North Carolina, newspaper about my helping Representative David Price from that state. Dave showed me the article, and I am sure he had been watching for it to appear because several evenings ago at the Tom Boggs party, I told Dave that I had spoken to a reporter from his local paper, and that I had told the reporter that Dave had a great deal to do with the funds for the new radar tower at the Raleigh-Durham Airport that he represents. I told the reporter also about Republican Tim Valentine of North Carolina, who likewise had worked to obtain funds for the airport.

Sue Perry stopped by the office, and together we went to Bob Mrazek's fundraiser at his home, which is a real fun place to be. The usual lobbyists were there and congratulated me on getting my bill out. We stayed for about half an hour, and then went to Washington's Union Station for an Amtrak reception. This reception will be written up in the *Washington Post* tomorrow, as thousands of dollars were spent on this gala event. Going through some of the private railroad cars, I stopped at Micky Wolfson's and he had the best food, drinks and party crowd of all. I saw Carter Brown of the National Gallery, Senator Packwood of Oregon, and Wolfson's friends from Miami. Micky played the grand host, giving me a special tour of his private car. In other private cars I saw Graham Claytor, President of Amtrak, John Riley, Federal Railway Administrator, and with them was Senator Frank Lautenberg. It was a black tie affair, but Frank was wearing regular clothes, as was I, and when I saw Dante Fascell in Wolfson's car, he too was in regular attire. But most everyone else was dressed in tuxedos and the women in evening wear. I stayed till 8:30 p.m., went back to the office to clear off my desk, and then went home.

SEPTEMBER 29 THURSDAY

Writing to Micky Wolfson this morning, I told him how much I enjoyed last evening, the party and special tour of his private railroad car. I did enjoy it, but it was a mob scene, and maybe a little too much for me. Joan called and said that all the catering arrangements had been made for my birthday party next week. I am having more of a celebration that I thought I would. I then went to the Air and Space Museum where the NASA people were having a reception for the space shuttle sendoff. Back at the office, Irv Kessler, Richard Strauss and Herman Markowitz from the United Israel agency, were in about arrangements for my trip to Israel in February for the dedication of the Kathy Lehman Weiner Absorption Center.

At noon I joined in the luncheon for the North Dade Chamber of Commerce. I spent a good deal of time with them a few days ago, and about two-thirds of them had already gone home. On the Floor I spoke to Charlie Wilson, and he is concerned about the fragile emotional state of the Speaker, who is confronting all the charges coming out against him on Nicaragua and other things, like selling his book with a fifty-percent royalty. We both feel bad for Jim. At the office Nan Rich was in. Nan is a friend of mine from Miami, and was in Washington regarding the refugee issue. Nan had once campaigned for the Dade County School Board; her father, Dan Herman, was a good tennis buddy of mine who died a few years ago, and seeing Nan brought back fond memories of Dan.

Going back and forth to vote kept me pretty busy today. I spoke to Bob Mrazek on the Floor about an unhappy intern I knew of in Bob's office, and he said he appreciated my telling him. John has kept me busy talking to other than the Miami media, including the *New York Times* about the MacKay/Gunter race and the *Los Angeles Times* about problems with the Los Angeles Transit Authority.

Everything was going fine on the Floor until about 7:00 p.m., when the DC Appropriations Bill fell apart, so there was a motion to recommit the bill back to committee. Presently two more appropriations bills have to pass the House - the DC Bill which is hung up on the abortion issue, and the Defense Bill. When these bills are passed, we will be finished in the House with the thirteen appropriations bills; then we will have the problem of what to do with the nonappropriations bills that are still awaiting action.

SEPTEMBER 30 FRIDAY

Barney Frank told me this morning that he thinks we will recess next week, but come back before Election Day in November to take care of any pending legislation. Transportation Secretary Jim Burnley called to tell me that he really tried hard to have a ceremony for the President's signing of my Appropriations Transportation Bill, but because there were so many bills before the President, it could not be done. Burnley did say, however, that in a serious conversation with the President about my bill, he told Reagan of my "brilliant management in bringing the conference report to a successful conclusion." Apparently my Transportation Bill is now signed, as the President has left for Illinois.

Steve Neal (D-NC) wants me to write a letter on his behalf concerning a road project in our bill for his district, but I told him I could not do it. If an opponent was trying to take credit away from Steve for the road project, I would certainly write a letter saying otherwise, but writing such a letter just to give Steve the credit, does not sit well with me - especially since the main person involved with this project, and who has worked with me to get the road project into the bill, is Bill Hefner of North Carolina, Chairman of Appropriations Military Construction Subcommittee.

At 11:45 p.m., we finished on the Floor and passed, before the midnight deadline, the last of the thirteen appropriations bills. In a conversation with Congressman Drier of California, Drier was apologizing for being one of the thirteen members to vote against our conference report. "That is okay," I said, "but subcommittee members did want to know why you voted against the bill when you had asked for all that money for Los Angeles mass transit." Not waiting for an answer, I said, "I don't have a 'shit list,' but you owe me one." Drier said, "Fine."

Chapter 22

OCTOBER 1, 1988   SATURDAY

Joan is to fly into Washington tomorrow, so this morning I was off to Eastern Market for a few groceries.

OCTOBER 2   SUNDAY

Joan arrived okay. She is primarily here for my birthday party on the 5th, and will have to leave the next day, as she still has her work to do on the Art in Public Places sculpture.

OCTOBER 3   MONDAY

Jewish members met this morning with Hyman Bookbinder, former Director of the American Jewish Committee, regarding the Dukakis campaign that has need of not only financial assistance, but people to work for his campaign throughout the country. For this I will give Jeff and Patrice time off to work in our

17th district; other members will do the same in their districts.

Thirty-four suspension bills are on the calendar, and later today there will probably be about ten recorded votes. Apparently we will have to vote out the drug bill before we can leave Washington hopefully by Friday. If the Senate does not vote out its version of the drug bill and send it to conference, then the Republicans are going to ask the President to call us back into session to "beat on us" for the lack of a drug program. Leaving the Floor, I went to the Speaker's office and spoke to his top aide, John Mack, who said that the Speaker was satisfied with the letter I wrote to the FAA Administrator McArtor about funding the control tower for the North Ft. Worth Airport in Wright's district.

In the evening Joan and I went to Washington's Union Station. Joan had not seen all the changes that had taken place at the station, and was excited upon seeing the renovations and the new environment that had been created there.

OCTOBER 4 TUESDAY

We were busy on the House Floor today with votes every five minutes on forty bills. According to the Majority Leader we will be in Washington next week because the Senate has not finished the Clean Air and Drug bills. I did get a chance to grab a bite to eat in the Rayburn Cafeteria while meeting with lobbyist Gary Hymel and Mr. Soysal, head of the Jewish community in Turkey. After our meeting, I walked them over to the Capitol's Rayburn Room and got Dave Obey and Claude Pepper to come off the Floor to also meet with them.

While on the Floor, I invited a few more members to my birthday party being held tomorrow, as I want to be sure of a reasonable turnout. Barbara Boxer said she would definitely be there. There will be no votes after 3:00 p.m. tomorrow, and a lot of the members I invited will be going to Omaha for the Bentsen/Quayle Vice-Presidential debate. Besides Joan, our sons Bill and Tom will be at the party, as will our late daughter's husband, Don Weiner and his wife Gene Beckwith. Tom has already arrived, coming a day early to attend the Dukakis party this evening, which I don't think I can make.

The party for retiring member Eddie Boland (D-MA) was held this evening in the House Appropriations Committee room, hosted by Appropriations Chairman Jamie Whitten. At age 77, and having served 36 years (18 terms) in Congress, this was Eddie's sentimental "farewell" party. My son Tom was with me and had a really good time there with his old friend Jim Molloy, Doorkeeper of the House. The party was fun, with me and Tom having our photo taken with Tip O'Neill. Afterwards, Tom dropped me off at home, and he went on to the Dukakis party at the Washington Hilton.

OCTOBER 5 WEDNESDAY

The Florida runoff elections were held yesterday, and Jeff called this morning to let me know that Buddy MacKay had won over Bill Gunter for the Democratic nomination in the Senate race. State Senator Ken Jenne won the Democratic nomination for State Insurance Commissioner over state Senator John Vogt, but Metro Commissioner Beverly Phillips lost to newcomer Charles Dusseau, a Chase Manhattan Bank executive. With the defeat of Phillips, three of the Metro Commissioners have now been defeated, and all three - Oesterle, Clark and Phillips - were on the Metro Transportation Committee chaired by Oesterle. With new members on the Metro Commission, a major shift in Dade County's transportation policy may take place, moving away from expanding the Metrorail.

Florida State DOT Secretary Bill Henderson was in the office this morning with some of his people to discuss the various problems and concerns of the State Department of Transportation. Henderson thanked me especially for the help I had given on the cost of building the Acosta Bridge in Jacksonville, and then I had to leave as Sid Yates was waiting for me and for my son Tom to drive us to the dedication ceremony of the Cornerstone for the U.S. Holocaust Memorial Museum. On the program booklet, I was listed as one of the museum board representatives from the House of Representatives, and it was a very impressive ceremony with the President making the keynote address. Florida Senator Bob Graham was there as were many other Senators and Representatives. Some members, however, left early because of a vote in the House, but Sid and I stayed; we missed the one vote, but it was worth it.

The party in celebration of my 75th birthday today was held

this afternoon, and it was a big success. Sharyn Fallick, who did much of the work in putting the party together, was also up from Miami. There would have been a larger turnout of my colleagues, but voting stopped today at 2:30, so that members could catch the plane from Dulles International for the Vice-Presidential debate. But most of my good friends on and off the Hill were there, including my tennis buddies and the State of Florida delegation, which made the party a very enjoyable and memorable time for me. Afterwards, Joan, Don, Gene and I went home, but stayed only a short while before going to New York member Tom Downey's house to watch the televised Vice-Presidential debate. We all got a kick out of Senator Lloyd Bentsen, who outshone Dan Quayle, and I wonder if the Dukakis campaign can take advantage of Bentsen's ability, status, and presidential character.

OCTOBER 6 THURSDAY

Ira Estis, a former intern in our Washington office, who now works for an AIDS group in Ft. Lauderdale, came in to urge me to do what I could to deal with the AIDS problem, saying that there was a geometrical expansion of the disease among children. Ira is quite an articulate and bright young man, and has done well since those early days as our intern. After Ira, Vice-Mayor Resnick of Miami Beach and some other South Florida people arrived. They were in Washington for the dedication of the Holocaust Cornerstone yesterday, and I had thought they wanted to see me about plans for the Miami Beach light rail, but instead they talked about Israel and the Holocaust Memorial on Miami Beach. I took the initiative and mentioned the light rail, but it seems a dead issue on Miami Beach.

At noon, Charlie Bennett hosted a luncheon for the retiring Florida Senator Lawton Chiles, but the luncheon unfortunately coincided with about ten votes on suspension bills running five minutes apart, and this really blew the luncheon out of the water. I did try to be there, going back and forth between votes, but I never got a chance to see Lawton. During one of those trips to the Floor, Ways and Means Chairman Dan Rostenkowski told me there was going to be a problem with the FAA regarding the tax on airline tickets, a proposal that originated in the Ways and Means Committee. As the money accumulates in the FAA trust fund and is not spent at a certain rate, the tax is mandated to be reduced, which may be a good thing. The reason our transportation subcommittee does not appropriate any faster is not because of budgetary restrictions, but that the software technology for improving air traffic control is slow to come online, and communities are not building airport expansions as rapidly as they should.

Back at the office, I met with Evelyn and Gordon Schmitt from my district, two of my old Miami Shores friends. I took them to see Bob Knisely on Appropriations Subcommittee staff on Labor, HHS, and Education, and we set up an appointment for tomorrow morning with liaison officials from the Education Department. Evelyn, founder of Broader Opportunities for the Learning Disabled (B.O.L.D.), is seeking a demonstration grant for a Learning Disabled Anti-Dropout Program for Dade County, and for her to get this grant is a long shot; but I said to her, "It doesn't hurt to try."

There were a lot of comments today about the Quayle/Bentsen debate. The Democrats were upbeat and the Republicans were a little uptight about the results. In the evening Sharyn and I went to the Florida House reception for Buddy MacKay, and here too the Democrats were upbeat, as we now have hopes of maintaining the Florida Senate seat for the Democratic party. Buddy thanked me for appearing with him in Miami, and together we had our picture taken. Sharyn and I stayed only about fifteen minutes before going on to the Brasserie for dinner; I was home by 8:30 p.m.

OCTOBER 7 FRIDAY

The morning was relatively quiet, so I had a chance to get off the Hill for tennis with my House buddies. In the afternoon, lobbyist Art Roberts came in with Eugene Suter and Tom Henderson from Broward County regarding funding for the Ft. Lauderdale-Hollywood Airport. They talked about a $10 million grant for the airport to build sound barriers along its perimeter. Afterwards, the Schmitt's and I met with two liaison officials from the Department of Education regarding a grant for South Florida to establish a summer program for dropout prevention among the learning disabled. We spent about an hour with the liaison officials, and surprisingly the possibility exists for a $100 thousand grant by the spring of next year.

Next in was Bob Kunst, who heads a gay rights group in Dade

County. Bob wanted to see if he could get something going for a coordinated program of housing/medical/food care for AIDS victims. I suggested that next year he get on the public hearing testimonies agenda in the relevant appropriations subcommittees, and I also talked to Patrice in my district office about the kinds of grants for which Bob could apply that would be pertinent for this effort.

The Weiner's remained in Washington for some extra days, and together with Katherine Karpoff, we went this evening to hear the National Symphony Orchestra at the Kennedy Center, and it was very enjoyable.

OCTOBER 8 SATURDAY

Charlie Wilson and I got together in the evening, and mostly we talked politics and discussed his trip in December to Baghdad.

OCTOBER 9 SUNDAY

Don Edwards and his wife Edie invited me to their home on the Eastern Shore. I had taken my tennis gear, but the weather prevented us from playing, so we just sat around the fireplace and talked for a while. I got back home early, settled in and read the Sunday paper.

OCTOBER 10 MONDAY

Federal offices are closed today for the Columbus Day holiday, but I went to the office and spent about an hour going through the mail.

OCTOBER 11 TUESDAY

Since I finished my bill I haven't much work pending. I did speak to an administrator at the North Dade General Hospital about funds in the drug bill that I had gotten Congressman Claude Pepper to agree on for Opa Locka, and presumably there will be a newspaper item on this.

OCTOBER 12 WEDNESDAY

While I was out of the office this morning lobbyist Dawson

Mathis, a former Democratic colleague from Georgia, came in and left four $1,000 checks from the UPS PAC , for me, Carr, Gray and Sabo, all members on my transportation subcommittee.

The House will close business for the week at 1:00 p.m. tomorrow so that members can fly out to California for tomorrow's second Presidential debate between Vice President George Bush and Michael Dukakis. I understand the session will not resume until Tuesday, and I have spent most of the day rearranging my schedule, particularly the evening meeting tomorrow with people from Memorial Sloan Kettering. Instead of the evening, I have arranged with Congressman Joe Early and Mike Stephens on Appropriations Labor, HHS, and Education Subcommittee staff to have a catered luncheon tomorrow in my subcommittee room. Joe Early oversees NIH funding on the aforementioned subcommittee, and he is crucial to Sloan Kettering's funding request.

The House passed the Leave Sharing Bill this afternoon. This is the bill that I had originated in 1986-87 for the benefit of Shannon Chiles. The bill went to the Senate which passed its version, and then back to the House which today passed the compromise version.

OCTOBER 13 THURSDAY

Democratic Vice-Presidential nominee Senator Lloyd Bentsen spoke today before the Democratic Caucus, and he was very good. Most of the Democrats are disturbed by the new polling results on the campaign and don't know exactly what to do. Bentsen had a lot of fun with Dennis Eckart from Ohio, saying to Dennis, "You know Dan Quayle, and I know Dan Quayle, and you are not Dan Quayle" and that relaxed everyone. Dennis had played Quayle in the debate practice sessions.

At the office the staff and I had a short meeting about my pending trip to Cuba on the 15th of this month, and then at noon the luncheon meeting began with Congressman Joe Early, Appropriations Labor, HHS Subcommittee staff, Jim Quirk and Jim Harding, both Vice-Presidents of Memorial Sloan Kettering. Quirk and Harding seemed most appreciative of the guidance provided, and Joe, along with telling them to solicit more grass roots support for cancer research, was very helpful and encouraging.

At 1:00, I met for about an hour with *Miami Herald* reporter

Ricardo Zaldivar concerning my trip to Cuba. What was most interesting and intriguing to Ricardo was the reaction of the Miami Cuban community to a liberal Democratic member of Congress going to Cuba to bring back Cuban prisoners. Ricardo knew that the basic Miami Cuban community was very opposed to my position on the Contras, but its reaction to this undertaking was no longer an issue for me. As I told Ricardo, I saw it as people suffering in prison and I had been given this opportunity to do something about getting them released.

My 3:15 p.m. flight on Eastern to Miami was on time, and I was happily moved up to first class. Sitting next to me was the Washington representative from the Nicaragua Contra group; we were cordial, but of course we were coming from different directions. Also sitting in first class was President Duarte of El Salvador, who was quite ill and very fragile; his wife said they had been at Walter Reed Hospital where Duarte had received treatment. Duarte has terminal cancer.

At home in Miami I took it easy, watching with Joan the evening televised Bush/Dukakis Presidential debate, which we both thought was quite pathetic, especially Dukakis. The kickoff question from one of the three panelists about the death penalty was obviously a challenge to Dukakis on his opposition to the death penalty, and when asked if he might change his mind about capital punishment if his wife were raped and murdered, Dukakis failed miserably in his response, saying only that he had been opposed to the death penalty all of his life and that there were better and more effective ways to deal with violent crime. The question gave him the perfect opportunity to wipe out the notion that he was soft on crime, and he responded with such a lame answer, which did nothing to strengthen his position. Also, the fact that Dukakis could not think of any heroes, really left George Bush in charge.

OCTOBER 14 FRIDAY

At the district office, I spoke to the staff about what I needed to have done for my trip to Cuba. I then called the front office of the Appropriations Committee to explain that I would not be in Washington Tuesday, in the event a meeting was held with the subcommittee chairs. There may be some votes I will miss Tuesday, but the main votes I believe will be later in the week. Plus, I am too far committed to the Cuban trip to worry about being back in Washington by Tuesday. John Schelble called last evening a bit concerned because he had received a call from Al Oliver of Airlift International, and Al had told John that he heard from my son Tom about my trip to Cuba. John is worried that too much information is out about the trip, prior to my departure, but I do not think so since we are leaving tomorrow. John also reminded me that the *Miami News* was closing down at the end of the year, so I called the paper this morning and, among other things, I told them of the nostalgia I felt when I remembered the time I first came to Miami in 1936 and worked in the old News Tower Building, which is now the Freedom Tower.

Later, with my ophthalmologist, Dr. Henry Clayman, we talked about the Adele Acosta story that he and St. Francis Hospital did for *Tropic Magazine*. Dr. Clayman and I will be meeting later in the month with the St. Francis people, Adele Acosta, and reporters for the story on how things work in the private sector to the benefit of a person without federal medical care.

Nancy Pollock invited me to a political campaign event this evening by one of her friends in North Miami, and if anything was wrong with the Nancy Pollock campaign, it was certainly evident there. About fifty people were coming and going, and all they did was eat and sign the guest book; Nancy never asked them to do anything in the way of raising campaign funds or putting signs in their front yards, or handing out posters, etc. She hasn't got her act together.

Meanwhile, Dave Samson from Winston Towers, chairman of the Northeast Dade Concerned Citizens, called to ask how strongly I wanted him to support Nancy in the November election. I told Dave that I was very much in support of Nancy, but he had to make up his own mind. I think what he wanted me to do was to ask him to support Nancy so that he could say "Congressman Lehman put impossible pressure on me," and I wouldn't do that. Many condo residents perhaps feel that Nancy was supportive of David Young for the State Senate, and they were very strong for the incumbent Gwen Margolis. It is one of those types of situations, and I don't know what will happen, as Nancy is in trouble without the *Miami Herald* endorsement and without the big condo vote in Northeast Dade that she got in the primary. Evelyn Schuengrund is another condo community leader who does not want to get involved at this time. I think, however, that Ruby Steiner and her group at Aventura still are with Nancy. Unfortunately, at this stage I cannot see any progress that Nancy has made, not even to hiring a campaign manager.

OCTOBER 15 SATURDAY

This morning, on the day that I am to depart for Cuba, I took time to play doubles at the Miami Shores Tennis Club with Jerry Willenborg and Tony Fernans, and I now have a regular 11:00 a.m., doubles match at the club. It was a lot of fun and I really enjoyed it. People at the club on Saturday mornings are not the usual people that I meet there late in the afternoon. They were happy to see me and made a little bit of a fuss over me, and I guess I am a political character there now. They were so respectful that it was almost a bit embarrassing to me.

In the afternoon Adele Liskov from my office and Myer from Mickey Leland's office flew in from Washington and met Joan and me at the Miami International Airport. With everyone accounted for, we were escorted out to the plane - a two-engine Cessna - which took off about 5:00 p.m., landing at the Havana airport at about 6:30 p.m. The plane with our group from Miami was the first to arrive in Havana; not long after, two planes from Texas arrived with Representatives Mickey Leland, Solomon Ortiz, and their entourage: House Sergeant-At-Arms Jack Russ, the Speaker of the Texas House of Representatives, a Judge Green from Texas, and various others - mostly Texas businessmen.

About ten of us were accommodated together in a beautiful government guest home, whose former owner is now in exile. Others were at another beautiful and more modern home, and some were at a hotel on the ocean. All of us, though, are in the same area. At the home where we were staying, a kitchen crew prepared a delicious dinner. After dinner, we sat around awhile and talked. The atmosphere was very relaxed and congenial, with the representative from the American Interest Section giving us the usual welcoming brochures. We then boarded a bus to pick up the other groups and went to the old Tropicana Nightclub. It was raining that evening, and since this was an out-of-doors club, there was no performance. Many tourists were there from Canada, Southeast Asia, Eastern Europe, etc., all waiting to get in. Because of the rain, we left the club and took a sightseeing tour. Havana is like a time capsule, as nothing much had changed since I was here thirty years ago. It was and still is a very beautiful city.

OCTOBER 16 SUNDAY

The coffee was so good at breakfast this morning that I went back for seconds. After breakfast, we boarded a bus for a sightseeing drive out to the country, stopping along the way at a few small towns to take pictures. During our visit to an amphitheater, we met some tourists from Argentina and took more photos. For lunch we stopped at Ruins Restaurant, so named because the restaurant had been made over from the ruins of an old sugar mill. The building was beautiful, but the food was only average and the service was slow. Leaving the restaurant, we went to the Hemingway Marina and bought souvenirs from several gift shops there. I bought some Cuban-slogan tee shirts and hats, and a case of rum that cost me $45.00. The ride was very interesting, and being an old automobile dealer, I couldn't help but notice the many 1949 through 1959 Chevrolets. All in all, the people seemed well and the farmland was beautiful. The problems don't seem too great, and though the people are not rich and the houses shabby, it really did not seem all that bad.

We had a very lovely evening with Jade and Betsy Taylor at their home. Jade is the Chief Officer of the American Interest Section, and was most gracious, as was his wife Betsy, putting us all at ease and in a good mood. We were there until rather late, 10:00 p.m., having arrived at 6:00, and the four hours went by quickly.

OCTOBER 17 MONDAY

After lunch today we went to the Bio-Technology Institute where there are millions of dollars worth of equipment. Not many people were at the Institute, and I was aware of all the empty rooms with all the unused high-tech equipment. Unlike Memorial Sloan Kettering or NIH, there is not the skilled manpower to use this high-tech equipment that comes from Japan and elsewhere, and I think the technicians are in over their heads trying to mass produce

Interferon, which presently, by many accounts, is not yet much of a proven use.

Everyone is keeping busy, some shopping and others like Joan going off to see some Cuban artists this morning. Adele reached John Schelble in Washington and told him we should be back tomorrow afternoon, but at the moment everything is problematical. We may be bringing in four or five prisoners and perhaps some family members, but everything is up in the air and not in our control. The Foreign Minister representative assigned to us is saying that they are releasing these prisoners mainly because of Mickey and me - and especially because I had come from South Florida to do this.

In the evening around 5:30, we left the house going to the Mayor's office in downtown Havana. Joan was not around when we left, as she had wanted to purchase some paintings from an "underground" painter, and was held up negotiating with the attache from the American Interest Section about what she should pay for the paintings. When we arrived at the Mayor's office, I called Joan at the house and instructed her to take a taxi to meet us, and, fortunately, her taxi arrived at the Mayor's office just as our bus was leaving. Now it seems hardly mentionable, but at the time it was a minor crisis. When I asked the Mayor about the bus service in Havana, he said they charge ten cents a ride, and that they have over 3,000 buses and several hundred on order from Italy, where the buses are made, to be assembled in Havana. This was a good subject for the Mayor, as he went on and on for an hour.

We then proceeded to the synagogue where we met several members of the congregation and learned a little about the community. The synagogue is very beautiful, and although they do not have a Rabbi they do conduct services - especially on the High Holy Days. While at the synagogue we received a message from President Fidel Castro that he was ready to see our group.

Before entering Castro's office, we first had to go through tight security. We were with Castro for about two and a half hours, and if we had not begun to stand, as an indication that we were preparing to leave, we would have been there all night. Part of it was non-serious, just a nice exchange of views, and then Castro turned more serious, telling us that much of his country's problems were related to oil. He mentioned the Cuban-American Foundation and said with Bush as President it would be a problem to move negotiations any closer because of Bush's ties to the Cuban-American

Foundation. He also said that he would like to see Bentsen as President. Castro is very knowledgeable, and even charming, and I witnessed this today firsthand; he really captivated the Texas businessmen who were with us. As he was giving me a signed photograph for my grandson Tommy, I expressed my appreciation for his willingness to free for us the political prisoners, and reminded him, since I knew that he had been informed, that I represented about 200,000 Cuban-American exiles in Miami.

The Cuban-American leadership in Miami, I believe, does not realize that just harassing Castro is not going to change things in Cuba. Castro, I feel, is in power and will remain in power as long as he lives, and although there is no great joy in Cuba, I did not see any evidence of great misery either.

OCTOBER 18 TUESDAY

This morning I sat outside on the lawn at the home where I was staying and admired the beautiful view. Looking back, I think that Egypt's Anwar Sadat and Cuba's Fidel Castro were the two most fascinating people I have talked to in my career as a Congressman.

We had a safe flight back to Miami, returning with three prisoners and several family members. One prisoner and four family members were on the plane with me, one prisoner was on the Texas group plane, and the other in a plane with Adele. In Miami there was a mob scene at the airport with lots of media present. I was feeling very good about getting the three people out of prison, and even though I was surrounded by close to a hundred of their family and friends, I was sure there would be some adverse comments from Anglos like, "We don't need any more Cubans coming in to the States." One prisoner we were able to have released returned to prison, as he would not leave Cuba without his son.

OCTOBER 19 WEDNESDAY

I flew to Washington this morning on a 7:45 flight. There were lots of phone calls congratulating me, and two front page articles in the *Miami Herald* telling of how the trip came about and how I had been talking to Mickey Leland for some time about political prisoners in Cuba, knowing that Leland was supportive of better ties with Cuba and a friend of Fidel Castro. When Mickey asked me for a list of political prisoners in Cuba, I asked Tony Costa of the Cuban-American Foundation if he could supply such a list, and everything snowballed from there. The trip might even make some people suspicious of me, but I would do business with anyone to relieve the suffering of people who have been in prison for 20 years. I appreciated the *Herald* article because not only did it talk about the Cuban trip, it also mentioned my smuggling a heart valve into the Soviet Union several years ago, and that I had helped the Jews of East Berlin get a rabbi last year, making this trip seem like just another humanitarian undertaking, which for me is exactly what it was. I just wished we could have gotten all the prisoners on the list released. The *Miami News* also had a big story.

It is quiet in Washington today, just a few minor votes, and no one seems to know just when we will recess. The Democratic leadership in the House does not want to adjourn until the House passes a drug bill, which means that we may be here until election day. Senator Dole's office called to let me know that space was available on the plane for his trip to Southeast Asia. Also, the date for the Neal Smith trip has changed from December 8 to December 22, and now I do not know which trip I want to take.

Maria Elena came in with her client from Hazeltine Corporation, which produces instrument landing systems. Hazeltine is concerned about the progress of a grant from the FAA that would help change inflight responders to the new high-tech microwave landing systems.

Mickey Leland and I have not had a chance to talk since our return to Washington, and I want him to know that I am thinking that perhaps we can go back to Cuba to get the prisoners on our list that Castro did not release. Joe Kennedy was in the gym, and I told him that Fidel Castro spoke very highly of his Uncle Jack as President, who had opposed U.S. air cover for the Bay of Pigs invasion. Joe said that his Uncle did not want to provide air cover over Cuba because it would have killed many innocent people, and that that was the primary reason his Uncle Jack did not support air coverage for the Bay of Pigs operation.

OCTOBER 20 THURSDAY

Alice Rivlin, the former Director of the Congressional Budget

Office, met me at the office this morning for breakfast in the Members Dining Room. We talked politics and discussed where the country was headed. She was concerned about the kind of president George Bush would make if he listened to the advisors he has had in the campaign. Because I had spent the morning with Alice, I missed Jesse Jackson who was speaking to the Democratic Caucus.

Lobbyist Tim Furlong came in with several lawyers and business officials from Dallas/Fort Worth about the commuter rail line that they hope to build on the old railroad bed between Dallas and Fort Worth, with a stop at the regional airport. I told them what to do and how to do it, pointing out the questions Texas members on our subcommittee should ask UMTA and the FAA in next year's hearings. When they left, I notified Senator Dole's staff that I would be going on the codel with Dole to Southeast Asia. His aide then informed me that there was no way to provide space for a House of Representative staff, which means that Adele or Terry Peel on Foreign Ops will not be able to join me on the trip. Joan and I are going regardless, and after speaking to Larry Coughlin about the trip, he and his wife Susan may also be joining us.

Claude Harris (D-AL) told me on the Floor today that the FAA had told him that there would be no funding for Selma in this year's bill. So now Claude and I are in the process of setting up a meeting with the FAA Administrator Allan McArtor to see what can be done about reinstating the priority for Selma in the bill.

In a meeting with the four other appropriations subcommittee chairmen who have a piece of the drug bill - Neal Smith, Bill Natcher, Jamie Whitten, and Ed Roybal - we divided the $500 million into $250 million for interdiction of supply, which is our part, and $250 million for treatment and education. Meanwhile, I have given the Armed Services Committee's Subcommittee on Readiness Chairman, Earl Hutto, our subcommittee's budget authority figures for the Coast Guard operations, and also the outlay numbers on the total Coast Guard appropriation.

On the Floor, Bob Mrazek asked if I could get him a $2,000 honorarium in Miami. I told him I would try, and that I would contact Jeffrey Berkowitz of a Jewish group in Miami that raises money for Congressional candidates. Also, I spoke with Mickey Leland about the other prisoners on our list who were not released from the Cuban prison. I told Mickey that I would be speaking to the Cuban-American Foundation to try to work out a deal, through

Mickey, whereby Jorge Mas and Tony Costa from the Cuban-American Foundation could go to Havana and meet with Castro in good faith, to encourage Castro to release the other four prisoners. The Cuban-American Foundation is the roadblock for the removal of the trade embargo with Cuba. If the trade embargo were removed, it would rejuvenate a lot of business in Miami, to the mutual benefit of Miami and Cuba.

I met with the full Appropriations Committee on my part of the drug bill. Larry Coughlin is already on board, and I tried unsuccessfully before the meeting to reach Bill Chappell, Chairman of Appropriations Defense Subcommittee, to make sure he had no problem with transferring a DOD aircraft to the Coast Guard to be fitted with radar equipment at the Coast Guard's expense. In the bill, we have $100 million for Coast Guard acquisitions, construction and improvement (AC&I) for helicopters, radar and the remodeling of Coast Guard vessels, in addition to $16 million for operating expenses. Silvio Conte questioned me on the fact that I earmarked the AC&I, instead of letting the Coast Guard make the determination as to how the funds would be used. My reply to Conte was, "We earmark in the regular bills, and there is no reason why we can't earmark in the supplemental."

On the House Floor, Claude Pepper told me he was going to Walter Reed Hospital tomorrow to have a growth removed from his groin. "I am telling you," he said, "but no one else is to know." I suggested to Claude that he go as I did to Memorial Sloan Kettering in New York or M.D. Anderson in Houston if he thought there might be a malignancy, and Claude said he wished he had come to me initially, as apparently this is a recurrence of a previous operation that was done at Walter Reed. He thinks now it is too late to go elsewhere.

OCTOBER 21 FRIDAY

The only visitor I had today was Sol Rudis from New York, my son Tom's father-in-law. Sol is in Washington for some legal work for a homeowner's loan corporation. We talked for a while and then had a photo together in front of the Capitol. I am now waiting to go to the Floor for about six suspension bills that are coming up. It looks as though we will be here until midnight or later as things are moving rather slowly. On the Floor, Larry

Coughlin said that he is definitely interested in going on the Dole codel to Southeast Asia. It would be good, as Joan and I have traveled with him and his wife Susan before, and we enjoyed them.

Bob Kastenmeier (D-WI) and I took a break for a game of tennis, and I won. Back on the Floor, I showed Mickey Leland the article that appeared today in the *Ft. Lauderdale Sun Tattler.* The article quoted Tony Costa as saying that it was okay for me to go to Cuba and get the prisoners out, but he criticized Mickey for embracing Fidel Castro. When Mickey read the article he became angry, but told me he is working on a deal for Tony and Jorge Mas to go to Cuba to get the other prisoners released. We may make Tony Costa and Jorge Mas an offer they cannot refuse. Bill Gray came up to me on the Floor and said that he wanted me to talk to Sonny Montgomery, Chairman of the Veterans Affairs Committee, about supporting him for Democratic Caucus Chair, which I of course will do.

At 6:00 p.m. we were in session so I went to dinner, then home for a short nap, and then back to the office. It was after 11:00 p.m. when we passed the drug bill, but the session did not end until 1:00 a.m. By the time I got home, I was so charged up that I had a hard time getting to sleep, finally doing so around 3:00 a.m., and back up at 7:30 a.m.

OCTOBER 22 SATURDAY

This morning, with less than five hours sleep, I was back on the House Floor for the end of the final session of the 100th Congress. No further legislation from now until the end of the year. Immediately after the last vote, I was off to the airport for a 10:30 a.m. flight to Miami, which landed at Miami International at 1:00, time enough to keep my tennis date with Nancy Pollock.

OCTOBER 23 SUNDAY

Today was easy - nothing political. I did go by the district office to review the mail and leave notes for the staff. In the afternoon John Meyerhoff and I played tennis in Miami Shores, and he congratulated me on what I had done for the Cuban prisoners. In the evening at home I listened to the tape that I did for Bill Bayer's radio show on the Cuban trip, and it was not too good a recording. I was pleased, however, that my speech impediment was not apparent. That evening the family went out to dinner, and Joan remarked about how much kinder some of the Cuban shop people had been toward her since our trip.

OCTOBER 24 MONDAY

At the district office, the check for $5,000 that I made out to the Dukakis campaign was returned to me, as you cannot contribute to a presidential campaign out of a congressional campaign fund. But a $1,000 check that was sent to Buddy MacKay's Senate campaign was acceptable. A constituent called and kept me on the phone for quite a while because he could not get over the fact that he was actually speaking to a Congressman; he was so surprised that I would get on the phone and talk with him personally. The caller was from Opa Locka and wanted help with his mother's social security check that was lost. Sharyn came in to tell me about some problems she is having with my bringing the transportation subcommittee to Miami for the Super Bowl; most problematical is getting the sufficient number of game tickets, but it will all work out. Then, when I called *Miami Herald* reporter Tom Fiedler to see if he wanted to play tennis with Gardnar Mulloy and me Wednesday on Fisher Island, Tom said he would be going to Washington Wednesday. This reminded me that I would not be returning to Washington until the second week in November, when Joan and I are scheduled to depart Washington on our overseas trip with Senator Dole's codel.

OCTOBER 25 TUESDAY

I visited with Annie Ackerman this morning. Annie is still bedridden and no longer cares about appearance. Her personality has changed a bit, understandably, but she seemed glad to see me. In the afternoon, I visited with my other critically ill friend, Marjorie Deutsch, a young brain tumor victim.

John called to confirm that the meeting with Adele Acosta, Dr. Henry Clayman, and members of the press was now set for Friday, October 28. In the evening I took it easy and tried to catch up on some rest, as it has been long hours and a busy end of session.

OCTOBER 26 WEDNESDAY

This morning I met with the new County Commissioner Charles Dusseau. Dusseau defeated Beverly Phillips in the runoff election, and I, frankly, was surprised today at how little he knew about the status of transportation in Dade County and the way the system works here, especially regarding full-funding contracts and the people he needs to contact as to future federal funding for the Metromover. He did not know about the two different UMTA funding pots, one for the buses and one for the Peoplemover, but he listened very well as I explained this, and seemed to favor building the two extensions for the Peoplemover. Afterwards, I met with Patrice and a group of exporters concerning trade issues and aid programs in Jamaica.

OCTOBER 27 THURSDAY

This morning I went to the bus garage to see how Joan's artwork is coming along, and the sculpture is coming together okay. We can go on the Dole codel and feel good about leaving the project behind. Many of the workers at the garage congratulated me on getting the Cuban prisoners released. Some had immigration problems concerning their relatives, and I referred them to Patty Diaz in our district office.

That evening Joan and I attended the Transition organization dinner. Marvin Rauzin heads the organization, which is a support system for convicts just out of prison. It was a long ceremony, but I was glad to be there and to be the recipient of a very lovely plaque.

OCTOBER 28 FRIDAY

10:00 a.m. I was at the *Miami Herald Tropic Magazine* office to meet with the editor Gene Weingarten and A.J. Montenari who ran the Montenari School thirty years ago when I sponsored Adele Acosta there. Dr. Henry Clayman who did the recent surgery on Adele's eyes was also there. To get the complete story, Gene spoke to all three of us, but because the story did not have much intrigue or complexity, he did not think it would be a good story for *Tropic*. Gene said he would talk to the people who run the *Living Today* section of the *Miami Herald,* and he thinks they would like to run the story as a human interest piece, based on the complex support system that Adele Acosta has had to use over the last thirty years.

Leaving the Herald building, I headed for Maria Elena's Dupont Plaza office to meet with her and Tony Costa, about plans for a future trip to Cuba. The most important thing I said was not to exaggerate the concern that Fidel Castro lightly expressed about the Cuban-American Foundation. We parted with the understanding that a meeting would be set up in Washington with Maria Elena, Tony Costa, Mickey Leland and myself in early December.

At the district office, I met with leaders from the Transit Workers Union and the Builders Trade Union to get their backing for the full-funding contract for the Metromover. I explained to them that whether they build the Metromover or not, federal bus subsidy for Metro-Dade would not be affected, and that bus funds come out of a different pot than the funds to build the Metromover. The labor unions are so worried that rapid mass transit funds will reduce UMTA aid to labor intensive bus transportation.

OCTOBER 29 SATURDAY

At 12:30 p.m. my two grandsons, Tommy and Matt, and I were picked up at the helicopter pad on 151st Street and Biscayne Boulevard, and flown to Opa Locka for the Air Show. The Golden Knights Parachutists did quite a spectacular jump, and when they landed I went out on the field to congratulate them. My grandson Tommy, who is only five years old, was beside me, and it was a warm touch for me to march out on the field to congratulate these parachutists and have my little grandson coming out alongside me holding my hand. The boys especially enjoyed the Blue Angels.

OCTOBER 30 SUNDAY

My son Tom picked me up late in the afternoon and we drove to the Florida Keys for fishing. I did nothing political today, just had a good time with my son fishing, and I caught the most fish ever.

OCTOBER 31 MONDAY

This morning I went to the Miami Chamber of Commerce for a meeting with the chairman of the Miami Chamber, the Assistant Manager of Dade County, and other people involved with my subcommittee's visit to Miami in January. Along with tickets to the Super Bowl, each subcommittee member will receive a $2,000 honorarium from various organizations. When the members arrive Saturday, January 21, they will be met at the airport and taken to their hotels; in the evening we will all go to Joe's Stone Crabs for dinner. The next day they will have some free time before a bus picks them up and takes them to the Super Bowl game. The day after the Super Bowl, they will be taken to the Dadeland Marriott Hotel Station to ride the Metrorail and later visit the Miami International Airport. The plans are beginning to come together.

Last night my Texas colleague Charlie Wilson was on the television show "*60 Minutes*," regarding the Soviet war in Afghanistan and how he singlehandedly made the difference in the war against the Soviet invasion. As a member of the Defense Appropriations subcommittee he got the DOD to send Stinger missiles to the Mujahaden which destroyed the Soviet helicopter gunships. It was a great segment, and I must call Charlie to tell him so.

Chapter 23

NOVEMBER 1, 1988 TUESDAY

Since I will be in Miami through November 8, the Washington office will be sending my mail to the district office. The package that I received today contained a lot of letters for my signature and other paperwork, which took most of the morning to go through it all. I had only one office appointment, and that was in the afternoon with ORT members, a group of Jewish women from my district that raises money for vocation education in Israel.

NOVEMBER 2 WEDNESDAY

At the office this morning Jeff and I went over my district schedule. He also brought me up-to-date on several rumors circulating in the district, including the one of him running for the Metro Commission if there is a change to single member districts, and the rumor that Metro Commissioner Barry Schrieber will be appointed to an Ambassadorship. Bea Moss, acting president of the Twelve Trees Condominium Association, came in to complain that our office had neglected her condo and some of the other smaller condos, while catering to the larger ones like Aventura and Point East. She is partly correct, and she is also a cranky old lady, but after assurance that I would be making up for this oversight, she was appeased, and left seeming to feel much better about our office.

Larry Coughlin called to let me know that space was available on the Air Force plane for him and his wife Susan to join us on Senator Dole's codel to Southeast Asia. The trip takes off from Andrews Air Force Base on Friday, November 11. Joan and I will be returning to Washington next Wednesday the 9th. Larry said he was very happy to be going, as was I, because another House member will be with me on the Senate trip.

In the evening I spoke at the Junior Chamber of Commerce meeting at the Holiday Inn in North Miami Beach. Most of these young chamber members were of very modest means, and several had spent time as Cuban political prisoners. After my speech and then the question and answer period, an appreciation plaque was presented to me. My staff also received a lot of praise for the help that they had rendered to many of these members. People mostly remember not what you do in Washington but what your staff does at the local level. Very rarely has anyone complained to me about the district office staff and how it handles casework, and I believe that is why I very seldom have any real opposition.

NOVEMBER 3 THURSDAY

Mostly at the district office today I was busy on the phone with calls from friends and constituents about all sorts of problems on which they needed help. Some calls were as routine as the one I received from Nate Lee, an old friend, about his grandson who wants to attend the Air Force Academy. Other calls, like the one from Charles Dusseau, the new Dade County Metro Commissioner, were more political. Dusseau asked for my help in setting up an appointment with the Transportation Workers Union, but I won't arrange for a meeting that would include me, Dusseau, and the transportation union. I will, as I told Dusseau, give him the names of people to call. The problem is the TWU has not signed off on the Metromover Federal Grant, and until it does Metro cannot proceed with the construction.

Jack Lovell also called. Jack heads the Chamber of Commerce

Metromover task force, and wanted to know what the situation was regarding the existing impasse to proceed with the Metromover. I told Jack that the grant contract should be signed while Dellibovi was still the UMTA Administrator, but that the real crisis would come when we mark up our bill next year if, at that time, Metro has not signed the full-funding contract. Then we will try to defend the money appropriated in past years for the Metromover, funds that have not yet been obligated by Metro-Dade, and also try for additional funding. Lovell said the problem is that Metro does not want to sign the full-funding contract until a dedicated source of local revenue is in place, and I told him that I am getting tougher with Metro officials to motivate them to act on this matter. If I do not give Metro some sort of "drop dead" deadline, the county will let this drag on forever, which eventually will be an embarrassment to me and also, delay construction indefinitely.

In the evening I went to Miami Shores to visit with the recently widowed Pat McIntosh. Don McIntosh, Pat's husband and a former Miami Shores Mayor, is to be interred tomorrow. Pat was holding up very well among her family and friends, many of whom I knew from when I lived in Miami Shores; her sister Joan Kunkel was my first administrative assistant in Washington. Joan was there, and we talked for a while. I soon left for a quiet evening at home.

NOVEMBER 4 FRIDAY

Midmorning I went to see Dr. Wilson, an orthopedic surgeon at the University of Miami Children's Hospital. Dr. Wilson had recognized me at the airport in Nuremberg when I went to East Germany last year with Rabbi Neuman. Today, as he handed me a campaign check from the Orthopedic PAC, we laughed and shared fond memories about the occasion. He also shared with me that Dr. Ketchum, head of Surgical Oncology at the University of Miami, had fallen and broken his hip. This was very sad news, for not only is Dr. Ketchum a good family friend, he was very instrumental in my going to Sloan Kettering for my tumor operation.

For lunch and then tennis I got with my former brother-in-law Harold Friedman. Harold had been very effective in the success of my first campaign, and I still value his friendship. For dinner Joan and I went out with Al and Esther Green, old friends and supporters of mine.

NOVEMBER 5 SATURDAY

The mail this morning from the Washington office was light, but it did contain the Congressional schedule for the coming year, which was important to me as it had all the dates that Congress would be in session.

NOVEMBER 6 SUNDAY

This morning I drove with Ruth from my staff to visit with the veterans at the VA rehabilitation halfway facility for drug and alcohol abuse. When we arrived, about twenty-five of the veterans who live at the facility had already gathered, along with a *Miami Herald* reporter. The reporter was there to get photos and the story on how this facility had been saved from closing down due to the budget cuts. The veterans came up and thanked me for the contribution I had made to extend funding so that their halfway facility could remain operative, and they all seemed so appreciative. The reporter spoke with me and some of the veterans, and I believe the story is to appear in tomorrow's paper.

NOVEMBER 7 MONDAY

Nancy Pollock and I met at Neighbors Restaurant this morning. She wanted to thank me for my help in advising her on her campaign for a Dade County judge position, as she knew that I would be leaving Miami for Washington the day after the election and we would probably not have a chance to speak before I left. Nancy said that she could very well cope if she lost the election, but she was very confident that she would win.

A photo and the story about my visit yesterday to the VA rehabilitation facility were in today's *Miami Herald*. It was a good story, and I was very pleased. More mail came from Washington, and that is what I worked on for most of the morning. Jim Burnley, I heard, is resigning as Secretary of Transportation, with the resignation to be effective January 20, when the new administration comes in. Although Jim and I have had our conflicts, it will be sad to see him go. I left the office to meet Sharyn for lunch at Clifford's Restaurant. We are planning my Washington fundraiser, and there are still some loose ends on bringing my subcommittee members to Miami during the Super Bowl.

NOVEMBER 8 TUESDAY

Today, election day, only a skeleton crew was at the district office when I came in this morning. Half of the staff took a vacation day to work in one of the Democratic party campaign offices. At my dentist's office in the afternoon, and later at tennis with John Meyerhoff, who thinks that Dukakis would make a good president, the feedback that I got was that Dukakis may have a chance. And, while I was at the video store to return some tapes, pollsters were checking on how people voted, and it was three to two in favor of Dukakis.

That evening I went to the Miami Shores Country Club to watch the election results, and it was rather sad for Dukakis. But Nancy Pollock was well ahead, and won by 30,000 votes. Yesterday at breakfast Nancy had said that if she won it would be my help that made the difference, and I was feeling good about that. Bill Chappell, though, Chairman of Appropriations Defense Subcommittee, was ahead in his reelection bid but, surprisingly, only marginally.

NOVEMBER 9 WEDNESDAY

Joan and I arrived in Washington this afternoon. Friday we will depart Washington on Senator Dole's codel to Southeast Asia. At the Rayburn Building Gym, the staff members were all happy that George Bush had won the Presidential election. Bush plays paddleball in the gym quite often, and the staff there really like him.

Seeing Donald Richbourg, staff head on Appropriations Defense Subcommittee, I asked about Bill Chappell, and Don said Chappell was about 1,500 votes ahead, but that about 17,000 absentee ballots had yet to be counted. I don't know how disappointed Richbourg would be if Chappell did lose, as John Murtha (D-PA), next in line for chairman of the Defense Subcommittee, is very popular on that subcommittee, and many of the members and staff, I believe, would like to see Murtha take over the Chair position.

In the evening Joan and I went to the Kennedy Center to see "Driving Miss Daisy," which we very much enjoyed, especially from the great box seats that Sid Yates's office got for us.

NOVEMBER 10 THURSDAY

Today was easy. After meeting with the few office appointments that I had, I got with Judge Abner Mikva in the afternoon for tennis. Returning to the office, I learned that both Bill Chappell and Buddy MacKay may have lost, although all the ballots have not been counted. [Both were ahead before absentee ballots were tallied.]

NOVEMBER 11 FRIDAY - NOVEMBER 13 SUNDAY

8:00 a.m. Joan and I were picked up at home by military transport and driven to Andrews Air Force Base. The plane took off at 10:00 a.m., but instead of going straight to Japan, listed as the first stop on our itinerary, we had to make a stop in Anchorage, Alaska, to pick up Senators Jim McClure of Idaho and Frank Murkowski of Alaska. Landing at Elmendorf Air Force Base in Anchorage, we could see the snowcapped mountains, and the weather was beautiful. Anchorage is only about 300 miles south of the Arctic Circle, but the climate is surprisingly pleasant - the winters are comparatively moderate and the summers mild.

After an officer's mess lunch of Alaskan king crab and halibut, we took off again, flying southwest over the Aleutian Islands for seven hours, and landed in Japan at a U.S. Air Force base, 400 miles north of Tokyo. It was around 8:00 in the evening when we arrived, and the base staff had already prepared our dinner, which was quite good. Apparently the restaurants off the base are too expensive, but I was glad not to have to go off the base so soon after the long trip.

The Commanding General of the U.S. Air Force base in Japan was very interesting. Along with U.S.-owned bases in Okinawa and Tokyo, the United States owns this base, and the $9 billion worth of real estate surrounding the base. Our largest military base in this region is in Okinawa, 900 miles southwest of Tokyo, and home for more than half the close to 50,000 U.S. troops in Japan. The United

States probably owns more military real estate in Japan than the value of Japanese private property in our country; and, I believe, at least $50 billion worth of real estate should probably be sold to Japan to offset some of our Japanese trade deficit. The U.S. security plan, however, rejects the call for any reduction of U.S. troops in the Pacific Rim region.

Leaving Japan, it took five hours to reach Clark Air Force Base in the Philippines. Landing at Clark, we were escorted to the Officers Quarters and briefed on the problems surrounding the air base, such as the 25,000 squatters camping on its outskirts. We then went in small planes from Clark to the airport in Manila.

For centuries Manila has been the economic, political, social, and cultural center of the Philippines, and widely known as the "Pearl of the Orient." Most Manilans are Filipinos, with small groups of Chinese, Americans, and Europeans, and about 90 percent of the population are Roman Catholics. From the Manila airport, we traveled by bus to the Manila-Westin Hotel. I had managed to get some sleep during the flight from Japan, sleeping in an upper level bunk on the plane, as did others.

Sunday morning I got up about 8:00, had breakfast and then played tennis for a bit. We do not drink the water here, and use U.S.-bottled water even to brush our teeth. In the afternoon, a large group of demonstrators assembled in front of the hotel calling for Senator Dole, saying that they had a message for us to take back. Senator Dole went out to meet them, and returning he said they were Marcos demonstrators who were paid seventy-five pesos a day plus a free lunch to create a big crowd. Senator Dole has impressed me on this trip.

Nothing was scheduled for us this evening, so Larry and Susan Coughlin and Joan and I went to the old Manila Hotel for dinner. The hotel has great atmosphere, as does much of Manila with the colonial Far Eastern architecture mixed with more modern structures. Larry talked about the possibility of his being nominated for Secretary of Transportation, and I told him that I would do what I could through Sonny Montgomery, who is close to George Bush, to push for him. Larry is not on the short list and knows it, but he is a friend of George Bush, and has been for many years.

NOVEMBER 14 MONDAY

This morning we had an early breakfast in our hospitality room, and then attended another breakfast with the Manila Chamber of Commerce and other business leaders. A woman member of the Manila chamber spoke, addressing primarily the other chamber members, saying that if nothing is done to support family planning, then economic problems would worsen, and I could not have agreed with her more. Base rights and the amount that the United States should pay the Philippine government were discussed, and it was fairly evident that some Filipinos there still have longings for Marcos.

After breakfast, we went to the Foreign Ministry, and again the discussion was about U.S. base rights. I interjected with a question to the Foreign Minister about what was happening to refugees from Cambodia since I was there in 1978, ten years ago, but the Foreign Minister avoided my question on the Southeast Asia refugee problem. Then, with the Defense Minister, the discussion was again about U.S. base rights. I made another point about the Nation of First Asylum, saying that it was a tragic problem that the world must not avoid. These refugees escaped to a country where they do not want to remain, nor does the country want them, and, technically, they are no longer political refugees. When I raised the question about Philippine vigilante abuses, Senator Arlen Specter (R-PA) picked up on that and was very supportive. Much of the Senator's Pennsylvania constituency comes to him about abuse in the Philippines.

Following our meeting with the Defense Minister, we drove through the cemetery where 17,000 American soldiers are buried, and then to the presidential palace for lunch with President Cory Aquino. She was very gracious but seemed a bit in over her head. The Marcos's had made elaborate expenditures for furniture, like the crystal chandeliers and the extravagant interior designs throughout the palace. Leaving the presidential palace, we headed for the airport; upon arrival, newspaper reporters were all over Senator Dole, and a huge press conference followed. I could visualize the stories in tomorrow's stateside newspapers about the trip, and how Senator Dole's visit related to the political stability of the Philippines and how much money the United States would pay between now and 1992 for base rights.

We boarded the codel plane about 2:00 p.m., and flew to Bangkok, the capital of Thailand and home to about 10 percent of

Thailand's population of 59 million. Whereas Manila is known as the "Pearl of the Orient," Bangkok is dubbed, mostly by Europeans, as the "Venice of Asia," because of its many canals carrying Bangkok's famous floating market - hundreds of small boats that come into the city every morning to sell fruits, vegetables, flowers and fish.

Our hotel accommodations were at the uniquely beautiful Oriental Hotel. Joan went out to dinner with codel members, but I needed some quiet time alone and opted not to go.

NOVEMBER 15 TUESDAY

After breakfast and then tennis with Larry Coughlin, I went with Joan to the River City Shopping Center and bought some souvenirs; for lunch, we dined at the Sheraton on delicious Thai food. That afternoon we went to the Grand Palace for our visit with "King Bhumibol the Great," also called King Bhumibol Adulyadej. We all sat in a large circle and King Adulyadej was about twenty-five feet away talking to Senator Dole. We could not hear the conversation as King Adulyadej spoke very softly, and our American Ambassador, a real idiot, did nothing to improve the situation for us and others who were also invited. It was not Dole's fault, but it was senseless to have us there and then to be so left out of the exchange. Everyone was disgusted with the Ambassador and wondered how he got the position.

Back at the hotel, David Narot had called and said he would be meeting me tomorrow morning at 9:00. Our evening was free, and Larry Coughlin and I went out on the town, alone, just to get away from the crowd. We had our own driver who knew well his way around the city, and so we got to experience some of the Bangkok night life, which was quite "educational."

NOVEMBER 16 WEDNESDAY

David Narot, the son of my former Rabbi in Miami, had come to Thailand, married here, and is now a Buddhist. The people of Thailand, as opposed to Europeans, call Bangkok the "Divine City" or "City of Angels." David and I were very happy to see each other, and had fun reminiscing about old times and our families. There is something very special about meeting someone from home when you are in a faraway country.

After my visit with David, our codel met with the Prime Minister and then the Foreign Minister in their offices. I asked the Prime Minister about the Peace Corps, and he said to keep sending them as they are doing a lot of good. Both the Prime Minister's and Foreign Minister's offices were more elaborate than the office of King Adulyadej.

At 12:30, Senator and Mrs. Dole, Senator and Mrs. Specter, and Joan and I were the codel members who traveled by bus to a U.N. refugee camp. We had box lunches on the bus, and the ride, which took about two hours through the countryside, was very beautiful. The refugee camp was a sad place, and my heart went out to these people. Many of the refugees, mostly Vietnamese, had been at the camp for over five years; particularly sad were the young children, who had no future, and it is said that the Vietnamese send their children out first as a sort of wedge to help get themselves out. A leader at the refugee camp works with a Catholic charity from Detroit, and I will keep in touch with him as perhaps adoptions are possible for some of the children through Lorri Kellogg's adoption agency in my district.

It was close to 6:00 p.m. when we arrived back at the hotel, so I had a quick shower before a dinner meeting hosted by Thai business leaders in honor of Senator Dole. At the 7:00 cocktail reception, a few business people from the United States were there, but at the dinner it was just our delegation and Thai business leaders - a total of about fifty people. The main things the Thais wanted were that the United States not get too protectionist in our trade policy, and that we provide the technological assistance needed for developmental purposes in Thailand. A young woman Thai economist sat on my left and on my right was a young woman Thai physician, both beautiful and fascinating. I thought I'd died and gone to heaven!

NOVEMBER 17 THURSDAY

This morning we flew south of Thailand to Singapore, which took about two and a half hours. Our accommodations are at a Westin Hotel. First there was a meeting for the codel's Republican members at a private club, so I had some free time. I am the only Democratic member on this codel.

At 3:00, we were all briefed by different U.S. Embassy officials on the economic, trade, political and military problems in Singapore, one of the most crowded nations in the world. Singapore is trying to control its population growth and, in fact, is the first Asian country to do so. Through official programs administered by a government agency with some 40 clinics, family planning has been very successful in Singapore. After this "country team" briefing, I got with John Reilly for tennis. Reilly is the Air Force physician assigned to our codel. In the evening Joan and I went to a Chinese restaurant for a quiet dinner.

NOVEMBER 18 FRIDAY

Our delegation was taken to a very beautiful hotel called the Shangri-la for a breakfast hosted by the American Business Council. Several hundred people, mostly Republican Americans, were there to hear Senator Dole, the guest speaker, and to take part in the question and answer period.

We met with the Minister for Foreign Affairs and I raised the question about Singapore being in the same position as Israel, a small nation surrounded by Moslem countries. Following our meeting with the Foreign Affairs Minister, we went into a meeting with the very impressive Acting Prime Minister, who will probably be the next Prime Minister. To my inquiries regarding the history of Singapore, especially as to how the Japanese captured Singapore by coming down the Malay Peninsula on bicycles, I learned that the Japanese do an annual ceremonial bicycle trip down the Malay Peninsula in celebration of the conquest. I also directed questions to the Acting Prime Minister about the old rubber plantations in Malaysia, and it impressed him that I knew so much about their history.

Back at the hotel Senator Specter and I, accompanied by American Embassy staff, drove to the Israeli Embassy to meet with the Ambassador. Senator Specter spoke to the Ambassador about the new Palestinian State that some Southeast Asian countries are now recognizing. I asked questions about the loss of Jewish presence and a Jewish community over the last ten years in Singapore, and about the mutual military assistance between Israel and Singapore and how the Israelis have helped train the Singapore military. There is the threat to Singapore of the rise of fundamentalism from the Moslem countries, both in Indonesia and Malaysia which surround Singapore.

I also wanted to find out what Israel had done recently in other parts of Southeast Asia, particularly with irrigation, land cultivation, and similar public works projects in which Israel is highly experienced. The Ambassador said that for many of these projects, Israel was bringing trainees to Israel from Southeast Asia, teaching them the different methods and techniques, and then the trainees return home to apply their new skills.

In the evening we had dinner at the home of General Lee, the Minister of Industry and Trade, who also happens to be the Prime Minister's son. General Lee is quite impressive - very self- assured - and he and the present Deputy Defense Prime Minister are on a collision course to be Prime Minister, as they are both ambitious young men. Also impressive were the General's Deputy Ministers all of whom were vital young men under thirty and all destined to be leaders. It was a good meeting. The dinner was a Chinese banquet, with delicious and exotic food; the Asian women there were dressed quite beautifully.

NOVEMBER 19 SATURDAY

This morning I met with two of the men that I had breakfast with yesterday morning at the American Business Council. The staff from the Embassy knew them and I was happy that I invited them to breakfast. Both are happily married to oriental women.

At the airport in Singapore, Senator Dole presided over another news briefing. There were at least a dozen newspaper reporters and a television crew. I raised the fact that democracy in Singapore was different from ours in that it does not have the same freedom of press and the same human rights levels that we do, especially in due process of law. It strikes me that the people of Singapore are much more disciplined, and perhaps we can learn something of the level of personal responsibility that is in their type of democratic system. Senator Specter also raised the human rights issue. We mentioned the problems of protecting intellectual copyrighting as to the use of U.S. copyright labels on Singapore products, and Senator Murkowski of Alaska, in particular, raised the issue of processing through Singapore of illegally caught salmon.

After this early afternoon news briefing, we boarded the plane and flew to Jakarta, Indonesia. In Jakarta we were met by American

Ambassador Wolfowitz, who is Jewish, an unusual assignment in a Moslem country. The Ambassador, however, is very well liked, and had an excellent staff. After a country-team briefing that lasted about forty-five minutes, people from the Agency for International Development (AID) and I got together and planned a trip for tomorrow to a population planning center, and then out to some villages the following day.

For the rest of the day we were pretty much free, so Joan and I did some shopping, and it was great fun. We even bought strange tropical fruit on the side of the road. The scenery is exotic, the food good, and every place that we have been I was there ten years ago, and the changes are unbelievable. Now there are skyscrapers, expressways, interchanges, and modern restaurants in Manila, Singapore, Bangkok and even Jakarta. But the old Orient is not hard to find beyond the skyscrapers.

NOVEMBER 20 SUNDAY

Today's arrangements were for me and Senator Specter to meet on human rights with Ambassador Wolfowitz and the Catholic Archbishop from East Timor Island, a Catholic island in a Moslem country. Indonesia invaded East Timor, a former Portuguese colony, in 1975 and annexed it the following year, a move still not recognized by the United Nations. Since the takeover, a small guerrilla force remains in the hills making occasional attacks on Indonesian forces, but the main thing the Indonesians are fighting is a possible Communist or Marxist presence on East Timor.

We talked about an hour with the Archbishop, who said that the human rights situation in Indonesia was bad, particularly in East Timor, but better than what it had been. I was satisfied that there was progress and there remains a predominant Catholic presence in East Timor.

I arrived back at the hotel in time for tennis with Larry Coughlin, and that evening he and Susan, and Joan and I had dinner together.

NOVEMBER 21 MONDAY

At 7:30, we were in a breakfast meeting with the American Chamber of Commerce in Jakarta. Senator Dole introduced our codel members, and when he introduced me, I stood and said that "Senator Dole is a genuine national treasure, and I appreciate the opportunity to travel with him." Jakarta is next to the last stop on our itinerary before we return to the States, and I thought this would be the best occasion for me to publicly express my appreciation to Senator Dole. My comments came as a surprise to Senator Dole and sort of embarrassed him, but several of his staff members on the trip with us came to me and said that I had done the right thing and that "the Senator" appreciated my statements, as no other member had recognized him publicly. Senator Dole has done a fine job, especially on refugee problems, and this trip has gone along without any problems.

Harvey Goldstein and I had a photo opportunity together. Harvey is Chairman of the American Chamber of Commerce in Jakarta, and a consultant to American businesses in Southeast Asia. We talked some, mostly about his parents who live in the United States, and then our codel had to leave for our visit with Indonesian President Suharto at his sumptuous palace. President Suharto spoke to us for over an hour on various issues, and I wished that we had had more time to raise questions about Vietnamese refugees being held on Indonesian islands.

As I left the palace, the U.S. AID staff were waiting to take me across town to the Indonesian family planning center. When we arrived, a slide show was presented, followed by lunch, and a press interview. Dr. Reilly and I agree on what the problems are and the unfortunate misinterpretation of abortion as part of family planning. Indonesia has made some progress in family planning, and the people from AID said that I did very well in the press interview on this issue.

By 4:30 p.m., I was back at the hotel in time for a press conference. Following the press conference we were off to the airport for our trip to Bali, only an hour's plane ride just east of Java.

NOVEMBER 22 TUESDAY

In Bali today we drove about an hour and a half into the boondocks to a small village. All of the codel members and their wives were on this trip except Senator and Mrs. Dole; Senator Dole was not feeling well. The villagers put on a very entertaining and beautiful Bali dance show for us, and Senator Specter and I were asked to make speeches about U.S. aid and family planning programs. I had promoted the visit to this village, which had lots of craftwork in its shops, crafts for which Indonesia is well noted, and the people were happy to see us.

For lunch, we went to one of the most beautiful spots that I had ever been. It was a small resort up in the hills, and it reminded me of one of the scenes from the film, "Bridge on the River Kwai." We then separated into different groups to drive back to the hotel, as some wanted to shop along the way. I would like to visit Bali again sometime, as Joan and I really enjoyed it. Our codel worked hard in Indonesia and learned a lot about the people and the country; I feel I made a good contribution, especially on the refugee problems, the family planning program, and on the question of East Timor.

Dinner was at a restaurant near the airport and, again, we were entertained by Bali dancers. It was a good show, but the village dancers that entertained us earlier today were better. At dinner the codel presented the Dole's with gifts and thanked them for leading the trip. After dinner we drove to the airport and were off to Japan, the first leg of our trip back. I slept most of the way from Bali to Japan. From Japan to Alaska I worked on a newsletter and wrote letters. In Alaska we went to the Officers Club and had a drink, got back on the plane, and I slept all the way from Alaska to Andrews Air Force Base.

NOVEMBER 23 WEDNESDAY

Our plane landed at Andrews around 7:00 a.m. this morning, and I was in the Rayburn Cafeteria having breakfast before my staff came in to work by 9:00. At the office Bernie Fogel, Dean of the University of Miami Medical School, Jay Weiss, Chair of the Metro- Dade Health Trust, and Ira Clark, President of Jackson Memorial Hospital, spoke with me in a conference call about their concern for the lack of operating space at Jackson Memorial due to emergency medical care, especially in neurosurgery. To solve this, they said, money was needed for a trauma building and for its operating costs, and they wanted to know what could be done at the federal level. I told them I would see what I could do and get back with them. I went to see Mike Stephens, and Mike will try to locate funds in the pipeline at Health and Human Services, and also see if any funds are available from some other appropriation subcommittee, such as the Energy and Water Subcommittee.

I returned to the office to go over my Southeast Asia notes with John and Adele, and we think there is enough material of interest to produce a really good newsletter, hopefully to be received as well as my previous newsletter on the distribution of food at the Camillus House.

NOVEMBER 24 THURSDAY

The Neal Smith trip to Eastern Europe is in December, but I cannot go, as I told John Osthaus this morning. John, as chief of staff on Neal Smith's Appropriations Subcommittee on Commerce, Justice, State, and Judiciary, is putting the trip together. He said they now have about eight members going, so they are okay. I then went to see Terry Peel at Foreign Ops about the trip to Israel. Terry showed me the schedule, which I took back to the office to show to Adele, and she was all excited even though I was only to be in Israel for five days.

NOVEMBER 25 FRIDAY

In the Rayburn gym I saw Chris Perkins (D-KY) and Bruce Vento (D- MN), but only a few members are around today. Leaving the gym I went to the Capitol expecting to do a few errands - first I stopped at the Sergeant-at-Arms to cash a check, but the bank was closed, and at the Members Dining Room to get a bowl of soup, the dining room was closed, and then stopping at the Capitol Physician's Office for medicine, that office was closed. Everything it seems is closed for the Thanksgiving weekend.

NOVEMBER 26 SATURDAY - NOVEMBER 27 SUNDAY

Deborah Benchoam arrived yesterday from Argentina and Friday evening Joan and I took her to dinner. This morning we took Deby to the Eastern Market and in the evening to a movie. Joan leaves Sunday for Miami.

NOVEMBER 28 MONDAY

At the office this morning I briefed the staff on my trip to Southeast Asia, as I do whenever I go on an overseas trip. I did not leave with Joan yesterday because of this briefing today, and I still had some correspondence to finish; but by 5:00 p.m. I was on a flight home.

NOVEMBER 29 TUESDAY

John is in Miami for a few days. This morning at the district office we discussed our Southeast Asia newsletter, and set up some appointments that John thought I should make. Real progress is being made on the subcommittee's visit to Miami during the Super Bowl, and Sharyn is handling this very well. The rest of the week seems easy.

NOVEMBER 30 WEDNESDAY

Jeff and I spent the morning going over my schedule and other pending matters, because tomorrow Jeff is going into the hospital for minor surgery. At noon, the American Jewish Committee is honoring me at its annual Awards Luncheon, and Jeff said that he would be accompanying me. When we arrived at the luncheon some minutes before it was to start, the tables were pretty much all filled. Members of the black community were there, and in my speech I stated the fact that, "We *have* to work together, and it is essential for us to continue building bridges between the black and Jewish communities in Miami."

Following the luncheon, I went to Fisher Island for tennis with *Miami Herald* reporter Tom Fiedler, Gardnar Mulloy, the tennis pro at Fisher Island, and John McDermott, formerly a *Miami Herald* reporter and now administrative aide to Metro Mayor Steve Clark. We played doubles with Ross Dubin, whom I knew when he was a kid. Ross is a graduate of Duke University and is now the tennis pro at North Shore Tennis Club on Miami Beach.

Later in the afternoon I was at Jackson Memorial Hospital for the 15th anniversary celebration of the Dade Health Trust. Our office continues to work for shock trauma appropriation funds, and from the vantage point of our transportation subcommittee, we have been successful in bringing funds for shock trauma to the forefront in Dade County. At the celebration all the "VIP's" were there like Bernie Fogel, Dean of the Medical School, and Jay Weiss, the new Chairman of the Health Trust as well as Ira Clark, President of Jackson. When I spoke with them, they continued to be concerned about the lack of operating space at Jackson Memorial.

The trouble is with the overwhelming emergency medical care requiring neurosurgery, which ties up the operating rooms. I told them about my efforts to provide funding in the next fiscal year appropriations, and "As we speak," I said, "efforts are being made to locate funds through Health and Human Services or through some other appropriation subcommittee to bring some relief to Jackson Memorial." Ruth Kassewitz, in public relations at Jackson, was at the celebration, and she is very much aware of our efforts.

Chapter 24

DECEMBER 1, 1988 THURSDAY

Patrice and I met early this morning at Neighbors Restaurant, and from there we went to meet Admiral Yost at the Opa Locka Airport Coast Guard station for the dedication of one of the seven new jet interceptors for drug interdiction.

Considerable publicity, generated mostly by Admiral Yost emphasizing the Coast Guard's inability to conduct a quality drug interdiction program without a supplemental appropriation put a great deal of pressure on our subcommittee. Both Admiral Yost and I were interviewed by Channel 10, and our remarks ran along the same line of how glad we were that additional funding had been worked out for the program.

At the office I received a call from John Schelble to call a *Miami Herald* reporter about a statement that the newly-elected Metro Commissioner Charles Dusseau had made at the Metro Commission. Apparently Dusseau had said that I would have a hard time protecting the $152 million appropriated to date for the

Metromover extensions unless Dade County moved on signing a full-funding contract. Dusseau made it seem as though I was issuing an ultimatum. Talking to the reporter, I told him that it was not an ultimatum, but that I could see the handwriting on the wall, and that it was essential that the Metro Commission make a decision, and soon, on the full-funding contract.

DECEMBER 2 FRIDAY

It is a very calm time for me in the district, but Joan and I are returning to Washington Sunday, December 4, for several meetings and events that I want to and need to attend. Patrice is managing the main office during Jeff's recuperation from his recent surgery; he is doing fine, but we do not expect him back to work until later in the month.

I stayed at the office until 2:30, breaking only for a short lunch with my son Bill. Ira Clark and I spoke on the phone and agreed that we would not go all out for funds for Jackson Memorial until next year when Ira can make the trauma center case before our subcommittee. Meanwhile, I will speak with Pete Stark, Chairman of the Ways and Means Health Subcommittee, about possible funds for Jackson.

At the campaign office Sharyn is constantly on the phone about plans for our subcommittee members when they are in Miami. Officially, the members will be in Miami for a hearing on Dade County public transportation, so expenses for hotel and travel are not a problem. Sharyn is working on obtaining Super Bowl tickets for the members, and confirming with the Greater Miami Chamber of Commerce and Metro-Dade County that each subcommittee member will receive a $2,000 honorarium, as promised. These and other details have to be ironed out, and all the principal parties involved will meet again next Tuesday.

DECEMBER 3 SATURDAY

Today was a day to just relax.

DECEMBER 4 SUNDAY

Groundbreaking for the new Turnberry/Aventura synagogue

was held this morning. Rabbi Salzman greeted me and Gina, our newest staff member, as we arrived, and then introduced me to those gathered, making some very flattering comments about me. Keeping my remarks brief I told them how glad I was to be there, especially for such an occasion. It was also important for me to be there, as constituents expect their Representative to share in such momentous events. Following the ceremony, which was very nice, I picked up Joan for a family brunch at our son Bill's house, and from there we headed for the airport to catch our 1:45 flight to Washington.

There are several events for which we have returned to Washington, but outstanding among them is the "*Kennedy Center Honors*" this evening. I think I enjoy this annual Kennedy Center extravaganza more than any other social event that I attend. Perhaps it is all the glamour of being among such famous actors, actresses, and musicians, etc., that impresses me, but, in any case, it is always fun.

This year's Kennedy Center honorees included the comedian/actor George Burns, actress Myrna Loy, the black American dancer Alvin Ailey, Lithuania-born violinist Alexander Schneider, and the founding chair of the Kennedy Center, Roger Stevens. Usually one honoree seems to receive more of the publicity than the others, and this year it was the actress Myrna Loy, about whom the *Washington Post* ran practically two biographical pages, along with one of her earlier, glamorous pictures. She is now 83 years old.

We arrived early at the Kennedy Center to attend General Motors' cocktail party, and then on to the Kennedy Center Opera House for what was, as usual, a wonderful gala. Later the show will be broadcast nationwide. After the show, we had a late supper at the Kennedy Center, with Phil Jones, President of CBS News, the host at our table. Phil talked about problems affecting the Coast Guard and the FAA. Joan and I got home late, but not tired.

DECEMBER 5 MONDAY

Other than a meeting with Jack Cooney, my one time used car business auditor, regarding his EPA problem, I had no further office appointments today. I saw Florida member Bill Nelson in the cafeteria, and we talked about his race for governor in two years. Most of my time was spent with the staff going over details for several projects we have pending, including the subcommittee's trip to Miami.

Several Capitol Hill receptions were held in the evening, but Joan and I turned "thumbs down" on all of them, preferring instead a nice, quiet dinner alone.

DECEMBER 6 TUESDAY

After breakfast in the Members Dining Room, I went to the Regional Caucus meeting where Ron Flippo of Alabama was elected to the Steering and Policy Committee. There are now only ten Democratic members out of the nineteen-member Florida Delegation.

At the office Chip Bishop, the Vice President of APTA, Robert Kiley, the General Manager of MTA of New York City, and Jack Gilstrap, Chairman of APTA, came in about funding problems for mass public transit. When they left, I got with the staff again to continue finalizing plans for the subcommittee's trip to Miami. The members will all be arriving at different times and, therefore, separate arrangements have to be made. Also, we are still trying to come up with the number of Super Bowl tickets needed.

Alan Porter of Senator Dole's staff sent me lots of great photos from the Southeast Asia trip. John is presently working on a newsletter about my recent experiences and findings in Southeast Asia, and the photos that Porter sent will be helpful.

That evening I went to the home of New York member Jim Scheuer and his wife Emily for a meeting with Secretary of State George Schultz. About a dozen Jewish members were there, many of whose parents now live in my district, having moved from up North to South Florida. We talked about Israel, Sri Lanka and other international topics, with the Secretary answering all of the questions put to him, including questions on what his daily life was like and on his meetings with leaders around the world. Regarding the Soviet Union, he said, "Now, the biggest problem in the Soviet Union is too much freedom, too soon, which is hard to handle." As to Jews in the Soviet Union, Schultz said they are being granted instant exit visas faster than we can grant them visas to come to the United States, as the INS does not have the manpower to process them, and added that most of the Soviet Jews are still entitled to U.S. refugee status.

When I told him about my recent trip to Southeast Asia and my visit to the refugee camps in Thailand, Schultz's only comment was: "It is a cruel world." He is optimistic about South Africa; as for the Middle East, "...The immediate real peril," he said, "is the danger of biological or chemical warfare and the present inability of the Israelis to form a government." The members were attentive and very responsive to the Secretary, viewing him as an effective and valuable leader. Schultz had to leave about 9:00 p.m., as tomorrow he will be meeting with Gorbachev in New York. It was a wonderful evening, very informative, but I was sorry not to have the opportunity to speak to the Secretary about my visit to Cuba, as our discussions were mostly on the Middle East.

DECEMBER 7 WEDNESDAY

About forty of us House members attended a breakfast discussion this morning with the Commissioner of Social Security, Dorcas Hardy. The meeting was held at the Hubert Humphrey Building, one block from my office in the Rayburn Building. Social Security is very big in my district, and the meeting this morning was very worthwhile and informative. I will use some of this information and material for a future newsletter, along with some photos I had taken with Dorcas Hardy and several of her deputies.

Charlie Wilson thanked me for the congratulatory telegram I sent following his appearance last month on "*60 Minutes*" with Harry Reasoner. I called the segment with Charlie, "Gary Cooper is alive and well," as Charlie is definitely the bold, Bengal Lancer type. I also gave Atlanta Representative John Lewis information on a page applicant, the granddaughter of my friend Sue Stevens. Sue's son and his family live in John's district, and the granddaughter seems to meet all the qualifications to become a page - high grade point average, excellent character references, etc., just the type of applicant I would seriously consider for a page position were she from my district.

Tom Bevill from Alabama may try for a possible vacancy on

my subcommittee. If so, this would give us extra leverage as Tom is Chairman of the Energy and Water Subcommittee and would be a very effective addition on our subcommittee.

After a very good time Joan and I left Washington today on an evening flight to Miami. We didn't want to leave, but Joan had to get back to her sculpture, and I had commitments in the district.

DECEMBER 8 THURSDAY

At the district office I kept busy writing "thank you's" and going through the paperwork that accumulated while I was in Washington. In the afternoon I got with my grandson Matt for tennis.

DECEMBER 9 FRIDAY

The Japanese Gardens Dedication and tea ceremony were held this morning at Watson Island. Members of the Japanese press and many Japanese business people were there. Before leaving, I made a commitment to bring in bonsai trees from the national arboretum for the Gardens. I saw Mayor Suarez and went over to speak with him. Patrice was with me, as we had another stop to make, so we did not stay long.

The National Urban League Conference on "How to Use the Legislative Process," was our next stop. The conference was being held at the Sheraton Bal Harbour, and had already begun when Patrice and I arrived. It was a good gathering of participants, and most impressive was the quality of people there. Florida State Senator Carrie Meek spoke on how to work at the State level. Then John Jacobs, President of the Urban League, introduced me, and I spoke on the workings at the Federal level. We were there for about an hour.

Returning to the office, I went first to meet with Sharyn upstairs in our campaign office for a status report, and she is still trying to get more Super Bowl tickets. I soon left, going downstairs to the district office to return phone calls. That evening Joan and I went to the bayfront mansion of Micky Wolfson for a cocktail party. It was a magical sort of evening, brought on by the elegant surroundings and the congenial atmosphere. It was fun seeing so many people there that I knew like Ed Fox and his wife from the State Department, Bronx member Bob Garcia, and Ruth Shack, Director of the Dade Foundation.

DECEMBER 10 SATURDAY

This is the weekend, so things are quiet at the district office this morning as I clear my desk. I left to meet Patrice at the Northside district office for the grand opening at noon of the Liberty City Market at the Northside Shopping Center. My speeches are brief at all of these events, and today was no exception, but it was a good turnout of the black community and its leadership, as well as the Koreans who funded part of the center.

At 7:00, I went to the Forum of North Dade for the Annie Ackerman Award dinner. This year the "Annie Ackerman Award" was presented to former Governor Reubin Askew. Governor Askew commented very favorably about me, saying that I would be measured by what I had done, not by what I said, when it comes to the evaluation of representatives in the political area. Annie was on the dais. Her faculties are still okay, but she did not speak. I kept my speech short, as usual, acknowledging the Governor and talking a little about politics. State Senator from Orlando, George Stuart, now running for governor, was the featured speaker. When it was over, I got with Nancy Pollock, and we talked some about her recent election victory.

DECEMBER 11 SUNDAY

Today was free to just spend with family.

DECEMBER 12 MONDAY

The morning was busy with phone calls. First I rang Bob Foster in Washington. Bob is on the staff of Jamie Whitten's Agriculture Subcommittee and is working to obtain the bonsai trees that we are hoping to get for the Japanese Gardens at Watson Island in Miami. Next was a call to Adele about a dinner meeting with Tony Costa and the Cuban-American Foundation. We may also include the Young Urban Cuban Americans organization. Adele and I discussed her coming to Miami for this meeting and doing a slide show presentation on my trip to Havana. Lucy and I discussed the meeting that we are trying to schedule with the Coast Guard legislative liaison and boater/developer Bill Broeder, a good supporter of mine, and a client of my son Tom.

I got off the phone to speak with Marvin Bacon, a friend and constituent who came in about a personal problem. It seems the ex-husband of the lady he is to marry is soon to be released from prison, and the ex-husband has threatened Marvin's life.

At noon we held our U.S. Service Academy Nominating luncheon; as usual, the event was at the Turnberry Isle Country Club. When I arrived, about a dozen nominees and the sponsors from their schools had already gathered. Patrice, who coordinates the academy nominations in our office, was there ahead of me. This year rather interesting is a nominee for the Merchant Marine Academy, which is unusual. We had a Vietnamese-born nominee, who is the stepdaughter of Peter Collins, the ABC network commentator; also, we had our first nominee from the Hebrew Academy on Miami Beach. Last year the press covered this event, but there is no reporter here today. It was a good event, in any case, and everything went very smoothly.

Back at the office I went through the mail and paperwork on my desk. Senator Dole has sent me the list of people that he thanked regarding the Southeast Asian trip. There are at least sixty names, and besides my own list, I have marked off quite a few names from his list, which means that I will be busy writing thank you's for several days. Adele has sent me information on the Anti-Defamation League, information that I will take home to review tonight, as I will be speaking tomorrow at their luncheon.

Before leaving the office I scanned the newspaper, which was a disappointment, as I am still waiting to see a story in the *Miami Herald* about the Munisport. Everytime I am interviewed by Jackie Swearington who reports for the *Herald*, nothing is printed. The *Herald* seems to be tightening up on news story space.

DECEMBER 13 TUESDAY

At the Turnberry Isle Country Club for the Anti-Defamation League Breakfast this morning, I received the Torch of Liberty

Award. The first part of the program was about the Neo-Nazis and the skinheads, with strong emphasis on the danger of these groups. Then I was introduced as the guest speaker. My speech was less frightening than what the more than 300 people in the audience had just heard, as I told them about the Jews in Southeast Asia, particularly the U.S. Ambassador to Moslem Indonesia and Harvey Goldstein, who heads the Chamber of Commerce in Jakarta. I also talked about the new Jewish members now in Washington, and generally painted a much brighter picture. Even though this was a fundraising event, and I may have cost the ADL a few donations, I thought it best to ease the minds of the people there.

Back at the district office, the staff told me that the *Miami Herald* had called, interested in the U.S. Service Academy luncheon and the young Vietnamese girl's nomination. The *Herald* may do a story on the event.

DECEMBER 14 WEDNESDAY

At the office this morning I had my photo taken with the nominee who was absent at our service academy luncheon yesterday, a young black man going to the Naval Academy. Apparently there was some conflict with another appointment, but his guidance counselor had been there. After the young man left, Alan Kaufman, who has a business called "Dr. Software," came in to see if there were any government agencies that could use his expertise or software in a demonstration project. I will look into it, as I told him, but he may need to bid for such a government contract.

Then Dr. Carmen Diaz, head of a moderate Cuban organization came in with the head of the ACLU office for this area to talk about alternatives to the Cuban-American Foundation's anti-Castro position. I assured them that I was willing to listen and to cooperate with them in any way I could. Dr. Diaz, a very attractive, intelligent young woman with American-born children serving in the U.S. military, has taken a courageous position that really puts her in physical danger from the ultra-right Cuban anti-Castro demagogues.

Commissioner Helen Miller, my good friend from Opa Locka, was in to give me a gift from Eunice Liberty, a longtime black activist in the Brownsville area. Helen said that Eunice was not feeling well, so I have marked on my calendar to go by to see her.

DECEMBER 15 THURSDAY

After some routine work at the office this morning, Patrice and I left to visit Eunice Liberty, a remarkable old lady in Brownsville. She was not feeling well, but she was managing. I thanked her for the lovely desk set that Helen had delivered, and soon left, not wanting to tire her. I dropped Patrice back at the office and headed for Coral Gables, stopping at a gun shop on NW 36th Avenue to pick up the Baretta pistol that Xavier Corbero, Joan's and my artist friend in Spain, had asked me to get for him. At the gun shop the pistol was registered in my name, but it will be transferred to Xavier when he comes to Miami.

At lunch in Coral Gables, Priscilla Perry briefed me on what was happening in Dade County regarding the Metromover extensions. Priscilla is a lobbyist for Westinghouse, the contractor, so she keeps current on the matter. After lunch I picked up my grandson Matt, who lives in Coral Gables, and we were off to the tennis court; that evening Joan and I took Matt to dinner to celebrate his 4.2 grade point average.

DECEMBER 16 FRIDAY

This morning I met condo leader Irving Levine and his wife Lillian at Gold Coast Helicopters on Biscayne Boulevard in North Miami, and the three of us flew in the Broward County Sheriff's Department helicopter. The Levine's are celebrating their 60th wedding anniversary, and I thought this would be something different to help them celebrate. Joining us was the public relations person for the Broward County Transportation Department.

After about a ten-minute ride, we landed at the Fort Lauderdale/Hollywood Airport and went into the airport conference room, where waiting for us were the Broward County Manager and the head of the Broward Engineering Department. First there was a slide presentation on their road needs and airport problems, and then they talked about the need for federal funds to build a sixty-foot high bunker to separate the airport from the residential district on one side of the airport to alleviate the noise problems with the neighborhood. They also want funds for a feasibility study for a Peoplemover from the Ft. Lauderdale-Hollywood Airport to Port Everglades, as both facilities are expanding and the number of airport and seaport passengers has grown.

It was a very effective hour, and although I had to be careful not to overpromise, I was not too concerned, as transportation matters have become quite instinctive to me now. Today I felt really sharp in my answers and in knowing what questions to ask.

With the Transportation Director we took the helicopter over Port Everglades to view the nature conservation problem and then over the new I-595 highway, which is complete but not in use as the interchanges are unfinished. We then flew west to I-75 and over Joe Robbie Stadium [now Pro Player] and back to the Ft. Lauderdale airport, where we dropped the Transportation Director and picked up the public relations person who began the trip with us. Flying back to the heliport in North Dade, the Levine's talked about how impressed they were with the entire event.

DECEMBER 17 SATURDAY

Today was restful - nothing political. I did stop by the office to sign some letters that Patrice had prepared for my signature, and answered a few phone calls that came in, as people still call the office on weekends, though, officially, we are not open.

In the evening Joan and I went out with Joe and Felice Davis and they told me there was, indeed, a Jackie Swearington story in the *Miami Herald*. I had apparently missed it.

DECEMBER 18 SUNDAY

No commitments today.

DECEMBER 19 MONDAY

This morning I met with Tima Burke and a Simone Axelrod from the Soviet Union on a Soviet Jewry family reunion problem, and we may be able to help by sending a cable to Axelrod's relatives in Russia and to the supervisor at his relatives' place of employment. Joining us in the meeting was Adele Liskov from my Washington staff, who is in Miami for the dinner this evening with the Cuban-American National Foundation. John Schelble is in from Washington as well. John will probably be at the dinner meeting this evening, but he is here particularly for several meetings we have scheduled today and tomorrow with newspaper reporters and officials.

Today we met with the *Miami Herald* Editorial Board, led by Jim Hampton and Bob Sanchez. We talked about the Metromover, the PLO/Israeli crisis, shock trauma, and even the forthcoming issue of the Congressional pay raise. I think I did well, as I was certainly informed. The one mistake I made was that I did not emphasize enough the need of a Metro-Dade director for the trauma agency and a director for the Metro-Dade transit. However, I did get across the message that transit funds could be in danger unless the Metro Commission signed the full-funding contract. During the next fiscal year, holding on to the $152 million already appropriated, but not obligated, would be unlikely if Metro has not signed by then.

Returning home, I freshened up a bit before leaving again with Joan to pick up Maria Elena Torano at her office. The three of us then headed for the home of Tony Costa for our dinner meeting with the Cuban-American Foundation. Adele was already there, having brought the photo slides of our trip to Cuba. Looking at the slides, they were delighted with what we had captured of Havana, but the highlight was near the end, which showed our return to the United States with the three prisoners. The slide presentation was a big hit, and everyone seemed really pleased that we were there. Before leaving, Tony Costa handed me a $2,000 check as part of the $3,000 that I had advanced for the chartered plane to go and bring back the Cuban prisoners. Joan and I got home about 10:00 p.m.

DECEMBER 20 TUESDAY

This morning John and I met with the *Miami News* Editorial Board, and it went quite well. Two of my grandsons were with us, and during the time that we were in the meeting, my grandsons were given a tour. The fate of the newspaper is now before a Federal judge, who is deliberating the newspaper's closing. A local community newspaper has requested that the 92-year-old daily remain open. A decision is expected imminently.

DECEMBER 21 WEDNESDAY

At the Miami Club this morning, I met with loan officers of the AmeriFirst Savings and Loan. Charles Stutzen of Citizen's Federal was also there. Their concern was with ASLIC and the federal bailout of the savings and loan institutions. Those there represented solvent thrifts and did not feel they should be charged by ASLIC for the mistakes of other loan institutions. One CEO, Hershel Rosenthal, said that half of his profits now go to pay the cost of his ASLIC premiums, which is punitive on the 95% of savings and loan institutions not in trouble.

When the meeting ended, I went to the Metro-Dade Commission Chambers to see Charles Dusseau about the need to move on the full-funding contract for Metromover extensions. Dusseau said he disagreed with the Mayor about a referendum on both this contract and on the dedicated source of revenue, and that he wished to put that vote off until July because "there is no way the referendum will pass at this time." Dusseau is coming to be a very dedicated, resourceful commissioner in behalf of the Metro system. When I told him that he needed a first-class transit manager, Dusseau said that, at my suggestion, he had been to see Carmen Turner, General Manager of the Washington Metropolitan Area Transit Authority, and that he wished he could get her to come to Miami. I saw Commissioner Sherman Winn there, and Bob Simms who, as Community Relations Director, worked with me when I was on the Dade County School Board. Bob now has his own consulting firm.

I then headed for Jackson Memorial to meet with Ira Clark, President of Jackson, Stan Tate from the Dade Health Trust, and Jay Weiss, to discuss the need for federal funds for the new wing Ira wants built for the Shock Trauma Center. It was a productive meeting. The goal, they said, was to raise $14 million, with the funds to come from a variety of sources: $1 million from Dade municipalities such as the City of Miami Beach and the City of Hialeah, $2 million from the State, probably $3.5 million from the feds, and contributions from local corporations. I told them to get me an inventory of what they were requesting in the way of equipment for the hospital, and that I would make this one of my main priorities in the transportation bill next year.

From Jackson Memorial I went to the *Jewish Floridian* and spoke to a reporter about my trip to Southeast Asia, noting especially the situation with the Jews there. Norma Orovitz is the paper's editor, and the story should be out in about a week. While there I saw the publisher, Fred Shockett, a longtime friend.

I soon had to get back to the district office for our holiday party, and it was very nice, with the staff in quite a festive mood, laughing and joking during the exchange of gifts. Patty Diaz, the immigration caseworker in our office, told me that she had a visit from Mike Bander, Chairman of the American Jewish Committee in Miami. Mike was concerned about the problems lawyers face in losing their special expedited position with the Immigration & Naturalization Office in Miami. I agree with the INS position, as lawyers serve clients for fees, whereas our office can often get the same results, with no charge to the applicant. I think Patty handled it very well, but I am sure Mike will want to see me on behalf of his lawyer friends.

Afterwards I played tennis at Quayside with my former brother-in-law Harold Friedman, and then went home for the rest of the evening. Al Moskovitz came by the house about a problem he is having with the Florida Department of Transportation concerning his property in Broward County. Al will get back to me in writing with a thorough explanation of the problem, and I will follow through with the Florida Department of Transportation's Kaye Henderson.

DECEMBER 22 THURSDAY

The lead editorial in the *Miami Herald* today was from the *Herald* interview I had last week regarding the full-funding contract for Metromover. The editorial basically said that I could not protect the unobligated appropriated funds forever, and this was the message that I wanted to get across.

Several newspaper visits and interviews were scheduled today, starting at 9:30 a.m. in my home with a *Ft. Lauderdale News* reporter about the Florida delegation and what life was like for us in Washington. Each delegation member will have a different view of Washington. The reporter was also interviewing Joan, as John Schelble and I left the house for our meeting at the *Miami Times*.

Patrice was at the *Times* building when we arrived, and the three of us went into a meeting with Mohammed Hamaludin, the *Times* Managing Editor. Mohammed wasted little time in raising the issue of Haitians who go to jail for illegally entering the United States, while the Nicaraguans are housed at the Miami Stadium and get work permits. Other issues discussed were the Yahweh's, a black Hebrew cult in Miami, and of course the drug problem.

Leaving the *Times*, John and I headed for the *Jewish Tribune,* the competing newspaper with the *Jewish Floridian,* and the last stop on our agenda.

DECEMBER 23 FRIDAY

As guest speaker today at Temple Israel, I covered several topics: namely, what life was like for me in Washington, the Congressional Jewish members, and the Jews in Southeast Asia. The congregation was very receptive and, surprisingly, my criticism of AIPAC's recent actions went unchallenged. I made some brief mention of the elderly and Medicare, and Jeff was there to record it all for future reference. Jeff is getting out gradually, still not fully recovered from his surgery, and his schedule at the office is on a very limited part-time basis.

DECEMBER 24 SATURDAY

Today, Joan and I just took it easy around the house. I did get out for tennis with my friends in Miami Shores, but this was mainly a day to relax.

DECEMBER 25 SUNDAY (CHRISTMAS DAY)

While I was at Jack Burstein's in Miami Beach, Jack told me during a break in our tennis game that he and Bob Marlin were going to "buy out" AmeriFirst Bank, the oldest federal banking institute in South Florida.

It is good to be with our friends during these holidays. Marvelle Colby and her husband, Selig, are in from New York, and Joan and I will be having dinner with them this evening; later we are going to designer Ton Luyk's party at his home in Coral Gables. Tomorrow we are having dinner at Joe's Stone Crab restaurant with New York Representative Jim Scheuer and his wife Emily. As a couple, the Scheuer's have really mellowed over the years since I first knew them in Washington.

DECEMBER 26 MONDAY

At Ton Luyk's party last evening, several Dade officials were there. I spoke to Ruth Shack, who heads the Dade Foundation, about problems of Dade County. I also spoke to the chief of the fingerprinting department of Dade County's Public Safety Administration who complained that Dade County had fifteen people to do its fingerprinting, while other cities like Washington, D.C., of equal population had 200 fingerprinters to fight crime. Yes, it is probably true that a city like Washington, D.C., does have a larger fingerprinting staff than does Dade County, but then it also has the prison facilities to handle more arrests. When I asked the chief what he would do with the greater number of people that could be arrested with the additional staff experts, he did not have an answer. As I said to him, "What is the point of making arrests if there is no facilitating space to put them." We all know what the problems are.

DECEMBER 27 TUESDAY

Around 10:00, I went to the district office and stayed until noon. Staff are working half shifts over the holiday season. Going through all the Christmas cards on my desk, there was a card from Robert Sanders. Sanders, a Jewish right winger with a big condo on Brickell Avenue, lives in El Salvador and had asked me to call him about the corruption in the El Salvador/U.S. AID Program. We now have an appointment to meet.

I was a little disturbed by the *Miami Herald* article today on the Munisport dump site in North Dade. In November the EPA ruled the Munisport harmless, and now the environmentalists are in an uproar. The article implied that the Florida Delegation, in letters to the EPA, "insisted" that the agency take the Munisport off the Superfund list, but as I said to the *Herald* reporter in our interview session, "My first priority has always been the environment and public health." The fact is we had only asked that the EPA "move quickly" in its decision, and we would have stood by the EPA's decision if it found that the site was a health hazard. EPA officials also denied that they had been pressured, saying that "Whatever the problems at Munisport, the state could handle them," and I agree.

DECEMBER 28 WEDNESDAY

Another day with my name in the paper, and again I am not happy with the criticism. Today's *Miami Herald* had a story on the scarcity of Super Bowl tickets, the headline reading: "The rich, important, lucky will attend championship game." The article referred to the Super Bowl tickets I had provided to the subcommittee members, whereas other "less important" ticket seekers were going without. It may be that preferential treatment is accorded to the subcommittee members, but these same Congressmen are the decision makers on where transportation dollars go, and the ones who will help bring to Dade County the funds to improve and expand its transportation system. I figure a Super Bowl ticket is a good tradeoff for what our subcommittee members can bring to Dade County.

There was also another story on Munisport, much like yesterday's article, criticizing the effort to take the Munisport off the Superfund list. The whole story, however, is not being told, particularly the fact that there was also the effort to prevent legislation mandating that the Munisport be taken off the Superfund list without any EPA involvement. My problem is that I do not know how to correct or change the *Herald* slant on the story without making it worse. What I have found when dealing with environmental issues is that the environmentalists are generally absolutists.

I got on the phone with John in Washington about the *Herald* article, and then Lucy about air safety, discussing the Pan American Airlines explosion over Scotland and the recent cabin decompressions on Eastern Airlines planes. I will be speaking tonight before the new North Dade Democratic Club on air safety related issues, and I needed some background information. Adele and I discussed AID's request to detail a person from its agency to our office. I have no problem with this, and told Adele to get back to them with our acceptance.

Lately, I have been writing a lot of condolence messages. Too many people I know have died over the past few weeks.

Tonight I spoke before the North Dade Democratic Club on problems concerning aviation safety. The event was held at the North Miami Beach City Hall Recreational Facility, with Bernie Levy, president of the club, acting as master of ceremonies. About fifty of the club members were there, along with State Representative Mike Abrams. After my address, I took questions from the audience. The primary questions concerned the cost of catastrophic health care legislation, but there were also concerns about the Democratic party. The Democratic party can only return to power at the national and state levels by having the right man at the top of the ticket, and the members there seemed to agree. It was a good event, and my many friends who were there seemed happy to see me. I went to the tables and shook hands with everyone, and photos were taken.

DECEMBER 29 THURSDAY

My schedule at the district office was busier today than at any time during the holidays. At 10:00 I met with Sam Opshular, formerly president of the North Beach Property Owners Association. Sam is concerned with the possible cost proposal of catastrophic health insurance legislation. He did not have anything in writing, so I helped him draft a letter, addressed to me, which I will give to the Ways and Means Committee staff working on this legislation. Telling Sam to expect a response, I added that he should get back to me if the response was not received within a reasonable period of time.

Betty Knight was next on the schedule. She had a project proposal to help the elderly with business and legal problems, "to prevent them from being taken advantage of," she said. She was requesting funds to conduct a demonstration project on the proposal. Again, such information needed to be in writing so that when I present the request to the relevant committee, in this case the House Select Committee on Aging, the staff will have all the information at hand. Afterwards, Evelyn Scheungrund came in, and we discussed the necessity of keeping the condo vote as a bloc. The last election showed that the condos lack leadership to keep the bloc-vote intact.

Carl Cochran, State Director of the United Transportation Union was in concerned about the Coal Slurry pipeline, and lobbied me to oppose the pipeline legislation when it comes to the House Floor. Basically I support this legislation, but Carl is right to be concerned about the loss of jobs on coal-carrying railroads.

And then George Koonce, Patrice's brother, came in. George is in charge of the Drop-Out Program in the Dade County school system, and is lobbying for funds for secondary education grants for black disadvantaged youths. Charlie Kirsh of the Machinists Union was in about the FAA regulation that permits the overhaul and maintenance of American planes at overseas repair stations. His main concern was about the loss of jobs to repair facilities in places like Singapore or Brazil where there is little quality control on inspection and maintenance.

Kirsh was my last appointment, and when he left I rang John at the Washington office about today's *Miami Herald* article on Munisport. With today's story, I have decided that enough is enough and that the newspaper is overreacting to this Superfund problem. John and I talked about a draft response to the *Herald*, one that would adequately refute the newspaper's slant on this issue. What we both realize, however, is that whatever our response, there are those who will vigorously maintain their adversarial position.

In the evening Joan and I went to her niece Suzy's pre-wedding dinner at a restaurant in South Beach. Suzy is the daughter of Joan's only sister Emily. Even at nonpolitical events such as this, I am never really offstage as people always ask questions and I have to be prepared with answers. As usual, Dr. George Kleinfeld at the dinner complained to me about federal medical policy, and when George sees me again tomorrow at the wedding, I will get more of the same complaints.

DECEMBER 30 FRIDAY

When I arrived at the office this morning the staff showed me the lead story in this week's issue of the *Jewish Floridian*, which stemmed from my interview with *Floridian* reporter Erin Stein. I was very pleased with the article as Erin is a tough interviewer, but a good writer, and parts of the article I can use next year in a newsletter.

In today's *Miami Herald* it was announced that Dewey Knight, the Deputy Dade County Manager, is retiring after a 30-year career and, according to the *Herald*, Dewey is the "highest ranking black in county government." The writeup was very complimentary, and Dewey deserves it, listing among his achievements several positions that Dewey held as the "first" black, such as Dade's first black department director, the first black assistant county manager, the first black deputy county manager, and the first black interim county manager.

The office closed about 1:00 p.m. today for the holiday, but before leaving I spent time writing an introduction to the news story on Dewey, to be placed in the *Congressional Record;* when the *Record* is printed, I will send it on to him. I was also able to get Super Bowl tickets for retiring Congressional member Ed Boland, quite an achievement considering all the flak in the newspaper about preferential treatment to congressmen in the requests for Super Bowl tickets. Boland is a subcommittee chairman on the Appropriations Committee, but he is not a member on our transportation subcommittee.

Joan's niece Suzy was married this evening - a lovely ceremony, with many of my constituents and campaign contributors among the guests. I had a chance to speak with Frank Callahan, head of the Chamber of Commerce Task Force on Transportation, about Metro-Dade transportation, especially the bus system. Bill Broeder and I talked about the meeting that Lucy had managed to schedule for him with the Coast Guard. Besides Bill's boating interest, he is a developer whom I have been successful in helping on several environmental and immigration problems. An in-law relative from Kentucky talked to me about a new bridge in Owensboro and wanted to be sure that there would be funding again next year. With subcommittee chairman Bill Natcher requesting it, I will of course earmark such funds. It was a good gathering, and a happy time all around.

DECEMBER 31 SATURDAY (NEW YEAR'S EVE)

I called Jeff this morning, and he is feeling better and will be back to work on a full-time schedule beginning January 3. It has been a quiet day - tennis in the morning and at my son Bill's house in the afternoon.

Joan and I brought in the New Year at the home of State Senator Jack and Myra McPherson. We arrived about 10:00 p.m., and did not get home until 3:00 a.m. Many of our friends were there, and we had a wonderful time. Jack wanted to hear about my trip to Southeast Asia, and I tried to give him an overall picture of what I had seen and experienced during the trip. Discussing the U.S. air bases in Japan and my findings there, I told him about the many billions of dollars worth of Japanese property that the United States owns that we should probably sell to the Japanese to help reduce our trade deficit and help balance our budget. Through the Congressional Research Office I will find out first the property value and then see if legislation is possible to dispose of these air bases for the reasons mentioned.

Jack and Myra are worried about the religious fundamentalist conservative right in our country. Jack and I both agree that Dukakis never satisfactorily explained his opposition to military aid to the Contras, which a majority in this country also opposed, and thereby let George Bush get by free on the issue. But that was only one of Dukakis's big mistakes. Jack thinks that Jim Baker who did all the dirty tricks in the Bush campaign should be held accountable in the Congress at his nomination hearing for Secretary of State. Personally, I do not think that will work as people do not care about what happened in the campaign now that it is behind us. There were other very stimulating conversations during the evening, and a good way to start the New Year.

JANUARY 1 SUNDAY (NEW YEAR'S DAY)

The *Miami Herald* reported yesterday that the Federal judge rejected the request to keep the *Miami News* open, and as of

December 31, 1988, the *Miami News* was officially closed.

JANUARY 2 MONDAY (1989)

Members are to be sworn-in tomorrow for the 101st Congress. I left Miami today, arriving in Washington about 1:00 p.m., in good time for a game with my tennis buddies: Ab Mikva, Sonny Montgomery and Bob Kastenmeier. We were glad to see each other, and had a really great time. It is also good to be back in Washington again.

JANUARY 3 TUESDAY

This morning I had breakfast with Gerald Cassidy of the lobbying firm Cassidy and Associates. Gerry has been a good fundraiser for me. We ate in the Members Dining Room, and joked and talked with many of my colleague friends - Dave Obey, Butler Derrick, and John Dingell.

A brief Democratic Caucus was held at 9:00 a.m., and shortly after noon I was sworn in for my ninth term. Later in the afternoon I was again nominated by the Appropriations Democratic Caucus to chair the Subcommittee on Transportation and, happily, all the Democratic members stayed on the subcommittee with me.

JANUARY 4 WEDNESDAY

On the House Floor this morning at the full Democratic Caucus, the Appropriations Committee's nomination was approved, and I was again Chairman of Appropriations Subcommittee on Transportation for the new 101st Congress.

This effort may seem self-centered and self-indulgent, but I wanted to be as honest as possible in the presentation of one member's activities, perceptions, relationships, failures and accomplishments. Much work over an interesting two years has gone into making notes, recording tapes, and gathering material, and I do not think I would want to do it for another term. I do, however, hope this effort is both informative as to the inner workings of the House of Representatives and also shows that someone in the seventy-something age bracket can have a very interesting, full and productive life: Be a "player." What I do find hard to believe is that this wonderful experience at this kind of old age is happening to me.

Serving in the 100th Congress for my country and for the 17th Congressional District of Florida has been a rewarding experience and a great privilege for me, and I am eagerly looking forward to what the 101st Congress holds.

INDEX